# THE AMERICAN WING

*at The Metropolitan Museum of Art*

# THE AMERICAN WING

## *at The* METROPOLITAN MUSEUM OF ART

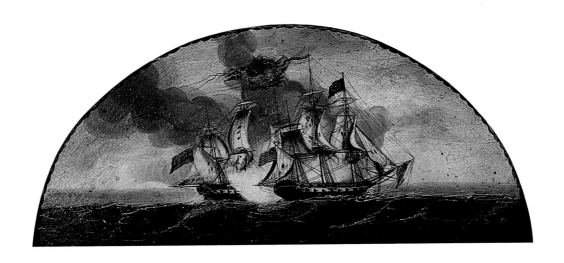

Marshall B. Davidson
and
Elizabeth Stillinger

**The Metropolitan Museum of Art**
**Alfred A. Knopf, New York**

*1985*

THIS IS A BORZOI BOOK

PUBLISHED BY THE METROPOLITAN MUSEUM OF ART, NEW YORK, AND ALFRED A. KNOPF, INC.

Bradford D. Kelleher, *Publisher*, The Metropolitan Museum of Art
John P. O'Neill, *Editor in Chief*
Polly Cone, *Project Coordinator*
Elizabeth Stillinger, *Editor*
Roberta Savage, *Designer*
Tammi Colichio and Roberta Savage, *Illustrators*

Type set by Graphic Composition, Inc., Athens, Georgia
Printed and bound in Italy by Amilcare Pizzi, s. p. a., Milan

*Photo Credits*

*Photographs by Paul Warchol commissioned especially for this book:*
Figs. 1–3, 5, 8–12, 14–17, 21, 24, 27–30, 33–36, 39–42, 44, 47, 49, 50, 53,
56–58, 60, 62, 64, 66, 68–71, 73, 76, 78–80, 82–84, 86, 88, 90, 93–96, 98,
99, 101, 102, 104, 105, 107, 110, 122, 123, 125, 126, 128, 130, 136, 139,
140, 143–46, 148, 149, 155, 156, 162, 168, 169, 172, 174, 176, 178–85, 188,
192, 194–96, 201–206, 211, 215–26, 229, 230, 233, 234, 236–39, 241–43,
246, 247, 249, 250, 253–61, 263–66, 268, 269, 275–86, 288–91, 302–304,
310, 313, 319, 320, 322–25, 329, 331, 333, 334, 337, 338, 343, 348–53, 355,
356, 360, 361, 366, 368, 369, 371–73, 376, 378, 380, 381, 384–91, 393, 395,
396, 398–403, 406–10, 412, 418, 421, 427, 430–37, 441–43, 446–48, 479,
482, 485, 488, 489, 499, 502, 507, 511, 518, 523, 524.

*Photographs by the Photograph Studio, The Metropolitan Museum of Art:* Figs. 4,
18, 19, 23, 25, 26, 31, 32, 38, 44, 46, 51, 52, 55, 59, 63, 65, 72, 75, 85, 89,
92, 97, 100, 103, 106, 108, 109, 111–16, 118, 124, 127, 129, 131–35, 137,
138, 141, 142, 150–54, 157–61, 163–65, 167, 170, 171, 173, 177, 186, 187,
189, 191, 193, 197–200, 207–10, 212–14, 228, 231, 232, 235, 240, 244, 245,
248, 251, 252, 262, 267, 270–74, 287, 292–300, 307–309, 311, 312, 314–18,
321, 326–28, 330, 332, 335, 336, 339–42, 344–47, 354, 357–59, 362–65,
367, 370, 374, 375, 377, 379, 382, 383, 392, 397, 404, 405, 411, 413–17,
419, 420, 422–26, 428, 429, 438–40, 444, 445, 449–78, 480, 481, 484, 486,
487, 490–98, 500, 501, 503–506, 509, 510, 516, 517, 521, 522. *By Jerry L.
Thompson:* Figs. 6, 7, 508, 512–15, 519, 520. *By Richard Cheek:* Figs. 13, 20,
22, 37, 43, 48, 54, 61, 67, 77, 81, 87, 91, 147, 190, 227. *By the Albany Institute
of History and Art:* Fig. 45. *By Cervin Robinson:* Figs. 117, 119–21, 305, 306.
*By Helga Studio:* Fig. 301.

LIBRARY OF CONGRESS CATALOGING IN PUBLICATION DATA

Metropolitan Museum of Art (New York, N.Y.). American Wing.
 The American Wing at the Metropolitan Museum of Art.

 Bibliography: p.
 Includes index.
 1. Art, American. 2. Metropolitan Museum of Art (New York, N.Y.). Amer-
ican Wing. I. Davidson, Marshall B. II. Stillinger, Elizabeth. III. Title.
N6505.M44      1985      709'.73'07401471      85–7250
ISBN 0–87099–309–7
ISBN 0–87099–424–7 (pbk.)
ISBN 0–394–54847–7 (Knopf)

# Contents

# Foreword

When they were opened in October 1924, The American Wing's sixteen period rooms, three exhibition galleries, and several alcoves caused a sensation. Here, virtually for the first time, American antiques were presented in an orderly, chronological way. In the period rooms, furniture, silver, paintings, glass, and other objects of more or less the same date were arranged together in spaces whose wood- and plasterwork were also of that date. Until this time, American antiques had most often been shown jumbled among curious, exotic, or historically interesting relics at charity fairs and patriotic celebrations. Under the circumstances, it is easy to see why Americans had not until now understood how their heirlooms related to one another or how they might have fit together in colonial and Federal households. Visitors to the new Wing were absolutely astonished to discover, as well, that the rooms were attractive and inviting. "Colonial America had good taste," exclaimed one headline just after the opening.

From its very beginning, The American Wing has had an enormous effect on American taste. Many people were on the verge of turning their attention from European art to the art of their native land, and The American Wing was the spark that set off the great burst of enthusiasm for American antiques and early houses that characterized the 1920s. World War I was over, Americans were feeling the confidence that accompanied their realization that their country was a world power, and many were primed to appreciate their own past and culture. The American Wing's accomplished and refined picture of home life in colonial and early Federal America showed enthusiasts how to use old houses and antiques together. At the same time, the period rooms greatly influenced the way antiques and department stores and other museums and historic houses across the country arranged their collections. Finally, The Metropolitan Museum of Art, the greatest museum in what was by then the greatest American city, endorsed the artistic validity of American arts and crafts by showing them proudly alongside the arts of antiquity, Europe, and the Near and Far East.

Even though there are today many more American art enthusiasts than there were in the 1920s, The American Wing still focuses Americans' interest on their own artistic heritage. In a survey taken at the Museum shortly after the expanded Wing opened in 1980, a number of visitors mentioned their surprise and pleasure at finding wide-ranging displays of American art: "The American Wing makes an important statement about American art," said one visitor. "For one thing, it says that our art is as good as European art. More important, however, it says that furniture, sculpture, and stained glass are as valued as paintings."

And indeed, it is the melding of art of a great variety of materials and levels of sophistication that has always distinguished The American Wing. It was a concept for which the period room was a perfect beginning and from which the Museum has branched into collecting in many different categories and periods of American art.

The first, and until now the most comprehensive, book about The American Wing was *A Handbook of The American Wing,* by R. T. H. Halsey, who oversaw the installation of the original Wing, and Charles O. Cornelius, his assistant; it was brought out in the fall of 1924. Henry W. Kent, the Museum's distinguished secretary and the man who conceived the idea of an American wing for the Metropolitan, had set forth his ideas about a handbook in a 1923 letter to Halsey. "This book should be written in a popular style, and the old-fashioned, dry-as-dust museum catalogue method forgotten," he advised. Both men must have been pleased by the result, for the *Handbook* sold nine thousand copies in its first year and eventually went through seven editions.

Although the *Handbook* was organized so that visitors could tour the galleries and rooms in sequence, beginning on the third floor with the seventeenth and early eighteenth centuries and descending through the mid-eighteenth century on the second to the late eighteenth and early nineteenth on the first, it remained for many years a foremost treatment both of domestic life in the colonies and of American antiques in general, with special emphasis on furniture.

Other important publications that deal with nearly all aspects of the collection have been brought out in book, pamphlet, catalogue, and other forms from time to time, and many of them are listed in the Selected Bibliography at the back of this volume. Metropolitan Museum *Bulletin* articles have announced additions to and presented research on aspects of the collection, beginning in 1910 with an article on the 886 pieces of furniture the Museum had just acquired from H. Eugene Bolles as the foundation of the American Wing collection. Many of these articles are also listed in the bibliography.

The present volume is different from the foregoing works, for it treats the

# Acknowledgments

whole of the expanded American Wing, rather than one of its parts. It is not a guide to the installation, but to the collection itself, and its illustrations have been selected to represent the remarkable range of that collection—from great paintings and sculptures to period-room appointments. Captions provide up-to-date information on each object illustrated, while the text offers the story of the development of the arts in America—not a "dry-as-dust" book, we hope, but one that will prove a worthy successor, sixty-one years later, to the *Handbook*.

John K. Howat
*Lawrence A. Fleischman Chairman of the Departments of American Art, The Metropolitan Museum of Art*

**M**any members of the Museum staff have contributed to this book—helping with everything from the correct credit line to tracking down an elusive chair in the storeroom—and we are very grateful to them all. Over the several years during which this work has been in preparation, the staff of The American Wing has been unfailingly helpful, responding generously to requests for advice, information, and photographs. Without their help, this book would not have been so up-to-date nor so rich. Jeanie James in Archives and David Kiehl in the Department of Prints and Photographs have also been extremely helpful. Robert Trent of the Connecticut Historical Society very kindly contributed information and suggestions on the Early Colonial Period. Bill Guthman was supportive at all stages, but especially during research, when he suggested (and lent copies of) source material.

In the beginning, Andrew Solomon and Peggy Kutzen spent summer internships digging out preliminary material for captions and Naomi Godfrey gathered pictures and information. As we were entering the galley stage, Kelley Forsyth capably tied up loose ends. Susie Saunders's hours of picture research and of digging for information in files and catalogues saved the authors months of work, and we extend heartfelt thanks. Paul Warchol spent many hours in a makeshift studio just off the galleries taking splendid photographs specifically for this book.

Besides providing good advice and comfort at crucial moments, Polly Cone, our executive editor, constantly smoothed the way and saw to it that our practical needs were met. Cynthia Clark's thorough and thoughtful copy-editing and proofreading have benefited both text and captions. Roberta Savage, our gifted designer, has worked with us almost from the beginning, and it is through her efforts that we have been able to present so much information so coherently and attractively.

Elizabeth Stillinger

**A**s the manuscript for this book was in preparation, I profited from the advice very generously given me by numerous staff members of The American Wing. The late Berry Tracy, Morrison Heckscher, Craig Miller, Alice Frelinghuysen, and Frances Safford were particularly helpful, and it is a pleasure to acknowledge my debt to them, one and all.

Marshall B. Davidson

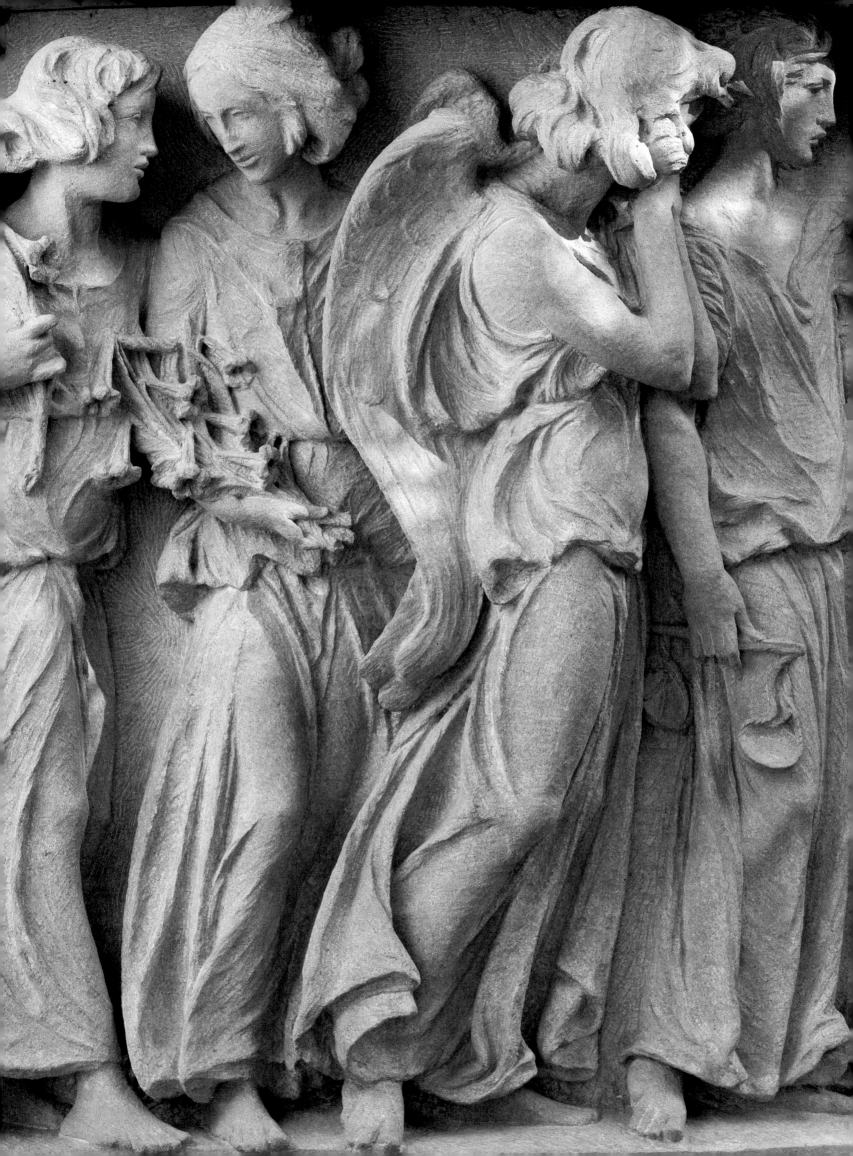

# INTRODUCTION

THE COLLECTIONS OF AMERICAN ART in the Metropolitan Museum are the most comprehensive and representative to be found anywhere. Here have been assembled significant objects in every medium and from all periods of American history, including acknowledged masterpieces in each of the many categories—painting, sculpture, prints, drawings, interior and exterior architecture, furniture, and other decorative arts of numerous kinds.

The first acquisitions were made almost immediately after the Museum was founded more than a century ago, and as it grew in size and importance its holdings of American art grew in proportion. To accommodate this ever-increasing wealth of material The American Wing, which had opened with great fanfare in 1924 and enjoyed mounting popularity over the following half century, has recently been substantially enlarged. This new construction, designed by the firm of Kevin Roche John Dinkaloo and Associates, provides for the very first time an area wherein virtually all the arts that have been practiced in America can be coherently displayed, seen in their intimate relationships, and enjoyed in their full variety. The present book is a tour of the collections, and not of the galleries alone. Material that is not on view is sometimes included—and is often accessible to students in nearby storage areas.

The Museum's large selection of outstanding and typical examples provides a fair opportunity to judge the true nature of our rich and distinctive artistic heritage. For a long time it was widely assumed that the early settlers of this country, preoccupied as they were with Puritan principles and with the no less demanding wilderness, were indifferent to beauty. But neither Puritanism nor pioneering blighted the creative side of human nature. Man's urge to create and to fashion works of art was conditioned but not stilled by his experience in the New World; and as the country expanded across a continent of immeasurable resources, that urge was continually stirred by new and challenging visions.

Quite aside from the purely visual attractions of its collections and exhibits, The American Wing presents what is in effect a pageant of our history as a people. It clearly demonstrates the varieties and degrees of skills that were called into play by the changing tastes and fortunes of Americans over the centuries. In doing that it evokes aspects of the past, remote and recent, that can be recalled in no other way, for the arts often speak to us when histories remain dumb. The corollary is equally true, to be sure; we must know history to understand the arts. History and art are closely interwoven strands in the seamless fabric of any culture.

In the pages that follow, examples of American arts and crafts are described, illustrated, and explained in terms of their style, their quality, and their historical interest. The talents of a great many artists and artisans—native and foreign born; some well known, some little known, others unidentified; men and women with varied skills and of different temperaments—are represented by the works discussed. The stories of their individual accomplishments add interesting and colorful sidelights to the story of life in America. That story as seen in the arts is the mirror of ourselves as a people. Year by year our lives and our outlooks are never less than the sum of our past. The better we know and understand this the better we know and understand ourselves.

## The Charles Engelhard Court

The ground-floor approach to The American Wing leads from the Museum's main building into a spacious, glass-roofed garden court dedicated to the memory of Charles W. Engelhard. As the visitor enters the courtyard his immediate impression is of space and light and greenery. But stone and marble, bronze, and brilliant colored glass contribute to the atmosphere as well. Here a melange of architecture, fine art, and decorative art is presented as a prelude to the rest of the Wing. This blending of the fine and applied arts is one of the important features of The American Wing, where paintings and furniture have always been displayed together in old rooms. The expanded space provides as well galleries for the chronological display of paintings and sculpture adjacent to similarly arranged galleries of furniture and cases of silver, glass, and ceramics. Until now, the paintings galleries and the decorative-arts displays have not necessarily been neighbors.

Although the courtyard contains only nineteenth- and early twentieth-century arts—giving continuity to the space but not indicating the range of centuries represented inside—it does reproduce the diversity of the collections within. From the severe classicism of the 1820s' bank facade through the romanticism of mid-century sculpture to the modernism of stained glass and architectural elements of the early 1900s, the court expresses the character of The American Wing.

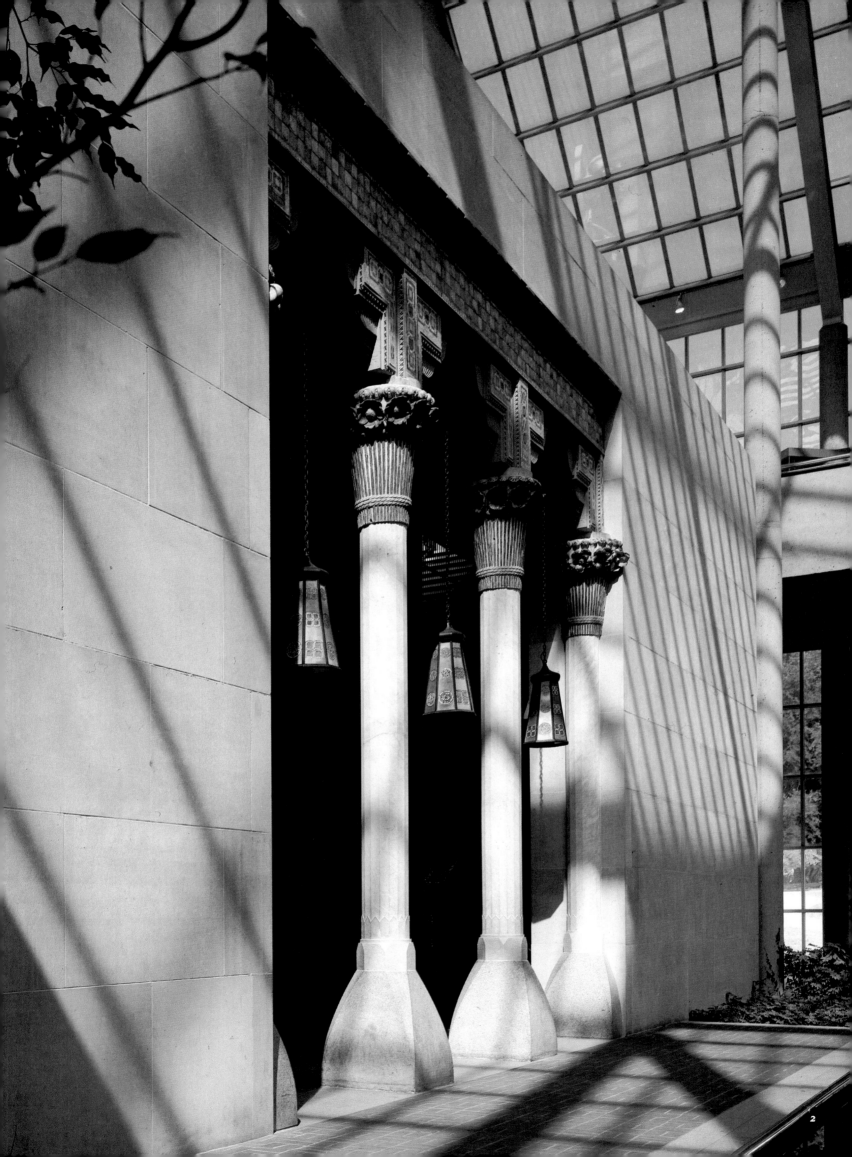

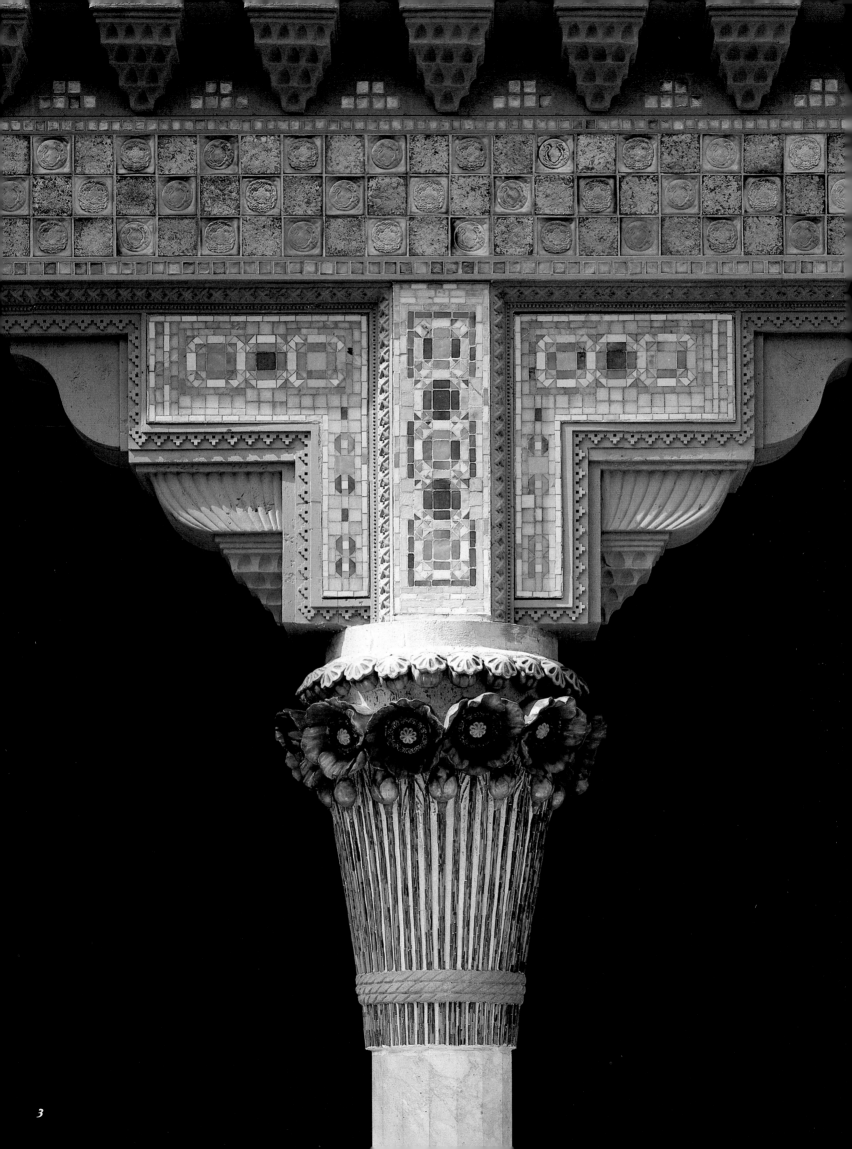

3

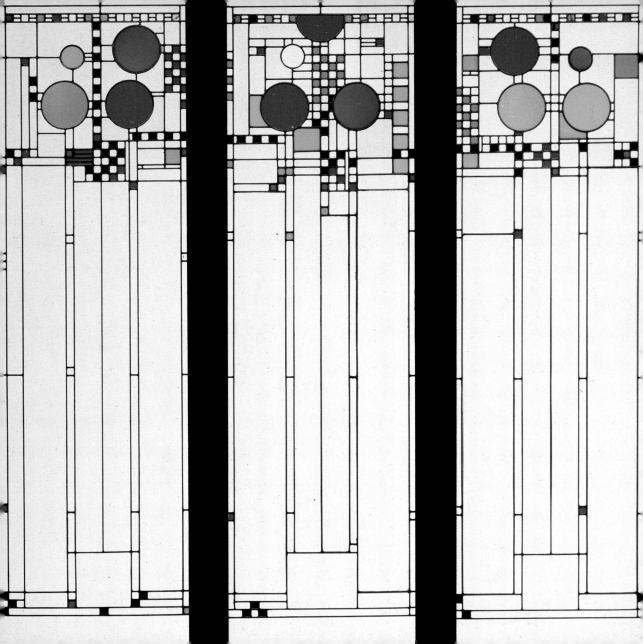

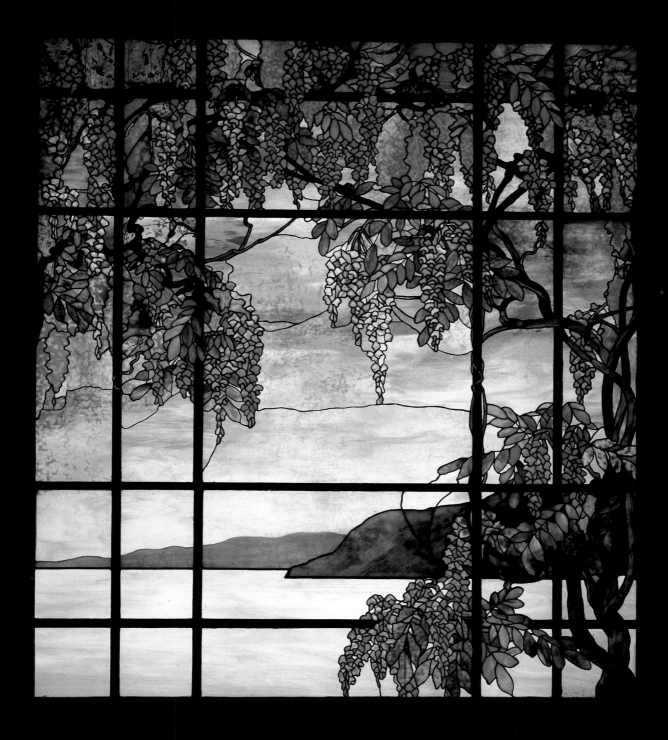

5

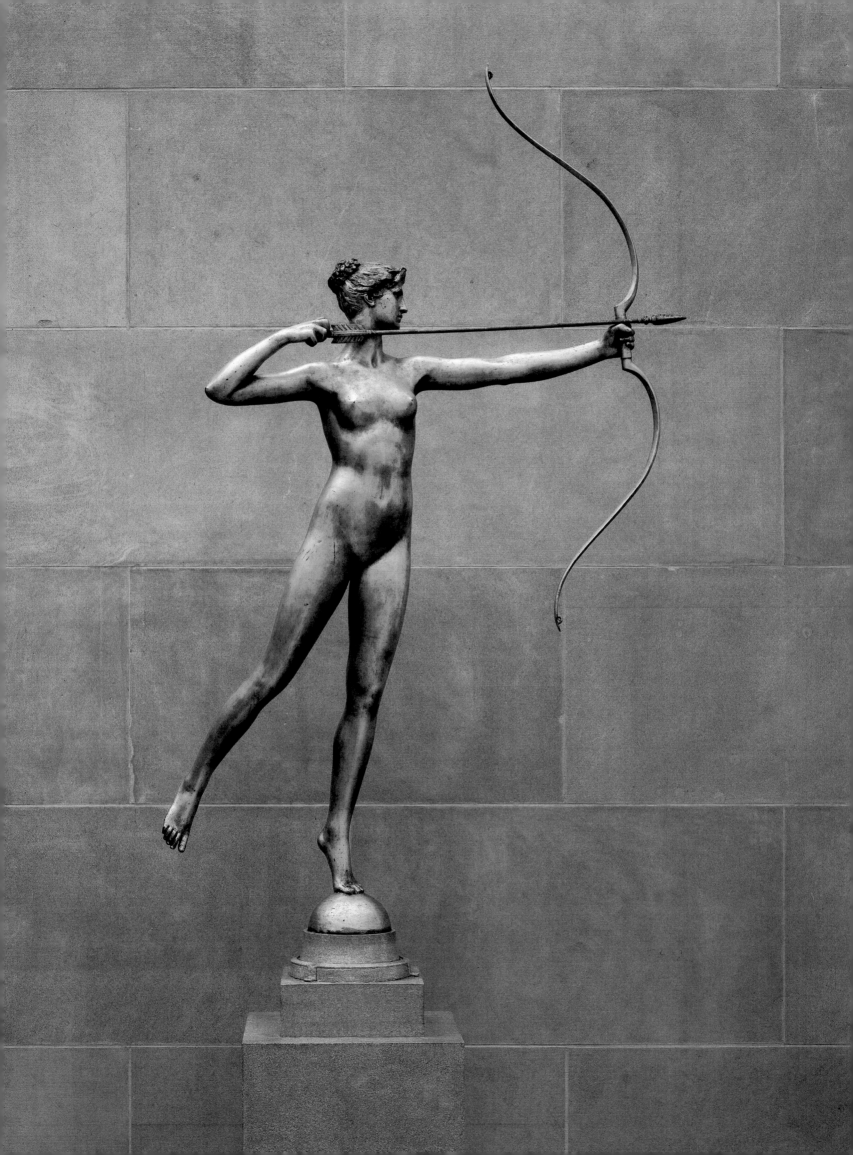

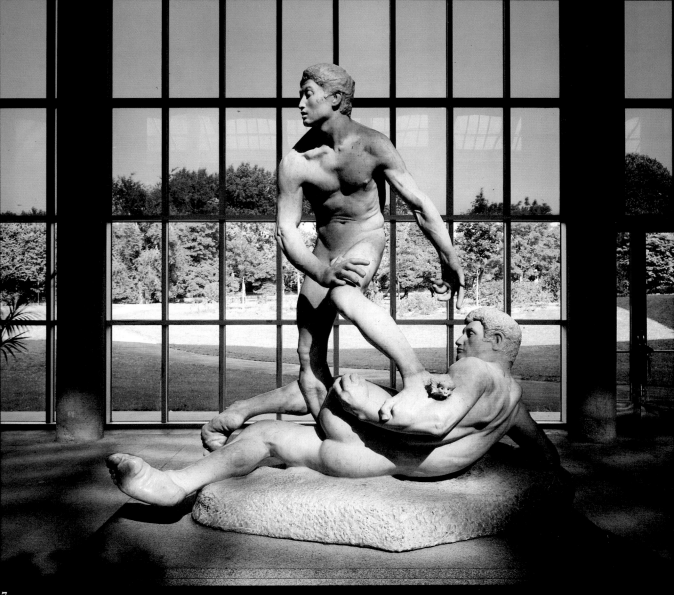

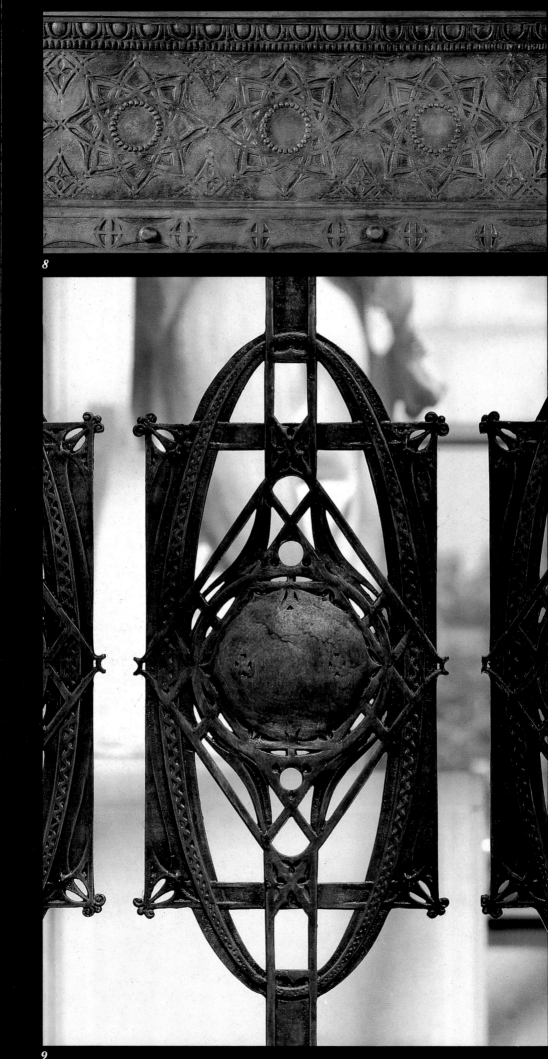

8

9

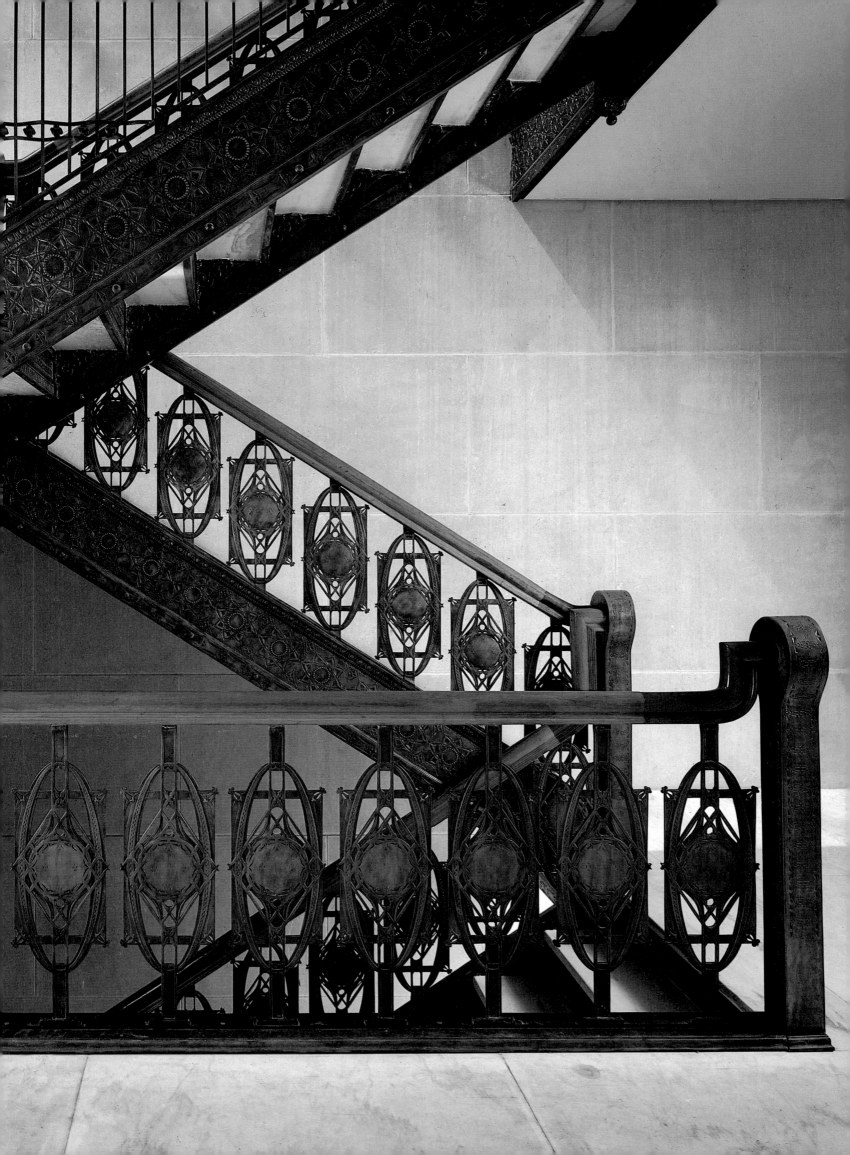

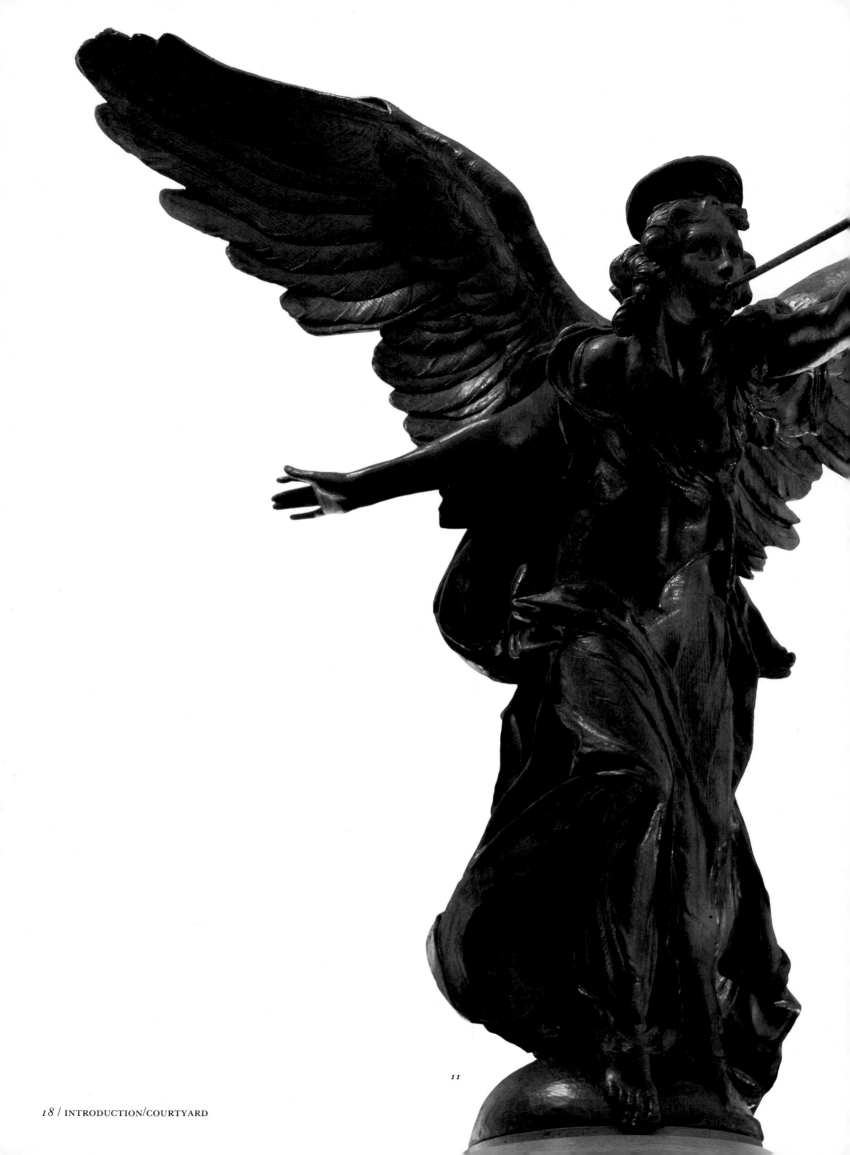

11

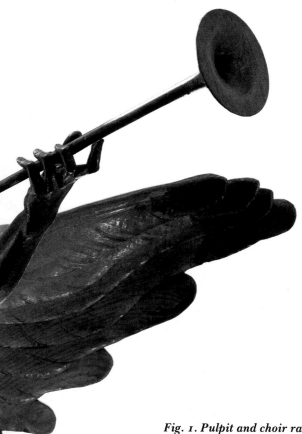

**Fig. 1. Pulpit and choir rail,** *detail, All Angels' Church (now demolished), by Karl Bitter (1867–1915), New York, 1900; limestone, oak.*
Rogers Fund, 1978 (L.1983.53.1,2)

**Fig. 2. Entrance loggia,** *Laurelton Hall, designed by Louis Comfort Tiffany (1848–1933), Tiffany Studios, New York, about 1905; limestone, ceramic, glass.*
Gift of Jeannette Genius McKean and Hugh Ferguson McKean, in memory of Charles Hosmer Morse, 1978 (1978.10.1)

**Fig. 3. Capital of column of entrance loggia,** *Laurelton Hall, detail of Fig. 2.*

**Fig. 4. Stained-glass triptych window,** *Avery Coonley playhouse, designed by Frank Lloyd Wright (1867–1959), Riverside, Illinois, 1912; leaded glass, height 86¼ inches (219.1 cm.).*
Purchase, Edgar J. Kaufmann Foundation and Edward C. Moore, Jr. Gifts, 1967 (67.231.1–3)

**Fig. 5. View of Oyster Bay,** *stained-glass wisteria window, Tiffany Studios (1900–38), William Skinner house, 36 East Thirty-ninth Street, New York, about 1905; leaded glass, 72¾ by 66½ inches (184.8 by 168.9 cm.).*
From the McKean Collection through the courtesy of the Morse Gallery of Art, Winter Park, Florida

**Fig. 6. Diana,** *by Augustus Saint-Gaudens (1848–1907), 1891, this cast 1928; gilded bronze, height 112 inches (284.5 cm.).*
Rogers Fund, 1928 (28.101)

**Fig. 7. Struggle of the Two Natures in Man,** *by George Grey Barnard (1863–1938), 1894; marble, height 101½ inches (257.8 cm.).*
Gift of Alfred Corning Clark, 1896 (96.11)

**Figs. 8, 9, and 10. Staircase** *(one of a pair) and details, Chicago Stock Exchange Building, designed by Louis H. Sullivan (1856–1924), 1893; cast iron with electroplated copper finish, mahogany.*
Purchase, Mr. and Mrs. James Biddle Gift and Emily C. Chadbourne Bequest, 1972 (1972.50.1–4)

**Fig. 11. Trumpeting angel,** *detail, pulpit and choir rail, All Angels' Church (now demolished), by Karl Bitter (1867–1915), New York, 1900; oak.*
Lent by All Angel's Church, 1978 (L.1983.53.1,2)

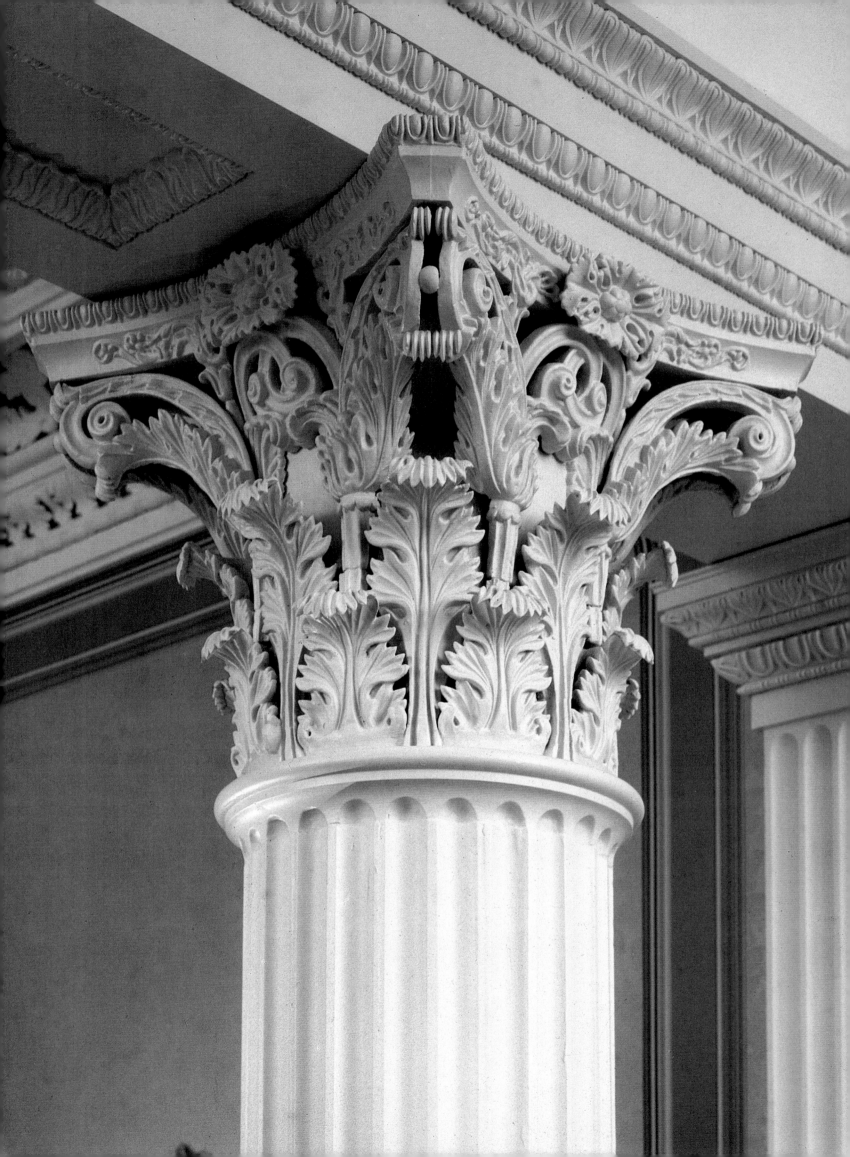

# PERIOD ROOMS

When The American Wing first opened in 1924 it consisted principally of a series of period rooms whose woodwork and other architectural features had been removed or reproduced from early dwellings that once stood in various colonies and states along the Atlantic seaboard. Thus preserved from neglect and destruction, these interior elements, ranging in date from the late seventeenth century to the early decades of the nineteenth, were installed to approximate their original appearance as closely as possible. Furniture and accessories were chosen and arranged so that the rooms reflected the purpose which the curators felt they had been planned and designed. Walls and woodwork were painted in colors that either matched those believed to have been used on them originally or known to have been popular at the time the rooms were built. Wherever possible, fabrics used for upholstery and for bed and window hangings were contemporary with the rooms. The designs of the hangings followed those shown in engravings and other illustrations from the various periods.

This was the first time a major museum had given such considerable, studious, and discreet attention to the American decorative arts. Little or nothing in history or art books had prepared either the press or the public for what was disclosed by The American Wing rooms. The general reaction was one of astonishment and acclaim. An occasional critic queried whether these "American things" deserved a place in the history of art alongside treasures from ancient Egypt, Greece, Rome, and all the other historic cultures of the East

and West. However, the passage of time has made such reservations seem like historical and pedantic curiosities. As the Wing became increasingly popular it attracted the growing interest of scholars and serious antiquarians as well as of decorators and dilettante collectors. One of the most important consequences was that the Wing provided an outstanding model for innumerable subsequent ventures in restoration and preservation across the land.

Most of the rooms included in the old Wing are still on display in the recently reopened building, although over the years a few of them were replaced with better examples from the same periods. In accordance with the original plans for the Wing, these are limited to material dating before about 1825. However, it has long since been apparent that achievements of the later years of the nineteenth century and the first decades of the twentieth were hardly less important to our cultural heritage than those of earlier times. Consequently, a number of rooms and galleries have been added to carry the presentation of historic styles forward for almost another hundred years. The Museum has now collected an impressive variety of fine furniture and accessories of virtually all the historical styles, and, like the interiors themselves, the objects that furnish these later rooms are on permanent view for the first time.

Attitudes toward period-room installations have evolved since The American Wing's rooms first opened in 1924. Then they were considered, in the words of trustee R. T. H. Halsey, who oversaw their installation and furnishing, "a visual personification of home life in this country from almost the beginnings of New England until the end

of the first quarter of the nineteenth century" (*The Homes of Our Ancestors*, 1934). In the intervening years it has become evident that such settings inevitably reflect the biases and tastes of the era in which they are installed at the same time as they convey information about interiors in earlier times and that the claim to transport modern viewers into a chamber that looks exactly as it would have in an earlier day must be qualified. The rooms today demonstrate the stylistic relationships among the objects and the architectural elements in a given period; furniture arrangements, colors, floor and window treatments, and so on are shown in accordance with the latest research without being presented as inevitable.

Another difference is that delicate dress and other rich fabrics previously used in the Wing for upholstery, while interesting contemporary documents themselves, were not always authentic furniture coverings; these have been replaced by faithful reproductions of early upholstery and curtain materials. Aside from the obvious advantages, using reproductions with full-strength colors makes it possible to provide a more accurate view of the rooms and furniture—so that they appear more as they would have during the periods being represented. The collection does contain a few rare, vigilantly preserved pieces with their original woolen needlework or leather upholstery.

---

*Fig. 12. Detail, Rococo Revival Parlor, see Fig. 102.*

# The Early Colonial Period, 1630–1730

In considering the earliest exhibits, it is helpful to recall that the seventeenth-century colonists who settled at widely separated points along the eastern seaboard intended to build and furnish their new homes as nearly like those they had left overseas as their skills and the materials at hand would permit. Not long after the first strains of settlement in a strange and sometimes hostile wilderness were eased, these colonists succeeded in providing for themselves dwellings, meetinghouses and churches, furniture, silver, and other necessities and conveniences that did not differ appreciably either in character or in quality from English and Continental models.

These first immigrants were largely of modest origins, and their craftsmanship was modest in pretension—at least in those examples that have survived—but it was by no means crude. The settlers came mostly from small towns and rural villages where, although they were removed from the fashions of the courts and capitals, they had become familiar with the heavy forms and grotesque and geometric ornament of the Mannerist style. This had arrived in England by way of the Netherlands during the sixteenth century. Early colonial work reflected also a way of life, rooted in old habits, that barely comprehended the comforts, the conveniences, and the more specialized arrangements that were soon to become as widely appreciated in America as they were in Europe. This advance toward a more modern concept of living and the changing styles by which it was accommodated can be traced in the succession of rooms and objects in The American Wing.

The first colonists to settle along the Atlantic coast brought precious little furniture with them. There was room in the holds of their tiny ships to store nothing more than the most necessary supplies and utensils for starting their lives in the New World. All the treasured heirlooms that allegedly came over on the *Mayflower* would have had to hang from the yardarms to have arrived on that epic voyage. "Before you come," the Reverend Francis Higginson, first minister at Salem, Massachusetts, warned prospective emigrants, "be careful to be strongly instructed what things are fittest to bring with you. . . . For when you are once parted with England you shall meete neither markets nor fayres to buy what you want." Higginson recommended such essentials as cloth and leather for clothing, "all manner of carpenters tools," agricultural implements, iron for nails, and glass for windows. He did not mention furniture. That, like the houses it was to serve, could be made on the spot with the proper tools.

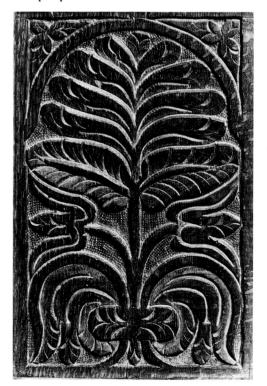

Until the immediate acute problems of settlement were overcome, the first arrivals had to put up in the most primitive shelters wherever they came ashore—at Plymouth, Salem, New Amsterdam, Jamestown, and later in the century at Philadelphia—in caves, holes in the ground, and even in empty casks. In the years immediately following settlement some colonists questioned their own judgment in crossing the sea to face the rigors they were at first forced to endure. "Wanting houses and other comforts," half the members of the Plymouth community died during the first bitter winter.

In good season, however, "orderly, fair, and well built houses" sprang up in each of the infant settlements. These early permanent structures owed their essential character to the particular origins of their owners and builders—whether they came from Ipswich, Dedham, Essex, or Cambridge in old England; from Amsterdam or elsewhere in the Low Countries; or from other parts of Europe—and to the nature of available building materials. Wood was everywhere, of course, and was used everywhere. But in spite of its abundance, the Dutch in New Amsterdam, like the Virginians and their close southern neighbors, showed a preference for brick construction. (There were bricklayers among the settlers at Jamestown in 1607, and bricks were being produced there or nearby almost immediately.) The early brick houses built on Manhattan Island, with their tile roofs and their stepped gables facing the street, resembled transplantations from the Low Countries. Although Virginians came almost entirely from England, they came from virtually all parts of the mother country rather than from one relatively limited area, as

New Englanders so largely did, and the houses they built in the New World took different forms that expressed their varied inheritances. There is no such thing as a standard seventeenth-century southern house.

Brick—and stone—were also used in New England, but wood was by far the favored building material. Contrary to the persistent legend that the earliest colonists built their own homes, trained carpenters built even the simplest houses in the Massachusetts Bay Colony. Most of them were young men who had completed their apprenticeship in England under master workmen skilled in traditional building practices. Almost 150 of these trained craftsmen are known to have arrived in Massachusetts before the middle of the seventeenth century. Even so, there was a shortage of skilled labor to meet the building boom of those days. This should be no cause for surprise, since during what is known as the Great Migration alone (roughly, the decade between 1630 and 1640) probably as many as twenty thousand discontented Englishmen left their homes to start life afresh in New England.

The typical framed houses that replaced improvised primitive shelters were made of stout oak timbers securely united by mortise and tenon joints. Raising a house frame about an ample chimney pile was a communal effort and was accompanied by spirited ceremony and ample potables. In both construction and design these dwellings were all but identical with English models. There was no such thing as a professional architect in the earliest colonial years; the very word "architect" was not in the common provincial vocabulary. Immigrant carpenters came equipped with neither plans, cross sections, scale models, nor pattern books. Without consciously striving to achieve a "style," but using traditional structural techniques that had been passed down from one generation to another, they built houses that served practical domestic needs according to the accepted standards of the day. For the most part, the individual elements used for construction were cut and hewn where it was most convenient for the carpenters, and the frames were then transported to the building site. Each piece was carefully incised with Roman numerals (which often can still be seen in early houses) to indicate its proper place when the frame was assembled and raised. In a sense these structures were early examples of prefabricated houses. (There were no log cabins built in the first English colonies in America. These were introduced by the Swedes who settled along the Delaware River in the late 1630s.)

Scattered about the New England countryside are several dozen seventeenth-century structures that have withstood most of the hazards to which such buildings have been subjected for

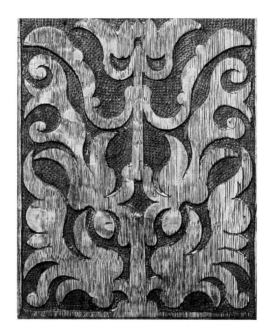

more than three centuries—fire, neglect, hurricanes, and wreckers' tools. Their number is diminishing, and few that have survived have escaped alteration. From time to time changes and additions—lean-tos and ells—were made until sometimes, as in the case of the House of the Seven Gables in Salem, the result is a picturesque agglomeration of different elements. On the other hand, some of these old structures have been carefully restored to their earliest state and others that had completely disappeared have been meticulously reconstructed. Enough evidence remains for us to recognize their essential character—foursquare floor plans; steep pitched roofs crowned by chimneys rising like capstones above the shingles; clapboard exterior walls pierced by small casement windows; and, often, overhanging upper stories with decorative pendents and knobs to add interest.

There were more than a few buildings, both private and public, that were much larger and more elaborate than any that have survived. It was reported in 1676 that among some 1,500 families in Boston there were fifteen merchants worth about £50,000 each—dramatic evidence of the flourishing trade that had already developed in and out of that little port. Theophilus Eaton, a well-to-do London merchant, came to Boston in 1637, moved to New Haven the next year, and became the first governor of that fledgling colony. There he soon built what must have been one of the most pretentious houses of the time. It was a U-shaped structure with a great central hall flanked by two gabled ells, and it had at least ten rooms and five chimneys. Old College at Harvard, constructed in 1642, was another extremely impressive pile; and there were other buildings scattered about the colonies that were of hardly less imposing size and interest. However, it is one of the sad accidents of American history that these have all disappeared, leaving few remaining traces.

In passing, the 1657 inventory of Eaton's New Haven establishment includes a startling variety of what would at the time have been considered luxurious accessories. Among these were clocks; glassware; tapestries, Turkey work and various other textiles; silver; and over 250 pounds of pewter utensils. This is of particular interest since at about this same time the English diarist Samuel Pepys complained that at a formal dinner in London he was obliged to eat from wooden trenchers and drink from earthenware pitchers.

One exceptional building that remains standing to testify to the ambitious architectural works of the early New England builders is the First Parish Church, also known as the Old Ship Meetinghouse, at Hingham, Massachusetts, erected in 1681 and still serving its community. The openly revealed timber framework of this venerable example is typical of seventeenth-century furniture as well as architecture. The heavy roughhewn trusses constructed above the large central gallery on the third floor of the Wing are adapted from those at Hingham, and the space serves as a sympathetic setting for the foursquare oaken chests, cupboards, tables, and stools of the seventeenth century.

# Hart Room

**Fig. 13. Hart Room,** *Ipswich, Massachusetts, before 1674. Edward Johnson was able to write of New England by 1642, "the Lord hath been pleased to turn all the wigwams, huts and hovels the English dwelt in at their first coming, into orderly, fair and well built houses, well furnished many of them." Fair and well-built Thomas Hart's house certainly was, and because its architectural framework is visible, as it was in all seventeenth-century New England buildings, the strength and solidity of each post and beam are revealed. The same molding planes that softened the sharp edges of the summer beam and the boards on the fireplace wall also shaped parts of cupboards, chests, and other wooden objects. Walls are whitewashed, the floor is bare, and comfort is at a minimum. Thomas Hart, the first owner of this room, was a tanner. He lived modestly and would not have had the number of sophisticated joined pieces seen here. Rather, the Hart Room has been used to give an idea of what kinds of objects were available in seventeenth-century New England and to bring together a group of furnishings that were made at about the same time the house was built. The ample cushions on the Carver chair and joint stool and the cupboard cloth, all of red wool fabric, show that although the lines of seventeenth-century furniture were uncompromising, cushions and cloths softened hard seats and added color to interiors. Using the top of the court cupboard—which was, with the press cupboard, the most important fur-*

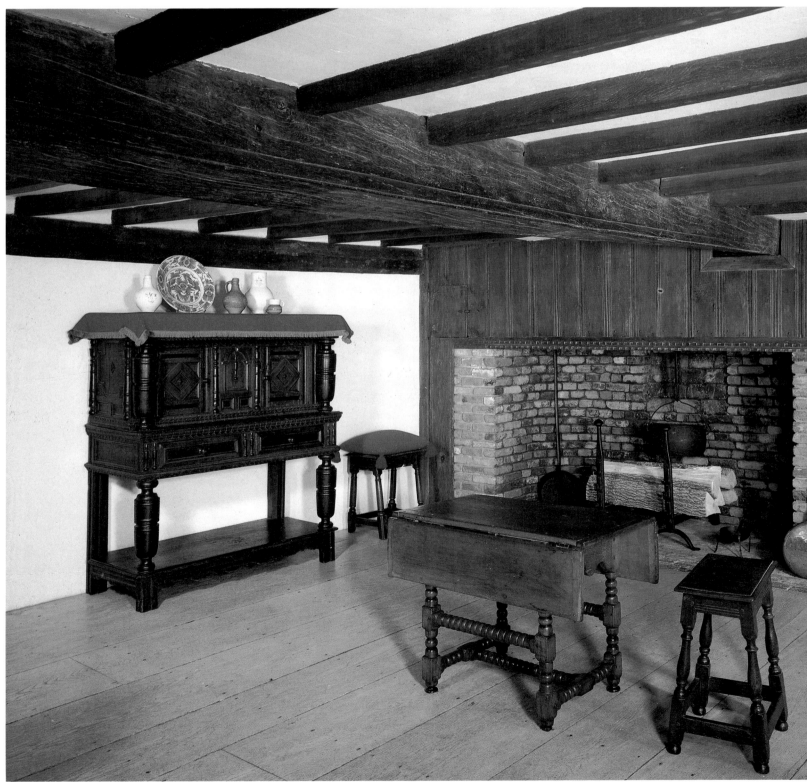

*13*

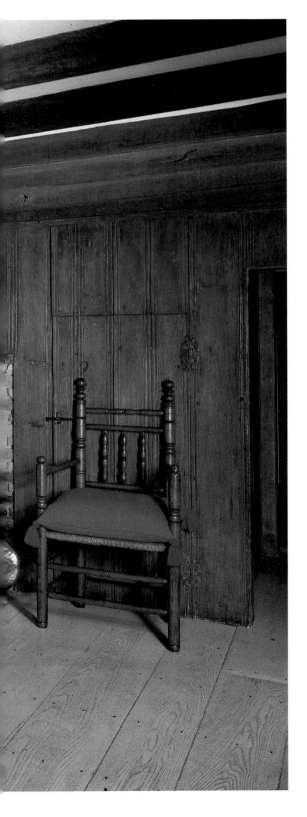

The earliest of the Museum's American rooms, from the Thomas Hart house, built in Ipswich, Massachusetts, before 1674, shares the central gallery's forthright architectural appeal (Fig. 13). Its massive fireplace lined with large, irregular bricks suggests the size of the central chimney pile about which the house was constructed. Hand-hewn oak corner posts, horizontal supports, or girts, and the huge chamfered summer beam that spans the room from the chimney to the end wall of the house and acts as a major framing unit, all securely joined by mortises and tenons, frankly reveal the structural skeleton of the building. Clay and sun-dried brick, now visible in one exposed section, were used to fill the walls between the studs. White plaster conceals this filling on three walls, and boards lightly molded at the joins sheathe the fireplace wall. In 1632 Thomas Dudley improved the walls of his house with similar vertical sheathing and was thereupon called to account for his extravagance by John Winthrop, first governor of the Massachusetts Bay Colony. "His answer now was," reported the governor, "that it was for the warmth of his house, and the charge was little, being but clapboards nailed to the wall in the form of wainscot."

Wrought-iron hinges of various designs support the boarded doors of the room. The small casement windows with their diamond-shaped leaded panes are facsimiles of the originals. Houses of this period were poorly heated and inadequately ventilated; their large fireplaces sucked in copious drafts of cold air. Benjamin Franklin once remarked that, seated close to a roaring fire of a winter night, one scorched before and froze behind.

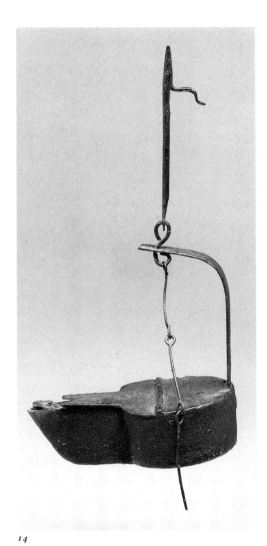

*14*

**Fig. 14. Betty lamp,** *American, eighteenth or nineteenth century; iron, height 10 inches (25.4 cm.). Betty lamps, which burn fat or oil from a variety of animals and fish, have a history that goes back at least as far as Roman times. They work very simply: a wick soaked in fat protrudes from the slanted spout and, when lit, gives off a dim light. The handle that curves up and over the betty is attached to a combination hook and spike, so that the lamp could either be hung on a piece of furniture or stuck into the wall or fireplace. Although this example is later than most of the other objects in the room, it represents similar lamps of earlier periods.*
Gift of Mrs. Russell Sage, 1909 (10.125.638)

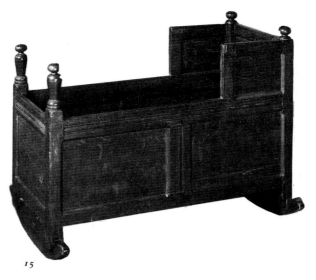

15

**Fig. 15. Cradle,** *eastern Massachusetts, 1640–80; oak, length 37 inches (94 cm). Two similar cradles set upon stiff rockers descended in families in the areas of Duxbury and Plymouth, Massachusetts, respectively, indicating eastern Massachusetts as the probable source of this example. These cradles, like all of the best seventeenth-century furniture, were "joyned"—that is, put together with mortise and tenon joints. They are constructed of panels held in place by frames mortised and tenoned together; straight horizontal and vertical lines made by a molding plane and turned finials at each corner are this example's only ornament.*
Gift of Mrs. Russell Sage, 1909 (10.125.672)

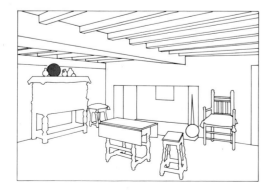

16

**Fig. 16. Delft dish,** *probably England, about 1680; earthenware with tin-enamel glaze, diameter 13 inches (33 cm). By the second half of the seventeenth century, colorful delftwares brightened the homes of many affluent colonists. Although they were of course used to hold food and drink, they also served decorative purposes, often residing atop a cupboard and sometimes hung on the wall. Both Dutch and English delftwares were used in colonial America. The technique involved in making them was the same in both countries: ordinary earthenware was covered with a tin-enamel glaze that turned opaque white in the kiln. Ornament, often blue, was added to produce a ceramic object inspired by the blue and white Chinese porcelain so admired by Europeans.*
Sansbury-Mills Fund, 1980 (1980.143)

There was little hope of warming the room throughout, and none at all of heating the whole house. The feeble glow of open grease or oil lamps (Fig. 14), candles of dubious quality, and rushlights was the only supplement to firelight. Nor did the small casement windows admit much light, for glass was costly and of poor quality. A truly satisfactory lamp was not contrived until the late eighteenth century, and earlier devices smelled more or less disagreeable according to the nature of the illuminant, be it animal fat, homemade tallow, or a similar substance.

This was the principal room of the Hart house, known as the hall, in which domestic life centered. It was a living area that recalled in its various functions the all-purpose "great hall" of early English manors. In such rooms most of the vital activity of the house took place, especially in winter when other rooms were closed off to conserve heat. Here the cooking was done (before separate kitchens were added) and here the family often ate, sometimes slept, and usually stored a miscellany of household and other gear that might have included anything from firearms to farming equipment. At a time when, as in Plymouth and other seventeenth-century communities, the average household consisted of nine or ten persons, the congestion can hardly be imagined. The Museum's installation therefore incorporates the types of objects that might have been used in such a room, but it does not attempt to simulate the flavor of life as it was lived by the Hart family in the seventeenth century—an impossible task at the distance of nearly three hundred years.

However, the varied character of the furnishings of the Hart Room does reflect the different uses to which this small area was put. The recessed bake oven and the cooking utensils at the fireplace speak for themselves. Most of the oak and pine furniture, such as the court cupboard and drop-leaf table, is of Massachusetts origin. The Hart Room also contains an oak chair whose back can be lowered to rest on the arms and serve as a tabletop (Fig. 17); this represents another space-saving form, one that was mentioned in Massachusetts inventories as early as 1644. And a rocking cradle (Fig. 15) stands beside the low bedstead that occupies the corner opposite the fireplace. Thomas Hart's inventory indicates that originally this room contained the best bed, a high-post example with curtains. Almost no seventeenth-century American bedsteads have survived, however, and this low-post bed of somewhat later date simply reminds one that every room of most seventeenth-century houses was used for sleeping as well as for many other things. It was probably in such a room that, in the winter of 1631, the aforesaid Thomas Dudley, trying to write by the light of the fire, explained that his whole family had congregated to keep warm, "though they break good manners, and make mee many times forget what I would say, and say what I would not."

**Fig. 17. Hart Room,** *detail. Chest, Massachusetts, Ipswich area, 1660–1700; oak, 28½ by 41½ inches (72.4 by 105.4 cm.). Chair-table, New England, 1675–1700; oak, pine, height of seat 19½ inches (49.5 cm.). One of a group of carved chests that are attributed to the school of joinery established in Ipswich by William Searle and Thomas Dennis, this chest is covered with low-relief carving. Its ornamental motifs, including stylized S-scrolls, leaves, flowers, and lozenges (diamond shapes), are characteristic of the Searle-Dennis vocabulary, which these men brought with them from their native Devonshire, England. Like the chest, the now rare chair-table is of framed construction. The shape of its original top is not known, for this is a replacement.*

*This form was made to perform the tasks of a table when the hinged top was down and of a chair when the top was swiveled up.*
Gift of Mrs. Russell Sage, 1909 (10.125.24), and Gift of Mrs. Russell Sage, 1909 (10.125.697)

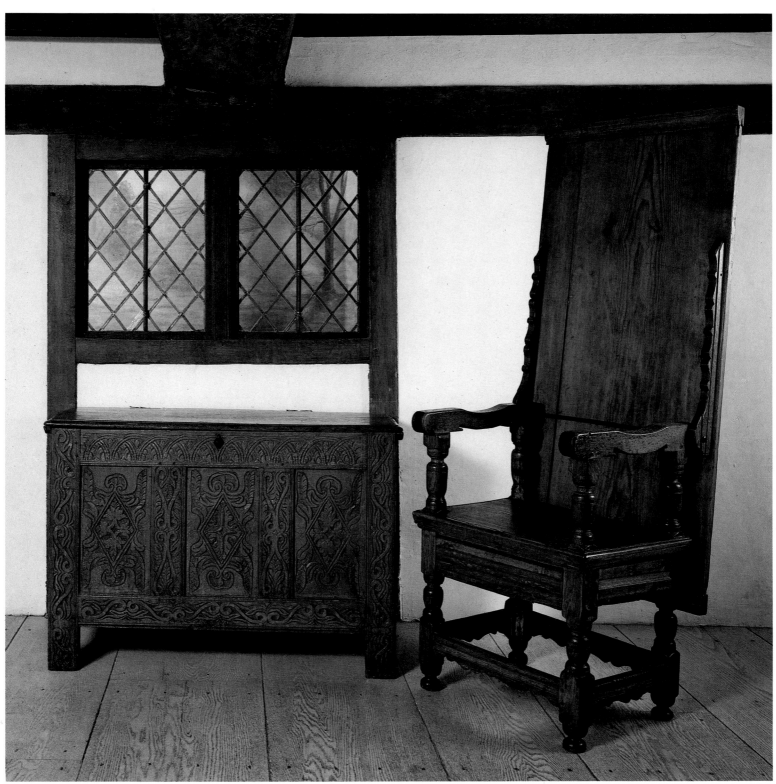

17

# Wentworth Room

**Fig. 19. House built by John Wentworth** of Portsmouth, New Hampshire, in 1695–1700. When the Museum bought it in 1926, the dwelling had been removed from this site on the grassy banks of Puddle Dock Creek and was sitting in a dump, "a grisly wraith of its former self." The Museum's Wentworth Stair was located just inside the front door; the Wentworth Room was on the second floor, above and to the right of the front door.
From The Homes of Our Ancestors, by Edwin Whitefield, 1886. Photograph courtesy of The New-York Historical Society

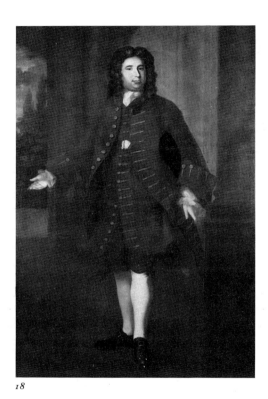

18

**Fig. 18. Lieutenant Governor John Wentworth** (1671–1730), by Joseph Blackburn (active in America 1754–63), 1760; oil on canvas, 92 by 57¼ inches (233.7 by 145.4 cm.). Joseph Blackburn painted this likeness in 1760, thirty years after Wentworth's death; the earlier life portrait from which it was probably copied is now lost. Merchant and sea captain as well as lieutenant governor, Wentworth was a member of a distinguished New England family: both his son Benning and his grandson John were governors of New Hampshire after its separation from Massachusetts. Wealth and position are indicated by the richness of Wentworth's dress and the formality of his pose.
Courtesy of the New Hampshire Historical Society, gift of Anne Wentworth Morss, Margaret Wentworth Whiting, and Constance Wentworth Dodge

The new standards of taste and design that evolved in the William and Mary period are handsomely demonstrated in the chamber (upstairs room) from the John Wentworth house, built in Portsmouth, New Hampshire (Figs. 20 and 22). Its woodwork dates from about 1700, and most of its furnishings are from the years just before and after that date.

The main staircase of this house, also in the collection, is a rare and exceptionally handsome survival (Figs. 25 and 26). Earlier, the upper floor of a house had been gained either by means of a ladder or, more commonly, by stairs immediately within the front entrance, set against the bricks of the central chimney and enclosed by a wall of unmolded vertical boards, or sheathing. Here that area has been opened up. The chimney is covered by attractive paneling that is also used for the soffit (the underside of the staircase) and for the walls of the entry. Bold moldings enframe the individual panels. The most distinctive feature of this steeply rising staircase with high treads is the ranks of unusual spiral-turned balusters that support the heavy molded handrails. It is perhaps the most impressive example of its kind to have survived from the William and Mary period. It is also an early harbinger of the development of the small entry into a central hallway with a large and prominent staircase—a feature that became a focal element of the house.

The Wentworth chamber has a higher ceiling and a good deal more space than the Hart Room, and its architectural features are more formally and deliberately treated. Structural elements—all of white pine—still intrude into the room, but two of the corner posts are neatly boxed in, the girts are

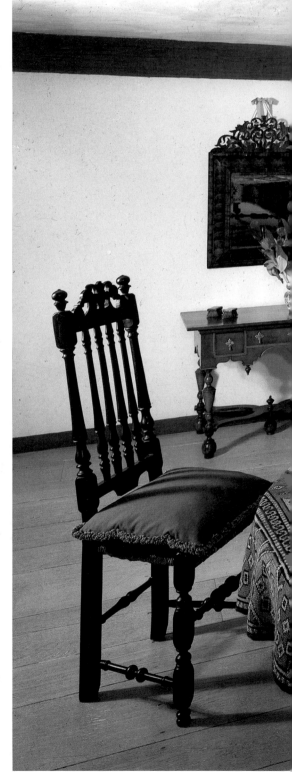

20

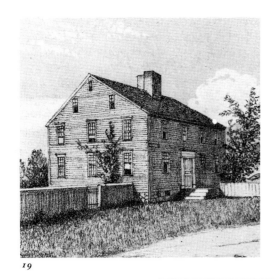

**Fig. 20. Wentworth Room,** Portsmouth, New Hampshire, 1695–1700. The newest fashions in American paneling and furnishing appear in this second-floor chamber from John Wentworth's house. With higher ceilings and fewer exposed posts and beams, this room brings us closer to the elegancies of eighteenth-century interiors. The variety of new forms signals the arrival of a new era too, for each specialized form makes the specific occupation for which it was designed a little easier. The dressing table, for example, has three handy drawers and an uncluttered surface on which to arrange powder, hairpins, and other necessities of the toilet. The couch, or daybed, serves as a sitting place by day and an extra bed by night. Using the same green fabric for the couch and other seating furniture as well as for the curtains was a practice that added a note of formality and a feeling of unity to the room. Although there are no surviving pictures to show us how rooms were arranged in America during the late seventeenth and early eighteenth centuries, European prints and paintings of that period depict interiors with all furniture not in use arranged around the walls. Since the colonists followed European furnishing conventions, we know that such room arrangements were customary in America too.

Sage Fund, 1926 (26.290)

19

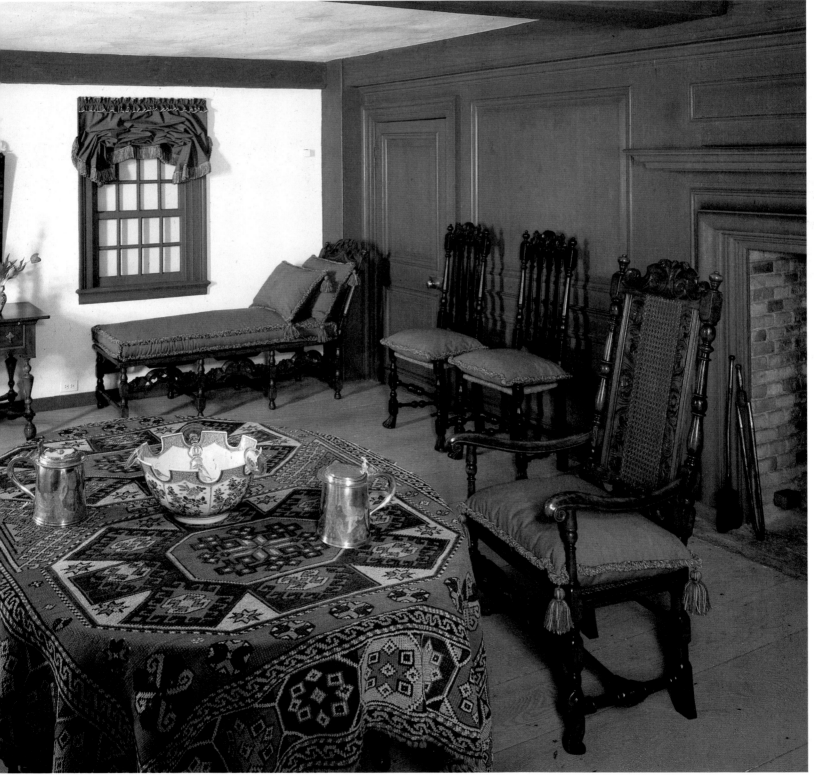

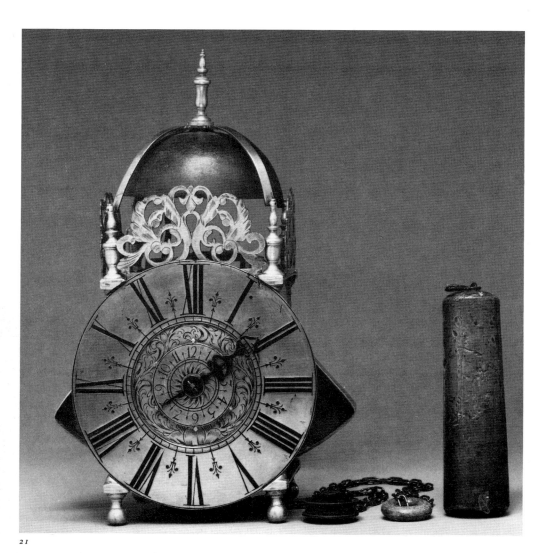

21

**Fig. 21. Lantern clock,** *England, about 1700; brass, height 14½ inches (36.8 cm.). Advertisements in the earliest colonial newspapers stating that old clocks could be "turn'd into Pendelums" indicate that a revolution had occurred in clockmaking: the addition of a pendulum, invented in 1657, made timepieces much more accurate. Even so, the single hand on this example indicates that seventeenth-century Americans didn't feel the need to be punctual to the minute. The high arching top and boldly scrolled fret of the clock case echo other arches and scrolls throughout the room. A triangular projection on either side of the face allows the pendulum to swing freely back and forth. Only wealthy colonists could own imported accessories like this.* Gift of Mrs. J. Insley Blair, 1942 (42.197.11)

**Fig. 22. Wentworth Room,** *Portsmouth, New Hampshire, 1695–1700. Raised, or fielded, panels surrounded by bolection moldings achieve a splendid boldness on the fireplace wall. Among the new forms that appeared during the William and Mary period are the six-legged high chest, the gateleg table, and the easy chair, and all imply a heightened concern with personal comfort and convenience. This was the best chamber, or bedroom—equal to the parlor in elegance and formality—and it would also have contained a richly hung bed. Since the collection does not contain an appropriate bed, the room is furnished to give a feeling for the variety of high-style forms and accessories available to prosperous colonists in about 1700. Among the signs of affluence are*

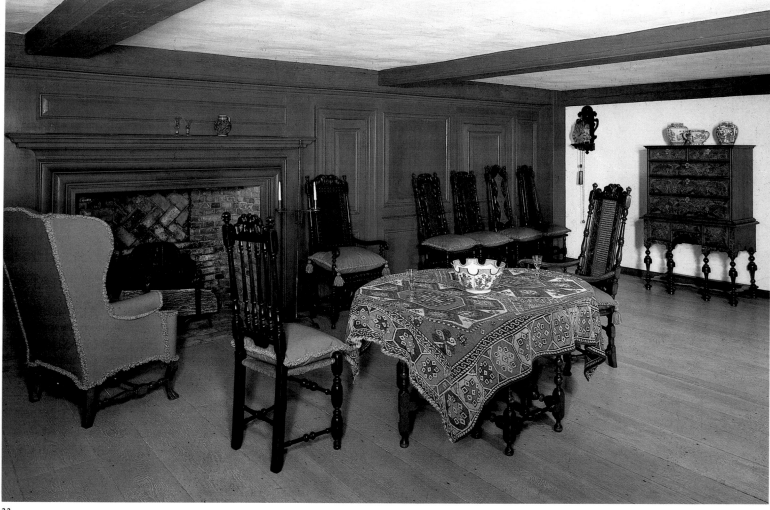

22

*the imported clock, blue and white ceramics, and Turkey carpet—the latter placed proudly on and not under the table. It was many years before such valuable weavings covered the floor.*
Sage Fund, 1926 (26.290)

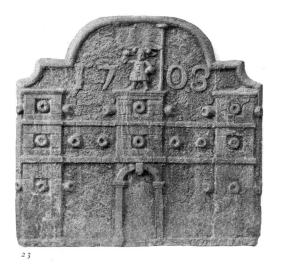

23

deeply and decoratively chamfered, and the ceiling joists are concealed by plaster. The gunstock shape of the two remaining corner posts provides a substantial bearing for the crosswise girts.

The fireplace wall (Fig. 22), like the walls of the stairway, is composed of wide panels with heavy moldings. The fireplace opening is itself framed by a robust bolection (projecting) molding and is capped by a boldly fashioned mantel. Within the fireplace old bricks are laid in a herringbone pattern copied from a surviving example of the period—another instance of the deliberate attention to decorative detail that increasingly characterized American architecture of the early eighteenth century (see also Figs. 25–36).

Double-hung sash windows with molded muntins (narrow wooden strips that divide panes) were introduced into America very late in the seventeenth century and have remained a standard treatment. Here the windows are still relatively small and have no side hangings, but they have been fitted with draw curtains that follow a fashionable design of the period. When they are raised the curtains admit a maximum amount of daylight. Contemporary brass door hardware—box locks fitted with their original knobs and keys—replace the shapely wrought-iron fixtures seen in the Hart Room.

The new fashions of the William and Mary period are appropriately featured in the Wentworth Room. Oak furniture all but disappears and is replaced by lighter forms of walnut, maple, and similar hardwoods. A six-legged maple-veneered highboy is paired with a lowboy, or dressing table, a custom that became more or less conventional at this time and persisted for years. A group of tall-backed William and Mary chairs with cushions of matching fabric and trimming further embody the sense of order and formality that was becoming a ruling principle in domestic arrangements. When they were not needed in other places, chairs were arranged against the wall, a practice that was customary until the nineteenth century.

Throughout the early years of the eighteenth century, Turkey "carpitts" were used as table rather than floor coverings by those who could afford such imported luxuries. The carpet was often laid over a gateleg table, a space-saving form that came into fashion during the William and Mary period. Its two large drop leaves, when raised, are supported by movable legs hinged to swing out from the fixed central frame. Tin-glazed pottery from Holland and England (broadly referred to as delftware) and such other imported items as looking glasses and small brass wall clocks became increasingly common accessories in well-to-do households (Figs. 20 and 21). Chinese porcelains that found their way to the wealthier American homes and silver plate fashioned both at home and abroad also testify to the colonies' growing affluence.

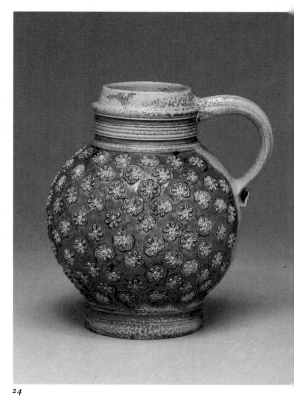

24

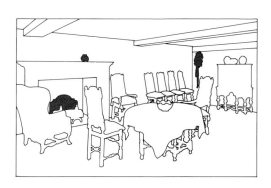

**Figs. 25–36.** *This group of vigorous turnings, moldings, and carvings shows that the same characteristic shapes appear in both the architecture and the decorative arts of the William and Mary period. Stretchers, crest rails, banisters, legs, and feet repeat and reinforce the robust profiles of wall and fireplace moldings. Juxtaposed highlights and shadows, swells and tapers, curves and straight lines, and solids and voids relate these diverse elements even though the formula is different in each case.*

Figs. 25, 26: Rogers Fund, 1926 (26.290); Figs. 27, 28: Gift of Mrs. Screven Lorillard, 1952 (52.195.8); Figs. 29, 30: Gift of Mrs. Russell Sage, 1909 (10.125.678); Figs. 31, 32: Sage Fund, 1926 (26.290); Figs. 33, 34: Gift of Mrs. Russell Sage, 1909 (10.125.133); Figs. 35, 36: Gift of Mrs. Russell Sage, 1909 (10.125.704)

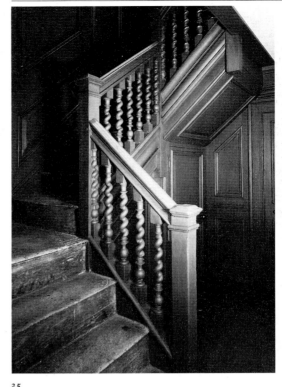

25

**Fig. 25. Wentworth Stair,** *Portsmouth, New Hampshire, 1695–1700. Twist balusters and boldly molded paneled walls enrich this small hallway. Before the advent of the center hall, stair entries like this were squeezed between the massive center chimney and the front door. These are the earliest twist-turned balusters known in New England.*

Rogers Fund, 1926 (26.290)

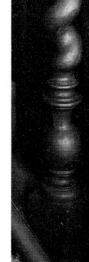

26

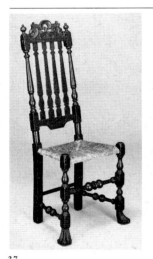

27

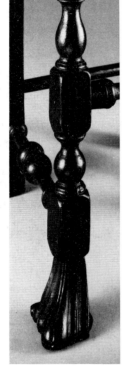

28

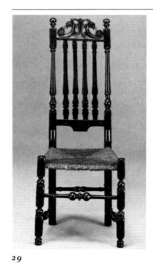

29

30

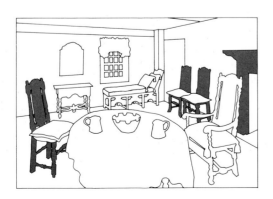

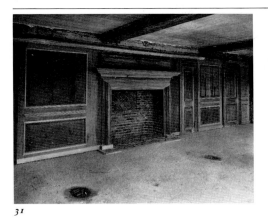

31

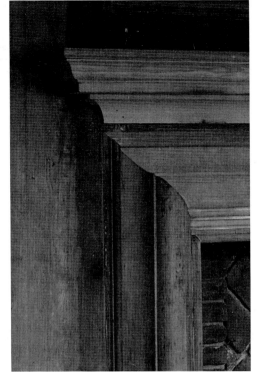

32

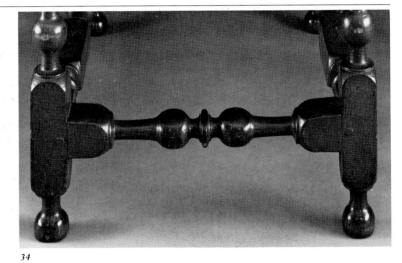

33

34

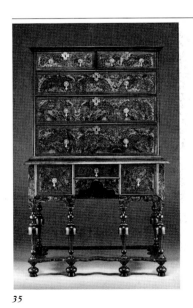

35

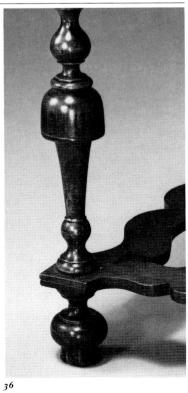

36

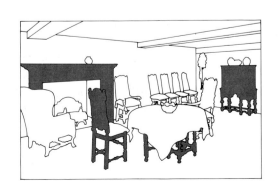

# Hewlett Room

**Fig. 37. Hewlett Room,** Woodbury, Long Island, New York, 1740–60.
The symmetry and careful proportions of classical architecture, where the inspiration for this fireplace wall ultimately lies, are not to be found here. Whimsical pilasters and an entablature that have become merely ornamental are what remain. The exaggerated moldings and cornice that top the pilasters and are a major feature of the wall are reminiscent of the pronounced cornices of Dutch *kasten,* or cupboards. The brilliant prussian blue of the paneling is the color originally used in this room, and an equally lively red highlights the interior of the built-in shell cupboard. Dutch tiles decorated with biblical scenes surround the fireplace opening; although there is no evidence that such tiles were originally used in this room, they did decorate many eighteenth-century fireplaces. Besides being decorative, the tiles could be used to illustrate stories to make the Bible come vividly alive in children's minds. The leather cradle is attributed to New York; the greater mid-Atlantic region is represented by the Pennsylvania slat-back armchair—a sophisticated Philadelphia version of an inexpensive everyday chair (see also Fig. 39).

Gift of Mrs. Robert W. de Forest, 1910 (10.183)

As the seventeenth century waned, more and more new elements were introduced into architecture. Renaissance influence found its earliest significant expression in America in the better houses then being built. Although most of them have disappeared or been altered beyond recognition, it was these houses, with their emphasis on symmetry and formal order, their uses of classical and baroque motifs, and their interior arrangements, that introduced the elements of style and comfort that prevailed throughout the remainder of the colonial period.

A tentative approach to such refinements is apparent in the Wentworth Room. Interiors from the mid-eighteenth century illustrate how the new modes were interpreted in different areas of the New England and New York countryside. More sophisticated developments are displayed in the late-colonial period rooms.

In the interior from the Metcalf Bowler house, built near Newport, Rhode Island, about 1763, we meet for the first time in the Wing features that recall, modestly but pleasantly, the formal practices of the Georgian architecture of England. These had been introduced into the colonies by English building and architectural manuals—manuals that were adapted from Renaissance publications that were in turn interpretations of classical designs of antiquity. Throughout most of the eighteenth century this classical spirit thrice removed was a persistent influence on American architecture, both exterior and interior, and this is evident in all the rest of the colonial rooms in the Wing.

For example, the woodwork of a room salvaged from the John Hewlett house, built at Woodbury, Long Island, about 1740–60 (Fig. 38), reflects the influence of English manuals. Fluted pilasters carried up into projections of the cornice represent in provincial fashion a classical entablature although, to be sure, it is not clearly understood (Fig. 37). In the Hart Room the structural needs of the house, frankly stated, made the "style." In this case the applied designs largely obscure the underlying framework of the house. The abbreviated pilasters over the fireplace, for example, rest on nothing and do not even suggest structural supports.

Dutch tiles painted under the glaze with scriptural subjects surround the fireplace opening (Fig. 44). Such decorative borders were advertised for sale in colonial newspapers from the early days of the eighteenth century. The fireplace is flanked by a shell-carved "beaufett," or cupboard, for the display of pottery, glassware, and other useful and decorative accessories. The room is painted a bright blue that painstaking analysis indicates was its original color. In 1748 the visiting Swedish naturalist Peter Kalm noted that blue was a usual interior-wall color in New York. Blue and white resist-dyed fabric was apparently widely used in and about New York for bed and window hangings and upholstery (Fig. 42).

A painted cupboard, or *kas,* from the New York area is a delightful reminder of the huge Dutch prototypes whose expensive woods and ornate carvings are here simulated by grisaille decoration painted on the pine carcass (Figs. 43 and 45). Such representations of fruit and vegetable forms could be considered the earliest American still-life painting.

A chair also characteristic of the New York area from Long Island to Albany

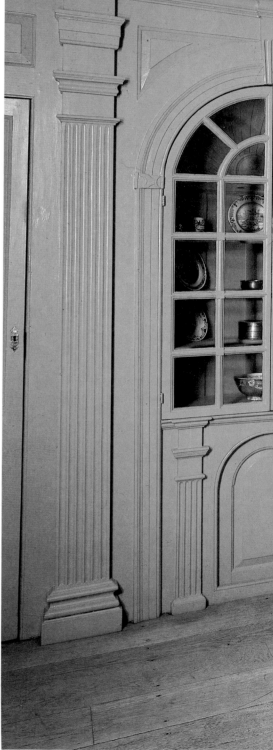

37

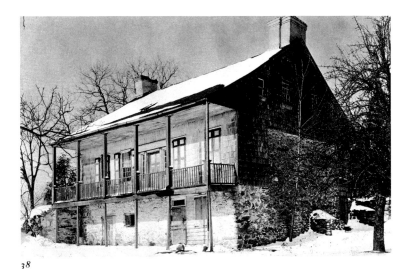

**Fig. 38. House built by John Hewlett** of Woodbury, Long Island, New York, 1740–60. Although Hewlett was English, his Dutch neighbors' building and furnishing styles were reflected in his home. The long low lines of the house, the sweeping roof line, and the stone chimney are characteristic of "Dutch colonial" architecture. The fireplace wall in the Museum's Hewlett Room was probably taken from one of the rooms on either side of the front door.

38

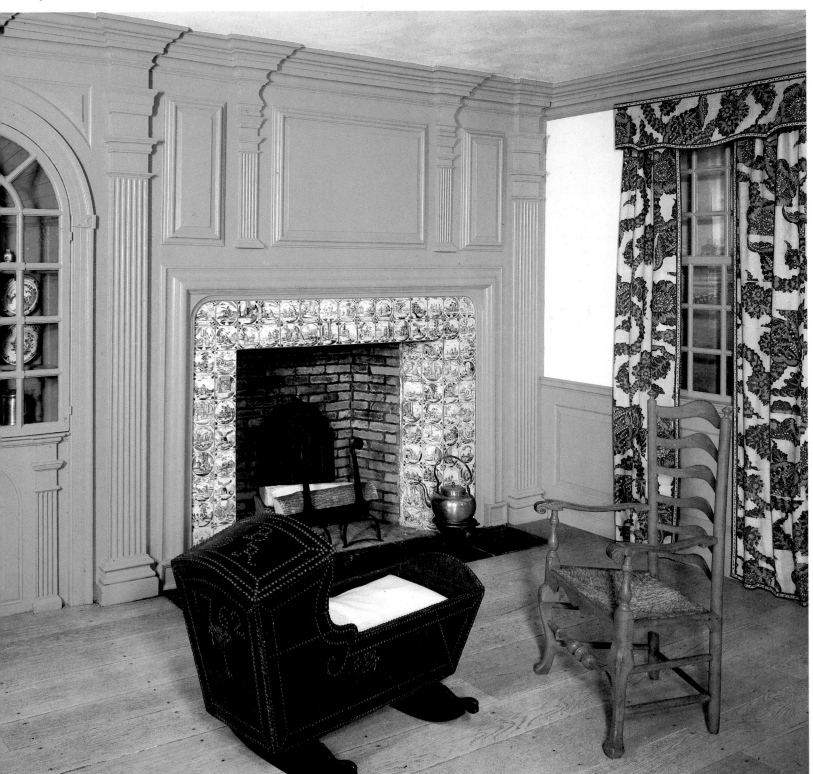

**Figs. 39–41. Chairs** from, left to right, *Pennsylvania or New Jersey, New York, and New England, 1730–80; maple, painted, height 48¾ inches (123.8 cm.); maple, painted, height 40¾ inches (103.5 cm.); and maple, ash, height 41½ inches (105.4 cm.).* Everywhere in the colonies seats that could be made quickly and bought cheaply were in demand, and chairmakers responded with different versions that have become characteristic of their regions. The Delaware River valley turned out a slat-back chair whose most characteristic features are graceful slats that curve upward at both top and bottom, rear stiles that taper slightly from foot to finial, prominent turned front stretchers, and onion-like turned finials and front feet. Hudson River valley makers produced a broad-splatted, chubby-legged chair with pad feet that rest on disks; this type was also popular in New Jersey, on Long Island, and in Connecticut, where it was referred to as a "York" chair because people associated it with New York. New Englanders, like New Yorkers, combined William and Mary and Queen Anne features in their inexpensive chairs. This example differs from its York cousin in having a serpentine curved back, a narrower splat, and block-and-vase turned front legs.

Purchase, Virginia Groomes Gift, in memory of Mary W. Groomes, 1975 (1975.310); Rogers Fund, 1933 (33.121.1); Gift of Mrs. Russell Sage, 1909 (10.125.263)

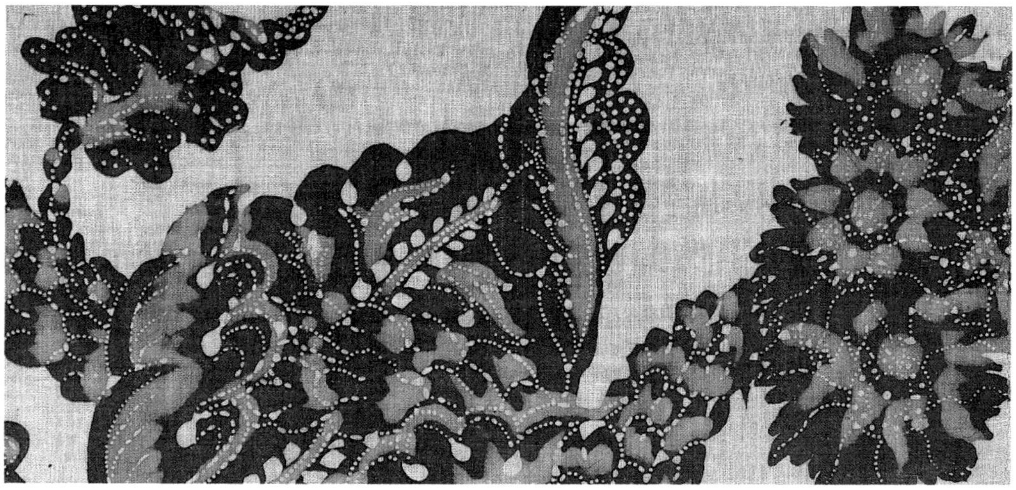

42

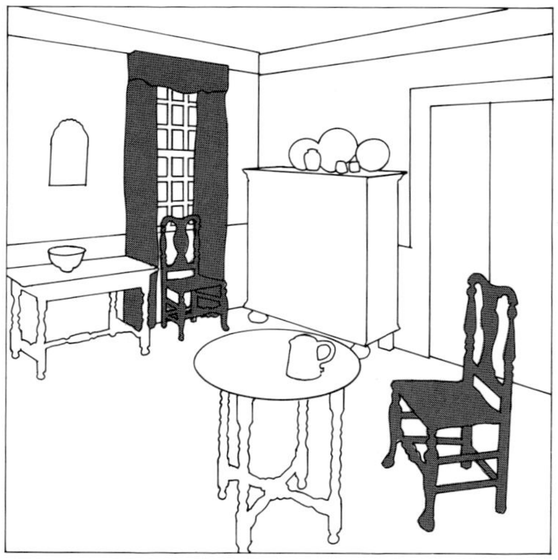

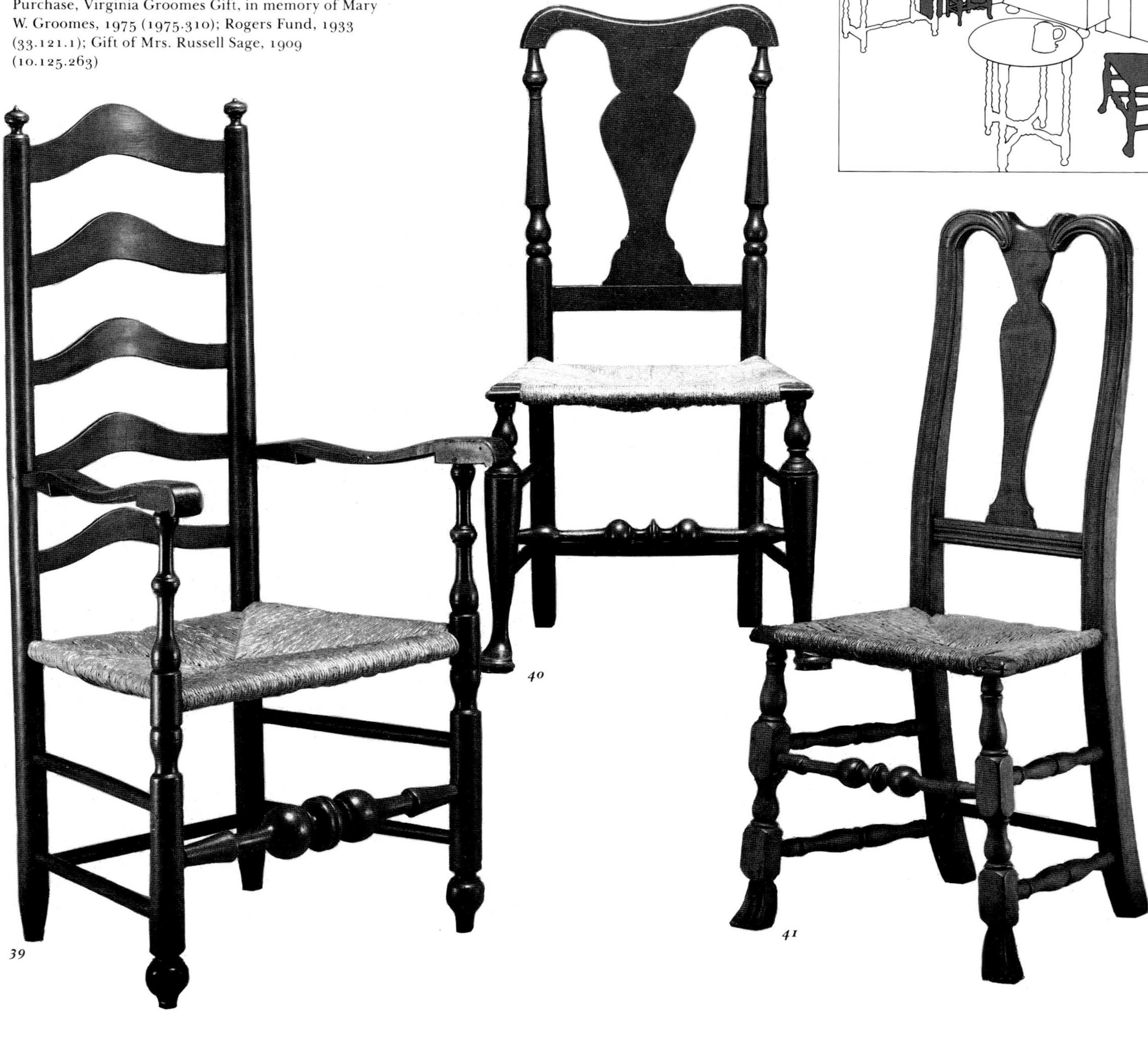

39

40

41

**Fig. 42. Hewlett Room curtains,** *detail, last half eighteenth century; cotton(?). Blue and white resist fabric like this was very popular in eighteenth-century New York and surrounding areas, but its origin is a mystery. Such fabric does not seem to have been used in England or on the Continent, and it is therefore tempting to believe that it is of American manufacture. This would be a mistake, however, for in our present state of knowledge, says scholar Florence Montgomery, ". . . it seems doubtful that American [textile] printers could have produced these patterns. . . ."*

**Fig. 43. Hewlett Room,** *Woodbury, Long Island, New York, 1740–60. In seventeenth-century New York the great two-doored kas was unquestionably the most important furniture form, as the press or court cupboard was in New England. The majority of kasten were made of joined hardwoods, but there is a fascinating group of eight softwood examples constructed more simply of boards nailed together and decorated with grisaille designs (painted in shades of gray). Two of these are in the Museum's collection, and the one shown here descended in the Hewlett family. In fact, it is said to have come from the same house as the fireplace wall. Somewhere along the way this* kas *seems to have lost its cornice and its original feet, which were simply extensions of the side boards. It was usual to*

*make* kasten *in three sections so that they could be taken apart and moved easily. The table between the windows and the chairs with wide vase-shaped splats were also made in New York.*
Gift of Mrs. Robert W. de Forest, 1910 (10.183)

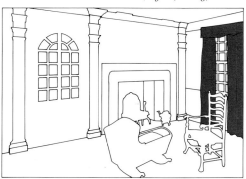

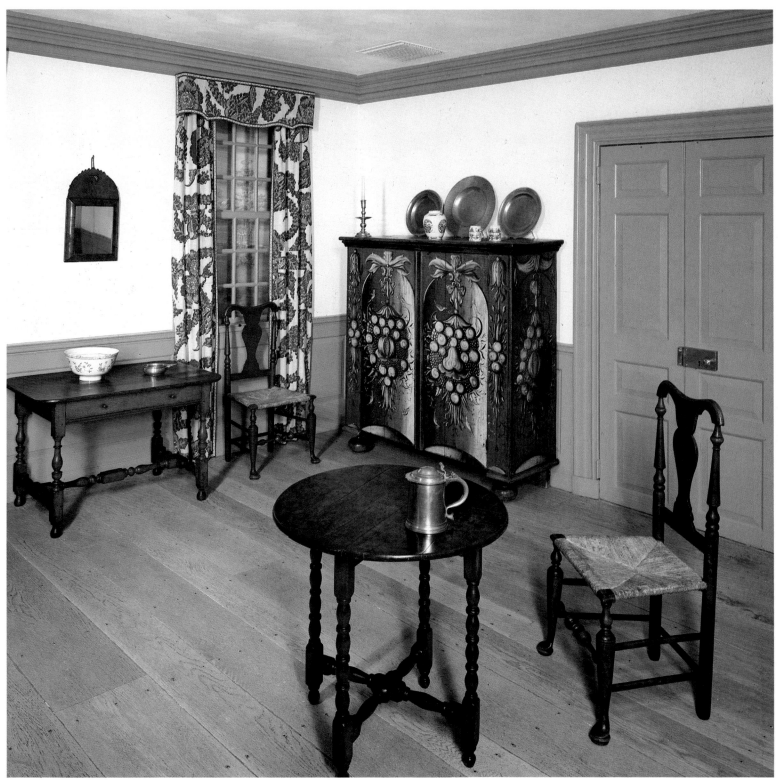

**Fig. 44. Tiles,** *Holland, 1700–50; tin-glazed earthenware, 6 by 6 inches (15.2 by 15.2 cm.). Handpainted delft tiles from Holland and England were advertised regularly in American newspapers from about 1720 to the 1770s. In 1738, for example, Captain Stephen Richards of Boston advertised "All sorts of Dutch Tyles viz, Scripture (round and square), Landskips of divers sorts, Sea Monsters, Horsemen, Soldiers, Diamond, &c." According to Ivor Noël Hume, archeologist at Colonial Williamsburg, the tin-glazed tiles we call "delft" were produced in a number of Dutch cities besides Delft and by Dutch potters working in England, making it very hard to say positively just where a given tile was made. It is possible to say that, although few*

*fireplaces survive with their original tiles intact, many eighteenth-century parlors were brightened by these ornamental and sometimes didactic ceramics. They came in a variety of colors, as indicated by Robert Crommelin's advertisement, "Plain white and Sculpture Tiles, handsome blue and white flower'd Tiles" and "Green and Yellow Hearth Tiles."*

Gift of Mrs. Frederick Allien, in memory of her mother, Julia Taber Martin, 1924 (24.122.1–102)

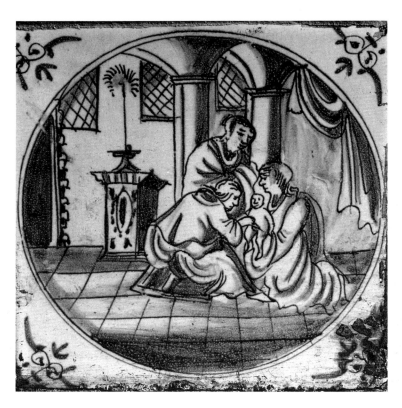

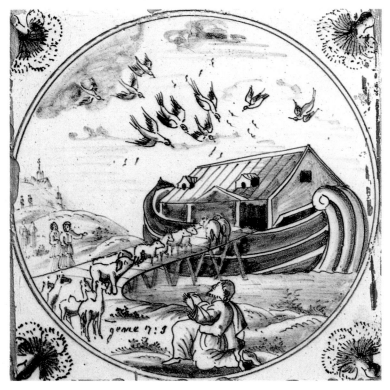

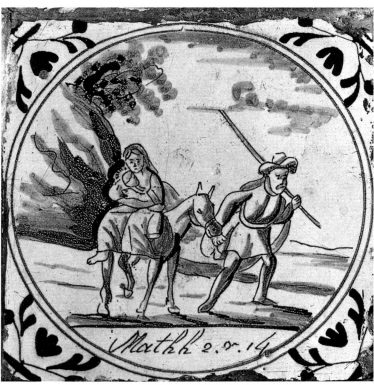

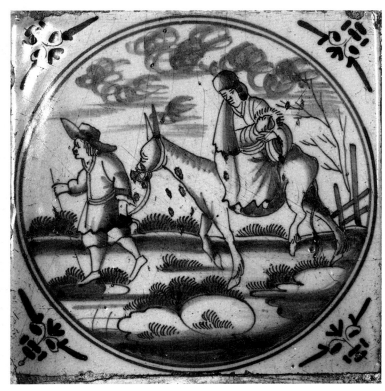

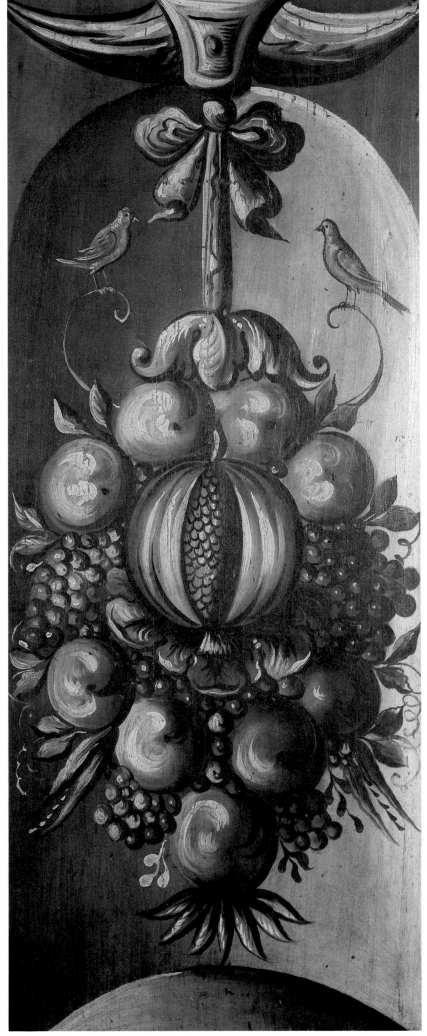

**Fig. 45. Kas,** *detail, New York region, 1690–1720; tulip poplar and oak with grisaille decoration. The* trompe l'oeil *painting on this* kas *door is more three-dimensional than that of the* kas *in the Hewlett Room. Following a Dutch tradition of furniture making for well-to-do rural and middle-class urban customers, these* kasten *are decorated with painted still lifes composed of fruit, flowers, and foliage to imitate the carved and inlaid patterns of ornate Dutch and Flemish cupboards (see also Fig. 43). The European practice, which was probably observed in the colonies as well, was to have a woodworker construct the piece and a painter who specialized in such work decorate it.*
Rogers Fund, 1909 (09.175)

ingenuously blends features of various early styles (see also Fig. 40). Such chairs were commonly painted black or brownish red. Their solid back splats and pad feet reflect Queen Anne fashions, whereas their straight stiles, boldly turned front stretchers, and rush seats continue traditions of an earlier period. In New England a related type combines Queen Anne and William and Mary features somewhat differently (see Fig. 41). Local craftsmen turned out such engagingly simple forms until the early 1800s. Another type of regional chair, this one identified with the neighborhood of the Delaware River valley in nearby New Jersey and Pennsylvania, has a tall back with arched slats arranged in graduated sizes (see also Fig. 39).

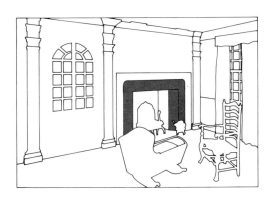

45

# The Late Colonial Period, 1730–90

**Fig. 46. Design for a doorway** *from William Salmon's* Palladio Londinensis. *The Italian Renaissance architect Andrea Palladio, whose ideas underlay the English Georgian style, never published a design showing a broken-scroll pediment like this one. That was a baroque embellishment supplied by English architects, and one very much in evidence in colonial America.*

Gift of W. Gedney Beatty, 1941 (41.100.74)

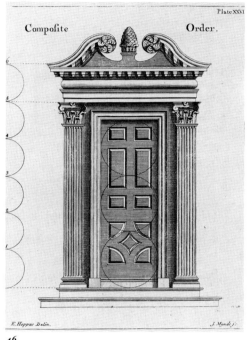

46

**Fig. 47. Doorway,** *from the Daniel Fowler house, Westfield, Massachusetts, about 1762; pine, painted. The architecture of Connecticut, like its furniture, often expresses the quirky individuality of the inhabitants of that state. Here, in what was originally an English Georgian design, the outlines and proportions are still more or less in place, but liberties have been taken with the decoration. Instead of the sedate fluting we expect on an applied pilaster, we find a wavy-leafed vine; where we look for a Corinthian capital, we find stylized leaves. Although the doorway in the Salmon design is the prototype for the Westfield door, its builder had probably never seen it. He was working from a vague knowledge of current styles, and even though he and his patron clearly wanted to be up-to-date, the builder was hampered by outdated tools and a strong conservative streak. He was competent and artistically gifted, however, and in the end he produced a delightful expression of his own and his neighbors' architectural ideals. Doors like this are characteristic of the Connecticut River valley and can be seen in that region from Deerfield to Hartford—the same area in which distinctively carved Hadley chests were made.*

Rogers Fund, 1916 (16.147)

A superb example of the woodwork peculiar to the Connecticut River valley, a pedimented doorway from Westfield, Massachusetts, demonstrates how effectively and distinctively craftsmen of that region could translate the stately language of English Georgian architecture into a lively vernacular (Fig. 47). Doorways of generally similar design were—and still are—a familiar sight up and down the valley.

The wooden frame of the Westfield doorway is carved and painted to simulate cut stone, but what were the fluted Corinthian pilasters of a Georgian model have been converted into a spirited exercise in flat carving. The outlines of the entire doorway are duplicated in miniature on the base of each pilaster in an ingenuous provincial pattern.

The primary source of the design for the Westfield doorway was probably an engraved plate in the architectural manual *Palladio Londinensis: or The London Art of Building*, published by the Englishman William Salmon in 1734 (Fig. 46). More than fourscore different English architectural manuals were known in America before the Revolution and in their various forms and editions served as indispensable guides to colonial builders. It is safe to say that every house and public structure of any pretension built in America in the eighteenth century owed some debt to one or another of these publications. Even when he was in the field leading the colonial troops in the cause of political independence from Britain, Washington carefully followed building developments at Mount Vernon, referring his workmen to English manuals for guidance. Although most such books used a

common grammar, so to speak, their designs were realized in different regional accents. Diverse climatic conditions and available building materials called for modifications of the English models. For example, most of the designs for exterior architecture in the English manuals were intended as guides to the stonemason; in America, where wooden construction was prevalent in many areas, the designs were perforce executed somewhat differently by carpenters and wood-carvers. This is conspicuously true in the case of the Westfield doorway.

Wherever such stylish architectural-guide features were employed, the emphasis was on symmetry and formal order and on a use of classic motifs and details. The designs are followed more literally and executed with better understanding of the principles involved than they had been in buildings of the early colonial period or in rural versions that, like the Westfield doorway, were far removed from the source of the design.

Interiors were now formally treated as well, for pattern books provided models that were sometimes scrupulously copied, sometimes adapted to the needs or tastes of a builder or his client. All this concerned more than mere formality of planning and designing, however: it involved new concepts of living in which comfort, convenience, and privacy played growing roles. The multiplication of rooms in larger houses led to increased specialization in domestic arrangements—to separate rooms for cooking, dining, entertaining, sleeping, and so forth. Relieved of kitchen duties, fireplaces became both more efficient and decorative.

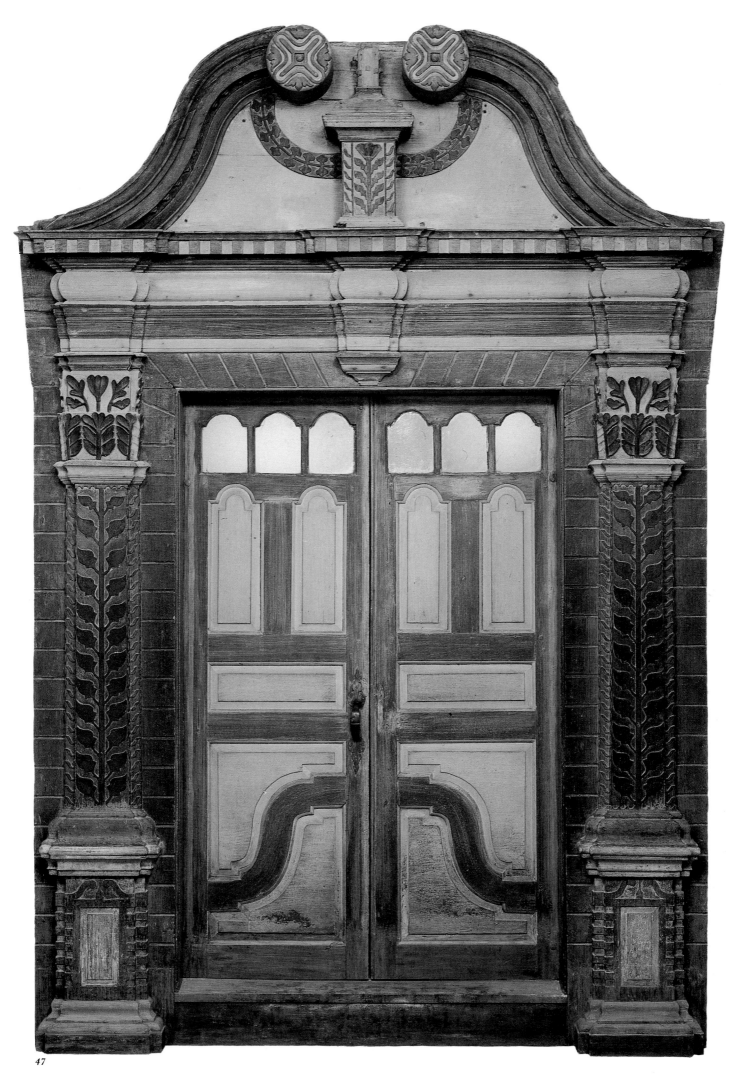

47

# Almodington Room

**Fig. 48. Almodington Room,** Somerset County, Maryland, 1730–60. Though taken from a country gentleman's seat rather than from a fashionable urban interior, these fully paneled walls provide a sympathetic setting for the high-style Boston furniture that fills the room.

The furnishings are of a type characteristic of a well-to-do Massachusetts resident's bedroom of the late colonial period. The kneehole bureau table between the windows served as a dressing table—and in New England this form seems to have been preferred over the lowboy popular in Philadelphia. The three matching side chairs seen here are part of a larger set, which would usually have been lined up against the walls—an indication that bedrooms were used for entertaining as well as for sleeping. Easy chairs, nearly always placed in the bedroom rather than in the parlor, continued to be reserved for the infirm and elderly. Many of them were originally fitted with chamber pots, though today it is rare to find one that retains this fixture.

Venetian blinds may seem surprising in an eighteenth-century interior, but they were advertised in Paris as early as 1757. Ten years later, a Philadelphia upholsterer advertised ". . . the newest invented Venetian sun blinds for windows . . . stained to any color, moves to any position . . . and is the greatest preserver of furniture of anything of the kind ever invented."

Rogers Fund, 1918 (18.99.1)

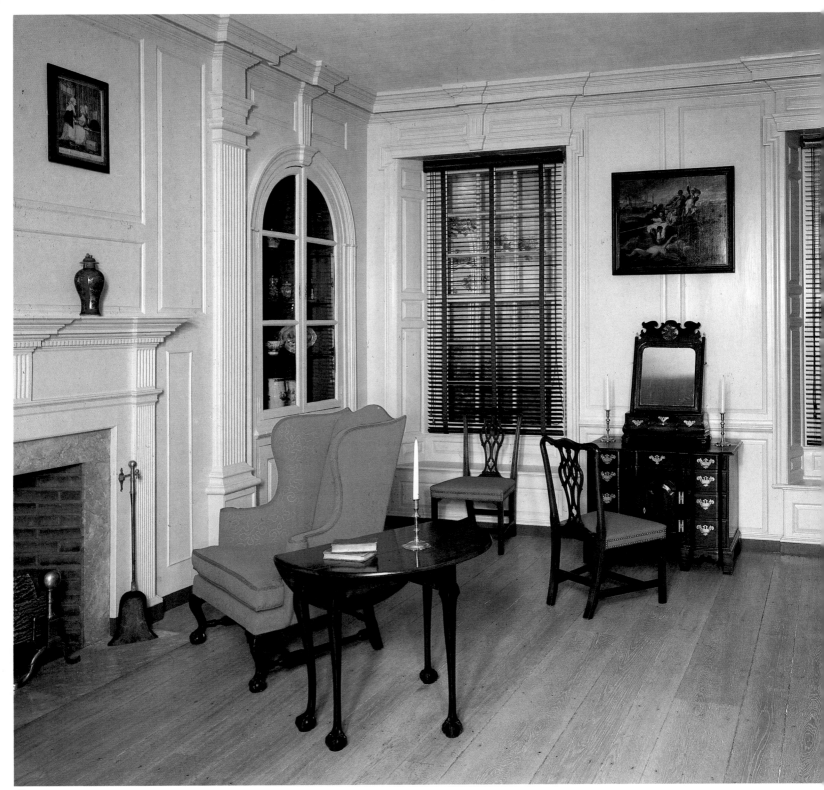

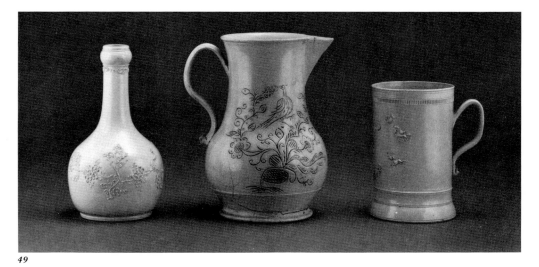

*Fig. 49. Group of salt-glazed stoneware, England, 1730–60.* Left to right: *bottle, height 8¾ inches (22.2 cm.); pitcher, height 9½ inches (24.1 cm.); mug, height 6⅝ inches (16.8 cm.). White salt-glazed stonewares made in molds and variously ornamented with blue-filled incised motifs ("scratch blue") and applied molded designs proved very popular in England and the colonies during the second third of the eighteenth century. They rivaled delft, according to expert Ivor Noël Hume, "as the best selling general purpose tableware" during that period.*
Gift of Mrs. Russell S. Carter, 1944 (44.110.2) and
Gift of Mrs. Russell S. Carter, 1946 (46.64.1, 46.64.13)

49

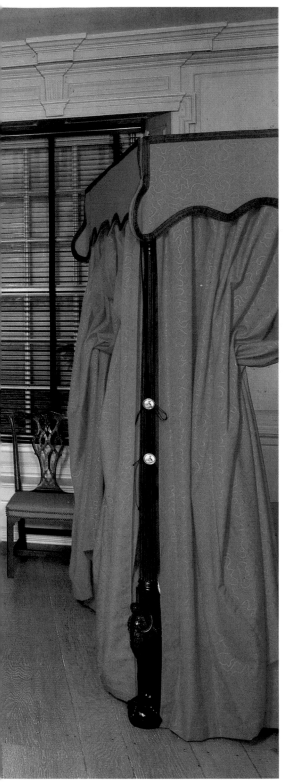

Ｎew England furniture was often shipped to the southern colonies, and examples of such northern exports have been installed in a room taken from a brick house known as Almodington in Somerset County, Maryland (Fig. 48). The walls of this interior, divided horizontally by a heavy chair rail, are paneled from floor to ceiling in a manner that was gradually going out of fashion by the middle of the eighteenth century. The present mantelpiece replaced an earlier one about 1814. The shell-top cupboards on either side of the fireplace might have contained Delft from Holland, salt-glazed wares from England, and possibly China Trade porcelains, all of which added decorative emphasis to many rooms of the time and, to be sure, also saw active use at dining and tea tables (Fig. 49). A painting on the wall, attributed to Copley, could be his original oil sketch for *Brook Watson and the Shark* (Fig. 52). This is the canvas that, when shown at the Royal Academy in London shortly after Copley had taken up his permanent residence abroad, was hailed as among the "first performances" of that prestigious exhibition.

The room is furnished as a gentleman's bedroom. The most conspicuous piece of furniture in it is a Boston-made four-posted bedstead with cabriole legs on the footposts that have detachable carved kneecaps and that terminate in boldly shaped claw-and-ball feet (Fig. 51). The bed hangings and the upholstery on an attendant easy chair and a suite of side chairs—also made in Boston—are all cut from the same stout cloth, a raspberry red wool moreen embossed in a vermicelli pattern (so named because it resembles a formal arrangement of strands of thin spaghetti). Both

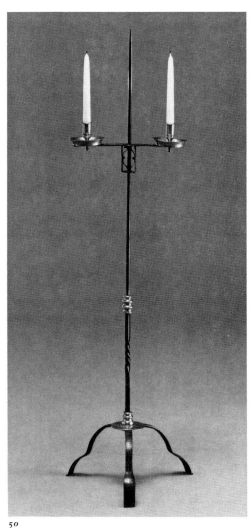

50

*Fig. 50. Candlestand,* inscribed by Benjamin Gerrish (about 1686–1750), Boston, about 1735; iron and brass, height 49¼ inches (125.7 cm.). *Delicate wrought-iron standing candle holders are rare, and signed examples are even rarer. This and one other stand, dated 1736, are signed by Benjamin Gerrish, gunsmith and brazier of Cambridge and Boston. The two candles held by this stand produced lavish illumination by eighteenth-century standards, when many households depended on the flickering flames of the fire to light the room.*
Rogers Fund, 1920 (20.110)

**Fig. 51. Bedstead,** *detail, Massachusetts, 1760–90; mahogany, height 89 inches (226.1 cm.). One of the surest signs of wealth in the eighteenth century was an impressive bed. The fluted footposts and carved legs and feet of this example are admirable, and the richly carved detachable kneecaps, added to conceal the bolts that join the side and foot rails, are particularly rare. The bedstead is one of a very small group of Massachusetts examples with such kneecaps. Their elegance is indisputable, but their precise origin is as yet unknown. However, the sharply raked side talons of the claw that grasps the ball foot is a feature that is associated with the finest furniture produced in eastern Massachusetts.*
Gift of Mrs. Russell Sage, 1909 (10.125.336)

**Fig. 52. Brook Watson and the Shark,** *by John Singleton Copley (1738–1815), 1782; oil on canvas, 24⅞ by 30⅛ inches (63.2 by 76.5 cm.). Most eighteenth-century American paintings are portraits, not historical scenes like this. The subject, Brook Watson being attacked by a shark in Havana harbor, was based on an actual occurrence. Watson lost part of one leg to the shark, and is shown being rescued just in time to prevent loss of the other leg. The painting is undeniably dramatic, but is unusual for its time in depicting a scene that, though vivid, has no marked historical importance.*
Gift of Mrs. Gordon Dexter, 1942 (42.71.1)

the pattern and the color are exact reproductions of eighteenth-century samples. Contemporary references to "the red room" or "the green room" indicate that as often as not a single fabric, or hue at least, served throughout a room, as it does here. Appropriately, a dressing table and a dressing glass stand between the windows (Fig. 53). A highboy or a chest-on-chest like the one against the wall opposite these windows served for the storage of wearing apparel, linens, and so forth in a day when closets were not yet common conveniences.

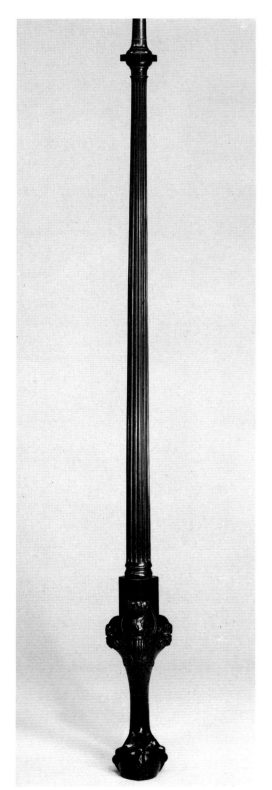

51

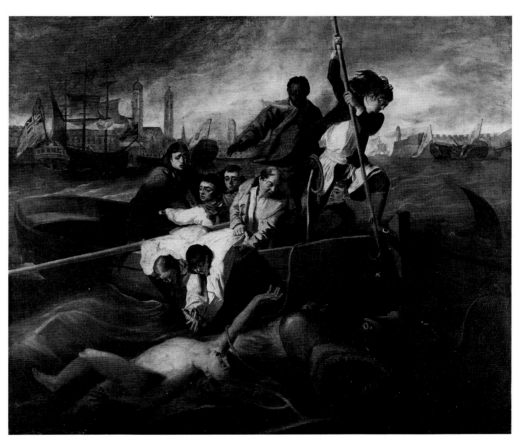

52

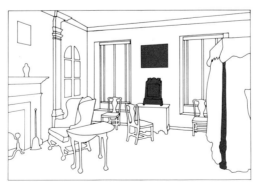

**Fig. 53. Dressing glass with drawers,** *Boston, 1760–90; mahogany, white pine, height 32½ inches (82.6 cm.). In an era before "the modern bureau with its expansive glass, capable of reflecting everything in the room except the hang of one's nether garments" had come into prominence, this sort of small standing mirror, with or without drawers, provided a convenient glass to use while making up. Meant to sit atop a dressing table as it does here, this glass incorporates a feature characteristic of a small group of the very highest-style Boston pieces—the bombé base. For reasons that are still unknown, the bombé, or kettle-shaped, form caught on in Boston and its immediate environment and provided a surprisingly baroque note in an otherwise staid group of case pieces. Its use in a dressing box is very rare.*
Bequest of Cecile L. Mayer, 1962 (62.171.14)

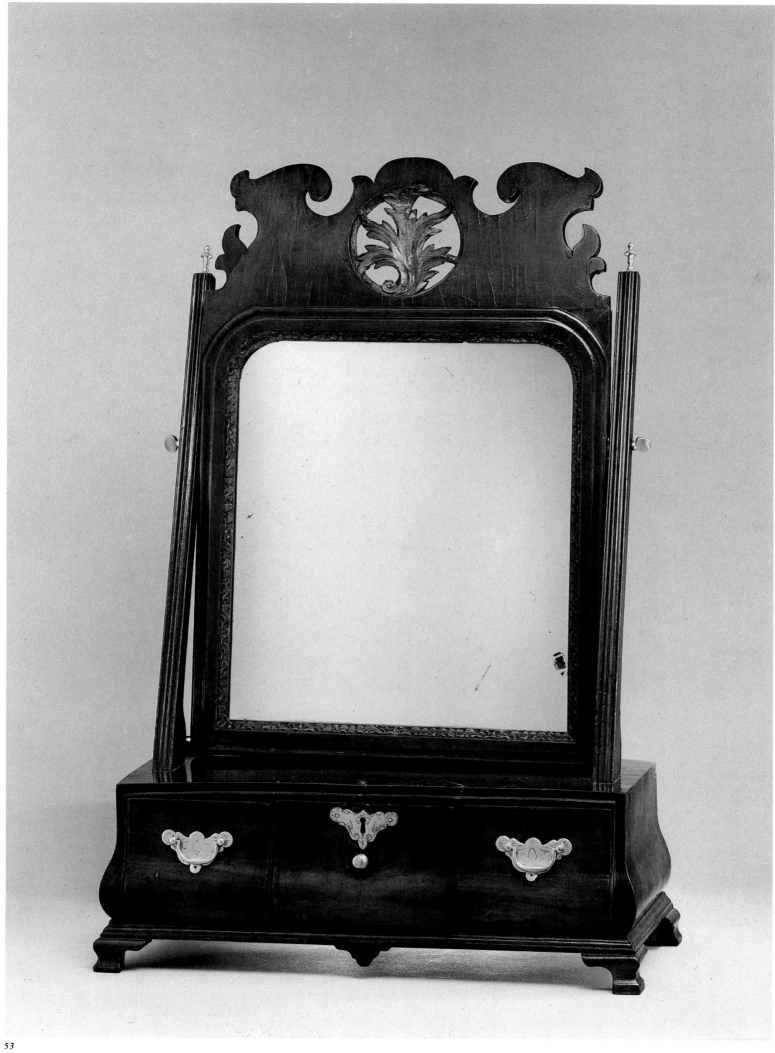

53

# Powel Room

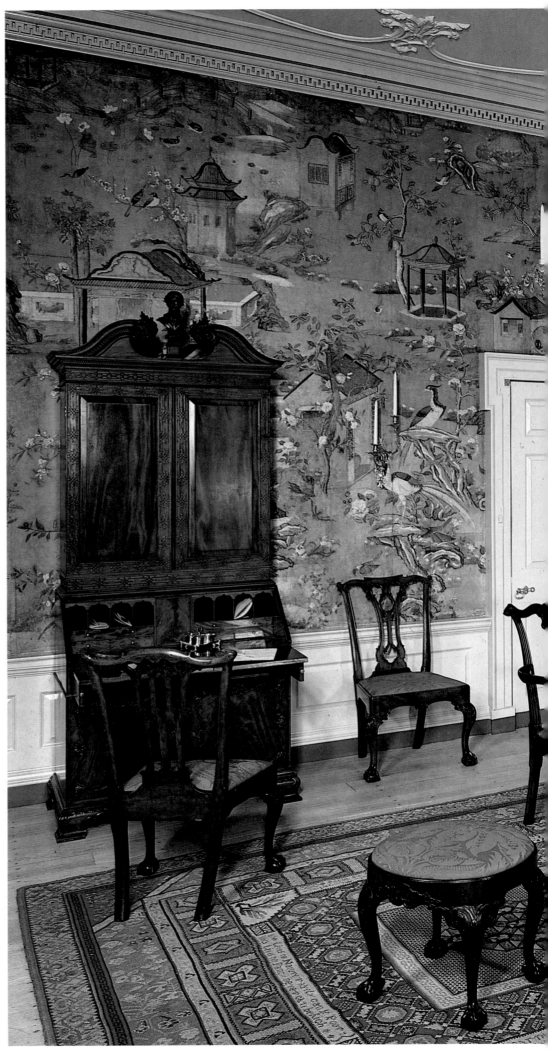

A parlor from a house built in Philadelphia about 1765 and owned by Samuel Powel, the last colonial mayor of that city, incorporates a rich display of scrupulously executed ornament drawn from contemporary English pattern books (Fig. 54). These highly decorative designs represent a culmination of the advanced stylistic trends of the late colonial period. Powel had traveled widely and was abreast of the latest fashions from abroad. He had made the grand tour of Europe, during the course of which he was presented to George III and to the king of Sardinia. In Rome he had numerous conversations with the duke of York and on his journey back from Italy he paid a visit to Voltaire.

Powel was also wealthy enough to command the finest craftsmanship in

**Fig. 54. Powel Room,** *Philadelphia; built 1765–66, remodeled 1769–71. The original use of the Museum's room—one of the two finest in the Powel house—is not known. It is seen here furnished as a parlor, with the numerous chairs and tables indicated as parlor furniture by eighteenth-century wills and inventories. The room contains some of the finest surviving carved woodwork of the late colonial period but, not content with the beautiful chimney breast and cornice, the curators who installed this room in the 1920s copied the elaborate ceiling design of the ballroom, the room originally next to this one on the second floor of the Powel house. To add further richness, they hung the walls with sumptuous hand-painted Chinese wallpaper, which is of the period but was not originally on these walls. Perhaps, knowing of the brilliant social events that took place in the Powel rooms, the curators were striving to create surroundings worthy of such luminaries as George Washington, who was a frequent visitor. Their additions have been retained by the current staff as a tribute to the taste and vision of collectors and scholars of the twenties, for they have had an enduring effect on later generations' views of the American past.*
Rogers Fund, 1918 (18.87.1–4)

54

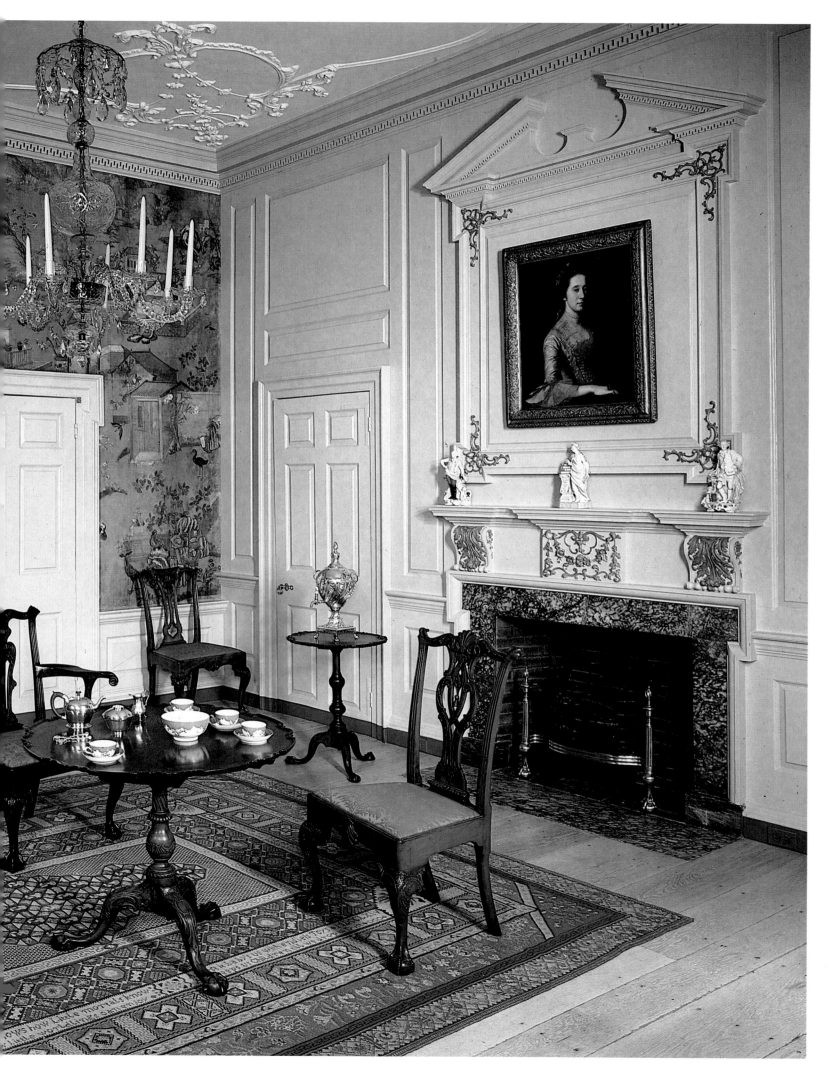

**Fig. 55. Powel house,** 244 South Third Street, Philadelphia; built 1765–66. The Museum's Powel Room came from the rear of the second floor of this elegant town house at a time when it was dilapidated and deteriorating; happily, the house was rescued and restored in the 1930s, and is now open to the public. Its second owner was well-connected and wealthy Samuel Powel, who was mayor of Philadelphia during the years just before and just after the Revolution. Mr. and Mrs. Powel's lavish hospitality was extended to all eminent Philadelphians and visitors. John Adams, writing of a visit to the Powels, noted that he "Drank madeira at a great rate," and lamented indulging as well in "A most sinfull Feast again! . . . Curds and Creams, Jellies, Sweet

meats of various sorts, 20 sorts of Tarts, fools, Trifles, floating Islands, whipped Sillabubs &c. &c." The Powels' paintings and furnishings were certainly as elegant as their refreshments—a situation that has been recreated in the Museum's room.

**Fig. 56. Coal grate,** probably North America, about 1760; brass, iron, height 26 inches (66 cm.). The transition from wood to coal was slow in America, where there were abundant wood supplies nearly everywhere except in the big cities. It was thus in such metropolises as New York and Philadelphia that coal—and coal grates—were in demand. This example, thought to be American rather than English and therefore unique, sets a fluted tapering column on claw-and-ball feet and tops it with urn-and-flame finials, both familiar elements of American Chippendale furniture. The resultant form is related to that of andirons.
Rogers Fund, 1938 (38.122)

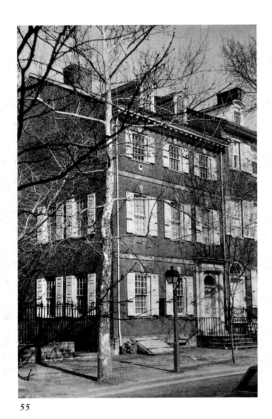

55

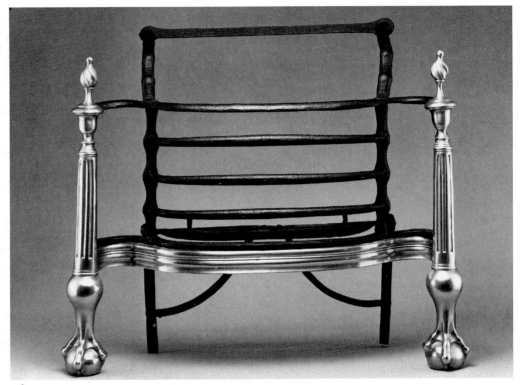

56

furbishing his elegant town house. The carved and molded decoration of the wood- and plasterwork are masterly interpretations of the style associated with Chippendale's adaptations of French rococo designs. The plaster relief of the ceiling, in a pattern of swags, flowers, musical trophies, and pendent masks in the French manner, is a cast taken from the ceiling of an adjoining room in the same house.

By now the fireplace, which in the earliest days of colonization had been in effect a hole cut in the fabric of the house for utility's sake, had become the most formally featured element of interior architecture. It was indeed the focus of a principal room, and in this age of highly stylized design it and what is termed chimney furniture were treated with full regard for their decorative quality and interest. The carving on the

overmantel resembles that which distinguishes fine Philadelphia furniture of the period. English statuettes on the mantelpiece include a fine one of John Wilkes, whose outspoken sympathy in the British Parliament for the American cause won him the gratitude of colonial patriots (Fig. 59).

Wilkes was far from being the only Englishman who supported the colonists in their grievances during the years immediately preceding the Revolution—and during the war itself. The people of the mother country were worried enough about their own liberties at that time (see Fig. 420). When Parliament was obliged to repeal the odious Stamp Act in 1766, one London artist made a small fortune satirizing the defeat of Parliament in a cartoon that was sold for sixpence and that was pirated in at least a half-dozen versions by rival

printsellers. (The original artist was Benjamin Wilson, whose portrait of Franklin was taken from his home as booty by Major André when the British evacuated Philadelphia, carried back to England, and finally returned—to the White House—in 1906.)

Within the overmantel hangs Charles Willson Peale's portrait of Mrs. Thomas Harwood of Maryland, probably completed about 1771. One authority has written that this painting is "the most vivid and charming of Peale's portraits of women, a personification of feminine grace and dignity." (For the fascinating story of Peale's many-sided career, see p. 295.)

Three walls of the room are covered with Chinese wallpaper that originally hung in another house of the same period. Such exotic wall coverings enjoyed a vogue among the fashionable gentry of the time. Robert Morris, Powel's cousin and the chief financier of the Revolution, ordered a set for his own sumptuous home, but for some reason never got around to hanging it. Copies and approximations of Chinese papers were made in England and these also found their way to America. Thomas Hancock ordered a set from London for a room in his very elegant Beacon Hill house, sending as a pattern a sample of a wallpaper that had recently been installed in the house of one of his wealthy friends and that, he wrote, "takes much in ye Town. . . . Get mine well Done & as Cheap as Possible, & if they can make it more Beautifull by adding more Birds flying here & there, with Some Landskip at the Bottom, should Like it well. . . ." By way of further advice to his agent Hancock continued, "In other of these hangings are great variety of different Sorts of Birds, Peacocks, Macoys, Squirril, Monkys, Fruit and Flowers, etc.," and he said he hoped his order might be executed by the same hand that had created his friend's model of fashion.

Here, as in so many other contemporary examples, the eclectic character of eighteenth-century design and decoration reveal the widening horizons of colonial culture. Within a house of typical Georgian style, its exterior arrangement reflecting Renaissance precedents drawn from classical sources (Fig. 55), individual rooms might display baroque broken pediments, decorative oriental features, and rococo embellishments derived from French sources, all agreeably and sensitively combined.

A unique series of paintings in the Chinese manner with scenes of the Buddhist hell, Chinese courts of punishment, and some more ordinary oriental birds and flowers was applied directly on the plaster walls of the parlor in a Newport house that Metcalf Bowler acquired as his city residence in 1759. The ingenious artist who created these fanciful chinoiseries has never been identified. For some reason of fashion they were at one point covered by wooden paneling, and were not rediscovered until 1937.

The brass-and-iron coal-burning fire grate was probably made in the colonies (Fig. 56). As early as 1667 the records of one New England community complained "that great waste is made in the

*Fig. 57. Side chair, Philadelphia, 1760–90; mahogany, height 46½ inches (118.1 cm.).* The modern name "strap splat" is sometimes applied to this type of chair back because the solid Queen Anne splat of the previous period has been carved into interlaced curved "straps" to make a graceful design. Here the straps are enriched by leaf carving, a decorative tassel provides a focal point for the central void, and flowing leafage and a sculptural shell enrich the boldly scrolled crest rail. Shells and leaves ornament the front seat-rail and legs, and stop fluting emphasizes the verticality of the rear stiles. This was one of the most popular Philadelphia chair-back patterns, though this example is especially richly ornamented. Tassel-back chairs were also produced in New York, Massachusetts, and Charleston. The Sylmaris Collection, Gift of George Coe Graves, 1932 (32.57.2)

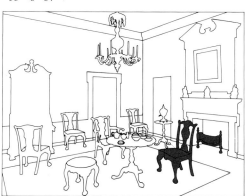

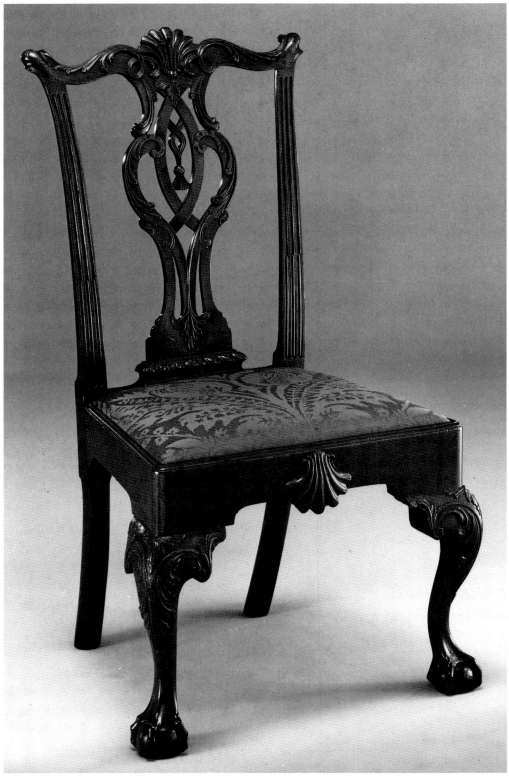

57

*Fig. 58. Stand table, Philadelphia, 1760–90; mahogany, height 28¼ inches (71.8 cm.). This lovely little table is both unusual, in being smaller than most others of its type, and typical, in having a round top supported by a turned column on a tripod base. During the late colonial period this was the preferred form for fashionable Philadelphia tea tables, and they bore as much or as little carved ornament as suited the customer's taste and pocketbook. The carving here is plentiful and particularly fine, enriching the eight-lobed "piecrust" top, the turned column, and the sinuous cabriole legs.*
John Stewart Kennedy Fund, 1918 (18.110.44)

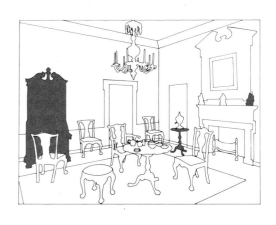

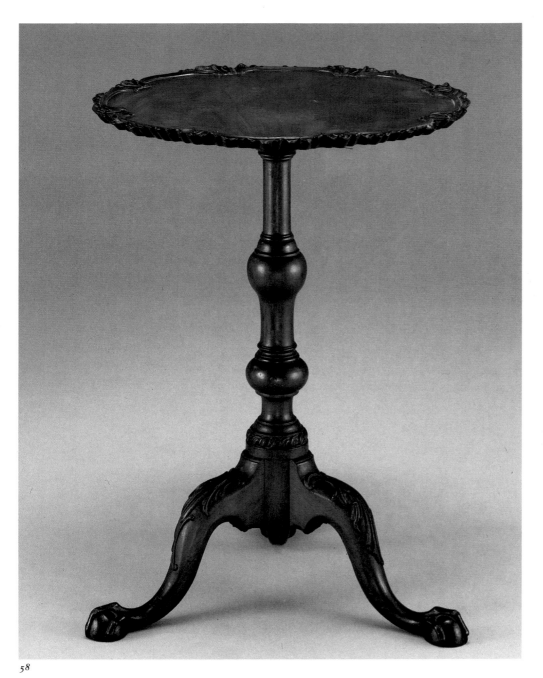

58

wood and timber in the Common Lands of the Throne," which was judged "very prejudiciall at present but especially for the succeeding generations which it concerne us to consider." There was then, of course, no visible end to the supply of firewood in the colonies. But as the forest receded from growing communities, wood gatherers had to go increasing distances for their harvests, and the cost of haulage mounted accordingly. In 1737 growing alarm over the continued recession of the forests led to the first proposal for conservation in this country, an alarm that has a typical ring in our own day. By the middle of the eighteenth century one contemporary reported that coal was now being increasingly used "both for kitchen fires and in other rooms."

All the furniture in the Powel Room is fashioned in the sophisticated version of the Chippendale style that was popular among the affluent gentry of Philadelphia and its environs. Between the two windows a tall, elaborately framed pier glass with gilded carving is hung above a slab table. A number of side and armchairs with carved splats of varying popular patterns (Fig. 57) complement a tilt-top table and a tripod stand, both supported by carved cabriole legs (Figs. 54 and 58). Such graceful forms were generally used for serving tea, which had by now become a formal social ritual that called for this and other special equipment. A handsome mahogany desk further contributes to the elegance that so deeply impressed John Adams when he first visited the homes of Philadelphians on the eve of the Revolution. To the staid New Englander Powel's "splendid seat," and his hosting a "most sinfull Feast" with an abundance of delicacies of all sorts, smacked of

*Fig. 59. Figure of John Wilkes, Derby, England, 1770–75; soft-paste porcelain, height 12¾ inches (32.4 cm.).* Although "burnt images and figures for mantelpieces" were a rarity even in wealthy pre-Revolutionary homes, the Powels' house, with its elegant parties and illustrious company, was as likely a place for these charming luxuries as any in the colonies. The figure shown here is of John Wilkes, a staunch defender of liberty for all Englishmen, including colonists, and he became something of a hero during the American Revolution. George III was so outraged by Wilkes's published criticism of the crown's policies that he had the author thrown into jail more than once.
Fletcher Fund, 1944 (44.89.2)

*Fig. 60. Desk and bookcase,* detail, Philadelphia, 1765–90; mahogany. One of the chief glories of the Chippendale period in America was high-style Philadelphia furniture. The combination of richly grained mahogany masses and free-flowing rococo carving worked particularly well on large pieces such as high chests and desks and bookcases. An impressive group within this category is ornamented with three-dimensional portrait busts (see desk and bookcase, left, Fig. 54), of which this female figure is an example. She appears to have been taken from a plate in Thomas Chippendale's famous design book, The Gentleman and Cabinet-Maker's Director, *first published in London in 1754. The modeling of this bust is considerably more deep and detailed*

than that of another such bust in the collection—the one nicknamed "Madame Pompadour" that graces the extraordinary high chest shown in Fig. 187.
Rogers Fund, 1918 (18.110.1)

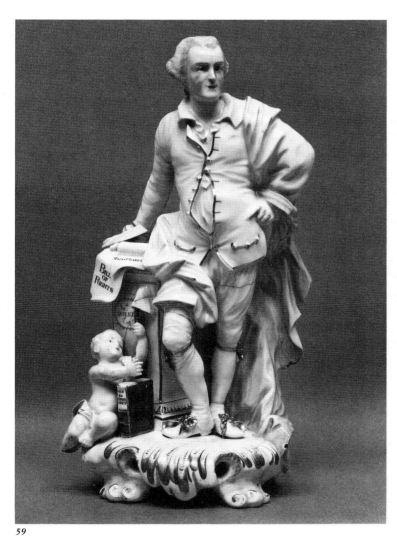

59

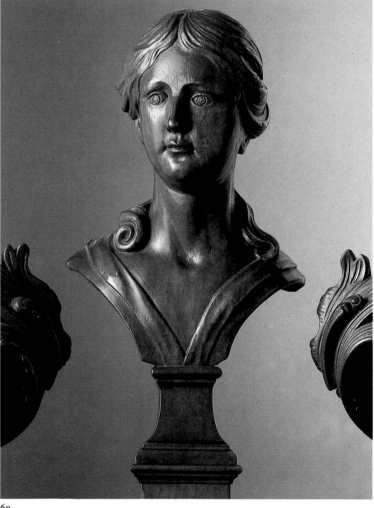

60

prodigality. Washington, another of Powel's many distinguished guests, was less awed by these surroundings and the ample hospitality they offered. At the Powels' on one occasion at least, he romped through a succession of dances with a number of younger ladies as his wife, Martha, who no longer danced, looked on—benignly, we can only hope. Nevertheless, it was reported that the "luxury and profusion" with which he was there surrounded gave the general "infinitely more pain than pleasure."

The elegance of this and other rooms

could hardly be imagined from the outside of the house. As the population of colonial urban centers increased rapidly, building space became restricted, and in the central sections of the larger cities houses were built in rows of adjoining or closely spaced structures. The Powel house, built in 1765–66 by Charles Stedman and sold to Powel in 1769, is an example of such a house. It still stands at 244 South Third Street, restored by the Philadelphia Society for the Preservation of Landmarks.

# Van Rensselaer Hall

Interiors from other geographical areas provide the opportunity to compare and contrast regional characteristics. A large and magnificent entry hall comes from the Van Rensselaer manor house, built at Albany, New York, between 1765 and 1769 by Stephen Van Rensselaer II (Fig. 61). The house was one of the most important examples of Georgian architecture in the middle Atlantic colonies.

The patroonship of Rensselaerwyck, which in 1637 had been granted by the Dutch administration to Kiliaen Van Rensselaer, a pearl merchant from Amsterdam, stretched for twenty-four miles on either side of the Hudson River in the vicinity of Fort Orange (Albany). In 1685, twenty-one years after the British take-over of New Amsterdam, this vast area became the manor of Rensselaerwyck. As a footnote to history, Stephen's son and namesake was to be "the last of the patroons." When he died in 1839, in the aftermath of Andrew Jackson's turbulent democratic upheaval, the spectacle of a landed gentleman living in semifeudal splendor among the 3,000 tenants who worked his 700,000 acres had become an insupportable anachronism. The estate was broken up and in time the great house was dismantled. Elements of its central hall came to the Museum from descendants of the patroons.

More than forty-six feet long and twenty-three feet wide, this extravagantly embellished and monumental high-ceilinged room offers a spectacular contrast to the tiny entrance halls of earlier colonial dwellings. Originally this hall ran from the front to the rear entrance, with a stairway to the upper story through an arch at one side. The intricate rococo carving in the spandrels

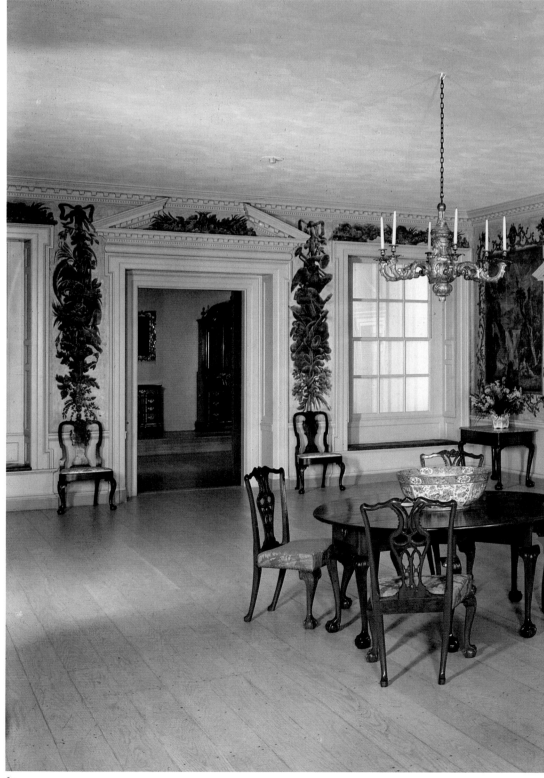

**Fig. 61. Van Rensselaer Hall,** *Albany, New York, 1765–69. Stephen Van Rensselaer II, eighth patroon and sixth lord of the Van Rensselaer manor, built the house from which this hallway and wallpaper came. One of the largest interiors to survive from the pre-Revolutionary period, it is enormously imposing, with its classical architectural details and striking painted wallpaper. A plan of the room was sent to London so that the paper could be designed and painted to fit the room exactly. Scenes of antique Italian ruins and such perennial favorites as the four seasons and the four elements were painted in grisaille (shades of gray) on a yellow ground and framed by lively rococo cartouches. This series of enframed scenes created an atmosphere not too different from that of the picture-hung halls of English manor houses that Stephen Van Rensselaer was emulating. Like the Marmion Room, which uses painted decoration in imitation of fashionable European salons, the Van Rensselaer Hall achieves its effect through ingenious simulation. Both this paper and the Marmion painted panels are rare survivals.*

Woodwork: Gift of Mrs. William Van Rensselaer, in memory of William Bayard Van Rensselaer, 1928 (28.143); *wallpaper:* Gift of Dr. Howard Van Rensselaer, 1928 (28.224); *doors:* Gift of Trustees of the Sigma Phi Society of Williams College, 1931 (31.95.1–6)

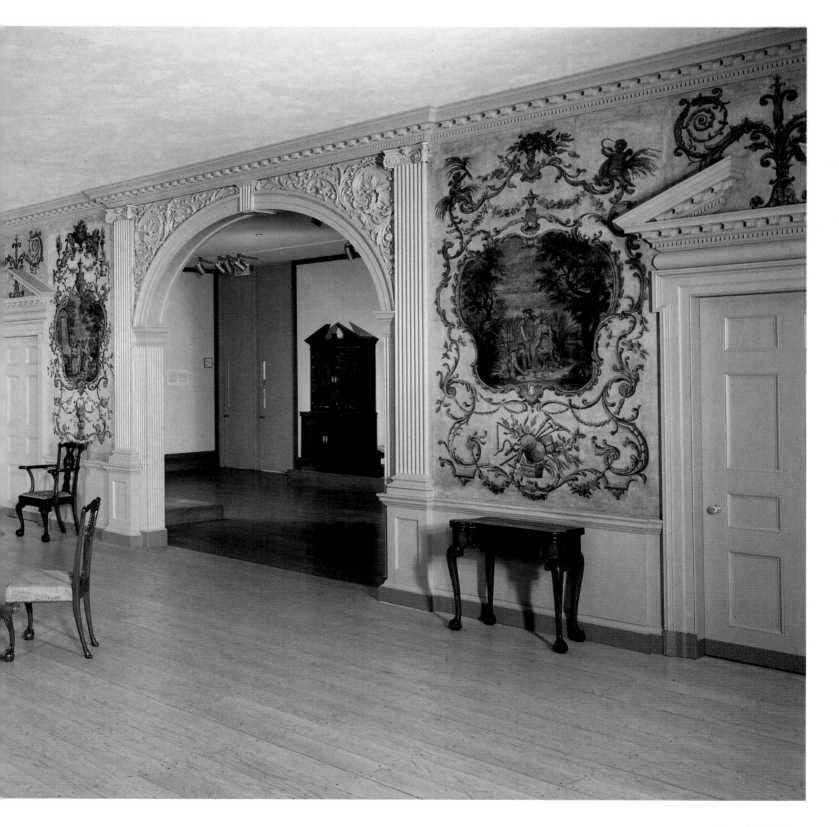

of the archway is derived from *A New Book of Ornaments* published at London by Matthias Lock and H. Copland in 1752 (Figs. 62 and 63). Both these men played important parts in developing the rococo style in England. A copy of their book may be consulted in the Museum's Department of Prints and Photographs, along with many of the original drawings made by Copland for the engravings in Chippendale's *Director*.

The most remarkable feature of this impressively spacious passageway is the scenic paper painted in England in 1768 especially for these walls (Fig. 64). Its landscapes and seascapes are done in tempera after engravings of popular eighteenth-century European paintings by such artists as Vernet, Lancret, and Pannini. They are surrounded by fanciful scrolls and rococo designs that echo the carving on the spandrels, and they alternate with smaller cartouches framing representations of the four seasons. The two end doorways are flanked by trophies that represent the elements—earth, air, fire, and water—hung from painted bowknots.

Nearly all the furniture shown in the Van Rensselaer Hall was made by New York craftsmen in the Chippendale style. A number of chairs with tassel-and-ruffle backs, gadrooned skirting, boldly fashioned claw-and-ball feet, and flat leaf-carving—all characteristics of New York workmanship—were once owned by the Van Rensselaers and Verplancks and may well have originally been used in this hall (Fig. 65). An upholstered settee, made between 1757 and 1760, bears the label of Joseph Cox, upholsterer from London, whose New

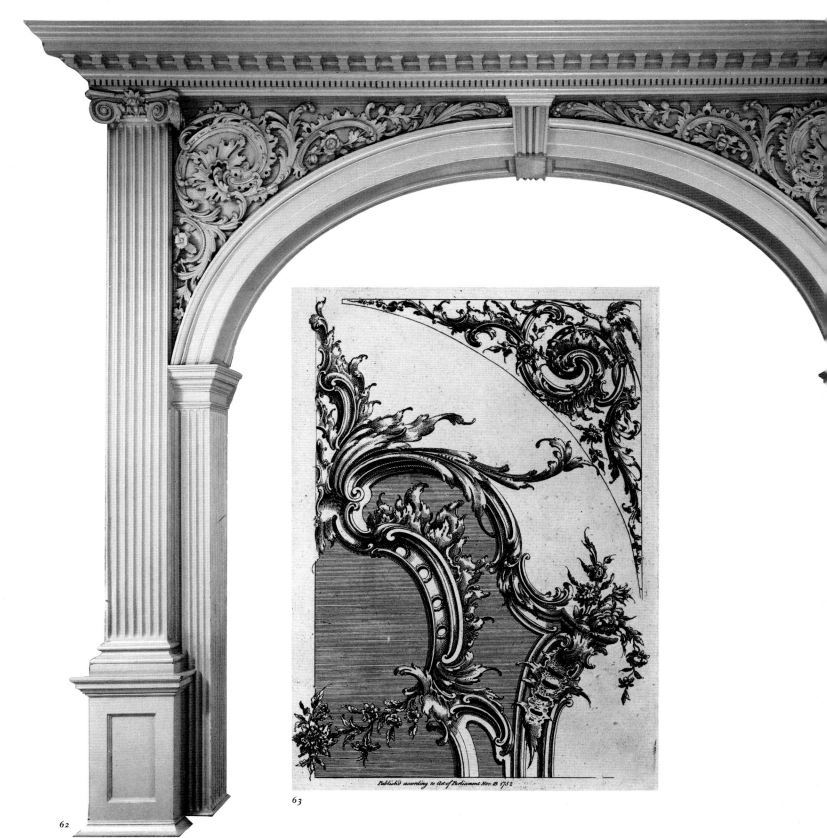

Publish'd according to Act of Parliament Nov.ᵗʰ 1752

62

63

York shop was then at the Sign of the Royal-Bed in Dock Street. Two pier tables and other chairs and tables, including a Van Rensselaer family card table, are also characteristic of the particular type of fine furniture produced by artisans of the New York colony in the years leading up to the Revolution.

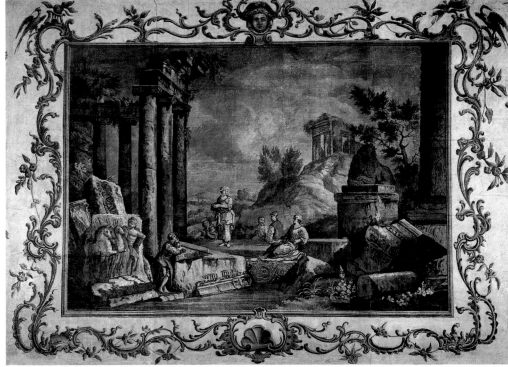

64

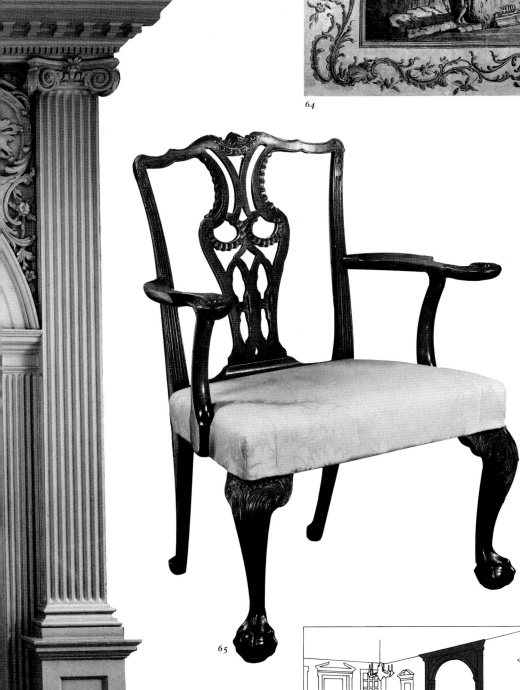

65

*Figs. 62 and 63. Archway, Van Rensselaer Hall, Albany, New York, 1765–69; and Plate 12, A New Book of Ornaments, with Twelve Leaves . . . , by M. Lock and H. Copland, London, 1752. Perhaps because they expected the wallpaper to outshine the woodwork, the designers of the Van Rensselaer Hall kept their plan simple—except in the case of the archway. Here, in the spandrels, or triangular areas above the arch, is some spectacularly free rococo carving whose source is the Lock and Copland design shown here within the arch. Freely and boldly executed, the carving contrasts vividly with the stately symmetry of the pilasters and cornice that surround it, but provides a link with the uninhibited scrolls and whimsies that ornament the wallpaper.*
Archway: Gift of Mrs. William Van Rensselaer, in memory of William Bayard Van Rensselaer, 1928 (28.143); *design:* Harris Brisbane Dick Fund, 1928 (28.887)

*Fig. 64. Wallpaper, detail, Van Rensselaer Hall, Albany, New York, 1768; tempera on paper.*
Gift of Dr. Howard Van Rensselaer, 1928 (28.224)

*Fig. 65. Armchair, New York, about 1770; mahogany, oak, height 39½ inches (100.3 cm.). This ample armchair, which came down in the Verplanck family, joins seven side chairs from the same set already in the Museum's collection. It is the finest eighteenth-century New York chair known with eagle heads carved into the armrests; this feature was adopted by New York chairmakers from English chairs of the early Georgian period.*
Bequest of Barbara Bradley Manice, 1984 (1984.287)

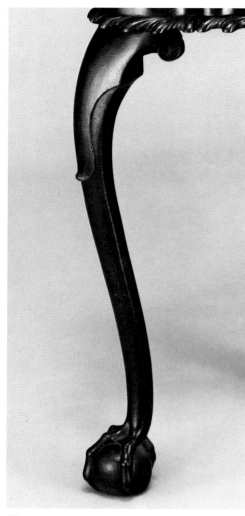

66

***Fig. 66. Card table,*** *detail, New York, 1760–65; mahogany, mahogany veneer. This simple cabriole leg is found on each object in the Verplanck parlor set. Carved gadrooning, which underlines the table skirt, and prominent squarish claw-and-ball feet are characteristic features of much New York Chippendale furniture, but the extremely simple carving on the knee is a holdover from the Queen Anne period—and is unexpected on such a sophisticated group.*
Gift of James De Lancey Verplanck and John Bayard Rodgers Verplanck, 1939 (39.184.12)

Still other examples of New York Chippendale furniture are shown in a parlor opening off the Van Rensselaer Hall (Fig. 67). By rare good fortune, all the furnishings have been reassembled from their original home, the eighteenth-century residence of Samuel and Judith Crommelin Verplanck at 3 Wall Street, New York City, which was long ago destroyed.

Samuel Verplanck belonged to the fifth generation of his family in New York. The first immigrant to the city to bear the name (then spelled Ver Plancken) came from Holland in 1638 to trade in beaver pelts. In 1758 Samuel graduated in the first class at King's College (much later to become Columbia University). He then went to Holland to study banking in the countinghouse of his uncle, Daniel Crommelin, and while there married his cousin Judith, a very young lady who brought with her a substantial dowry. Back in New York, in 1763 the couple settled near the old city hall in the brick house that had been a bequest from Samuel's father.

Samuel was an active patriot, and when the British occupied New York in 1776 he retreated to his country place at Fishkill Landing in Dutchess County. Judith chose to remain in the city and often entertained her close friend Sir William Howe, commander in chief of the British forces. After Howe's recall to England on charges "of dissipation and high play," he sent Judith several presents in appreciation of her warm friendship and hospitality. These included a French porcelain tea service decorated with sprigs of cornflowers and gold bands and a pair of paintings representing Venus and Eros by the English artist Angelica Kauffmann. When Judith died in 1803 the furnishings of

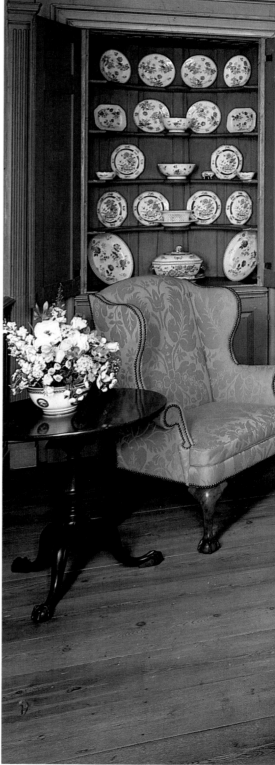

67

**Fig. 67. Verplanck Room,** *Coldenham, Orange County, New York, 1767. Although this room was taken from a house in the heart of country heavily settled by the Dutch, it embodies English Georgian, rather than local provincial Dutch, building traditions. The paneled fireplace wall is symmetrically divided, with a built-in cupboard on either side of the fireplace—that at right for clothes, and that at left for china. The open doors of the left-hand cupboard reveal China Trade ceramics that came down in the Verplanck family. The room is arranged as a parlor, and among its furnishings is the only known intact set of American Chippendale parlor furniture, donated to the Museum by members of the Verplanck family, in which it descended. The set is thought to have oc-cupied the large Verplanck town house at 3 Wall Street in New York City in the eighteenth century. Each object in the set, which consists of the settee, side chairs, and card table, has the same leg—a smooth Queen Anne cabriole that ends in a boxy claw and ball. The pumpkin-yellow wool damask that covers the chairs and settee is a reproduction of a Verplanck family fabric.*

Purchase, The Sylmaris Collection, Gift of George Coe Graves, by exchange, 1940 (40.127)

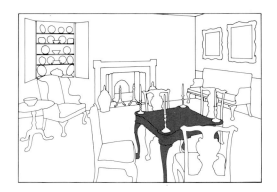

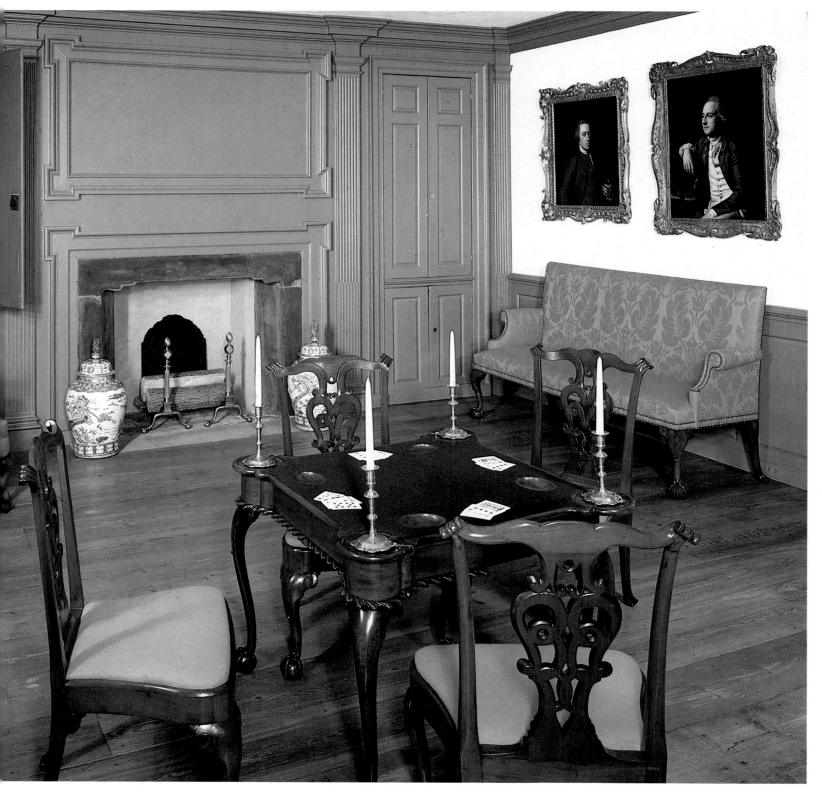

**Fig. 68. Side chairs,** *New York, 1760–70; walnut, height 38¼ inches (97.2 cm.). Two of a set of six, these chairs are part of the Verplanck parlor suite. Their front legs are like that in Fig. 66, and their back legs are prettily shaped and finished with a little square foot, as those of so many finely made New York chairs were in the Chippendale period. The broad splat retains its original Queen Anne vase shape, now pierced and given a design of thick loops. The breadth of the splat and of the seat, as well as the characteristic legs and feet, give this chair a feeling of strength and sturdiness that mark it as being from New York.*
Gift of James De Lancey Verplanck and John Bayard Rodgers Verplanck, 1939 (39.184.3–8)

**Fig. 69. Gulian Verplanck,** *by John Singleton Copley (1738–1815), 1771; oil on canvas, 36 by 28 inches (91.4 by 71.1 cm.). Brother of Samuel Verplanck, for whom the parlor set was probably made, Gulian was painted by Copley in 1771, during his only visit to New York. After graduating from King's College (now Columbia University), young Gulian set off for Holland to gain experience in business and banking in his uncle's firm. Upon his return to New York, he served with success in both the business and political arenas: he was president of the board of directors of the Bank of New York from 1791 until his death in 1799, and speaker of the New York State Assembly in 1791 and again in 1796.*
Gift of Mrs. Bayard Verplanck, 1949 (49.13)

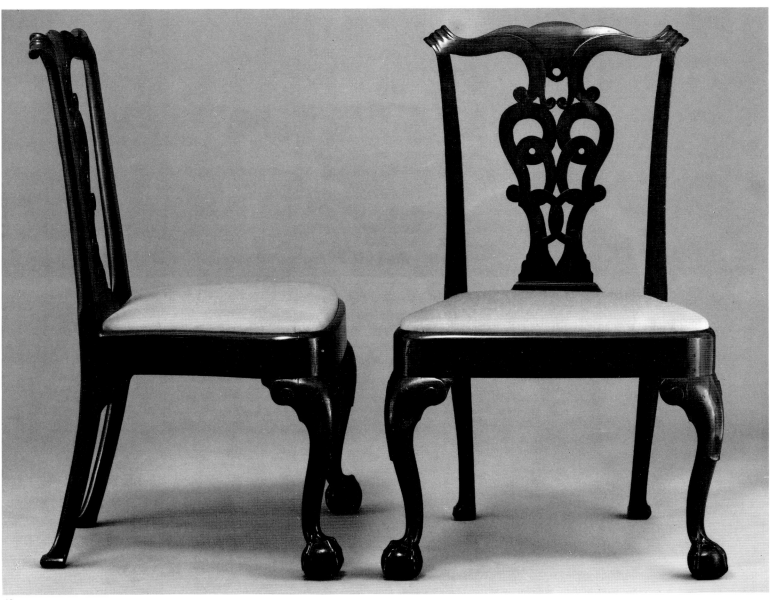

68

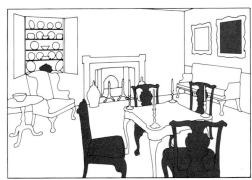

the city house were shipped up to Fishkill. When the New York house was demolished in 1822 it was replaced by the United States Branch Bank, whose facade now graces the courtyard of the Wing.

A proper setting for the Verplanck furnishings has been provided by a room from another house of comparable date, built in Orange County by Cadwallader Colden, son of the famous naturalist and lieutenant governor of colonial New York. Considering the uniform style of these pieces, it seems likely that most of them—particularly the card table, settee, and set of six chairs, all with legs of similar design (Figs. 66 and 68)—came from the shop of the same local maker. No other matching set of American Chippendale parlor furniture is so intact. Two obvious exceptions, a red-and-gold japanned secretary and a gilt-framed looking glass in the Chinese Chippendale style, were imported from England.

As may be seen in the cupboard flanking the fireplace, the Verplancks owned a complement of China Trade porcelain (Fig. 70), a coveted ware that was brought to America via England and the Continent in growing quantities as the eighteenth century advanced. Family portraits by John Singleton Copley (Fig. 69), colonial America's finest artist, recall this Boston portraitist's observation, made as he journeyed along the Atlantic seaboard in search of commissions from well-to-do patrons, that the New York gentry were so discerning that he could "slight nothing" in taking their likenesses. On November 27, 1771, the artist wrote his stepfather in Boston, "We have just come from Mr. Verplanck's where we have spent the Even'g."

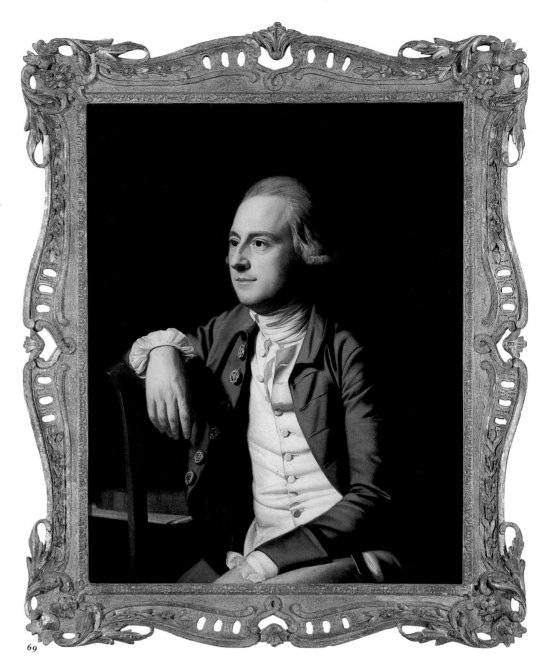

69

*Fig. 70. Tureen, China, made for the Western market, 1765–70; porcelain, height with cover 9 inches (22.9 cm.). As the eighteenth century progressed, large dinner services were shipped from China to the West in great quantities, and many found their way to the colonies. Sometimes composed of as many as 350 pieces, these sets included plates and bowls of several sizes, platters, dishes, and tureens, among other forms. This tureen is from the set of such porcelain that descended in the Verplanck family. It is also visible in Fig. 67, where it is displayed with other pieces from the same set in the cupboard to the left of the fireplace.*
Gift of James De Lancey Verplanck and John Bayard Rodgers Verplanck, 1939 (39.184.37)

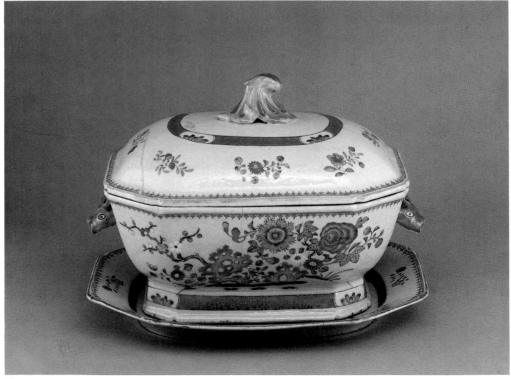

70

# Marmion Room

**Fig. 71. Marmion Room,** *King George County, Virginia, paneled 1735–70, painted 1770–80; pine, painted.* By far the most elegant room at Marmion was this, the back parlor, whose windows looked out toward the Potomac. The house was built by John Fitzhugh some time in the first third of the century, and the pine paneling of this room was given its present painted decoration at a later date. The rococo mirror above the fireplace was obviously ordered for this space; it descended in the Fitzhugh family. Rococo and neoclassical motifs and scenes ornament the large panels, and where there is no other decoration marbling enriches the woodwork. An entablature and cornice supported by beautifully carved Ionic pilasters unify the oddly shaped room. Other painted rooms are known in Virginia houses, but none is so fine nor so engagingly romantic as this one.

Rogers Fund, 1916 (16.112)

**Fig. 72. Marmion,** *King George County, Virginia, built about 1719.* Although the exact date of the construction of this house is not known, it is regarded as important because it is an early version of what was to become the standard Virginia plantation house. In its plan—a center hall with four rooms opening off it and with stairs to one side—and in the size of its rooms, it is very similar to Mount Vernon. Its plain exterior makes the paneled interior a surprise—and the painted parlor now in The American Wing a very special treat.

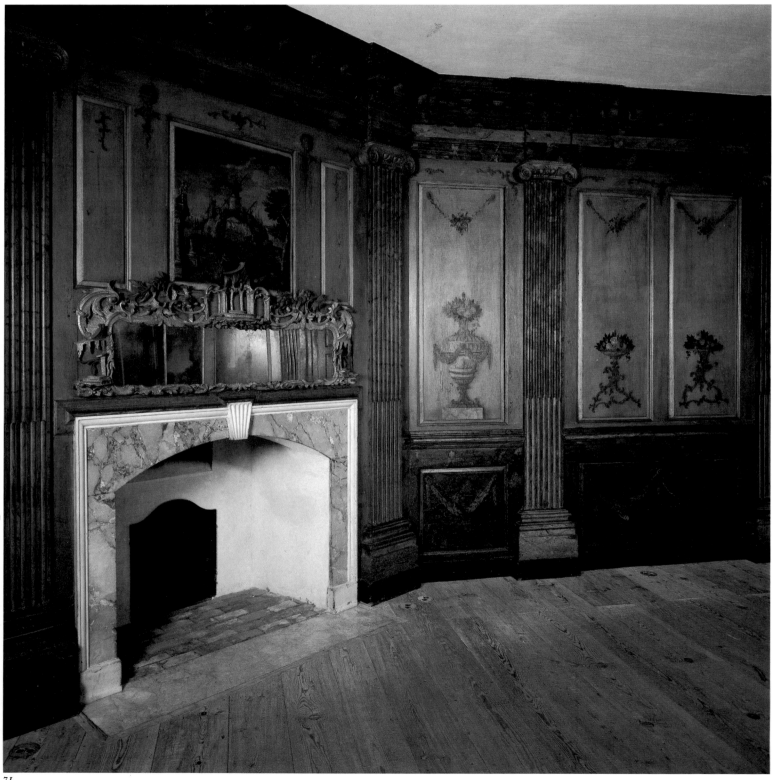

71

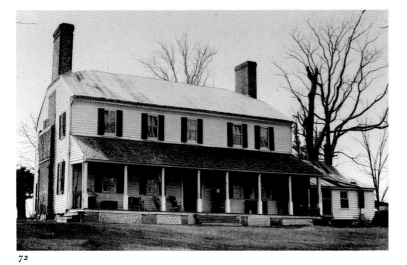

72

One of the most interesting of all surviving early American domestic interiors is that from Marmion, the Virginia plantation home of the Fitzhugh family (Figs. 72 and 74). Here the architectural treatment of Ionic pilasters and entablature conforms with unusual fidelity to the Renaissance conception of the classical order (Fig. 71). Part of the woodwork is painted to simulate marble; the larger wall panels show landscapes suggestive of Dutch painting, representations of urns with flowers (Fig. 71), festoons of leaves, and asymmetrical scrolls. These may be the work of one of the itinerant artists who advertised in newspapers that they could do all sorts of paintings, including landscapes "in the neatest Manner." The Siena-marble-lined corner fireplace is thus placed to enable the end chimney to serve two fireplaces on each floor of the house.

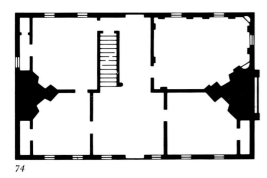

74

Fig. 74. Plan of Marmion, *showing the central hall with two rooms opening off either side. This became the standard arrangement for Virginia houses, first for the large ones and then for the smaller ones as well. The Museum's room is paneled with woodwork from the large back parlor on the right in this plan.*

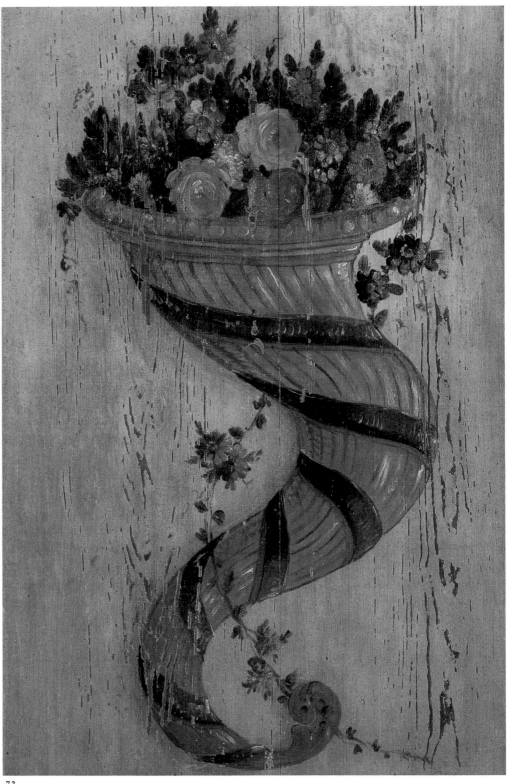

73

# The Federal Period, 1790–1820

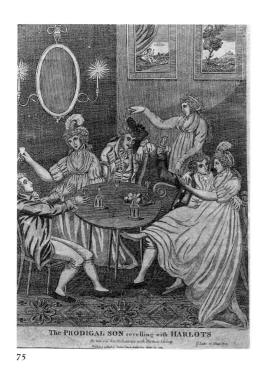

75

*Fig. 75.* **The Prodigal Son Revelling with Harlots,** *by Amos Doolittle (1754–1832), 1814; engraving, 14 by 10⅜ inches (35.6 by 26.4 cm.). Although Doolittle may have been inspired by contemporary English engravings of a similar subject, he set the scene in his own New England, providing us with fascinating details of dress and interior decoration during the Federal period.* Gift of Mrs. J. Insley Blair, 1948 (48.95.2)

In the several decades following the Revolutionary War, years that are broadly referred to as the Federal period, fresh currents of taste and design flowed into the new republic from European countries, notably England and France. The convulsions of the war had delayed the appearance of these new trends in America, and by the time they appeared here they had become firmly rooted abroad. A second classical revival was taking place—this time based not on Renaissance concepts, as in the earlier Georgian period, but on a more direct and accurate knowledge of ancient art and architecture. Among other remains scattered throughout the Mediterranean world and accessible for study by archeologically minded adventurers were the recently excavated ruins of Pompeii and Herculaneum. Suddenly buried (and preserved) under ash from the volcanic eruption of Mount Vesuvius in the first century A.D., these cities provided a new vocabulary of ornament and decoration that was translated into the delicate neoclassical styles of France and England.

The architect-designers Robert Adam and his brother James were the foremost English exponents of this fashion. Their *Works in Architecture*, published at London in 1773–79, had an electric effect on the development of both architecture and the decorative arts. Robert Adam had toured Italy and Dalmatia, carefully studying classical remains at first hand. With the designs he created after his return to England, his professed aim was "to transfuse the beautiful spirit of antiquity with novelty and variety." This he did in highly personal fashion, including in his proposals every kind of household equipment from inkstands and fire grates to sideboards and bookcases, as well as architecture. These light and graceful adaptations of ancient Roman ornament quickly won him the patronage of wealthy and aristocratic clients throughout the British Isles.

In fashionable American houses of the Federal period, rooms tended to be more spacious than ever before and to have higher ceilings and larger windows (which sometimes extended, French style, to the floor). In 1790, when Abigail Adams was living in New York while that city was the new nation's temporary capital, she wrote her sister that all the rooms of her present residence were eleven feet high, which caused her some inconvenience in furnishing it adequately. Oval, round, and octagonal rooms added variety to floor plans. (The oval room of the White House is a historic example.) By the end of the eighteenth century the up-to-date American home might have had numerous rooms for special purposes—a dining room, a parlor, a library, a ballroom, as well as kitchen and bedrooms (but rarely a bathroom)—creating a domestic environment far removed from the all-purpose seventeenth-century hall, and calling for furnishings of a different order from those of the colonial period.

# Haverhill Room

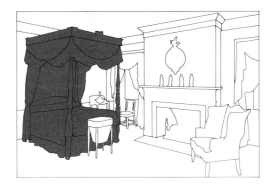

**Fig. 76. Bedstead,** Boston, 1808–12; mahogany with painted and gilded cornice, height 106¾ inches (271.1 cm.). Bedstead attributed to workshop of Thomas Seymour (active 1794–1843); carving attributed to Thomas Whitman (active 1809); cornice attributed to John Doggett (1780–1857); painted decoration attributed to John Penniman (active 1806–28). This bedstead is said to have been made for Elizabeth, daughter of Elias Hasket Derby, one of the grandest and wealthiest of New England's merchant princes, and if its richness and excellent workmanship are any indication, it was. It is the finest of a very select group of carved, painted, and gilded bedsteads made in Salem and Boston whose inspiration seems to have been Thomas Sheraton's design for a similar bed in the Appendix to his Drawing Book (Pl. 9, London, 1802). The group of artisans who cooperated to produce this bedstead includes some of the most talented craftsmen of the period, and this is a most interesting instance of such cooperation among specialists to produce a masterpiece.
John Stewart Kennedy Fund, 1918 (18.110.64)

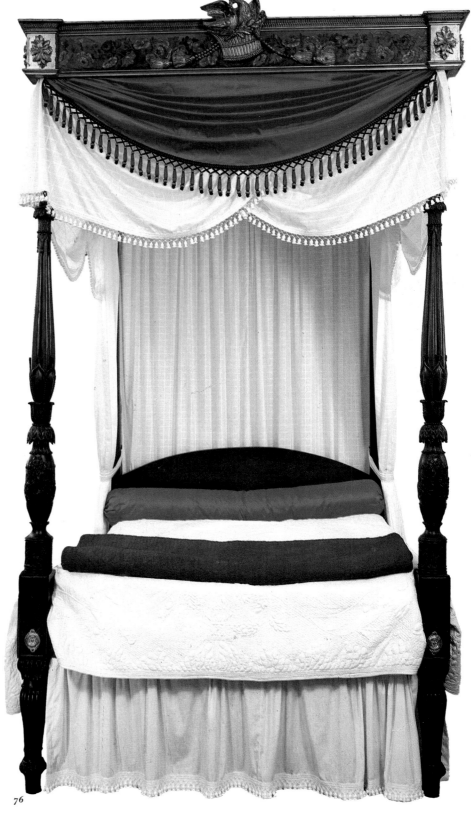

**B**oston's North Shore was an area where superb craftsmen found ample and discriminating patronage during the Federal period. For more than a generation after the Revolution Salem was one of the celebrated ports of the world. Its seamen, wrote one historian, "were despatched to every part of the world, and to every nook of barbarism which had a market and a shore." In some remote areas where its ships seemed everywhere to be seen it was believed that the small town *was* the United States—an immensely rich and important country. As another historian has written, the list of exotic freight brought home to Salem conjures up an oriental bazaar—ivory and gold dust from Guinea, gum copal from Zanzibar, iron from Gothenburg and St. Petersburg, coffee and palm oil from Arabia, whale oil from the Antarctic, silks and pepper from the Far East, hemp from Luzon, hides from the Rio de la Plata, silk slippers from somewhere east of Good Hope, and among the interminable variety of other things, one elephant in good condition, the first to be seen in America.

Merchants in Salem and neighboring towns grew wealthy from their foreign ventures, and their demands for the best in houses and furnishings were ably met by the consummate craftsmen of the area. Visible evidence of their good fortune endures in their dwellings and in the furniture that was made for them. An interior with woodwork from the Duncan house, built twenty miles from Salem in Haverhill, Massachusetts, about 1805, is furnished as the bed-sitting room of a New England merchant prince (Fig. 77). Details such as thin, reeded columns with brass bases and capitals on the mantel, plaster or-

76

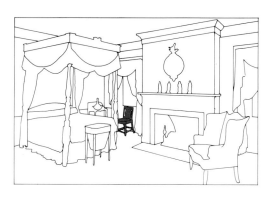

**Fig. 77. Haverhill Room,** *Haverhill, Massachusetts, about 1805. After the Revolutionary War, New Englanders sailed off to the four corners of the globe, trading as they went. Many made large fortunes, and it was not unusual for a man of thirty to retire from the sea, leaving the sailing and trading to his employees. The wealthy young man was then free to build himself a fine house and fill it with the best of everything. The Haverhill Room is arranged to show what luxurious and elegant objects were available to furnish the bed-sitting room of a New England merchant prince. Furniture echoes the symmetry and delicacy, straight lines and geometrical shapes of the newly fashionable Federal architecture, and among the new forms that appeared* were those represented by the sewing or worktable at the end of the bed, the washstand in the corner, and the girandole mirror over the mantel. Beside the fireplace is an easy chair whose symmetrical serpentine curves and straight tapered legs are typical of this form in the early neoclassical period. While it contrasts markedly with the delicacy of everything else in the room, the wall-to-wall ingrain carpet with its bold geometrical pattern of squares and crosses is of a type that was popular throughout most of the nineteenth century. *Rogers Fund, 1912 (12.121)*

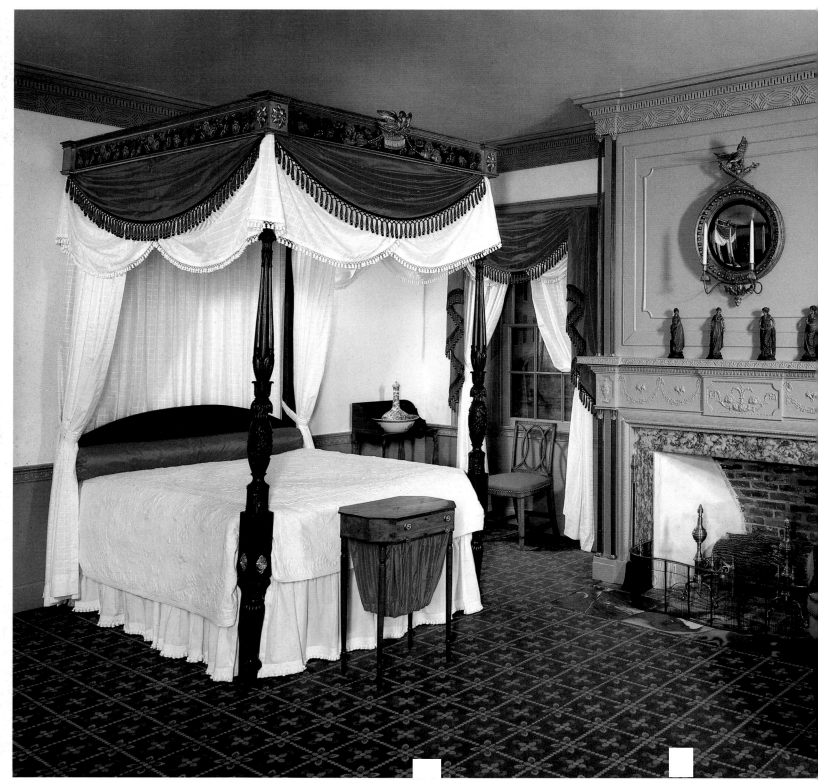

77

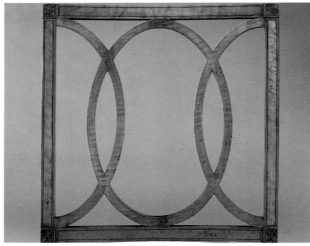

**Fig. 78. Side chair,** detail, Boston, 1795–1810; bird's-eye and striped maple. Part of a set of fourteen that descended in John Hancock's family, these unusual square-backed chairs express the spirit of neoclassicism in general and of New England neoclassicism in particular. The design of ovals within a square is in the early Federal tradition of strict symmetry. The shape of the square back is emphasized at each corner by a smaller square enclosing a carved rosette on a punchwork ground. The use of light woods with a rich grain is characteristic of northern New England.
Lent by Kaufman Americana Foundation
(L.1979.26.1)

78

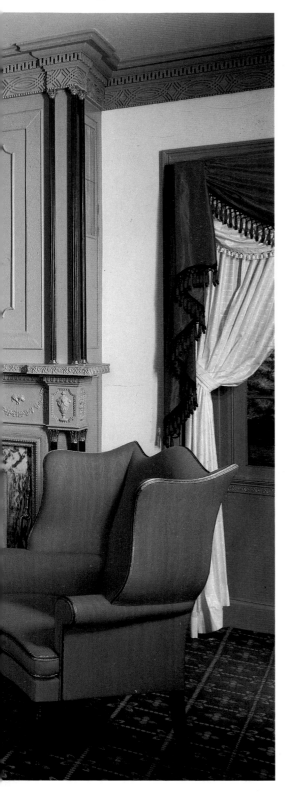

nament on the chair rail and chimney breast, and cornice with fret design copied from the 1792 edition of William Pain's *Builder's Companion* combine to produce a harmonious early nineteenth-century North Shore interior. The room is dominated by what is generally considered the finest surviving American bed from this period—a magnificent joint accomplishment of thoroughly proficient craftsmen that descended in the Derby family (Fig. 76). Its cornice, original in conception and decorated in colors and gold, was the combined achievement of John Doggett, a celebrated looking-glass-frame maker of Roxbury, Massachusetts, and John Ritto Penniman, an ornamental painter who, along with other gifted artisans, worked with Doggett on some of his many commissions. The bedstead itself was fashioned in the workshop of Thomas Seymour; the exquisitely carved details on the foot posts are attributed to Thomas Whitman.

**Fig. 79. Pole screen** with hinged shelf, Salem, 1785–95; mahogany, holly and ebony inlays, height 61½ inches (156.2 cm). Elegant little forms like this indicate America's prosperity in the second half of the eighteenth century. Only a household that was completely fitted up with the necessities would contain such a luxury as a pole, or fire, screen—it was an extra, an expensive nicety that made life more comfortable. The purpose of such a screen was to shield the person next to it from the heat and glare of the fire. This example has, in addition, a folding shelf for a candle, a refinement found only on the finest examples. The style of this screen is transitional—it combines the snake feet of the Chippendale period with the oval screen and inlay of the Federal era.
Gift of Mrs. A. Goodwin Cooke, in memory of her mother, Mrs. Frederic C. Munroe, and Purchase, Anonymous Gift and Friends of the American Wing Fund, 1977 (1977.425)

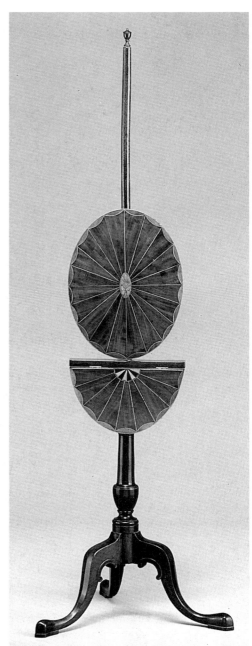

79

# Baltimore Room

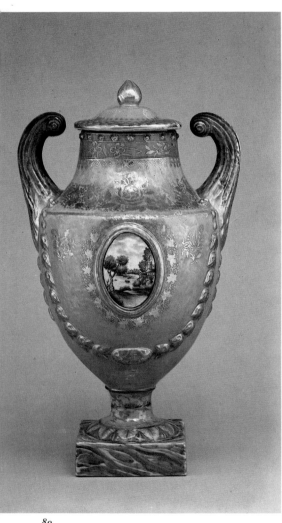

80

*Fig. 80. Urn, one of a pair, China, 1785–1815; porcelain, height 16³/₁₆ (41.5 cm.). The symmetrical pistol-handled urn form and its idealized landscape in an oval are characteristic of neoclassical design. The antecedents of the form are a late sixteenth-century Italian urn and, more immediately, a late eighteenth-century version by the English potter Josiah Wedgwood. Such oriental porcelains designed for the Western market were made in great numbers in the Federal period when, for the first time, American ships began to make the long journey to Canton. Once there, they traded goods that ranged from furs and tobacco to ginseng for coveted Chinese tea, silks, and ceramics.*
Gift of Mrs. W. Murray Crane, 1954 (54.87.34)

By the beginning of the nineteenth century the port of Baltimore, commanding the shipping on Chesapeake Bay, had become a principal market town for most of the South and a good portion of Pennsylvania. One European visitor commended the city's "American frankness and French ease." Its rocketing prosperity brought an influx of skilled craftsmen, many from Great Britain, and their work was more English in character than that of any other American city.

In the dining room removed from a house built in Baltimore just before the War of 1812 the architectural elements—pilasters, colonnettes, and cornice worked in solid pine—are all delicate in scale and refined in detail (Fig. 81). The relationships between the wall openings—arched recesses flanking the fireplace, windows, and doors—and the wall surfaces, whose oval panels echo those of the alcoves and the mantel, reveal a studied composition and a restrained elegance typical of the revived classicism of the early republic.

In the center of the Baltimore Room are a sectional dining table (Figs. 84 and 85) and a set of square-back Sheraton-style chairs (Fig. 83) that exemplify the regional characteristics of Baltimore and of the mid-Atlantic or southern regions, respectively. On the card tables in the arched recesses are a pair of beautifully colored and gilded urns (Fig. 80). Above them a remarkably handsome pair of carved and gilded Massachusetts wall mirrors with *églomisé* inserts make it evident that painted-glass decoration was not exclusively a Baltimore device (Fig. 82).

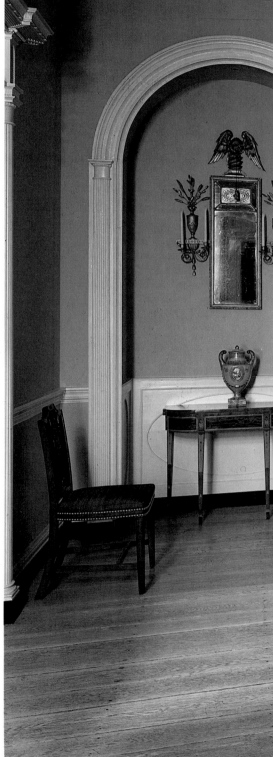

81

**Fig. 81. Baltimore Room,** *913 East Pratt Street, Baltimore, about 1810. "Some forty years ago," wrote the Russian diplomat Paul Svinin about 1812, Baltimore "consisted of several fishermen's huts. Now it is one of the fairest cities of North America, in point of wealth and trade occupying the first place after Philadelphia, New York, and Boston." The architecture and moldings of this Baltimore room are simple but elegant, emphasizing ovals and rectangles. The furniture is mainly from the Baltimore area, with imported accessories: the chandelier and candelabra are from England, the porcelain dinner service from France, and the pistol-handled urns were made in China for the Western market. The floor covering of such a room, however, might* either have been imported from England or made in America. This one is a reproduction floorcloth—a decorative but eminently practical alternative to a carpet or painted floor. Made of canvas or some other heavy cloth and covered with several layers of oil paint, floorcloths were remarkably durable. Charles Carroll of Annapolis certainly expected those he ordered from England in 1767 to stand up to hard wear, for he stipulated that they be able to "bear mopping over with a wet mop and Put up Dry and so as not to be Cracked or to have the Paint Rubbed of [ f ]."
Rogers Fund, 1918 (18.101.1–4)

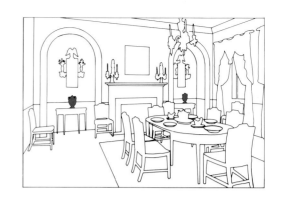

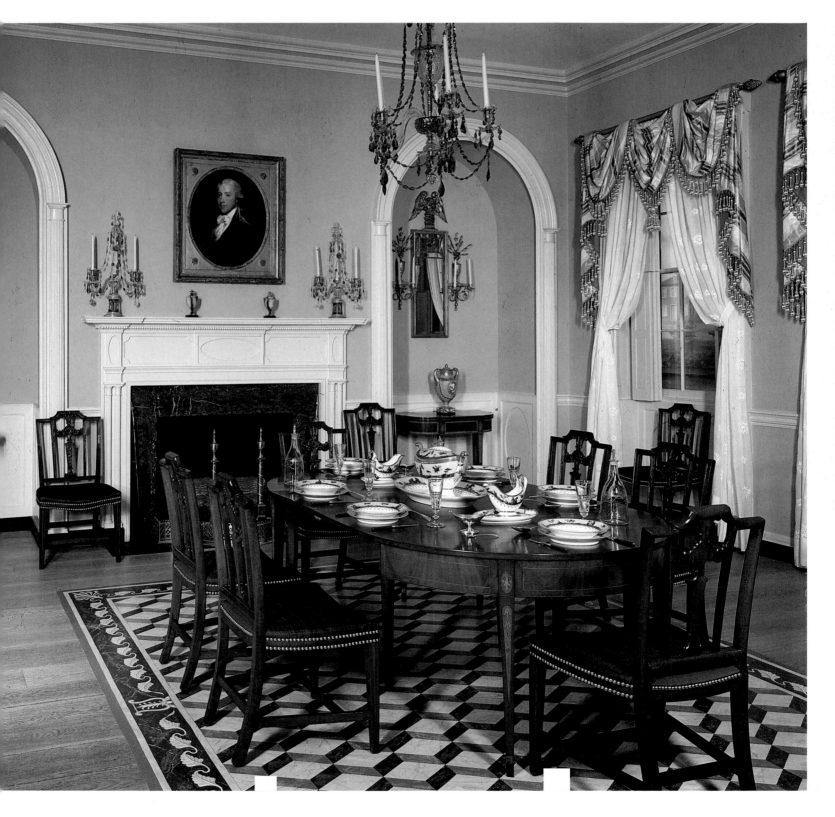

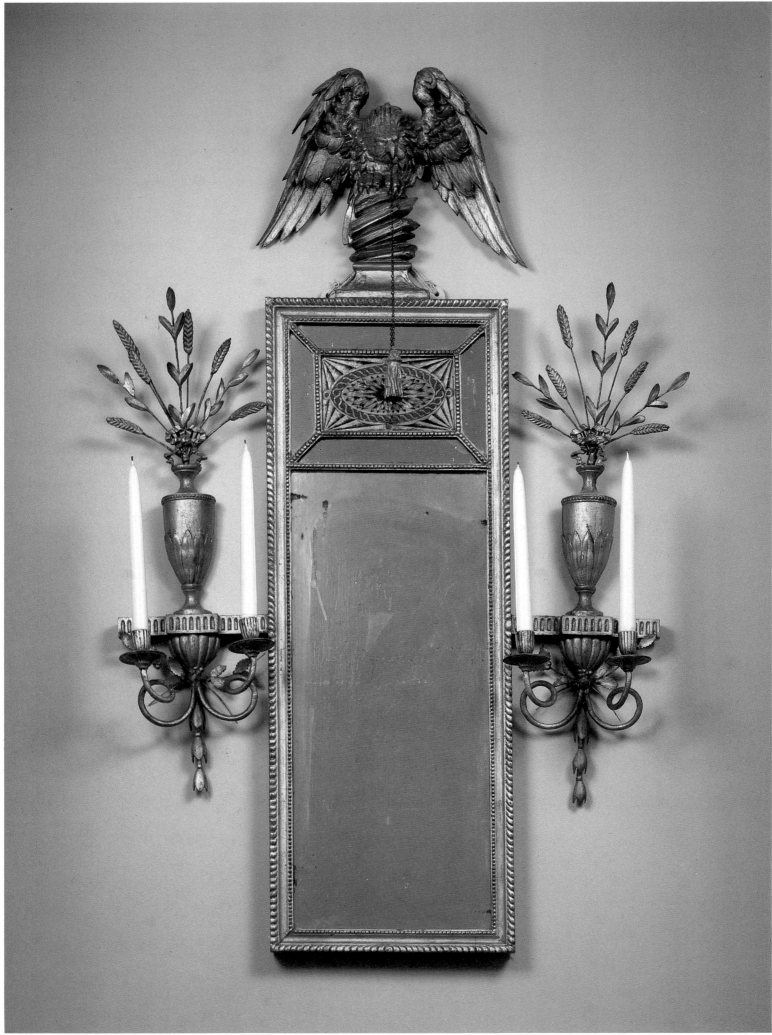

82

**Fig. 82. Looking glass,** *one of a pair, Boston, 1795–1810; gilt gesso on pine and wire, églomisé tablet, height 50½ inches (128.3 cm.). Although églomisé decoration, or reverse painting on glass, is usually associated with Baltimore furniture, it was used by Boston and Salem craftsmen as well. Here it forms the central ornament of the upper mirror section of this extraordinarily decorative looking glass. Gilded vases of wheat sprays, pendent husks, and a splendid feathery eagle are executed with skill and combined to produce a supremely elegant object that, like the bedstead in the Haverhill Room, epitomizes the symmetry, delicacy, and refinement of the early Federal period.*
Sansbury-Mills Fund, 1956 (56.46.1)

**Fig. 83. Square-back side chairs,** *two of a set of ten, southern or mid-Atlantic states, 1795–1810; mahogany, heights 36¾ inches (93.4 cm.). Straight lines, square outlines, and chaste stylized ornament carved in low relief are features that place these seats in the early Federal period. The splat is composed of characteristic motifs—three feathers, drapery swags, and urn—used together here to create an unusual silhouette.*
Bequest of Flora E. Whiting, 1971 (1971.180.16–17)

**Figs. 84 and 85. Dining table,** *details, Baltimore, 1795–1810; mahogany, sycamore inlay. Between 1790 and 1810 Baltimore furniture was richly and distinctively ornamented. Inlay was particularly popular, and a light-wood "teardrop" used as a background for further inlay was a favorite device. The pendent husks, or bellflowers, that descend this teardrop are one of the best-known Baltimore motifs. Each petal is very clearly delineated, with the middle one unmistakably longer than the other two. The eagle in a patera, or oval inlay, is a simplified version of the bald eagle on the Great Seal of the newly formed United States of America.*
Rogers Fund, 1919 (19.13.1,2)

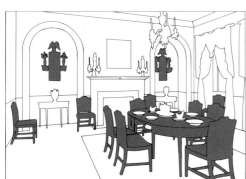
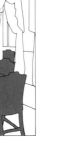

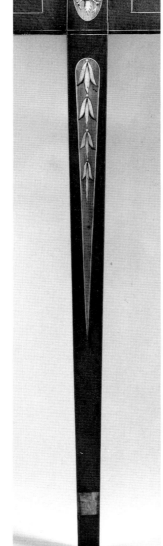

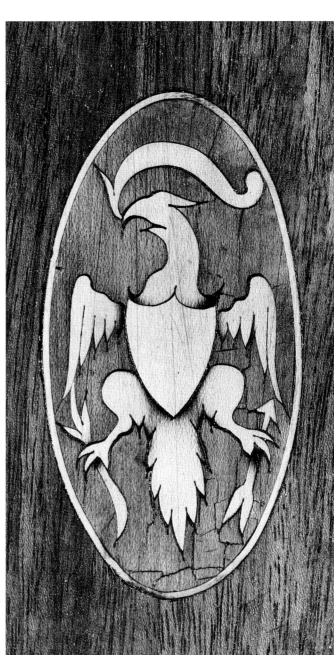

83

84

85

# Richmond Room

**Fig. 87. Richmond Room,** *Richmond, Virginia, 1810. A new boldness has replaced the delicacy of proportion and restraint in scale and ornament that were principal characteristics of the Haverhill and Baltimore Rooms. Here both architecture and ornament have taken on a grand—even showy—aspect. Door and window openings are larger, made important by substantial friezes. The use of mahogany, an unusual but eminently suitable choice for an interior in this style, increases the impact of the woodwork; another unexpected choice is seen in the King of Prussia marble baseboards. Marble is used again for the mantel, whose caryatid supports and anthemion border are larger and more boldly sculptured than the linear Adamesque ornament of the earlier rooms. Furniture and accessories are suit-ably rich: mahogany, gilt bronze, and cut glass complement the woodwork and wallpaper. Since the French Empire style was a decided influence on its American counterpart, it is not surprising that the* bouillotte *lamp on the card table and the clock on the mantel are both French. Above the clock is a girandole mirror made in either England or America after a French design. The assertively figured Aubusson carpet carries out the theme of substantial classicism, but the wallpaper, a copy of a popular French pattern called "Monuments of Paris," supplies a lighter, more open feeling. The electric blue silk at the windows and on the sofa and chairs is a reproduction of the Chinese-export silk that originally covered these seats.*
Gift of Joe Kindig, Jr., 1968 (68.137)

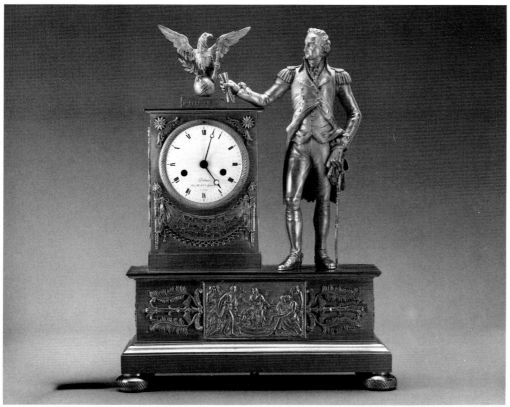

86

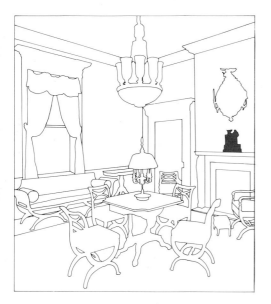

**Fig. 86. Clock,** *works by Dubuc (active about 1780–1819), Paris, 1792–1819; bronze, gilded, height 19 inches (48.3 cm). Like many other European artists and craftsmen, the firm of Dubuc produced goods especially for the American market, taking advantage of Americans' taste for objects whose ornament commemorated their new independence. This clock features George Washington in a pose borrowed from John Trumbull's painting* Washington Before the Battle of Trenton, *well known in Europe through engravings, and an American eagle perched on a globe. The frieze on the base shows Washington relinquishing his commission as commander in chief of the American army. The clock is inscribed "Dubuc/Rue Michel-le-Comte No. 33/A PARIS."*
Bequest of Jane E. Andrews, in memory of her husband, William Loring Andrews, 1930 (31.41.1)

**E**xamples of the work of leading New York cabinetmakers Phyfe and Lannuier are displayed in a room from a house built in Richmond, Virginia (Fig. 87). The wainscoting and door and window units are most unusually made of solid mahogany; the woodwork is signed by one "Theo. Nash, Executor," presumably the joiner. Baseboards are of a stone known as King of Prussia marble, quarried only in the Philadelphia area.

Two caryatids support the mantel of the marble fireplace, which is carved with anthemia and other classical motifs. A French gilt-bronze clock (Fig. 86) on the mantel displays a freestanding figure of George Washington (modeled after a portrait by John Trumbull), and patriotic motifs relating to his fame. The other walls are covered with a facsimile of a colorful French scenic wallpaper, a popular embellishment of Federal American homes from New England to Virginia. Made by the Dufour firm of Paris and first published in 1815, the paper celebrates the monuments of Paris. More than a thousand separate silk screens were required to produce the exact copy displayed here. An ornamental plaster rosette in the ceiling is adapted from a design in Asher Benjamin's *American Builder's Companion*, a widely used reference book published at Boston in 1806.

For decades after the Revolution most American households continued to rely upon candles for illumination at nighttime. Good candles were never really inexpensive, and as a matter of domestic economy even such an eminent householder as George Washington kept an account of what it cost him to burn them. In the late eighteenth and early nineteenth centuries glass

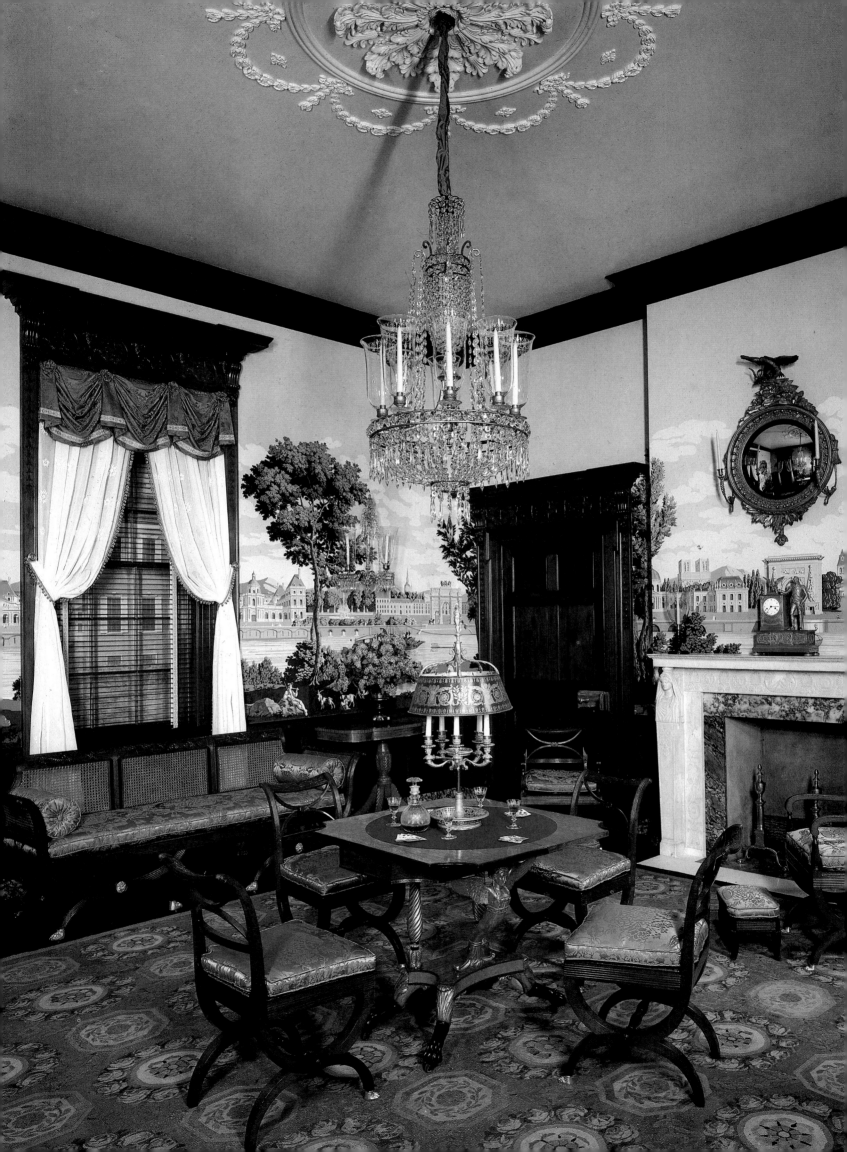

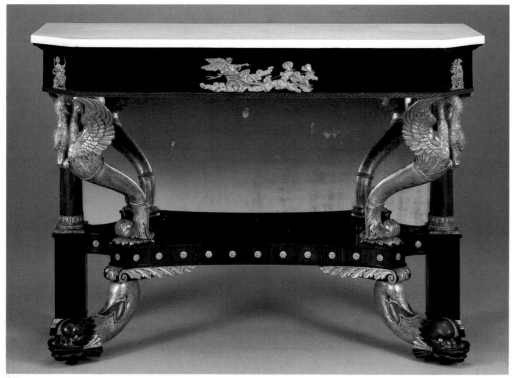

88

shades, often handsomely cut and engraved, were placed over candles to protect their flames from drafts. An unusually elaborate pair of wall lights, each with three candle sockets, and a central chandelier are all equipped with these so-called hurricane shades. Each is also embellished with faceted glass arms and with chains and borders of cut-glass pendent drops and prisms that sparkled with reflections of the flames.

About 1810, according to family tradition, Thomas Cornell Pearsall ordered from Duncan Phyfe a large suite of mahogany chairs with "Grecian-cross" legs. Chairs from this set of twelve, now in the Museum's collection, are shown here (Figs. 87 and 89), as is a sofa of the same design. Also in the room are two tables by Charles-Honoré Lannuier, Phyfe's French-émigré contemporary (Figs. 88 and 90). Although each man could—and did—work in the style usually associated with the other, Lannuier's more sculptural approach may be contrasted here with Phyfe's restrained, reeded treatment.

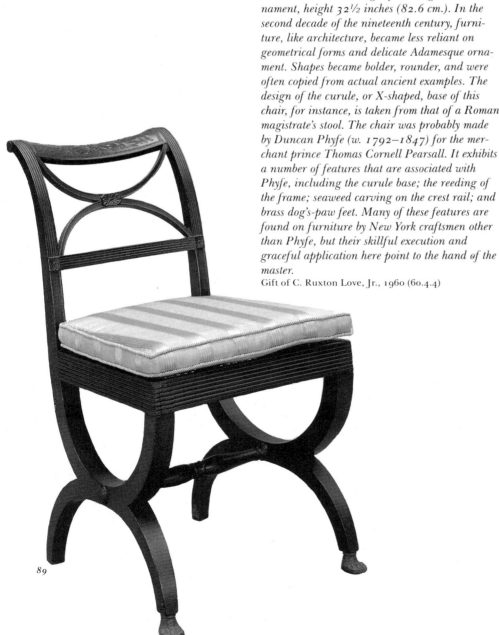

89

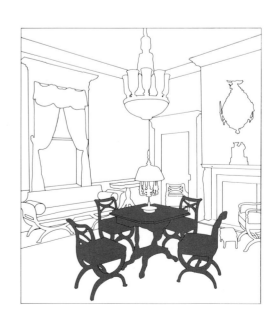

ing, naturalistic carved swan and dolphin supports, and a mirrored back. Besides being the most lavish furniture produced in New York at this time, Lannuier's products were also beautifully constructed of the finest woods.

Friends of the American Wing Fund, 1968 (68.43)

**Fig. 90. Square card table** with hollow corners, attributed to Charles-Honoré Lannuier (active New York 1803–19), New York, 1810–15; bird's-eye-maple, rosewood, satinwood, and mahogany veneers, gilt gesso and verd antique, brass inlay, gilt-bronze mount, mahogany, white pine, height 31 inches (78.7 cm.). Naturalistic carving, highly figured woods, gilding, and metal inlay and appliqués distinguish this second example of Lannuier's work and show how elegantly he adapted the French Empire style to his American patrons' needs. Winged figures, like that of the woman seen here, were a favorite of Lannuier's, as were carved animal paws with leafy hocks. The table belonged to Philip Hone, diarist, leading citizen, and mayor of New York, who described his house, which the table probably furnished, as "one of the most genteel residences in the city."

Funds from various donors, 1966 (66.170)

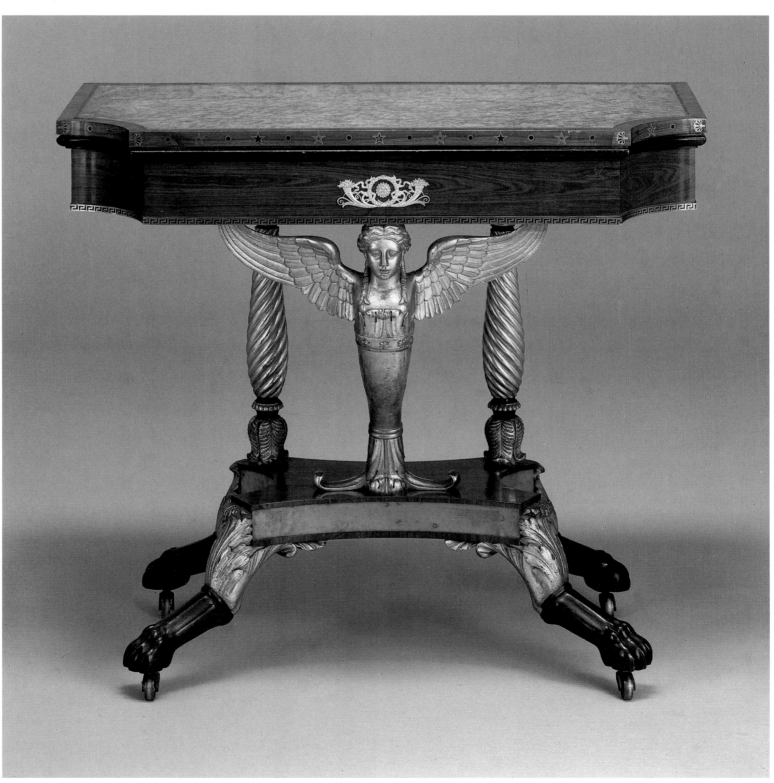

90

# The Shaker Vernacular

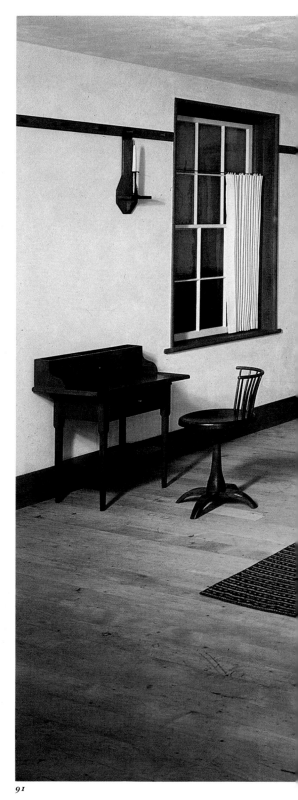

A retiring room from the North Family Dwelling at New Lebanon, New York, dating from the 1830s, has been installed to display the Museum's collections of Shaker material (Figs. 91 and 92). Here, as in all Shaker structures, there is complete economy of detail; architectural elements are reduced to essentials, without embellishment of either the wooden trim or the plaster walls. Flawless techniques, used to construct everything, were unsurpassed by those of any of the leading worldly craftsmen of the time who catered to the most demanding and wealthy clients. The plain doors and drawers of an inconspicuous built-in cabinet with simple wooden knobs and without moldings function with rare perfection, securely fitted yet opening, closing, or sliding at the lightest touch. Window sashes were designed to be easily removed for cleaning.

Both a utilitarian wooden tripod stand and a neatly boxed cast-iron stove are typical of those workaday objects fashioned by the Shakers that, isolated from their domestic setting, can stand as examples of pure design in wood and metal. One of the Shakers' precepts held that "order is the creation of beauty," and visitors to Shaker communities often commented on the immaculate tidiness of their interiors. Within the general uniformity of Shaker design there was a purposeful diversity in individual forms according to the specific function each was made to serve. With some exceptions paint or varnish on woodwork was generally eschewed as a disguise for shoddy workmanship. Most surfaces were lightly stained for preservation and an unpretentiously agreeable appearance.

The ingenuity exercised by Shaker craftsmen led to numerous inventions, which as a matter of principle were rarely patented. The list is long and impressive, from the common clothespin to a turbine waterwheel. At the International Centennial Exposition held in Philadelphia in 1876 a washing machine invented by the Shakers won a gold medal. It did the work of fourteen washerwomen.

The efficient spareness of Shaker designs, which was scrupulously maintained over the years, caught the attention and won the admiration of the outside world, providing a profitable market for many different products—brooms, leather goods, baskets, silk-lined straw bonnets, and other practical articles including various types of furniture (Figs. 93–95). The Shakers were probably the first in this country to produce rocking chairs systematically, both for the use of the brethren in their own communities and for sale.

*Fig. 91. Shaker Retiring Room, New Lebanon, New York, 1830–40. Serenity, order, and practicality—important goals in the Shaker world—are exemplified in this room. Each evening the Shakers withdrew after the day's work to "banish from the mind all thoughts of a secular nature, as well as all vain imaginations or worldly temptations." After half an hour's "retiring time," they were prepared for worship. Four brothers or sisters shared a room like this one, which was used both for sleeping and retiring. Its furnishings were prescribed in the Millennial Laws, a set of rules governing nearly every aspect of life in the Shaker community. Because part of the Museum's purpose is to show a variety of forms against the proper background, and because it would be very difficult to obtain the prescribed objects, this is not an exact replica of a Shaker retiring room, but a display combining authentic architecture and appropriate furnishings.*
Emily C. Chadbourne Fund, 1972 (1972.187.1–3)

91

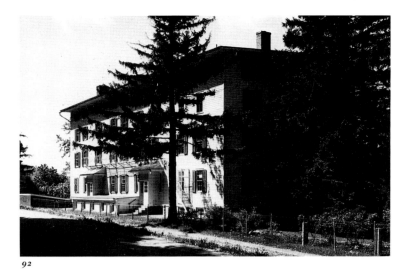

92

**Fig. 92. North Family Dwelling,** *New Lebanon, New York, 1830–40. The Mount Lebanon community, established in 1785, was the Shakers' spiritual and organizational center. Once described by a visitor "as a place where it is always Sunday," what is left of the Shaker community today is occupied by the Darrow School. This building, torn down in 1973, contained the sisters' retiring room, now in the Museum's collection.*

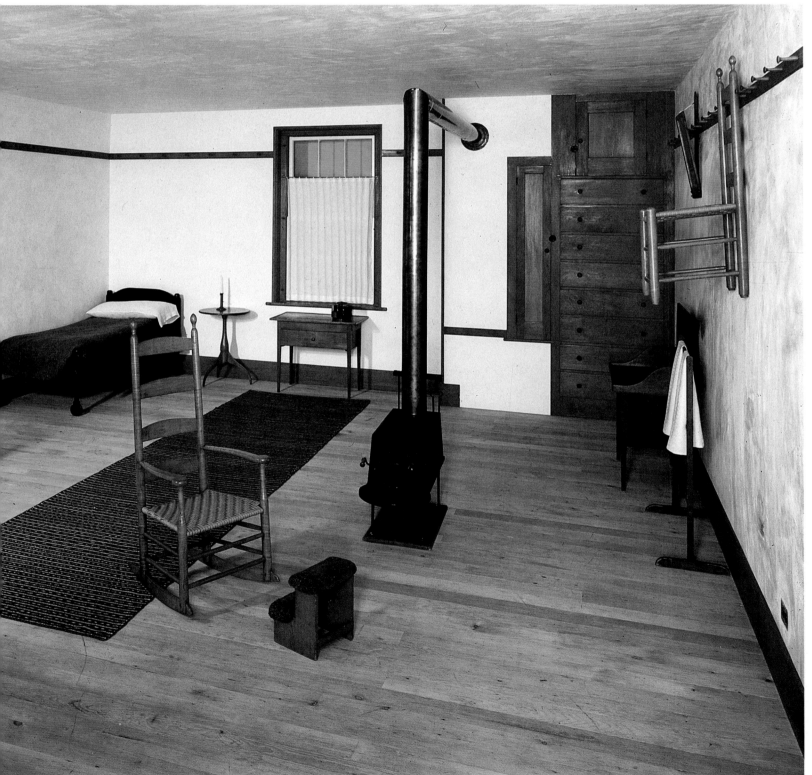

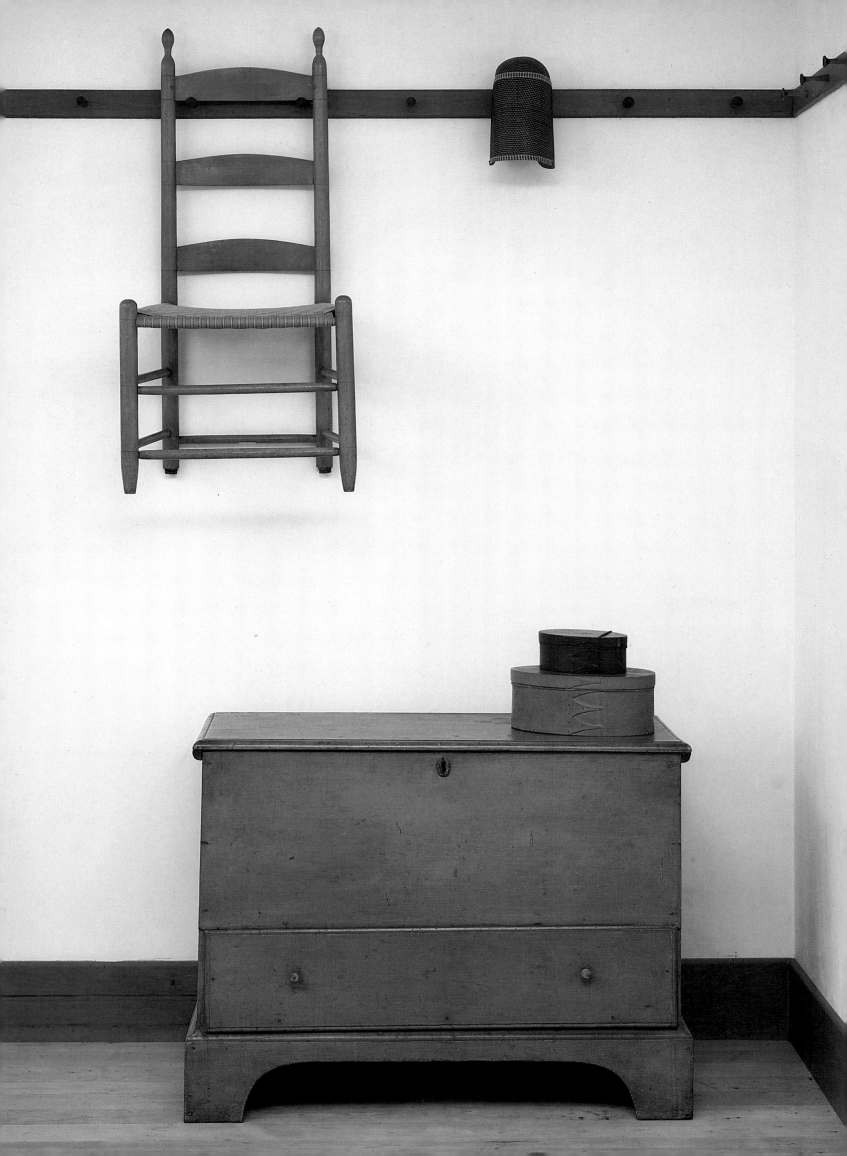

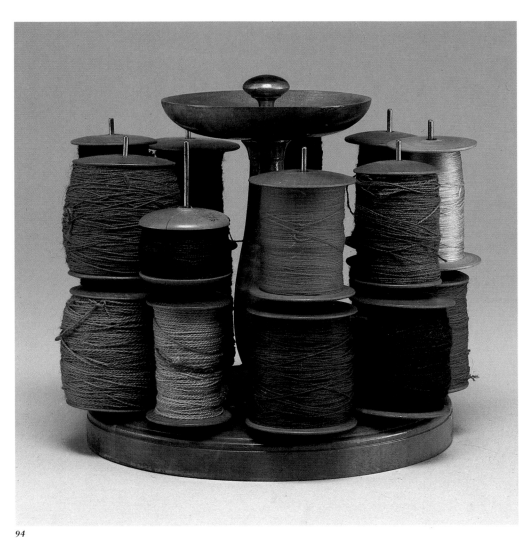

**Fig. 93. Corner of the Shaker Retiring Room,** *detail, showing representative objects. The Shakers are famous for oval bentwood boxes of the kind seen here; these are not only lovely to look at but, like all the sect's crafts, beautifully and simply constructed with delicate "fingers" to hold them together. The slat-back chair and the bonnet hung from pegs exemplify the observation of one reporter, who wrote of Shaker interiors that their halls and rooms were "lined with pegs, on which spare chairs, hats, cloaks, bonnets, and shawls are hung." The Shakers themselves explained that they hung "everything but people, and that we leave for the world to do."* Emily C. Chadbourne Fund, 1972 (1972.187.1–3)

**Fig. 94. Spool stand,** *United States, 1830–50; maple, height 5¾ inches (14.6 cm.). The Shaker notion of "a place for everything and everything in its place" fostered the creation of simple yet eminently graceful objects like this spool stand. Thread probably spun and dyed by the sisters remains wound on the spools.* Rogers Fund, 1966 (66.165.3)

**Fig. 95. Basket,** *United States, nineteenth century; wood, wicker, diameter 9¾ inches (24.8 cm.). The New Lebanon Shaker community was apparently a great center of basketmaking. At first made for the use of the brethren, the baskets were eventually produced for sale as the Shakers began to interact with the outside world and the beauty and durability of their products became known. Made from strips of ash especially chosen by experienced Shaker woodsmen, the baskets were woven over molds of many different shapes.* Rogers Fund, 1966 (66.165.1)

94

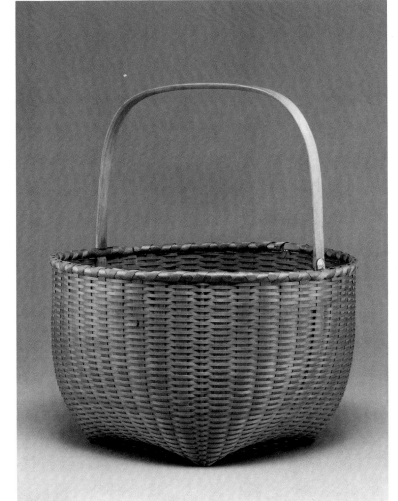

95

93

# The Pre–Civil War Period

## *The Greek Revival, 1820–45*

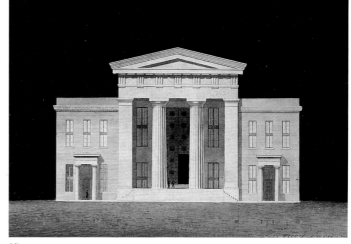

97

Although the Greek Revival style had precedents in European architecture, it was in America that the fashion struck its deepest roots and won the most popular favor. In the second quarter of the century the landscape from Maine to the farthest western outposts sprouted buildings of every description—city mansions and banks, state capitols and outhouses, modest dwellings, wayside stores and saloons—that in one way or another borrowed forms and ornament from the vocabulary of ancient Greek architecture and expressed them in a native idiom. When Samuel Francis Smith wrote "My Country, 'Tis of Thee" in 1832, he referred to the "templed hills" that were then so characteristic of America's countryside; hills dotted with generally temple-like buildings, many of them made of wood or brick but painted "the whitest of white," as Charles Dickens observed, to suggest gleaming marble.

Books by such leading proponents of the style as Asher Benjamin and Minard Lafever provided models and instructions for city architect and country carpenter alike. Benjamin's works, published at Greenfield, Massachusetts, were widely circulated in numerous editions and had a profound influence on the development of architecture throughout much of New England. Alexander Jackson Davis, a prominent and very versatile architect of the time, designed a number of imposing structures in the Greek Revival style (Fig. 97). Among these were the old New York Customs House (1832–42) on Wall Street (now the Federal Hall National Museum), and Colonnade Row, also known as La Grange Terrace, on Lafayette Street in New York. The latter was originally a continuous row of nine ele-

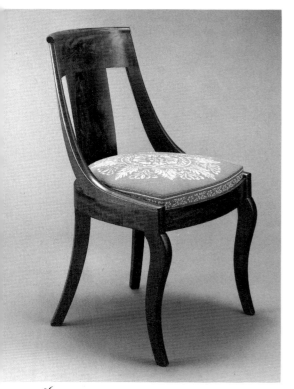

96

**Fig. 96. Gondola chair,** *workshop of Duncan Phyfe (w. 1792–1847), New York, 1837; mahogany, mahogany veneer, mahogany, ash, height 31 inches (78.7 cm.). Broad, simple curves and plenty of richly grained mahogany give this chair from the Foote suite (see also Fig. 98) its character. The cabinetmaking firm of Joseph Meeks and Sons pictured a very similar chair in their broadside of 1833 (see Fig. 254, No. 12).*
Purchase, L. E. Katzenbach Fund Gift, 1966 (66.221.4)

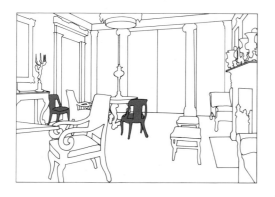

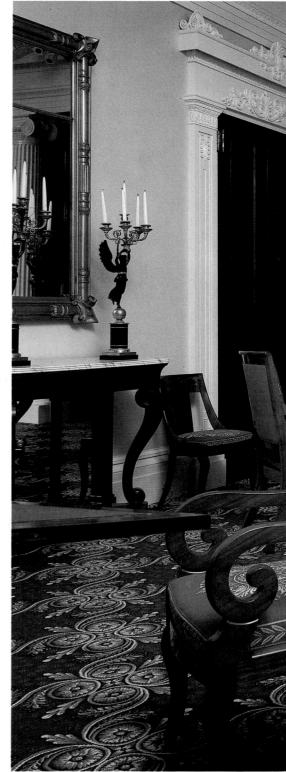

98

**Fig. 97. Design for a public building,** by Alexander Jackson Davis (1803–92), 1835–40; pen and ink, pencil, and watercolor, 12³/₁₆ by 17¹/₂ inches (32.4 by 44.5 cm.). Bold squares and rectangles sparingly ornamented with elements borrowed from Greek temples are characteristic of the Greek Revival style in America. In this design Davis used Doric columns, the plainest of the classical orders, to support a simple triangular pediment. The monumental dignity of the resultant stone facade contrasts strongly with the delicate wood and brick fronts of the earlier Federal style. Much Greek Revival furniture was correspondingly boldly shaped and simply ornamented.
Harris Brisbane Dick Fund, 1924 (24.66.457)

**Fig. 98. Greek Revival Parlor.** *Composed of elements salvaged or copied from Greek Revival houses, this room represents the front parlor of a high-style New York town house of about 1835. The columnar screen with mahogany doors, taken from a New York house, is a particularly fine example of an architectural treatment often found in dwellings with connecting front and back parlors. It is very similar to the design in Plate 60 of Minard Lafever's popular* Modern Builder's Guide *of 1833. The parlor's expanses of unadorned plaster and mahogany embody the Greek Revival aesthetic and serve as a congenial setting for the parlor suite made in 1837 by Duncan Phyfe for New York lawyer Samuel A. Foote and his family. The suite contains couches, pier tables, stools, window seats, and side chairs, all with the broad lines and uncarved mahogany surfaces that succeeded the high-relief naturalism of the 1820s. A set of armchairs that descended in Phyfe's family and a drop-front desk in the French manner that is also very likely Phyfe's work complete the furnishings. Upholstery fabric copied from the original Foote suite and a Brussels carpet woven according to a watercolor pattern of 1827 found in the archives of an English carpet mill carry out the Greek Revival theme of bold stylized motifs and strong colors.*

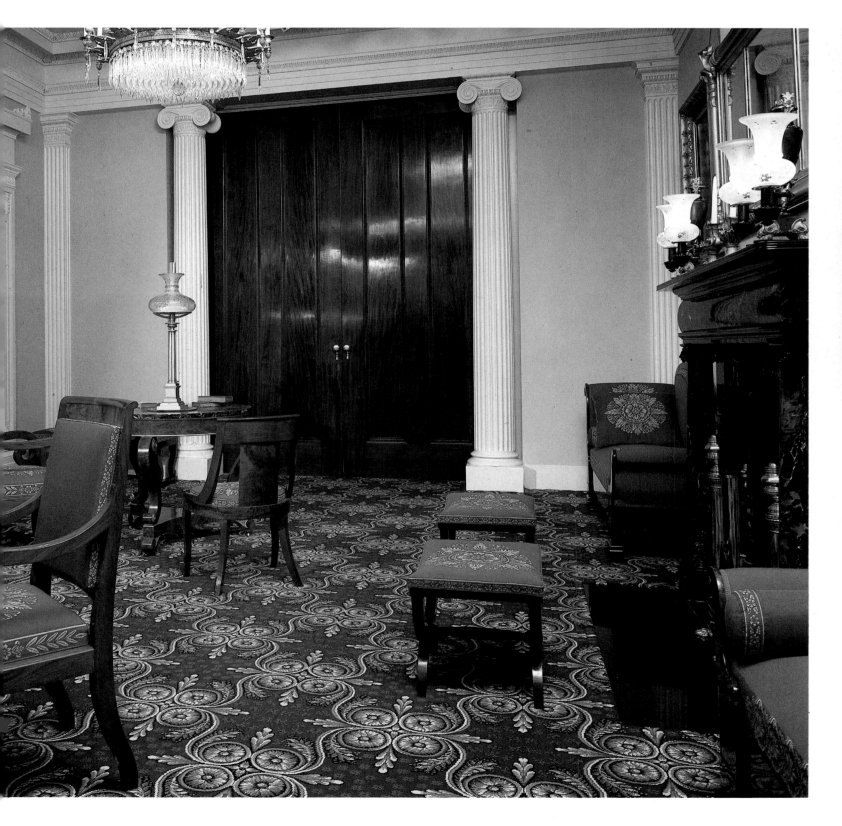

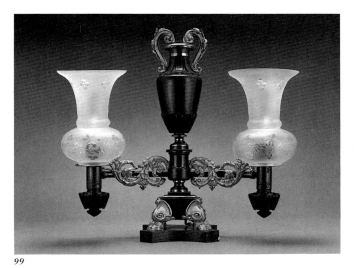

**Fig. 99. Argand lamp,** *labeled "B. Gardiner/N. York," 1835–40; bronze, gilded brass, glass, height 17⅞ inches (45.4 cm.). By using fuel more efficiently than ever before, Argand lamps revolutionized interior lighting. Brighter light and less smoke were its most important features. This example, one of a pair, combines a classical-vase shape and paw feet with flowing acanthus scrolls that foretell the naturalistic curves and foliage of the oncoming rococo style.*
Gift of John C. Cattus, 1967 (67.262.6)

99

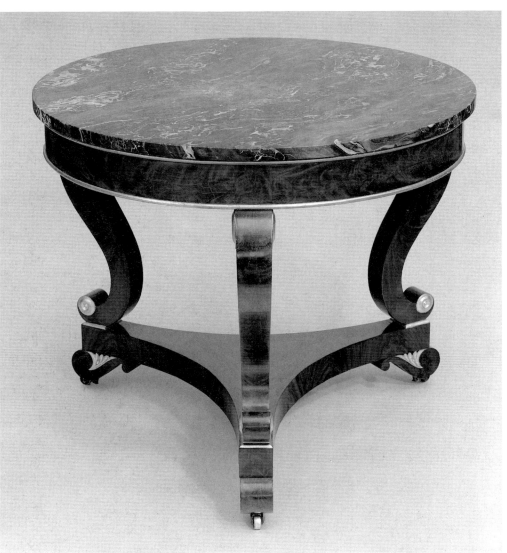

100

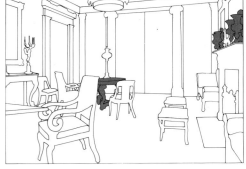

**Fig. 100. Table,** *New York, 1830–35; mahogany, mahogany veneer, marble, height 28½ inches (72.4 cm.), diameter 33⅜ inches (84.8 cm.). The broad, plain scrolls that support the handsome black marble top of this center table are echoed by the smaller scrolls that serve as feet. The table's rich marble, mahogany, and gilt surfaces and its pleasing combination of circles and simple scrolls are characteristic of the finest Greek Revival furniture.*
Bertha King Benkard Memorial Fund, 1974 (1974.146)

gant town houses screened by a monumental Corinthian colonnade.

The Museum's Greek Revival room recreates the front parlor of a fashionable New York City town house of about 1835 (Fig. 98). Such a house, built in the 1830s and still standing on West 11th Street, provided the models for the doorways, window casements, and overall proportions of this room. The screen of Ionic columns came from another New York City house of the period, and the black marble fireplace, typical of Greek Revival architecture, was taken from a Rye, New York, house of about 1825. Cornice and ceiling-rosette designs are based on Lafever's *Modern Builder's Guide* of 1833.

Furnishing the room is an Empire parlor suite, thought to have been made by Duncan Phyfe in 1837 for Samuel A. Foote, which illustrates the late, broadly curving Empire fashion at its best. In spite of their heaviness, a pair of méridiennes (daybeds) with asymmetrical backs and arms achieve a monumental grace. Window benches with plain scrolled legs, so-called gondola chairs (Fig. 96), and curule stools are all simple but elegant accompaniments to the daybeds. Crimson linen-and-wool rep upholstery with woven gold medallions, a facsimile of the original fabric, brilliantly sets off the rich color and grain of the mahogany used for these pieces. The plain scrolls and broad uncarved surfaces of the marble-topped center table (Fig. 100) echo those of the Foote suite. Imposing proportions and richly figured mahogany are also distinguishing characteristics of the *secrétaire à abattant* (Fig. 101), which, like the table, is attributed to the shop of Duncan Phyfe.

During this period virtually all the decorative arts made some reference to

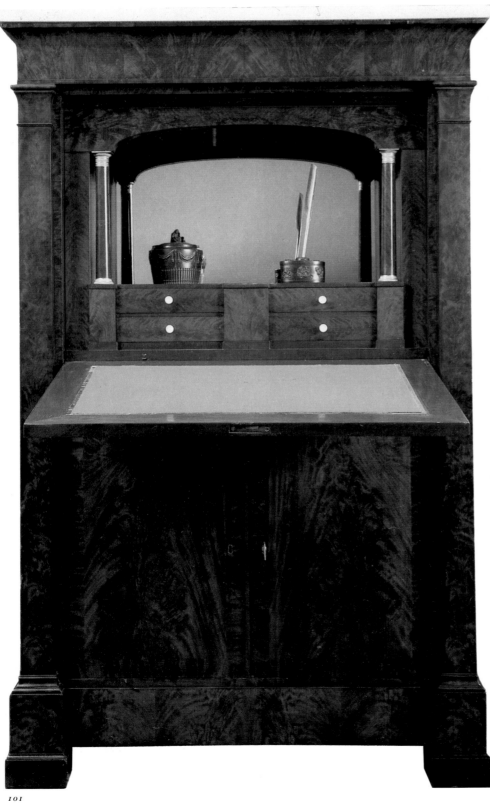

101

ancient Greek designs. An exceptionally handsome bronze Argand lamp made and labeled by Baldwin Gardiner, a well-known New York retailer, is a case in point (Fig. 99). The oil font is made in the shape of an amphora, the two-handled jar used by Greeks and Romans for carrying oil and wine. The neck is ringed by an egg-and-dart molding in the ancient style. Ormolu paw feet similar to the carved and gilded ones of contemporary furniture emerge from sockets derived from Greek architectural ornament. The lamp was made about 1835 or 1840, and the loose, feathery acanthus scrolls along its oil pipes suggest the rococo styles soon to come into fashion.

# The Rococo Revival
# 1840–60

The fading authority of classical styles opened the way for a variety of others, each inspired by a different period of the past. Never in history had there been such a medley of disparate vogues competing for attention, succeeding one another, and often mingling their different designs—a situation that caused confusion which persisted throughout the rest of the nineteenth century. "All we can do," conceded one well-known practitioner, "is to combine, using bits here and there, as our education affords more or less acquaintance with the models from which we steal our material." None of these revival styles was presented without an attribution to a historic style represented by some suggestive element of design—usually employed with imagination and abandon—but these styles tell us more about the nineteenth century than they do about the more distant past.

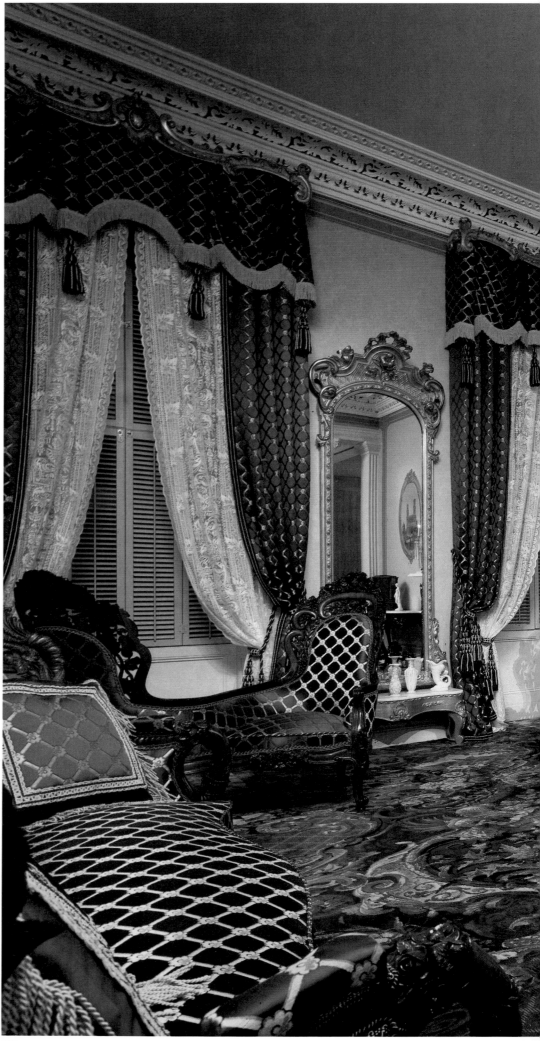

*Fig. 102. The Richard and Gloria Manney, John Henry Belter Rococo Revival Parlor,* about 1852. *Architectural elements taken from a late Greek Revival house built in Astoria, Queens, New York, in about 1852 are used here in a room that recreates a fashionable mid-1850s parlor such as the one published by Minard Lafever in* The Architectural Instructor *(New York, 1856, Pl. LXIII). A set of rosewood furniture by the preeminent New York cabinetmaker and manufacturer John Henry Belter furnishes the parlor. Sets had become popular by the mid-nineteenth century, and one such as this with elaborately carved side and armchairs, sofas, tête-à-têtes, and center and side tables proclaimed the wealth and fashionableness of its owner. The high curving chairbacks are lavishly pierced and carved with characteristically Rococo Revival fruit, flower, and other naturalistic motifs. They are complemented by the richly scrolled carpet, the voluminous and assertively patterned draperies and upholstery, and the gilded, scrolled, and glassornamented chandelier.*

102

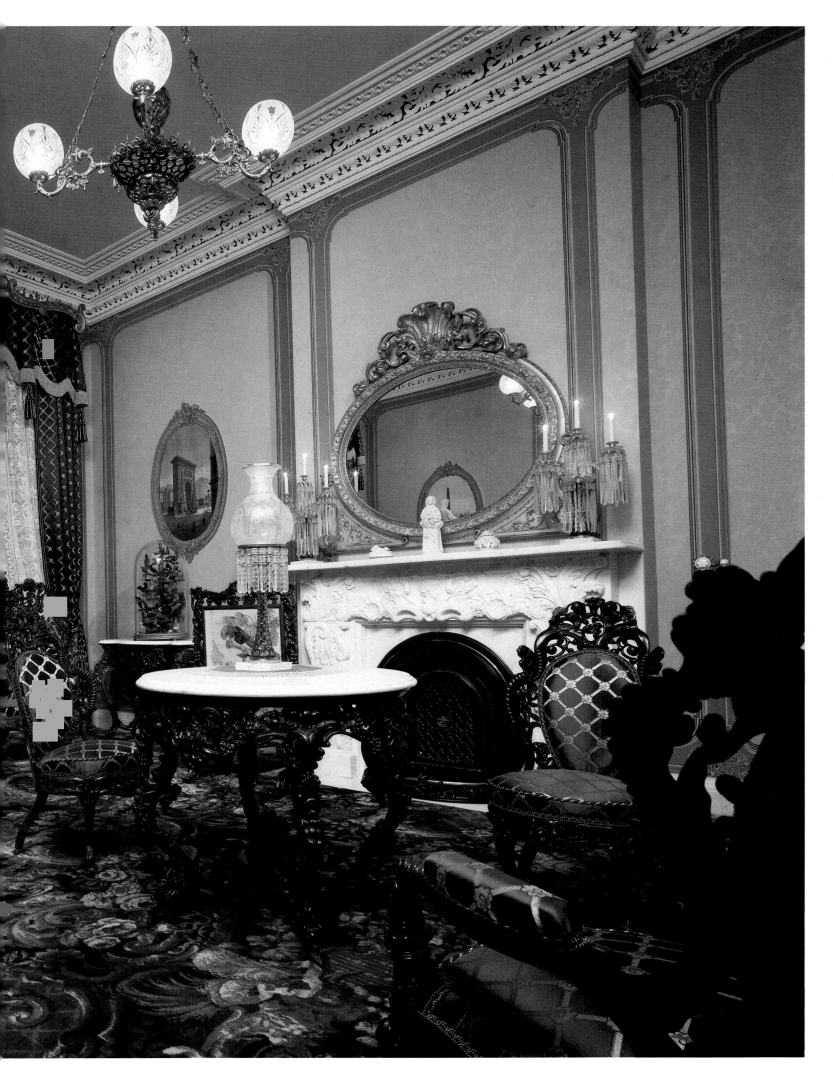

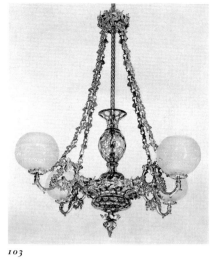

103

*Fig. 103. Chandelier, possibly by Henry N. Hooper and Company, Boston, about 1850; lacquered brass, glass, height 54 inches (137.2 cm.). By mid-century gas was available to city dwellers, and manufacturers were only too happy to supply such elegant fixtures for gaslight as this chandelier. Its central baluster-shaped column and bowl are made of fashionable blue over clear Bohemian glass, and its gilt-bronze arms and chains are composed of rose, leaf, and scroll motifs.*
Rogers Fund, 1969 (69.170)

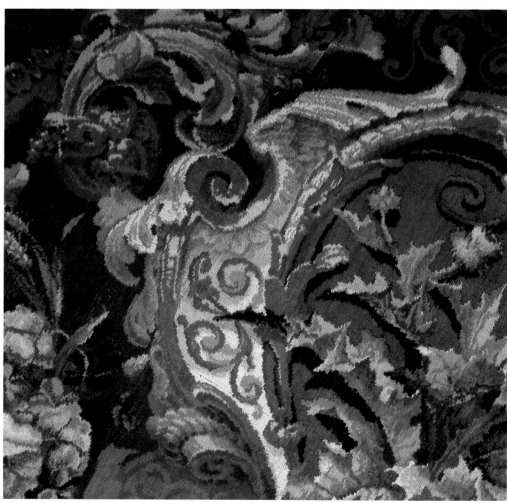

104

*Fig. 104. Tapestry velvet rug, detail, French or English, about 1855. Webster's* Encyclopedia of Domestic Economy *(1844) reported that "Velvet pile carpets are a kind lately introduced. . . . Nothing can surpass their beauty and rich effect. . . ." And, indeed, elaborately patterned floral rugs of this kind carried out the spirit of the pierced, carved, and curved Rococo Revival furniture that sat upon it.*
Rogers Fund, 1963 (63.6)

When the Rococo Revival arrived, at the end of sixty years of classical symmetry and order, people were delighted with its curvaceous lines and highly naturalistic carved ornament. The taste maker Andrew Jackson Downing tells us that by 1850, when his *Architecture of Country Houses* was published, "Modern French furniture [the revived Louis xiv and Louis xv styles] . . . stands much higher in general estimation in this country than any other. Its union of lightness, elegance, and grace renders it especially the favorite of the ladies. . . ."

To display some of its ample collec-

tion of Rococo Revival furnishings, the Museum has installed wood- and plasterwork from the double parlor of a late Greek Revival house built in Astoria, Queens, New York, about 1852 (Fig. 102). In an era when cheap machine-made furniture was becoming the rule, the most opulent Rococo Revival examples were expensive because of their profuse hand-carved ornament, and a Rococo Revival suite was a status symbol. Furniture of this type was considered most appropriate for parlors, living rooms, and bedrooms—often in houses like this that were late, somewhat florid versions of the tenacious neoclassical style.

Two large fluted columns with elaborately carved Corinthian capitals (see p. 20), flanked by pilasters of the same order, separated this from the adjoining half of the parlor. A deep, richly modeled plaster cornice borders the ceiling. A floor covering of flamboyant Wilton carpeting (Fig. 104), typical of the time, indicates how contradictory tastes frequently coexisted in contemporary interiors—as, in fact, they always have. The curved and floral shapes that epitomize the rococo are again employed in the gilded-bronze elements of the chandelier (Fig. 103). Blue over clear- and frosted-glass elements are charmingly combined in the central baluster and the globe-shaped shades. New techniques in glassmaking made such colorful ornamental accessories an important aspect of later nineteenth-century decorative art.

The rococo style as it was developed in this country during the 1850s is sumptuously represented by a laminated rosewood armchair that is almost certainly a product of John Henry Belter's shop (Fig. 106). A label he used between 1856 and 1861 states that he and his workmen were "manufacturers of all kinds of fine furniture." This and the other laminated pieces in the room are not labeled, but they exhibit all the characteristics associated with Belter's manufacturing techniques and are quintessential examples of what we think of as "Belter." The whole repertory of S- and C-scrolls, the cabriole legs, the deeply carved flowers and other natural forms, and the sinuous outlines are all present in the full richness of design and craftsmanship upon which his reputation rests.

Part of a suite that also includes side chairs and a sofa, the armchair is constructed of intricately carved and pierced laminated woods whose assembled motifs, as William Hogarth had remarked about rococo design a century earlier, lead the eye in "a wanton kind of chase." Visually it is indeed a restless piece of furniture: the eye cannot linger on any detail without being distracted by an adjoining curlicue. Yet the allover effect is of a remarkably coherent design without any comparable historical precedent. That same creative vision is seen again in a richly ornamented pier table (Fig. 105) with deeply curved and carved skirt, cabriole legs, and undulating saltire stretcher centering a lavish floral bouquet. In each piece frippery and vigor have been brought together with telling effect.

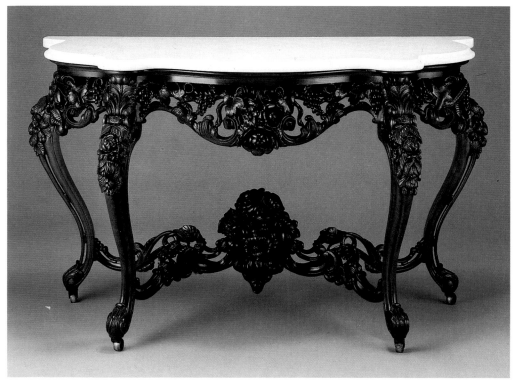

105

*Fig. 105. Console table,* attributed to John Henry Belter (1804–63), New York, about 1855; rosewood, height 54½ inches (138.4 cm.). This table, one of a pair, exhibits the deep, rich scrolling and curving forms and the luxuriant fruit, flower, and leaf decoration that distinguish Belter tables. "Belter's signature," according to expert Marvin Schwartz, "is the very high quality of the design and carving, the vitality with which the parts are juxtaposed, and the richness of the details."
Gift of Richard and Gloria Manney, 1980 (1980.510.2)

*Fig. 106. Armchair,* attributed to John Henry Belter (1804–63), New York, about 1855; rosewood, ash, pine, walnut, height 50 inches (127 cm.). Part of the suite of furniture that is displayed in the Belter Parlor, this armchair is elaborately pierced and carved in the Rococo Revival manner. It had not previously been possible to create furniture with such elaborate lacy crests, but the revival of the technique of steaming and bending into curved shapes thin layers of veneer laid at right angles created very strong surfaces that could be carved into the most delicate motifs. Along with the scrolls and twisted cornucopia shapes that form the back are oak leaves and acorns and naturalistic roses. In true nineteenth-century fashion, the cabriole legs are vigorously curved and fitted with casters.
Gift of Mrs. Charles Reginald Leonard, in memory of Edgar Welch Leonard, Robert Jarvis Leonard, and Charles Reginald Leonard, 1957 (57.130.2)

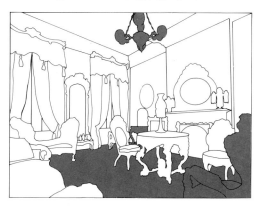

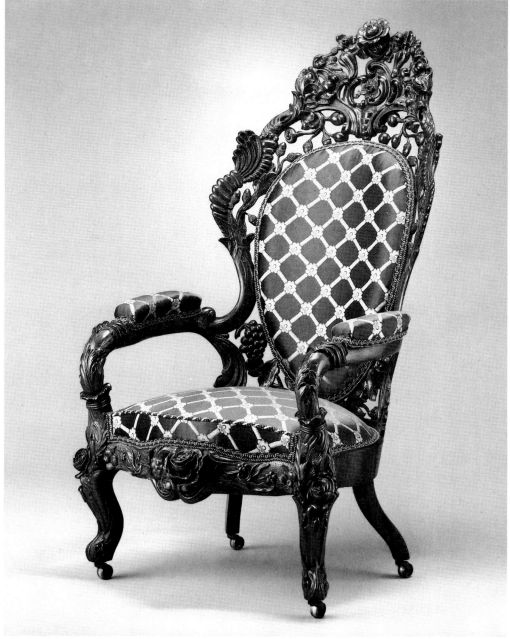

106

# The Gothic Revival, 1830–75

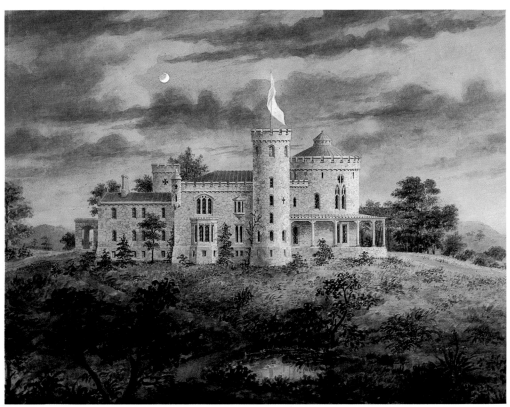

107

*Fig. 107. Design for Herrick House, by Alexander Jackson Davis (1803–92), 1855; watercolor, pen and ink, 30 by 25⅜ inches (76.2 by 64.5 cm.). Pointed windows with Gothic tracery, a crenelated roof line, and round towers add atmosphere and romance to this comfortable country villa. Davis's goal was not moral or philosophical, like that of many nineteenth-century reformers who promoted Gothic design, but rather the creation of a charming and romantic dwelling. Gothic details transformed a building that was essentially solidly modern.*
Harris Brisbane Dick Fund, 1924 (24.66.10)

In England a "Gothic" strain in furniture, decoration, and architecture had lingered through the centuries since medieval times, surviving even the overwhelming popularity of the styles introduced by the brothers Adam and their followers in the late eighteenth and early nineteenth centuries. Horace Walpole, a brilliant and somewhat eccentric man of letters, disparaged the Adams's concoctions as being all "gingerbread, filigraine, and fan-painting" and built himself a fantastic house, Strawberry Hill at Twickenham, in what it pleased him to call the Gothic style. As he once wrote a friend, however, "every true Goth must perceive that [my rooms] are more the works of fancy than imitation." A few years earlier his somewhat older contemporary the ornamental designer Batty Langley had written a book known as *Gothic Architecture, Improved by Rules and Proportions in Many Grand Designs of Columns, Doors, Windows.* . . . Here Langley set down wildly inaccurate versions of what he considered to be in the "Gothick taste," and they were copied as such. The same antiquarian enthusiasm led Sir Walter Scott to build his celebrated residence, Abbotsford. Washington Irving spent four memorable days with Scott and returned to America to remodel his home, Sunnyside, at Tarrytown, New York, as a Gothic "nookery."

In eighteenth-century America, at least one country retreat, like Strawberry Hill a sort of architectural "folly," had been built by Benjamin Latrobe on the outskirts of Philadelphia; it was followed by occasional other adventures in the same spirit. Even earlier, that confirmed classicist Thomas Jefferson had considered placing a Gothic "temple" in his garden at Monticello.

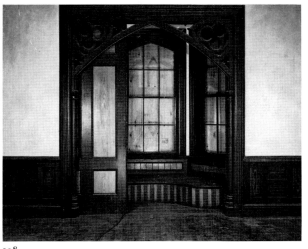

**Fig. 108. Interior detail** (*photograph taken before installation*), *window embrasure from a house built by Frederick Clarke Withers (1828–1901), 1859. The screen that frames the embrasure is composed of Gothic colonnettes whose capitals support an openwork pointed arch with pierced tetrafoils in the two spandrels. Beneath the central window, also topped by a pointed arch, a spacious curved seating surface rests on a support faced with vertical strips of alternating light and dark woods.*

Gift of Mrs. Hamilton Fish, 1977 (Inst. 1977.7.1)

*108*

But it was Andrew Jackson Downing, a generation later, who gave the Gothic Revival style its great impetus in America. Downing was not only an eminent landscape architect in a day when that profession was barely recognized, but he was also one of the most perceptive and widely esteemed taste makers of the time. His career was tragically brief but his books on horticulture, domestic architectural and furniture design, and the art of landscaping won him an international audience and renown. (The queen of Denmark, for example, sent him a "magnificent ring" in appreciation of his works.)

Downing had an almost religious belief in "the power and virtue of the individual home," placed in the right setting and sensitively furnished to support and preserve human dignity. A number of his books were illustrated by his friend Alexander Jackson Davis, whose many structures in the Gothic Revival style were as felicitous as those he designed in the classical mode. Davis's architectural exhibits at the New York Crystal Palace won him a number of diplomas and medals. He was an excellent draftsman, and his renderings of the buildings he designed are works of art in themselves (Fig. 107). It was in no small part due to the influence of these two highly accomplished men that during the several decades preceding the Civil War the American scene burgeoned with cottages, "palaces," and churches that, with some stretch of the imagination, could be associated with the spirit of the Middle Ages.

Around the middle of the century Downing wrote that the ambition of almost every person building in America was to put up a Gothic cottage. "The Greek Temple disease has passed its cri-

sis," he exulted in 1846. "The people have survived it." Instead of the gleaming white of the Greek-style structures, Downing urged his readers and clients to use the colors of grass, stone, and moss that would blend into the natural landscape. Once again the nation's architectural face was radically changing its expression. Aside from cottages, every conceivable type of structure from university buildings to garden houses, from penitentiaries to park shelters, and from railroad stations to clubhouses were built in the new style.

To design such a miscellaneous assortment of buildings, their interior decoration, and their furnishings required ingenuity and imagination. The problem was akin to the one that affected Nathaniel Hawthorne in his writing. "No author, without a trial," he observed in *The Marble Faun*, "can conceive of the difficulty of writing a romance about a country where there is no shadow, no antiquity, no mystery, no picturesque and gloomy wrong, nor anything but a commonplace prosperity, in broad and simple daylight, as is happily the case with my dear native land."

Gothic furniture was generally considered especially appropriate for libraries and halls, and the library of a house in Newburgh, New York, has been chosen to serve as a background for a number of representative and outstanding examples. At one end of the interior is a recessed window embrasure (Fig. 108) that can be closed off by a sliding door. A paneled wood dado extends from the embrasure around the rest of the interior to the fireplace opposite. The central area of the floor is covered by an unusual English needlework carpet of

the same period as the room. Its pattern of multifoil designs surrounded by a running border of entwined leaves and tendrils is a handsome reflection of the Gothic taste. Rosettes, each the center of a frame of molded ribs, decorate the ceiling. A deeply and boldly molded cornice is fringed by a colorful stenciled design of floral motifs. The interior is in general a remote echo of the work of that insistent French revivalist Eugène Emmanuel Viollet-le-Duc, who played such an important role in the restoration of French Gothic monuments in the middle years of the last century, and whose efforts have been both praised and damned for their independence from strict historical accuracy.

In his book *The Architecture of Country Houses*, published in 1850, Downing noted that the firm of Burns and Trainque of New York made "The most correct Gothic furniture that we have yet seen executed in this country. . . ." These cabinetmakers may have made the rectangular oak and walnut library table illustrated here (Fig. 109)—a solid and eminently handsome piece that thoroughly justifies Downing's confident belief that capable designers could "unite a simple and chaste Gothic style with forms adapted to and expressive of our modern domestic life."

Bookcases were, of course, essential to such rooms, and they lent themselves especially well to decoration in the Gothic style (Fig. 111). That such forms were highly valued is attested by the fact that at least one family of Forty-Niners attempted the almost impossible task of taking one with them across the continent. They eventually had to abandon the piece along the trail, but a succeeding group of adventurers discovered it—"a very handsome and new Gothic

**Fig. 109. Library table,** *attributed to Burns and Trainque, New York, about 1855; oak with walnut panels, cherry, poplar, height 29¼ inches (74.3 cm.). Made about the same year that Belter produced some of his most lavishly curved, beflowered, and befruited pieces, this table expresses an entirely different style. Where the Rococo Revival is frivolous, the Gothic is solid, sober, and worthy. This example stands on four sturdy, ringbanded cluster columns that terminate in square molded plinths, reminiscent of some Gothic architectural constructions. On the drawer fronts are inset dark walnut panels with trefoil designs that contrast agreeably with the surrounding lighter oak frame.*
Gift of Berry B. Tracy, 1979 (1979.484)

**Fig. 110. Girandoles,** *by William F. Shaw (active about 1845–1900), Boston, 1848–51; gilt on brass, marble, glass, height 14 inches (35.6 cm.). Cast in the form of the Gothic chapel at Mount Auburn Cemetery in Cambridge, Massachusetts, these girandoles exemplify the Victorian love of the picturesque, incorporating numerous Gothic forms and motifs. Mount Auburn was America's first planned cemetery, with landscaping so impressive that the great landscape architect Andrew Jackson Downing called it "the Athens of New England."*
Purchase, Mr. and Mrs. H. O. H. Frelinghuysen Gift and Friends of the American Wing Fund, 1983 (1983.97.1–3)

**Fig. 111. Bookcase,** *United States, about 1855; oak, pine, height 71 inches (180.3 cm.). Imposing Gothic-style pieces like this were considered suitable for the library by popular mid-nineteenth-century architect Alexander Jackson Davis. Impressive in its size, given Gothic verticality by pairs of narrow rectangular doors on both top and bottom sections, and ornamented with lavish carving inspired by medieval Gothic architecture, this bookcase creates the proper serious and studious atmosphere.*
Sansbury-Mills Fund, 1977 (1977.310)

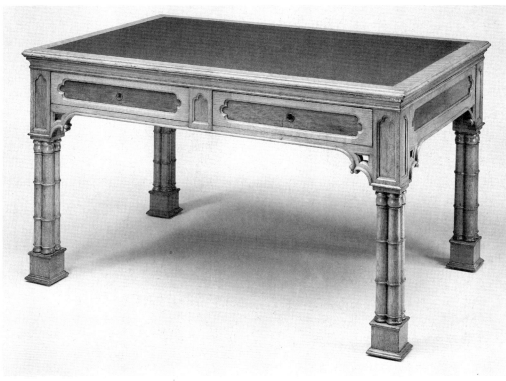

109

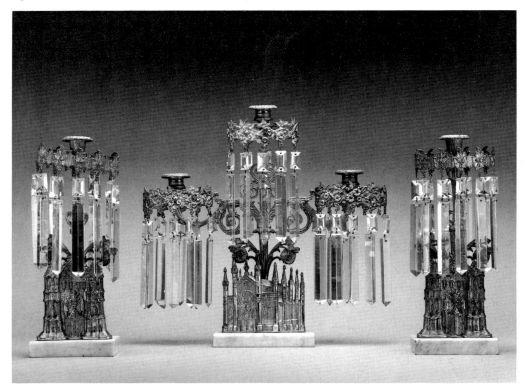

110

bookcase!" as they recorded their find—and in that treeless terrain they quickly dismembered it to feed the fires that boiled their coffee kettles.

Flickering light was particularly suitable for Gothic-style interiors, whose ambience greatly depended on the romantic contrasts of light and shadow. The prisms of three girandoles (Fig. 110), whose bases are cast into the shape of the Gothic Revival Bigelow Chapel at Mount Auburn Cemetery in Cambridge, Massachusetts, reflect light and create moving shadows, while at the same time they serve as souvenirs of the famous cemetery.

Although it eventually waned as a popular fashion in domestic design, the medieval strain continued to assert itself in various ways for many years. The towering Woolworth building in downtown Manhattan with its Gothic-like flourishes is one prominent example. To our own day the style has determined the design of religious buildings with their peaked roofs, spires, and stained-glass windows. And in "collegiate Gothic" architecture the chapels and dormitories of many of our leading universities remind us of the scholastic and spiritual zeal that we associate with our ideal vision of the medieval world. The heritage is deeply rooted and probably will never be forgotten or neglected. After many years of interrupted labor, the world's largest church in the Gothic style, the Cathedral of St. John the Divine, is still rising on Morningside Heights in New York, and it very likely will be growing toward its completed size for years to come.

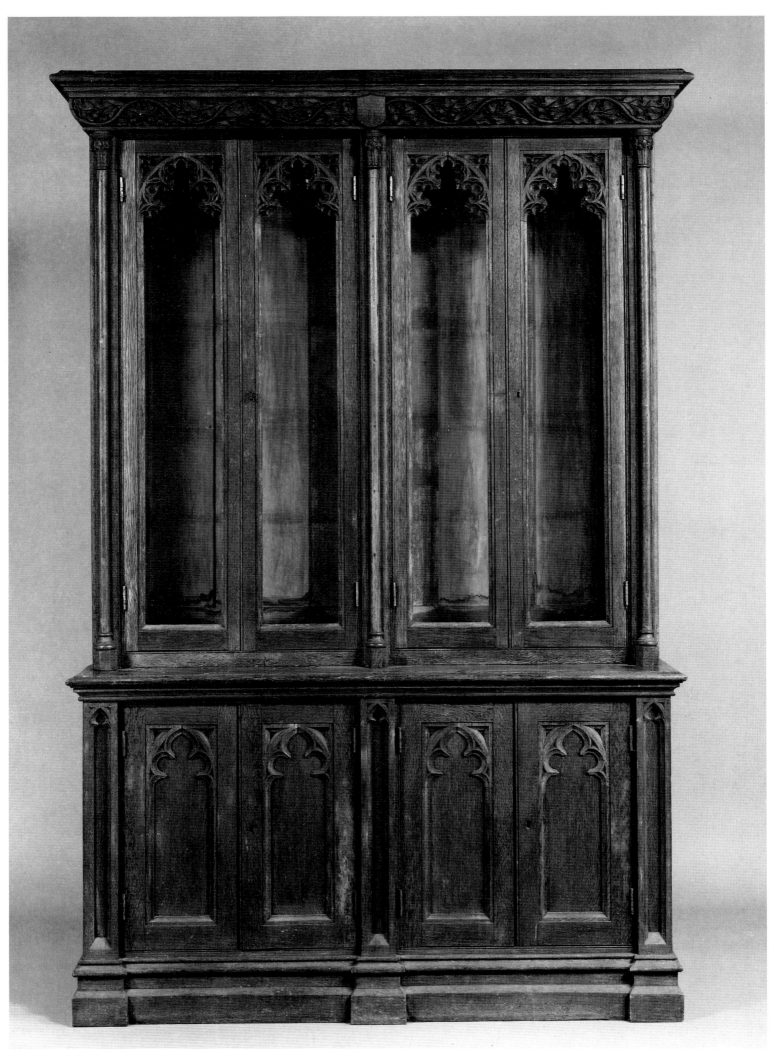

111

# The Post–Civil War Period
## The Renaissance Revival, 1860–80

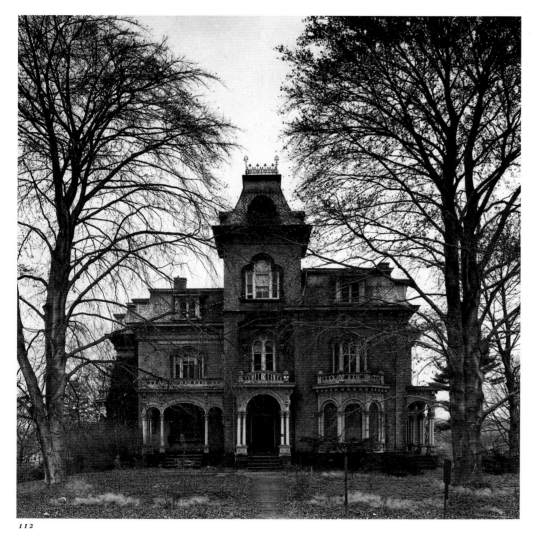

112

**Fig. 112. Beechwood Lodge,** built for Jedediah Wilcox, Meriden, Connecticut, 1868–70; the Museum's room was taken from this mansion before it was demolished in the 1960s.

In 1870, as the popularity of the Renaissance style was still growing, one Jedediah Wilcox of Meriden, Connecticut, built what the press termed a "princely residence" of forty rooms (Fig. 112). Everything in it, the report continued, was "grand, as the French say" and "rich in design and appearance." (Among its other features, it was the first house in Meriden to have running water, a phenomenon then virtually unheard of.) The sitting room and some of its original furnishings have been installed in The American Wing, and to add to the confusion in terminology already mentioned, a local paper reported that the interior had been "fitted up in the Marie Antoinette style of art" and the soft furniture "upholstered in the Grand Duchess style," generally of scarlet satin (Figs. 113 and 114).

Here, in any case, may be seen other examples of what we choose to refer to as the Renaissance Revival style. The ornate woodwork itself, including the overmantel mirror and the architectural surrounds of a doorway and window, essentially repeats the design that embellishes the furnishings of the room. A sofa (Fig. 114), the central piece of seating furniture, was conceived as three separate chair backs brought together in a unified design. The central element of the crest rail is a framed mother-of-pearl medallion flanked by a pair of carved, draped-urn-like knobs. Arm and side chairs are designed en suite— they share ornamental skirts beneath seat rails, turned tapered legs in the shape of "trumpets" (not unlike those found in seventeenth-century designs), and curvilinear back legs and stiles. All are made of rosewood and are further ornamented with thin, gilded incised lines—a common practice at the time.

**Fig. 113. Armchair,** *probably New York, about 1870; rosewood, gilt, height 44½ inches (113 cm.). The assertive symmetrical nature of Renaissance Revival design is clearly apparent in the bold triangular medallion, the focal point of the crest rail on this and the other seating furniture in this suite (see also Fig. 114). Incised lines in the Eastlake tradition of flat linear ornament reinforce and elaborate the shape of the angular medallion, which centers a mother-of-pearl profile in the Louis XVI tradition. Such richly tufted and buttoned upholstery, characteristic of the most fashionable Rococo and Renaissance Revival seating furniture, had come into fashion before mid-century, with the invention of the coiled inner spring.*
Gift of Josephine M. Fiala, 1968 (68.133.3)

**Fig. 114. Sofa,** *probably New York, about 1870; rosewood, gilt, length 76¾ inches (195 cm.). This sofa and the armchair in Fig. 113 belong to a large suite of furniture commissioned by Jedediah Wilcox for the sitting room of his forty-room mansion at 816 Broad Street, Meriden, Connecticut. In describing the house, a November 1870 newspaper article stated that the "sitting room . . . is fitted up in the Marie Antoinette style of art, the crimson curtains, sofas, lounges, chairs and furniture generally, being covered with scarlet satin." The symmetrical design and classical motifs such as the mother-of-pearl head carved on the medallion, the draped urns, and the tapering turned front legs are no doubt what caused the reporter to name this style after Marie Antoinette, for she was queen during the late eighteenth century, when the neoclassical style dominated France.*
Gift of Josephine M. Fiala, 1968 (68.133.1)

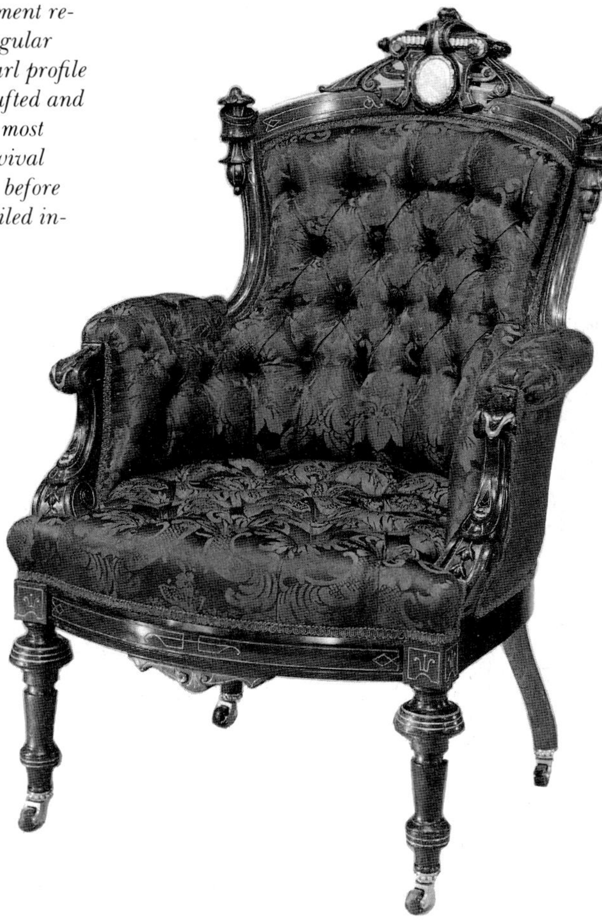

113

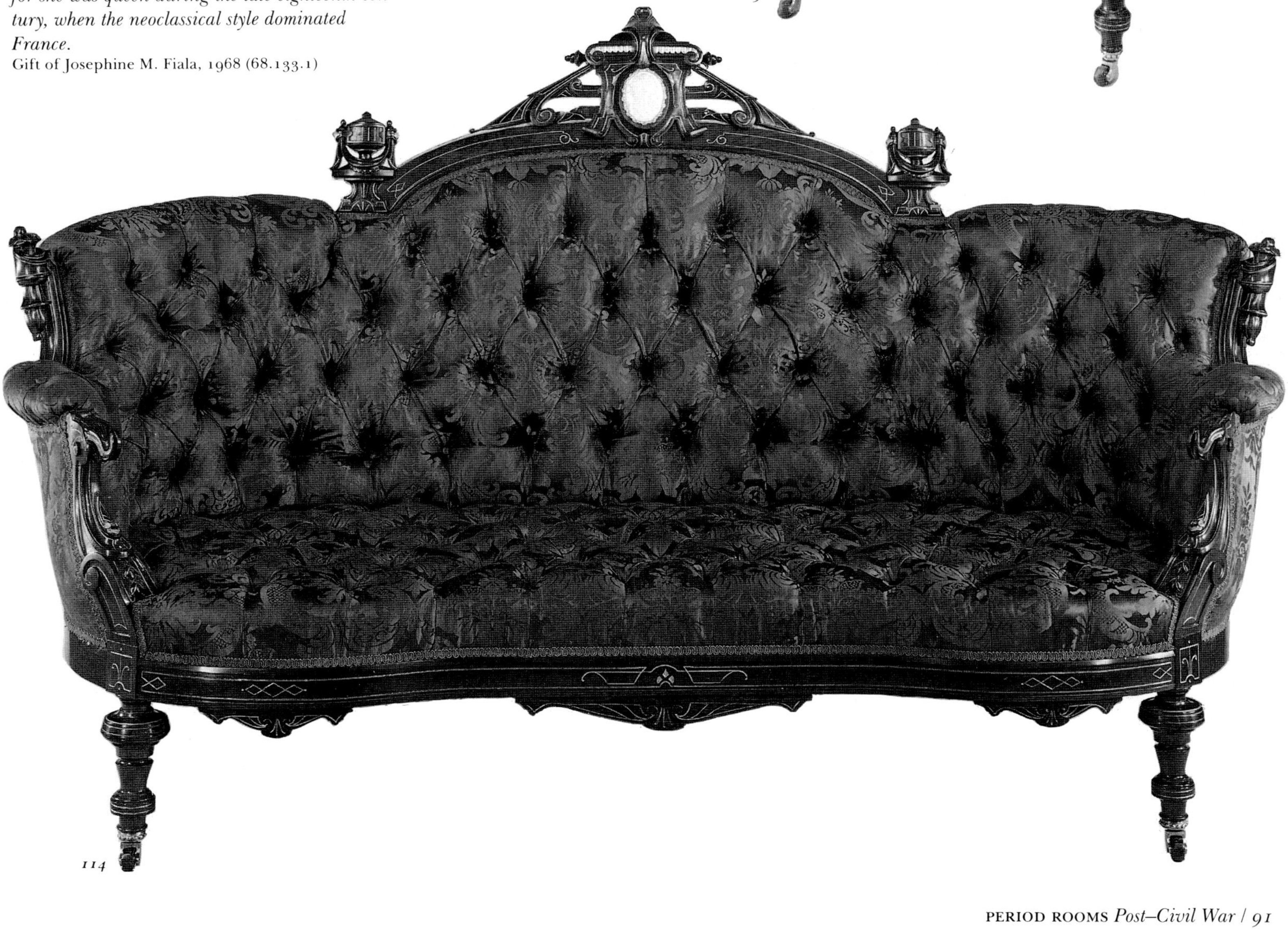

114

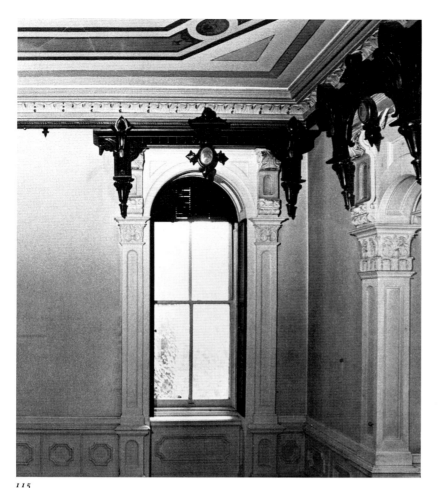

*Fig. 115. Architectural detail,* at Beechwood
Lodge, Meriden, Connecticut.
Gift of Josephine M. Fiala, 1968 (68.143.1)

These amply padded tufted seats indicated a trend that soon caused most of
the important furnishing houses to refer to themselves as "upholsterers." This
development was, in part, supported by
the oncoming popularity of Moorish
dens, oriental divans, and Turkish cozy-
corners with their abundance of soft, inviting upholstered furniture.

As might be expected, the twelve-
branch bronze gas-burning chandelier
in the sitting room, a design by Mitchell,
Vance and Company, was completely
consonant with the rest of the decor
(Fig. 116). It has twenty gas jets of different sorts, the light from which was
refracted by engraved- and cut-glass
globes.

115

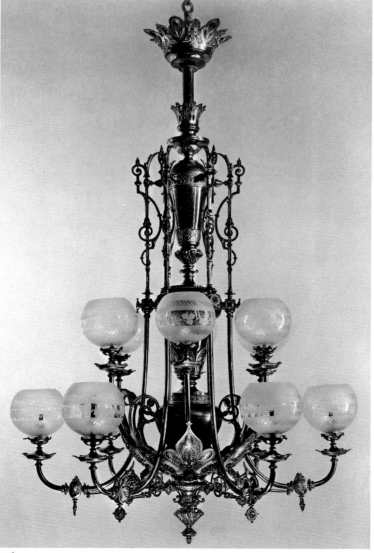

116

*Fig. 116. Chandelier,* by Mitchell, Vance and
Company (established 1854), New York, about
1870; bronze, engraved and cut glass, height 68
inches (172.7 cm.). Gas for heat and light was
not generally available until after the Civil War,
when the cities began to install pipe lines. This
gas-burning chandelier, from the sitting room of
the Wilcox house, is a typical nineteenth-century
eclectic concoction mixing a variety of motifs from
different periods, including classical Greek,
Gothic, and—for want of a more precise word—
"Renaissance." The last of these is conspicuously
represented by the vase-shaped urns that form the
central shaft—they are comparable to the urns
used in decorating cabinets, tables, and other
pieces of furniture during this period.
Purchase, Anonymous Gift, 1968 (68.143.5)

# The Twentieth Century

**Fig. 117. Wall lamp,** *designed by Frank Lloyd Wright (1867–1959), 1912–14; oak, frosted glass, height 32 inches (81.3 cm.). The emphasis on verticals and horizontals that is so apparent in Wright's architecture is also present in the design of the wall lamps for the Littles' living room (see Fig. 119). The lamps are made of the same light-colored oak as that used for the woodwork of the room; thus, like most of Wright's furnishings, both their form and their surfaces echo those of the architecture.*
Purchase, Emily Crane Chadbourne Bequest, 1972 (1972.60.2)

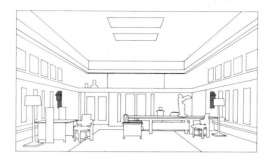

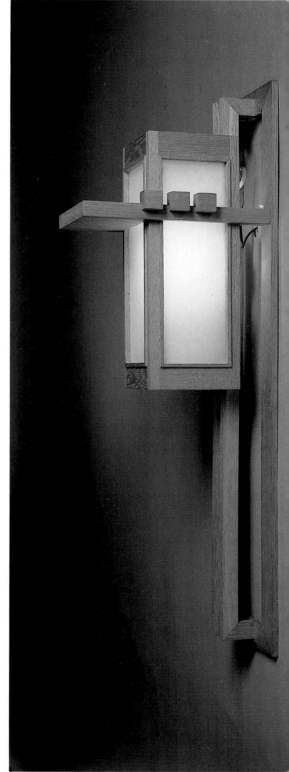

The most recent period interior installed in The American Wing comes from a residence built by Frank Lloyd Wright, widely considered America's most influential architect. When he was a young man Wright had become a disciple of Louis Henri Sullivan, that prophet of modern architecture who in the 1880s and 1890s was transforming the architectural profile of Chicago with his innovative, handsomely conceived skyscrapers. After a few years with Sullivan, the younger man went his own way, though he continued to look on Sullivan as his *Lieber Meister*—beloved master.

Throughout his long life Wright's restless imagination and accumulating experience led to a constant renewal of his vision. In industrial and public buildings he was a pathfinder with radical solutions to different problems in design and construction. His contributions to domestic architecture were no less original and important. His novel approach to the timeless but ever-changing requirements of human shelter cleared the way for others to follow his lead.

About the turn of the century Wright introduced what quickly became known as his "prairie houses." These low-lying structures, cunningly adapted to their sites in the flat midwestern countryside, altered the course of twentieth-century architecture. Within, Wright completely eliminated the boxlike arrangement of rooms that had for so long been standard building practice, opening the interior into a free-flowing series of spaces, doing away with what he considered unnecessary partitions and doors. He used light and space as the equivalent of natural building materials (as had medieval cathedral builders). At

the same time, Wright eschewed all reference to traditional form and ornament, never violating the natural colors and textures of wood and stone with uncalled-for embellishment. As Henry James observed of one of these structures, it was a house "all beautiful with omissions."

The great living room now incorporated in the Wing (Fig. 119) is from a house Wright completed as a summer residence for Francis W. Little at Wayzata, a suburb of Minneapolis, in 1914 (Fig. 118). It was the second house he built for this demanding client, and it combined elements of prairie-house design with new ideas Wright began implementing after 1910. The Littles used this large room set in its own freestanding pavilion for entertaining and for the musical recitals they frequently held. High above the floor floats a hipped ceiling lighted by five stained-glass skylights that serve as a glowing central focus for the interior below.

Glass played a prominent role in Wright's houses. There were almost three hundred windows in the Little house, and the necessary window openings in the walls, Wright insisted, must be tightly integrated with the structural elements surrounding them. Each side wall of the room has a continuous bank of twelve interrelated window panels made up of multiple, geometrically arranged, leaded (or, more accurately, electroglazed) glass segments spotted with bits of colored glass. Those geometric motifs are repeated in a bank of square clerestory windows above and again in windows at each end of the room. At the insistence of his client, Wright made the main areas of the window of clear glass instead of using the tinted panels he had originally pro-

117

posed. One of the most important aspects of the Little living room is that it exhibits so clearly one of Wright's seminal contributions to modern architecture: his concept of dynamic spatial continuity. The glass walls and skylighted ceiling allowed a harmonious combination of light and unrestricted open space that created the kind of total effect that contributed to Wright's international reputation. One Dutch architect who came to America early in the century to see Wright's buildings left "with the conviction of having seen a genuinely modern work, and with respect for the master able to create things which had no equal in Europe."

Wright considered the furnishings and other domestic equipment of his houses integral elements of his architectural program. Wherever possible he chose to do away with "fixtures of every kind, and to incorporate into the architecture all means of lighting, heating, or ventilating" (Fig. 117). That program was made more practical by such advances in domestic technology as central heating, electricity, and other more or less recent developments. Except as ornamental and gracious accessories, the fireplace and the candle had long since headed the way of the parlor and the outhouse—toward obsolescence.

Wright believed that the furniture that cluttered the average interior was quite unnecessary. Most of the chairs, tables, lamps, and other objects displayed in the Museum's room are from the architect's designs, and made of white oak. Like the furniture he conceived for his other houses these forms are architectonic—relentlessly rigid. Even his occasional upholstered, freestanding seating furniture (Fig. 121) follows the strong horizontal and vertical lines of his architecture, rather than the curved lines of the human body.

Some pieces, such as a print table (Fig. 120), two plant stands, armchairs, and a large reading table, had probably been created for the earlier Little house. They are stained a dark brown. Others, fashioned specifically for the Wayzata house, are treated with a blond wax finish and are more severe in conception. Unlike the furniture and built-in fixtures, some of the accessories used in the room were not among the Littles' original furnishings. However, objects such as the candlesticks by Robert Jarvie

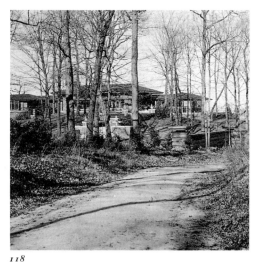

**Fig. 118. Francis W. Little house,** *designed by Frank Lloyd Wright (1867–1959), Wayzata, Minnesota, 1912–14. When this house was torn down in 1972, the Museum bought the interior woodwork, fittings, and the furniture from the living room, which is now installed in The American Wing.*

118

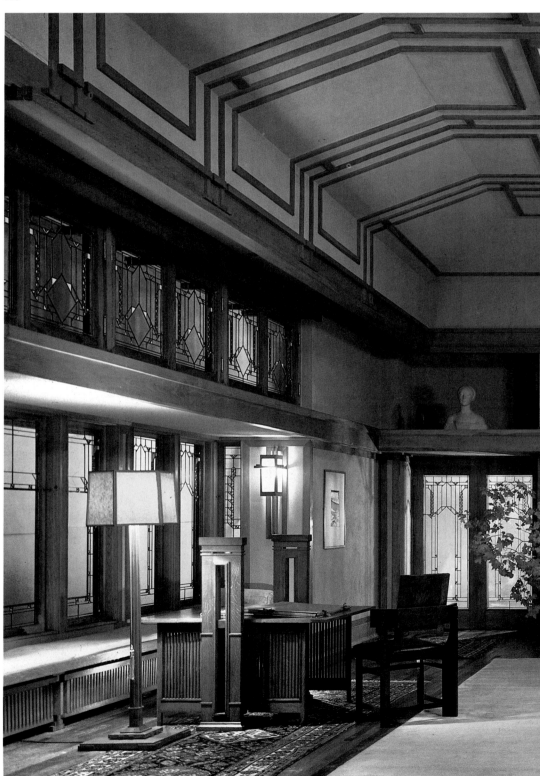

119

**Fig. 119. Living room,** *Francis W. Little house, designed by Frank Lloyd Wright (1867–1959), Wayzata, Minnesota, 1912–14. Wright's prairie houses, so called because their horizontal lines and open interior spaces repeat the contours and spaces of the Illinois plains where they were first built, incorporated most of the ideas considered characteristic of twentieth-century American houses. The Little living room encloses space to provide, in architectural specialist Peter Blake's words, "a succession of experiences so varied and yet so continuously related that the interior became a symphony of space and light." The furnishings and accessories, many of which were designed by Wright himself, reflect the same concerns as the architecture, and they are arranged to preserve the flow of Wright's spaces. The windows, which allow the interior spaces to merge with the exterior, are of leaded glass, broken up into small panes that catch and reflect fragments of light instead of appearing dark and blank, as a picture window would.*

Purchase, Emily Crane Chadbourne Bequest, 1972 (1972.60.1)

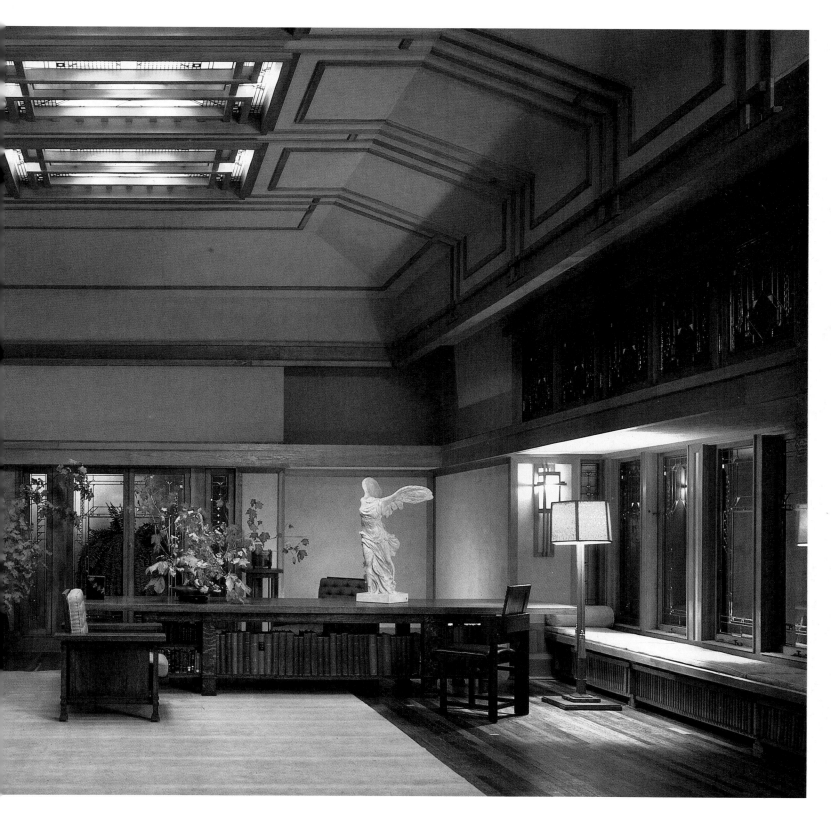

**Fig. 120. Print table,** *by Frank Lloyd Wright (1867–1959), probably 1902–03; oak, overall height 45⅜ inches (115.3 cm.). Probably made for the earlier house Wright had built for the Littles, this table was designed to store prints vertically and to open to a flat horizontal study surface. At once bold, with its strong vertical posts, and elegant, with many refined details, such as the delicate spindles within the gates that swing out to support the broad leaves, the table is among Wright's finest achievements as a furniture designer.*
Purchase, Emily Crane Chadbourne Bequest, 1972 (1972.60.8a,b)

**Fig. 121. Armchair,** *designed by Frank Lloyd Wright (1867–1959), probably 1902–03; oak, height 33¼ inches (84.5 cm.). Like all Wright's architecture and furniture of this period, this chair is uncompromisingly rectilinear. Thin bands of horizontal molding on sides and legs provide a graceful link between vertical and horizontal lines. Wright is thought to have designed this and three matching armchairs for the first house he built for the Littles, in Peoria, Illinois. When the new house in Wayzata was finished, Mr. and Mrs. Little installed these chairs in the living room.*
Purchase, Emily Crane Chadbourne Bequest, 1972 (1972.60.4)

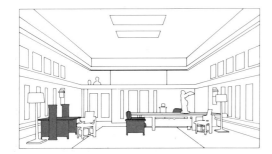

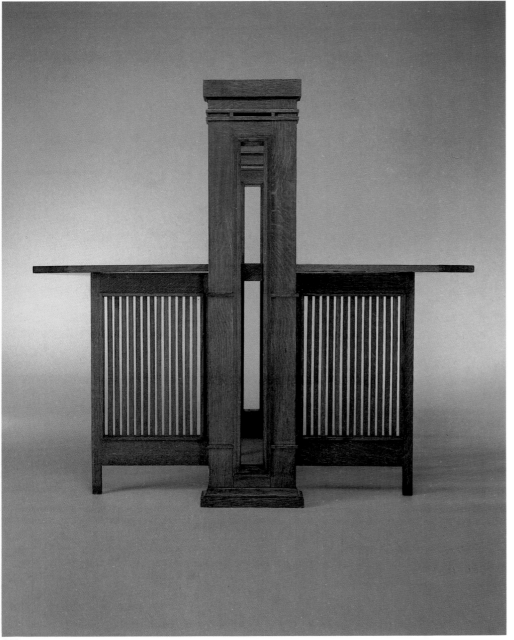

120

(Fig. 122) are interesting and representative examples of work by another gifted designer of the time.

There were, of course, many other American architects, craftsmen, and designers who were turning their backs on traditional and European forms in favor of concepts that were particularly related to American and modern ways of life. Notable among architect-designers were the brothers Charles Sumner Greene and Henry Mather Greene, exact contemporaries of Wright. While Wright was developing his prairie house, the Greenes were creating a distinctive type of domestic architecture in and about Pasadena that was peculiarly well suited to the southern California landscape. Like Wright, who admired their work, they were interested in Japanese architecture, and although its influence was much more obvious in their designs than in Wright's, this exotic strain was thoroughly domesticated in the Greenes' work. Like Wright, too, they opened up the interiors of their houses with carefully integrated spacious areas, designed fixtures and furnishings as part of the total scheme for a dwelling, and played up the qualities of the natural materials used throughout. The grounds and gardens surrounding their exquisitely fashioned structures were also part of their overall plan. Again like Wright (and many other architects of the time) the Greenes made effective use of colored glass, sometimes depending on panels provided by Louis Comfort Tiffany.

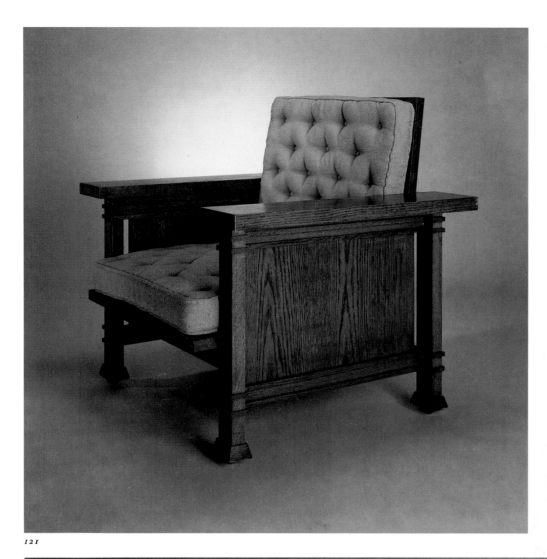

121

*Fig. 122. Table,* designed by Frank Lloyd
Wright (1867–1959), 1912–14; oak, height
26⁵/₁₆ inches (67.1 cm.). Wright probably designed this library table specifically for this room,
and like the other furnishings he designed for the
Little house, it is composed of strong horizontals
and verticals. The pair of marked bronze candlesticks were designed by Robert Jarvie about 1901
for The Jarvie Shop in Chicago. They were not
among the Littles' original furnishings, but are
included in the display to illustrate the work of a
gifted Arts and Crafts designer to whom Wright
gave numerous commissions.
Purchase, Emily Crane Chadbourne Bequest, 1972
(1972.60.3); Purchase, Mr. and Mrs. David Lubart
Gift, in memory of Katherine J. Lubart, 1944–1975,
1981 (1981.157.1,2)

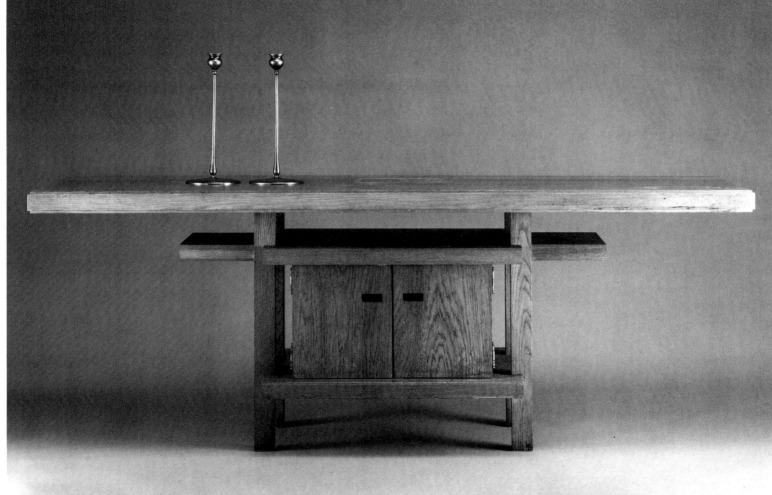

122

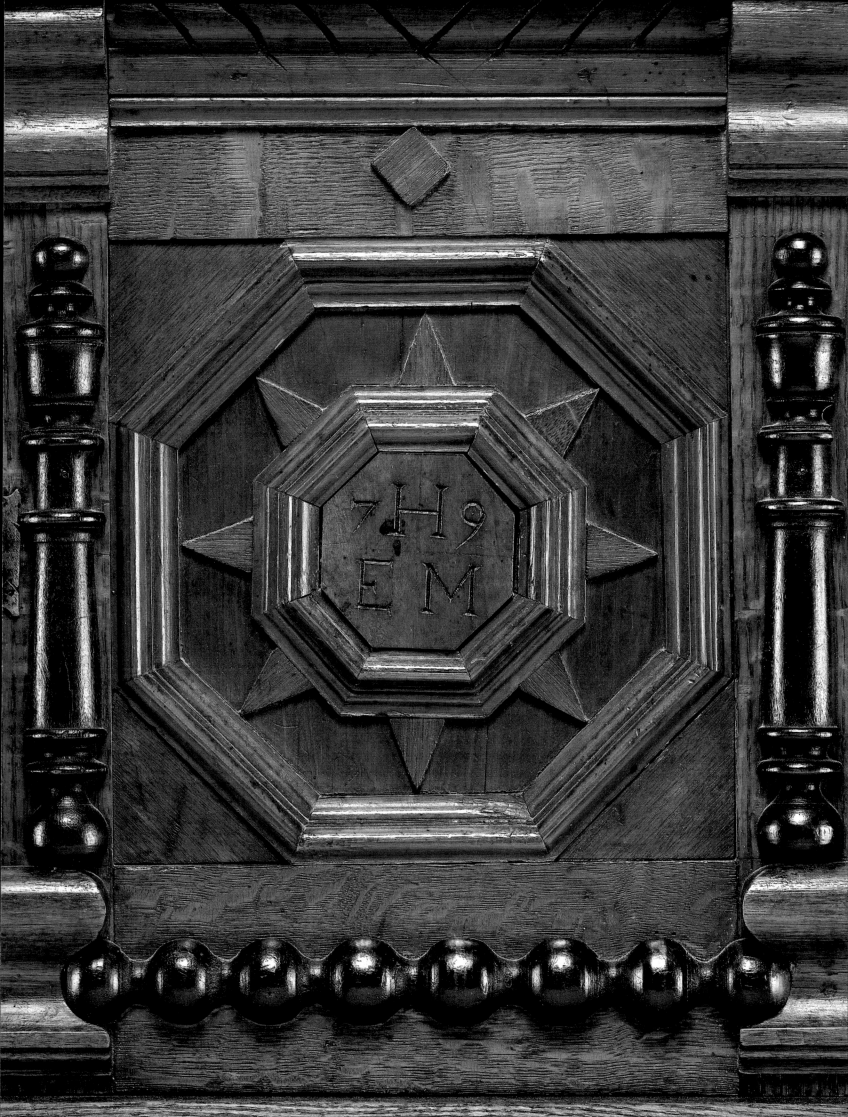

# FURNITURE

Fig. 123. Detail, cabinet attributed to the Symonds shops, see Fig. 127.

# The Early Colonial Period 1630–1730

*Figs. 124–29. Joined furniture, the most expensive type of the seventeenth century and the most durable, was decorated with carving, painting, and applied ornament. Sometimes only one of these decorative techniques was employed, sometimes two, and sometimes all three. Although only a handful of pieces survive with their original paint, we know that much seventeenth-century furniture was painted. Fortunately, even when the paint has worn off or been removed by an overzealous collector, the carving remains. Motifs were derived from a varied provincial English vocabulary that blended medieval and Renaissance influences. The examples shown here are all shallowly carved, and most show traces of their carvers' scribe lines, made when the designs were being laid out. Flowers and leaves, paired S-scrolls, arches and guilloches (intertwined circles), and geometrical shapes like diamonds and circles are some of the motifs that are often seen. All of these, interpreted and combined differently, may be picked out in the examples shown. The fluid leaves on the Thurston box contrast strongly with the simplified guilloche-and-rosette pattern that ornaments the Buel box, and both are very different from the complicated combination of geometrical and Renaissance-derived motifs of the New Haven Colony chest.*

The forms and designs of seventeenth-century furniture are referred to as Jacobean, after Jacobius, the Latin name for James, because James I reigned in England when the first permanent American settlements were made. The chest was one of the most typical forms of seventeenth-century furniture, as indeed it had been in ages past. In addition to serving as a storage place, it sometimes doubled as a seat, and, since it was portable, as a kind of luggage. Like virtually all case furniture of this early period, chests were uncompromisingly rectangular, constructed of vertical stiles and horizontal rails solidly joined at right angles to frame slightly recessed panels. From the earliest days of settlement, distinctive local and regional differences appeared in the designs applied to this basic form. The front of one example

(Fig. 129) is covered with flat carvings that combine late Tudor and Jacobean motifs in the manner associated with William Searle and Thomas Dennis of Ipswich, Massachusetts.

What are commonly referred to as sunflower chests because of the nature of their stylized floral carvings were fashioned exclusively in the Connecticut River valley in the neighborhood of Wethersfield (Fig. 128). These pieces are also decorated with applied split spindles and bosses stained black to simulate ebony. The bosses, reminiscent of generally similar decorations on Elizabethan furniture, are sometimes referred to as "jewels." Still other regional variations in design can be attributed to the furniture makers of such separate centers as Hadley, Salem, Boston, and other New England towns and villages (Figs. 124–27). A point to be made here

is that these local differences, so early apparent, were slight but clear indications of the diverse cultural strains that contributed to colonial society and that continued to characterize American craftsmanship in the changing styles of years to come.

The most complex seventeenth-century furniture form was the cupboard—the court cupboard and the press cupboard—used for the display of silver, pewter, brass, and pottery, as well as for storage (see Fig. 13). In America such large and important pieces reached a peak of elaboration late in the century and then quickly went out of fashion, to be replaced by more specialized forms. At the other extreme of size, miniature chests, cabinets, and boxes used for the storage of small objects display essentially the same type of carved and applied ornament that

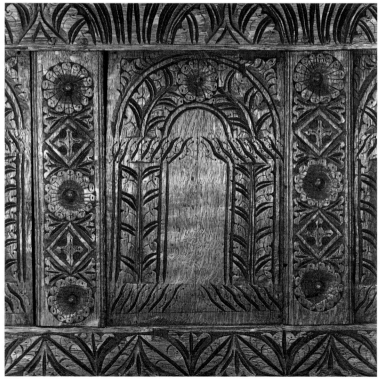

124

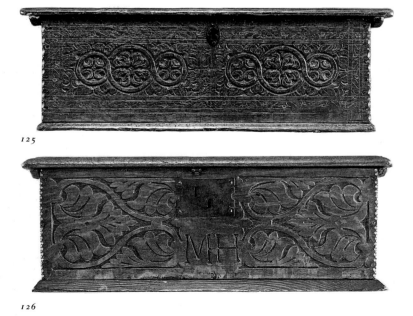

125

126

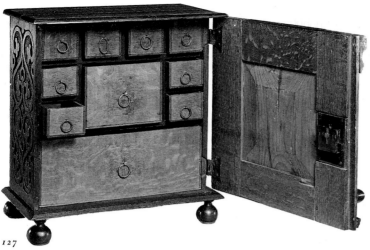

127

**Fig. 127. Cabinet,** *attributed to the Symonds shops, Salem, Massachusetts, dated 1679; red oak, white pine, walnut, maple, height 18 inches (45.7 cm.). This diminutive chest, whose center door (see detail, p. 98) conceals ten little drawers for valuables, is a rare form, made for Ephraim and Mary Herrick of Beverly. Like a seventeenth-century child, who was always dressed as a miniature adult, small chests resemble their elders in every detail except size. Applied ornament in the form of pillar-like split spindles flanking an octagonal sunburst formed of moldings and flat triangles, gives a strong architectural effect. Carving is used too, to create the paired S-scrolls that decorate the sides.*
Gift of Mrs. Russell Sage, 1909 (10.125.168)

**Fig. 124. Chest,** *detail, New Haven Colony, 1640–80; oak, pine. Found in Cheshire, Connecticut.*
Gift of Mrs. George C. Bryant, in memory of her husband, 1947 (47.133.3)

**Fig. 125. Box,** *attributed to John Thurston (1607–85), Dedham, Massachusetts, 1660–85; oak, pine, height 9½ inches (24.1 cm.).*
Gift of Mrs. Russell Sage, 1909 (10.125.680)

**Fig. 126. Box,** *attributed to William Buel (here 1630–d. 1681), Windsor, Connecticut, 1640–80; oak, pine, height 9½ inches (24.1 cm.).*
Gift of Mrs. Russell Sage, 1909 (10.125.2)

**Fig. 128. Chest with two drawers,** *Connecticut, Wethersfield area, 1675–1705; oak, pine, cedar, maple, height 39⅞ inches (101.3 cm.). Chests and cupboards of the so-called sunflower type share panel-and-frame construction with other well-made case pieces of the period, but they combine distinctive low-relief carving with applied moldings and split spindles. Here the usual arrangement of stylized tulips with wavy petals and leaves in the two side panels and "sunflowers"—spiky geometrical Tudor roses—in the center panel is varied, for this example has tulips in all three front panels and the original owner's initials, DC, in the center. Peter Blin of Wethersfield is credited with originating the sunflower form.*
Gift of Mrs. J. Woodhull Overton, 1966 (66.190.1)

**Fig. 129. Chest,** *Ipswich, Massachusetts, 1660–80; oak, height 29¾ inches (75.6 cm.). In basic form this chest is typical of seventeenth-century colonial work—it is rectangular, made of oak, constructed of panels and frames held together by mortise and tenon joints, and ornamented with motifs taken from geometry, nature, and architecture. But the elaborate combinations of patterns that decorate the facade and its deep, rich carving place the chest in a small, celebrated group of objects attributed to William Searle (1634–67) and Thomas Dennis (1638–1706), both of whom were trained in Devonshire, England, came to America, and worked in Ipswich. The strong rectangular outline of the chest is balanced and softened by the rounded forms of much of its ornament.*
Gift of Mrs. Russell Sage, 1909 (10.125.685)

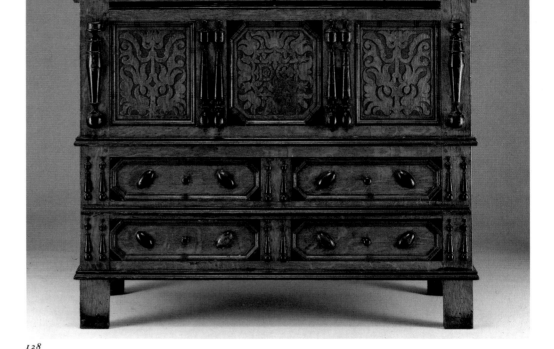

128

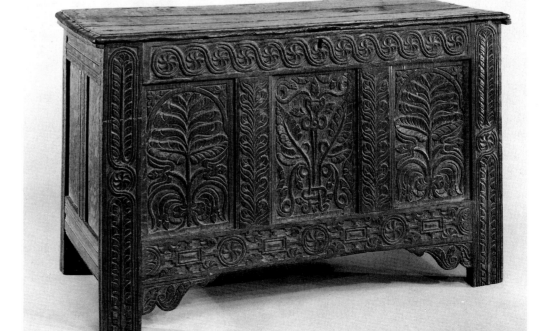

129

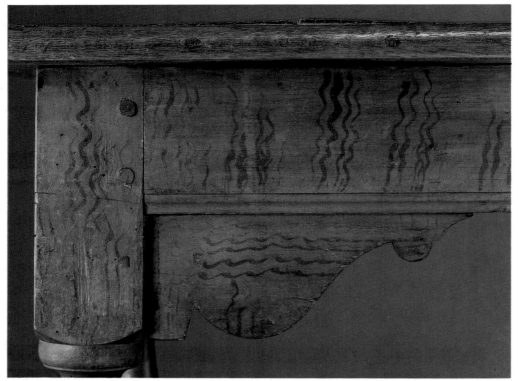

130

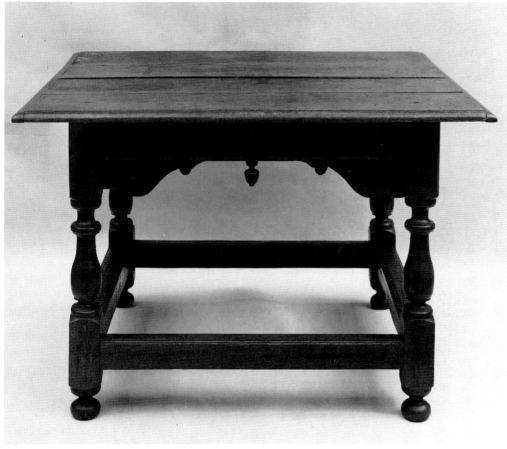

131

Fig. 132. **Turned great chair,** eastern Massachusetts, 1640–80; ash, height 44¾ inches (113.7 cm.). Imposing, even stiffly elegant, this chair was a symbol of authority and status in the home of its owner and would have been used only by the head of the household or an honored guest. Made entirely of parts turned on a lathe and decorated with spindles below both arms and seat as well as in the back, chairs of this type have been nicknamed "Brewster" after the example now in Pilgrim Hall, Plymouth, that is said to have belonged to Elder William Brewster of the first Plymouth settlement. Only a few turned chairs of this quality survive.
Gift of Mrs. J. Insley Blair, 1951 (51.12.2)

appears on larger pieces (Fig. 127).

The collection also includes one of the earliest known American tables, consisting of trestles supporting a removable board that could be put aside to clear space when the table wasn't in use, and an oaken table tightly joined in a boxlike form with turned legs and a skirt molded and underlined by a decorative edging (Figs. 130 and 131).

The progression of styles from the last decades of the seventeenth century through the first decades of the eighteenth, and the influences that conditioned their design, are succinctly summarized in seating furniture. Seventeenth-century chairs made few concessions to comfort and even the frequent addition of loose cushions provided little respite. These straight-lined, firm, and often elaborately turned and carved chairs did however impose upon the sitter a measure of dignity and importance. (At a time when tables often consisted of removable boards set upon trestles, he who occupied the principal seat had the distinction we recall in the phrase "chairman of the board.")

Among examples that illustrate these points is a chair that is today sometimes called a Brewster chair because Elder William Brewster (d. 1644) of Plymouth Plantation is said to have owned one of this type (Fig. 132). With its eight banks of turned spindles and its massive posts, this very rare survival from the seventeenth century is one of the most venerable relics in early American furniture.

One of the earliest and grandest types of seating furniture made in colonial America is the wainscot chair (Fig. 133). Characterized by a solid wooden back and seat and an almost formidably solid basic structure, chairs of this kind were

**Figs. 130 and 131. Square table,** eastern Massachusetts, 1670–1700; oak, maple, pine, and ash, partly grained, height 29½ inches (74.9 cm.). Turned legs connected by plain rectangular stretchers form the base of this table. This was the usual pattern for joined tables in seventeenth-century America, though the top could be round, oval, or oblong, as well as square. Like all joined furniture of this period, this table's aspect is foursquare; its only decoration derives from the

simple shapes of its turned legs, its sedately scrolled brackets, and its pendent drops. The several different woods used in its construction were originally concealed by a painted grained surface—quartets of squiggly black lines over a red base were meant to suggest the rich grain of an expensive imported wood. Although most of it has worn off, some of the graining is still visible on the skirt and brackets.
Gift of Mrs. J. Insley Blair, 1949 (49.155.1)

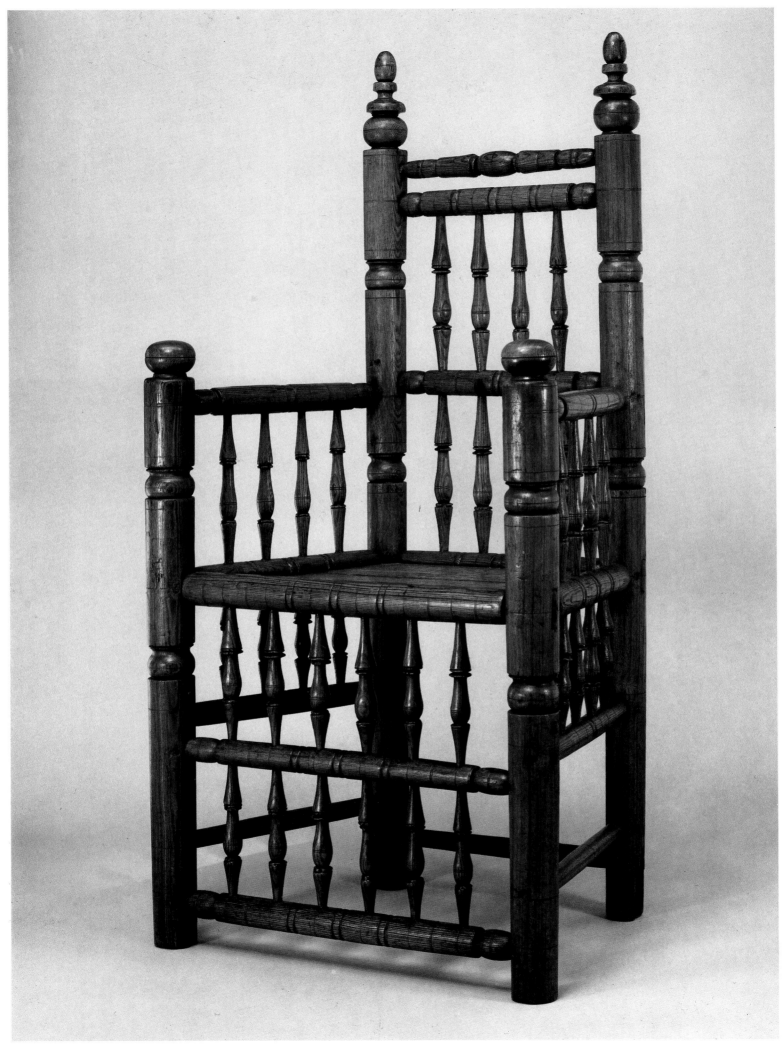

132

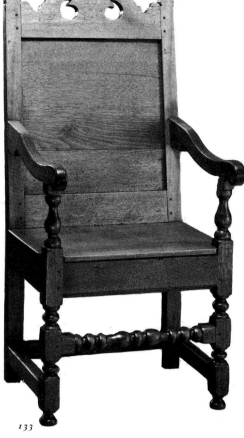

**Fig. 133. Joined, or wainscot, chair,** *Pennsylvania, 1690–1720; walnut, height 49½ inches (125.7 cm.). The most dignified article of seating equipment in colonial America was the wainscot chair, whose frame-and-panel back was like an enlarged section of a joined chest. The backs of oak wainscot chairs made in New England were often just as elaborately carved as a chest facade, but Pennsylvania makers preferred expanses of uncarved walnut. The distinctive decorative cresting of this example is the same as that of wainscot chairs made in Lancashire, England.* Anonymous Gift, 1948 (48.61)

*133*

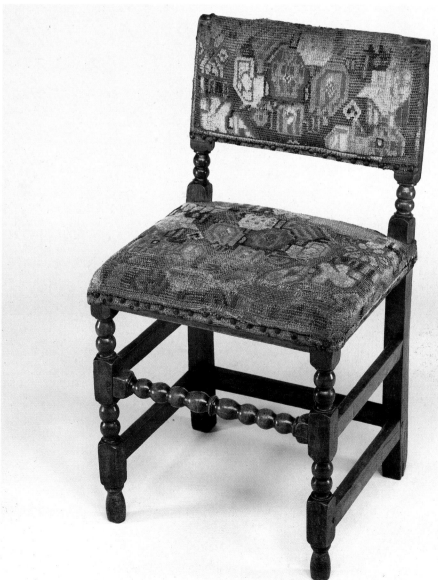

*134*

produced in most of the early colonies. The word "wainscot" derives from the Dutch *wagenschot,* referring to a fine grade of oak panel that for centuries was floated down the Rhine from Russia and Germany to Holland, whence it was shipped to England and other countries. With its own vast stands of white and red oak, America obviously had no need of such imports—or of any other woods, for that matter—at least until later, when exotic materials such as mahogany came into favor.

The American Wing collection includes as well two chairs with built-in upholstery (Fig. 134). They represent a type sometimes termed "Cromwellian" because they became popular in England during Cromwell's protectorate of the mid-1600s. There were at least four upholsterers' shops in Boston before the end of the seventeenth century that specialized in chairs, stools, and couches both for sale locally and for export to other English colonies. The seats and backs of these examples, rare because they retain their original upholstery, are covered with Turkey work, a Western imitation of Eastern pile carpets. Such upholstered pieces signaled the beginning of new standards of comfort that were soon realized so successfully in the special case of the easy chair. Stools, often referred to as "joyned" or joint stools, remained a common form of seating furniture in homes and taverns, as they had been from time out of mind (Fig. 135). The relative scarcity of such pieces today suggests the hard use to which they must have been put.

**Fig. 134. Turkey-work chair,** *Massachusetts, probably Boston, 1670–1700; maple, oak, height 37 inches (94 cm.). Turkey work, like delft and japanned wares, was a European imitation of an exotic Eastern—or in this case Near Eastern—product. Turkey-work covers, which copied the designs and textures of oriental rugs, were exported from England to the colonies in sets—seventeenth-century inventories contain many entries like "6 Turkie worke chayres, £3" and "In the Hall, one dozen of Turkey work Chayrs, £5"— and furniture scholar Margaret Swain has recently concluded that the chairs were then made up to fit the covers, not vice versa. The form was always like that of the example shown here, with a rectangular back separate from a square seat. Multicolored fringe (now lost on this chair) and brass nails finished the edges. This example, which is one of two in The American Wing collection, retains not only its original Turkey work, but also its original marsh-grass stuffing, and is therefore a great rarity.* Bequest of Mrs. J. Insley Blair, 1951 (52.77.51)

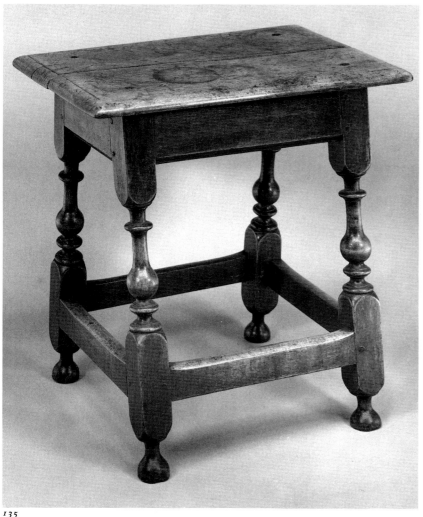

135

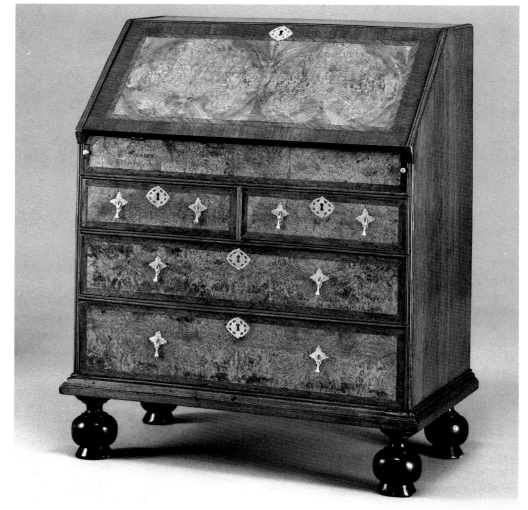

136

**Fig. 135. Joint stool,** *New England, probably Rhode Island, 1700–30; maple, height 22½ inches (57.2 cm.). The stool is among the most ancient of forms, having been in use since the time of ancient Egypt. Until the eighteenth century, it was far more common than any other type of seat. In the seventeenth century, joint (joyned) stools and benches (forms) were the usual seats for those lucky enough to sit down at all. Even though they were constructed as solidly as other joined furniture of the period, few American joint stools have survived.*
Gift of Mrs. Russell Sage, 1909 (10.125.329).

**Fig. 136. Scrutoire or desk,** *eastern Massachusetts, 1700–30; olivewood veneer, walnut banding, walnut, poplar, height 40 inches (101.6 cm.). Aside from its boxiness, everything about this desk is different from Jacobean forms. The introduction of dovetailed board construction made possible furniture with large, uninterrupted wood surfaces very different from the heavy frame-and-panel arrangement of earlier pieces. Shimmering veneers were now often glued to the surface of a cheaper wood, as is the case here. The framework of the desk is further outlined, and the veneered sections emphasized, by crossbanding and molding. The maker's use of imported olivewood, rather than burl-maple or burl-walnut, veneer is exceptional.*
Gift of Mrs. Russell Sage, 1909 (10.125.75)

A number of pieces in the collection provide an introduction to the new standards of taste and style and to the new forms that developed as the seventeenth century gave way to the eighteenth. Such changes largely reflected the fashions that became popular in England during the reign of William and Mary, although in America what has come to be known as the William and Mary period lasted long after the deaths of both monarchs.

Among the new forms that were introduced during these years was the slant-top desk with drawers, a convenient successor to the primitive portable desk boxes that had served writers since before the Middle Ages (Fig. 136). A typical example is handsomely finished with highly figured veneers, a fashionable feature of much William and Mary cabinetwork that is also displayed on several high chests of drawers, later known as highboys (see Fig. 22). This was another innovative and convenient form of the period; the turnings of its six legs and the shape of its connecting stretchers signal the introduction of curvilinear elements into furniture de-

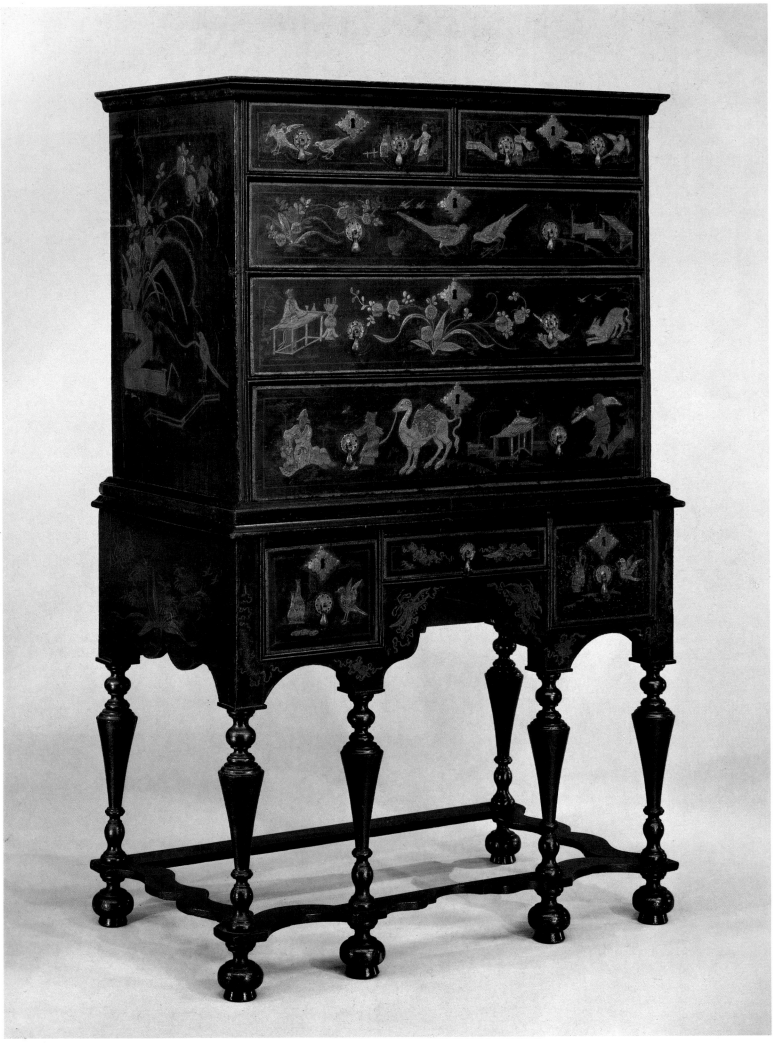

137

**Fig. 137. High chest of drawers,** *Boston, 1710–30; maple and pine, japanned, height 62½ inches (158.8 cm.). Nowhere is the William and Mary love of contrast more apparent than here, in the mounting of a substantial rectangle on a sextet of slender trumpet-turned legs. By about 1700 the high chest had superseded the cupboard as the most important case piece in a stylish household, and the brilliant japanned finish of this example must have made it even more fashionable. The technique of japanning, or using paint and varnish to imitate oriental lacquer, came to America from England at the end of the seventeenth century, and this charmingly decorated chest is one of the earliest surviving examples of American japanned work.*
Purchase, Joseph Pulitzer Bequest, 1940 (40.37.3)

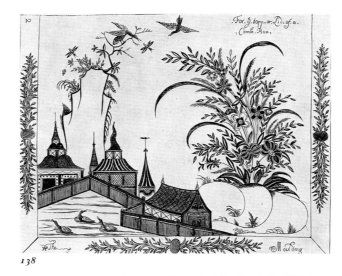

138

sign, providing a welcome change from the unremittingly rectangular character of earlier forms.

Highboys of this period were also decorated with japanning (Fig. 137), a term coined to designate a relatively inexpensive Western substitute for true oriental lacquer. Exotic figures and scenes in low relief, taken from imported objects and from pattern books fancifully concocted in Europe and naïvely recalling Chinese and Japanese designs, were modeled in relief, painted with colors and metal leaf, and varnished. In 1688 two Englishmen, John Stalker and George Parker, published an influential illustrated manual in which they described the various ways this could be accomplished (Fig. 138—and see Fig. 318 for a rare instance of the use of similar motifs on American silver). The vogue for these decorative fantasies, produced in America primarily by Boston craftsmen, endured until the middle of the eighteenth century. In 1712 one Nehemiah Partridge of Boston advertised that he could provide "all sorts of Japan work," and there were other local practitioners who somewhat extravagantly claimed that "no damp air, no moulding worm or corroding time" could ever deface their handiwork.

Such pieces were provincial equivalents of stylish English models of some years earlier. Other contemporary forms evolved that had a decidedly native American character. A small maple table with scalloped skirt, neatly turned raking legs, and well-carved "Spanish" feet (a scroll foot with vertical carved grooves) has a grace that owes little to the influence of foreign fashions (Fig. 141). Its oval top provides a further re-

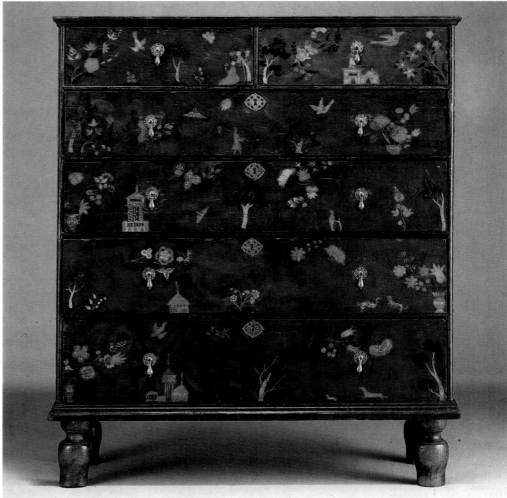

139

**Fig. 138. A Treatise of Japaning and Varnishing,** *detail, by John Stalker and George Parker, Oxford, England, 1688. Craftsmen who wished to decorate their work with japanning found this book an important source of both information and designs. The scene here, with fanciful pagoda-topped buildings, birds, and exotic vegetation, was labeled "For ye topp or Lid of a combe Box."*
Harris Brisbane Dick Fund, 1932 (32.80.20)

**Fig. 139. Chest of drawers,** *Connecticut, Windsor area, 1720–50; yellow pine and maple, painted, oak, height 49¾ inches (126.4 cm.). Just as American japanned work was a simplified version of European, this Connecticut chest is a simplified painted version of the japanned Boston high chest on the opposite page. One of a group of Windsor-area pieces with imitation japanning, this chest of drawers employs a simple palette of cream, red, and black on an olive-brown background. Diminutive animal and human figures occupy a landscape dominated by giant vases of flowers, for here, as on much japanned furniture, the laws of perspective have not been invoked.*
Gift of Mrs. J. Insley Blair, 1945 (45.78.3)

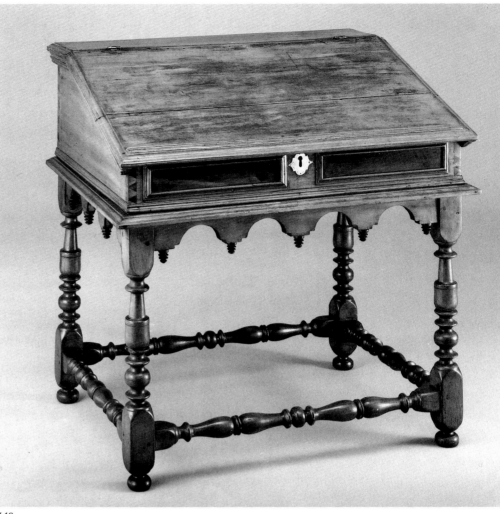

**Fig. 140. Desk on frame,** *New York, 1695–1720; gumwood, walnut(?) veneer, tulip poplar, height 35¼ inches (89.5 cm.). This desk appears to be unique—it combines as no other piece does crisply turned legs and stretchers with an unusual scalloped skirt punctuated by pendent drops. It bears an early Dutch inscription recording a business transaction and this, along with the fact that it is made of gumwood—popular in New York—makes that city its logical place of origin. The turnings are related to those of some French examples, and the piece may be the work of French Huguenots who had fled the Old World.*
Rogers Fund, 1944 (44.47)

**Fig. 141. Oval table,** *New England, 1700–30; maple, painted base, height 27 inches (68.6 cm.). The combination of curved skirt and turned legs and the bold sweep of legs and feet give this little movable table a rakish grace. The finish of the top has been worn off over the years, but the base has an old finish of black paint. Remarkably, the table has no repairs or restorations.*
Gift of Mrs. Screven Lorillard, 1952 (52.195.4)

*140*

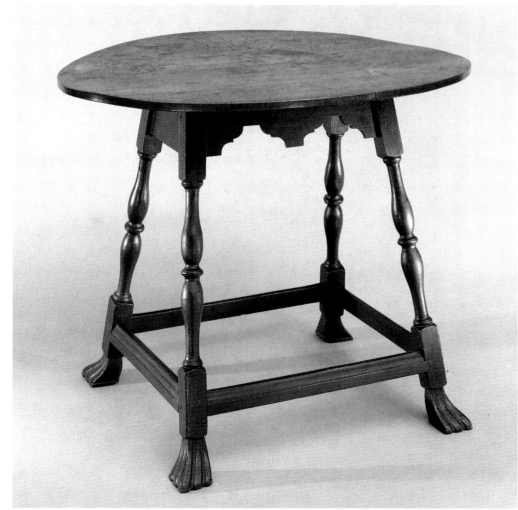

*141*

minder that curved lines were becoming increasingly evident in the decorative arts. Soon they would dominate the design and influence the construction of furniture.

A radical change in design had been under way in England before William and Mary took the throne. Following the overthrow of Oliver Cromwell's Puritan protectorate in 1660 the "merry monarch," Charles II, returned to England as king after his exile on the Continent. He took as his wife Catherine of Braganza, who brought with her from her native Portugal a host of skilled craftsmen and the richest dowry in Europe. When the Stuart dynasty was in turn overthrown in the Glorious Revolution of 1688, the Dutchman William of Orange came to the throne as joint sovereign with his wife, Mary Stuart, daughter of the deposed James II.

These several monarchs brought in their train fresh ideas from the Continent. Portugal and Holland stood at the crossroads of world trade, and the furniture forms and designs produced in those countries amalgamated influences from all parts of the globe. These were transplanted to England's courtly circles and set new standards of style and taste that undermined the old insular traditions of Britain. In modified form these standards soon found their way to the colonies and broke through the conventions that had held sway here through most of the seventeenth century.

In William and Mary seating furniture the departure from Jacobean practice is startling and reflects the influence of both the European continent and, indirectly, the Orient (see Figs. 20 and 22). Crests on backs and stretchers joining legs sometimes elaborately conceived in what are called Flemish scrolls characterized English chairs of the Restoration period; the scrolls that often served as front legs are baroque in the Continental manner, as are richly carved backs "cut with scrowles all over"; caning derives from Far Eastern models. Those features are notably displayed again in a daybed (see Fig. 20) with back canted for comfort, a novel form of the period and a prototype of what would later be commonly known as a chaise longue. A number of these seats, including the daybed, are of English origin and clearly illustrate the influence of imported examples on colonial craftsmanship. It is often difficult, if not impossible, to distinguish American-made examples of these caned chairs from those known to have been sent to this country from England. About 1700 one English visitor to Boston observed, "There is no Fashion in *London* but in three or four Months is to be seen in *Boston.*"

The fashion lingered. In 1720 the noted Boston diarist Samuel Sewall ordered "a Duzen of good black Walnut Chairs, fine Cane, with a Couch," a suite that must have been in the William and Mary style. Furniture of this sort was still being offered at auction twelve years later when the Queen Anne style had become eminently fashionable.

During this period the wing chair, or easy chair as it was then called, was introduced to the colonies (Fig. 142). No more completely comfortable chair has ever been devised: its frame is padded on four sides and its "wings" both ward off drafts and provide restful corners for a nodding head. The essential design remains unchanged to the present day.

Although the radical innovations in chair design that we associate with the William and Mary style were readily adopted in the colonies, and their elegant refinements were sometimes faithfully copied by local craftsmen, the new fashion was commonly modified in relatively simple versions of sophisticated English models. As in provincial England, durable and more readily available leather was substituted for cane. Local rushes made serviceable and inexpensive seats, and split spindles, or banisters, served for backs. The elabo-

Fig. 142. **Easy chair,** *Massachusetts, probably Boston, 1710–30; maple, tulip poplar, and oak, height 49¼ inches (125.7 cm.). The easy chair appeared in America during the William and Mary period. It was used originally for sick or elderly people—a halfway station between bed and the bustling household. Examples of this early period are scarce. William and Mary characteristics are apparent in the tall, narrow back that rises in a cut-off arch, the block-and-vase turned legs, Spanish feet, and vase-turned medial stretcher. The striking blue and white upholstery fabric is contemporary with the frame, but the chair would probably have been covered with solid color wool, as the example in the Wentworth Room has been.* Gift of Mrs. J. Insley Blair, 1950 (50.228.1)

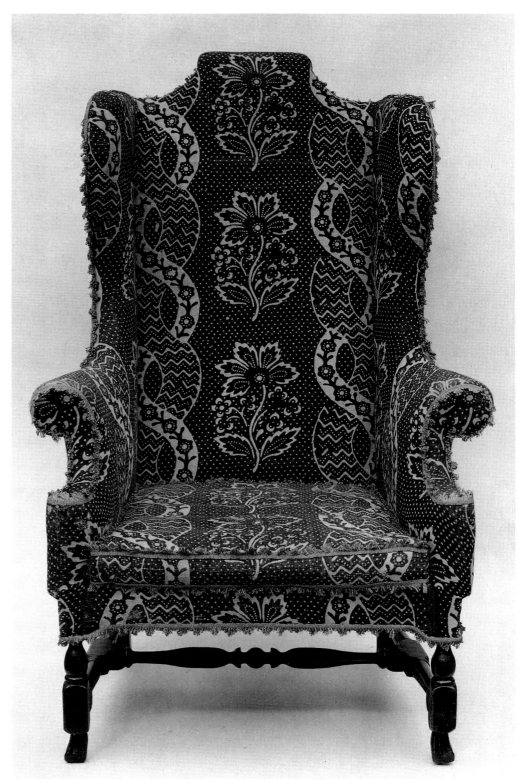

142

**Fig. 143. Leather chair,** *Massachusetts, Boston area, 1720–50; maple, oak, height 45¾ inches (116.2 cm.). Just as London sent thousands of cane chairs to America to satisfy the demand for fashionable lightweight seats, so too Boston shipped a somewhat later and certainly less elaborate, but still handsome and lightweight chair to colonies from Connecticut to Virginia. Characterized by a William and Mary understructure and a "crooked" (serpentine curved) and molded back in the oncoming Queen Anne style, these were called Boston chairs because they were produced assembly-line fashion in sizable quantities in the Boston area. Chairmakers in other colonies found it hard to beat the price of the Boston chairs being offered in their territory. However, Plunkett Flee-* son from Philadelphia advertised in 1742 that he had "black and red leather Chairs, finished cheaper than any made here, or imported from Boston."
Gift of Mrs. Russell Sage, 1909 (10.125.698)

**Fig. 144. Armchair,** *eastern Massachusetts or New Hampshire, 1730–50; maple and poplar, painted, height 40⅝ inches (103.2 cm.). Chairs in this distinctive style, with ram's-horn handrests, sweeping Spanish feet, and an unusual carved and pierced crest rail, are attributed to the Gaines family on the basis of four very similar side chairs that descended in that family. The design of the armchair is wonderfully compelling, with its boldly turned and carved forms and the* dramatic sweep of its arms. Though there may have been other, as yet unknown, members of the Gaines family who qualify, John, the father, and John II and Thomas, his sons, are known to have been turners. As was customary in the colonial period, they also applied themselves cheerfully to nearly any task their neighbors needed done. Besides supplying chairs and other parts of furniture such as table legs and bed posts, they made handles for kitchen and farm utensils, plowed fields and sold the crops when they were ready, looked after livestock and sold it if desired, and thatched buildings.
Bequest of Mrs. J. Insley Blair, 1951 (52.77.55)

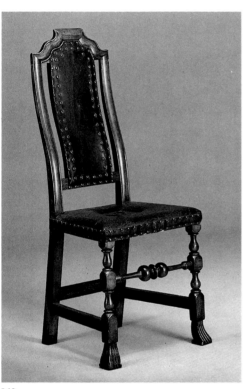

143

**Fig. 145. Roundabout chair,** *New England, 1730–60; maple, hickory, height 31½ inches (80 cm.). An unusual form, the roundabout chair was used at desks and card tables and very often had a deep skirt and easily removable slip seat to conceal a chamber pot. In many cases the deeply scalloped seats of such chairs were cut off by nineteenth- and early twentieth-century dealers and collectors who felt they were awkward looking. The form began to be made very early in the eighteenth century and continued in fashion during the Queen Anne and Chippendale periods. In rural areas, the roundabout chair was made up and into the nineteenth century. This example is in the William and Mary style, with turned vertical members and Spanish feet. Slats in the back increased the sitter's comfort.*
Gift of Mrs. Russell Sage, 1909 (10.125.706)

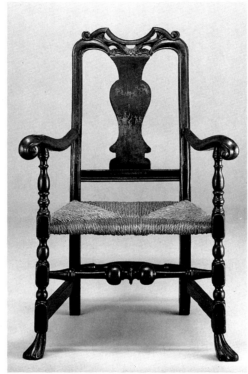

144

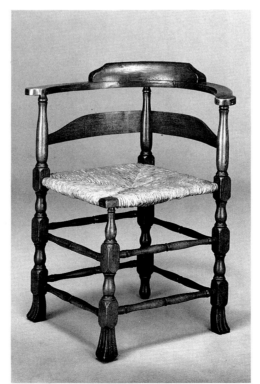

145

rate carving that distinguished the most fashionable urban models was limited to the crest rail. Banister-back chairs continued to be made throughout the eighteenth century (see Figs. 27–30).

One of the last and most enduring of these colonial variations was a simple and handsome descendant of the William and Mary line known as the Boston chair (Fig. 143). Devoid of elaborate carved ornament, these were usually upholstered in leather with a comfortable scooped back, a feature associated with the oncoming Queen Anne style. The maple frames were often painted red or black. Boston chairs were copied in Philadelphia and probably in other cities. The type continued to be popular throughout the colonies until the Revolutionary era.

In rural towns and villages elements of the William and Mary style lingered, merging with features from both earlier and later modes and often resulting in a vernacular expression of highly individual charm. Chairs with splat backs and yoke-shaped top rails show variant ways in which colonial makers successfully combined elements of the two styles (Fig. 147). A handsome armchair of this type is attributed to John Gaines of Portsmouth, New Hampshire, on the basis of specific features (Fig. 144)— most of which recall William and Mary precedents. Its solid vase-shaped back splat, on the other hand, was a customary feature of chairs in the then fashionable Queen Anne style.

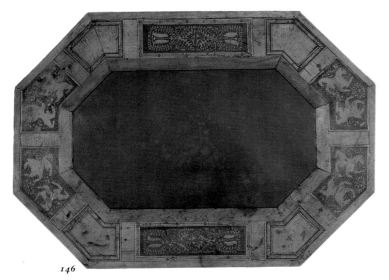

146

**Fig. 146. Slate tabletop,** *Switzerland, about 1720; slate and inlay of various European woods, length 35⅛ inches (89.2 cm.). Most furniture used in colonial America was made here, although occasionally English pieces were imported, so it is unusual and interesting to come across a small group of slate-topped tables whose bases were made in America, but whose elaborate slate-and-inlaid-wood tops seem to have come from Switzerland. It has been suggested that the tabletops were imported as a group by some enterprising merchant, to whom they were shipped via the Rhine to Rotterdam and then to New England.*
The Sylmaris Collection, Gift of George Coe Graves, 1930 (30.120.56)

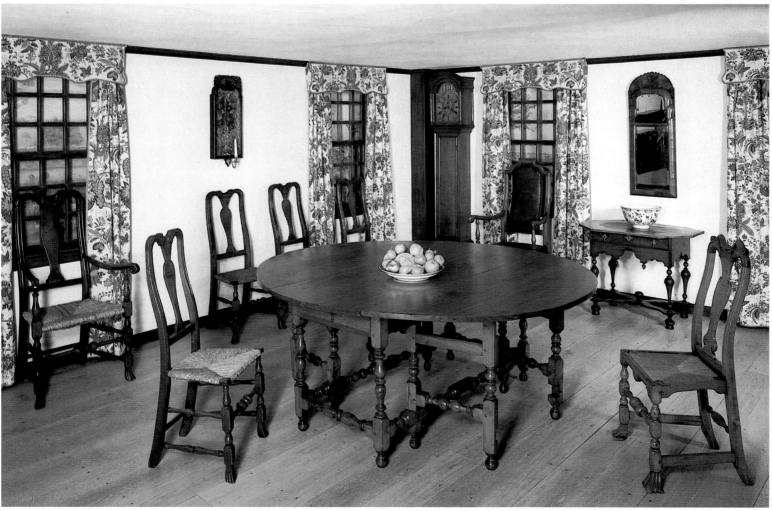

147

**Fig. 147. William and Mary furniture** *ranging from very special to standard for the eighteenth century is shown in the Metcalf Bowler Room. The walnut gateleg table, a space-saving form that became popular in this period, was made in New England between 1700 and 1730. It is surrounded by several rush-bottomed chairs that combine William and Mary bases with Queen Anne backs—a type that was made in large numbers throughout the middle years of the eighteenth century, and very possibly later. To the right is an elaborate Gaines version of the standard rush-bottomed chairs across the table (see Fig. 144), and in the background is a leather chair of the Boston variety. Next to it is a slate-topped table, a rare form in America. Nowadays*

*sometimes called a mixing table because its slate top permitted mixing drinks without worrying about spills, this form consisted of a base with trumpet-turned legs and arched skirt like that of a dressing table and a slate-and-inlaid-wood top imported from Switzerland (see Fig. 146).*
Rogers Fund, 1916 (16.120)

# The Late Colonial Period, 1730–90

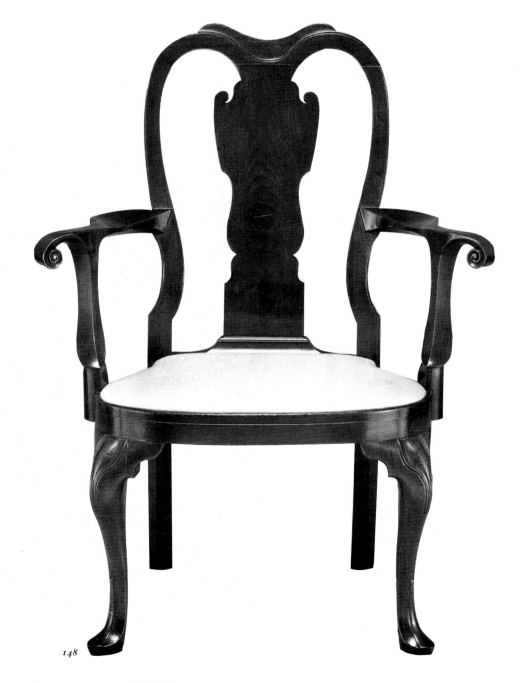

148

**Fig. 148. Armchair,** *Philadelphia, 1740–60; walnut, height 41 inches (104.1 cm.). Much of the richest Queen Anne and Chippendale furniture made in the colonies comes from Philadelphia, which by 1750 had become, after London, the most prosperous city in the English-speaking world. Prosperity and sophistication are reflected in the suave curves of this armchair—in its generously scrolled splat, inviting outward-curved armrests, and cabriole legs ending in dainty slipper feet. Its rear legs are the stumplike posts characteristic of Philadelphia seating furniture.*
Rogers Fund, 1925 (25.115.36)

The late colonial interiors and furniture that superseded those of the William and Mary period date largely from the middle decades of the eighteenth century, a period culminating in the Revolutionary War. The increasing use of mahogany along with handsomely grained black walnut made for more opulent appearances.

With the introduction of the Queen Anne style in furniture every trace of Tudor and Puritan stiffness vanished. The elaborate ornamental scrolls, turnings, and pierced carvings of high-style William and Mary furniture gave way to undulating curved elements that both please the eye and serve the needs of solid comfort. Decorative carving played only a secondary role in this suave harmony of form and function. In 1712 Lord Shaftsbury rationalized this newly conceived simplicity and unity in design: "In short we are to carry this remembrance still along with us," he wrote, "that the fewer the objects are besides those that are absolutely necessary in a piece, the easier it is for the eye by one simple act, and in one view to comprehend the sum or whole."

The single most conspicuous element of this graceful construction was the cabriole leg, a reverse-curved support with a shaped foot (Fig. 148). The term cabriole comes from the Italian *capriola*, goat's leap, and the form itself from a type of support derived in ancient times from the profile of an animal's hind leg. Curves were often repeated in serpentine stretchers, horseshoe-shaped seats, and solid vase-shaped splats molded to the contours of the human spine and framed by rounded supporting stiles continuous with arched crest rails. Colonial furniture makers first employed the cabriole leg about 1730. Boston,

Newport, New York, and Philadelphia—as well as other regions—each had its own distinctive interpretation of the style. Chairs made in Philadelphia during the middle years of the century, some departing into Chippendale flourishes, reached a peak of sophistication.

The basic elements of style of any period are probably more immediately visible in a piece of seating furniture than in any other form. The transition from earlier fashions was often gradual, however, and elements of a fading style may be combined with those of one on the rise. An extremely rare walnut settee in the Wing has a tall back whose curved outlines recall chair backs of the late seventeenth century (Fig. 149). On the other hand, its cabriole legs with shell carvings on the knees announce the newer style of the Queen Anne period. (The legs terminate in trifid feet, a re-

finement often adopted by Philadelphia furniture makers.) This exceptional piece descended in the family of James Logan, at one time William Penn's secretary and the builder of Stenton, a handsome country seat that still stands near Germantown, Pennsylvania. Logan, a scholar and a botanist as well as a statesman, had amassed a fortune in land investments and in trade with the Indians. He was so content to remain in his suburban retreat that he retired from public service to enjoy life there.

Generally speaking, lean proportions and restrained ornamentation are regional characteristics of furniture made in New England (Fig. 150). The relatively slender legs and narrow backs of chairs are typical features of this form in both the Queen Anne and Chippendale styles. An easy chair in the Queen Anne style retains its original uphol-

*Fig. 149. Settee, Philadelphia, 1740–60; walnut, yellow pine, height 48 inches (121.9 cm.). A few sofas and settees were made as early as the William and Mary period, and during the Queen Anne and Chippendale eras they gradually replaced their predecessor, the daybed, but the form was not frequently made until the Federal period. This rare early settee gracefully unites William and Mary and Queen Anne design with its high, boldly scrolled back and shell-carved cabriole legs and trifid feet (the latter characteristic of only the finest Philadelphia Queen Anne furniture). It descended in the family of James Logan, scholar, statesman, merchant, onetime secretary and lifelong friend to William Penn. It is both the earliest known American settee and the only known Philadelphia example in the Queen Anne style. Rogers Fund, 1925 (25.115.1)*

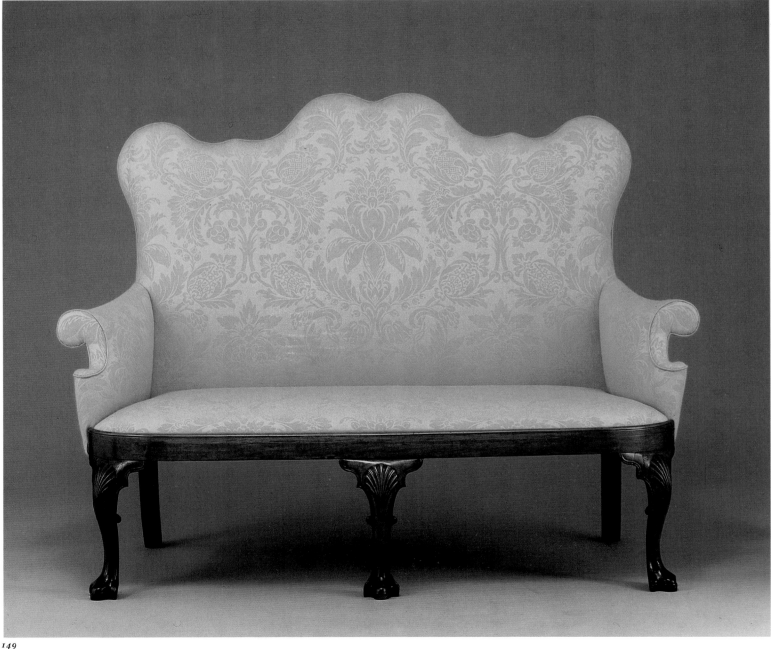

149

**Fig. 150. Side chair,** *Connecticut, 1740–70; maple, painted, height 43¼ inches (109.9 cm.). One of a set of four in the Museum's collection, this chair belongs to a group that has recently been associated with the Lothrops, cabinetmakers of Norwich and Wallingford, Connecticut. A set of similar chairs descended in the Lothrop family, and the needlework seat on a similar example in the collection of the Henry Ford Museum is signed by one of the Lothrop girls, so since many of the Lothrops were joiners, an attribution to their shops seems justified. Although simplicity and restraint are characteristic of New England chairs in general, Connecticut examples are often straighter and stiffer than chairs from neighboring colonies. The pinched splat, straight stiles, and high shoulders seen here are characteristic of Connecticut, as is the square seat.* Gift of Mrs. J. Insley Blair, 1946 (46.194.1)

**Fig. 151. Crewel-embroidered linen chair seat,** *perhaps by a member of the Lothrop family of Norwich and Wallingford, Connecticut, detail of Fig. 150. Any chair that retains its original fabric covering is a rarity, and if the decoration of that covering is as fresh and charming as this crewelwork scene, it is a great bonus. The placid lion and the frisky dog and the deer in this crewelwork scene gambol in a landscape stitched in red, blue, yellow, and green. The other three chairs in this group have equally engaging, but different, crewelwork seats.* Gift of Mrs. J. Insley Blair, 1946 (46.194.1)

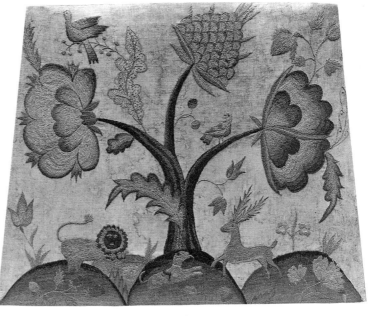

151

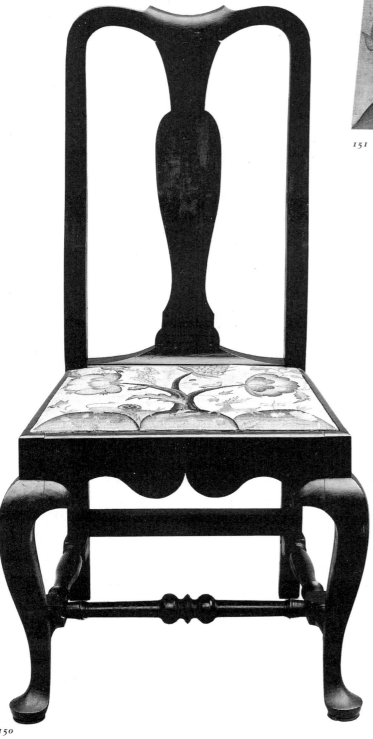

stery, the front and sides covered with finely worked needlepoint and the back with a colorful landscape worked in crewel (Figs. 153 and 154). The chair is unique in being signed and dated by the upholsterer, "Gardner Junr" (Fig. 152).

The cabriole curve that transformed Queen Anne chairs lent the same grace to tables of the period, and examples from New England have a delicacy that sets them apart from tables of other regions (Fig. 155). Case furniture is more dainty, too. A mahogany spinet supported by four cabriole legs with pad feet in the Queen Anne style is the earliest American work by an immigrant member of a family of eminent London musical-instrument makers (Fig. 157). A panel above the keyboard of this exceptional piece bears the inscription "John Harris Boston New England fecit." When it was completed in 1769 and shipped off to a Newport customer (probably to the merchant Francis Malbone, in whose family it subsequently descended) the Boston press daily and proudly reported that this "very curious Spinnet" was "the first ever made in America." Actually this distinction belongs to another spinet in the Museum's collection, made thirty years earlier by Johann Clemm of Philadelphia.

A walnut-veneered and inlaid high-

150

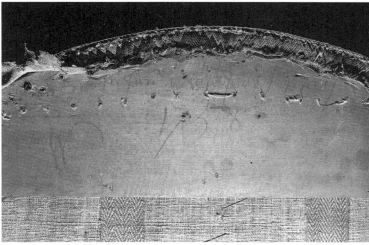

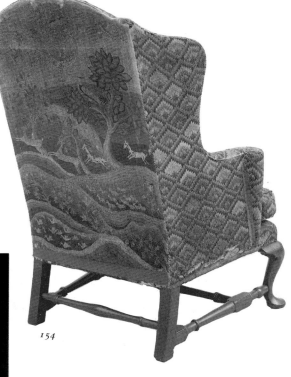

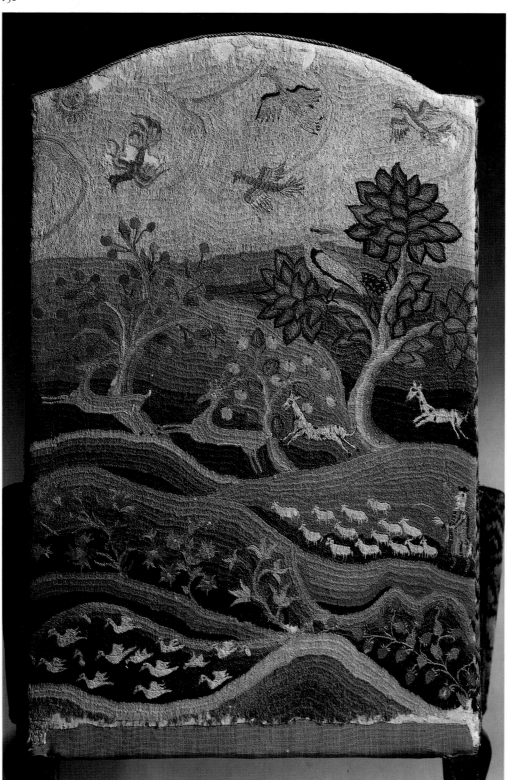

**Fig. 152. The frame of the easy chair,** *Fig. 154, is inscribed "Gardner Junr/ Newport May/ 1758/ W."*
Gift of Mrs. J. Insley Blair, 1950 (50.228.3)

**Fig. 153. Back panel of easy chair,** *Fig. 154. Like designers of the chinoiserie that was play-fully disposed over japanned furniture, the de-signer of this splendid scene ignored the laws of both probability and perspective. Tiny ducks float in the foreground, while large deer frolic in the middle distance. The whirling bird-filled sky turns the whole naïve rural scene into an artistic triumph.*
Gift of Mrs. J. Insley Blair, 1950 (50.228.3)

**Fig. 154. Easy chair,** *Newport, 1758; walnut, maple, height 46¾ inches (118.8 cm.). Growing concern for comfort had produced the easy chair in the William and Mary era, and its popularity increased throughout the late colonial period. This example, which displays characteristic New England features—vertically rolled cones to sup-port the armrests, plain cabriole legs and pad feet, and turned stretchers—is outstanding among American easy chairs in preserving its original upholstery in remarkably fine condition. The "Gardner Junr" who signed the frame (see Fig. 152) covered the front and sides in a dia-mond, or flame, pattern worked in an Irish stitch and the back with a brilliant crewelwork scene.*
Gift of Mrs. J. Insley Blair, 1950 (50.228.3)

**Fig. 155. Tea table,** *New England, 1730–60; maple, height 26 inches (66 cm.). When tea was introduced into England in the seventeenth century, it received a mixed reception. Thomas Garway asserted that "Tea removeth lassitude, vanquisheth heavy dreams, easeth the frame, and strengtheneth the memory," while the poet Colley Cibber denounced the beverage as "the universal pretence for bringing the wicked of both sexes together in the morning." Despite its detractors, tea soon became the rage, and many new forms were created to be used in the tea-drinking ritual. In New England rectangular tea tables were preferred to round ones, and this is a particularly appealing example with long slender cabriole legs, pad feet, and a liltingly curved apron.*
Gift of Mrs. Russell Sage, 1909 (10.125.135)

**Fig. 156. Dressing table,** *Boston, 1747; maple, japanned, white pine, height 30½ inches (77.5 cm.). Like highboys, lowboys—as dressing tables are often called—had been softened by gracefully curved elements as the Queen Anne style succeeded the William and Mary. This example retains its original japanning, or painted decoration inspired by oriental lacquerwork. Just as Western craftsmen imitated oriental porcelain by using the materials and technology at hand, so they imitated the velvety lacquer wares of the East by substituting paints, varnishes, and gesso for true oriental lacquer. When it came to appropriate motifs, Westerners felt not a bit inhibited. They applied whimsical people, buildings, animals, and flora and fauna freely adapted from oriental porcelains, fabrics, and from lacquer ob-*

*jects themselves. In 1688 the enterprising Stalker and Parker published their* Treatise of Japaning and Varnishing, *which contained detailed instructions for japanned decoration (see Fig. 138). "Perhaps," they wrote of their suggested motifs, "we have helpt [the orientals] a little in their proportions, where they were lame or defective, and made them more pleasant yet altogether as Antic."*
Gift of Mrs. Russell Sage, 1909 (10.125.68)

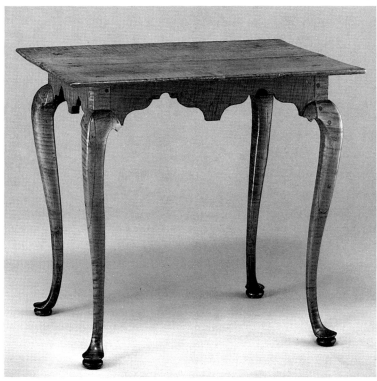 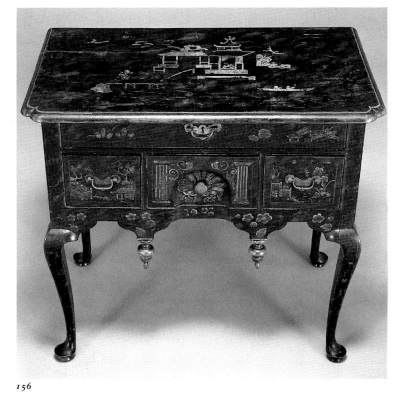

155  156

boy (Fig. 161) and matching lowboy are ornamented with carved and gilded shells and supported by slim, delicately shaped cabriole legs terminating in pad feet. This rare pair is an example of the highly developed Queen Anne style as it was realized in Boston in the second quarter of the eighteenth century.

The rather tricky art of japanning seems to have been practiced mainly but not solely in Boston. Because of the fragile nature of its built-up surfaces, furniture with this sort of whimsical and exotic decoration has survived in relatively small numbers. It is therefore an unusual circumstance that, besides the William and Mary highboy mentioned earlier (Figs. 137 and 158), the Museum also owns two japanned highboys with matching lowboys in the Queen Anne style (Figs. 156, 159, and 160). These rare pieces display an odd combination

of carved and gilded shells, classical architectural motifs, and pseudo-oriental ornamental designs—all applied to typically regional forms—and they provide another and singular witness to the crosscurrents of interest and taste that contributed to the pattern of life in colonial America. Before the fashion for japanning waned around the middle of the eighteenth century, the technique was apparently applied to many different forms of furniture. A japanned looking glass and a shaving glass, the latter having been imported from England by the owner of the dressing table on which it stands, are also in the collection.

By the middle of the century the relatively quiet curves of the Queen Anne style were gradually being converted into much more exuberant designs in the Chippendale manner. The term

"Chippendale" is loosely used to describe much of the furniture made in the last decades of the colonial period, owing to the fame acquired over the years of *The Gentleman and Cabinet-Maker's Director.* Issued by the London cabinetmaker Thomas Chippendale in 1754 and again in 1755, and then in an enlarged edition in 1762, this was the first published manual devoted entirely to furniture designs. Chippendale's books were quickly followed by others with comparable designs issued in London by such men as Robert Manwaring, Thomas Johnson, William Ince, and John Mayhew.

Actually, the style so widely associated with Chippendale's name originated in England before Chippendale was heard from. It had developed as a gradual translation of the French rococo style into an English idiom. "Rococo" is de-

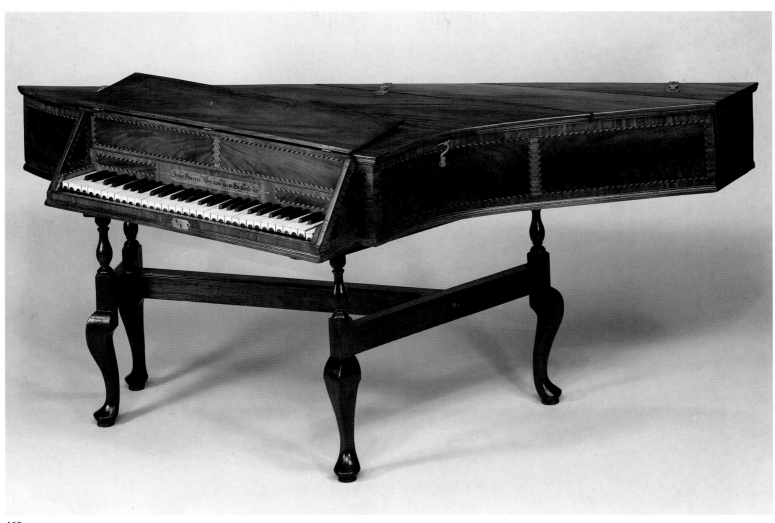

157

rived from *rocaille*, a word that refers to the combinations of rock and shell forms and C- and S-shaped curves that were popular in French ornament during the reign of Louis XV.

The development of the Chippendale style was stimulated by the increasing use of mahogany. This worm-resistant wood, which is almost as strong as metal and can be carved into the most intricate patterns, significantly affected the design and construction of chairs particularly. However, the great width of the boards obtainable from mahogany also made it an ideal wood for tabletops and case pieces with broad surfaces. Producers of the manuals had these working properties specifically in mind in proposing their designs. Most of the books referred to above were accessible to colonial craftsmen (as they were to craftsmen of other lands). Furniture

makers followed the designs more or less faithfully according to their ability and their individual preference or that of their patrons, who often also owned copies of the books. Virtually every piece pictured on the trade card of Benjamin Randolph, master craftsman who worked for the leading families of Philadelphia, is derived from one of three different English pattern books, including Chippendale's.

Among other advertisements of furniture was one in a Boston newspaper on New Year's Day 1767 offering for sale a copy of Robert Manwaring's *The Cabinet and Chair-Makers' Real Friend and Companion*. It was very likely shortly thereafter that a Boston chairmaker fashioned a side chair now in the Museum (Fig. 165), designing its carved back after one of Manwaring's plates (Fig. 167), but subtly altering the pro-

*Fig. 157. Bentside spinet, made by John Harris (active 1730–69), Boston, 1769; mahogany, mahogany veneer, white oak, birch, height 32½ inches (82.6 cm.). Because the musical instruments played in America were usually made in Europe, it is not surprising that the maker of this splendid Boston spinet was newly arrived from England. The case, of richly figured mahogany banded with patterned inlay, is supported by a base with Queen Anne legs, and the maker's name and geographical location are inlaid above the keyboard in flourishing letters. "It is with pleasure we inform the Public," reported* The Boston Gazette *in 1769, "That a few days since was shipped for Newport, a very curious Spinnet, being the first ever made in America, the performance of the ingenious Mr. John Harris, of Boston (Son of the late Mr Joseph Harris, of London, Harpsichord and Spinnet Maker), and in every respect does Honour to that Artist. . . ."* Purchase, Anonymous Gift, Friends of the American Wing Fund, Sansbury-Mills, Dodge, and Pfeiffer Funds, and funds from various donors, 1976 (1976.229)

**Figs. 158–64. The highboy** developed more fully and over a much longer period in America than in England. The earliest version, made during the William and Mary period, was a rectangular case supported by six trumpet-turned legs. Most examples were made of walnut or another native hardwood such as maple and many were veneered, but some of the most fashionable were japanned. Gradually the form acquired grace and grandeur: the six legs were reduced to four (though for some time after two of the four front legs disappeared the tripartite division of the skirt recalled them), turned legs became cabrioles, the flat top acquired a broken-scroll pediment, shells appeared on upper and lower drawers—in the beginning sometimes painted, and then carved. Japanned and walnut surfaces gave way to mahogany, whose strength inspired complex carving. The apotheosis of the highboy occurred in Philadelphia. The area below the broken-scroll pediment was gradually filled in with luxuriant carved leafage and the center finial became an asymmetrical rococo cartouche. Finally, the cornice, instead of rising to form the curved pediment, extended across the length of the crest, while the scroll arched above it. The space between pediment and cornice was filled with a delicate filigree.

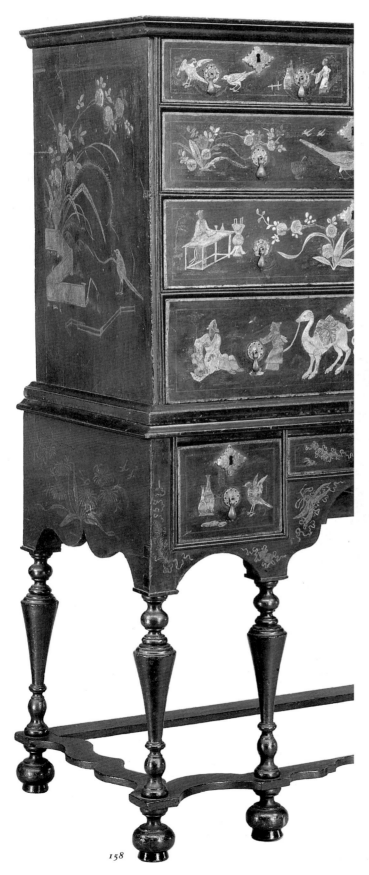

158

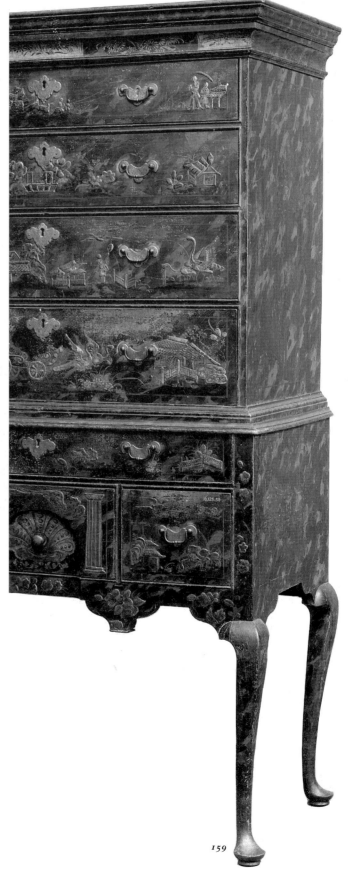

159

**Fig. 158.** *High chest of drawers, Boston, 1710–30; maple and white pine japanned, white pine, height 62½ inches (158.8 cm.). See also Fig. 137.*
Purchase, Joseph Pulitzer Bequest, 1940 (40.37.3)

**Fig. 159.** *High chest of drawers, Boston, about 1747; maple, japanned, white pine, height 70 inches (177.8 cm.).*
Gift of Mrs. Russell Sage, 1909 (10.125.58)

**Fig. 160.** *High chest of drawers, Boston, 1730–60; maple and birch, japanned, pine, height 85¼ inches (216.5 cm.).*
Purchase, Joseph Pulitzer Bequest, 1940 (40.37.1)

**Fig. 161.** *High chest of drawers, Boston, 1730–60; walnut, walnut veneer, white pine, height 89½ inches (227.3 cm.).*
Gift of Mrs. Russell Sage, 1909 (10.125.62)

**Fig. 162.** *High chest of drawers, Newport, 1760–80; mahogany, chestnut, white pine, height 84⅛ inches (213.7 cm.).*
Lent by Mrs. E. P. Moore, 1980 (1980.139)

**Fig. 163.** *High chest of drawers, Philadelphia, 1760–80; mahogany, tulip poplar, yellow pine, height 89¼ inches (226.7 cm.).*
John Stewart Kennedy Fund, 1918 (18.110.6)

**Fig. 164.** *High chest of drawers, Philadelphia, 1762–90; mahogany, mahogany veneer, tulip poplar, yellow pine, height 91½ inches (232.4 cm.). See also Figs. 186–87.*
John Stewart Kennedy Fund, 1918 (18.110.4)

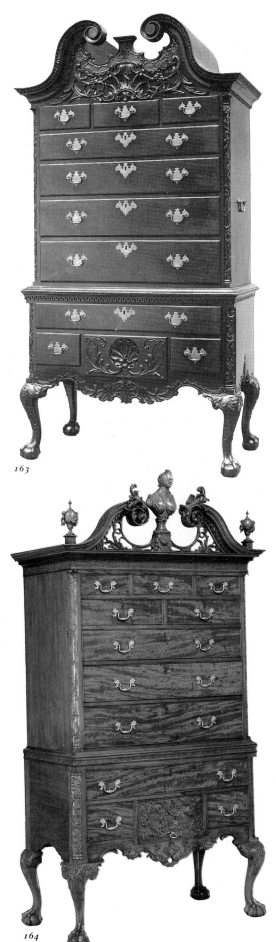

160

163

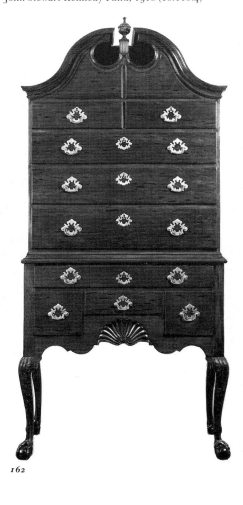

161

162

164

**Fig. 165. Side chair,** *Boston or Salem, 1760–80; mahogany, maple, white pine, height 38⅝ inches (98.1 cm). In the Chippendale period chairmakers brought the rounded Queen Anne shoulder to a right angle; pierced the solid vase-shaped splat; and embellished splat, cupid's-bow crest rail, and legs with carving. This particular chair, whose design was taken from Manwaring's Plate 9 (Fig. 167), exhibits both general Chippendale features and specific Massachusetts ones. The overall air of delicacy, the squared-off cabriole legs, claw-and-ball feet with side claws raked sharply backward, and delicately shaped rear feet are all indications of Massachusetts manufacture. This was a very popular chair pattern in the Boston-Salem area.*
Gift of Mrs. Paul Moore, 1939 (39.88.2)

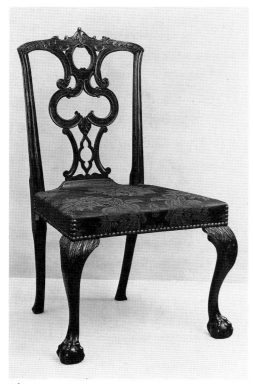

165

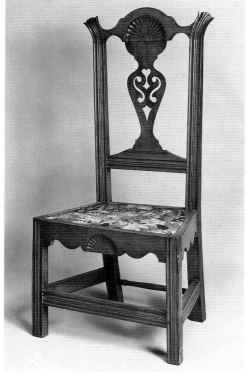

166

**Fig. 166. Side chair** *(one of a pair with original crewelwork seats), rural New Hampshire, 1770–90; maple, height 44⅞ inches (114 cm). Elements of all the eighteenth-century styles up through Chippendale are blended in this engagingly naïve masterpiece attributed to Major John Dunlap (1746–92). Major John was the central figure in a cabinetmaking family that, situated far from urban high-style developments in rural New Hampshire, created its own immensely distinctive style. Paired S-scrolls, seen here trimming the seat rails, piercing the splat, and shaping both crest rail and splat, are a constant Dunlap theme. Deeply incised fans—here on crest rail and front seat-rail—are another favorite Dunlap motif. Besides chairs, chests of drawers both high and low, chests-on-chests, and interior paneling*

*were made by the Dunlaps and their followers. Like other eighteenth-century craftsmen, Major John took payment in kind as well as in cash. In 1782 he recorded that he had agreed that for "one desk" he would be paid "Twenty Seven Bushels of corn or the Vealue thairof in fish or Eals or money."*
Gift of Mrs. J. Insley Blair, 1943 (43.149.1)

**Fig. 167. Plate 9, The Cabinet and Chair-Makers' Real Friend and Companion,** *by Robert Manwaring, London, 1765.*
Harris Brisbane Dick Fund, 1932 (32.9.6)

portions and substituting cabriole legs with claw-and-ball feet for the square-section examples shown in Manwaring's pattern.

Regional variations in the new style were as many and as marked as in earlier fashions. In the decades preceding the Revolution the most ambitious pieces were produced in Philadelphia, then the most progressive and populous of colonial cities. At the other extreme, in small towns, villages, and rural farming areas, country craftsmen turned out simplified versions in local woods. In both cases square seat frames, pierced back splats, bow-shaped cresting rails, and cabriole legs with claw-and-ball feet were the main distinguishing features of the style. Oddly, the cabriole leg and claw-and-ball foot, considered almost a hallmark of colonial furniture in the Chippendale style, is virtually ignored in the *Director*.

Many of the fine Chippendale case pieces made in Massachusetts in the decades immediately preceding the Revolution were of blockfront construction. Blocking, in which a flattened concave section on the front is flanked by two convex sections, was by no means restricted to Massachusetts cabinetwork, but it was apparently first practiced in that colony and enjoyed a long popularity there. (It is worth noting that this feature rarely occurs in English furniture.) The excellent examples in the collection include several desks and secretaries. One of the latter, distinguished by crisply carved scallop shells on the skirt and top, by perfect proportions, and by a lustrous patina, bears the cryptic phrase, "Nath. Gould not his work" (Fig. 168). Discreetly inscribed on the top of the lower section, this strange abbreviated message is concealed from all

but the most prying eyes by the upper carcass, which was placed over it when the finished work was assembled. When Nathaniel Gould died in 1781 he was the richest cabinetmaker in Salem, a community that supported a sizable group of flourishing woodworkers.

The staggering volume of correspondence and record keeping sustained by many prominent eighteenth-century figures underlines the importance of commodious and elaborate desk accommodations. We find it difficult to understand how men like Benjamin Franklin, John Adams, and Thomas Jefferson could have found time in otherwise very busy and productive lives to write such endless streams of letters, notes, and essays as flowed from their quill pens. The publication of their various papers in recent times has required hundreds of stout printed volumes. To facilitate keeping a record of his enormous load of correspondence, Franklin made a duplicating machine—"a rolling press, for taking the copies of letters or any other writing," a visitor to his house reported in 1787. "A sheet of paper is completely copied in less than two minutes, the copy as fair as the original, and without effacing it in the smallest degree." As his eyes grew weary with age, Franklin also invented bifocal eyeglasses to ease the strain of writing and reading.

An especially interesting slant-top desk of cherry wood, a provincial version of the blockfront, was made at Colchester, Connecticut, by one Benjamin Burnham (Fig. 169). According to an inscription on the piece (not hidden in this case), Burnham had "sarved his time in Felledlfey"—a quaint reminder of the itinerant habits of many colonial craftsmen. In his enthusiasm Burnham

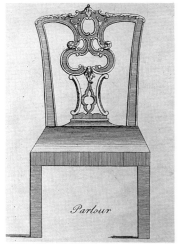

167

*Fig. 168. Desk and bookcase, Salem, 1770–90; mahogany, white pine, height 101 inches (256.5 cm.).* Large, impressive mahogany case pieces are typical of the Chippendale period, when successful merchants and sea captains up and down the eastern seaboard were building spacious houses and furnishing them elegantly "in the newest fashion." Blocked furniture, with alternate raised and receding vertical sections like those on the lower half of this piece, was a sign of affluence and status. Dignified proportions, discerningly chosen mahogany, and a glowing old finish make this secretary the finest of its type. It is attributed to the shop of Nathaniel Gould, Salem's wealthiest cabinetmaker, on the basis of a startling inscription: "Nath. Gould not his work." One theory is that a disgruntled employee left the message to indicate that he—and not Gould—had created this masterpiece.
Gift of Mrs. Russell Sage, 1909 (10.125.81)

included an unusual three-tiered bank of interior drawers with such robustly curved contours that niches had to be cut in the lid to permit it to close over the drawers.

A totally different, more restrained but extremely sophisticated style of furniture of the same period was peculiar to the area in and about the little seaport of Newport, Rhode Island (Figs. 171 and 172). The most prominent feature of this style was the blockfront of case pieces, with their alternately raised and recessed panels surmounted by carved convex and concave shells of a highly distinctive character. Neither blockfront furniture nor carved shells was peculiar to colonial Rhode Island, but nowhere else were these two elements more successfully integrated into a distinctive organic pattern. The blocking, usually fashioned from solid wood, extends in successive stages from shaped panels in the pediments of tall pieces down through the door and drawer fronts, through the moldings, and even into the bracket-shaped feet, where the line of the blocking is accented by delicately carved scrolls. These features are well illustrated by a tall secretary with six shells and a closed bonnet top. In these and certain other distinguishing characteristics, colonial Rhode Island cabinetwork owes nothing either to Chippendale or to any other contemporary English designer whose work was known in America.

Most of the prime surviving examples of such furniture were produced by one or another of the members of the interrelated Goddard and Townsend families, several of whose signed and labeled pieces are in the Museum's collection, among them a chest of drawers and a tall-case clock, both made by John

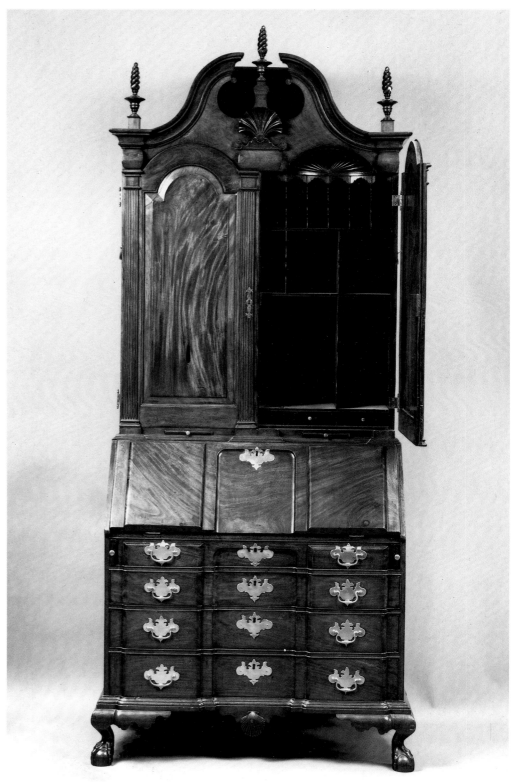

168

**Fig. 169. Desk,** *inscribed by Benjamin Burnham (1729–99), Colchester, Connecticut, 1769; cherry, white pine, tulip poplar, height 49¾ inches (126.4 cm.). Connecticut furniture has fascinated collectors and students for decades, and this desk is one of the premium pieces in that category. Its maker wrote on the bottom, "This Desk was maid in the year 1769 Buy Benjn Burnham, that sarved his time in Felledlfey." It has thus become important as a document—a master work whose distinctive features may be taken as characteristic of both one man's work and the work of neighboring cabinetmakers in the Colchester region. Among its special features are a blocked front, obviously inspired by similarly constructed Massachusetts and Rhode Island pieces; short cabriole legs ending in claw-and-*

*ball feet with very distinctive incised S-scroll carving; and a splendidly assertive array of small drawers and cubbyholes in the desk section. The drawers undulate in bold baroque curves reminiscent of the strong curving line of Massachusetts bombé furniture. The whole effect is one of a beautifully crafted piece that is imaginatively and somewhat unconventionally embellished—a combination that sets Connecticut furniture apart from its New England brethren.*
John Stewart Kennedy Fund, 1918 (18.110.58)

**Fig. 170. Chest of drawers,** *Newport, 1750–90; mahogany, chestnut, white pine, height 34⅜ inches (87.3 cm.). This rare chest of drawers has a serpentine front, serpentine sides, and a serpentine skirt, giving it something of the look of a*

*French commode of the Louis XV period—a "French message," as one expert put it, "conveyed with a strong Yankee accent." The undulating movement of the serpentine line is related to that of the blockfront pieces for which Newport is famous. A possible explanation for the appearance of this rococo form in conservative New England may be the existence of a similar chest with serpentine front and sides, said to have been ordered from a Newport cabinetmaker by a French sea captain. The Frenchman would have had the curvaceous commodes of his native country in mind when he ordered his chest, and its lines may have inspired those of this example. There is nothing of the French taste in the way this chest is ornamented, however: it is uncarved except for claw-and-ball feet and relies for its effect on the*

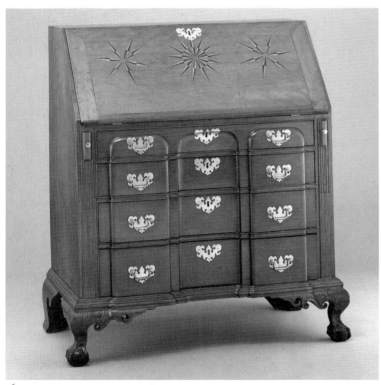

169

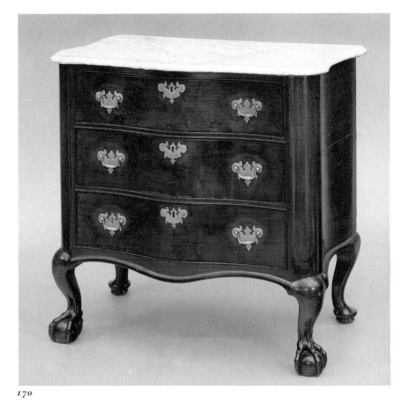

170

Townsend. Although their makers are as yet unidentified, a card table and marble-topped pier table also display features peculiar to the Newport area in their sharply contoured and carved cabriole legs and undercut claw-and-ball feet (see Fig. 178). The last was a refinement sometimes practiced in England but not elsewhere in the colonies.

One exceptional piece, a marble-topped commode, or bureau, with serpentine front (Fig. 170), follows a design markedly different from any of the others and more French than Anglo-American in spirit. It is attributed to John Goddard. We noted earlier that circumstances in the colonies did not encourage the kind of intensive specialization in any of the crafts that contributed to the most refined creations of European ateliers. Like all other master woodworkers of the era in other cities

along the coast, the Townsends and Goddards did not confine their efforts to the production of fine furniture. They also did odd jobs for their friends, neighbors, and patrons. The ledger of one of the Townsends, for example, lists among his miscellaneous output a "wigg box, a checkerboard, a 'Wooden Horse,' billiard sticks, and a coffin." He also built hen coops, cow pens, and pigsties; mended cellar doors; and bartered with his customers. At one point he gave three tables and a corner cupboard to a local barber in exchange for "A Year's Shaves, a Cutt Wigg, a foretop to the Wigg, and 24 feet of Mahogany."

Occasionally—less often than might be wished—artists included representations of furniture in their single or group portraits. One painting in the collection portrays Jeremiah Platt with his

hand resting on the crest of a handsome chair in the Chippendale style (Fig. 173); Platt commissioned the work from John Mare, a native New York painter, in 1767. It is the finest of a handful of identified works by this little-known artist. The opulence of the background in the painting seems justified by the inventory of Platt's well-furnished house.

Such a house might also have contained a gaming table, one of the elegant specialized forms that became popular as the eighteenth century moved along. The folding tops of these tables are frequently equipped with depressions at the four corners for candlesticks and with oval "fishponds" to hold counters used in the play. One of the Museum's several examples descended in the Van Rensselaer family and represents a type popular among New York's aristocracy—the five-legged card, sweep of its curves and the contrasts of its richly grained mahogany, shining brasses, and white marble top. Several features bespeak the chest's Newport origin, among them the front feet with long, thin claws grasping an elongated ball and the combination of carved claw-and-ball feet in front with plain pad feet in back. Furthermore, John Goddard produced pieces with legs and skirts like those of this piece.

Purchase, Emily Crane Chadbourne Bequest, Gifts of Mrs. J. Amory Haskell and Mrs. Russell Sage, by exchange, and The Sylmaris Collection, Gift of George Coe Graves, by exchange, 1972 (1972.130)

**Figs. 171 and 172. Desk and bookcase,** *Newport, 1760–90; mahogany, chestnut, white pine, height 99½ inches (252.7 cm.). One of the most impressive, and certainly one of the most charac-* teristically American, forms of the Chippendale period is the block-and-shell case piece from Rhode Island. Blocked furniture was popular elsewhere in New England, but it was in Rhode Island that this particular combination, with its sinuously curved shells, was brought to perfection. Great skill was required to create such pieces, whose strong vertical thrust is balanced by the horizontal lines of the drawers and the rows of shells. A number of block-and-shell pieces signed or labeled by the related families of Goddard and Townsend are known; this one bears the incised inscription ZH AM, but its maker is not known.

Rogers Fund, 1915 (15.21.2)

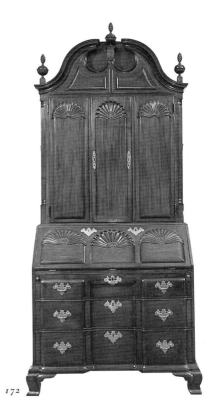

172

or gaming, table (Figs. 174 and 175). After a late dinner, when candles provided too little light to encourage reading, games of chance offered a pleasant diversion. George Washington frequently enjoyed the play. His account book records many winnings and losings at the table, and not always at games played in the evening. One entry in his diary reads, "At home all day over cards."

It was during the late colonial period that the high chest of drawers, or highboy, reached its ultimate and most elaborate development, most conspicuously in Philadelphia. There lofty examples, often with matching lowboys, were ornamented by master carvers with pierced shells, scrolling leaves, flowers, vines, and other naturalistic details in the rococo spirit of the day. "After all," wrote Nathaniel Hawthorne more than a century ago, "the moderns have invented nothing better in chamber furniture than those chests which stand on four slender legs, and send an absolute tower of mahogany to the ceiling, the whole terminating in a fantastically carved ornament." There are no English equivalents of such extreme treatment of the form.

In the disposition of its carved elements and the quality of its execution the "Pompadour" highboy and its companion lowboy are unsurpassed examples of eighteenth-century Philadelphia

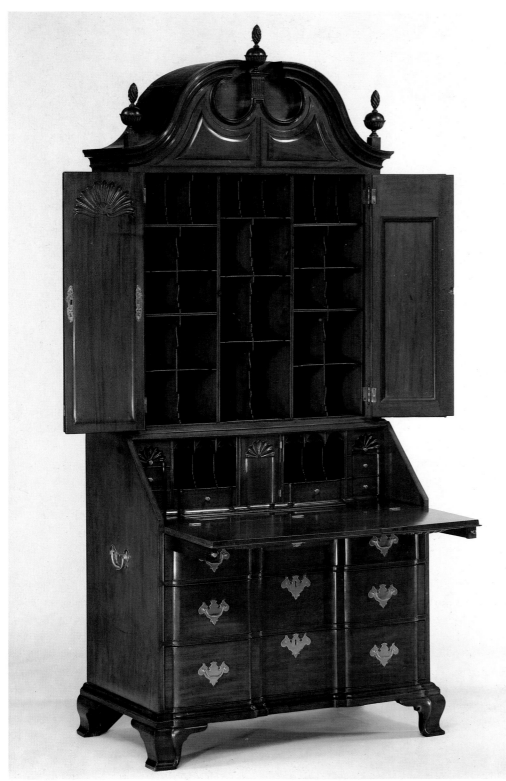

171

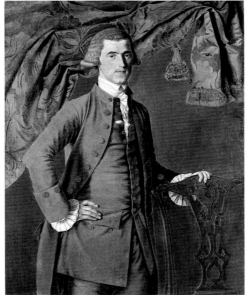

173

**Fig. 173. Portrait of Jeremiah Platt,** *by John Mare (1739–after 1795?), 1767; oil on canvas, 48½ by 38½ inches (123.2 by 97.8 cm.). This portrait of the prosperous New York merchant Jeremiah Platt came to the Museum in 1955 as a portrait of an unidentified man, purchased because it was the finest known likeness by John Mare. Mare's biographer, Helen Burr Smith, was fascinated by the portrait and set out to discover the identity of its subject. After sixteen years of hard and frustrating research, she succeeded. Platt was prominent in New York and later in New Haven, turning during the Revolution to outfitting ships for privateering. His inventory indicates that his house was finely furnished, containing a large number and variety of furniture, silver, ceramics, and glass, as well as "One large framed Picture—$100." Perhaps this is that picture, and perhaps the "3 red window curtains, 4 red ditto, red cord and tassels" are those shown in the portrait—although it was usual for painters to include drapery in the background of formal portraits. Perhaps, too, the handsome chair on which Platt rests his left hand was among his parlor furniture.*
Victor Wilbour Memorial Fund, 1955 (55.55)

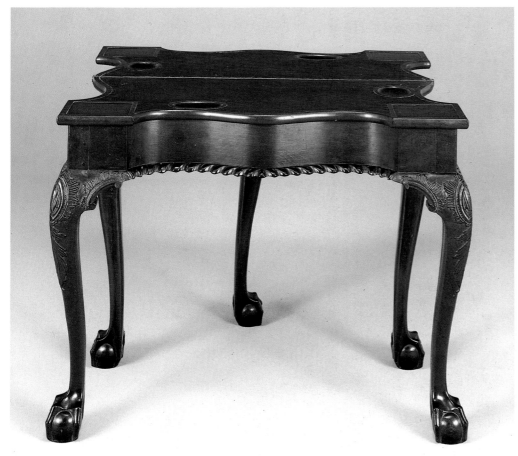

174

**Fig. 174. Card table,** *New York, 1760–90; mahogany, oak, tulip poplar, height 27 inches (68.6 cm.). The taste of eighteenth-century New Yorkers was for solid, well-made, but plain furniture. The showy carved highboys of Philadelphia and the magnificent bombé case furniture of Boston have no counterpart in New York. There is, however, the five-legged card table, which makes up in decorative impact whatever New York's case pieces lack. The boldness of the tables' swinging serpentine curves on both front and sides is reinforced by the S-curve of the substantial cabriole legs. Rich carving of C-scrolls and acanthus leaves, rendered with more grace and fluidity than on other New York forms, enriches knees, and gadrooned and foliate moldings edge aprons. Although not all superior New York card tables have the fifth, swinging, leg that serves as a support when the card table is in use, a group of more than twenty-five have, and they are considered American masterpieces. A number of these tables have New York histories, and this example is said to have descended in the Van Rensselaer family.*
Purchase, Joseph Pulitzer Bequest, 1947 (47.35)

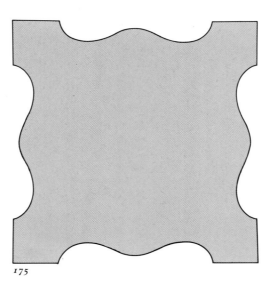

175

**Fig. 175. Outline of New York card-table top,** *Fig. 174. The strength of this table's bold serpentine curves is especially obvious when the top is opened out. The contrast between the exuberant curves of the sides and the strong squares at the corners gives the design its impact.*

**Fig. 176. Looking glass,** *New York, 1770–1800; mahogany veneer, gilt gesso, pine, height 45 inches (114.3 cm.). With this looking glass we bridge the gap between the uninhibited naturalism of the Chippendale, or rococo, period and the strictly controlled geometry of the Federal, or neoclassical, period. Neoclassical in its oval shape and its air of delicacy, this glass is ornamented with the frets, scrolls, and tattered leafage of the Chippendale era. The spirited phoenix that serves as its central finial exhibits all the asymmetry and vitality of the finest American rococo work. In New York oval looking glasses began to supplant rectangular Chippendale ones as early as 1774, when John Stites advertised "A Very elegant assortment of both oval and square [mirrors], of various sizes. . . ." This example descended in the Cortelyou family of Staten Island, and is thought to have been made in New York rather than in Europe, where most looking glasses used in eighteenth-century America were made.*
Sansbury-Mills Fund, 1952 (52.86)

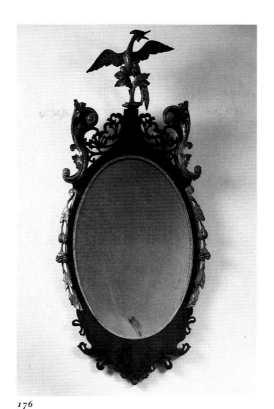

176

**Fig. 177. Chest on chest,** *New York, 1760–80; mahogany, white pine, poplar, height 78¾ inches (200 cm.). The broken-scroll pediments typical of large Pennsylvania and New England pieces were never popular in New York—perhaps because of the continuing influence of the great flat-topped wardrobes known as* kasten. *Thus, in the Chippendale period, as in earlier eras, important pieces like this double chest were straight lined and flat topped. The effect is one of solid handsomeness, the only decorative accents being the very architectural cornice and frieze and the carved brackets ending in claw-and-ball feet. Elaborate brasses and rich mahogany with a lively grain add to the effect of dignified good looks. The combination of claw-and-ball feet in front with thick bracket feet in back is characteristic of New York work.*
Gift of Mr. E. M. Newlin, 1964 (64.249.3)

cabinetwork (Figs. 164, 186, and 187). Carved details on the drawer fronts were taken from designs published by Thomas Johnson, a contemporary English rococo furniture maker, and were apparently based on such fables as those of La Fontaine.

The virtuosity evident in these examples of Philadelphia cabinetwork is also brilliantly demonstrated in the chairs, tables, and other forms fashioned in that populous and flourishing city, then the most eminent urban center in the British colonial world. At Princeton in 1771 two young Philadelphia undergraduate poets hailed their city as the "mistress of our world, the seat of arts of science, and of fame," an effusion that even a New England almanac of the same year virtually echoed. After a visit there a few years later, John Adams referred in hardly less glowing terms to "the happy, the peaceful, the elegant, the hospitable, and polite city of Philadelphia"—and Adams was not given to extravagant statements.

A remarkable side chair (Fig. 188), easily one of the finest examples of seating furniture to have been produced in the colonies, was once owned by the Cadwalader family. John Adams referred to John Cadwalader as "a Gentleman of large Fortune [with] a grand and elegant House and Furniture." The house was indeed one of the most sumptuously furnished dwellings in pre-Revo-

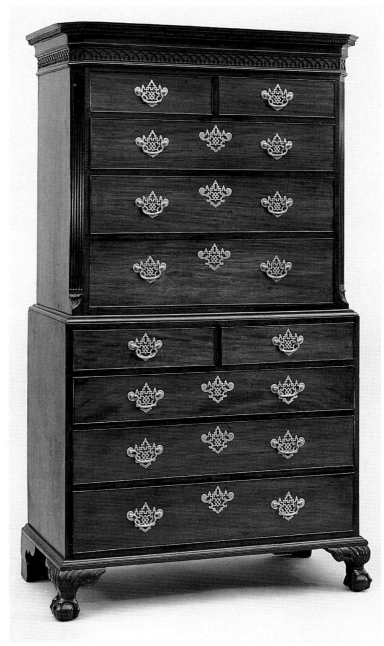

177

**Figs. 178–85. Feet and knees.** *Recognizing distinctive features that are characteristic of a particular region can be very helpful in identifying furniture. Here the carved claw-and-ball feet and knees of four beautifully executed high-style objects illustrate outlines and ornament typical of four mid-eighteenth-century regional style centers. Figs. 178 and 182 belong to a card table that represents Newport craftsmanship at its very finest. The crisply modeled talons curve out and away from the ball, so that there's a space between claw and ball. The accompanying knee is carved in a distinctive stylized scroll design. Figs. 179 and 183 show the foot and knee of a side chair that has been described as "perhaps the most nearly perfect of all Philadelphia Chippendale*

*chairs." The sturdy claws grasp the flattened ball firmly; the rounded knee is richly carved with flowing leafage. Figs. 180 and 184, from a delicate Boston settee, show the characteristic high ball with long slender claws spaced widely around it; the side claws bend sharply backward, as they do on many of the finest examples from eastern Massachusetts. The knee carving is remarkably unfettered for New England, with C-scrolls and flowing acanthus foliage. The New York pair from a serpentine card table, Figs. 181 and 185, show the powerful, squarish foot characteristic of this region. C-scrolls and tattered acanthus carved on the knee give the substantial table an unexpectedly elegant touch.*

Friends of the American Wing Fund, 1967 (67.114.1); Purchase, Bequest of W. Gedney Beatty and Rogers Fund, by exchange, 1951 (51.140); The Sylmaris Collection, Gift of George Coe Graves, 1930 (30.120.59); Joseph Pulitzer Bequest, 1947 (47.35)

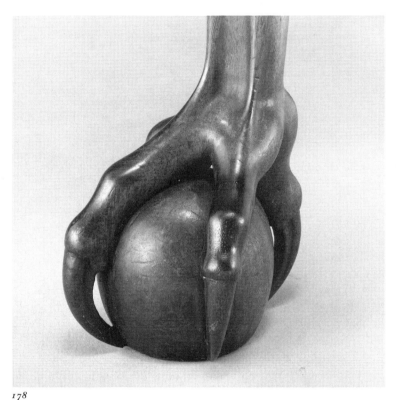

178

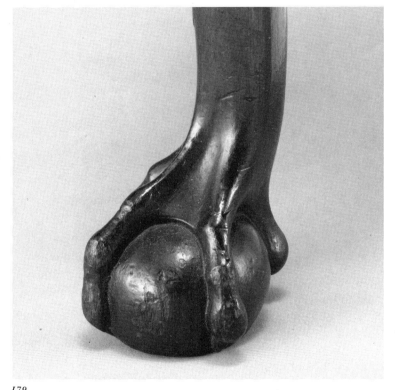

179

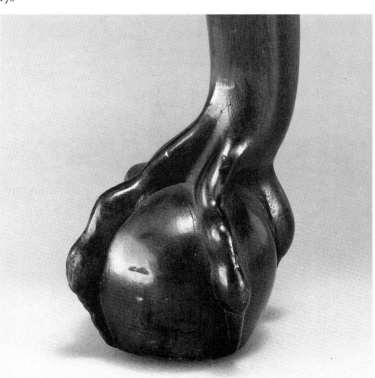

180

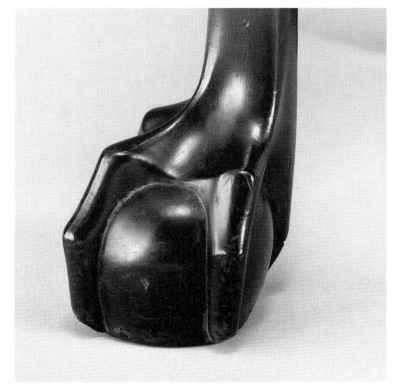

181

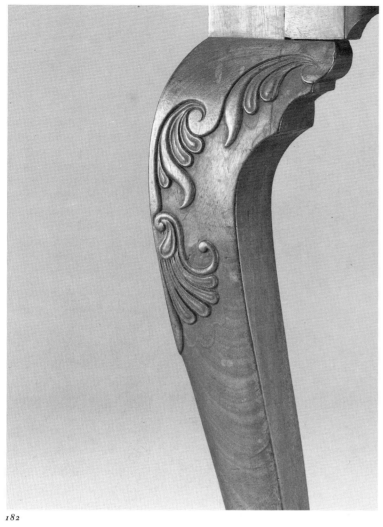

182

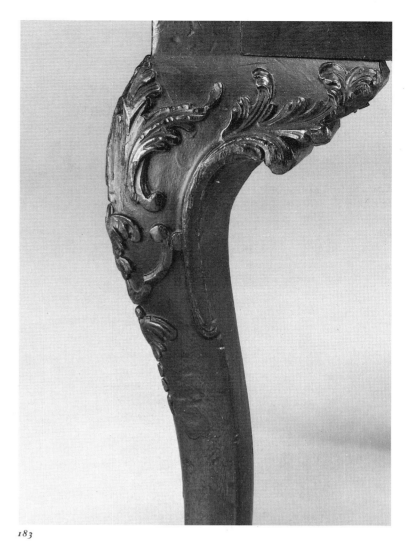

183

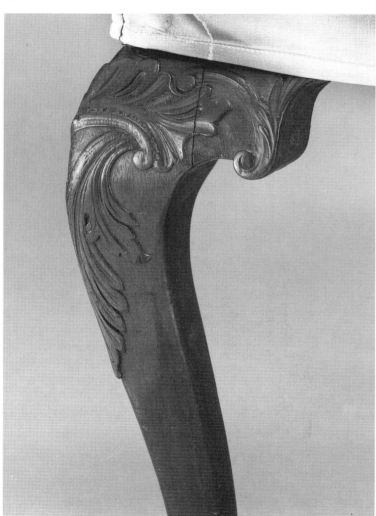

184

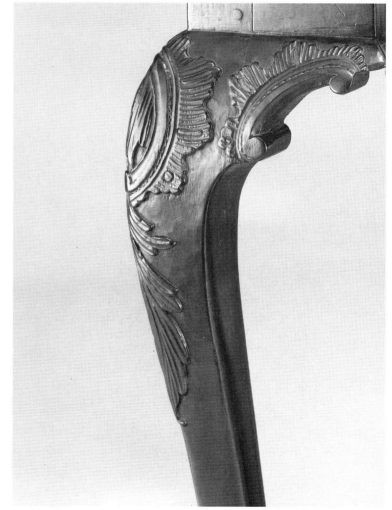

185

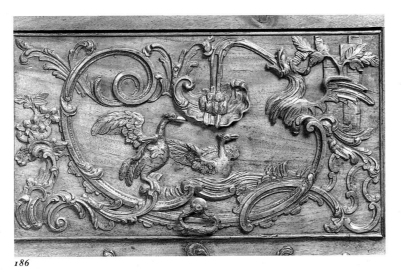

186

lutionary Philadelphia. Strictly English in its design and all but indistinguishable from the finest imported models, this chair was made locally at a time when imports of fashionable London furniture were being boycotted by patriotic colonists.

In 1765 Samuel Powel, who was planning to return from a sojourn in London with a shipment of fine English furnishings for his new house in Philadelphia, was advised by his uncle Samuel Morris: "Household goods may be had here [in Philadelphia] as cheap and as well made from English patterns." And he added (it was the year the Stamp Act had been passed by the British Parliament), "In the humour people are in here, a man is in danger of becoming Invidiously distinguished, who buys anything in England which our Tradesmen can furnish. I have heard the joiners here object this against [those] . . . who brought their furniture with them."

Other pieces in the collection, a tripod table, an easy chair, a pole screen with hairy-paw feet, and a pembroke table (Fig. 189) among them, amplify the impression of opulence and supreme craftsmanship typical of Philadelphia furniture at its best.

During those years when master craftsmen in the neighborhood of Philadelphia were producing superb furnishings, German-speaking immigrants from the Rhine valley and the Palatine, who had been settling in the southeastern counties of Pennsylvania, were turning out totally different simple and colorful forms that harked back to old traditions of their homeland. The earliest of these settlers came to the New World in response to William Penn's of-

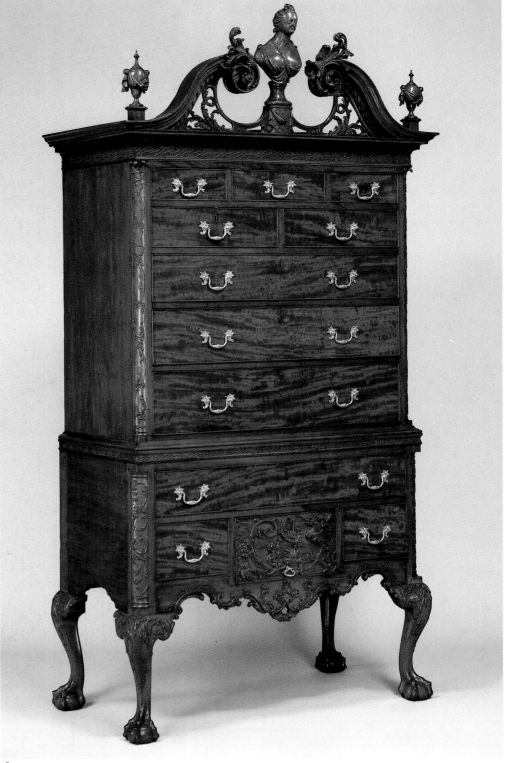

187

dition of lavish rococo carving. Perhaps the richest and most beautifully proportioned of all such pieces is this, known as the Pompadour high chest because its carved female bust reminded some romantic early collector of Louis XV's mistress. The design for urn finials on either side of the central bust is a modified version of a design taken from Chippendale's The Gentleman and Cabinet-Maker's Director, while the design of the central bottom drawer is taken, again with some modification, from another pattern book of the period, Thomas Johnson's New Book of Ornament. Finials and drawer, as well as all other carved ornament on this splendid piece, are of the highest order and were very possibly executed by English craftsmen who had immigrated to Philadelphia. A nineteenth-century chronicler reported that towering chests of drawers like this were often found in eighteenth-century parlors or sitting rooms, and, he added, "It was no sin to rummage them before company!"
John Stewart Kennedy Fund, 1918 (18.110.4)

**Fig. 188. Side chair,** *Philadelphia, about 1770; mahogany, southern white cedar, height 37 inches (94 cm.). Chairs of this degree of richness are extremely rare in American work, and for many years such a piece would have been identified either as simply "English," or as a member of a group of "sample chairs" attributed to Benjamin Randolph. Lately, however, these chairs (so far six others from this set have come to light) and a card table with similar carving have been attributed to Thomas Affleck, like Randolph an outstanding Philadelphia craftsman. The chairs, table, and a number of other pieces were apparently ordered between 1770 and 1772 by General John Cadwalader, leading citizen and fervent patriot, for his elegant town house in Philadelphia. The lavishly scalloped skirt, hairy-paw feet, and wide saddle seat are much more English in feeling than American, but the stump rear legs and the construction techniques, as well as the flowing naturalistic carving, bespeak a Philadelphia origin. Because of the richness and rarity of this set, one of these chairs recently established a world auction record in New York.*
Purchase, Sansbury-Mills and Rogers Funds, Emily C. Chadbourne Gift, Virginia Groomes Gift, in memory of Mary W. Groomes, Mr. and Mrs. Marshall P. Blankarn, John Bierwirth and Robert G. Goelet Gifts, The Sylmaris Collection, Gift of George Coe Graves, by exchange, and funds from various donors, 1974 (1974.325)

**Fig. 189. Pembroke table,** *Philadelphia, 1765–90; mahogany, oak, white pine, height 28 inches (71.1 cm.). The Pembroke, or breakfast, table was a new form in the Chippendale period and was named, according to Sheraton in his Cabinet Dictionary of 1803, for the lady who first ordered one. These useful small tables reverse the proportions of the earlier drop leaf, making the midsection wider than the leaves. This example is one of the finest of its type, but it relies for its effect on overall form and proportion instead of on the lush carving that gives so much Philadelphia Chippendale furniture its character. The curves of the scalloped leaves are repeated in the rising crossed stretchers; both provide a contrast to the straight, square-sectioned Marlborough legs.*
Purchase, Emily C. Chadbourne Gift, 1974 (1974.35)

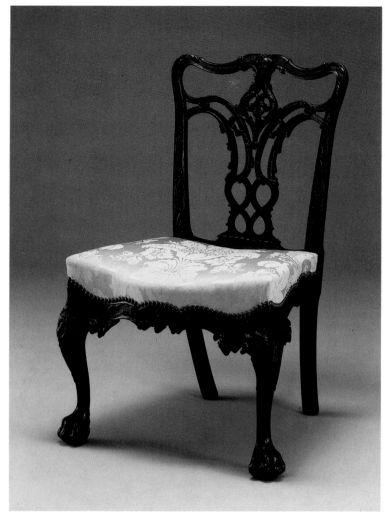

188

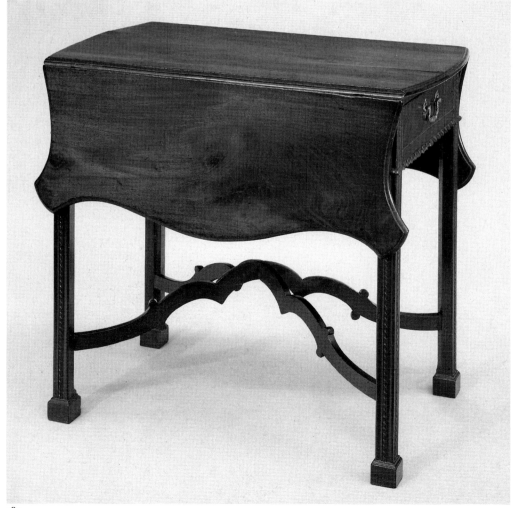

189

**Fig. 190. Group of Pennsylvania German furnishings** in the Pennsylvania German room from Morgantown, Lancaster County, about 1761. Simple, useful forms that would have served well in a bustling Pennsylvania German household are gathered here. The unpainted tables and open-shelved dresser are of walnut, a wood often used in Pennsylvania furniture even during the Chippendale period, when mahogany had become the fashionable wood. The corner fireplace retains its original blue paint, now much faded, and its overmantel painting—a rather grim scene with crosses marking wayside graves, copied from an English book on drawing and engraving. Pewter and woodenware dishes, as well as brightly decorated (and today much col-lected) slip- and sgraffito wares, indicate what would have appeared on a typical eighteenth-century Pennsylvania German table.
Chimney breast and chair rail: Morris K. Jesup Fund, 1934 (34.27.1,10)

**Fig. 191. Dower chest,** Berks County, Pennsylvania, about 1780; yellow pine, painted, tulip poplar, height 28⅝ inches (72.7 cm.). In Pennsylvania German country, painted-pine furniture was the alternative to the type seen in Fig. 190. Traditional German construction and decorative techniques were used, but the influence of the English who had first settled Pennsylvania is seen in the choice of motifs. The unicorns in the center were copied from the unicorn on the British coat of arms, while the horsemen with raised swords in the two side panels are English cavalry officers. The batwing brasses on the two lower drawers are English, too. In joining influences from both German and English cultures, Pennsylvania German furniture was a joyful and unique expression of the environment of the new land.
Rogers Fund, 1923 (23.16)

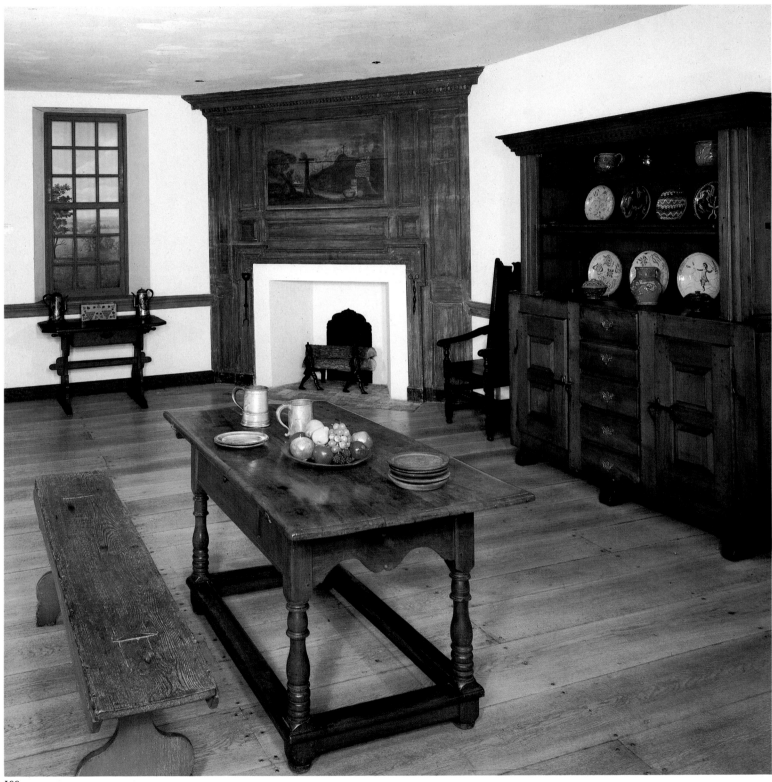

190

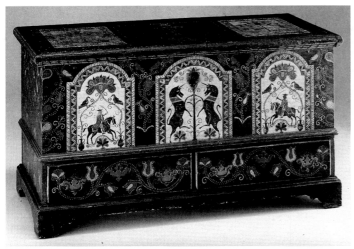

191

fer of a refuge from persecution and hardship, and over the years they came in growing numbers as Penn's promises were abundantly fulfilled.

The painted dower chests of the Pennsylvania Germans, their cupboards and boxes, sgraffito and slipware pottery, objects in wrought iron, textiles, and illuminated writing, or fraktur, all recall German prototypes, but do not lack originality. A large open dresser, or cupboard, resting on trestle feet, its shelves lined with a variety of locally made earthenware, suggests the ample living these people reaped from the rich soil they so shrewdly selected for their farms and so zealously cultivated (see Fig. 190). The trestle table is a direct if distant descendant of medieval north European forms. A dower chest from Berks County (Fig. 191) made about 1780 and decorated with tulip motifs and figures of unicorns is typical of the painted-furniture tradition these people carried with them from overseas and of the homely skills with which local artisans enlivened even the most commonplace accessories of daily living.

From early in the eighteenth century tall cases were devised to house and protect the works of clocks from dust and dirt and to accommodate their long pendulums that, controlled by an anchor escapement, improved their accuracy. Such impressive timepieces were thus the joint product of the cabinetmaker and the clockmaker, only very occasionally combined in one person. They retained the same general appearance for a century or more, but variations in details indicate their approximate date and regional origin. (The term "grandfather clock," commonly used to designate such pieces, was de-

rived from a popular song of the 1880s.) As the century advanced, timepieces of this sort appeared in household inventories with increasing frequency. However, they continued to be relatively expensive, and it may be surmised that while ownership of these decorative accessories remained limited it was as smart to be on time for an engagement as it is to be fashionably late now that everyone owns a watch.

Few clocks were made in the colonies before the 1720s, and of these hardly any have survived. One of the earliest colonial clockmakers was English-born Benjamin Bagnall, who emigrated to Boston sometime before 1712 and was perhaps the first to practice the craft in that city. One example of his work, dating from the second quarter of the century, is enclosed in an attractive walnut-veneered case in the William and Mary fashion (Fig. 192). Its flat top is surmounted by a domed superstructure, for some reason termed a sarcophagus top, that promises the greater elaborations that were soon to follow. As was common at the time, the spandrels of the dial surrounding the maker's nameplate are filled with cast-brass ornaments similar in design to some of the applied decorations on silver tankards of the period.

Most such timepieces had brass eight-day movements hammered, turned, cut, and shaped with quite simple hand tools. When kept in condition (or restored to their original condition), these clocks continue to keep good time, as visitors to the Wing will realize when they check their watches as the clocks' bells strike the hour. In 1768 Gawen Browne of Boston devised a "superb stately Town-Clock . . . [with] a curious mathematical Pendulum" that could be

altered to the thirty-five-hundredth part of an inch. That degree of precision was probably of more interest to astronomers, and possibly the horse-racing gentry, than to ordinary householders.

It should be repeated that a clock's mechanism and its wooden casing were rarely the work of the same individual; each required a separate expertise. One exceptionally fine tall-clock case bears the label of the master Newport cabinetmaker John Townsend (Fig. 194) and displays the carved block-and-shell design characteristic of the Newport school of woodworkers and so highly developed by the Townsend-Goddard families. It houses works by an English clockmaker. A good case often cost somewhat more than the works it protected, as it probably did in this instance. The same thing might be said of the mahogany case enclosing works by John Wood of Philadelphia, with the elaborate rococo carved embellishments of its hood (Fig. 197). As time passed, the hands told the minutes as well as the hours and small dials indicated the days of the month. Occasionally the arch above the dial contained a rotating painted representation of the phases of the moon.

In later colonial models the brass dial was replaced by a flat, silvered-metal dial, usually with engraved decoration. A clock made in 1772 by Benjamin Willard and his young brother Simon of Roxbury, Massachusetts, has such a dial (Fig. 193). In all there were four Willard brothers who made outstanding clocks well into the post-Revolutionary period.

**Figs. 192–98. Tall clocks.** *A tall clock was a luxury item throughout the 1700s. The form had evolved in the previous century as a solution to the problem of encasing and protecting the long pendulums that made clocks much more reliable and accurate than they had ever been before. The pendulum was such an improvement that Isaac Webb, "Watch-Maker and Clock-Maker at the Sign of the Clock Dial in Boston," advertised in 1708 that "if any Person or Persons wants any Clock to be made, or any Old Clocks to be turned into Pendelums, or Watches and Clocks to be Mended . . ." Let them repair to the said Webb. . . ." Usually specialists like Webb made and repaired the works, while cabinetmakers supplied the cases—though occasionally both crafts were practiced in the same shop. Tall-clock cases, like other furniture forms, reflect changing styles and regional variations, seen here in examples that range from the William and Mary to the Federal periods.*

**Fig. 192.** *Works by Benjamin Bagnall (1689–1773), Boston, 1725–50; walnut, walnut veneer, white pine, height 90 inches (228.6 cm.).* Gift of Mrs. Russell Sage, 1909 (10.125.388)

**Fig. 193.** *Works by Benjamin Willard (1743–1803) and Simon Willard (1754–1849), Roxbury, Massachusetts, 1772; mahogany, cherry, white pine, height 84 inches (213.4 cm.).* Gift of Dr. and Mrs. Brooks H. Marsh, 1976 (1976.341)

**Fig. 194.** *Case bearing the label of John Townsend (1732–1809), works by William Tomlinson (active London 1699–1750), Newport, 1789; mahogany, cherry, chestnut, and oak, height 99½ inches (252.7 cm.).* Rogers Fund, 1927 (27.57.2)

**Fig. 195.** *Detail, Fig. 196, showing the capture of the British frigate* Guerrière *by the American frigate* Constitution *painted above the dial.*

**Fig. 196.** *Case attributed to John Doggett (1780–1857), works by Aaron Willard, Jr. (active 1823–50), dial attributed to Spenser Nolen and Samuel Curtis (working together 1807–20) or Samuel Curtis's Manufactory (1824–about*

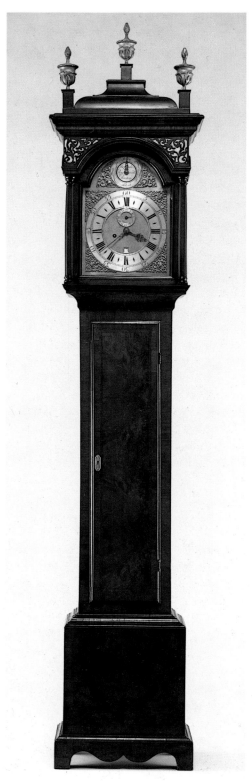

192

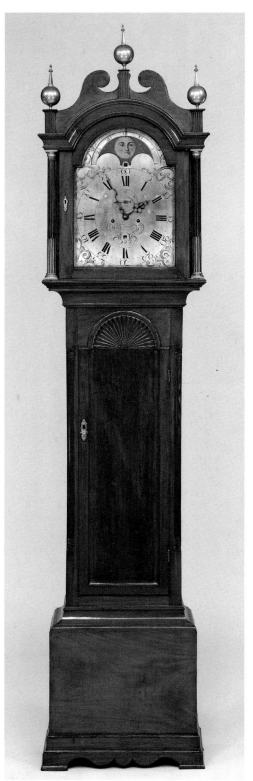

193

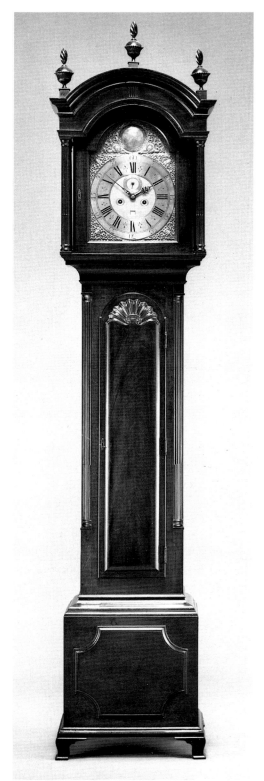

194

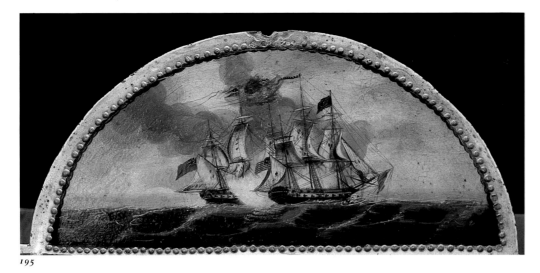

195

1855), Boston, about 1825; mahogany, mahogany veneer, maple, and white pine, height 99¾ inches (253.4 cm.).
Joseph Pulitzer Fund, 1942 (42.76.1)

**Fig. 197.** Works by John Wood, Philadelphia, 1755–65; walnut, white pine, tulip poplar, height 104⅓ inches (265 cm.).
Bequest of W. Gedney Beatty, 1941 (41.160.369)

**Fig. 198.** Works by Jacob Diehl (1776–1858), Reading, Pennsylvania, about 1800; walnut, pine, height 96½ inches (245.1 cm.).
Purchase, Douglas and Priscilla de Forest Williams, Mr. and Mrs. Eric M. Wunsch, and The Sack Foundation Gifts, 1976 (1976.279)

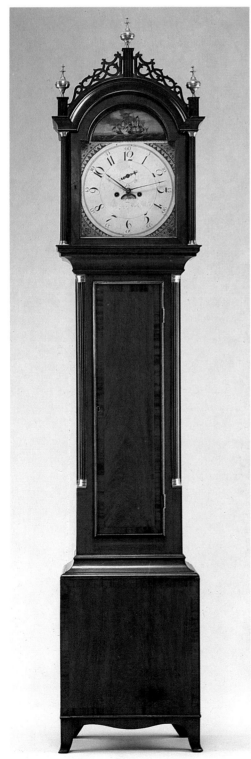

196

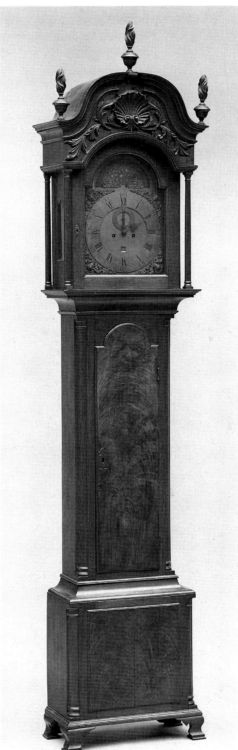

197

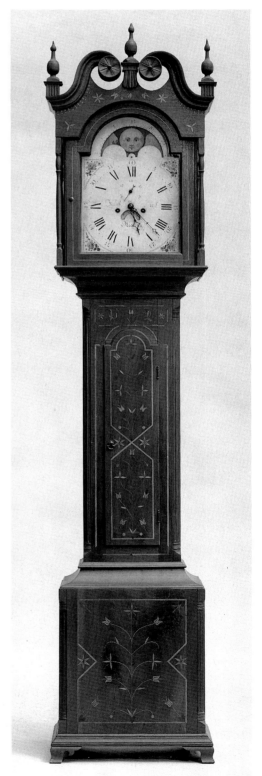

198

# The Federal and Early Empire Periods, 1790–1820

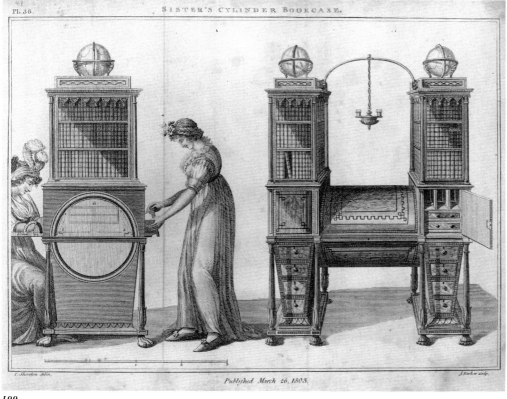

199

The regional characteristics so markedly apparent in the pre-Revolutionary decorative arts were even more pronounced in the decades following the war. No one of the cities of the new republic was to America what London, Paris, or Rome was to its country—at once the largest city and the center of government, as well as the principal center of wealth, fashion, and culture. Each of the half dozen or so larger urban centers along the Atlantic seaboard was conscious of its own distinctive character and its potential for future development. In and about each one evolved recognizably different styles in furniture and other decorative arts—or, more accurately stated, interpretations of styles that prevailed abroad.

The political independence America had won with the Revolution had not radically reduced the new nation's reliance upon Europe—upon England principally, but increasingly France as well—for cultural guidance and for manufactures. Immediately after the war imports from Great Britain were far greater in volume than they had been earlier. Noah Webster might plead for a whole new American way of life: the young nation, he insisted, must become "as famous for *arts* as for *arms.*" But ties with the Old World were too strong to be quickly severed.

The impact of Robert Adam's translations of the antique was very soon reflected in the illustrations of other English books on design produced by Thomas Shearer, George Hepplewhite, and Thomas Sheraton. In these manuals, the seminal, austerely elegant Adam furniture designs were modified to the point where it was practical to offer them to a wider public. Hepplewhite's *The Cabinet-maker and Upholsterer's Guide* was published posthumously in 1788 and was later produced in two other editions that illustrated some three hundred designs. Sheraton's *The Cabinet-Maker and Upholsterer's Drawing Book* was issued in four parts between 1791 and 1794 and was followed by two other publications by the same author. (Interestingly, no piece of furniture has ever been attributed to either man.)

As promulgated by such pattern books, the new style was at once ostensibly simple and dignified. The robust exuberance of the Chippendale style with its asymmetrical and eclectic accents gave way to lighter forms of measured symmetry and delicate grace. Carving was subdued in favor of inlay and veneer arranged in geometric patterns. Along with the development of the new style as such, there evolved dif-

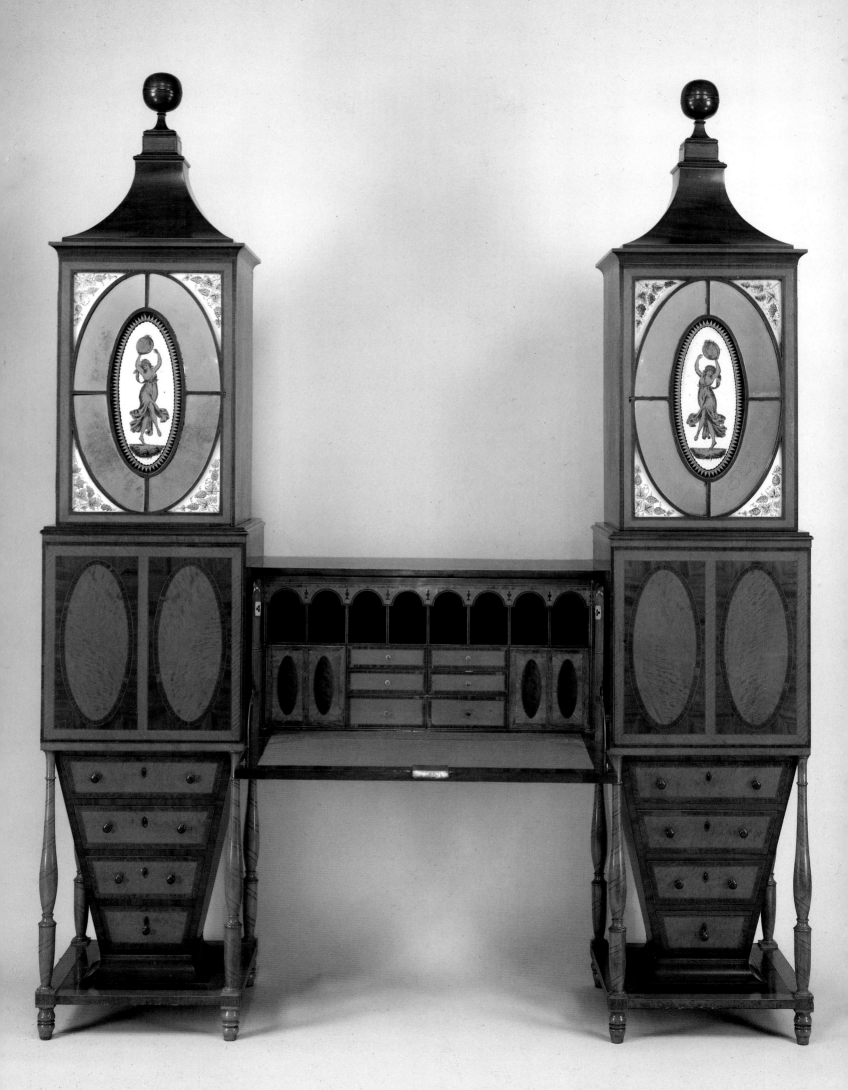

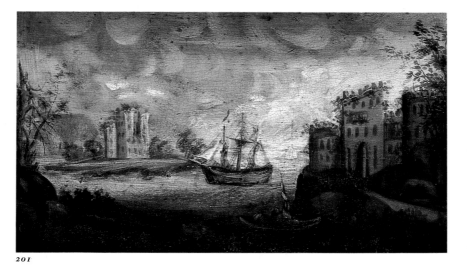

201

**Fig. 201. Detail of Fig. 202,** *showing the romantic harbor view centered on the apron of the table.*

**Fig. 202. Side chair** *(one of a pair)* **and table** *with ovolo corners attributed to John and Hugh Finlay (active 1800–37), Baltimore, 1800–10; mahogany and maple painted black with gilt and polychrome decoration, cane seat on chair (secondary woods, chair: tulip poplar; table: oak and tulip poplar), heights 33⅝ inches (85.3 cm.) and 28⅞ inches (73.3 cm.). These two pieces represent the finest in Baltimore painted furniture. On the basis of their general form and ornament, which are similar to those of thoroughly documented Finlay pieces, they have been attrib-*

ferent types of furniture designed to further the comforts and conveniences of life—sideboards, washstands, wine coolers, sewing tables, bookcases, and other household appurtenances that had earlier played little or no part in the domestic routine.

The styles popularized by Sheraton and Hepplewhite were introduced into this country not only by their publications, but also by immigrant craftsmen with some training and experience who came here largely from the British Isles. They brought with them or here developed their own personal interpretations of the prevailing styles. Pieces in the two early Federal styles are often referred to as either Hepplewhite or Sheraton, acknowledging some debt to one or another of the publications of these influential designers. Actually the styles overlap in both time and treatment, often so subtly that a distinction is difficult to make. Sheraton favored turned legs and square backs on chairs and sofas. However, he illustrated many square-sectioned tapered legs, which are often associated with Hepplewhite.

The latter's designs also featured shield- and heart-shaped backs for chairs, but showed square-backed chairs as well. In American cabinetwork the term "Hepplewhite" is used when the ornament includes light-wood stringings and small inlays of marquetry designs on a dark ground. "Sheraton" connotes color in fields and crossbandings of richly contrasting grains of light and dark woods.

Baltimore Federal furniture made constant and colorful use of light-wood inlays and painted glass, often with clas-

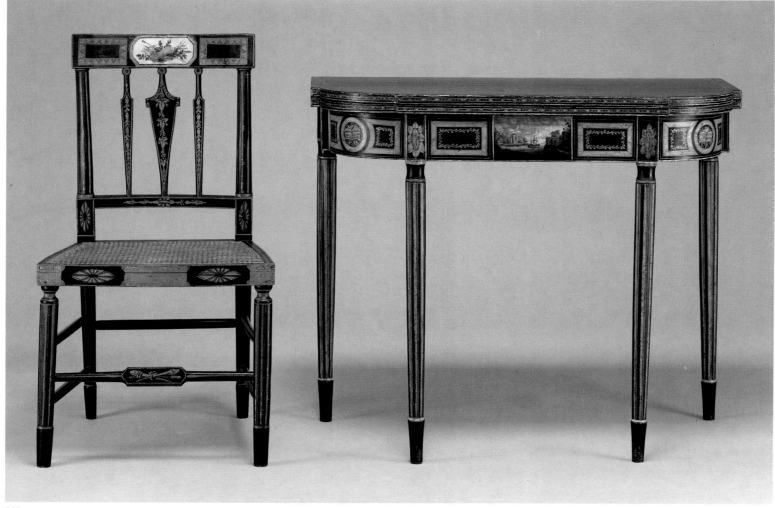

202

uted to John and Hugh Finlay, brothers who were trained in Ireland, emigrated to Baltimore probably in the 1790s, and produced elegant "fancy" (painted) furniture there for many years. The "icicle"-shaped splats in the chair back, the delicate grapevine ornament, and the panels containing floral trophies and romantic scenery are all characteristic Finlay features.

Purchase, Mrs. Paul Moore Gift, by exchange, 1974 (1974.102.1), and Purchase, Mrs. Russell Sage Gift, 1970 (1970.189)

**Fig. 203. Square-backed armchairs:** left, perhaps by Ephraim Haines (active 1799–1811), Philadelphia, 1800–10; mahogany and cane, height 33¾ inches (85 cm.). Right, attributed to Henry Connelly (active about 1800–40), Philadelphia, 1800–10; mahogany, ash, height 35½ inches (90.2 cm.). The quietly handsome banister-back chair on the left is nearly identical to those in a famous set of ebony furniture made in 1807 by Ephraim Haines for merchant and banking millionaire Stephen Girard. Turning, reeding, and low-relief carving ornament it. Its companion, attributed to Connelly, also has reeded front legs and the high-rising arms called "French elbows" in the Philadelphia furniture price book of 1795; a linear design of an urn surrounded by loops ornaments its back. Both designs were popular in Philadelphia.

Purchase, Mrs. Russell Sage Gift, 1970 (1971.15.2), and Rogers Fund, 1944 (44.106)

sical motifs, set into the wood. Pictorial and otherwise decorative glass panels of this sort have an ancient history, but are commonly referred to as *verre églomisé*, after an eighteenth-century Parisian picture framer, Jean-Baptiste Glomy, who used the process conspicuously in ornamenting his work. A large, elaborate, and colorful desk and bookcase has been artfully worked in a manner that is both personal and that identifies it with Baltimore or Philadelphia (Fig. 200), although its design derives ultimately from a plate in Sheraton's *Cabinet Dictionary* of 1803, where it is termed the "Sister's Cylinder Bookcase" (Fig. 199). The inlaid satinwood ovals and banding and the two panels of glass with neoclassical painted decorations are devices that have been particularly associated with Baltimore furniture in the Federal style. An attribution to that lively port city is fortified by a penciled inscription on the bottom of one of the drawers noting the marriage of Margaret Oliver of Baltimore to Roswell Lyman Colt on October 5, 1811.

"CANE SEAT CHAIRS, SOFAS, RECESS, and WINDOW SEATS of every description and all colors, gilt, ornamented and varnished in a stile not equalled on the continent—with real Views, Fancy Landscapes, Flowers, Trophies of Music, War, Husbandry, Love, &c. &c."—so advertised the brothers John and Hugh Finlay in 1805, and to judge by a card table and pair of chairs in the Museum's collection (Fig. 202), their claims were justified. These pieces exhibit careful, skillful construction and delightfully imaginative decoration. There were other makers of painted, or "japanned," fur-

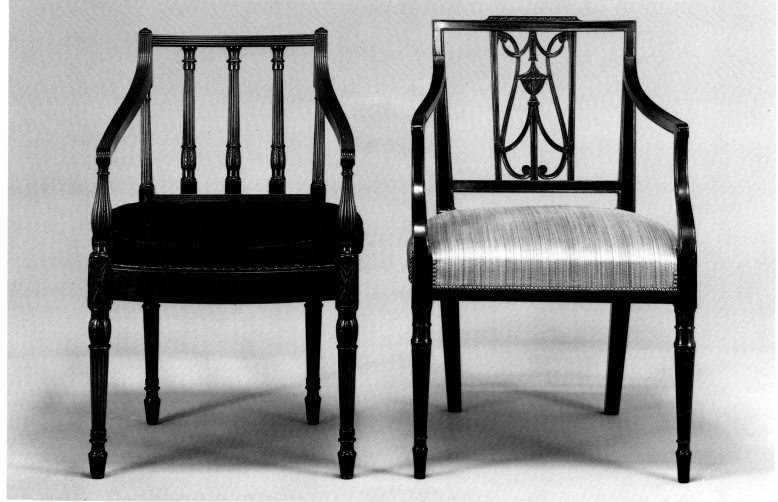

203

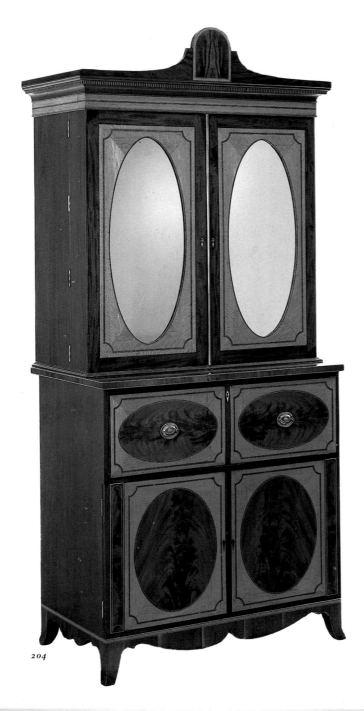

204

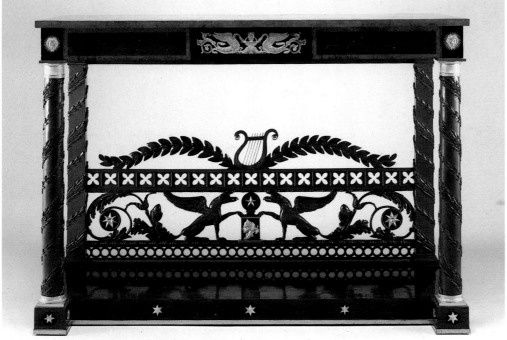

205

**Fig. 204. Desk and bookcase,** *made by John Davey (w. 1797–1822), Philadelphia, 1805–10; mahogany and satinwood veneers, mahogany, glass, white pine, tulip poplar, height 95⅞ inches (243.6 cm.). These dazzling mirrors and dark ovals framed by light rectangles conceal a very practical desk and bookcase. The middle drawer-like section pulls down to reveal pigeonholes and small drawers and to form a writing surface; the bottom doors open to disclose drawers; and behind the mirrored doors are shelves. The secretary's makers, John Davey, who inscribed the piece seven times, and the more restrained "John Davey Junr." (probably his father's apprentice), who signed it only twice, were obviously extremely accomplished craftsmen, so it is more than a little surprising that no other piece of furniture is known to have been made by either of them.*
Fletcher Fund, Rogers Fund, Gift of Mrs. Russell Sage, The Sylmaris Collection, Gift of George Coe Graves, 1962 (62.9)

**Fig. 205. Pier table,** *bearing the label of Joseph B. Barry (active 1794–died 1838) and Son, Philadelphia, 1810–15; mahogany, satinwood, and amboyna veneers; mahogany; gilt-bronze mounts; cast-brass ornament; tulip poplar; height 38⅝ inches (98.1 cm.). One of the most striking examples of early nineteenth-century furniture, this pier table is also a visual textbook of Federal-period cabinetmaking techniques. Here are veneer, ormolu (applied gilt-bronze ornament), gilding, carving, and turning—all used to spectacular advantage. The table's most outstanding feature, the friezelike ornament that forms its back, includes griffins, Pompeiian scrolls, laurel sprays, and a lyre taken from Sheraton's Drawing Book, and these relate it to the delicate Adamesque design of the early neoclassical period. The size and weight of the table, on the other hand, align it with more massive Empire forms. Its maker, Joseph Barry, was born in Ireland and emigrated to Philadelphia before 1790. He was successful enough to maintain a branch shop in Baltimore for a short time.*
Purchase, Friends of the American Wing Fund, Anonymous Gift, George M. Kaufman Gift, Sansbury-Mills Fund, and Gift of Mrs. Russell Sage, Gift of the Members of the Committee of the Bertha King Benkard Memorial Fund, John Stewart Kennedy Fund, Bequest of Martha S. Tiedeman, Gift of Mrs. Frederick Wildman, Gift of F. Ethel Wickham, Gift of Edgar William and Bernice Chrysler Garbisch, Gift of Mrs. F. M. Townsend and Bequest of W. Gedney Beatty, by exchange, 1976 (1976.324)

**Figs. 206 and 207. Square-backed sofa,** *carving attributed to Samuel McIntire (active about 1782–1811), Salem, 1800–10; mahogany, white pine, birch, length 84 inches (213.4 cm.); and detail of crest rail. Plate 35 in Sheraton's Drawing Book (1791–94) provided the design for this and a number of other square sofas made by Salem cabinetmakers and carved in the McIntire manner. Although Sheraton noted in his description of this form that if it "be thought to have too much work" a plain crest rail could be substituted, McIntire applied his carved design to great advantage. The eagle that is the central ornament, found on only three other sofas attributed to the great carver, indicates an interest in*

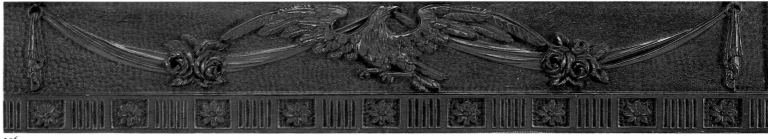

206

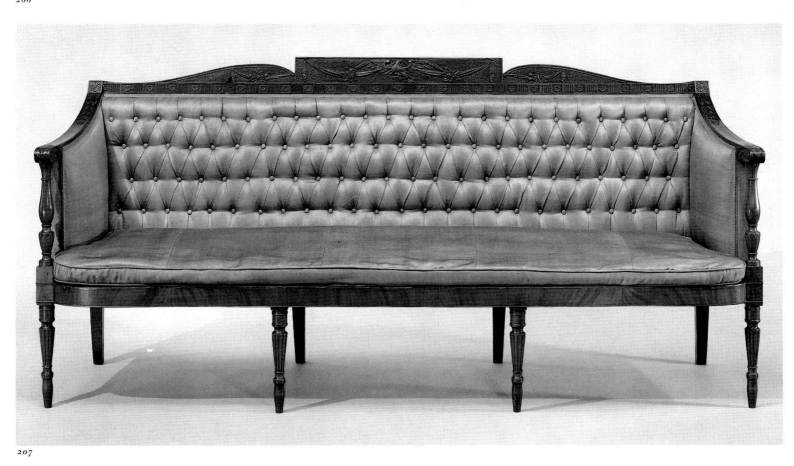

207

decoration with a patriotic overtone. The swags
with roses and the border of alternating flutes
and flowers, all seen against a star-punched
background, are found time and again on furniture believed to have been carved by McIntire.
There were a number of other carvers working in
late eighteenth-century Salem, however, and they
undoubtedly employed these motifs as well.
Fletcher Fund, 1926 (26.207)

**Fig. 208. Side chair,** *Salem, about 1795; mahogany, height 37⅞ inches (96.2 cm.). Samuel
McIntire is thought to have designed and carved
this chair as part of a set that furnished Salem
merchant Elias Hasket Derby's superbly elegant
mansion, of which McIntire was also the architect. This particular chair pattern was popular in
Salem. It came directly from Hepplewhite's Guide
(see Fig. 209), and it is in the details—the masterful carving of bunches of grapes and wheat
sheaves on the back and legs especially—that
McIntire's hand is visible. The fine carving is
complemented by the feet, which are of the frequently seen spade shape, but here are given the
immense refinement of ebony veneer.*
The Friends of the American Wing Fund, 1962
(62.16)

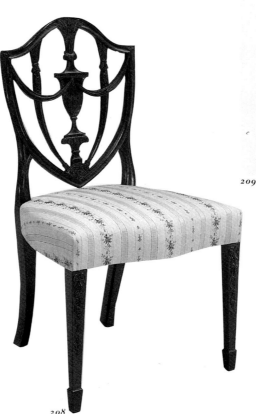

208

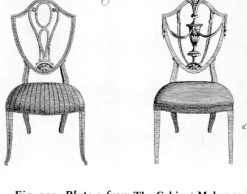

209

**Fig. 209. Plate 2 from The Cabinet-Maker and
Upholsterer's Guide** *(London, 1788), by George
Hepplewhite. McIntire's chair for Elias Hasket
Derby follows Hepplewhite's design remarkably
closely. Among his few changes are the confining
of the drapery swags within the shield; the addition of finely modeled bunches of grapes to the
vertical bars on either side of the urn, to the base
of the splat, and to the legs; and giving the tapering legs spade feet. McIntire's version is at once
less ornate and richer than Hepplewhite's.*
Rogers Fund, 1952 (52.519.187)

niture at work in Baltimore, the most important center for this type of very elegant and sophisticated furniture in the Federal period, but the Finlays seem to have been preeminent.

The special distinction of Philadelphia neoclassical furniture can be seen in a number of highly representative examples. Both Henry Connelly and Ephraim Haines made square-backed chairs with turned, reeded upright supports (sometimes referred to in contemporary records as "Spanish back"

chairs) like the one on the left in Fig. 203. This example is attributed to Haines, its companion to Connelly. At one time or another both men supplied furniture to the French-born Stephen Girard, merchant, financier, philanthropist, and distinguished Philadelphia citizen.

With understandable pride, Philadelphia's John Davey penciled his name seven times in inconspicuous locations to establish his authorship of what remains the only known documented example of his craftsmanship: an eight-

foot-tall secretary that presents a brilliant arrangement of mirrored panels and satinwood and mahogany veneers on door and drawer fronts (Fig. 204). Concealed in the satinwood interior are neatly and conveniently disposed bookshelves, pigeonholes, drawers, and an adjustable writing surface. Like the desk patterned after the "Sister's Cylinder" design, another elaborate piece of furniture, a pier table made by the Irish immigrant Joseph B. Barry and his son (Fig. 205), also owes a debt to Sheraton's designs.

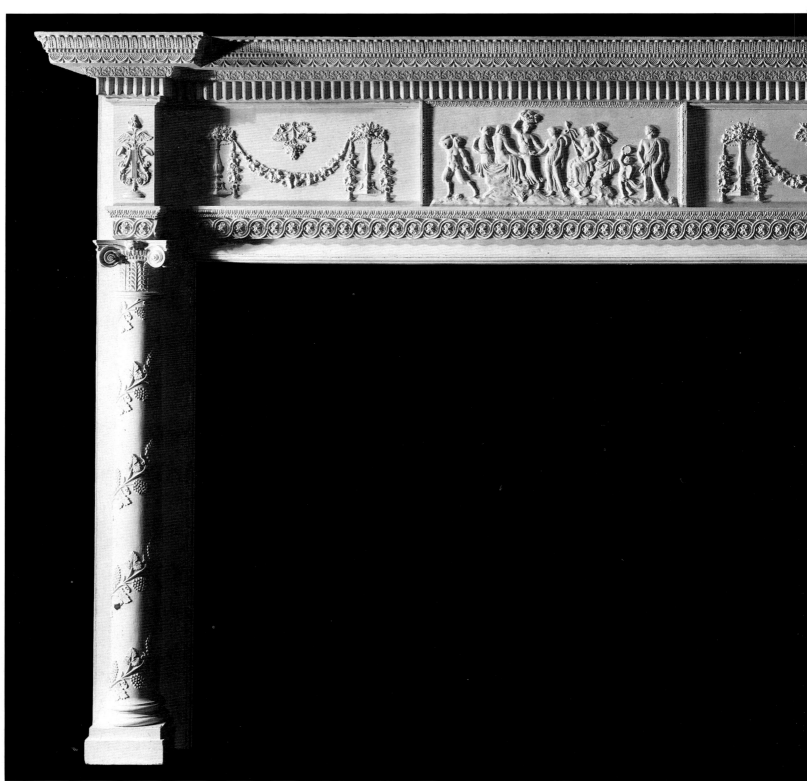

210

**Fig. 210. Mantel,** *carving by Samuel McIntire (active about 1782–1811), Salem, about 1795; wood, composition, height 54¾ inches (139.1 cm.), length 77 inches (195.6 cm.). When Elias Hasket and Elizabeth Derby's mansion was torn down in 1815, the eminent clergyman and diarist William Bentley lamented that "It was the best finished, most elegant, and best constructed House I ever saw. . . . The heirs could not agree to occupy it and the convenience of the spot for other buildings bought a sentence of destruction for it. . . ." After it was taken down many of its elegant architectural elements were advertised in the Salem* Gazette, *including "8 richly ornamented Chimney Pieces," of which this is believed to be the only survivor. It was not the most mag-*

*nificent mantel in this very grand house, however, for the advertisement also offered "2 marble Chimney Pieces, one very elegant." The ornament here is of composition (a plaster-like substance that could be molded into very delicate shapes) except for that on the columns, which McIntire is said to have carved. Garlands composed of the grape bunches and leaves associated with the master's work spiral down each column.*
Rogers Fund, 1946 (46.76)

**Fig. 211. Oval-backed side chair,** *Philadelphia, 1796 or 1801; maple painted dark brown with polychrome decoration, white pine, height 38½ inches (97.8 cm.). This charmingly painted chair is thought to be one of the twenty-four that*

*Elias Hasket Derby ordered for his magnificent new house in Salem. Others thought to be part of Derby's order have the same oval back enclosing a beribboned bouquet of feathers but are painted white instead of blackish brown. Possibly their maker-decorator had recently come to America from England, where similar chairs had been produced by the prestigious London firm of Gillow before Hepplewhite published his version of the design in 1788.*
Gift of Mrs. J. Insley Blair, 1947 (47.103.1)

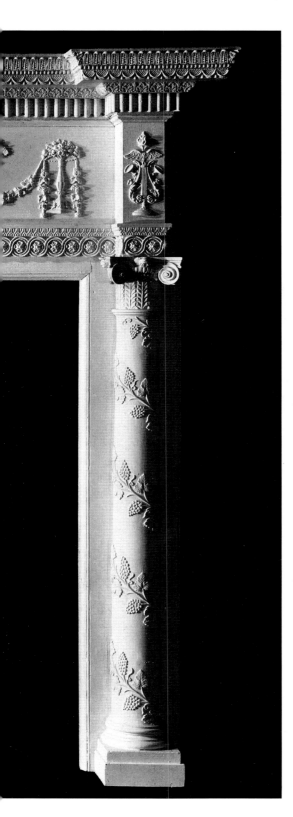

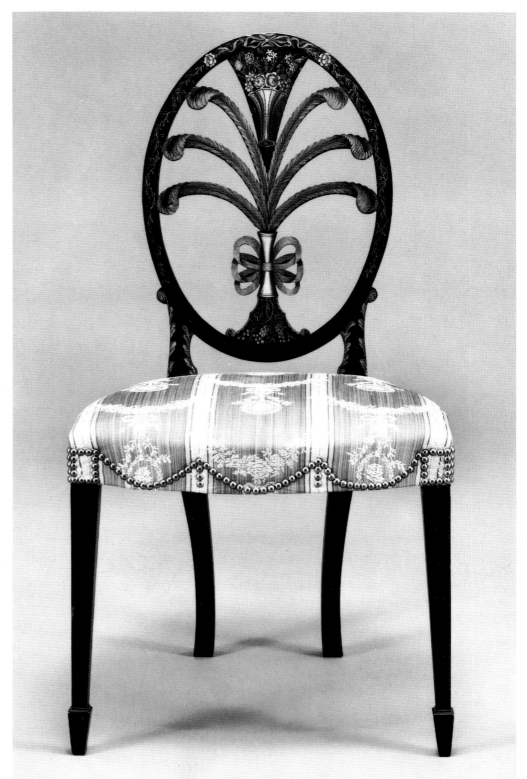

211

**Fig. 212. Sideboard,** *attributed to the workshop of Thomas Seymour (active 1794–1843), Boston, 1805–15; mahogany and birch veneers; birch, cherry, and holly inlays; white pine and cherry; length 73 inches (185.4 cm.). The sideboard was a new form in the Federal period— one so useful that it became popular immediately. Each prosperous center produced a characteristic* version, and this example represents Boston cabinetmaking at its best. Its beautifully matched veneers, each set off by light-wood banding; tambour section with flat alternating light and dark strips; turned and carved legs; and delicate inlaid ivory urns that serve as keyhole escutcheons (see also Fig. 221) are some of the many elegant details that contribute to the very high quality of this sideboard. The Seymours, who are believed to have made it, were Boston's outstanding furniture makers in this period, producing pieces comparable in quality and stylishness to those Duncan Phyfe was turning out in New York.
Gift of the family of Mr. and Mrs. Andrew Varick Stout, in their memory, 1965 (65.188.1)

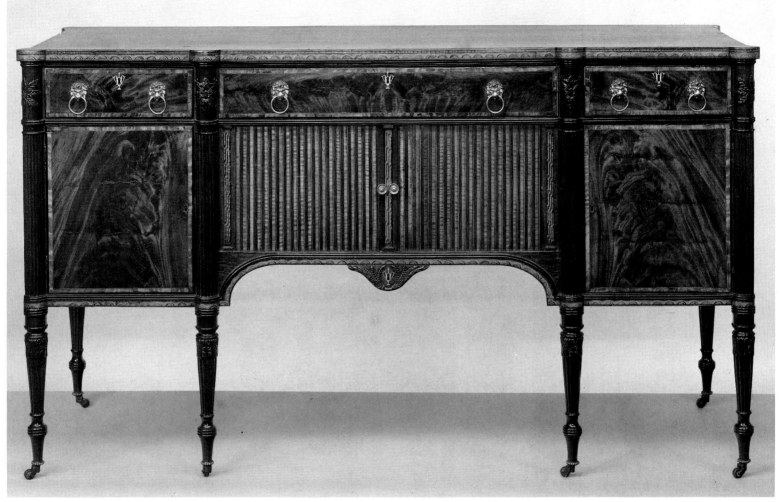

212

**Fig. 213. Worktable,** *attributed to Lemuel Churchill (active 1805–about 1828), carving attributed to Thomas Whitman (active 1809), Boston, 1810–15; mahogany veneer, mahogany, brass stringing, ebony turnings, ivory inlay, mahogany, tulip poplar, height 28⅝ inches (72.7 cm.). The worktable was newly created in the Federal period to provide convenient storage and work space for sedentary activities like sewing, reading, and writing. This example has the rounded outlines of the later, archeologically oriented neoclassical period. Its lyre-shaped pedestal, curved legs with brass paw feet, and segmentally reeded ovolo corners are all features of the oncoming Empire style, taken in this case from English designs of the Regency period. Lemuel Churchill, to whom the table is attributed because the name "Churchill" is scrawled on its underside, was also the maker of a labeled lolling chair that is now in the Winterthur Museum collection.*
Gift of Solomon Grossman, 1980 (1980.508)

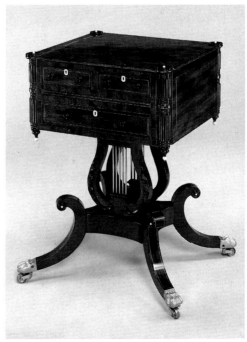

213

**Fig. 214. Tambour desk,** *labeled by Reuben Swift (active 1802–early 1820s), New Bedford, Massachusetts, about 1805; mahogany, burl walnut; flame-grain birch, tulip, and maple veneers; white pine, birch; height 55 inches (139.7 cm.). It was not until Reuben Swift's tour de force surfaced a few years ago that we had any inkling of the production of such fashionable furniture in New Bedford. So far, this is the only labeled piece by Swift to come to light, and the only piece of such magnificence to have a documented New Bedford history. This desk, made about 1805, was the most fashionable type of desk made in New England during the Federal period except for the much larger breakfront; its tambour closing, a newly fashionable feature, and its brilliant contrasting veneers, are characteristic of New England. It is unusual, however, in substituting a full case of drawers beneath the desk section, for most tambour desks have only one or two long shallow drawers. Swift's use of dazzling veneers is unexpected as well. An unusually refined detail is the diaper design executed in marquetry on the two top drawers.*
Bequest of Cecile L. Mayer, 1962 (62.171.6)

Up in Salem, Massachusetts, woodworkers were deriving inspiration from English design books too. A Salem-made chair carved by the ingenious Samuel McIntire, for example, is lifted from a plate in Hepplewhite's *Guide* practically without a change (Figs. 208 and 209). Such literal copying was not the rule, however. More frequently, cabinetmakers merged the elements suggested by design books so variously that the result is most aptly referred to simply as being in the Federal style.

Samuel McIntire was one of the most prominent and versatile of the artisans who worked in the Federal style, a superb craftsman who applied his skills to ships and buildings as well as to furniture. Like other fine woodworkers of his own and earlier times he also mended fences and built pigsties, and he may have made such commonplace necessities as washtubs and ironing boards. However, he was primarily an accomplished architect, designer, and carver—and a competent musician. When he died in 1811, an obituary affectionately characterized him as "one of the best of men." Thanks largely to his art and industry Salem became the handsomest New England town of the late eighteenth century.

The carved eagle and swags, raised elements set against a stippled background on a Sheraton "Square Sofa" (Figs. 206 and 207), are in McIntire's individual style. His gifts as an architect enabled him to design, on an entirely different scale, the house of Elias Hasket Derby, an adventurous and successful shipowner who became New England's first millionaire. The Derby residence was "more like a palace than the dwelling of an American merchant," according to a visitor from Baltimore. McIntire personally worked on many of the details that distinguished that celebrated but short-lived structure (it was demolished in 1815 and its furnishings dispersed). Apparently all that remains of the mansion is a mantelpiece ornamented with classical scenes and motifs, preserved in the Museum (Fig. 210). Fortunately, other Salem houses built by McIntire still stand in testimony to the man's architectural skills. The Peirce-Nichols and Pingree houses, one of frame construction and the other of brick, are among the outstanding Federal residences.

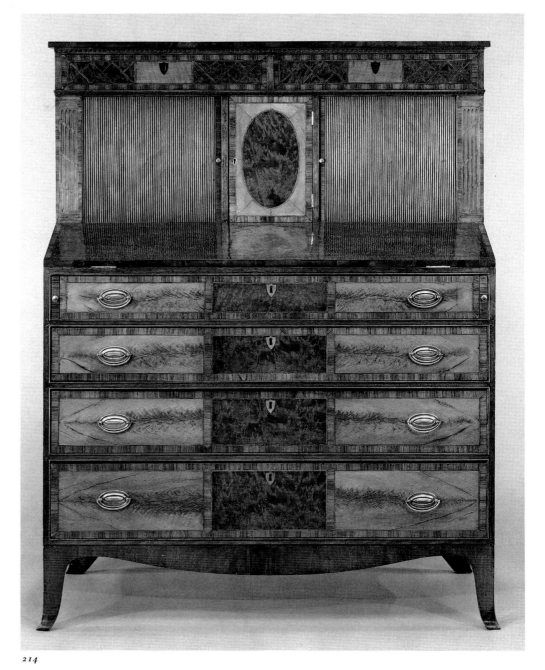

214

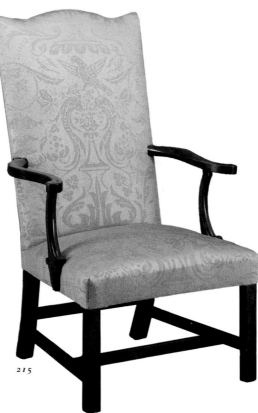

215

*Fig. 215. Lolling chair, Massachusetts, 1790–1800; mahogany, birch, height 44½ inches (113 cm.). Made almost exclusively in New England, the lolling chair (sometimes also called the Martha Washington chair) is a descendant of earlier French and English open-arm chairs with upholstered back and seat. Joseph Nichol Scott's A New Universal Dictionary of 1764 defines "to loll" as "To lean lazily against, or lie idly upon any thing"—a definition that conjures up a picture of an elegant gentleman lounging in such a chair. The term is contemporary with the chairs, for it turns up in advertisements and inventories. This example exhibits the high back with serpentine crest that is characteristic of many Massachusetts lolling chairs. The serpentine curve is repeated in the line of the arms, which are skillfully fashioned with a hollow for the elbow to rest in.*
Bequest of Flora E. Whiting, 1971 (1971.180.15)

**Figs. 216–26. Furniture and architectural details** *from the Museum's collection illustrate, on the left-hand page, the early Federal taste for flat surfaces with symmetrically disposed ornament. Motifs were idealized or stylized, like the églomisé, inlaid, painted, and carved classical and naturalistic forms illustrated here. By the* end of the first decade of the nineteenth century, delicacy was giving way to the highly sculptural carved ornament of the later Federal period. Now the trend was toward high-relief renderings of naturalistic motifs like the swan, paw feet, and the eagle atop a rock pile seen on the right-hand page. Paint was still fashionable, but colors grew deeper and richer, and gilding was frequently lavishly applied to create the boldly assertive forms of the 1810s and 1820s.

Eglomisé panel, desk and bookcase: Gift of Mrs. Russell Sage and various other donors, 1969 (69.203); shell inlay, gentleman's secretary: Joseph Pulitzer Bequest, 1967 (67.203); painted feather detail, side chair: Gift of Mrs. J. Insley Blair, 1947 (47.103.1); carved feather detail,

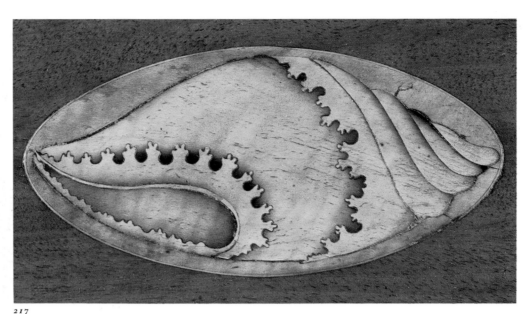

217

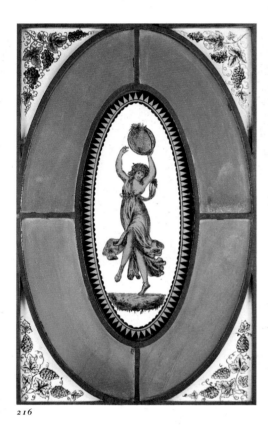

216

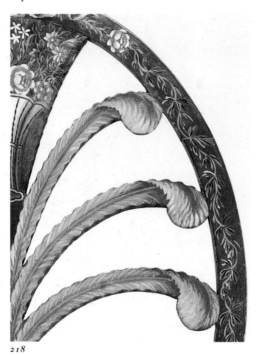

218

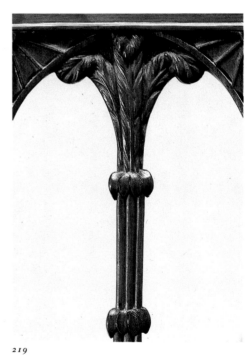

219

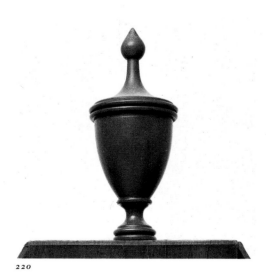

220

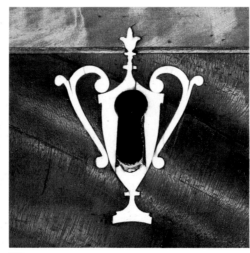

221

square-back side chair: Gift of the Members of the Committee of the Bertha King Benkard Memorial Fund, 1946 (46.67.102); urn finial, gentleman's secretary: Purchase, Gift of Mrs. Russell Sage, Bequest of Ethel Yocum, Bequest of Charlotte E. Hoadley, and Rogers Fund, by exchange, 1971 (1971.9); inlaid urn, sideboard: Gift of the family of Mr. and Mrs. Andrew Varick Stout, in their memory, 1965 (65.188.1); swan support, pier table: Friends of the American Wing Fund,

1968 (68.43); carved paw foot, Phyfe pier table: Gift of John C. Cattus, 1967 (67.262.2); carved and gilded paw foot, Lannuier pier table: Rogers Fund, 1953 (53.181); marble fireplace detail: Gift of Joe Kindig, Jr., 1968 (68.137); carved and gilded eagle crest, girandole mirror: Rogers Fund, 1921 (21.44.2)

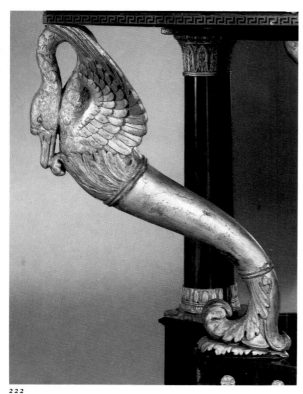

222

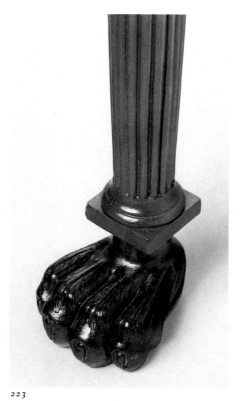

223

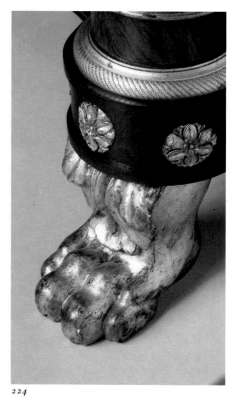

224

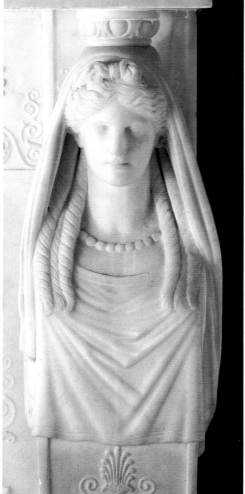

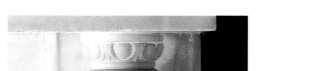

225

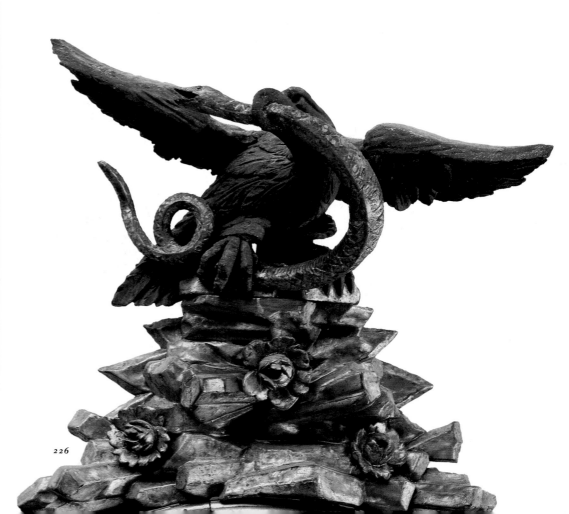

226

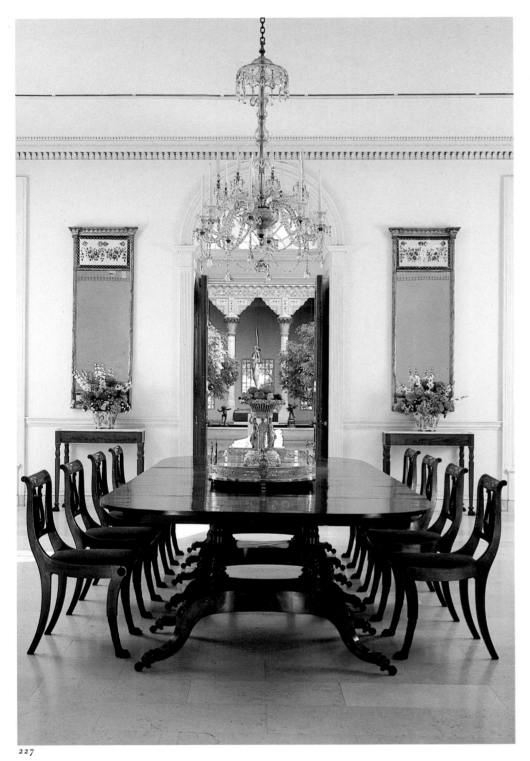

227

**Fig. 227.** *View of the Federal Gallery showing a pillar-and-claw dining table attributed to the workshop of Duncan Phyfe, a set of lyre-back chairs by Phyfe, and a pair of marble-topped pier tables perhaps also made in Phyfe's workshop. Although the parlor was still the most elegant room in the house, the dining room was becoming a close second and required the creation of specialized pieces like these. Instead of the flashing veneers of New England and the Middle Colonies, Phyfe favored solid mahogany ornamented with low-relief carving of stylized motifs taken from the classical vocabulary. Characteristic examples are paw feet, hairy shanks, lyres, and ribbons of waterleaves—all of which may be seen here.*

**Fig. 228. Side chair,** *made by Duncan Phyfe (w. 1792–1847), New York, 1810–20; mahogany, height 32¼ inches (82.6 cm.). Delicate klismos chairs of this type represent a transition from Phyfe's earliest chairs with round, reeded legs and square backs to the more fully archeological curule chairs (see Figs. 87 and 89). Here we have an ancient shape—the curving klismos with both front and back legs sweeping away from the chair in an arc—and details found on ancient furniture, such as dog's-paw feet with hairy shanks and lyre splat, but the proportions are still those of the early Federal period, and the whole is executed with a very light touch. This is one of a set of chairs Phyfe made for the family of New Jersey governor William Livingston. The Museum's collection contains thirteen of the original set of twenty-four (see Fig. 227).*
Gift of the family of Mr. and Mrs. Andrew Varick Stout, in their memory, 1965 (65.188.2)

A pair of exceptional painted chairs with open oval backs framing six curved plumes and other decorative motifs, generally patterned after a design in Hepplewhite's *Guide*, were probably made in Philadelphia for a member of the prominent Derby family of Salem (Fig. 211). It is certain, at least, that in 1796 Elias Hasket Derby ordered two dozen chairs of similar design from Philadelphia, and these could have been part of that shipment.

A sideboard that was probably made in the workshop of Thomas Seymour of Boston offers an individualistic variation of the Sheraton style (Fig. 212). Sideboards were introduced to America during the Federal period, as dining rooms assumed an increasingly important role in social life. In the words of Robert Adam, they had become "apartments of conversation." (Some English sideboards, and probably some American ones, were supplied with a small cupboard containing a chamber pot for the immediate relief of those who drank too much during the course of a long, drawn-out, possibly garrulous dinner party.) Seymour was an English immigrant, but the American work attributed to him speaks with a decidedly personal, New England accent. Another elegant Boston piece is a worktable attributed to Lemuel Churchill (Fig. 213). This form was new in the Federal period, and is another indication of that era's growing interest in specialized objects for specific functions—in this case that of holding a lady's sewing and writing equipment.

Until a few years ago when the Museum acquired a desk bearing his label (Fig. 214), the name of Reuben Swift of New Bedford had been all but forgotten. An original and sophisticated interpretation of prevailing styles with, among other highly refined details, tambour closings and richly contrasting woods in plain and marquetry surfaces, this piece alone is enough to establish Swift as a cabinetmaker of imagination and rare competence.

One of the most graceful and distinctively American chairs ever made, with a high upholstered back and open arms, was known to contemporaries as a "lolling" chair; sometimes in this country, for no known reason, it was called a Martha Washington chair (Fig. 215). This example was made in Massachusetts, although the form was popular throughout New England.

A sectional dining table represents one of the new forms characteristic of Federal furniture (Fig. 227). It is composed of three separate divisions, each with four-column platform supports and gracefully outsweeping legs with carved knees. When the table is fully assembled, brass clips hold its sections together. As separate dining rooms became increasingly fashionable, such sectional tables especially designed for dining rooms were popular in all areas of America. This sort of specialized convenience was a far remove from previous arrangements, such as those of about a hundred years earlier when Boston's Samuel Sewall noted in his diary that he had entertained nine guests for dinner in his bedchamber (probably at a gateleg table with the leaves raised). The suave curves of this example and the skilled disposition of a few decorative elements of carving and turning are features associated with the work of the Scottish immigrant Duncan Phyfe, whose superior craftsmanship and individual versions of English styles were in his own lifetime hailed far beyond the environs of New York.

Duncan Phyfe's establishment produced furniture in a succession of styles until almost the middle of the last century. His celebrated shop and warehouse on Fulton Street are pictured in an engaging watercolor seen in Fig. 229, a sketch that also provides an interesting look at the architecture of the time. Phyfe was not only a highly skilled craftsman but an industrious and practical spirit—and a disciplinarian. According to one reminiscence, he sent the members of his family to bed by nine o'clock each night. Both his skill and his industry paid off. When he died in 1854, his estate was appraised at almost half a million dollars—an awesome figure at the time.

Characteristic features are seen in the matching chairs from an original set of twenty-four with lyre-shaped backs and carved front feet in the shape of paws—both fashionable references to ancient models (Figs. 227 and 228).

Also typical of New York's version of the English Regency style, and also possibly from Phyfe's celebrated shop, are the pair of unusual marble-topped pier

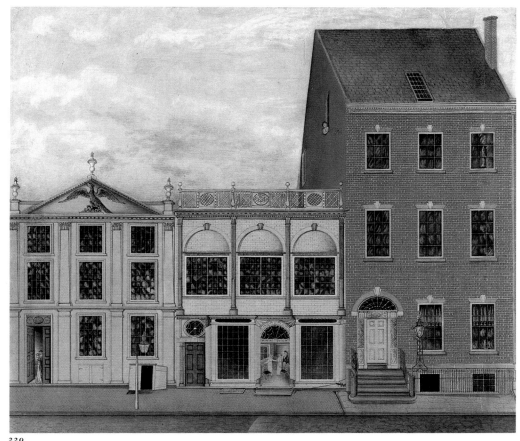

229

*Fig. 229.* **Shop and Warehouse of Duncan Phyfe,** *by John Rubens Smith (1775–1849), 1816–17; watercolor and pen and brown ink, 15¾ by 18⅞ inches (40 by 48.3 cm.). Phyfe occupied these buildings on Fulton Street in lower New York from 1803 to 1847, when he retired. It is thought that the ornamental woodwork on the central building, his salesroom, and the carved eagle and urns on his workshop at left were the products of that workshop. The tall brick building at right was Phyfe's warehouse. Two ladies stand in the doorway of the salesroom debating the qualities of ogee-cross versus lyre-back side chairs.*
Rogers Fund, 1922 (22.28.1)

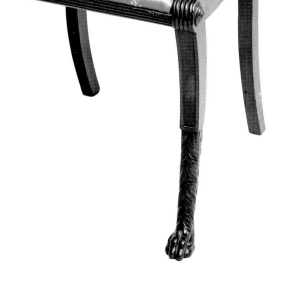

228

tables seen in Fig. 227. They are distinguished by turned, reeded, and carved legs, all four terminating in massive paw feet (see also Fig. 223), and by brass-trimmed apron edges. These handsome pieces originally graced one of New York's finest Federal houses, the home of Moses Rogers at 7 State Street, across from the Battery.

The later classical style of Phyfe and his New York contemporaries, dating from about 1815 to 1825, reflects an increasing awareness of Greco-Roman architectural forms and decoration as these had been adapted to what the French called *le style antique* during the Directory, Consulate, and Empire periods (see Figs. 222–26). A variety of new publications issued in France and England and, as always, the continued immigration of experienced craftsmen familiar with the currents of fashionable taste abroad introduced these to Americans.

One of the many highly skilled émigrés was Charles-Honoré Lannuier, who came to New York from France and produced many opulent carved, gilded, ormolu-mounted, and brass-inlaid pieces that provide a summary of the rich vocabulary of ornament that characterized American interpretations of the French Empire style. They reflect as well the exuberant antiquarianism that dominated stylish design of the period. Lannuier enjoyed the patronage of such diverse personages as Stephen Van Rensselaer of Albany and Henri Christophe, the self-styled king of Haiti.

Some outstanding pieces may have been made by either Lannuier or Phyfe. Such a one is a mahogany cheval glass, the finest American example of this form that is known (Fig. 230). A piece

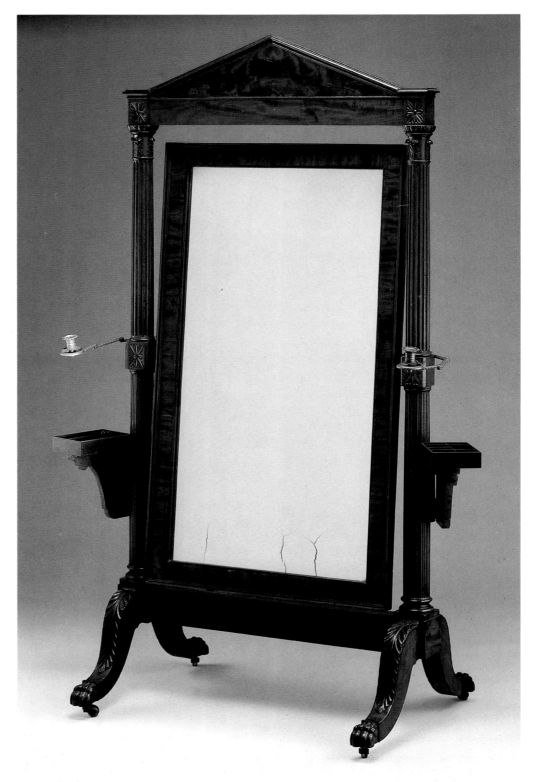

230

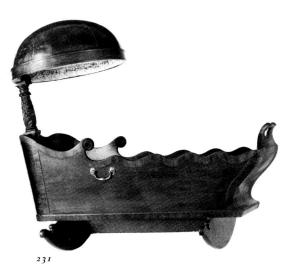

231

**Fig. 232. Desk and worktable,** by Michael Allison (active 1800–45), New York, 1823; mahogany veneer, mahogany; mahogany, tulip poplar; height 29¾ inches (75.6 cm.). So many features characteristic of Sheraton-style New York furniture may be seen on this elegant desk and worktable that it might very well be assigned to the vast pool of furniture simply called "Phyfe." Fortunately for our understanding of New York furniture, however, this piece bears the label of Michael Allison, Phyfe's neighbor and competitor. Obviously Allison learned and applied well the lessons of Phyfe's furniture. The reeded half-round storage spaces on either end, the waterleaf carving on the legs, the lyre supports—with their less usual swan-neck carving—and the careful choice of beautifully grained mahogany are all features we associate with the Phyfe school. Many makers besides Phyfe were at work in New York at the end of the eighteenth century and the first half of the nineteenth, however, and Allison was among the most skilled. More pieces labeled or stamped by him survive than for any other New York cabinetmaker of the Federal period. Rogers Fund, 1933 (33.160)

of particular interest that has just recently been attributed to Lannuier is a charming cradle with mahogany and rosewood veneers (Fig. 231). Suspended over the head of this utterly delightful infant's sleeping compartment is a semispherical hood, its interior upholstered with the original silk. Only the most indulged child would have enjoyed such a luxurious accommodation.

Unless it is labeled or otherwise documented, the work of Michael Allison, another New York furniture maker of the Federal and Empire periods, is often indistinguishable from that of Phyfe. Fortunately Allison's label does appear on a small, sensitively conceived desk and worktable with swan-neck lyres, carved eagle-head feet, and tambour-fronted storage spaces beneath its drawers and writing surfaces (Fig. 232).

Expert craftsmanship in all mediums abounded in New England, but the clockmakers of that region were unsurpassed. The Museum's collection includes clocks made in other areas as well, showing some regional differences in case designs, although the basic tall-clock form that had been established earlier persisted everywhere for some decades after the Revolution. An example of what is called the "Roxbury" type, made and labeled by the very well-known Massachusetts clockmaker Aaron Willard, Jr., has the painted dial, fluted corner columns on the waist, bracket feet, arched head with scrollwork, and vase-shaped brass finials that characterize his work (see Fig. 196). Other clocks, made in different states, share the same general appearance but vary in the treatment of details.

During the Federal period American

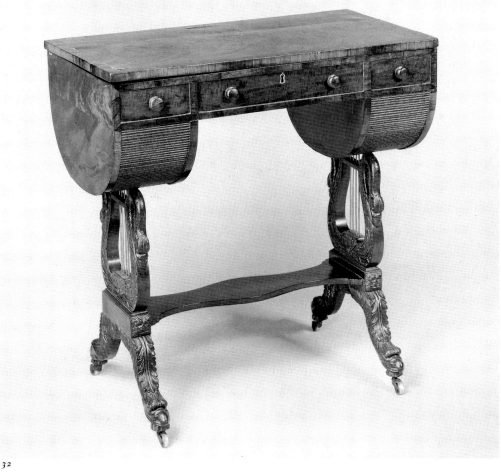

232

clockmaking took a vital new turn with the development of small and relatively inexpensive wall and shelf clocks of a strictly native character. What is known as the Massachusetts shelf clock, made in a variety of designs over the years, remained popular from the Revolutionary period until about 1830 (Fig. 233). The case of this type of timepiece consists of a box on a box, the upper one housing the mechanism, the lower one accommodating the weights and pendulum. Around 1802 Simon Willard, Aaron's brother, invented his "Improved Patent Time Piece," as he named it. With its gilt case, painted-glass panels, delicately fashioned hands, and, most importantly, its precise workmanship and fine proportions, this eight-day banjo clock (so called because of its shape) immediately won well-deserved success (Fig. 234). The design is still being copied. This skilled craftsman is said to have made more than 5,000 timepieces during the first four decades of the nineteenth century. The cases for a number of Willard's clocks were fashioned by John Doggett of Roxbury, Massachusetts, who was at once a carver, gilder, cabinetmaker, and looking-glass maker. An entry in Doggett's account books indicates that he provided the clockmaker with one "Clock case wood-work and Gilding complete" for seventy dollars, along with a "piece of Looking glass for timepiece" for thirty-seven cents.

Despite Willard's patent, his model was quickly copied by other makers. Twenty years later Willard also patented his "Eddystone Lighthouse Alarm Time Piece," named after the famous structure built upon the Eddystone Rocks near Plymouth, England, a reef "obnoxious to navigation" (Fig. 235). This model was also quickly copied, although no two surviving examples are exactly alike.

About this time, Connecticut Yankee clockmakers were initiating cheap clocks whose works consisted of interchangeable machine-made parts, produced in an assembly-line system. In the early nineteenth century Eli Terry had first manufactured wooden clocks by machinery, then adopted the idea of interchangeable parts, and finally, about 1816, reduced his product to the size of his famous pillar-and-scroll shelf clock. Seth Thomas of Plymouth, Connecticut—a name still familiar to clock buyers—was among those who adopted this popular design (Fig. 236). Slender feet support the case with its flanking pillars, a broken-arch or double-scroll pediment, brass finials, and a painted-glass panel showing a view of Mount Vernon.

An important factor in the change of clock design and cost was the introduction of inexpensive coiled springs that eliminated the need to accommodate weight-driven works. A so-called acorn clock made at the Forestville Clock Manufactory in Bristol, Connecticut, about the middle of the century is an early example of such a timepiece (Fig. 237). Like the Belter furniture of the same period, the case is made of laminated rosewood and is composed of exaggerated curves.

By mid-century veneer and mortising mills and circular saws had still further reduced the cost of the cases, and common shelf clocks could be produced for less than fifty cents apiece. That unique salesman, the Yankee peddler, had another item he could successfully hawk throughout the land. Some American clocks of modest size and price were winning ready markets around the world, including the ports of China.

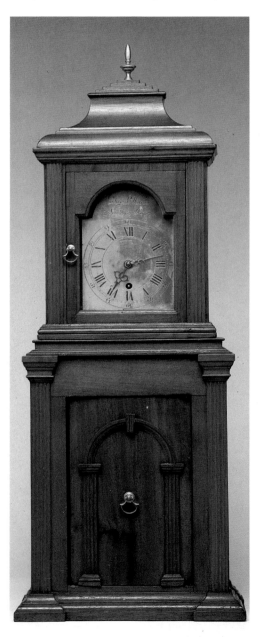

233

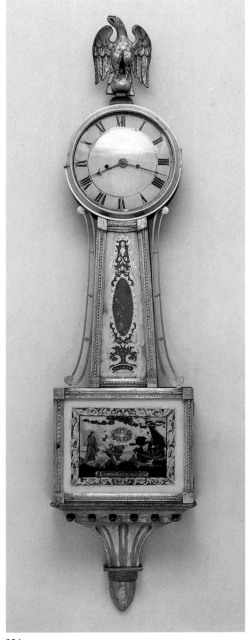

234

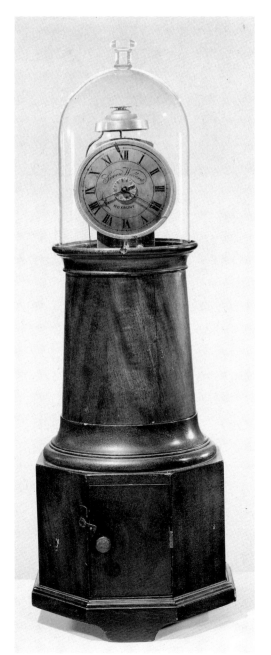

235

**Figs. 233–37. Shelf and wall clocks.** *Time-pieces were expensive and scarce in America until mass-produced clocks were developed in the nineteenth century. New types that were somewhat less expensive than the traditional, or "grandfather," clocks had begun to appear in the second half of the eighteenth century, however. These were shelf and wall clocks, which were cheaper because less brass was required for their works than for a tall clock and because their cases were much smaller and therefore less expensive to make. One of the first was the Massachusetts shelf clock, developed by Aaron Willard, one of the renowned clockmaking Willard brothers, but also produced by a number of other Massachusetts makers. The example shown here (Fig. 233), by David Wood, represents the type at its finest. The banjo clock (Fig. 234) was the invention of another Willard brother, Simon, and it, too, was made by many other clockmakers. Another of Simon Willard's apparently original inventions is the "Eddystone Lighthouse Alarm Time Piece," patented in 1822 (Fig. 235). The works of this unusual form didn't function very well, however, and production was soon discontinued. By about 1816 Eli*

*Terry of Connecticut had developed simple wooden works whose parts could be mass produced and housed in the popular pillar-and-scroll case. Like the Willards before him, Terry found that other makers quickly picked up his ideas and produced similar clocks. The pillar-and-scroll example shown here is by Seth Thomas (Fig. 236). A later development produced the "acorn" clock, in which tightly coiled springs replaced the weights of previous examples. The top of its case is shaped like an acorn and is flanked by two acorn finials (Fig. 237). The painted decoration of the lower section shows a sailboat drifting by a Gothic Revival house of about the same period as the clock itself.*

**Fig. 233.** *Shelf clock, works by David Wood (active 1792–1824), Newburyport, Massachusetts, 1792–1800; mahogany, mahogany veneer, white pine, height 27¾ inches (70.5 cm.).*
The Sylmaris Collection, Gift of George Coe Graves, 1930 (30.120.53)

**Fig. 234.** *Wall (banjo) clock, Massachusetts, 1815–25; mahogany, gilt gesso, églomisé tablets, white pine, tulip poplar, height 43 inches (109.2 cm.).*
Bequest of William B. Whitney, 1937 (37.37.3)

**Fig. 235.** *"Eddystone Lighthouse Alarm Time Piece," works by Simon Willard (active 1766–1839), Roxbury, Massachusetts, 1825–30; mahogany, mahogany veneer on white pine, white pine, height 28½ inches (72.4 cm.).*
Gift of Mrs. Richard M. Lederer, in memory of her husband, 1957 (57.57)

**Fig. 236.** *Shelf clock, pillar-and-scroll type, works by Seth Thomas (active about 1806–59), Plymouth, Connecticut, 1820; mahogany, mahogany and maple veneers, white pine, height 27⅞ inches (70.8 cm.).*
Rogers Fund, 1962 (62.195)

**Fig. 237.** *Shelf clock, "acorn" type, by the Forestville Clock Manufactory, Bristol, Connecticut, 1847–50; rosewood laminated to pine, height 24⅜ inches (61.9 cm.).*
Gift of Mrs. Paul Moore, 1970 (1970.289.6)

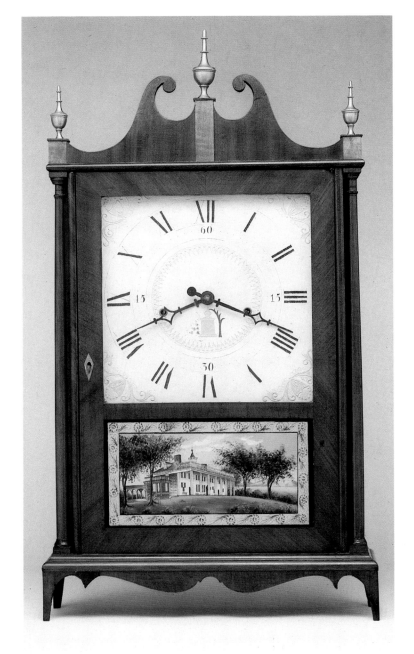

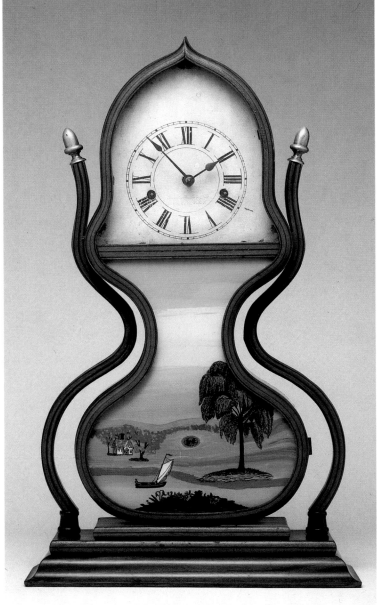

236

237

# The Shaker Vernacular

**Fig. 238. Double counter,** *New Lebanon, New York, about 1825; pine, length 68 inches (172.7 cm.). This convenient combination of chest of drawers and table was originally used in the sisters' weaving room at New Lebanon. The Shaker commitment to a life of honesty and purity led to their making objects that were simple, sturdy, and unassumingly graceful. Plain pine finished only with a light coat of red paint, simple moldings and turned knobs, and the utterly serviceable rectangular shape of this counter are characteristic of Shaker humility and practicality.*
Friends of the American Wing Fund, 1966 (66.10.14)

**Fig. 239. Sewing table,** *stamped "Jas. X. Smith, New-Lebanon, N. Y." and "1843"; cherry, butternut, pine, height 28 inches (71.1 cm.). Shaker furniture, household utensils, and gadgets often included ingenious features that made their user's task easier and smoother. This sewing table, for example, combines a case of drawers, an ample sewing surface, and a yardstick—which is marked off on the front edge of the top. Like the double counter, this table eschews all ornament in favor of straight lines, natural finish, and unobtrusive turned wooden knobs, one to a drawer. Brasses and escutcheons were never used on Shaker furniture—they were unnecessary ornament and therefore unacceptable.*
Friends of the American Wing Fund, 1966 (66.10.18)

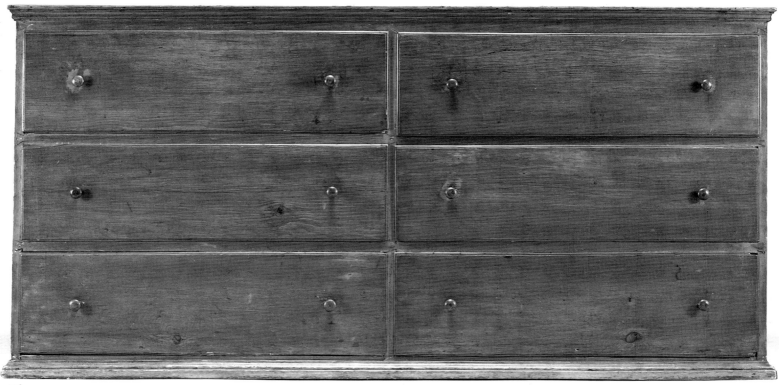

238

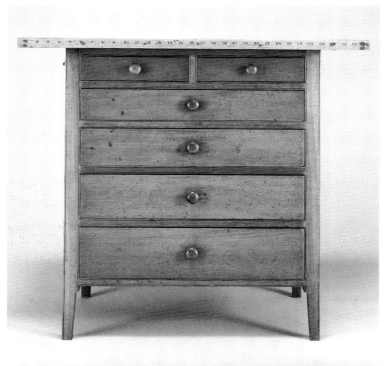

239

For almost a century following the American Revolution the various Shaker communities scattered about the countryside were building structures and creating artifacts of unique character and quality. While successive generations of non-Shaker architects, craftsmen, and manufacturers worked to keep abreast of ever-changing fashions, Shaker craftsmen motivated by religious ardor unalterably dedicated their hearts and hands to the production of useful objects stripped of all pretense to formal style. The utter simplicity of their designs and the unhurried, meticulous workmanship by which they were realized resulted in functional objects of singular and delicate grace.

The first small contingent of Shakers, led by "Mother Ann" Lee, came to America from England just before the

**Fig. 240. Revolving chair,** *United States, 1840–70; maple, white oak, pine, birch, height 28 inches (71.1 cm.). Swivel chairs both high and low were made for use at desks, workbenches, sewing tables, or anywhere else their revolving seats would make the sitter's task easier. They are scrupulously simple, with backs in the Windsor tradition.*
Friends of the American Wing Fund, 1966 (66.10.26)

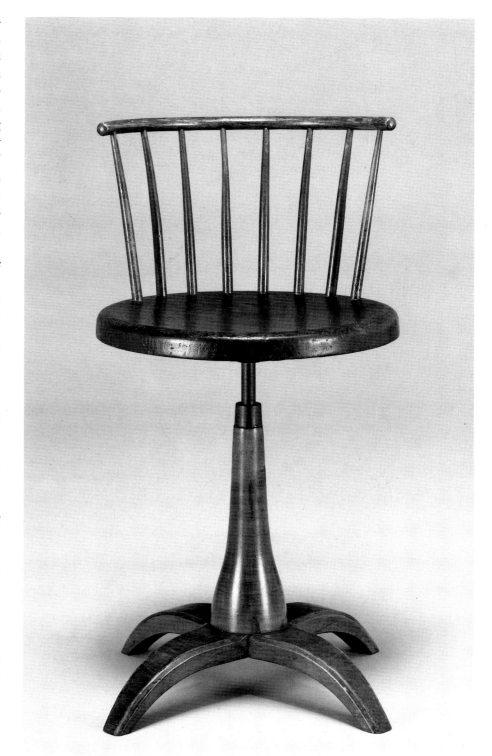

outbreak of the Revolution and eventually settled at Watervliet, New York. Mother Ann was an illiterate, slum-born millworker who had been imprisoned in England because of her zealous preachments against prevailing social mores. But she was an inspired leader. Among her homely injunctions were "Put your hands to work and your hearts to God" and "Do your work as though you had a thousand years to live, and as if you were to die tomorrow." Her followers grew in number with the passing years, as did the communal Shaker societies. An outgrowth of the Quakers, the Shakers were so named because they expressed their religious enthusiasms in agitated dancing, marching, and singing.

By 1840 some thirty Shaker colonies had been established from Maine to Indiana. The sect had reexamined the problems and responsibilities of men and women who must live together in a human association and had eliminated from their lives all that they considered unnecessary. They were frugal, industrious, and celibate. Their typical garb was utterly plain and completely unfashionable. Their austere concept of what made for a good life on earth (with heavenly rewards) was reflected in everything they produced. For them, to labor faithfully, painstakingly, and diligently was akin to praying. As one student of their craftsmanship has observed, Shaker furniture was religion in wood. Indeed they believed, wrote one visitor to the Watervliet community, that the furniture they made was originally designed in heaven (Figs. 238–40).

240

# Windsors

Shaker furniture designs and practices were rooted in the vernacular of eighteenth-century America, as the swivel chair with Windsor-like back, an innovation developed in certain Shaker communities in the third quarter of the nineteenth century (Fig. 240), makes clear. Of all forms of vernacular furniture made in America, the Windsor chair was probably the most conspicuous example (Fig. 241). Obviously related to English models of the same general sort, such "stick" furniture assumed a special—and especially graceful—character as it was developed in this country. In its various regional interpretations it departed sharply from any of the fashionable designs of successive periods. No other type of furniture made in America enjoyed such wide and enduring popularity in all ranks of society. George Washington used Windsors on his Mount Vernon porch, Benjamin Franklin had them in his Philadelphia home, Thomas Jefferson ordered four dozen of them for Monticello, and members of the Continental Congress sat in Windsors as they deliberated the cause of American independence. Over the years large quantities of them were shipped to various parts of the world.

One wit has observed that these light, inexpensive, durable, and highly functional forms had "an infinite capacity for taking strains." Adaptations of Windsor principles of construction persisted over many years, and variations of the form are still being made.

*Fig. 241. **Windsor writing-arm chair,** United States, eighteenth century; wood, painted, height 46⁹/₁₆ inches (118.2 cm.), depth at writing arm 32 inches (81.3 cm.). By the period of the American Revolution the most popular inexpensive all-purpose chair was the Windsor. Although its antecedents were European, the American Windsor evolved in its own distinctive way. Simply constructed of spindles stuck into a plank seat, it was lightweight, strong, and cheap. Because Windsors were easily movable, they were especially popular for use in the garden, on the porch, and in the hall, as well as for public rooms, but they could be useful anywhere in the house, be it rich or poor. Different kinds of wood with different properties were used for each part of the chair, which was then painted to unify the various wood grains and colors and to provide a protective coating. Combining a writing surface and storage space for reading and writing implements with a Windsor armchair resulted in the eminently practical, but today very rare, form seen here—a compact, movable desk and chair.* Gift of Mrs. Screven Lorillard, 1952 (52.195.11)

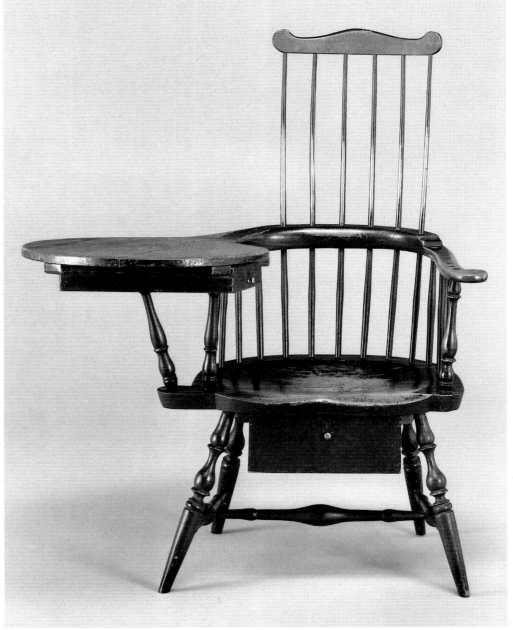

241

# Folk Art

There never has been a time when American furniture has not been painted either in plain colors or in decorative designs of various kinds. Painting inexpensive wood with graining to simulate costly materials was common practice from an early date. So, too, was the more or less elaborate ornamentation of flat surfaces with pictorial subjects of one sort or another—traditional folk themes, peopled landscapes, purely decorative patterns, and the like. The painted furniture of the Pennsylvania Germans offers conspicuous examples,

standing distinctly apart from the other early decorated forms in the collection of the Wing (see Fig. 191).

The dividing line between what might most properly be called folk furniture and other forms, traditional and sometimes innovative, cannot always be sharply drawn, but there should be no question about these two bold, ingenuous pieces (Figs. 242 and 243).

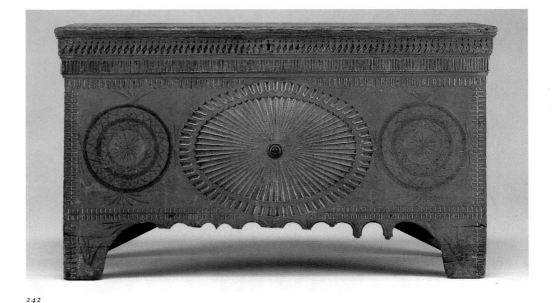

242

**Fig. 242. Chest,** *attributed to Nehemiah Randall (1770–1850), Belchertown, Massachusetts, 1800–20; pine, painted, length 37¾ inches (95.9 cm.). The maker of this lively chest would seem to have trained as a carpenter rather than a cabinetmaker, for the motifs he chose belong to the house-builder's repertoire. The fluted central oval and the borders of painted dentils and rosettes may be seen on mantelpieces, overdoors, and cornices of Federal-period houses. The oval and the arches that originally finished the skirt were laid out with a compass and ruler.*
Gift of Mrs. E. Herrick Low, Nelson Holland and Hudson Holland, in memory of their mother, Mrs. Nelson Clarke Holland, 1955 (55.84)

**Fig. 243. Table,** *New York State, about 1800; pine, painted, height 29½ inches (74.9 cm.). The maker of this stand used paint to simulate lively wavy and scalloped inlay on the two drawers and varicolored stringing on the legs. Although his stiff cabriole legs ending in squared-off shod feet and overhanging top with scalloped corners indicate a reluctance to give up elements of the previous Chippendale style, the simulated inlay and bail drawer handles are characteristic of the Federal period.*
Purchase, Virginia Groomes Gift, in memory of Mary W. Groomes, and funds from various donors, 1976 (1976.175)

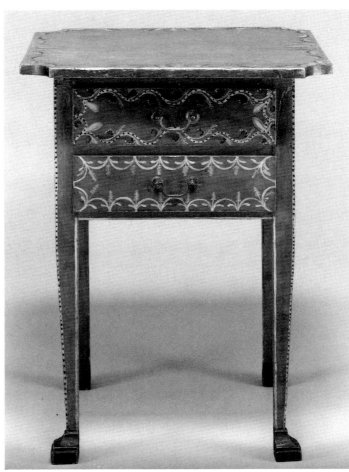

243

# The Pre–Civil War Period

## The Greek Revival, 1820–45

Obviously styles in art and fashion do not change overnight, and no period in history has been uniform in appearance. The past lingers and dies slowly; the future is born in the present. Often the old and the new are freely mixed to produce a separate, transitional style worrisome to those who prefer to confine art in neat categories. This has probably never been so clearly demonstrated as in the later decades of the nineteenth century. Before the end of that era the terminology used to categorize the many styles that were competing for public attention had become thoroughly confused.

For more than half a century after the end of the Revolution neoclassical designs in one variation after another had led American fashions in architecture and the decorative arts. No other basic style, before or after, endured for so long. As late as 1850 one observer noted that "the furniture most generally used in private houses is some modification of the classical style," even though totally divergent fashions were already securing a strong position in the marketplace at the time.

Toward the end of the early Federal period the relatively light, delicate forms and geometric shapes inspired by the initial publications of Hepplewhite and Sheraton gave way to bolder contours and more richly carved decoration reflecting French Empire and English Regency taste. The transition may be seen in an elegant New York armchair painted red and gold (Fig. 244). The straight lines and delicate ornament of the early Federal period began to give way to curves and decorative motifs that are broader and bolder. Some of the examples by Phyfe, Lannuier, and others that have already been described exemplify this more assertive neoclassicism as well. There was also an increasing tendency to rely upon ancient Greek, Roman, and Egyptian patterns of form and decoration. These were copied or construed from a variety of English and French publications that were available to the American public and, of course, to the craftsmen who served its wants and needs. Important sources for the new style were Sheraton's later designs; the designs of Thomas Hope and George Smith, which shaped the course of the English Regency; and such periodicals as Rudolph Ackermann's *The Repository of Arts* . . . , and Pierre de la Més-

angère's *Collection de Meubles et Objets de Goût*, published in France.

An outstanding illustration of this trend is a chair, one of a set of eleven made in Baltimore between 1815 and 1820, possibly by John and Hugh Finlay (Fig. 245). The curves of its backrest and back rails are modeled on those of the klismos form of ancient Greece, often depicted in vase paintings of the fifth century B.C. Its painted decoration, gold with green and black, includes ancient Greek motifs, some of which vary from piece to piece in the set. Benjamin Henry Latrobe, architect of the Capitol, designed a similar suite of furniture, probably based on designs in Hope's publications, for a room in Dolly Madison's White House. He commissioned the Finlays to make the suite, for which the drawings still exist. In 1811 Washington Irving described the finished room as one of "blazing splendor"—unfortunately a prophetic phrase, for three years later, during the War of 1812, all those appointments went up in flames when the British put a torch to the building.

What was called a "Grecian" sofa in an early nineteenth-century London price book shows this interpretation of the antique style in its most graceful form (Fig. 246). The continuously and gently flowing curves of the back and arms, the latter lightly carved in a scaly pattern, epitomize the inherent grace of the style. The shape of the dolphin legs and of the carved and gilded leafy sprays that join them to the seat-rail complement the curves of arm and back. An inlaid brass Greek-key pattern whose bright color is echoed in the brass rosettes that terminate the scrolled ends of the back rail provides a strong accent. In its sophisticated conception and the

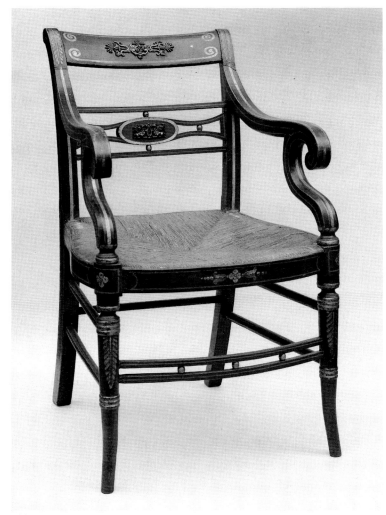

244

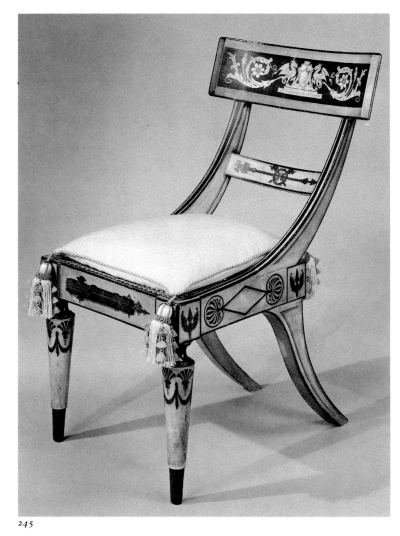

245

**Fig. 244. Armchair,** *New York, about 1820; maple, beech, painted and gilded, height 33½ inches (84.5 cm.). Delicacy of line and proportion triumph in this chair, even though it contains robust elements of the oncoming Greek Revival style. The curved crest rail and the sweeping curves of the arm and arm supports are both features of the later style, but the tapering legs and refined ormolu and painted ornament remain to testify to the linear elegance of early Federal design. The chair belongs to an early nineteenth-century category called "fancy furniture"—highly decorative painted pieces that, at their best, are among the most elegant survivals of the period. They were often made in sets for use in the parlor or dining room. About 1815,*

*both Thomas Ash and John Cowperthwaite advertised similar painted furniture in New York newspapers.*
Rogers Fund, 1945 (45.151.1)

**Fig. 245. Side chair,** *attributed to John and Hugh Finlay (w. 1799–1833), Baltimore, 1815–30; maple painted gold with black and green decoration, height 34 inches (86.4 cm.). The broad, sweeping curves of the Greek Revival style are masterfully employed in this modified klismos chair. Its classical prototype, a Roman version of the original Greek klismos chair (today most readily visible in ancient vase paintings), substituted round, tapering front legs for the*

*vivid saber curve of the Greek version. One of a set of eleven equally dashing chairs (undoubtedly there were originally twelve), this belongs to a group of distinguished fancy furniture made in early nineteenth-century Baltimore. The design on the broad crest rail of this and the other chairs in this set was very probably taken from Plate 56 of Sheraton's* The Cabinet-maker and Upholsterer's Drawing-Book, *1802 edition.*
Purchase, Mrs. Paul Moore Gift, 1965 (65.167.6)

**Fig. 246. Sofa**, *probably New York, about 1820; mahogany, ash, maple, pine, brass, length 97⅜ inches (247.3 cm.). Flowing curves and a variety of rich and colorful materials are expertly combined in this "dolphin" sofa to create one of the most interesting and graceful pieces of the Greek Revival period. The form itself was shown in an 1802 edition of the* London Chair-Makers' and Carvers' Book of Prices for Workmanship, *but this version, with polished mahogany, inlaid brass Greek key, carved and gilded leaf sprays, and carved verde antique dolphins and scales, is a distinctive high-style New York interpretation.* Friends of the American Wing Fund, 1965 (65.58)

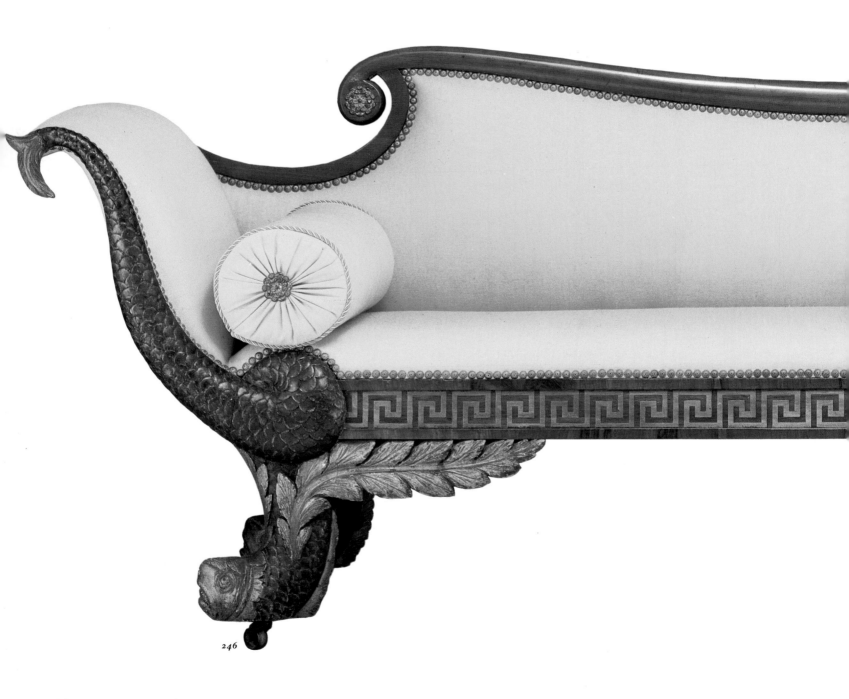

246

superb virtuosity of its workmanship, this piece represents a high point in the development of the Greek Revival, or American Empire, style. With the passing years pieces became heavier in construction and bolder in outline, a drift that can be detected in a mahogany sofa that, in comparison with the dolphin sofa, is a form of impressive bulk (Fig. 247). It was made in Boston about 1825–29. The brass rosette pulls on the arms open cylindrical drawers, each labeled by William Hancock. A half dozen other known pieces carrying Hancock's label are of the style and period of this piece.

Except for some continued references to Greek motifs in decoration, the dependence upon antique forms became less and less visible as the years passed. The piano was, of course, an instrument unknown to the ancients, but an example acquired by the Museum almost a century ago stands on heavy legs and is ornamented by stenciled designs inspired by classical motifs. Made of rosewood about 1825, this handsome instrument displays a gilded tablet with black script letters indicating that it was made by Loud and Brothers, whose firm had been making pianos in Philadelphia since 1816 (Fig. 248).

About the same time the piano was made, a New York cabinetmaking firm, possibly Joseph Meeks and Sons, fashioned a large mahogany secretary that

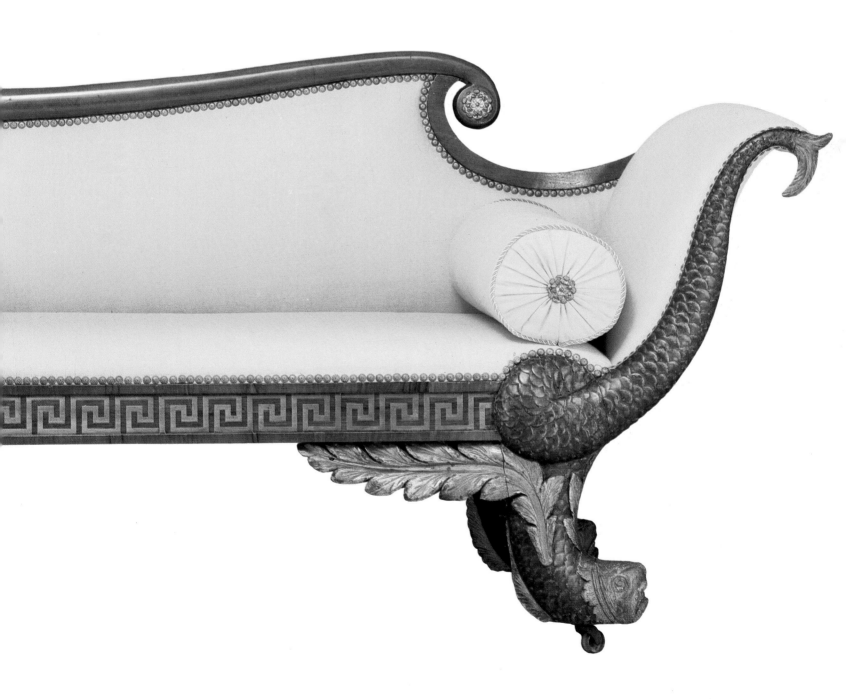

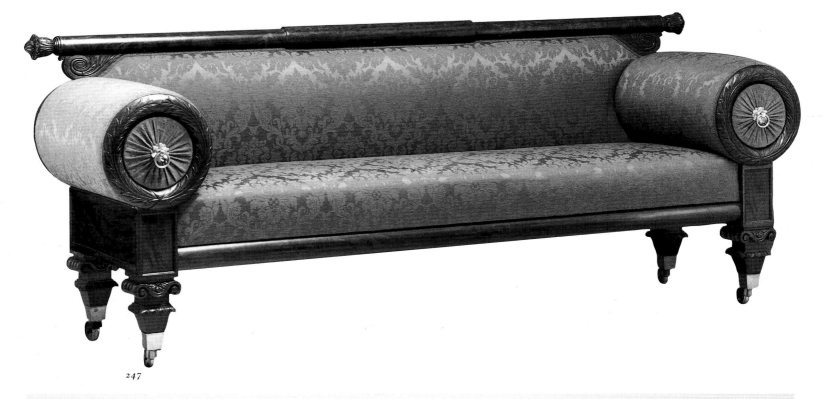

247

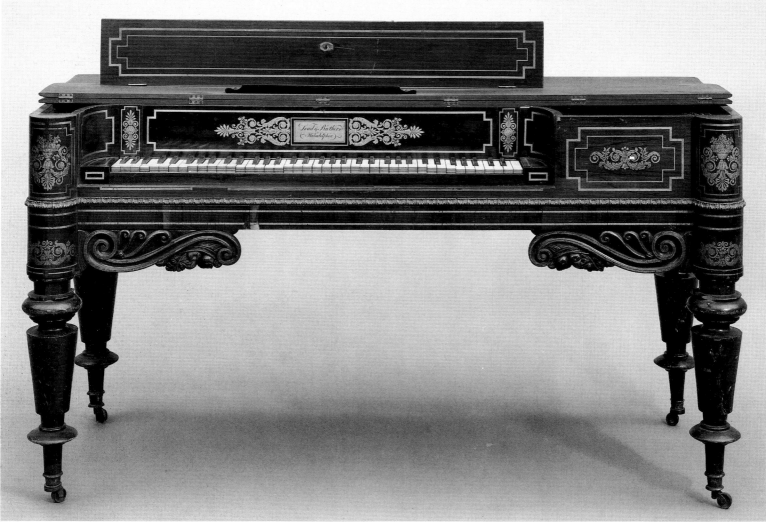

248

**Fig. 247. Sofa,** labeled "WILLIAM HANCOCK,/ *Upholsterer, 39 & 41* MARKET STREET,/BOS-TON," *1825–29; mahogany, maple, chestnut, length 89½ inches (227.3 cm). No exact prototype has been found for this sofa, with its assertive cylindrical arms containing drawers, but* Sheraton's *Cabinet Encyclopaedia of 1805 includes a design for a related sofa with upholstered cylindrical arms (Plate 2, sofas). The sofa's bulk is undeniable, but its design is cohesive, and its workmanship is the very best. Although it bears Hancock's label, his advertisements indicate that he was an upholsterer who did not make furniture, but sold that of other people.*
Gift of Mrs. William W. Hoppin, 1948 (48.164.1)

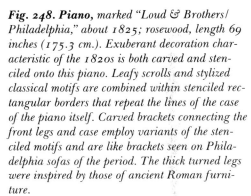

**Fig. 248. Piano,** *marked "Loud & Brothers/ Philadelphia," about 1825; rosewood, length 69 inches (175.3 cm). Exuberant decoration characteristic of the 1820s is both carved and stenciled onto this piano. Leafy scrolls and stylized classical motifs are combined within stenciled rectangular borders that repeat the lines of the case of the piano itself. Carved brackets connecting the front legs and case employ variants of the stenciled motifs and are like brackets seen on Philadelphia sofas of the period. The thick turned legs were inspired by those of ancient Roman furniture.*
The Crosby Brown Collection of Musical Instruments, 1889 (89.4.2812)

**Fig. 249. Secretary,** *possibly by Joseph Meeks and Sons, New York, about 1825; mahogany, brass, height 101 inches (256.5 cm). Dazzling decorative effects derive from carving, stenciling, and gilding on the case of this piece and from the patterns of the brass mullions and the elegant pleated silk behind the glass. The overall effect is of sophistication, but the stenciled designs vary from tight, precise running patterns that imitate brass inlay to much more casual, countrified flower and fruit designs of the kind that were used on Hitchcock chairs a few years later. The classically inspired columns and symmetrically disposed ornament are balanced by the naturalism of the large carved paw feet, leafy hocks, and fruit-filled cornucopia brackets. Such a brilliant ornamental effect is not seen often, but its elements are typical of New York furniture of the 1820s.*
Gift of Francis Hartman Markoe, 1960 (60.29.1)

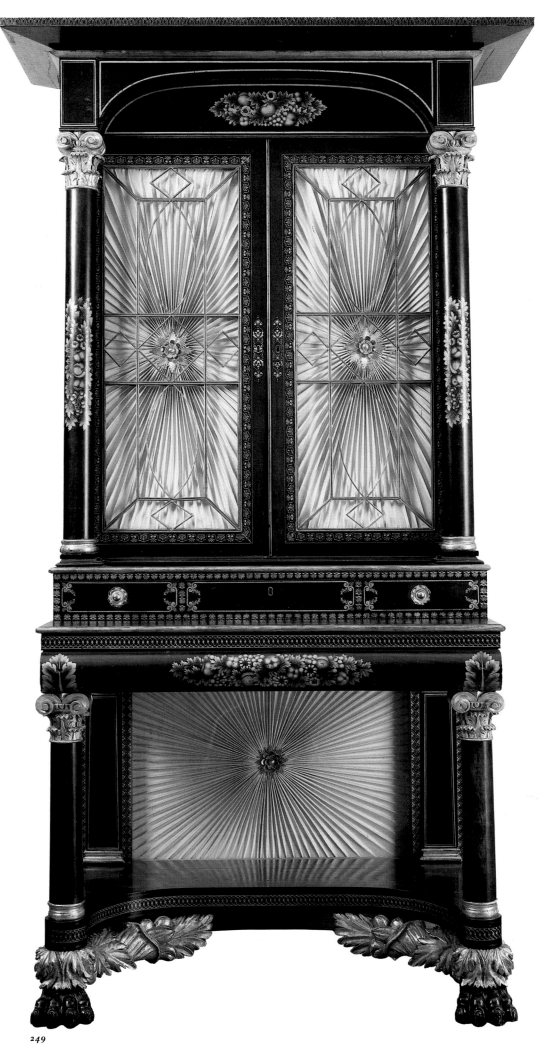

249

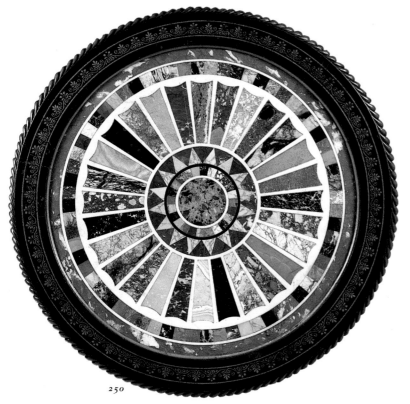

250

**Figs. 250 and 251. Pedestal table,** labeled
twice "*126/ANTHONY G. QUERVELLE'S/CABI-
NET AND SOFA MANUFACTORY,/SOUTH SECOND
STREET, A FEW DOORS BELOW DOCK,/PHILA-
DELPHIA,*" about *1830; mahogany, gilt brass, ormolu, marble, height 29¹³/₁₆ inches (75.7 cm.),
diameter 34½ inches (85.1 cm.). The deeply
carved paw feet and leafy hocks that are characteristic of American furniture of the Greek Revival period appear here on an elegant and richly
decorated variant of the pillar-and-scroll style
that dominated the 1830s. The colorful inlaid-
marble top, an unusual feature that was probably
imported from Europe, adds great richness. The
table belongs to a small group based on designs
in George Smith's* Cabinet-Maker and Upholsterer's Guide *of 1826; Quervelle made three very
similar examples for the White House in 1829.*
Purchase, The Edgar J. Kaufmann Foundation Gift,
1968 (68.96)

**Fig. 252. Card table,** *New York, about 1825;
rosewood, mahogany, brass inlay, ormolu, height
29½ inches (74.9 cm.), length of top 36 inches
(91.4 cm.). This supremely elegant example of
late classical furniture has linear brass inlay, one
fine imported French ormolu mount, and circular
leaf-carved verde-antique and gilt feet to complement its polished rosewood surfaces. During the
1830s the Empire style divested itself of most
carved ornament and let expanses of broad, plain
surfaces, pillars, and scrolls speak for themselves.
The style had originated in France during the
restoration (Restauration) of the Bourbon mon-
archy after Napoleon's last exile in 1815.*
Purchase, The Edgar J. Kaufmann Foundation Gift,
1968 (68.94.2)

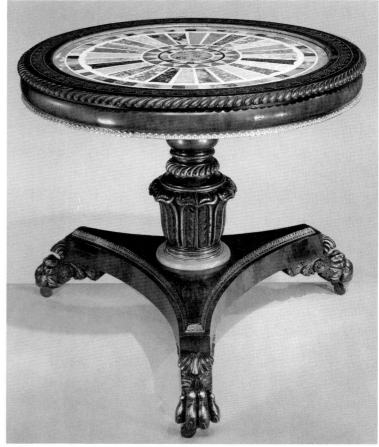

251

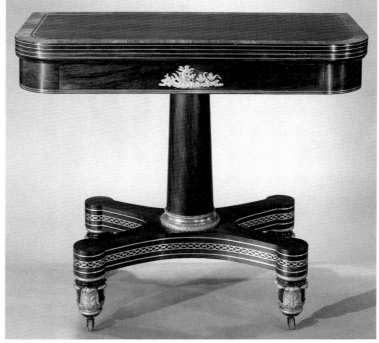

252

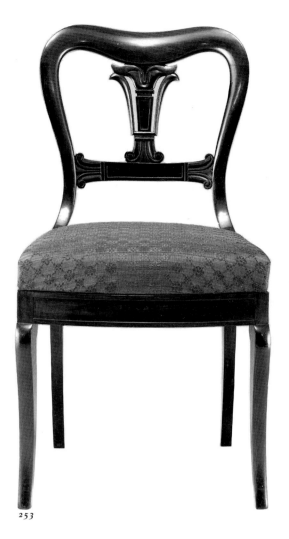

stands more than eight feet tall (Fig. 249). In this boldly conceived piece the later Empire style reached an unsurpassed opulence. The various painted and stenciled gilt designs that add measurably to its elegant appearance were employed as an alternative to much more expensive ormolu (gilded brass) mounts. The use of painted or stenciled decoration was characteristic in these years, most conspicuously in ornamenting the widely popular Hitchcock and other "fancy" chairs that, beginning in the late 1820s, were mass produced by the thousand.

A circular mahogany pedestal table whose elaborately patterned marble top is enclosed within a stenciled gilt border and whose boldly carved pedestal and paw feet are enriched by touches of gilt also clearly illustrates the use of paint in high-style as well as mass-produced furniture (Figs. 250 and 251). This exceptional piece bears the label of Antoine-Gabriel Quervelle, a French émigré craftsman who practiced his trade in Philadelphia from 1817 until his death in 1856.

The prevailing emphasis on solid forms is again demonstrated by a rosewood card table, one of a pair that may have been made in Duncan Phyfe's famous workshop (Fig. 252). Unusual distinction accrues to this relatively simple form because of the combination of painted gilt decoration with elegant inlaid and applied metal ornament. The top of the table swivels on a carefully fitted edge cushion of velvet. When the top is flipped over it centers on the columnar pedestal. The design of the table was influenced by the Restauration style, so called because it was introduced in France during the restoration of the Bourbon monarch after Napoleon's last

defeat in 1815. Influence from that same French source is apparent in the design of a rosewood chair made in New York about 1830 (Fig. 253). The inverted lotus design of the back splat and stay rail shows a lingering trace of the Egyptian influence that had long played a part in European decorative art, but that was especially important in the years following Napoleon's celebrated campaigns in North Africa. References to Egyptian themes continued to crop up for decades.

With the French Restauration style came the culminating stage of the classical revival in furniture design, which was quickly observed in the United States by the foremost artisans and manufacturers. As always, the foreign fashion was transmitted by imported trade publications, by immigrant craftsmen, and by examples from abroad. In 1835 French furniture was being imported in such volume that New York journeymen who felt it interfered with the selling of their own products descended on a salesroom and defaced the alien goods "in such a diabolical manner that the injury exceeds a thousand dollars," according to a reporter of the scene of vandalism.

In this last phase of neoclassicism the rich carving and gilded decoration of previous Empire pieces were replaced by flat, often veneered, mahogany or rosewood surfaces. Forms assumed an almost geometric simplicity (Fig. 252 and see Fig. 98). In 1833 the New York firm of Joseph Meeks and Sons published a broadside that shows popular furniture forms of the day (Fig. 254). Dominant features of most pieces illustrated are broad, plain surfaces, scrolls, and pillars, which explain the style's nickname—"pillar and scroll." The in-

253

**Fig. 253. Side chair,** *attributed to the workshop of Duncan Phyfe (w. 1792–1847), about 1830; rosewood, ash, height 32³⁄₄ inches (83.2 cm.). This is an early and very elegant example of what became the most popular form of mid-Victorian side chair. In America the curving outline of the back resulted in its being called a balloon back, and it was made in many degrees of quality for many decades. This example is attributed to Phyfe on the basis of its fine workmanship and materials. It is similar to chairs in a set Phyfe made for his daughter Eliza Vail.* Purchase, The Edgar J. Kaufmann Foundation Gift, 1968 (68.202.1)

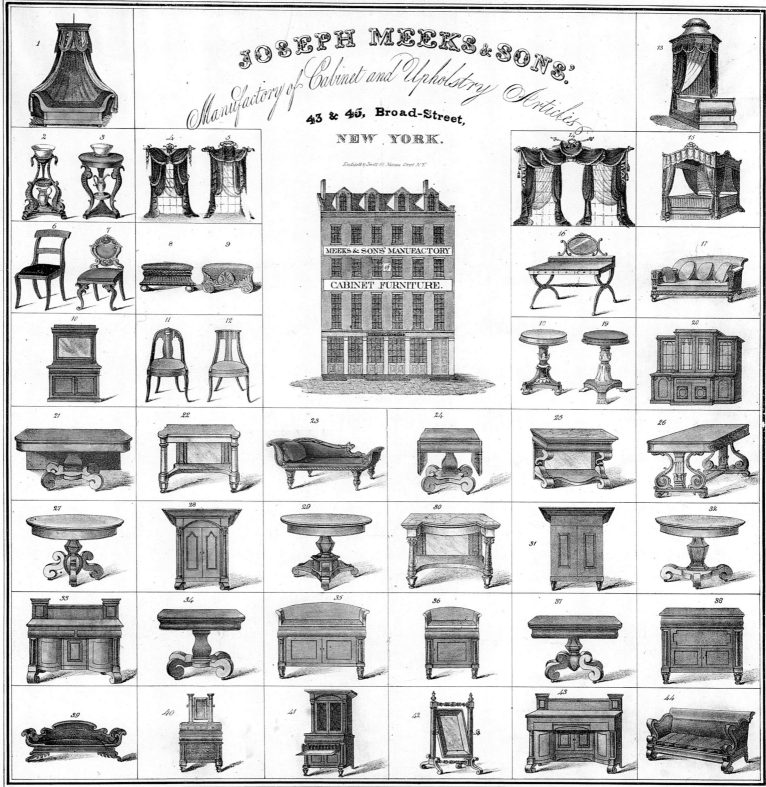

## JOSEPH MEEKS & SONS,
### Manufactory of Cabinet and Upholstry Articles
### 43 & 45, Broad-Street,
### NEW YORK.

MEEKS & SONS' MANUFACTORY
of
CABINET FURNITURE.

*Entered according to Act of Congress in the year 1833 by Joseph Meeks & Sons, in the Clerks Office of the District Court of the S.D. of N.Y.*

### CIRCULAR.

THE above constitute but a small part of the variety of Furniture made by the subscribers; it would be impossible to exhibit all the patterns on this sheet, as we are obliged to keep so great a variety, to suit the taste of our numerous purchasers—the patterns in this and foreign countries are so constantly varying, as to render it necessary for us to make alterations and improvements, and we are constantly getting up new and costly patterns, much to the satisfaction of the public, all of which are warranted to be made of the best materials and workmanship, and will bear the makers' card and names inside, as a guarantee to that effect. Our establishment being one of the oldest, and now the largest in the United States, we are able to execute orders, at wholesale prices, to any amount, and at the shortest notice.

| | |
|---|---|
| No. 1—A Canopy Bedstead, | $90 |
| Do. do. with Curtains and Top, | $250 to 500 |
| No. 13—A Canopy Bedstead, | 100 |
| Do. do. with Curtains and Top, | 300 to 600 |
| No. 15—A High Post Bedstead, | 50 |
| Do. do. with Curtains, | 300 to 300 |
| No. 2—A Rosewood and Gilt Washstand, | 75 |
| No. 3—A Mahogany Washstand, | 50 |
| No. 4, 5 and 14—Window Curtains, each, | 300 to 300 |
| No. 10—A French Dressing Bureau, | 150 |
| No. 16—A Dressing Table, | 35 |
| No. 6—A Mahogany Chair, each, | 7 |

| | |
|---|---|
| No. 7—A Mahogany Chair, silk seat and back, | 25 |
| No. 11 and 12—Rosewood Chairs and Silk Seats, each, | 15 |
| Mahogany do. hair cloth Seats, each, | 12 |
| Nos. 8 and 9—Foot Stools, Mahogany, and covered with hair cloth, each, | 10 |
| Do. do. Rosewood and Gilt, and covered with Silk, each, | 15 |
| No. 17—A Mahogany Sofa, covered with hair cloth, | 100 |
| Do. do. covered with silk, | 150 to 200 |
| No. 23—A Mahogany Couch, covered with hair cloth, | 90 |
| Do. do. covered with silk, | 140 |
| No. 39—A Mahogany Sofa, covered with hair cloth, | 80 |
| No. 44—A Mahogany Sofa, | 100 |
| Nos. 18 and 19—Piano Stools, Rosewood and Gilt, each, | 7 |

| | |
|---|---|
| No. 20—A Library, Secretary, and Book Case, | 200 |
| No. 21—A Mahogany End Dining Table $30—three in a set, | 150 |
| No. 24—A Breakfast Table, | 40 |
| No. 26—An occasional Table, | 100 |
| Nos. 22 and 30—A Rosewood or Mahogany Pier Table, white marble top and columns, | 90 |
| Do. do. Egyptian marble, | 100 |
| No. 25—A Mahogany Pier Table, white marble top, | 90 |
| Nos. 27, 29 and 32—Mahogany Centre Table, white marble top, each, | 96 |
| Do. do. Egyptian marble top, | 110 |
| No. 28—A Mahogany Wardrobe, | 110 |
| No. 31—A Mahogany Wardrobe, | 70 |

| | |
|---|---|
| No. 33—A Mahogany Sideboard, | 90 |
| No. 37—A Mahogany Sideboard, | 130 |
| No. 34 and 77—Mahogany Card Tables, each, | 50 |
| No. 35—A Double Washstand, with a white marble top, | 20 |
| Do. do. Egyptian top, | 60 |
| No. 36—A Single Washstand, with white marble top, | 20 |
| Do. do. Egyptian top, | 25 |
| No. 38—A Mahogany Bureau, | 40 |
| No. 40—A Mahogany Dressing Bureau, | 40 |
| No. 41—A Secretary and Book Case, | 120 |
| No. 42—A Mahogany Dressing Glass, with brass candle sticks complete, | 80 |

☞ We would observe, that when any Furniture is wanted of the above patterns, by referring to the above table or card, and giving the number of the same, or by giving a description of any other peice of Furniture in our line, to the Proprietors of the above establishment, the orders will be punctually attended to.

**JOSEPH MEEKS & SONS.**

Figs. 255 and 256. **Sewing table,** *attributed to Peter Glass (1824–95), Sheboygan County, Wisconsin, 1865–75; marquetry, height 28½ inches (72.4 cm.), diameter 27½ inches (69.9 cm.). This extraordinary table was probably made by Peter Glass, a craftsman trained in Europe to make both furniture and marquetry. In 1844 he emigrated to America—first to Boston and then to Wisconsin—and the work he produced, alone and by hand, over the next half century reflects both the styles of the 1830s, when he was an apprentice, and traditions of hand craftsmanship that were dying out. This sewing table is as* painstakingly crafted inside as out. Its interior *contains small drawers with ivory knobs and a drawer that lifts to reveal a mirror and two more rows of small drawers. Glass's known work includes several pedestal tables, work boxes, and work stands, all covered with lavish marquetry designs.*
Purchase, Mr. and Mrs. William H. Hernstadt Gift, 1978 (1978.284)

troduction of steam-driven band saws, which could cut out from wood of any thickness scrolls and other contoured elements such as those that distinguish this style, made it possible to produce these forms at relatively low cost, and with some modifications the style persisted for decades—even after other styles had won popular favor. By the time the vogue expired, evidence of its classical ancestry was almost completely lost.

At an exhibition held at Boston in 1850 one Peter Glass was awarded a blue ribbon for a pedestal worktable covered with elaborate marquetry inlays (Figs. 255 and 256). The square-section curved supports attached to its central pedestal relate the piece to pillar-and-scroll furniture, except that here the unusual and detailed refinement of the workmanship put the piece into a category quite its own.

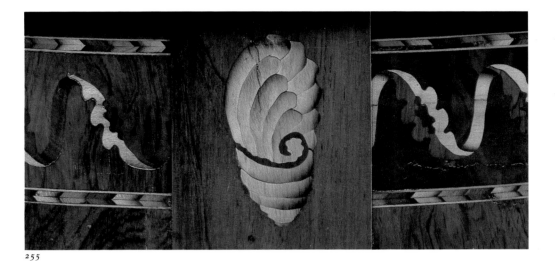

255

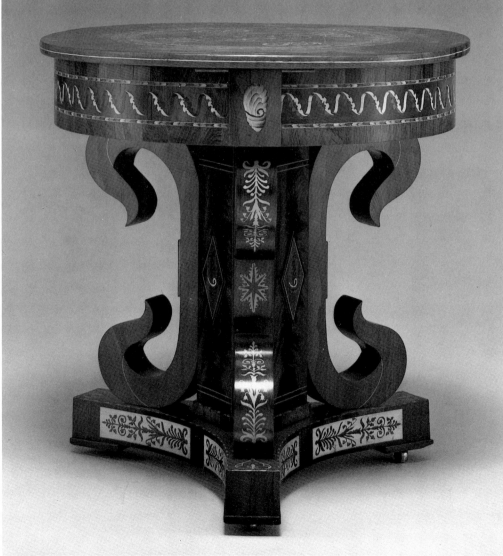

256

**Fig. 254.** *Broadside,* Joseph Meeks and Sons' *advertisement, New York, 1833; hand-colored lithograph by Endicott and Swett, 21½ by 17 inches (54.6 by 43.2 cm.). A varied selection of substantial pillar-and-scroll forms of the 1830s is illustrated here by Phyfe's competitors Joseph Meeks and Sons—in the first detailed publication of American furniture design. Based on the French Restauration style, which was popular in France from about 1815 to 1830, furniture of this heavy, plain sort complemented the simple high-ceilinged rooms of contemporary Greek Revival houses. Also included in the illustration, which the Meeks firm asserted showed "but a small part of the variety of Furniture" they had for sale, were lavishly carved tripod tables (Nos. 2 and 3) and a sofa (No. 39) in the manner most characteristic of the previous decade.*
Gift of Mrs. R. W. Hyde, 1943 (43.15.8)

# The Rococo Revival 1840–60

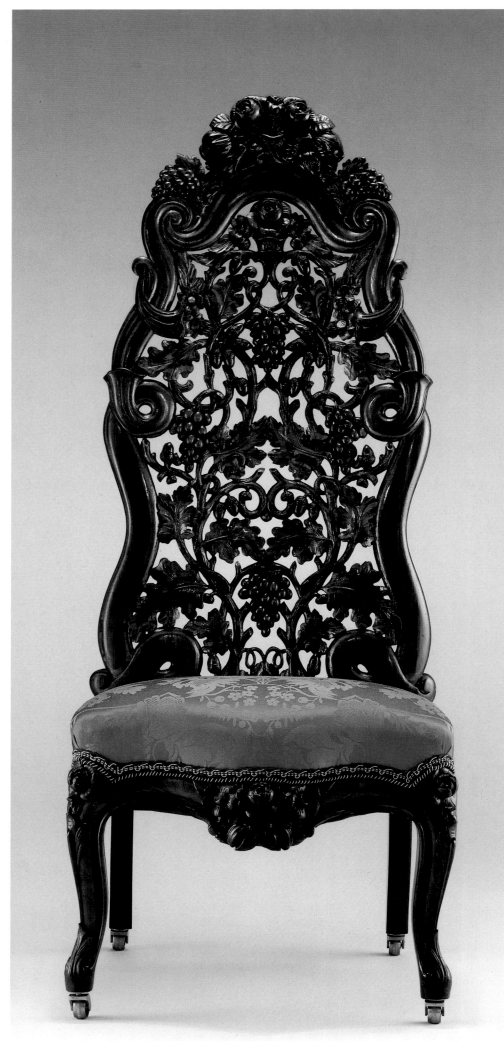

As the middle of the last century approached, A. J. Downing observed that in matters of taste, America was in an experimental stage. "With the passion for novelty, and the feeling of independence that belong to this country," he wrote, "our people seem determined to *try everything*." The commonplace prosperity of Americans noted by Nathaniel Hawthorne was abundantly advertised by New York's Crystal Palace exhibition of 1853, and the common man was becoming something of a prince in his own right. He probably enjoyed a greater degree and variety of material comfort and satisfaction than his like had known in any other society. He also enjoyed the reasonable expectation of joining the ranks of the more opulent—and faith in that possibility was constantly renewed by the numbers of self-made men who did precisely that. At practically every level of society citizens of the booming democracy confidently looked for more, better, and different things to enrich their lives. It was a time of great expectations.

Shortly before he lost his life in a steamboat disaster on the Hudson River in 1853 (at the age of thirty-seven), Downing conceded that in spite of his persuasive polemics supporting the Gothic style, a new fashion that followed "modern" French designs was gaining favor. He referred to a revival style that looked back to the rococo forms of the Louis XIV and Louis XV periods. Like those earlier designs, the nineteenth-century version featured cabriole legs, sinuously curving contours, and intricate arrangements of S- and C-shaped scrolls. However, in the later interpretation chairs, tables, étagères, and other indispensable house-

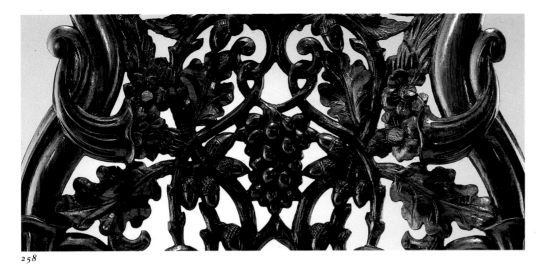

258

**Fig. 257. Side chair,** *attributed to John Henry Belter (1804–63), New York, about 1855; rosewood (secondary woods unidentified), height 44¼ inches (112.4 cm.). Part of a large parlor suite, this slipper chair illustrates the remarkable strength of the laminated wood that Belter steamed and pressed into the shapes he desired. The cabriole legs, scroll feet, and casters, as well as the curved and carved front seat-rail, are typical of much Rococo Revival furniture, but the lush and intricate vines, leaves, and bunches of grapes that make up the back of this chair are found only in Belter's furniture.*
Gift of Mr. and Mrs. Lowell Ross Burch and Jean McLean Morron, 1951 (51.79.9)

**Fig. 258.** *Detail, carved back of Belter side chair.*

**Fig. 259.** *Back view, Belter side chair, showing flat uncarved laminated surface.*

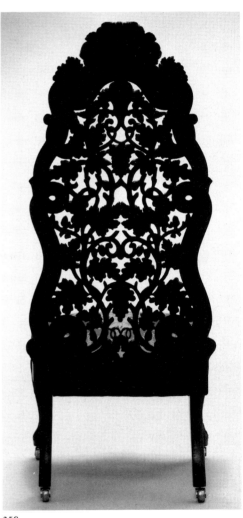

259

hold furnishings were embellished with rich, deeply carved clusters of fruit, flowers, and other natural forms in a variety of combinations and of a general character unlike anything produced in the eighteenth century.

The new fashion was prominently on display at various international fairs of the 1850s including, of course, the one held at New York's Crystal Palace. That very influential periodical *Godey's Magazine and Lady's Book* gave its stamp of approval with the reservation that "honest country folk" might decry such emphasis on modishness and novelty. However, the editors advised, an appreciative witness would be "especially struck . . . with the varied, in fact ever changing, curves of artistic carving of some beautiful wreath, with the boldness, depth, and sharpness of a *bouquet* or cluster; in another [piece], with the hanging foliage, budding flowers, and waving scrolls, many of which are triumphs of the chisel." In further explanation, the editors provided the English equivalents of the French terms for the forms in the new fashion that were to be seen in the better shops; a toilettinette was a lady's toilet table, an étagère was a whatnot or set of shelves for bric-a-brac, a tête-à-tête was a sofa, and so on.

As Benjamin Franklin had observed a century earlier, the newcomer to America was always welcome if he had any useful art, and, during the decades preceding the Civil War, Old World craftsmen were lured to this country by the prospect of increasing their fortunes. Many of them came directly from France, adding impetus to the mounting popularity of the new style. Such émigrés—men named Charles A. Baudouine, François Seignouret, Alexan-

der Roux, Auguste Eliaers, Prudent Mallard, and Leon Marcotte—dominated the fine furniture trade in New York and other cities, and helped to perpetuate the fashion for French-born styles for several decades.

Although the resulting form and ornament were predominantly French in inspiration, the actual production was for the most part handled by German craftsmen. The name of John Henry Belter (Johann Heinrich Belter, as he was christened), a German immigrant who came to New York in the early 1840s, is the one most commonly associated with the American Rococo Revival style. Belter's method of furniture construction, in which a number of thin layers of veneer were glued together at right angles and pressed and steamed into the desired curved shape, was not a new one, but was improved considerably in his hands. From 1847 to 1858 he patented his various improvements that, besides producing a strong, lightweight curved form, had the further advantage of creating a laminated element that could be carved in delicate detail not so easily accomplished in solid wood (Figs. 257, 258, and 259). This had been understood in the eighteenth century, as Belter himself was apparently aware. Although the chairback, with its pattern of grapevines, leaves, and fruit, is an extraordinary tour de force, the carving on the crest rail of the Belter sofa is equally remarkable (Fig. 260). Swirling leaves and C-scrolls form a lacy base for the solid carvings of flowers flowing from urns.

Many of the workmen who carved such ornamental features, both at Belter's manufactory and at other furniture-making establishments, had been recruited from Alsace-Lorraine and

*Fig. 260. Sofa, by John Henry Belter (1804–63), New York, about 1855; rosewood (secondary woods unidentified), length 66 inches (167.6 cm.). The division of sofa backs into three parts was commonplace in the mid-nineteenth century. The delicate high-relief carving that ornaments this crest, however, was a remarkable achievement, equalled only by a Belter sofa recently acquired by the Victoria and Albert Museum in London. Blocks of wood were glued to the laminated frame to allow the carving extra deepness and richness.*
Lent by The Manney Collection (L.1983.109.7)

Germany's Black Forest area—and many had been shaken loose from their homelands by the European revolutions of 1848. In spite of Belter's patents, furniture of a very similar type was quickly turned out by others, and was often even referred to as "Belter furniture." Much was constructed of rosewood because of its attractive color and handsomely figured grain. (It was called rosewood not because of its reddish color but because the freshly sawed wood smelled like roses.) In spite of Belter's meticulous craftsmanship and great popularity, his firm was undermined by increasing mass production of simplified, inexpensive, and popular versions of his creations; by ever-changing styles; and by infringements on his patents. He died poor in 1864.

The carving on the laminated rosewood set that includes a sofa (Figs. 261 and 262) and chairs generally resembles that of Belter, but is more restrained in its curves and scrolls than documented pieces by the master. The firm of Joseph Meeks, Belter's industrious contemporary and competitor, made the set for Meeks's daughter Sophia Teresa when she was married in 1859.

Three generations of the Meeks family were active in New York for more than seventy years (see Figs. 249 and 266). In 1833 the firm was called the largest of its kind in the United States and was said to turn out "the most expensive, elegant and durable cabinet work." Under Joseph Meeks, who lived from 1771 to 1868 and whose sons were also active in the firm, it grew and flourished, doing business on an international scale. Among innumerable other commissions, the firm supplied some furniture for the White House. Unlike

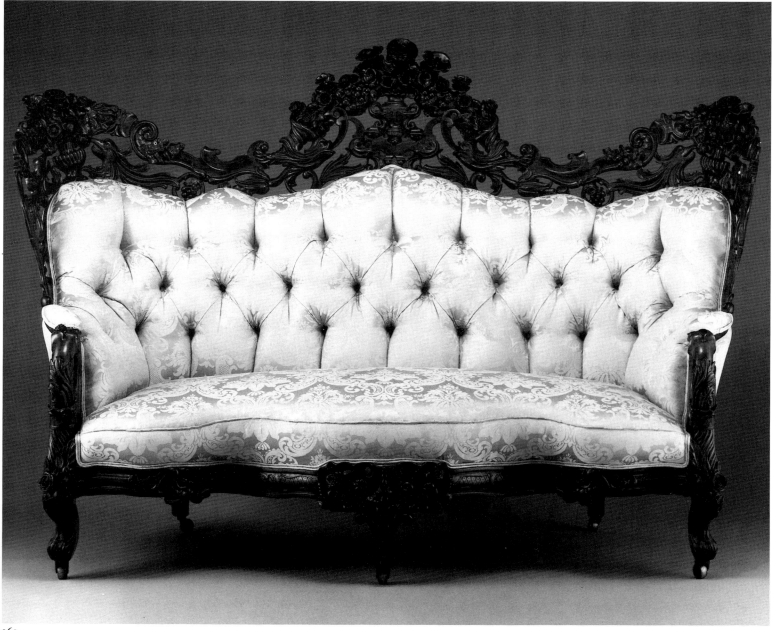

260

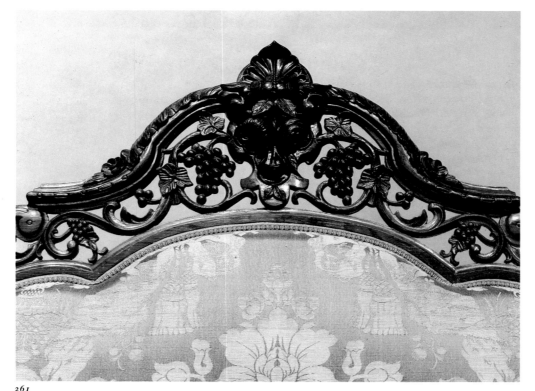

261

**Figs. 261 and 262. Sofa**, *by J. and J. W. Meeks
(active partnership about 1836–59), New York,
1859; rosewood (secondary woods unidentified),
length 63 inches (160 cm.). Although for many
years all Rococo Revival furniture was attributed
automatically to John Henry Belter, it has become
clear that a number of other firms made pieces
similar to Belter's. This sofa, part of a parlor set,
was made by the Meeks firm for the marriage of
Joseph W. Meeks's daughter Sophia Teresa
to Dexter Hawkins. It is therefore very important
because it provides a touchstone that helps to
distinguish Meeks's furniture from Belter's.*
Gift of Bradford A. Warner, 1969 (69.258.2)

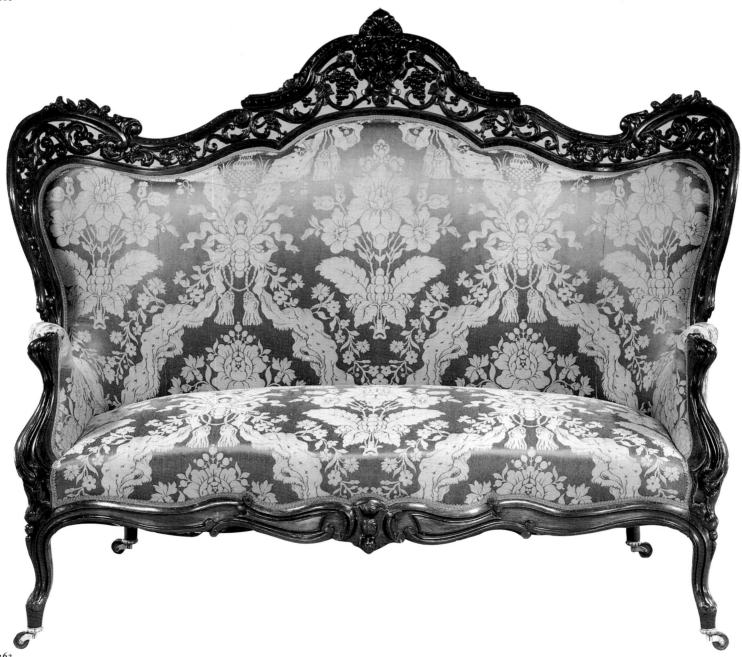

262

*Fig. 263. Etagère, by Alexander Roux (w. New*

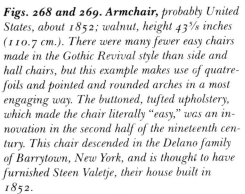

**Fig. 267. Side chair,** *United States, 1840–60; walnut, height 42½ inches (108 cm.). Ample chairs of this sort, made perhaps for a hallway or a dining room, lent themselves well to the addition of Gothic details. Here the back rises to a pointed arch, enclosing a cresting of Gothic tracery. The rows of arches below the upholstered oval and on the seat-rail provide further Gothic details. The spiral-twist front legs and rear stiles are often associated with a concurrent revival style, the Elizabethan.*
Gift of Mrs. Charles J. Bryan, 1965 (65.189)

**Figs. 268 and 269. Armchair,** *probably United States, about 1852; walnut, height 43⅝ inches (110.7 cm.). There were many fewer easy chairs made in the Gothic Revival style than side and hall chairs, but this example makes use of quatrefoils and pointed and rounded arches in a most engaging way. The buttoned, tufted upholstery, which made the chair literally "easy," was an innovation in the second half of the nineteenth century. This chair descended in the Delano family of Barrytown, New York, and is thought to have furnished Steen Valetje, their house built in 1852.*
Rogers Fund, 1967 (67.148)

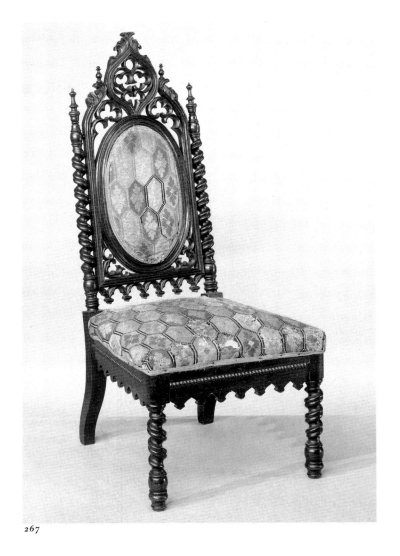

267

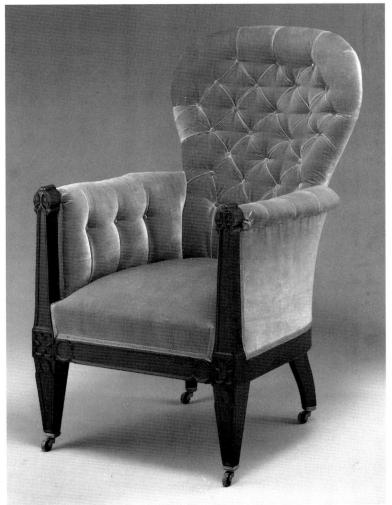

268

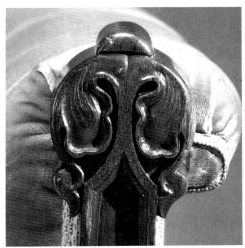

269

261

*Figs. 261 and 262. Sofa, by J. and J. W. Meeks (active partnership about 1836–59), New York, 1859; rosewood (secondary woods unidentified), length 63 inches (160 cm.). Although for many years all Rococo Revival furniture was attributed automatically to John Henry Belter, it has become clear that a number of other firms made pieces similar to Belter's. This sofa, part of a parlor set, was made by the Meeks firm for the marriage of Joseph W. Meeks's daughter Sophia Teresa to Dexter Hawkins. It is therefore very important because it provides a touchstone that helps to distinguish Meeks's furniture from Belter's.*
Gift of Bradford A. Warner, 1969 (69.258.2)

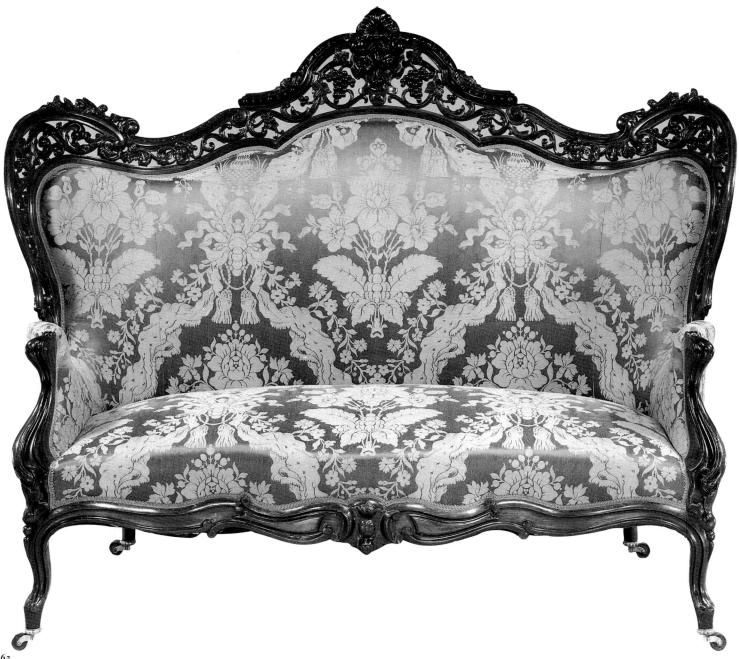

262

**Fig. 263. Etagère,** *by Alexander Roux (w. New York 1837–81), New York, about 1850; rosewood, chestnut, poplar, maple, height 86 inches (218.4 cm.). Elaborate shelves like this became popular in the Victorian period as repositories of oddities, curiosities, and objets d'art—symbols of travel or taste, or both. This lavishly carved example, obviously meant for an elegant parlor, is the work of Alexander Roux, a gifted Parisian cabinetmaker who emigrated to New York.* Sansbury-Mills Fund, 1971 (1971.219,220)

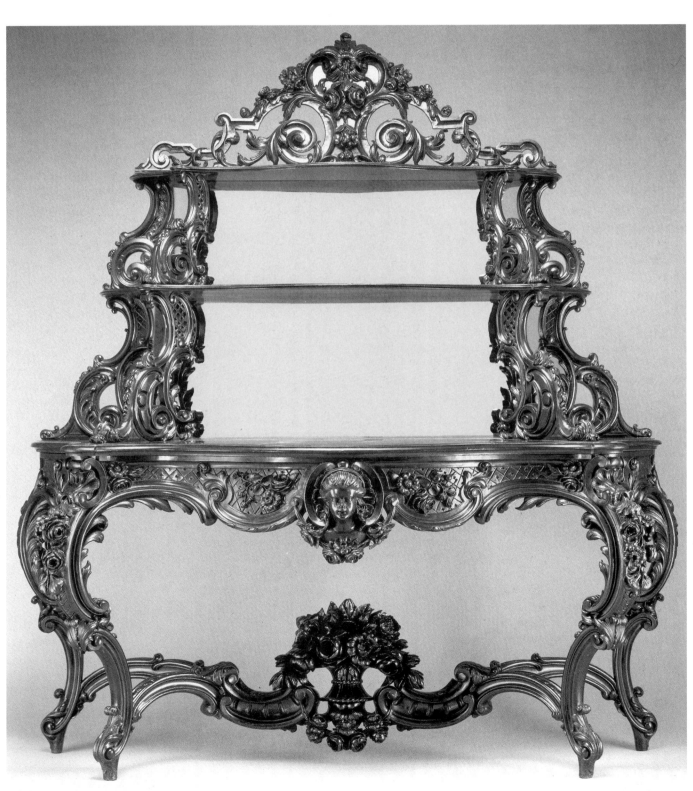

263

**Fig. 264. Slipper chair,** *by Alexander Roux (w. New York 1837–81), New York, about 1860; ebonized maple, ash, walnut, height 30⅝ inches (77.8 cm.). This chair was designed to rely on the curve and recurve of the "line of beauty," just as its eighteenth-century counterparts were. Almost the only embellishment allowed on this daringly sinuous seat is the chain of gold beads that dips and curves along the edge of its gleaming black frame. While the inspiration for its lines was obviously rococo furniture of the Louis XV period, the delicate simplicity of its ornament is characteristic of the succeeding Louis XVI period.* Gift of Zelina G. Brunschwig, 1968 (68.158)

the unfortunate Belter, Meeks not only made but kept a fortune. He died rich enough to own a vault with "eighty separate apartments" for him and his family in Brooklyn's Greenwood Cemetery.

Downing singled out the émigré cabinetmaker Alexander Roux for his "most tasteful designs" in the rococo as well as other styles. That this distinction was well deserved is apparent in an elaborate étagère labeled by this Paris-born and -trained craftsman (Fig. 263). It too is of laminated rosewood ornately carved in the Belter manner with scrolls and naturalistic forms that include a bouquet in a basket at the center of its stretchers and the likeness of a human face on the skirting. Here again is early Victorian exuberance in design, presented with imagination and masterful skill. The word "whatnot" came into popular use in the mid-nineteenth century to refer to forms for displaying decorative objects of one sort or another.

All Rococo Revival furniture was not made of laminated woods nor was it necessarily characterized by lavishly carved ornamentation. In extreme contrast to the highly elaborate whatnot is a slipper chair also made by Roux that shows how the rococo style could be modified into a form of suave simplicity (Fig. 264). Roux advertised that he made both "Plain and Artistic Furniture," and here the ornament is limited to simple rounded moldings (sometimes described as "finger rolled") and brass beading that trim the gracefully curved outlines of the ebonized maple frame of the chair.

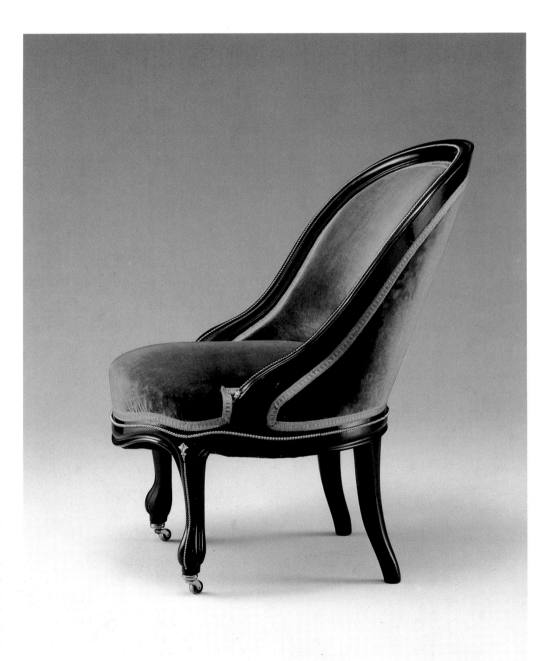

264

# The Gothic Revival, 1830–75

**Fig. 265. Side chair,** *New York, 1840–60; rosewood, rosewood veneer, ash, height 34 inches (86.4 cm.).* **Table,** *United States, 1840–50; rosewood, height 28¾ inches (73 cm.). Although they were not made en suite, these two pieces have many similarities. The chair combines, delicately and gracefully, aspects of two concurrent revivals—the Rococo and the Gothic. The undulating curves of the rococo, seen here especially in the cabriole legs, seat-rail, and back of the chair, blend with Gothic elements that are much less architectural than usual. Diminutive turned pendents, leafy carving on columnar supports, and rounded arches appear on both table and chair. The latter retains its original red and gold needlework seat with Gothicized fleurs-de-lis.* Purchase, The Edgar J. Kaufmann Foundation Gift, 1968 (68.202.2), and Gift of Ronald S. Kane, 1967 (67.269.1)

**Fig. 266. Desk and bookcase,** *by J. and J. W. Meeks (active partnership about 1836–59), New York, 1836–50; rosewood, satinwood, height 91¾ inches (233.1 cm.). Mid-nineteenth-century taste makers decreed that while Rococo Revival furniture was suitable for parlors, Gothic Revival pieces should be used in hallways and libraries. Objects like this desk and bookcase with glass doors lent themselves well to decoration with such Gothic elements as the tracery in the glass doors and the quatrefoil molding on the lower all-wood doors. The Meeks firm, best known for its Restauration-style furniture (see Fig. 254), produced all the other fashionable styles of the time as well. The beautiful workmanship evident in this desk, with its rosewood exterior and contrasting satinwood interior, indicate the high standards of the Meeks firm.* Rogers Fund, 1969 (69.19)

I n the area of household furnishings, the task of designing objects in the Gothic Revival style was complicated by the fact that the times called for conveniences and forms that had not been dreamed of in the Middle Ages—secretaries, bookcases, dressers, clocks, whatnots, upholstered furniture, and the like.

The inventive ways in which these demands were met resulted in forms and designs that would have bewildered people of the Middle Ages. But such an inconsistency was not important—this was a romantic phase in American history, and any device that could be asso-

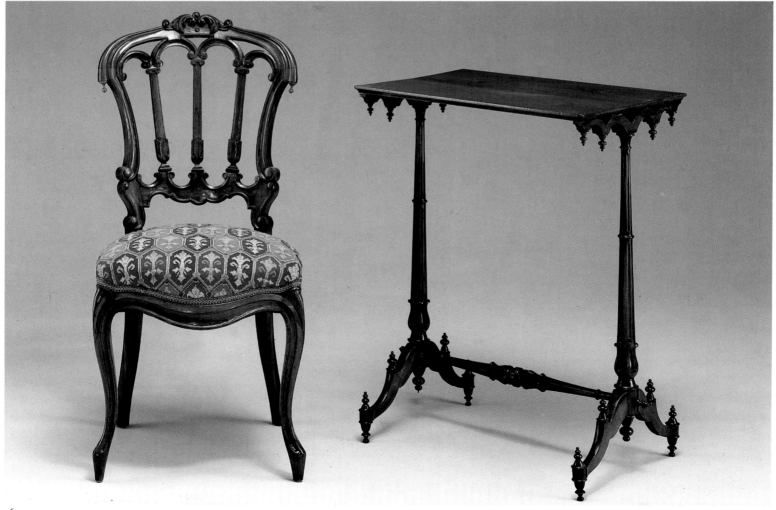

ciated with a remote, dimly perceived medieval past served the purpose. The formal order that had given the classical revival its essential character was rejected by Gothic Revival stylists in favor of picturesque arrangements of pointed arches, cusps and crockets, trefoils and quatrefoils, towers and turrets, and other features freely adapted from Gothic precedents.

In a side chair and a stand, both made of rosewood about mid-century (Fig. 265), elements of Gothic design are combined with rococo features. The chair expresses rococo mannerisms in its curving planes, C-scrolls, and cabriole legs; but pointed-leaf carving at the base of its balusters and pendents on either side of the crest rail, which is in turn ornamented with scrolls that suggest arches, call to mind Gothic motifs. The chair is still upholstered with its original red and buff needlepoint, worked in a pattern of repeated fleur-de-lis motifs. The arched apron of the stand, the leaf carving at the center of its stretcher and at the base of its channeled columnar supports, and again, pendents, represent a similar combination of the two styles.

A rosewood desk and bookcase stands out among the most important pieces of Gothic Revival furniture (Fig. 266). Probably fashioned in the 1840s, it bears a stenciled inscription indicating that it came from the prominent and highly industrious firm of J. and J. W. Meeks of New York. The pointed-arch and quatrefoil tracery of the glass doors enclose an interior of satinwood, which is used again for the drawers, pigeonholes, and compartments of the desk section. The rosewood panels of the lower case are set off by moldings with Gothic cusps.

Chairs were the most commonly produced form in the Gothic Revival style. The chair back and crest rail offered the designer excellent opportunities for showing off his vocabulary of Gothic motifs (Fig. 267). Side chairs were best for this, and many were produced to line large Victorian entrance halls and to furnish imposing Victorian libraries. A small number of easy chairs were made as well (Figs. 268 and 269), but since these consisted mainly of springs, buttons, and tufts, they provided more scope for the upholsterer than for the designer. Sofas and settees were also oc-

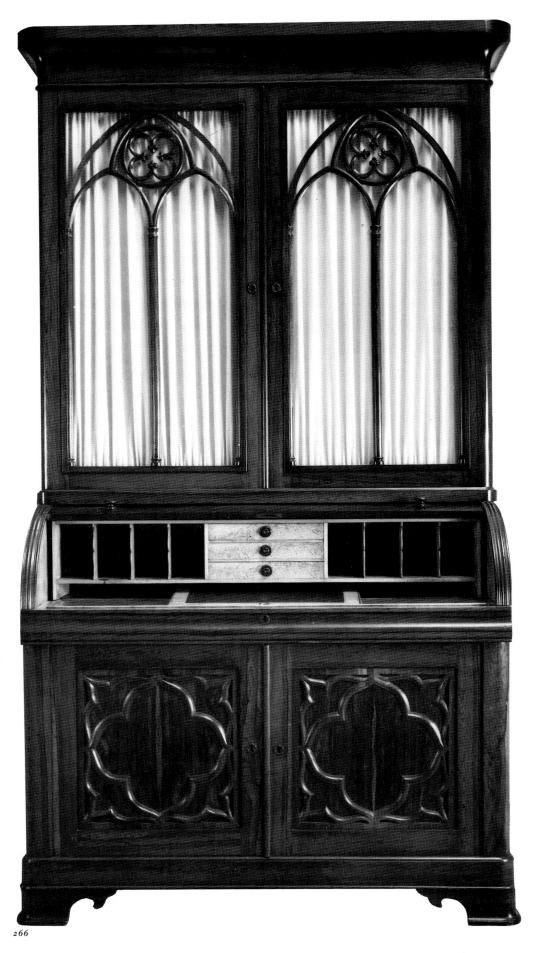

266

**Fig. 267. Side chair,** *United States, 1840–60; walnut, height 42½ inches (108 cm.). Ample chairs of this sort, made perhaps for a hallway or a dining room, lent themselves well to the addition of Gothic details. Here the back rises to a pointed arch, enclosing a cresting of Gothic tracery. The rows of arches below the upholstered oval and on the seat-rail provide further Gothic details. The spiral-twist front legs and rear stiles are often associated with a concurrent revival style, the Elizabethan.*
Gift of Mrs. Charles J. Bryan, 1965 (65.189)

**Figs. 268 and 269. Armchair,** *probably United States, about 1852; walnut, height 43⅝ inches (110.7 cm.). There were many fewer easy chairs made in the Gothic Revival style than side and hall chairs, but this example makes use of quatrefoils and pointed and rounded arches in a most engaging way. The buttoned, tufted upholstery, which made the chair literally "easy," was an innovation in the second half of the nineteenth century. This chair descended in the Delano family of Barrytown, New York, and is thought to have furnished Steen Valetje, their house built in 1852.*
Rogers Fund, 1967 (67.148)

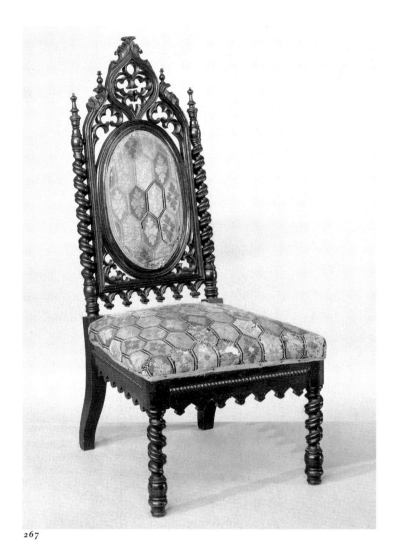

267

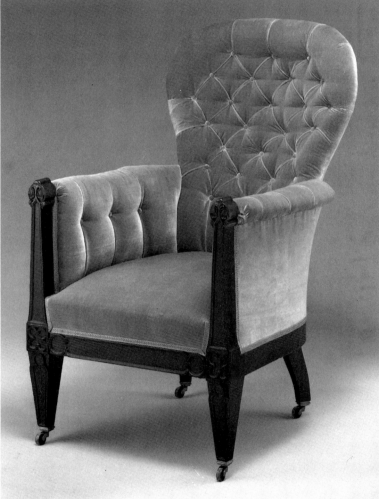

268

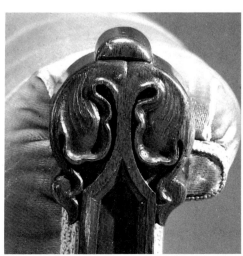

269

casionally produced in the Gothic Revival style (Fig. 271). This example, in the form of the earlier "Madame Récamier" sofa, perhaps substitutes Gothic exuberance for Grecian grace.

Tables often followed current shapes and achieved a Gothic look through ornament (Fig. 270). The impact of this example, with its boldly shaped skirt and feet, derives from both its Gothic decoration and its brilliant gilded surface.

At one point or another during these years every household form and accessory, whatever its function, was invested with some reminder of Gothic inspiration. Shelf clocks, for instance, were designed with features recalling the spires and steeples of medieval cathedrals. These relatively inexpensive timepieces were very popular in the 1840s and were manufactured in large quantities.

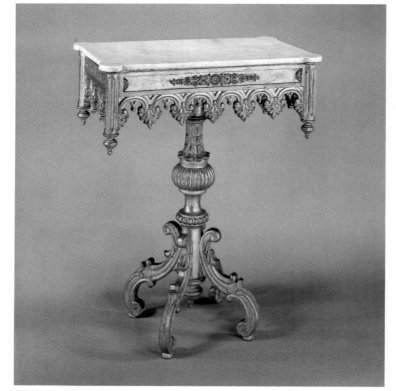

270

*Fig. 270. Table, by George Platt (1812–73), New York, about 1855; pine, gilt, marble, height 35¾ inches (90.8 cm.). One of a pair, this table originally furnished the drawing room of Benjamin C. Webster's Gothic Revival cottage in East Orange, New Jersey, designed in 1855 by Alexander Jackson Davis. Rococo and classical elements may be seen in the feet and baluster support, while the tabletop is edged with unmistakably Gothic motifs.*
Lent by I. Wistar Morris III (L.1982.99)

*Fig. 271. Couch, United States, 1851–56; oak, chestnut, cedar, length 73 inches (185.4 cm.). This couch is of the Madame Récamier type, with one end enclosed and the other open. The format allowed the designer to make spectacular use of the long straight side for creating a medley of Gothic ornament. Pierced stiles, leafy carving, and soaring clustered finials above a trefoil are among the high Gothic motifs the couch exhibits. Four chairs whose stiles, finials, and ogee rear legs are identical to those of this couch were among the original furnishings of Stanton Hall, Frederick Stanton's lavishly decorated antebellum mansion in Natchez, Mississippi.*
Friends of the American Wing Fund, 1983 (1983.148)

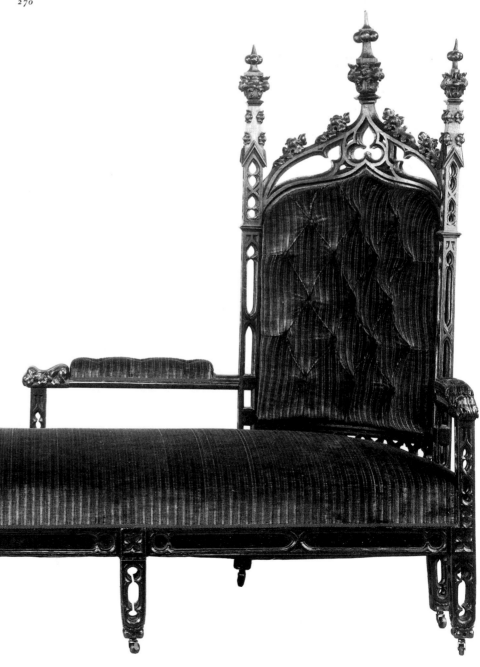

271

# The Post–Civil War Period

## Renaissance, Egyptian, and Related Revivals 1860–80

Fig. 272. **Cabinet,** by Alexander Roux (w. New York, 1837–81), New York, 1866; rosewood, tulipwood, ebonized cherry, ebonized poplar, pine, poplar, height 53⅝ inches (136.2 cm.). Large imposing pieces of this kind delighted cabinet-maker and patron alike, for their makers had plenty of scope for displaying their skill and their buyers had pieces that showed their good taste and proved their wealth. While this cabinet's form is based on that of a Renaissance credenza, its ornament is characteristically eclectic. Louis XVI, classical, and oriental motifs are used together—but in a particularly harmonious way. Alexander Roux, the maker of this luxurious piece, was a French émigré, and one of the leading New York cabinetmakers of the day.
Purchase, The Edgar J. Kaufmann Foundation Gift, 1968 (68.100.1)

During the years surrounding the Civil War the political, social, cultural, and industrial aspects of the American scene underwent enormous changes. When Charles Francis Adams, grandson of the second president of the United States and son of the sixth, returned to this country in 1868 after a ten-year sojourn abroad he felt almost as if he were visiting an alien land. Particularly in the North, the war effort had released a titanic vitality and spirit of enterprise that carried over into peacetime pursuits. Even while the war was in progress the visiting English novelist Anthony Trollope was impressed by the flourishing activity in "the ordinary pursuits of life." Men who had once talked of thousands now talked of millions of dollars in calculating their incomes. Edwin Godkin, founder and editor of the *Nation*, wrote that plenty of Americans knew how to get money, but not many knew what best to do with it.

Books and articles advised Americans in matters of taste and household economy at every level, from that of the nouveau riche to that of others still climbing the ladder to success. The advice was not always consistent, for in the postwar years even more than in the fifties, the recommended furnishings represented not so much a style as a medley of styles—identified by a miscellany of names that often had no specific meaning even for those who bestowed them. The past was continually pillaged for models to accommodate the changing fashions of the day, and the differing advice caused one reporter to conclude in 1877 that the subject of style and design was in a state of "hopeless confusion." A contemporary periodical commented that to give a name to the principles of art recognized by most

American manufacturers would be "extremely difficult, and in some cases, impossible."

As the century wore on a fashionable home might be furnished in styles variously labeled Gothic, Renaissance, Elizabethan, Jacobean, Louis XVI, Pompeiian, Moorish, or "modern"—terms that could sometimes be interchangeable according to the inspiration of the vendor, the maker, or the "authorities" in such matters. Trollope had noticed with some dismay the prevalence of French influence in American furnishing, as in American cuisine and conversation, and in the comforts and discomforts of life in general. The observant New York diarist George Templeton Strong had earlier complained of the "tyranny of custom" that obliged so many people with extra money to spend it on furnishings in the latest French taste. But in spite of his reservations, Strong himself went to Leon Marcotte for the interior decoration of his own palatial residence, as the parents of Theodore Roosevelt apparently also did.

One of the most favored labels for this furniture was "Renaissance style," a term that one critic cautioned "would seem to cover almost anything." Freely adapted design sources came from different European countries and ranged in date from the fifteenth century to the eighteenth.

Never since the Renaissance had furniture assumed such large, bulky forms. "We have been making our furniture so heavy of late," one observer reported in 1877, "that the amount of solid wood in it added to the carving, inlaying, and veneering with different woods, has made it very expensive." His remark aptly applies to a magnificent cabinet labeled by

Alexander Roux (Fig. 272). Many of the varied ornamental features of this piece—its bright ormolu moldings and mounts, painted porcelain plaques, and marquetry of contrasting woods—are improvisations on themes in the Louis XVI style, applied to a case of architectural character.

Such sophisticated cabinetwork was featured in 1876 at the Philadelphia Centennial, the largest of the international fairs yet to be held, and it marked a point at which the Renaissance Revival style was reaching its peak. According to one French witness, American (often Franco-American) craftsmen were producing furniture that compared favorably with some of the finest French work. In 1878 Marcotte exhibited an ebony cabinet at the Paris Universal exhibition that, a cataloguer of the fair stated, richly deserved the gold medal it was awarded. Such superior examples were obviously not intended for America's growing mass markets. They were made for special occasions like the fairs, or for wealthy customers. One shown at the Philadelphia Centennial was priced at $8,000—more than it cost to build a comfortable country house. A library table that is very elegant but still of more modest dimensions than the exhibition pieces may well have come from Leon Marcotte's shop, as family tradition alleges (Fig. 273). The workmanship of the piece corresponds to that described in a report of one witness who recalled that this shop "worked principally in the pure Louis XVI style and done the very best work. The style is really the best of all and will never go out of fashion, and, if not over done . . . is simply grand." Although the design is not "pure Louis XVI," and could not be mistaken as a product of that earlier pe-

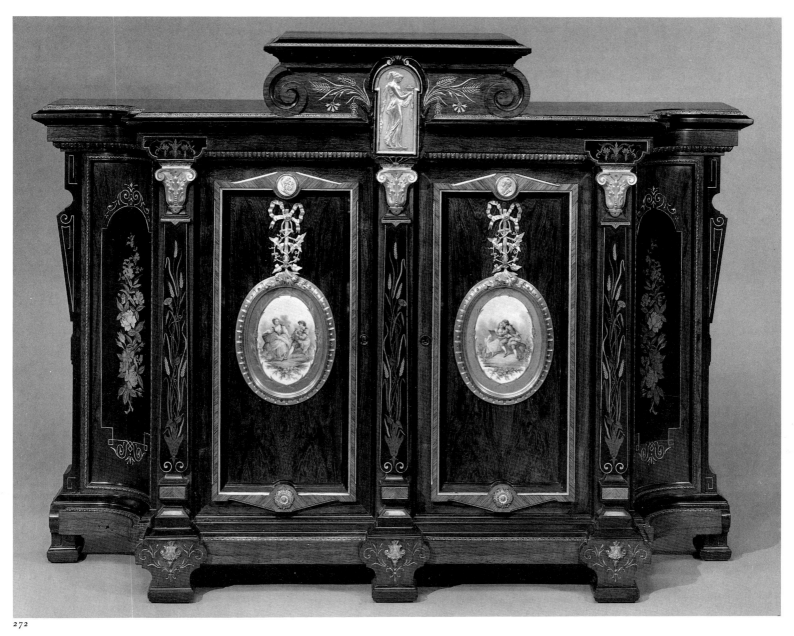

272

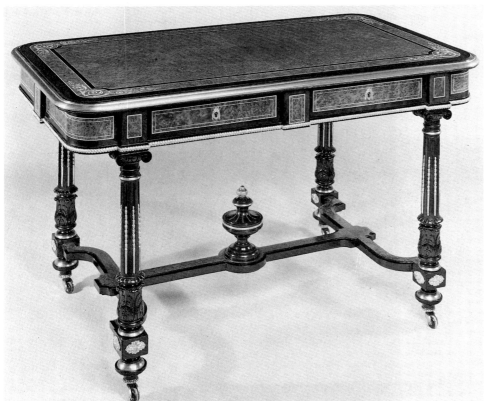

273

**Fig. 273. Library table,** *attributed to Leon Marcotte (w. New York 1848–about 1880), New York, about 1860; amboyna wood, bird's-eye maple veneer, stained hornbeam, ebonized black cherry, walnut, ash, length 49⅞ inches (126.7 cm.). More restrained than the cabinet in Fig. 272, but bolder than the Louis* XVI *style on which it was modeled, this elegant table was perhaps part of a set that included chairs, a sofa, and cabinets as well. Leon Marcotte was another of the French émigré cabinetmakers who produced most of the finest furniture in Victorian New York. This table and related pieces are in the Louis* XVI *Revival style, which had become popular in France before 1840 and was introduced to America by the French and German cabinetmakers who set up business in New York.*
Gift of Mrs. Robert W. de Forest, 1934 (34.140.1)

riod, it is nevertheless an excellent simulation of the French classical mode of the late eighteenth century. The table's most outstanding feature is its top of amboyna veneer bordered with alternating bands of stained hornbeam and amboyna outlined in ivory stringing, with ivory leaves and scrolls inlaid in the corners. This kind of decorative marquetry had been popular in France during the reign of Louis XVI and was revived in France before Marcotte came to the United States in 1840.

The romantic nostalgia that had bred and sustained the Gothic Revival went ever further afield for its satisfactions as the century progressed. No style was too bizarre or too exotic to find its place in the vocabulary of design. Whatever was remote in time or space appealed to the sensibilities of a generation that was be-

ginning to face the unsettling realities of the Industrial Revolution. The mechanization of America had been rapidly accelerated during the years surrounding the Civil War and had brought those realities into sharper focus. "It was no accident," wrote Lewis Mumford, "that caused romanticism and industrialization to appear at the same time. They were rather the two faces of the new civilization, one looking towards the past, and the other towards the future; one glorifying the new, the other clinging to the old; industrialization intent on increasing the physical means of subsistence, romanticism living in a sickly fashion on the hollow glamour of the past."

Among nostalgic and exotic references Egyptian motifs played a persistent role, in architecture as well as in

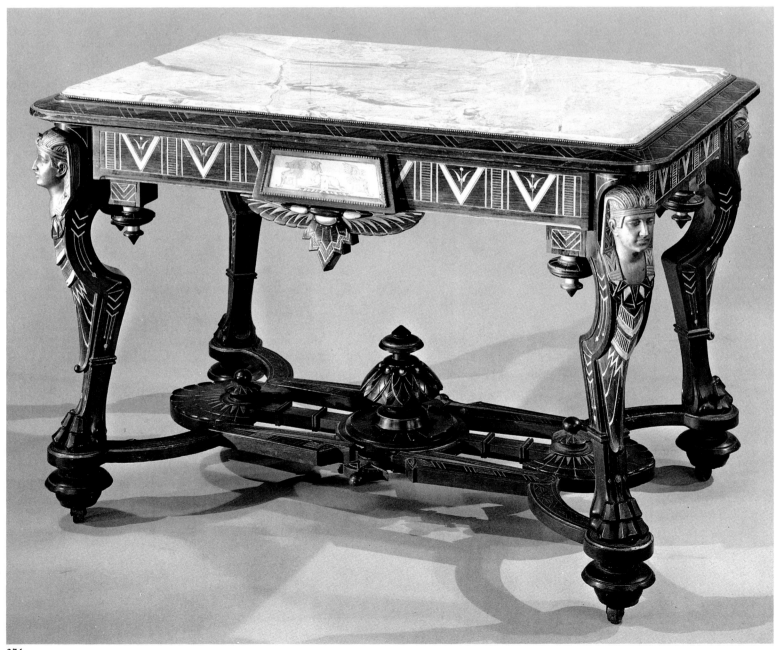

274

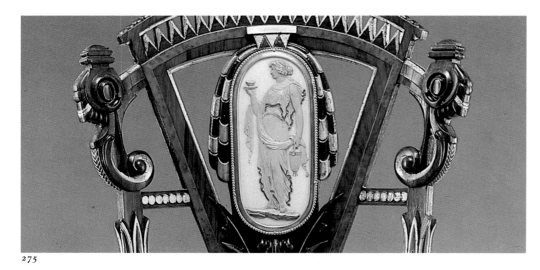

275

furnishings. In 1831 an impressive gate in the Egyptian manner was raised at the entrance to the famous Mount Auburn Cemetery at Cambridge, Massachusetts—to be followed by numerous analogous constructions at other graveyards across the country. Towns along the Mississippi River, "the American Nile" as it was sometimes called, were given names like Cairo, Karnak, Thebes, and Memphis.

In 1852 the first major collection of Egyptian art and artifacts was brought to New York. And about that same time a series of systematic excavations was undertaken in Egypt. Verdi's *Aida*, commissioned to celebrate the opening of the Suez Canal in 1869, was first performed in New York three years later. In 1881, the obelisk commonly known as Cleopatra's Needle was erected in New York's Central Park. The combination of these events encouraged a revival of interest in Egyptian decoration during the 1860s and 1870s. A rosewood table with a variegated marble top, probably made in New York about then, displays carved and gilded sphinx heads at the tops of its four corner supports (Fig. 274). Carved animal paws, a hawklike winged ornament on the apron, and palmette and lotus designs are additional Egyptian Revival details that are superimposed upon this otherwise Renaissance Revival form. It is one of the most impressive examples of this exotic type of furniture in the Museum's collection, which is rich in Egyptian Revival material.

Egyptian motifs also dominate a low side chair (Fig. 277) whose basic form is Renaissance Revival, but whose stylized wings, animal paws, sphinx heads, and geometric motifs were unmistakably inspired by Egyptian design; they are

combined to produce an arresting and exotic object. Equally eye-catching is a side chair also attributed to the high-style firm of Pottier and Stymus (Figs. 275 and 276). It is of laminated and inlaid wood with an enameled porcelain plaque containing a low-relief Greek maiden centered in the back.

The delicate low-relief classical ornament inspired by the Louis XVI period is seen again in an ebonized armchair with ormolu and gilt ornament (Fig. 278) and in a slipper chair that was possibly made by Herter Brothers, like Pottier and Stymus one of Marcotte's competitors and an outstanding New York firm (Fig. 279). While the ultimate inspiration for this chair was eighteenth-century France, its immediate inspiration was the furniture made for Eugénie and Louis Napoleon during France's Second Empire. Light woods and classical designs delicately applied were hallmarks of the style, which was introduced to wealthy Americans by firms such as Herter Brothers that had close connections with European furniture makers. A chair that makes more lavish use of inlay is the ebonized-maple side chair with delicate mother-of-pearl designs (Fig. 280).

By the 1870s the day of the professional interior decorator, designer, and supplier had dawned. "We generally get a house from the mason, that is when the mason work has been finished, and have charge of the entire woodwork decoration," wrote a representative of one firm that specialized in such commissions. ". . . Sometimes we get *carte blanche* for everything—style, design, quality and price." He spoke for Pottier and Stymus, examples of whose output may be seen again in two walnut chairs made for exhibition at the Centennial

celebration (Fig. 282). Pottier described the chairs as "in the style of Henry II," who reigned over France in the sixteenth century; their only readily apparent connection to Henry, however, is the use of his cipher and that of his mistress, Diane de Poitiers, in the designs of the tapestry upholstery. For the rest, they provide another example of the nineteenth-century inventions that were arbitrarily labeled Renaissance.

The eclectic character of the period can be seen in a number of other forms. The design of a particularly handsome stool (Fig. 281) made and labeled by the versatile Alexander Roux about 1865 is of a style termed by one contemporary "neo grec." It recalls the ancient curule seating forms that had influenced Duncan Phyfe earlier in the century. Here, however, hocked animal legs with waterleaf carvings terminate in gilded hooves. On either side of the piece is a pointed arch filled with turned-spindle ribs, shapes that resemble highly stylized palmettes. Polychrome decoration and the original tufted brocade upholstery give added distinction to this unusual and exotic example of stylish furniture.

**Figs. 275–82. Chairs.** *Along with a continuing fascination with revival styles, Americans of the last third of the nineteenth century felt an increasing interest in the exotic. This gallery of chairs, of the Renaissance, Louis XVI, and Egyptian Revival styles, as well as the Neo-Grec, were all very fashionable and were made more or less concurrently. Materials and decorative techniques vary widely and this, too, is characteristic of the age.*

**Figs. 275 and 276.** *Side chair, attributed to Pottier and Stymus (established 1859), New York, about 1875; detail (Fig. 275) on p. 179; laminated woods, including walnut and mahogany, enameled porcelain medallion, height 37⅛ inches (94.3 cm.).*
Purchase, Charlotte Pickman-Gertz Gift, 1983 (1983.68)

**Fig. 277.** *Side chair, attributed to Pottier and Stymus (established 1859), New York, 1870–75; rosewood, prickly juniper veneer, ash, height 28⅛ inches (71.4 cm.).*
Funds from various donors, 1970 (1970.35.2)

**Fig. 278.** *Armchair, attributed to Leon Marcotte (w. New York 1848– about 1880), New York, about 1860; ebonized maple and fruitwood, ormolu, height 39 inches (99.1 cm.).*
Gift of Mrs. D. Chester Noyes, 1968 (68.69.2)

**Fig. 279.** *Slipper chair, attributed to Herter Brothers (mid-1860s–1882), New York, about 1865; maple, rosewood, height 30¼ inches (76.8 cm.).*
Gift of James Graham and Sons, 1965 (65.186)

**Fig. 280.** *Side chair, attributed to Leon Marcotte (w. New York 1848– about 1880), New York, 1865–70; ebonized maple, brass, mother-of-pearl, height 35¾ inches (90.8 cm.).*
Gift of Ronald S. Kane, 1968 (68.198.2)

**Fig. 281.** *Stool, by Alexander Roux (w. New York 1837–81), New York, about 1865; painted beech, height 23¾ inches (60.3 cm.).*
Purchase, The Edgar J. Kaufmann Foundation Gift, 1969 (69.108)

**Fig. 282.** *Armchair, by Pottier and Stymus (established 1859), New York, about 1875; black walnut, height 51¾ inches (131.5 cm.).*
Gift of Auguste Pottier, 1888 (88.10.3)

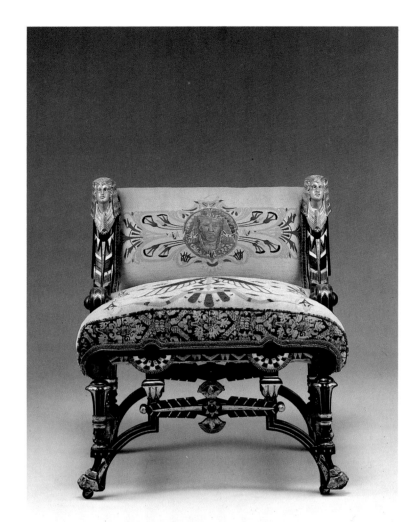

277

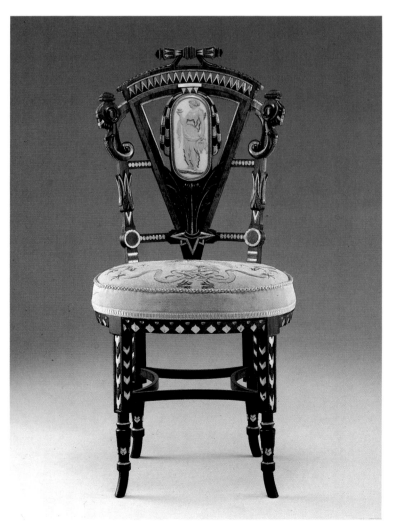

276

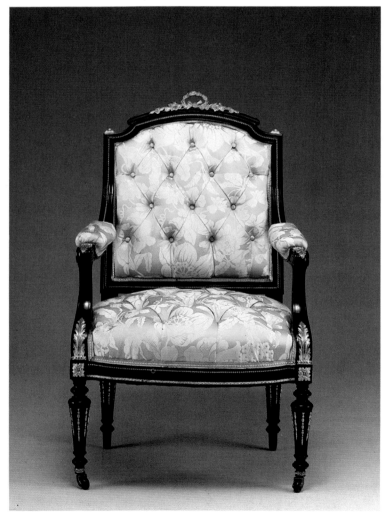

278

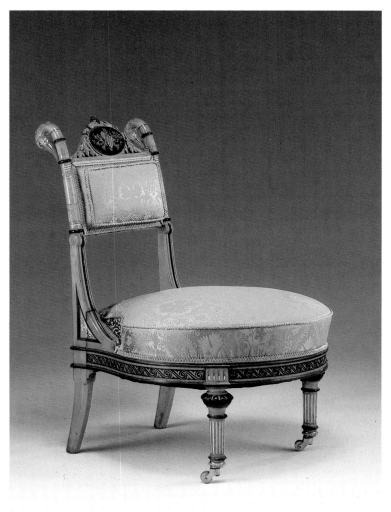

279

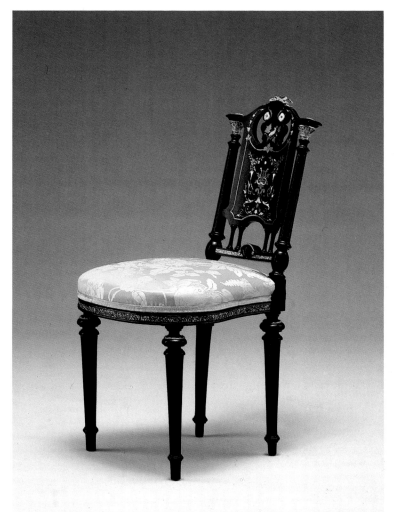

280

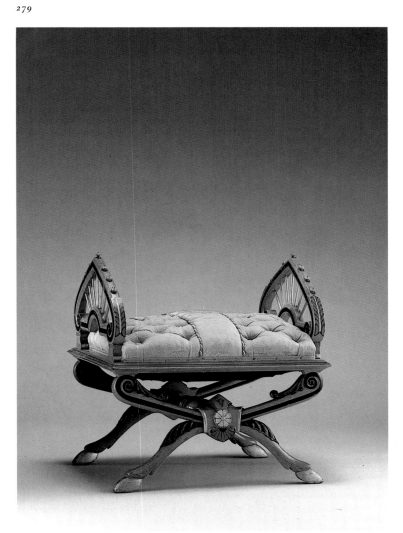

281

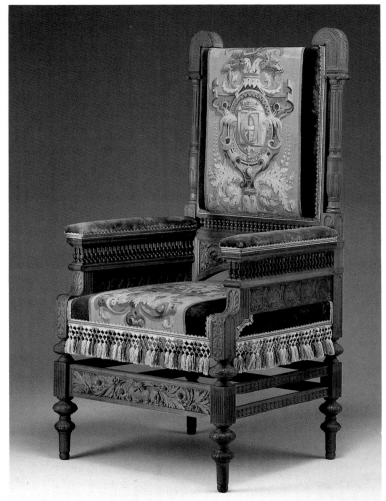

282

# Innovative Furniture

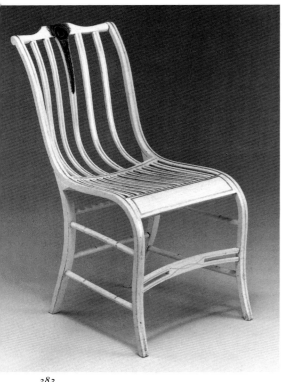

283

***Fig. 283. Side chair,*** *attributed to Samuel Gragg (1772–probably 1855), Boston, about 1810; painted bentwood, height 33⅞ inches (86 cm.). The dramatic curves of this chair were achieved by steaming and bending—the same technique used by Belter and Thonet many years later. Gragg advertised as a maker of "all kinds of Fancy and Bamboo* CHAIRS, *of the newest fashion, . . ." and seems to have been the only member of his generation to employ the innovative technique of bending wood. The result, a klismos-style chair whose rear stiles flow into the seat-rails and thence into the front legs, is both dramatic and graceful. It is also fragile, and few have survived.*
Friends of the American Wing Fund, 1980 (1980.496)

Throughout the nineteenth century a variety of furniture was made in America that had little or no reference to the prevailing formal styles of the period. As early as the first decade of the century one Samuel Gragg of Boston patented a uniquely conceived chair (Fig. 283) whose seat and legs were single pieces of wood bent into graceful shapes, forecasting the bentwood furniture that became vastly popular later in the century.

What may well be a unique piece, probably intended for use as a barber's chair, combines a variety of disparate elements (Figs. 284–86). Most prominently, the right arm broadens out into a writing surface similar to those occasionally found on Windsors. In this case the surface displays an inlaid design of a mariner's compass, indicating that it may have served on shipboard. As an added convenience a drawer is fitted beneath the seat, also a feature of some Windsors. The painted crest rail resembles those that were commonly used on the so-called Boston rockers that evolved in New England in the 1820s and remained popular for years to come. The chair's raking front legs are connected by a carved and gilded stretcher.

It was an inventive age, and some furniture makers, with typical American aptitude for mechanical improvisation, took advantage of newly developed techniques and newly available materials to create unprecedented forms that added diversity and fresh interest to the decorative arts of their time.

Cast iron was an inexpensive and durable material for all kinds of utilitarian objects. Always less expensive than wrought iron because it was made in molds rather than hammered by hand,

cast iron had been used in the eighteenth century for such small necessary objects as pots, andirons, firebacks, and stove plates, and it was a natural material from which to manufacture stoves as increasingly efficient models were developed during the late eighteenth and early nineteenth centuries. As the nineteenth century progressed the material began to be used for a wider variety of forms. A small, useful cast-iron object that combines classical and rococo motifs is the music rack of 1835–50—the only known example of this form (Fig. 287).

Advances in iron founding and milling techniques in the middle decades of the nineteenth century made it possible to fashion an increasing variety of forms in designs that followed any and all of the prevailing styles. Chairs, settees, urns, and many other elaborately patterned forms were made in cast iron for use in the garden. The Museum's collection of such pieces contains representative designs in the eclectic styles that succeeded one another and intermixed from the 1840s to the end of the century.

The use of metal in the fabrication of chairs led designers in diverse experimental directions. The point is illustrated by an unusual patented side chair intricately put together of cast- and wrought-iron and wood with an upholstered seat (Fig. 288). This ingenious construction, a so-called centripetal chair, was produced by the American Chair Company of Troy, New York, manufacturer of reclining seats for railroad passenger cars. The crown-shaped wrought-iron base acts as a spring that permits the occupant to recline or sit up as he chooses. The iron frame of the back is "japanned" (covered with a

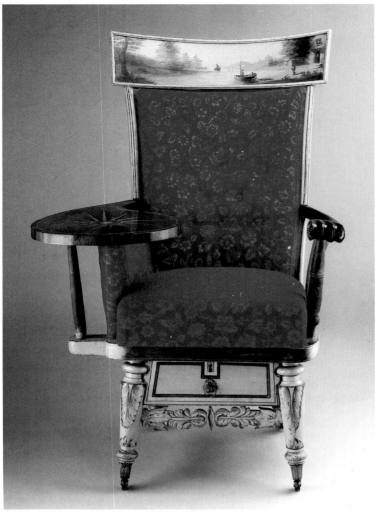

284

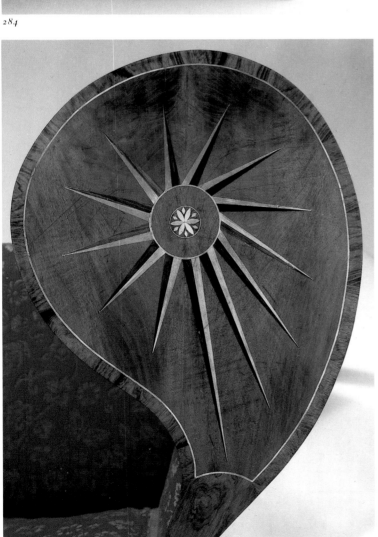

285

**Figs. 284–86. Writing/barber chair,** *Boston, 1820–25; mahogany, inlay, and painted decoration, height 42 inches (106.7 cm.). Multipurpose furniture has always intrigued buyers, and this chair is an odd mixture of writing-arm Windsor and barber chair. The curved, painted crest rail is removable, and there is an insert with a curving headpiece that could be used when the sitter needed a shave. The mixture of decorative techniques is odd, too: fancy-chair painted ornament is joined, on the writing arm, with mahogany and light-wood inlay in the shape of a compass. The back and seat are upholstered in a cut-velvet fabric that is a close facsimile of the original, over the original coil springs, a highly unusual feature on a chair of this early date.* Sansbury-Mills Fund, 1976 (1976.50)

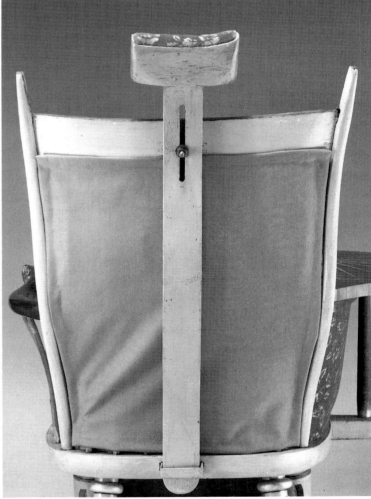

286

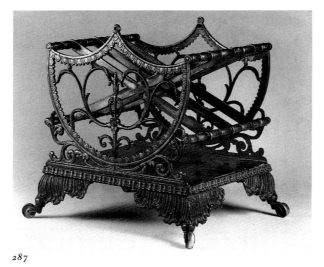

287

**Fig. 287. Music rack or canterbury,** by Gasper Godone (w. 1830–70), New York, 1835–50; tulip poplar and cast iron, height 18½ inches (47 cm). Though this is a very unusual form—at present it is the only known American cast-iron music rack—it belongs to a group of objects of varied uses that manufacturers introduced in cast iron during this period. It combines the earlier classical style—in its basic symmetry and shield-shaped sides—with the oncoming rococo style—in the scrolling leaves that fill and support the shield and in the leafy brackets that connect the stand to its casters. It is marked "GODONE'S STANDS N.Y." and is thought to have been manufactured as well as sold by this piano and musical instrument maker.
Purchase, Wunsch Foundation Inc. Gift, 1966 (66.100)

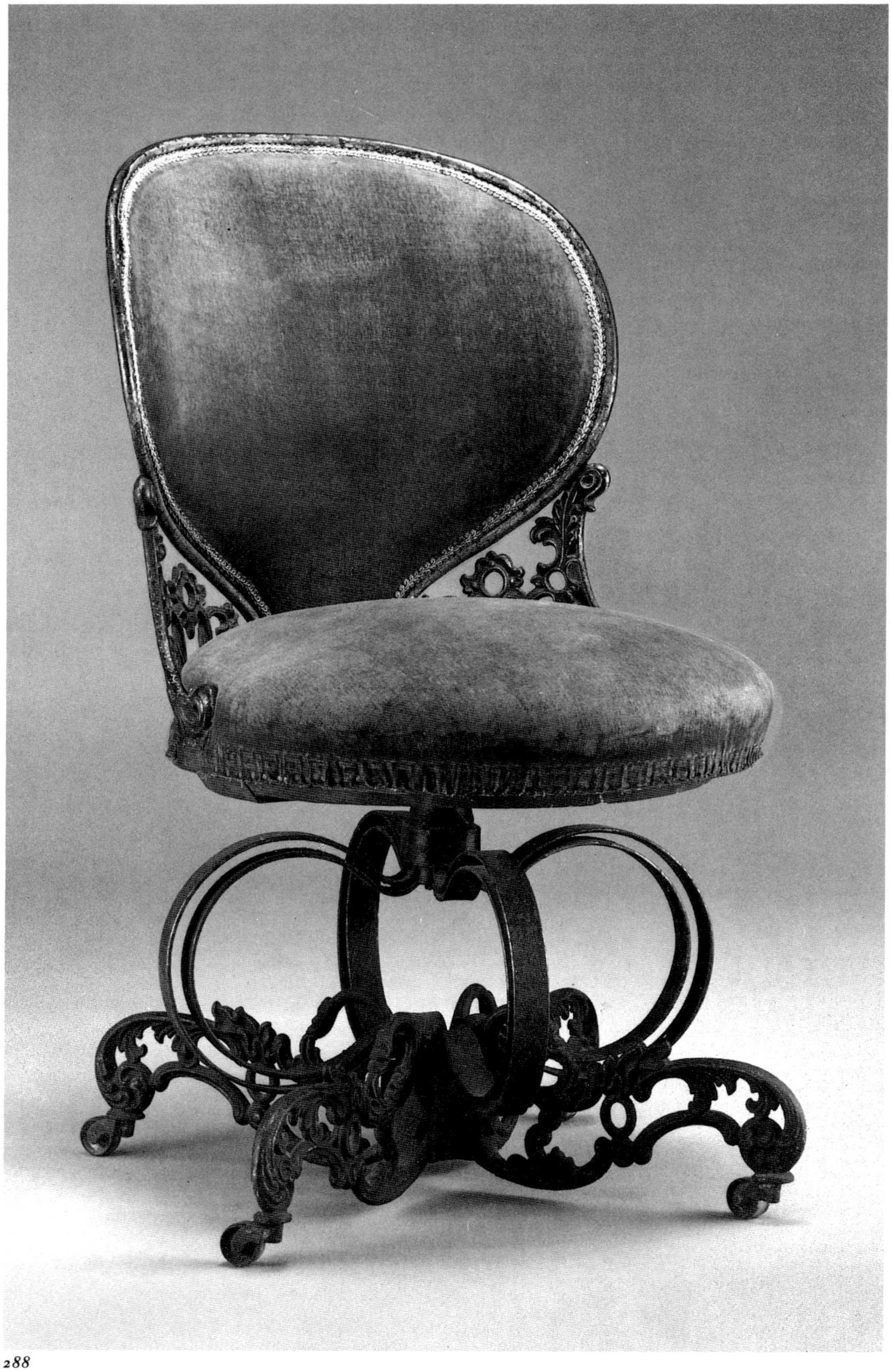

**Fig. 288. Centripetal spring chair,** by the American Chair Company, Troy, New York, about 1849; cast iron, wood, upholstery, height 31⅛ inches (79.1 cm). Innovation is apparent in all aspects of this exuberant chair. Its cast-iron base was new, as were its wrought-iron springs. It swiveled and turned in the manner of a modern desk chair, impelling one reporter, writing about a similar chair that was exhibited at the London Crystal Palace exhibition of 1851, to observe that: "The freedom with which the chair may be turned on its center, renders it very convenient to a person who may want to turn to his library-shelf or side table, as he can do so without leaving his seat."
Gift of Elinor Merrell, 1977 (1977.255)

hard, brilliant varnish) with polychrome decoration surrounded by gilt scrolls. Several variations of this remarkable contrivance were represented at the London Crystal Palace exhibition of 1851.

Folding furniture of one kind or another was in use from ancient times. Earlier in this book it was noted that from the first days of settlement American colonists had resorted to such space-saving features, as indeed we continue to do today. In the meantime, the nineteenth century provided fresh opportunities for mechanical inventions along these lines. In 1876 the Marks Adjustable Folding Chair Company of New York patented a reclining armchair with a strap-metal frame and folding foot piece (Fig. 289). This seat, which might aptly be called a chaise longue, has an arched, paneled, and incised top rail crowning the adjustable back—a decorative touch reflecting the Renaissance Revival style of the period.

New wire-making machines provided elements for the twisted-wire garden furniture that was another popular novelty in the years following the Civil War

288

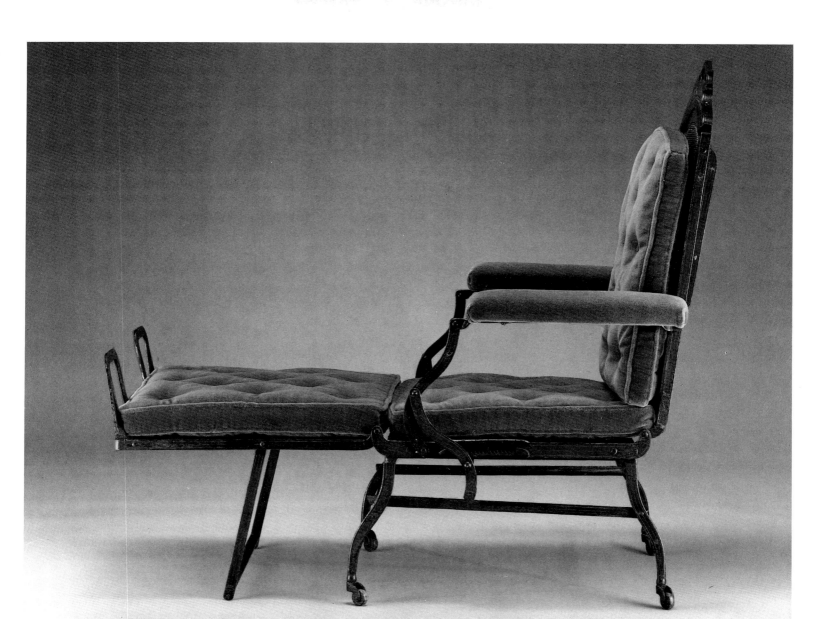

289

**Fig. 289. Armchair,** by the Marks Adjustable
Folding Chair Company (1877–97), about
1876; walnut, metal, cane, height 45¾ inches
(116.2 cm.). Folding stools and chairs were
known to the Egyptians, the Greeks, and the Romans. Later civilizations occasionally employed
the form but, in the last quarter of the nineteenth
century, the adjustable folding chair reappeared
in a dramatically increased number of versions.
This one, with adjustable arms and a folding foot-
rest, is constructed of lightweight materials and
mounted on casters so that it can be moved easily
from place to place. Its maker listed a number of
uses for the chair, including that of supporting
an invalid—for which it seems especially well
suited.
Sage Fund, 1975 (1975.157)

**Fig. 290. Settee,** United States, about 1870;
wire and solid metal rod, height 38 inches (96.5
cm.). This twisted-wire garden seat, which retains
its original blue-green finish, belongs to an innovative group made possible by the invention of
wire-making machines. The malleability of wire
invited designers to indulge in extravagantly curvaceous designs. Like cast-iron furniture, these
whimsical wire seats were eminently practical for
the garden, but they were also fairly fragile and
relatively few have survived.
Sansbury-Mills Fund, 1982 (1982.122)

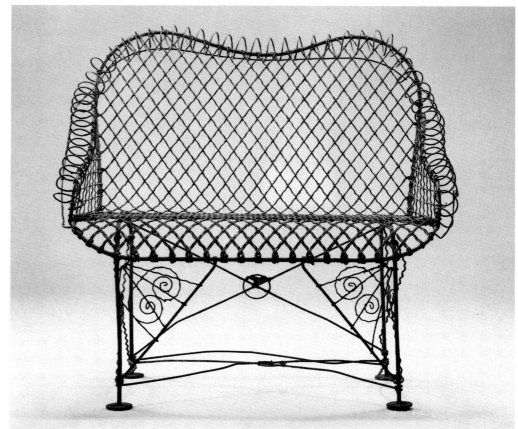

290

**Fig. 291. Armchair,** by George Hunzinger (1835–98), New York, about 1876; maple, fabric-covered steel mesh, height 34 inches (86.4 cm.). About mid-century, Hunzinger came to New York from Germany, where his family had been furniture makers for centuries. He was fascinated with furniture that actually had moving parts, or seemed to, and he patented many innovations, including that of using woven-steel bands instead of conventional upholstery. The bands of this chair are covered with blue fabric and the wooden frame is composed of elements that look like parts of machines—a Hunzinger trademark. Another innovation is that of cantilevering the seat from the back legs—a technique that became important in twentieth-century chair construction.
Sansbury-Mills Fund, 1982 (1982.69)

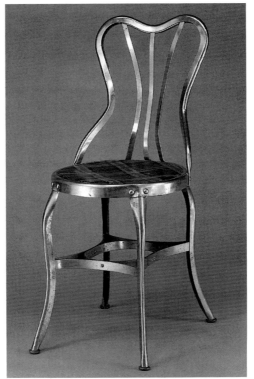

292

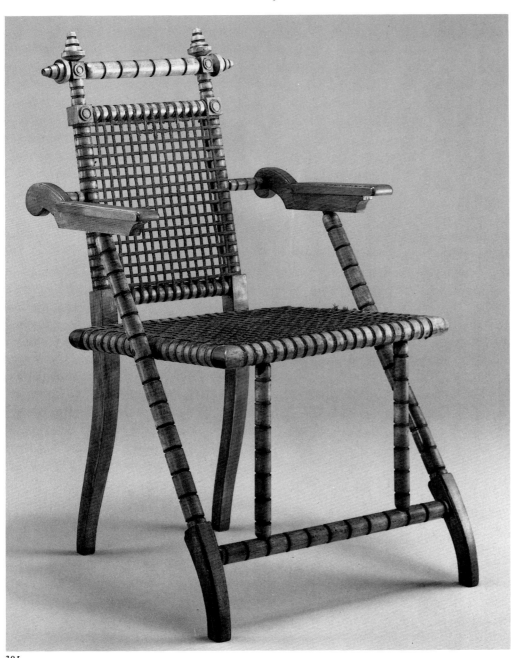

291

**Fig. 292. Side chair,** Toledo Metal Furniture Company, 1900–15; chrome on steel, Leatherette, height 34½ inches (87.6 cm.). This handsome metal version of the graceful, lightweight bentwood chair introduced by Michael Thonet retains its paper label and original Leatherette seat. The steel strips of which it was made were produced by machine, and the chair was thus inexpensive enough for ice-cream parlors across the land to use—thus its nickname "ice-cream parlor chair."
Gift of Jonathan Holstein and Gail van der Hoof, 1979 (1979.189)

(Fig. 290). The fanciful designs of these pieces recall those of Rococo Revival objects; the use of wire foreshadows that of designers like Harry Bertoia, whose welded-wire "diamond chairs" became popular after World War II.

Another innovative metal form was the "ice-cream" chair, so called because its portability and inexpensiveness made it practical for use in luncheonettes and ice-cream parlors everywhere. Some were made of wire and others, like this one, were made of wider metal strips curved like Thonet's bentwood (Fig. 292).

In the 1860s George Hunzinger of New York, one of the many German furniture makers who emigrated to America in the middle years of the century, patented an assortment of chairs, some of which could be folded up (Fig. 291) and some that only appeared to be collapsible. All were inventive in their unusual and complicated designs, which suggested the cogs, wheels, and shafts of a machine that might be set in motion at a moment's notice. The example here illustrated is made of walnut and carries the label "Hunzinger/N.Y./ Pat. March 30/1869." It bears an unmistakable imprint of the machine age, and at the same time of a highly individualistic designer.

Intricately structured furnishings made of rattan and wicker had been imported from the Orient from the first days of America's trade with China. Even earlier, examples had found their way to this country: it is said that a wicker cradle was among the limited cargo of household gear in the *Mayflower*; and an inventory from the Adam Thoroughgood house, the oldest surviving house in Virginia, lists "one wicker chair for a child." "Wicker" is a

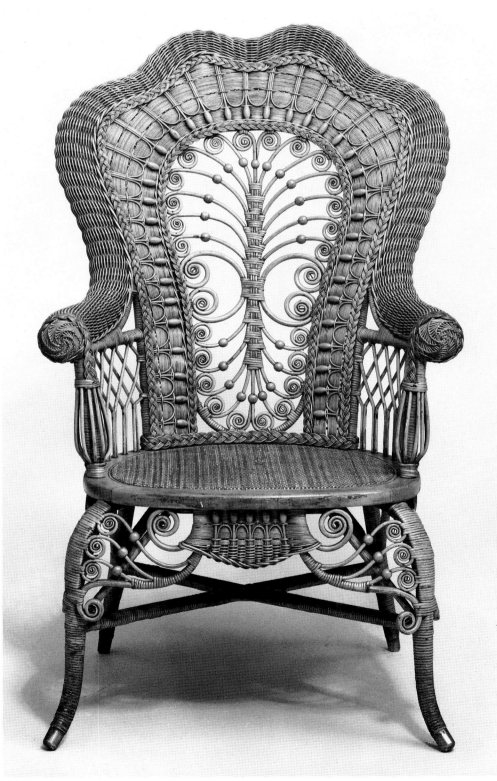

293

catchall term applied to furniture and furnishings woven from fibrous material grown principally in the Far East. In the second half of the last century it became both a popular and a fashionable vogue in America, and domesticated adaptations of what had originally been an exotic import were produced here in large numbers. Even the very wealthy and socially preeminent Mrs. Potter Palmer of Chicago placed wicker furniture among the Renoirs, Monets, and other avant-garde paintings that the artist Mary Cassatt had advised her to acquire.

The light, open forms that were manufactured—everything from rocking chairs to plant stands, from whatnots to sewing baskets—were flexible and all but indestructible. In 1886 it was reported that such types of furnishings were "indispensable in modern apartments." A generation later it was claimed that they made "housekeeping possible when a maid is impossible." An armchair made by Heywood Brothers and Wakefield, a firm that dominated the trade in the years after 1897, typifies the finest wickerwork that was produced during the height of fashion (Fig. 293)—a fashion whose popularity endures to this day in modern reproductions of all kinds.

# Reform Styles, 1875–1915

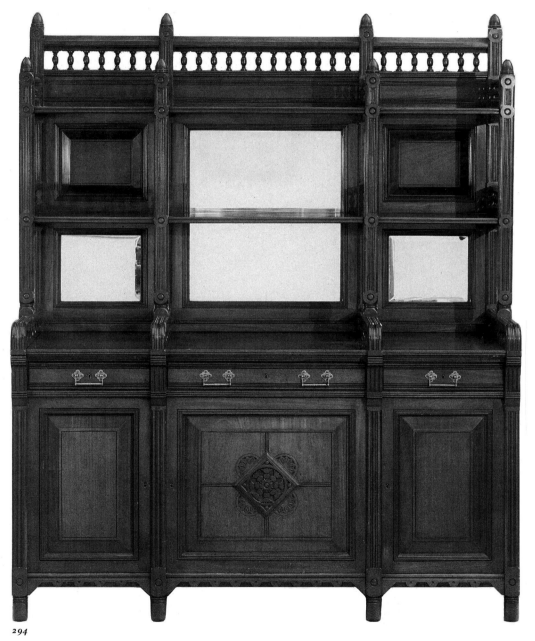

294

**Fig. 294. Sideboard,** *New York, 1877–80; mahogany with beveled-glass inset mirrors, height 81½ inches (207 cm.). Part of a dining-room set that includes a table and chairs as well, this sideboard embodies the rectangular form; simple incised, turned, and low-relief carved decoration; and straightforward "honest" construction that are marks of the style advocated by Charles Locke Eastlake. The care with which this set is con-* *structed suggests that it is from a leading New York cabinetmaker's shop.*
Gift of Richard T. Button, 1970 (1970.290.1)

The reforming Aesthetic and Arts and Crafts movements were essentially English transplants, having taken root in America about the time of the Centennial exhibition and flourishing for a little less than half a century, developing national strains of a distinctive order. That period included the years of extravagant fashions and social pretences that Mark Twain and Charles Dudley Warner aptly labeled "the Gilded Age" in their novel of that title. The Arts and Crafts movement stood for values exactly opposite to those that produced the aping of European fashionableness found in the grand chateaus that lined Fifth Avenue in New York and that overlaid the natural landscape of Newport and other summer resorts. In those wealthy enclaves were approximations of princely dwellings of the past filled with imported luxuries or costly imitations of them.

Such indulgences were made possible by profits from this country's highly industrialized economy, which depended upon increasing mechanization for its capital. The leaders of the Arts and Crafts movement turned their backs on all this, choosing to revert to basic principles of design and construction that produced objects of soundness, honesty, and simplicity.

The principles that underlay these new design ideas developed before the middle of the century in a revolt against what some critics considered the growing and dehumanizing mechanization of life that accompanied the Industrial Revolution. England had been faced with such problems long before they became apparent in the United States, and earnest English reformers like John Ruskin, William Morris, and A. W. N. Pugin recited the menace to human val-

Fig. 295. **Cabinet,** by Charles Tisch (w. New York before 1870–1890), New York, 1884; rosewood, with ivory, mother-of-pearl, and brass inlays, height 82¾ inches (210.2 cm.). Marquetry and border inlays, low-relief carving, turned spindles, and latticework are applied in eclectic patterns that reinforce the rectilinear character of this piece. Curio cabinets were very popular in Victorian times for displaying objects of all kinds. Taste maker Clarence Cook, author of The House Beautiful (1878), wrote of a cabinet like this: "The object of the irregular arrangement is first, I think, to avoid monotony, but it finds a better excuse in the accommodation it gives to articles of different sizes and shapes. Here are places for little things and places for larger things, and each is at home in its own compartment. . . ."
Gift of Charles Tisch, 1889 (69.245)

ues when the machine took command from the traditional individual artisan. A reversion to the handicrafts for producing those things that are intimate accompaniments of daily life, they asserted, would restore sanity and satisfaction to the domestic scene.

However it was accomplished, such work was to be guided by sound, honest principles of construction and with "sincerity." This suggestion that good design has a moral as well as a utilitarian purpose sounds a bit odd to modern ears, but it was repeated again and again through the second half of the nineteenth century. The apostle of that way of thinking whose message reached the largest American audience was the Englishman Charles Locke Eastlake. His book, *Hints on Household Taste in Furniture, Upholstery, and Other Details,* ran through eight editions in this country from 1872 to 1890. He was in fact more widely read here than in England. For large numbers of Americans he was the prophet of a new "Kingdom of the Tasteful," and his name was uttered with reverence. Although Eastlake designed some furniture, he was more concerned with the elemental importance of "constructive principles" and "sincerity" of purpose than with external forms or styles (Fig. 294). He emphasized the importance of simplicity and usefulness, which made it possible for manufacturers to travesty his ideas in shoddy and inexpensive merchandise that they freely labeled "Eastlake" to capitalize on the magic of his name. In the hands of conscientious craftsmen, however, his doctrines were interpreted in good faith and with consummate artisanry.

In 1884 Charles Tisch, a New York cabinetmaker about whom little is as yet

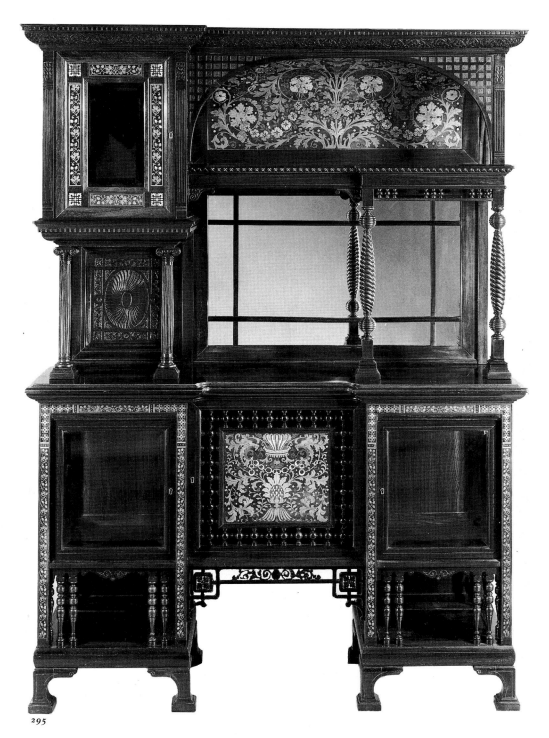

295

known, executed a construction that was elaborate but that still exemplified the principles of Eastlake; he proudly gave the piece to the Museum several years later (Fig. 295). This massive cabinet is distinguished by turned balusters and spindles, marquetry panels and trim, and shallow surface carving. It is further embellished by a mirrored panel and fretwork of vaguely oriental character. In his book *The House Beautiful,* Clarence Cook, one of the foremost critics of the day, wrote that such cabinets were designed for "the preservation of all the curiosities and pretty things gathered in the family walks and travel." The nation was experiencing an "artistic craze," as it was called at the time, and the quest was on for domestic trappings that were in "good taste" and "artistic."

Such master craftsmen as New York's Herter Brothers also applied Eastlake's ideas with sensitivity and skill. Their products were never mass produced, and they were expensive. Between about 1877 and 1882 Herter Brothers provided a desk (Fig. 296) for the financier and railroad magnate Jay Gould—a man who could easily afford the best. Eastlake's tenets are carried out in the relatively simple rectilinear forms of this and matching pieces: curved lines and deep carving are all but eliminated. The flat, ebonized cherry surfaces are inlaid with a colorful pattern of floral and leaf designs that reflect the pervasive influence of Japanese art. Even the drawer pulls and other hardware were carefully integrated into this allover pattern. Besides the marquetry, the desk's ornamental features consist of thin incised lines, low-profile moldings, and turned supports, all character-

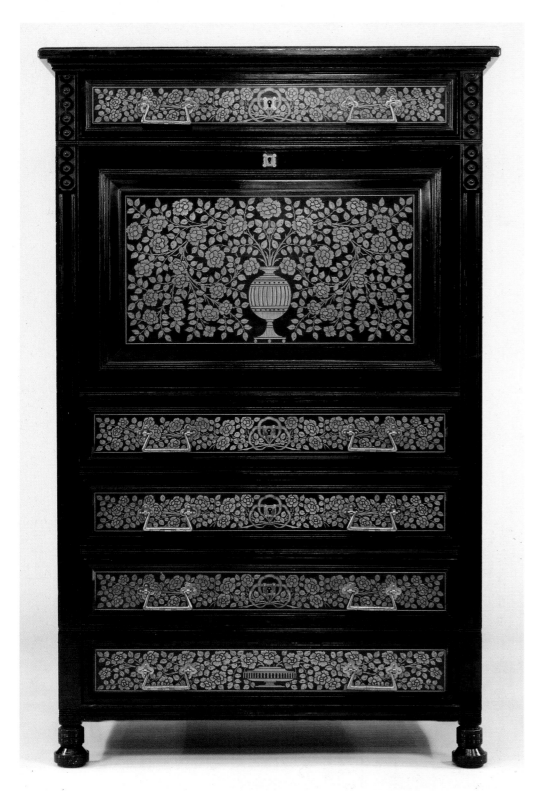

296

stars inlay on the ends and top of the table to create a stunning centerpiece for the library.
Sage Fund, 1972 (1972.47)

**Fig. 298. Library table,** detail, Fig. 297. *Mother-of-pearl stars inlaid in irregular patterns gleam from the dark, velvety tabletop, recalling in a most luxurious way the experience of gazing at the sky on a starry night.*

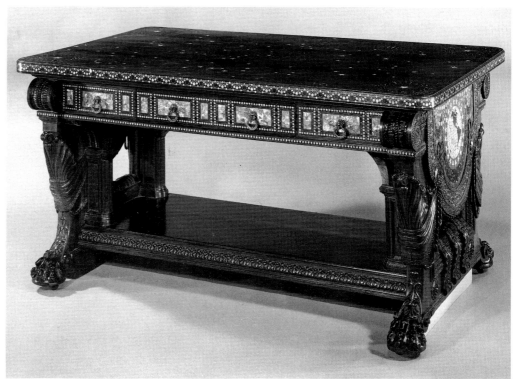

297

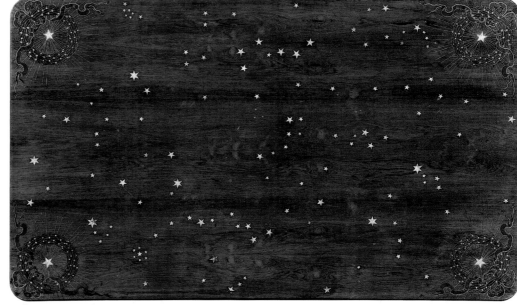

298

istic of the Eastlake style as it was interpreted in this country.

Christian Herter became the leading member of the firm after he bought out his elder half brother in 1870. Although born in Germany, he had been trained in Paris at the Ecole des Beaux-Arts and was well instructed in the arts of design and decoration. He had a versatile and wide-ranging talent, and under his direction the firm became one of the foremost decorating establishments in the United States. He was the interior designer for William H. Vanderbilt's great mansion on Fifth Avenue—a building that, incidentally, owed little to Eastlake principles in most of its very elaborate appointments.

Like most other prominent firms of the time, Herter's worked in a variety of styles. For the library of the Vanderbilt house they fashioned a huge table of rosewood, lavishly and handsomely carved, and inlaid with gleaming mother-of-pearl and brass, all in the eclectic Beaux-Arts style of the day (Figs. 297 and 298). Freely interpreted classical volutes and palmettes are whimsically combined with such inlaid ornaments as globes surrounded by stars and other decorative motifs. In its highly stylish way the table is a superb example of American craftsmanship. Such formal embellishments were set aside, however, in the Japanese parlor, which was done in a lacework of bamboo with enormous jeweled dragonflies, motionless among innumerable reeds, "as if the tropical summer were too warm to let them stir."

Another facet of Herter's virtuosity is revealed in an exceptionally graceful side chair (Fig. 299), which he probably made about 1880 and whose simple but

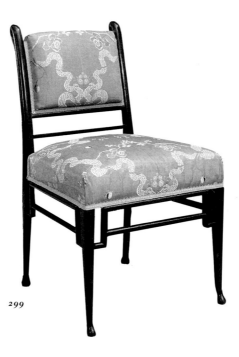

299

**Fig. 299. Side chair,** *attributed to Herter Brothers (mid-1860s–1882), New York, about 1880; rosewood, height 31½ inches (80 cm.). During the second half of the nineteenth century, the interest in simplicity of form and ornament led naturally to a fascination with seemingly simple oriental objects that Westerners saw at international exhibitions. Such a piece as this graceful side chair falls into the "Anglo-Japanese" category that is associated with the English designer W. E. Godwin. The beautiful lines and proportions of this chair rival those of the best of Godwin's production.*
Purchase, The Sylmaris Collection, Gift of George Coe Graves, by exchange, 1975 (1975.277)

**Fig. 300. Dressing table,** *possibly New York, about 1885; maple, bird's-eye maple, height 59½ inches (151.1 cm.). Like the Anglo-Japanese chair (Fig. 299), this dressing table makes specific reference to oriental design and materials. Here plain maple has been turned and tinted so that it resembles bamboo, and panels of bird's-eye maple form drawer fronts for the table as well as the head- and footboard of the bed that is part of the same bedroom suite. The motif is oriental, but the forms themselves are Western. Taste maker Clarence Cook called such furniture "capital stuff" for furnishing a country house.* Purchase, Anonymous Gift, 1968 (68.97.10)

**Fig. 301. Tall clock,** *by Tiffany and Company (1837–present), New York, 1880s; mahogany, pine, metal, height 105 inches (266.7 cm.). Near and Far Eastern influences are joined with Eastlake-style spindles to ornament this remarkable timepiece. Besides its colorful and unusual decoration, the clock's works are most elaborate: dials show the year, month, period of the zodiac, phases of the moon and sun, date, and day of the week, as well as the hour, minute, and second. Tiffany and Company made only two of these.* Gift of Mary J. Kingsland, 1906 (06.1206)

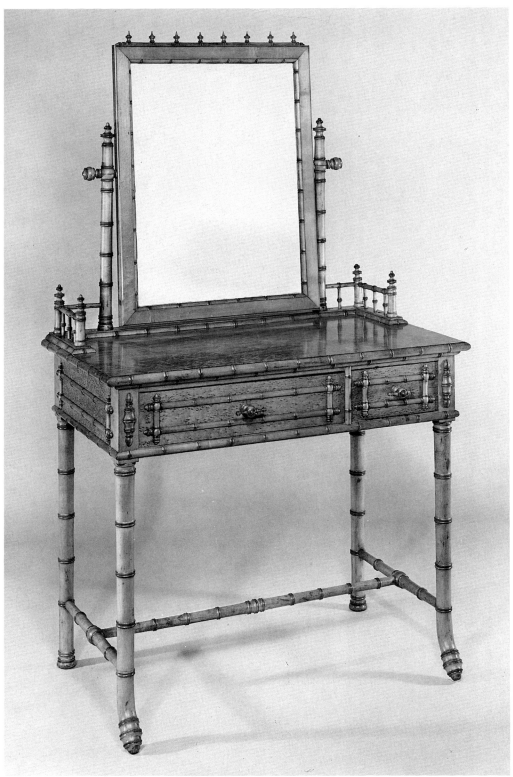

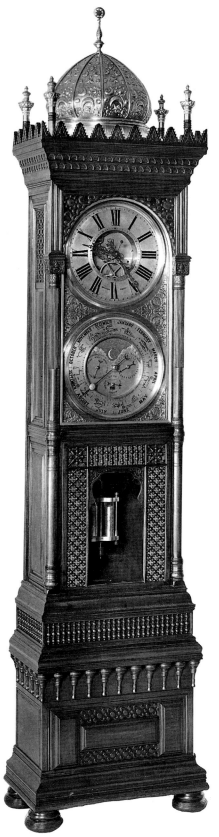

300

301

subtle outlines were influenced by the Anglo-Japanese designs of E. W. Godwin, a leading English figure in the Aesthetic movement and an enthusiastic admirer of Japanese arts and architecture. Oscar Wilde, who along with Whistler was one of Godwin's patrons, called him "the greatest aesthete of them all."

Bamboo furniture from the Orient was an absorbing fashion of the time, and rising demand for this exotic product very soon resulted in the domestic manufacture of simulated-bamboo pieces. Generally made of maple turned and ringed on a lathe to resemble the natural fibrous material, "bamboo" elements were combined to produce conventional stylish Western forms of the period. The point is emphatically made by a bedroom suite probably made in the 1880s and consisting of a bed, a chest of drawers, a dressing table, chairs, and other pieces unknown in oriental art but suitable for Western comfort and convenience (Fig. 300). Each element of the suite follows the rectilinear lines of the current mode, with panels of figured bird's-eye maple and galleries of spindles in the Eastlake manner. Such mixtures of material and motifs, according to one contemporary observer, resulted in an interior that was "light and bright, summery and inviting."

Another example of the variety of exotic influences that affected late nineteenth-century styles is a clock, almost nine feet high, that was fashioned by Tiffany and Company in 1882 (Fig. 301). This extraordinary timepiece in the Near Eastern style is almost the last word in eclecticism. The case is topped by a brass dome ornamented with stars and crescents following Turkish, Persian, and Indian models; and an almost indescribable variety of other design elements ornaments the case. Quite aside from these fanciful features brilliantly executed in wood and metal, the clock is a horological phenomenon in its mechanical ingenuity. A pendulum containing mercury regulates the movement regardless of the fluctuations of temperature and barometric pressure.

Louis Comfort Tiffany, son of the founder of Tiffany and Company, began his varied career as an artist. As he was turning twenty-one he went to Paris to study painting, and then on to North

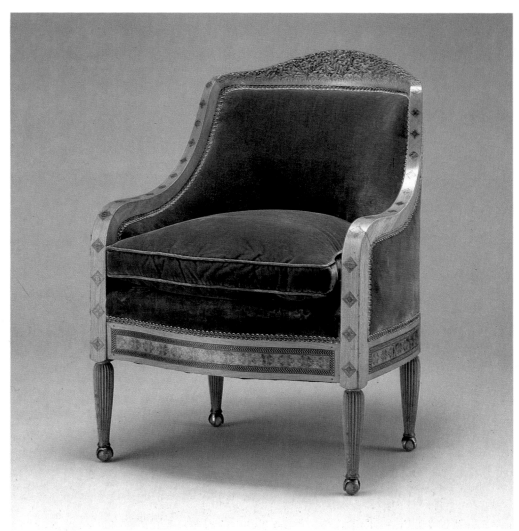

302

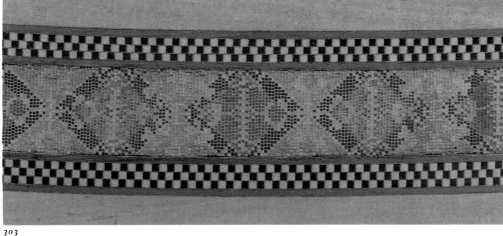

303

**Figs. 302 and 303. Armchair,** *attributed to Louis Comfort Tiffany (1848–1933), New York, 1890–1900; ash, wood and brass inlay, height 35⅝ inches (90.5 cm.). Tiffany endowed this French bergère (closed-arm chair) with Art Nouveau and exotic Eastern motifs, so that it became a form totally of its time. Low-relief carved flowers on the crest rail suggest asymmetrical Art Nouveau designs, while the inlaid geometrical motifs that descend the arms and form a band across the front and side seat-rails employ the east Indian technique of inlaying minuscule pieces of wood in fine patterns. The legs, tapered and reeded in the eighteenth-century tradition, end in feet made of glass balls held in place by brass* claws—*a type of foot found on other pieces associated with Tiffany.*
Gift of Mr. and Mrs. Georges E. Seligmann, 1964 (64.202.1)

**Fig. 304. Cabinet,** by George C. Flint and Company, New York, about 1910; mahogany, glass, velvet, height 58¾ inches (149.2 cm.). This curio cabinet in the Art Nouveau style was copied almost exactly from a piece by the well-known French designer Louis Majorelle of Nancy. The Art Nouveau style, which had become popular in Europe before the turn of the century, was never so successful in America, and examples made here tend to be stiffer and to lack the sensuous grace of European designs. This cabinet is closer to European models than most, for American pieces were frequently at least partly machine made and were therefore not so elegantly hand finished as European ones, but even this example lacks the suave flow of the best European pieces. Purchase, Anonymous Gift, 1968 (68.132)

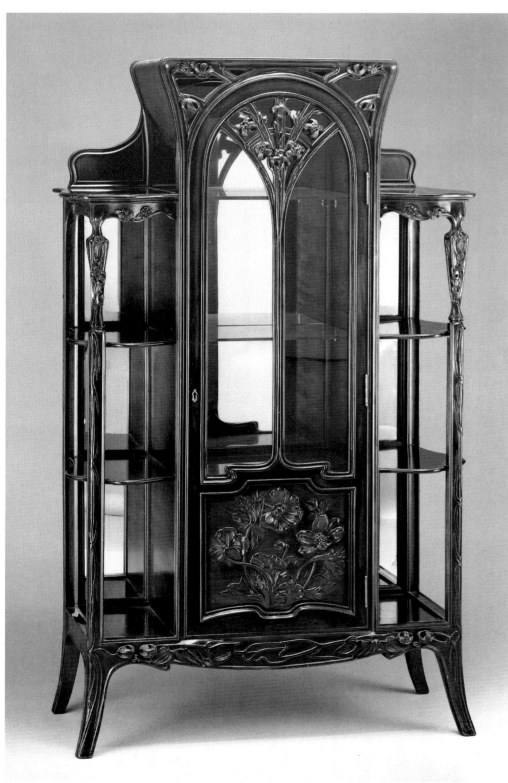

304

Africa and the Near East to widen his vision. In 1875, after returning from a second visit to Paris, he decided to make "decorative work" his main profession. In 1879 he organized the firm Associated Artists, with Samuel Colman, Lockwood de Forest, and Candace Wheeler as the associates. De Forest was an artist and orientalist who founded shops for the revival of woodworking in India to supply his New York studio-salesroom with "artistic creations."

Tiffany's romance with Eastern art, which he so imaginatively and variously expressed in contemporary idioms, was not an exclusive preoccupation in spite of the obvious influence it had on his work. The variety of forms in different mediums that issued from his company and studios is almost incalculable, and is barely suggested by the group of disparate objects shown in this book (see also Figs. 2, 3, and 5). Two ash chairs with reeded legs (Figs. 302 and 303), which may well be from Tiffany's studios, are in the shape of late eighteenth-century French bergères, although their light-wood frames, inlaid motifs, and shallow flower-and-leaf carving are very much in the spirit of the late nineteenth century.

An Art Nouveau cabinet whose flowing lines are related to those of Tiffany's bergères was made by George Flint and Company (Fig. 304). Very similar to a cabinet by the French designer Louis Majorelle, it belongs to what so far seems to be a small group of American furniture in this curvilinear style.

Both L. C. Tiffany and his remarkable younger contemporary, Frank Lloyd Wright, won international renown for their quite different contributions to the artistic movements of their time, contradicting Henry James's snobbish pronouncement that true art must wither in the "cruel air" of America. Among other Americans who also gave a flat lie to that observation was Louis Henri Sullivan, an almost exact contemporary of Tiffany's. In his adopted city of Chicago Sullivan represented a new and vital trend in American architecture, and his structures contributed to the unique distinction the Chicago skyscape was soon enjoying. By reconciling technology and utility with poetry and beauty, Sullivan transformed the steel-framed

**Figs. 305 and 306. Side chair,** by Frank Lloyd Wright (1867–1959), about 1902; oak, height 55½ inches (141 cm.). The flowing, swirling lines of the Art Nouveau cabinet are completely antithetical to this chair, with its emphasis on verticality and right angles. It was made, like all Wright's furniture, to occupy a specific space in one of his houses, the Ward W. Willits residence in Highland Park, Illinois, and it carries out the ideas that shaped the architecture. Pulled up to the dining table with several identical examples, this chair helped to create an island of privacy for those seated at dinner.
Purchase, Mr. and Mrs. David Lubart Gift, in memory of Katherine J. Lubart, 1944–1975, 1978 (1978.189)

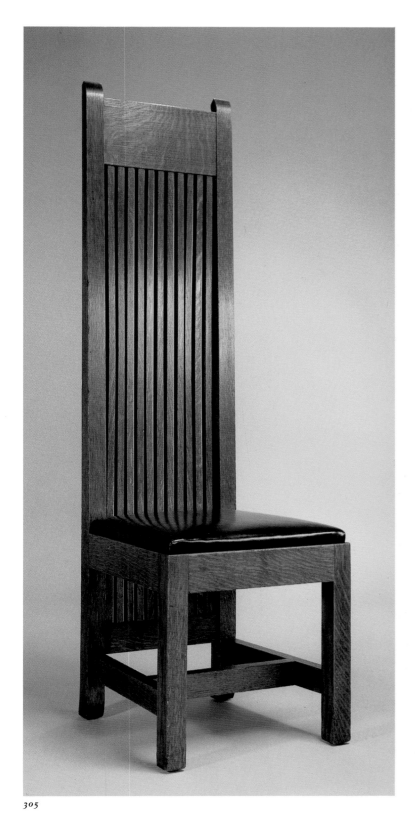

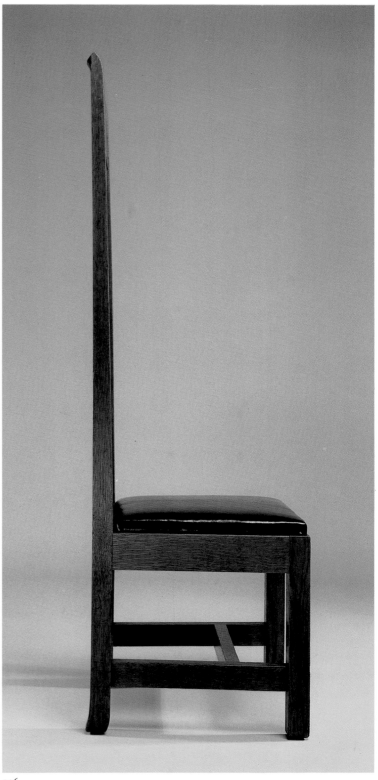

305

306

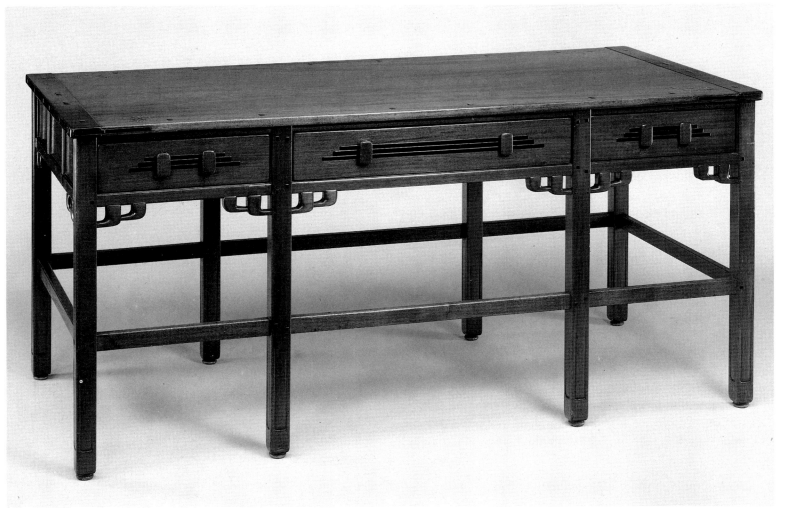

307

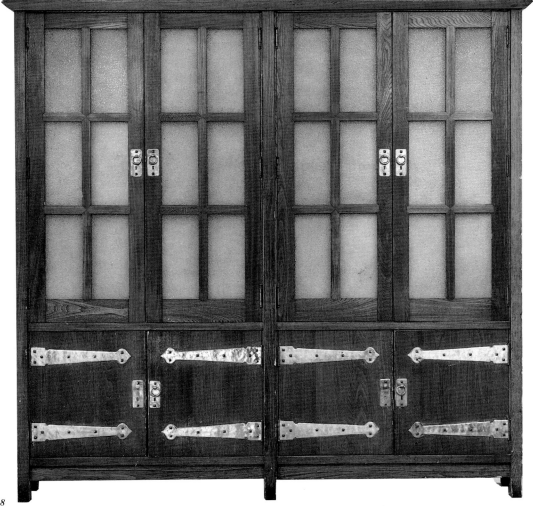

**Fig. 308. Linen press,** by Gustav Stickley
(1857–1942), about 1905; oak and copper,
height 72½ inches (184.2 cm.). One of the most
prolific makers of Arts and Crafts furniture was
Gustav Stickley, manufacturer of Craftsman furniture, of which this linen press is an example.
The use of oak, considered an "honest" and un-
pretentious wood, the rectilinear form, and the
hand-hammered copper hardware all conform to
the Arts and Crafts tenet of simplicity, utility, and
honesty. This handsome piece, whose pebbled-
glass doors conceal shelves held in place by
movable copper pegs, was made to stand in the
upstairs hallway of Stickley's Morris Plains, New
Jersey, home, known as Craftsman Farms.
Gift of Cyril Farny, in memory of Phyllis Holt Farny,
1976 (1976.389.2)

308

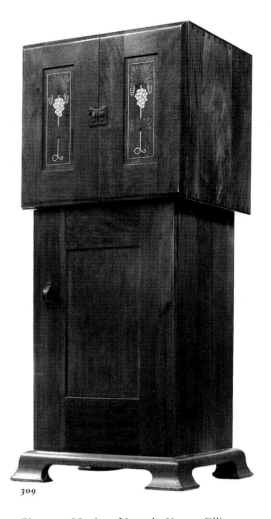

309

mass of the high-rising skyscraper into "a proud and soaring thing."

One of the several architectural masterpieces Sullivan designed in association with the brilliant engineer Dankmar Adler was the Chicago Stock Exchange Building, built in 1893. When that structure was demolished in 1972, several elements were salvaged and are now installed in The American Wing. A pair of functioning metal staircases (see Figs. 8, 9, and 10), each of two flights, now rise on either side of Tiffany's wisteria window (see Fig. 5). Except for the replaced mahogany handrails and marble treads, the stairs are made of iron cast into highly original stylized-plant patterns with an electroplated copper finish. They demonstrate clearly the unique skill with which Sullivan integrated utilitarian construction and handsome ornament.

Since Frank Lloyd Wright felt that "The most truly satisfactory apartments are those in which most or all of the furniture is built in as a part of the original scheme considering the whole as an integral unit," his early furniture was designed for specific rooms in the houses he built. The side chair from the Willits house (Figs. 305 and 306) was created as part of a set for the dining room; it was meant to be seen with others in an architectural setting whose lines and effects it repeated and reinforced. Despite that, the chair makes a strong sculptural statement standing alone. Another distinguished architect-designed piece is the library table by the brothers Charles and Henry Greene (Fig. 307). Made of mahogany rather than oak—the wood preferred by so many Arts and Crafts practitioners—and displaying delicate Japanese-inspired lines, the table nevertheless shares with Wright's oak chair a dignified rectangularity characteristic of the "Mission" furniture being produced at the time.

One of the outstanding proponents of sturdy furniture based on straight lines and made of oak or other strong, light-colored wood was Gustav Stickley, a contemporary of Wright and the Greenes, who occasionally turned to him for furnishings. In 1900, at a furniture exhibit in Grand Rapids, Michigan, Stickley introduced what he referred to as his Craftsman furniture—which became popularly known as Mission furniture. He claimed that these simple, heavy foursquare forms of solid white oak were "the first original expression of American thought in furniture." Since his designs were founded on basic structural principles rather than on considerations of style, he thought it unlikely that they would ever go out of fashion. They were a response, he wrote, not to the "cultivated taste of man learned in the great styles of the past, but [to] the need suggested by the primitive human necessity of the common folk." And because his products were made of superior, durable materials by skilled and conscientious craftsmen, Stickley believed they would withstand hard use for generations. Those hopes and intentions were in sharp contrast to the attitudes of many modish people whose aim was to keep abreast of the ever-changing fashions of the time. Not a few of these shied away from soundly made furniture and had no wish to spend money on things that would last even a lifetime. "What is life," one woman asked, "without new furniture?"

A large double linen press that was made about 1905 and that once stood in Stickley's own house handsomely exemplifies the man's craftsmanship (Fig.

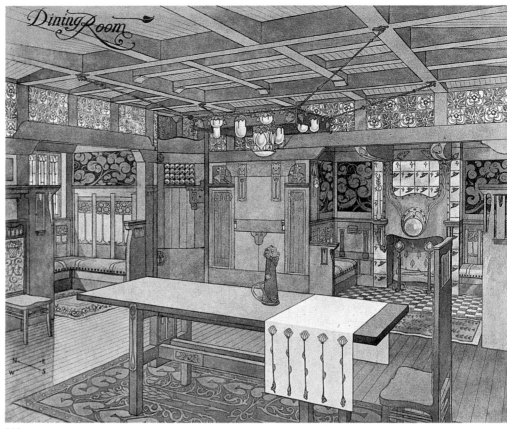

**Fig. 310. Design for a dining room,** *by Will H. Bradley (1868–1962) for* The Ladies' Home Journal, *about 1901; commercial printing process, 10 by 12⅞ inches (25.4 by 32.7 cm.). As part of editor Edward Bok's campaign to promote good design in domestic architecture and furnishings, this dining room reveals oriental, Arts and Crafts, and Art Nouveau inspiration. The table and chair in the foreground are obviously in the simple rectangular Arts and Crafts tradition, while the fabrics and wall and floor coverings show more interest in multiple patterns and in curved naturalistic forms, as does the fireplace in the room through the door at the right. Bradley was described by the* Boston Globe *in 1897 as "a many-sided genius [who] seems to be equally at home designing an initial or a font of type or a poster, and he also designs furniture—in fact there appears to be no limit to his ambition."* Gift of Mrs. Fern Bradley Dufner, 1952 (52.65.88[6])

308). The exterior, which was given an attractive greenish finish, is accented by handwrought patinated copper strap hinges and lock plates. These "honestly" reveal the marks of the hammer by which they were fashioned. Behind the pebbled glass doors are rows of shelves resting on copper pegs that can be moved to any level—an important innovative arrangement at the time.

A remarkable music cabinet was also produced by Stickley's workshop (Fig. 309). Made of mahogany and enriched by refined inlay, this elegant storage piece was designed by Harvey Ellis, a gifted designer about whom we know little as yet. The forthrightness and geometrical spareness of the design are very much in the Arts and Crafts mode, but the choice of mahogany and the unusual juxtaposition of forms set it far apart from most contemporary objects.

Encouraged by the large success of his enterprise, Stickley overextended himself and was forced into bankruptcy in 1915. His enterprise was matched by that of Elbert Hubbard, a flamboyant individual who claimed *he* had originated the Mission style. "Fra Elbertus," as he sometimes called himself, was a Harvard dropout who had been a soap salesman before he turned to furniture making. At his Roycroft Shops in East Aurora, New York, he produced furni-

ture in the Stickley manner. Besides furniture, the Roycroft community produced books and household objects whose range extended from metalwares to leaded glass and table mats. Among the creative and committed members of the community were artisan-designers Dard Hunter and Karl Kipp. Hubbard's fame was advanced by *The Philistine*, a little magazine he published that was widely read throughout the nation. In 1899 Hubbard printed his "Message to Garcia," an inspirational piece that, according to the author, sold forty million copies. Aside from his preachments, Hubbard was a very practical man. "Be kind," he advised, "—but get the mazuma." His life ended in 1915 with a tragedy, when he went down with the ill-fated *Lusitania*.

One of the most influential of the taste makers of those years was the Dutch-born Edward William Bok. Beginning as a young man in 1889, Bok served as editor of *The Ladies' Home Journal* for thirty years. He was dismayed by what he considered the "wretched" design of the average American home. To improve this state of affairs, he launched a campaign to "make the world a better place to live in." In 1895 he began to publish plans for dwellings prepared and certified by reputable architects. Among the latter was Frank

Lloyd Wright, who in 1901 drew up an elevation with specifications for what was an early model of his prairie-style house.

The same year Bok commissioned the internationally known commercial designer Will H. Bradley to prepare colored renderings of interiors and furnishings for a complete model home in a modern style. Bradley's drawings skillfully combined geometric forms with curvilinear ornament and color used with refined intensity. In concept they are strongly reminiscent of the ideas propounded by the celebrated English designer M. H. Baillie Scott, a prominent figure in the international Art Nouveau movement (Fig. 310).

The international design movement was slowly taking shape in the early years of the century, and a table by Joseph Urban (Fig. 311), made in America but reflecting Urban's Viennese training, provides concrete illustration of the progressive ideas of the influential Wiener Werkstätte.

A side chair (Fig. 312) made for the Imperial Hotel, designed by Wright in the years 1916–22, is another example of Wright's continuing evolution as a designer—and a reminder that this extraordinary man was one of the first Americans to influence design on an international scale.

**Fig. 311. Table,** *by Joseph Urban (1872–1933)*
*for the Wiener Werkstätte of America, New York,*
*1921; black lacquer, silver leaf, silk panel inset*
*on top, height 23⅞ inches (60.6 cm.). The ex-*
*quisite workmanship for which the Wiener Werk-*
*stätte stood is present here, in this elegant table*
*made for the Wiener Werkstätte Showroom on*
*Fifth Avenue in New York. Severe geometric*
*shapes are employed in the design, but the orna-*
*ment is less rigid: a bead-and-reel motif edges the*
*base of the supporting column and fills in the*
*narrow slits on the lower half of the column so*
*that it serves as a kind of stop fluting. Delicately*
*drawn flowers, leaves, stems, and insects are*
*gracefully disposed on the tabletop.*
Purchase, Gifts in memory of Emil Blasberg, 1978
(1978.492.1)

**Fig. 312. Side chair,** *by Frank Lloyd Wright*
*(1867–1959), 1916–22; oak, cane, height*
*37¾ inches (95.9 cm.). The only example with*
*cane panels in an American collection, this chair*
*was designed by Wright to furnish a promenade*
*in his Imperial Hotel in Tokyo. Its angled forms*
*repeated the lines and angles of the space it occu-*
*pied. The Imperial Hotel was one of Wright's*
*great engineering triumphs; it was designed so*
*that it could—and did—withstand severe earth-*
*quakes. It was, unfortunately, torn down in*
*1968 and only a fragment of the building and*
*some of its furnishings survive.*
Gift of Dr. Roger G. Gerry, 1968 (68.20.1)

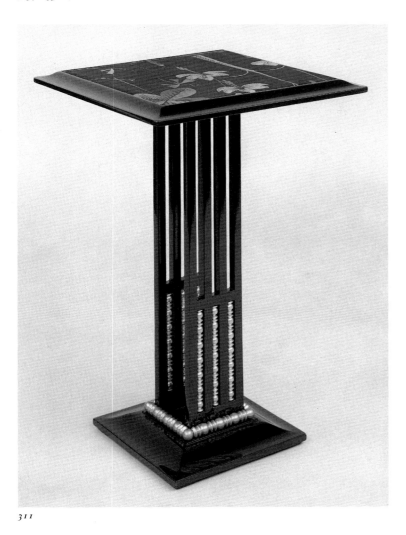

311

312

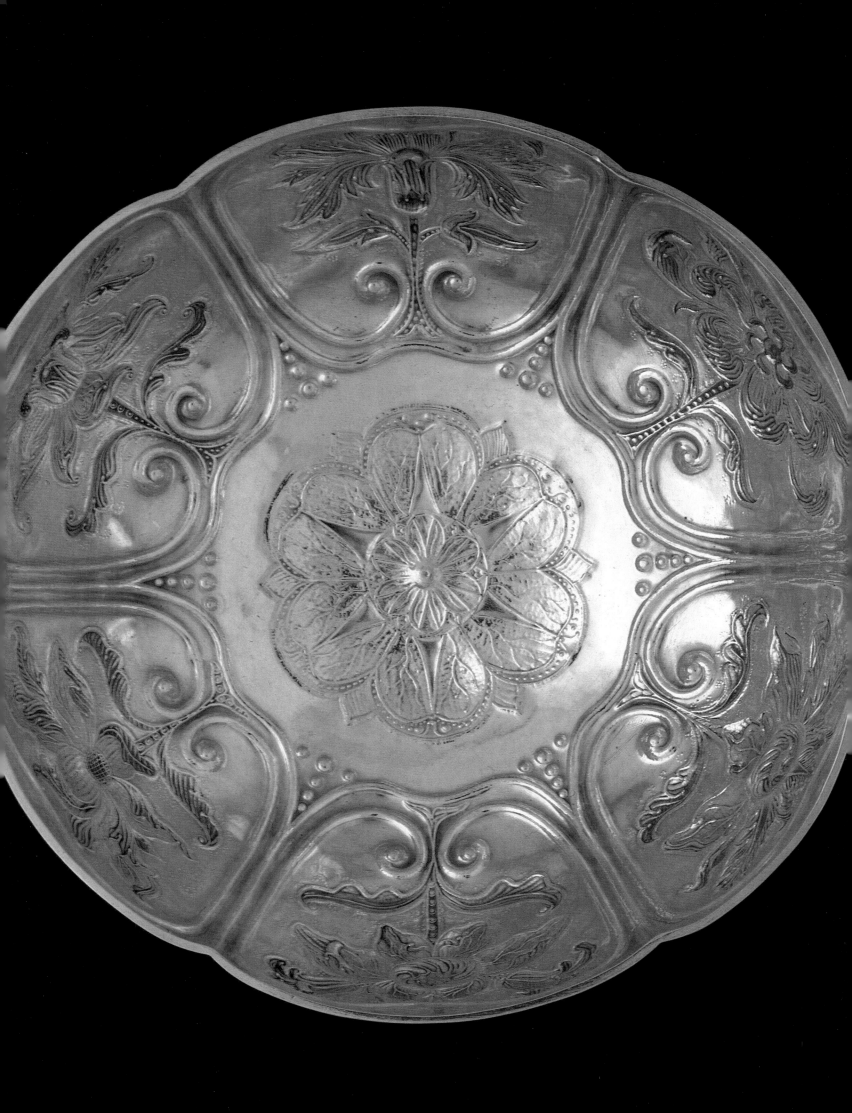

# SILVER

Fig. 313. Detail, bowl by Cornelius Kierstede,
see Fig. 316.

# The Colonial Period
# 1630–1790

*Fig. 315. Chocolate pot,* by Edward Winslow (1669–1753), Boston, about 1700–10; silver, height 9⅛ inches (23.2 cm.). New both in its tall lantern shape and in its function of serving chocolate, a recently introduced drink in the colonies, this pot is also decorated in the newly fashionable baroque style. Like the standing salt, it has surfaces that are alternately boldly ornamented and plain, creating highlights and shadows and contrasting smooth and ribbed areas. Cut-card work, in which a flat design is cut out of a separate sheet of silver and applied, is another typical baroque embellishment, used here at the base of the spout and the finial of the domed lid.
Bequest of Alphonso T. Clearwater, 1933 (33.120.221)

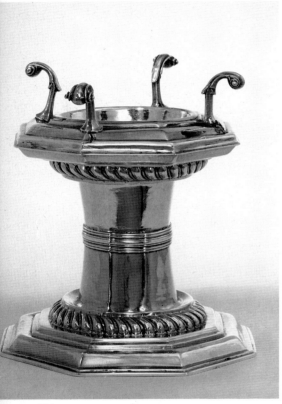

314

*Fig. 314. Standing salt,* by John Allen (1671/ 72–1760) and John Edwards (1671–1746), Boston, about 1700; silver, height 5⅞ inches (14.9 cm.). The spool shape of this standing salt is common to all three surviving American examples of the form and to the earlier seventeenth-century English salts that inspired them. Grand containers of this kind went out of style in America about 1700 as salt became more plentiful and fashionable hostesses began to serve it in individual dishes. The phrase "below the salt," which still denotes lack of status, arose in medieval times when salt was a luxury affordable only by the very rich. It meant that the guest was not seated near the host and the salt, but farther away.
Gift of Sarah Hayward Draper, 1972 (1972.204)

Long before the colonies produced a portrait painter or a landscapist of any consequence, they supported scores of master craftsmen in the precious metals whose work was handsomely designed and scrupulously wrought. The silversmith—or "goldsmith," as he was often termed—was a banker of sorts through whose skills the miscellaneous foreign coins that flowed into America in the course of trade might be converted into useful objects of silver, or, occasionally, gold. The weight and purity of this plate was certified by the integrity of the smith who made and marked it. Such marks and engraved decorations, which often included the initials of the owner, enabled him to clearly identify his tankard, porringer, or spoon in case of loss or theft, as he could never hope to identify coins. The objects could also be put to practical use at table or displayed as conspicuous wealth on a cupboard, and they could easily be reconverted into bullion or coin if need be.

Boston and New York (New Amsterdam until 1664) were the first New World centers of this highly practical art. As might be expected, work turned out in these two separate areas showed marked regional differences in design. Among the earliest colonial items in the collection are several silver shillings and sixpences coined at Boston by English-born John Hull and Robert Sanderson by order of the General Court of Massachusetts, but in defiance of restrictions imposed by Britain. These pioneering smiths worked both in partnership and individually, turning out forms that, except for the marks stamped on them, were indistinguishable from the relatively plain objects produced in England at the time.

By the end of the seventeenth century baroque features associated with the William and Mary style were being expressed in silver—a development clearly observable in a spool-shaped standing salt made in Boston around the turn of the century by John Edwards and John Allen (Fig. 314). Descended from the great architectural salts that were a conspicuous feature of medieval and Renaissance dining boards, this example is ornamented with two bands of spiral gadrooning—that is, convex, or inverted, fluting. Similar bands distinguish a rare chocolate pot made in Boston by Edward Winslow about that same time (Fig. 315). The salt represents a form that was being held over from earlier days and would soon be abandoned, while the chocolate pot is an early example of a form that evolved in England only late in the seventeenth century, when drinking chocolate first became fashionable. Both pieces, however, strongly remind us of the degree of affluence and the taste for luxury that had developed in New England less than a century after the settlement of that Puritan land.

The silver fashioned in New York in the late seventeenth and early eighteenth centuries reflects the mingling of Dutch, English, and French traditions. Cornelius Kierstede, probably the most individualistic of early American craftsmen, was the maker of a boldly embossed six-panel bowl whose design is peculiar to New York (Fig. 316) and a unique pair of stop-fluted candlesticks (Fig. 318). The sticks and a matching snuffer stand have splayed bases chased with fantastic chinoiserie designs. A beaker made by Jurian Blanck, Jr., in about 1683 (Fig. 317) and engraved with a Dutch inscription and figures of

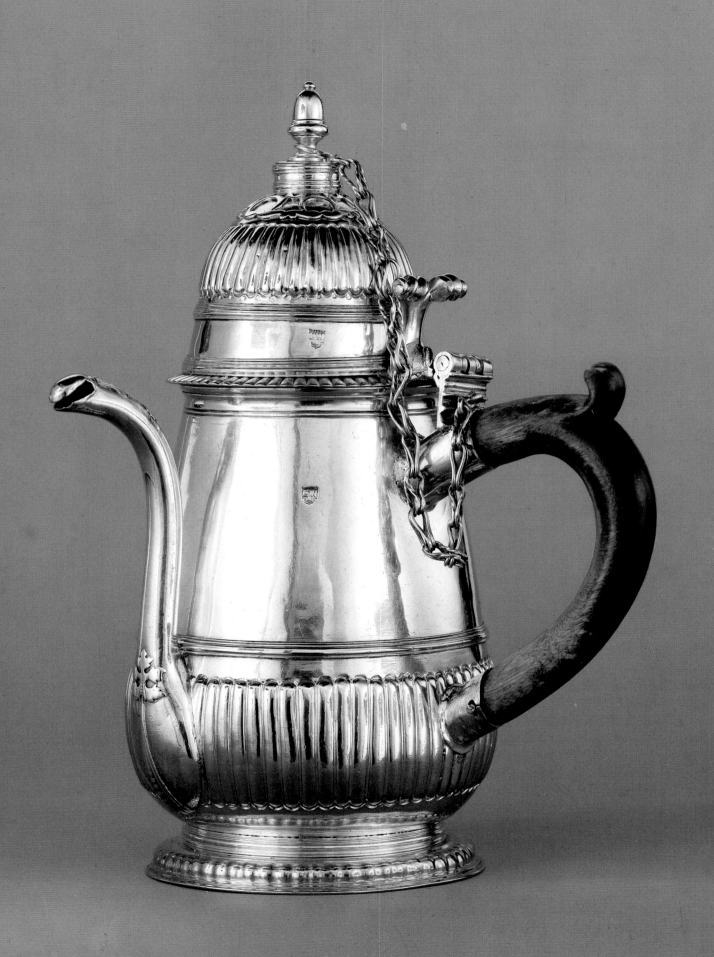

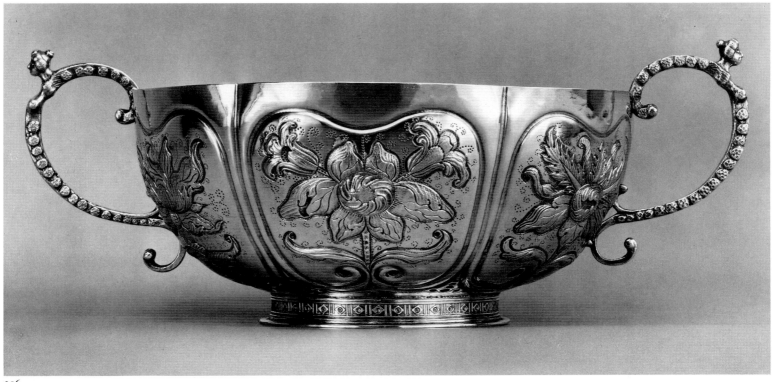

316

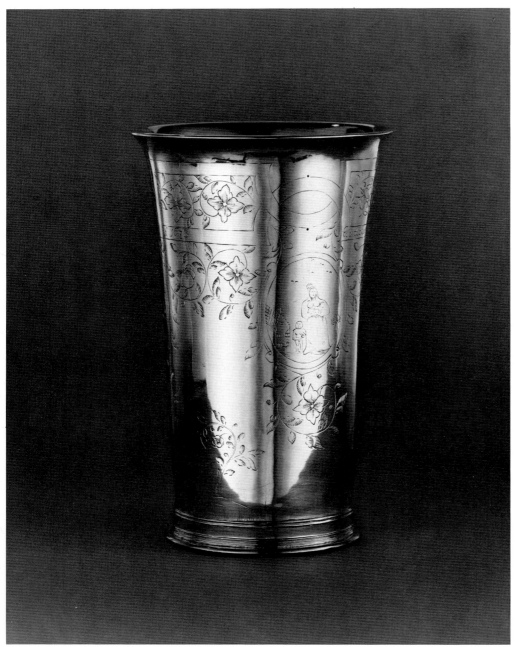

317

**Fig. 316. Bowl,** *by Cornelius Kierstede (1675–1757), New York, 1700–10; silver, diameter 10 inches (25.4 cm.). This bowl, with six clearly defined lobes filled with repoussé (relief) flowers and leaves and equipped with caryatid handles, belongs to a group of at least eighteen lobed bowls of New York manufacture. The Dutch and Huguenot silversmiths who made them were remembering similar pieces characteristic of northern European silverwork, especially as it was interpreted in Holland, and these in turn had been inspired by Italian mannerist silversmiths of the Renaissance. Their original use, according to John N. Pearce, who studied the group and published his findings in* The Magazine Antiques *(October 1961), was as a container of brandy and raisins. The bowl was passed from one guest to another, and each dipped himself a helping of the compote with the silver spoon supplied by the host. This particular bowl, the most lavishly decorated and one of the largest of its type, bears initials said to be those of New York baker Theunis Jacobsen Quick and his wife, Vroutje, married in 1689.*
Samuel D. Lee Fund, 1938 (38.63)

**Fig. 317. Beaker,** *attributed to Jurian Blanck, Jr. (about 1645–1714), New York, about 1683; silver, height 7¼ inches (18.4 cm.). Beakers, a common form of drinking vessel in the seventeenth century, were used for both domestic and ecclesiastical purposes. This example is inscribed, in Dutch, "A token of devotion and loyalty to the church in Kingston, 1683." Its graceful tapering shape and its engraved decoration combining rigid strapwork and whimsical floral scrolls are typical of New York beakers which, in turn, reflect seventeenth-century Dutch traditions. The beaker's engraved ovals, containing representations of Faith, Hope, and Charity, are characteristic of New York church-silver ornament.*
Jointly owned by the Reformed Protestant Dutch Church of Kingston, New York, and The Metropolitan Museum of Art, 1933 (33.120.621)

**Fig. 318. Candlestick and snuffer stand,** *by Cornelius Kierstede (1675–1757), New York, 1700–10; silver, height of candlestick 11½ inches (29.2 cm.), height of snuffer 8¼ inches (21 cm.). Kierstede, one of the finest silversmiths of his time, made this snuffer stand and candlestick (which is one of a pair—the other is also in the Museum's collection) for Johannes and Elizabeth Schuyler of Albany, New York. Schuyler was prominent in civic affairs, serving as mayor of Albany from 1703 to 1706. The impressive height of the candlesticks is matched by the boldness of their ornament. Stop-fluted columns, gadrooning, and chinoiserie vignettes combine in a way that both unifies the whole object and provides the contrasts that are so important in baroque design. The snuffer stand, which originally held a scissors-shaped snuffer for cutting and trimming the wick, has an acorn-shaped support reminiscent of the huge turnings on European state beds and cupboards of the sixteenth and seventeenth centuries. The snuffer stood vertically in the rectangular holder.*

*Candlestick:* Gift of Robert L. Cammann, 1957 (57.153a,b); *snuffer stand:* Gift of Mr. and Mrs. William A. Moore, 1923 (23.80.21)

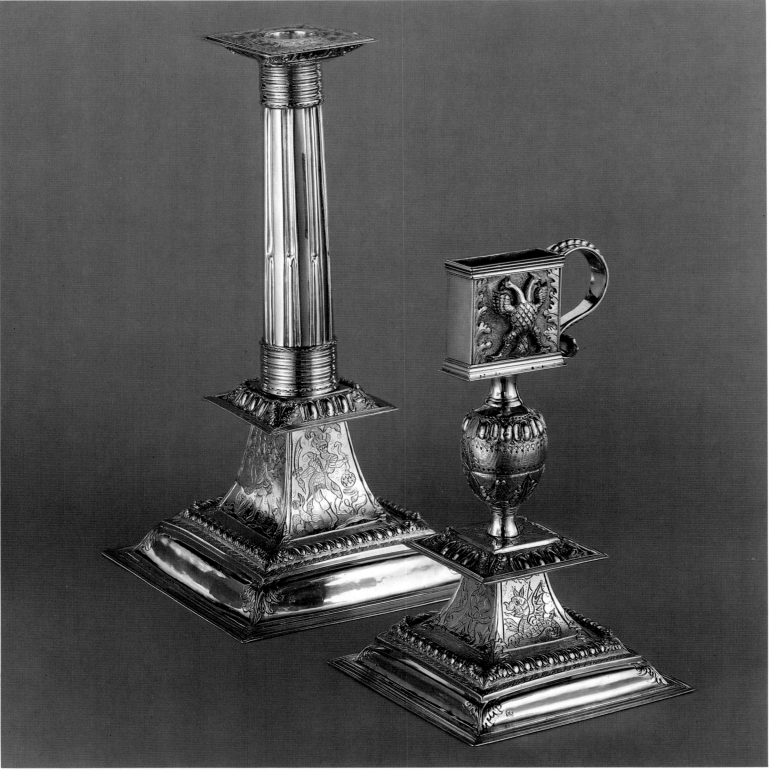

318

**Figs. 319 and 320. Group of tankards:** left, by Simeon Soumain (1685–1750), New York, 1705–25; silver, height 7⅛ inches (18.1 cm.); center, by Jeremiah Dummer (1645–1718), Boston, 1690–1705; silver, height 7 inches (17.8 cm.); right, by Benjamin Burt (1729–1805), Boston, 1760–70; silver, height 8½ inches (21.6 cm.). Throughout the colonial period and well into the Federal, widely separated American cities produced similar forms but decorated them differently. That point is brought out here, where two tankards of the early colonial period share a low, broad body, wide curved handle, and flat stepped top. The New England example on the left, however, lacks the rich ornament of the New York version, having only cut-card ornament at

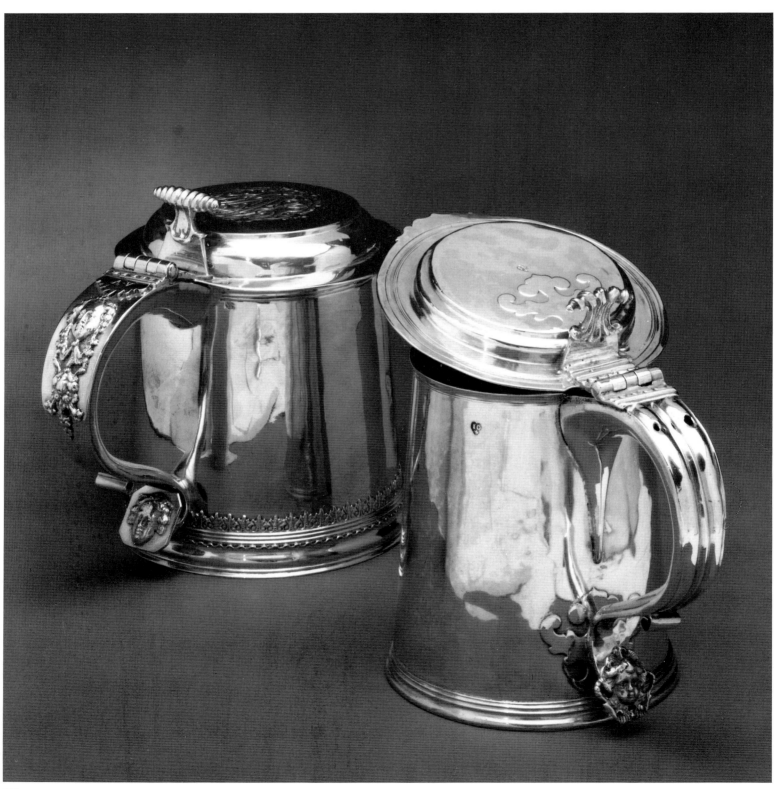

319

the base of the handle and on the lid as opposed to the band of leaf molding and meander wire at the base and rich cast ornament on the handle of the New York piece. Both have cast masks applied to their handle terminals and scrolled thumbpieces on their lids, but the tight single scroll of New York is quite different from the more relaxed double scrolls of New England. Such differences were very likely the result of craft specialization, in which one craftsman made thumbpieces and sold them to his fellow workers. The later example, on the right, made in Boston in the late colonial period, shows the preferred tankard form in that city after mid-century. The body is now elongated, the thrust is vertical, and the lid has become a high dome and acquired a

decorative finial. Rococo engraving provides the only other embellishment, except for the single horizontal band that encircles the tankard slightly below midpoint. By comparison, New York tankards of this period remain low and broad and look much as they had earlier. Their trend was toward simplicity, away from the earlier decorative leaf bands and cast ornament.

Gift of Annie Clarkson, 1927 (27.85.1); Anonymous Gift, 1934 (34.16); Gift of Robert S. Grinnel, 1970 (1970.287.1)

Faith, Hope, and Charity represents a type of vessel used for both domestic and sacramental purposes. A small, handsomely decorated globular teapot by Jacob Boelen is the earliest known American example of this form (Fig. 321). It was made at a time when tea, like coffee, was still a rare, exotic, and expensive commodity.

From the beginning American colonists preferred beer and ale to water, though they were not always able to indulge their preference. Describing his own situation in 1629, the Reverend Francis Higginson of Salem wrote: "Whereas my stomach could only digest and did require such drink as was both strong and stale, I can and ofttimes do drink New England water very well." Silver tankards, capacious and broad based to hold generous draughts of spirituous beverages, were at first straight sided and flat topped. The earliest New England examples often have cut-card ornament (flat designs cut into decorative shapes and applied), gadrooning, plain ribbed moldings, and cast thumbpieces (Fig. 319, right). Early tankards made in New York were also capacious, flat topped, and broad based (Fig. 319, left). With their engraved lids, corkscrew-shaped thumbpieces, handles with applied cast masks and garlands, and ornamental base moldings, these handsome drinking vessels display a combination of decorative features peculiar to New York. Flat tops for their tankards continued to please New Yorkers, but New Englanders came to prefer drinking from examples with domed tops (Fig. 320).

The suave simplicity of the Queen Anne style is handsomely demonstrated in two silver teapots—one with a pear-shaped body, the other globular (Figs.

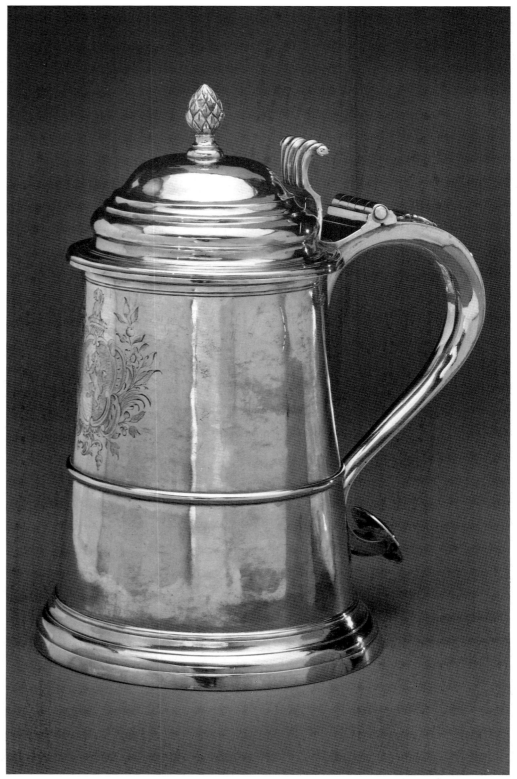

320

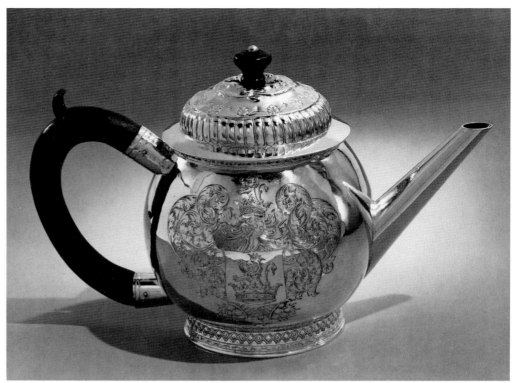

321

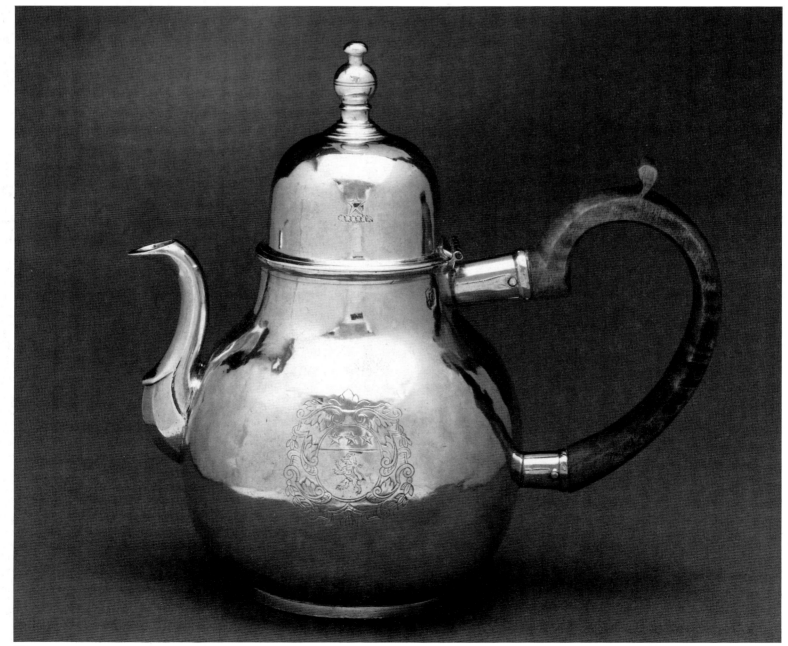

322

**Figs. 321–23. Group of teapots:** left-hand page, top, *by Jacob Boelen (about 1657–1729), New York, about 1700–15; silver, height 6½ inches (16.5 cm.); left-hand page, bottom, by John Coney (1655/56–1722), Boston, 1710–22; silver, height 7½ inches (19.1 cm.); right-hand page, top, by Benjamin Wynkoop, Jr. (1705–66), Fairfield, Connecticut, 1730–35; silver, height 6³⁄₁₆ inches (15.7 cm.); right-hand page, bottom, by Josiah Austin (1719–80), Charlestown, Massachusetts, 1745–55; silver, height 6³⁄₁₆ inches (15.7 cm.). This group of teapots spans the first half of the eighteenth century, after which the globular form seen in three examples here was superseded in fashionable circles by the inverted-pear form of the sugar bowl in*

Fig. 334. *The earliest known instance of the globular teapot in America is that seen here in the upper portion of the left-hand page. Its expansive engraved cartouche and coat of arms and its stepped gadrooned cover proclaim its manufacture in the William and Mary period; the meander wire and stamped band around its foot associate it with early New York tankards (see Fig. 319). Below it is the only teapot by John Coney that has so far turned up, embodying the popular Queen Anne pear shape. Here the S-curve dominates the design, and ornament is subordinate to form and proportion. A different Queen Anne form (upper right-hand page) is a continuation of the globular tradition seen in the William and Mary example. Now the beauty of*

*the globe shape is paramount—with the simple geometric outlines of its body, spout, and cover the main focus of our attention. This same shape was used for the earliest rococo teapots, an example of which is seen below. Lavish ornament is now back in style, visible in the engraved cartouche and decorative shells and leaves that encircle the shoulder of this pot, and in the extravagantly curved S-shaped spout. The cover is now set flush with the shoulder of the teapot.*

Gift of Mrs. Lloyd K. Garrison, in memory of her father, Pierre Jay, 1961 (61.246); Bequest of Alphonso T. Clearwater, 1933 (33.120.526); Purchase, Robert G. Goelet Gift and Friends of the American Wing Fund, 1980 (1980.89); Bequest of Charles Allen Munn, 1924 (24.109.7)

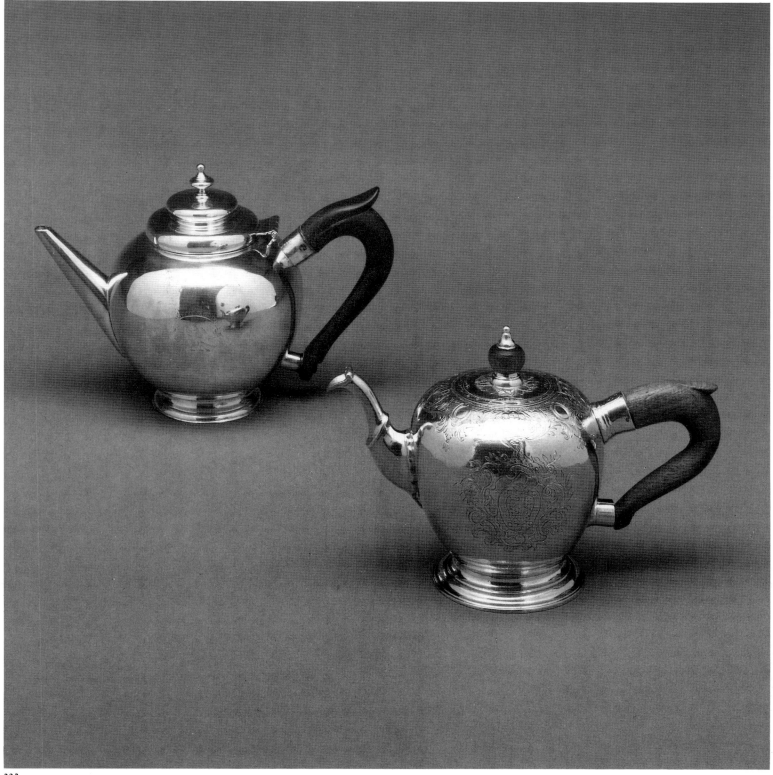

**Fig. 324. Pair of candlesticks,** by Edward Winslow (1669–1753), Boston, 1715–25; silver, height 7¼ inches (18.4 cm.). Simple graceful lines and a minimum of ornament distinguish these very fine Queen Anne sticks. The metal sparkles and shines as the S-curves flow in and out of the baluster—the only distraction is the simply engraved coat of arms of Edward Hutchinson, half brother of Thomas, for whom Winslow is said to have made the chocolate pot in Fig. 315.
Friends of the American Wing Fund, 1973 (1973.152.1,2)

322 and 323). Except for the very simple engraving, there are no embellishments to distract the eye from the plain graceful shapes. As the ritual of drinking tea developed, new forms evolved for serving the beverage— sugar bowls and tongs, milk and cream pitchers, teaspoons, tea caddies, and other novelties that were fashioned with the same sober restraint as the teapot.

The functional beauty of the Queen Anne style can also be seen in a pair of trimly modeled candlesticks by Edward Winslow (Fig. 324). There is no orna-

ment on these sticks except for a simple engraved coat of arms—their effect derives almost entirely from the dips and swells of the curving form itself.

With the gradual emergence of the rococo style in the middle years of the eighteenth century, greater elaboration of form and decoration once again became the fashion. The rococo influence that spread from France to England and America developed at a time when new patterns of domestic life were emerging in the colonies. Changing customs in living arrangements called for

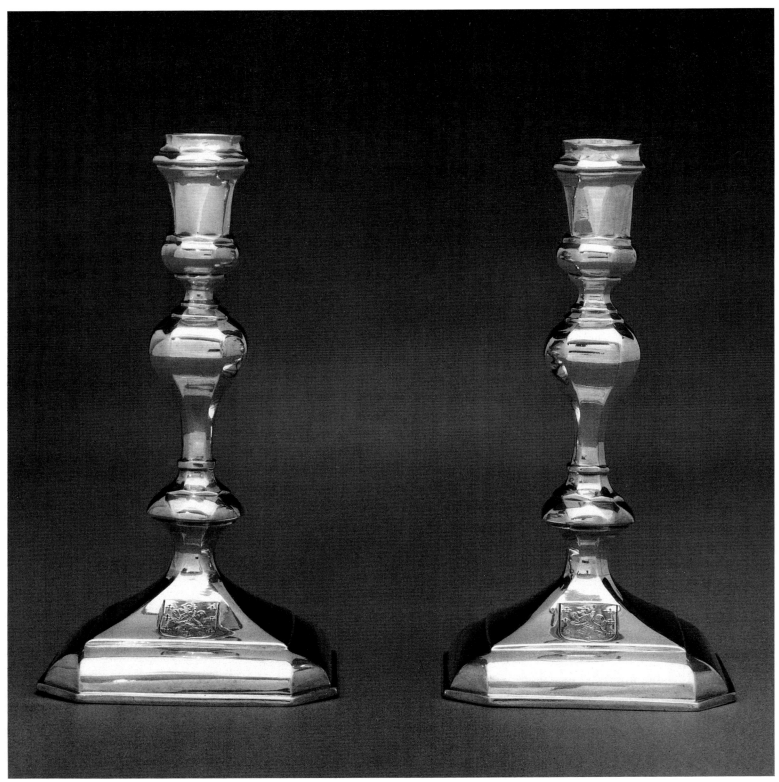

324

**Fig. 325. Whistle and bells,** by Nicholas Roosevelt (1715–69), New York, 1755–65; gold and coral, length 6⅛ inches (15.6 cm.). This rare object was made as a gift for some lucky colonial child. He could blow the whistle or rattle the bells, both fashioned in solid gold with repoussé rococo ornament, or teethe on the coral. Many more of these luxurious toys were imported from England than were made in America, but this example belongs to a small group of New York manufacture.
Rogers Fund, 1947 (47.70)

**Figs. 326 and 327. Cake basket,** by Myer Myers (1723–95), New York, 1760–70; silver, length 14½ inches (36.8 cm.). The rococo style swept away restraint in line and ornament, substituting swirling C- and S-scrolls, shells, flowers, and acanthus leaves. This cake basket exemplifies these trends at their most successful. Made for Samuel Cornell, a wealthy New York merchant, and his wife, Susannah, the basket indicates a taste for the new rococo style, the means to indulge it, and a society sophisticated and elegant enough to show it off to. Only a few American cake baskets survive from this early period and all were made in New York; later, in the Federal period, many more were made. As scholar Martha Gandy Fales has written in Early American

Silver, the pattern the basket casts "in the shadow is ephemeral and fleeting, as Rococo design was meant to be."
Morris K. Jesup Fund, 1954 (54.167)

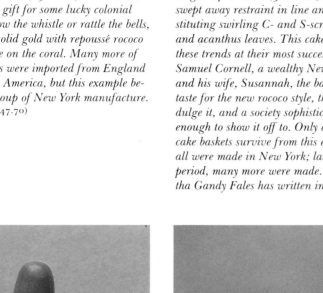

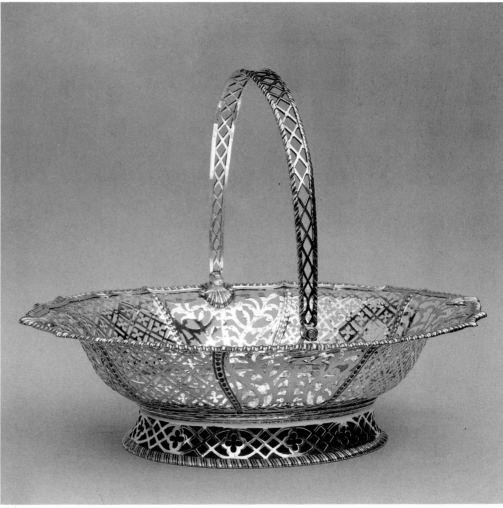

326

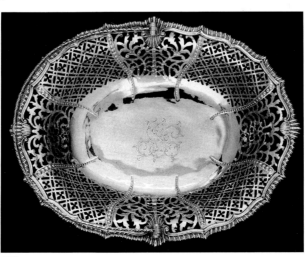

325

327

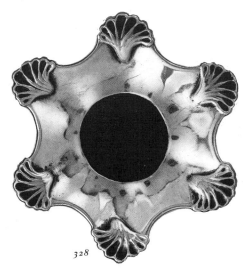

Figs. 328 and 329. **Pair of candlesticks,** *by Myer Myers (1723–95), New York, about 1759; silver, height 10⅛ inches (25.7 cm.). Shells and stylized leaf designs ornament the curved and knopped balusters of these candlesticks. Although they are severely restrained in comparison with swirling English and French models, the undulating movement of the scalloped bases combined with the suave curves of the fluting between shells gives these sticks a dignified rococo air. Part of a set of four, they were a gift to Catharine Livingston from her grandparents Peter and Sarah Van Brugh. Silver candlesticks are rare in American work, and a set of four was a sign of great affluence.*
Sansbury-Mills Fund, 1972 (1972.3.1ab,2), 1977 (1977.88)

328

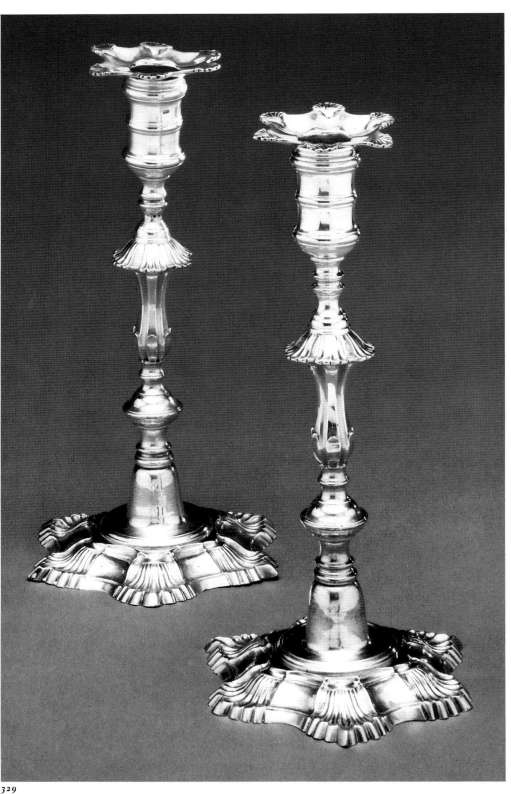

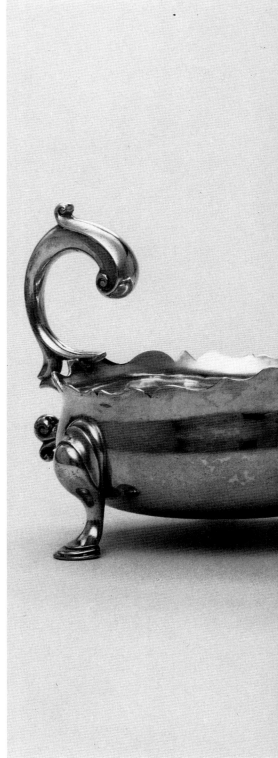

329

330

types of furnishings that had not been necessary before, and these changes were reflected in the design and decoration of all the household arts. One of the most engaging examples of precious metalwork in the rococo style is a very rare child's whistle and bells or rattle (Fig. 325). An ornately fashioned hollow gold stem decorated with two rows of bells terminates in a whistle at one end and in a handle of coral—from ancient times considered to have medicinal and magical properties—at the other. The rattle was made by Nicholas

Roosevelt, a New York craftsman of Dutch descent.

Another rococo example is the rare, intricately pierced cake basket (Figs. 326 and 327) by Myer Myers, another New York silversmith of Dutch descent. Undulating outlines, delicate cutout patterns, and shells on the rim give this piece an airy elegance that characterizes the rococo spirit. (Myers produced a variety of other forms for colonial synagogues, and still others for Protestant churches.) That same spirit is expressed in more solid form in a pair of candle-

*Fig. 330. Pair of sauceboats, or butter boats, by Paul Revere II (1735–1818), Boston, about 1765; silver, length 7 9/16 inches (19.2 cm). Lively curves and high scrolling handles give the low, broad bodies of these boats an air of vivacity. Such highly specialized forms were available only to wealthy colonists, but their presence indicates that the general level of affluence in the colonies was much greater than it had been in the seventeenth century. These boats—they were usually made in pairs—bear the initials of Mungo and Ruth MacKay, who were married in 1763.* Gift of Mr. and Mrs. Andrew Varick Stout, 1946 (46.40.1,2)

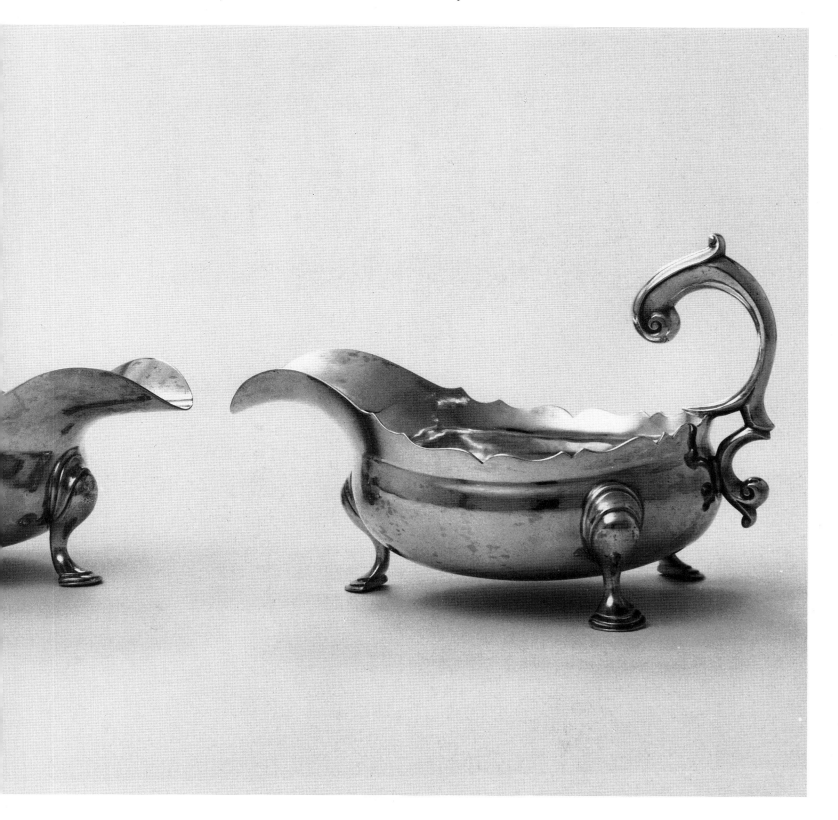

*Fig. 331. Salver or tray,* by Daniel Christian
Fueter (1720–85), New York, 1754–69; silver,
diameter 15⅝ inches (39.7 cm.). The salver was
introduced to England in the second half of the
seventeenth century, when it was described as a
"wrought plate . . . used in giving Beer, or other
liquid thing, to save the Carpit or Cloathes from
drops." By the mid-eighteenth century, when this
example was made, the form was much in use.
The serpentine lines that form the scallops of its
gadrooned rim echo the curves of all kinds of
fashionable furniture, silver, and ceramics of the
period. Flourishes and curves are used with
greater freedom, however, in the salver's finely
engraved central cartouche.
Bequest of Charles Allen Munn, 1924 (24.109.37)

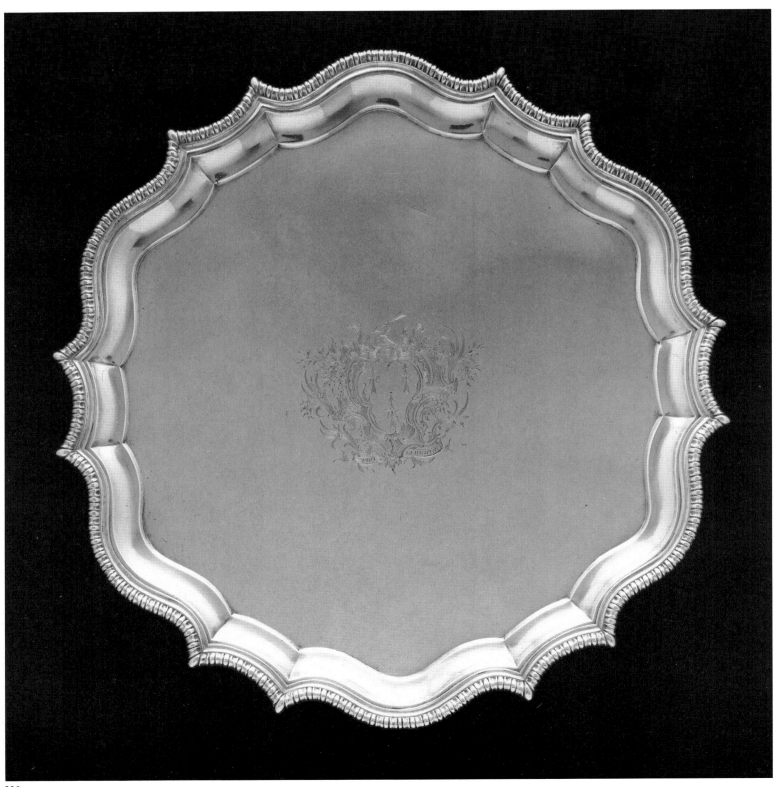

331

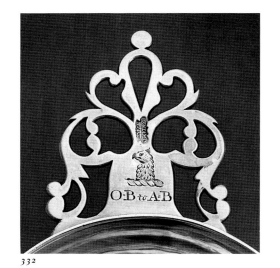

332

**Figs. 332 and 333. Porringer,** *by Benjamin Burt (1729–1805), Boston, 1750–1800; silver, diameter 5¼ inches (13.3 cm.). Porringers, whether of silver or pewter, were simple, attractive bowls for plain, everyday food, including porridge, as the name suggests. After about 1730 the regional designs that had until then determined porringer-handle shapes gave way, for the most part, to the keyhole pattern seen in this example. This porringer bears an engraved crest and initials, which may be those of Obadiah Brown of Providence and his daughter Anna.* Bequest of Alphonso T. Clearwater, 1933 (33.120.330)

sticks by the same maker (Figs. 328 and 329).

Paul Revere, as famous for his midnight ride as for his silver production, made a pair of sauceboats whose jaunty stance derives from the rococo (Fig. 330). The curves that enliven the vessels are seen again in the graceful outline of a salver by New York smith Daniel Christian Fueter (Fig. 331). Juxtaposed curves were also employed to create actual rococo forms like that of the double-bellied sugar bowl by Jacob Boelen II (Fig. 324). Here the S-curve creates a pear shape that, when turned upside down, makes this characteristic high-style rococo form; its unexpected proportions throw us a little off balance, increasing the effect of the design.

Porringers and spoons remained the most familiar forms in silver throughout the colonial period. Porringers were used for porridge, broth, berries and milk, and other comestibles. Their simply shaped bowls showed few variations in design, but the piercing of their flat handles differed from region to region until a "keyhole" pattern became popular almost everywhere late in the colonial period (Figs. 332 and 333).

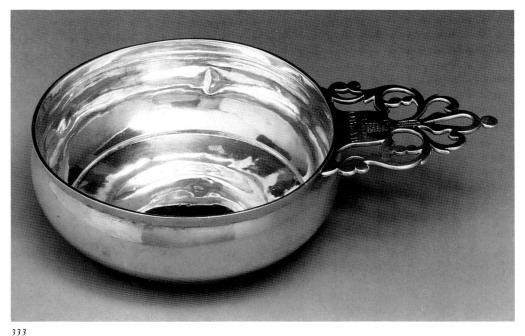

333

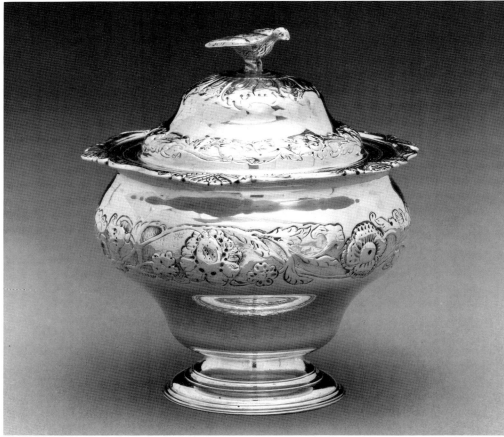

334

**Fig. 334. Sugar bowl,** *attributed to Jacob Boelen II (1733–86), New York, 1760–75; silver, height 5½ inches (14 cm.). Fully developed rococo design encompassed shape as well as decoration, and this double-bellied, or inverted-pear, shape was popular for the most fashionable coffee and teapots, for matching sugar bowls, and occasionally, for creamers. Its lines are sinuous, made up of combined S-curves, and it bears bands of repoussé leaves and flowers that accentuate the curves at their most prominent point. The cast bird finial is unusual in American silverwork.* Rogers Fund, 1939 (39.23)

# The Federal Period, 1790–1830

I n the rococo period tea sets had occasionally been made en suite, with teapot, creamer, sugar bowl, and other accessories designed as related elements. This practice became commonplace with the introduction of classical-revival styles in the years following the Revolution. Outstanding among the numerous examples in the collection is a four-piece tea service attributed to Philadelphia silversmith Christian Wiltberger (Fig. 335). The set is an impressive example of the Federal, or neoclassical, style in silver with its urn and helmet shapes, its shallow alternating convex and concave panels with bright-cut engraved designs, and its patriotic eagle finials.

The neoclassical mode is again employed, directly and simply, in a pair of candlesticks whose form is that of fluted columns fashioned by Isaac Hutton of Albany, New York (Fig. 336). Strong French influence is apparent in a pair of elaborate late neoclassical, or American Empire, sauceboats made in Philadelphia by the émigré smith Anthony Rasch (Fig. 337). The sinuous serpents that serve as handles, the ram's-head spouts, and the winged-lion feet are ornamental forms derived from classical antiquity. Clearly, as the influence of French Empire and English Regency styles increased, American silversmiths were introducing more robust versions of classical design.

The form of one of a pair of presentation vases made for Governor DeWitt Clinton, for example, is that of an ancient—and famous—vase excavated in Italy (Fig. 338). However, while a number of classical motifs ornament the vessel, specifically American scenes and references appear as well. And although the piece remains balanced and symmetrical, its overall appearance bespeaks nineteenth-century exuberance rather than classical calm.

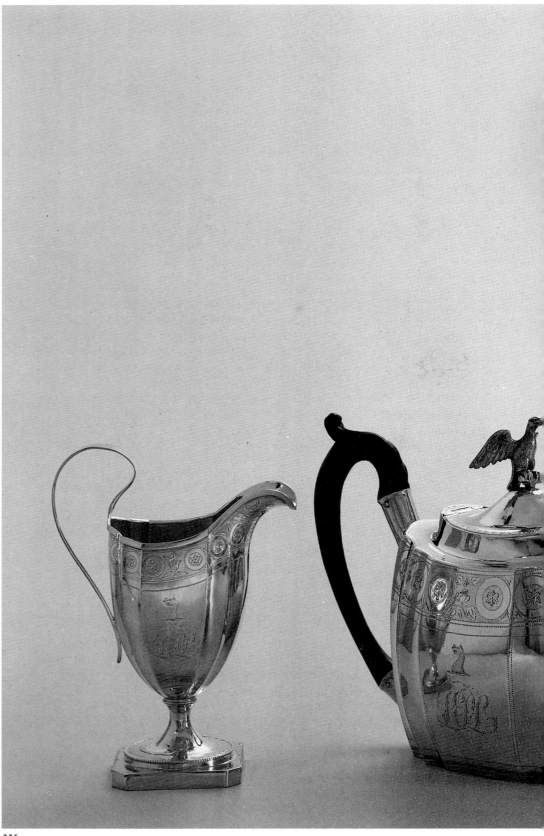

335

**Fig. 335. Tea service,** *attributed to Christian Wiltberger (1766–1851), Philadelphia, about 1800; silver, heights, left to right, 6½ inches (16.5 cm.), 7 inches (17.8 cm.), 14½ inches (36.8 cm.), 9⅞ inches (25.1 cm.). It is not surprising to learn that Philadelphia was America's cultural as well as political center when this superbly crafted tea set was made. It descended in the Lewis family, whose crest it bears, and is said to have been a wedding gift from General Lafayette and his son to Martha Washington's granddaughter Nelly Custis upon her marriage in 1799 to George Washington's nephew Lawrence*

*Lewis. By the time this set was made, the neoclassical shapes and motifs that came into fashion after the Revolution had entirely superseded rococo designs, so that these shapes are constructed of straight lines and strict symmetrical curves. The coffeepot, teapot, and sugar bowl are splendid vertical forms topped by cast eagle finials; the creamer is of the popular helmet shape taken from classical antiquity. Restrained bands of geometrical engraving are executed in the shallow brightcut tradition.*

Gift of H. H. Walker Lewis, in memory of his parents, Mr. and Mrs. Edwin A. S. Lewis, 1980 (1980.503.1–4)

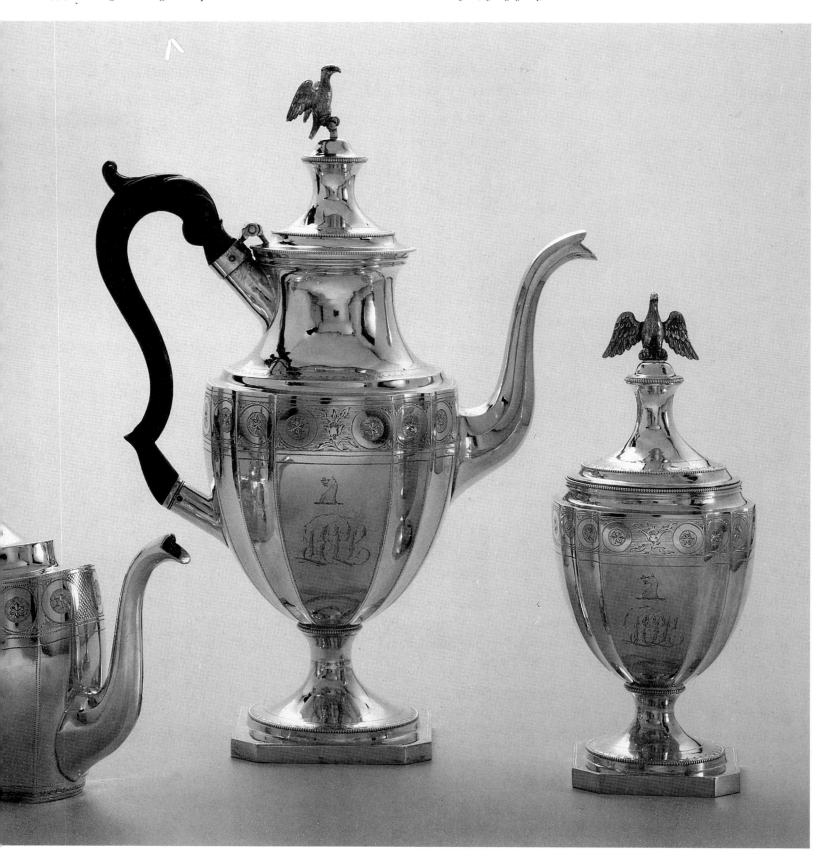

**Fig. 336. Pair of candlesticks,** *by Isaac Hutton (1766–1855), Albany, New York, 1800–15; silver, height 8½ inches (21.6 cm.). The forthright simplicity of these columnar candlesticks contrasts with the delicately shaped and engraved silver of the earlier Federal period, foreshadowing the more massive shapes and unadorned surfaces of Empire silver. Isaac Hutton was a leading silversmith and citizen of Albany from the 1790s to 1817, when he and his brother George—apparently because of overextension in their mercantile business—declared bankruptcy.*
Bequest of Alphonso T. Clearwater, 1933
(33.120.204,205)

**Fig. 337. Sauceboat** *(one of a pair), by Anthony Rasch (w. about 1807–25), Philadelphia, 1808–19; silver, length 11³⁄₁₆ inches (28.4 cm.). The strong boat shape of this piece is emphasized by the forward and horizontal thrust of the bold serpent handle and ram's-head spout. The use of these graphic animal motifs, seen again in the winged lion's-paw feet, is characteristic of French Empire design. Rasch was one of a number of highly skilled French craftsmen who emigrated to Philadelphia in the years after the French revolution, bringing with him the shapes and motifs of the high Empire style.*
Fletcher Fund, 1959 (59.152.1)

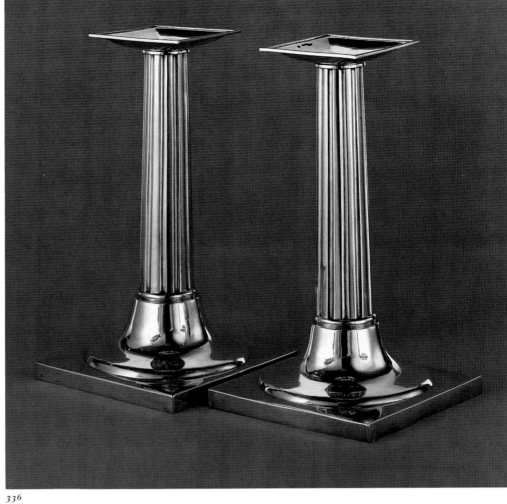

336

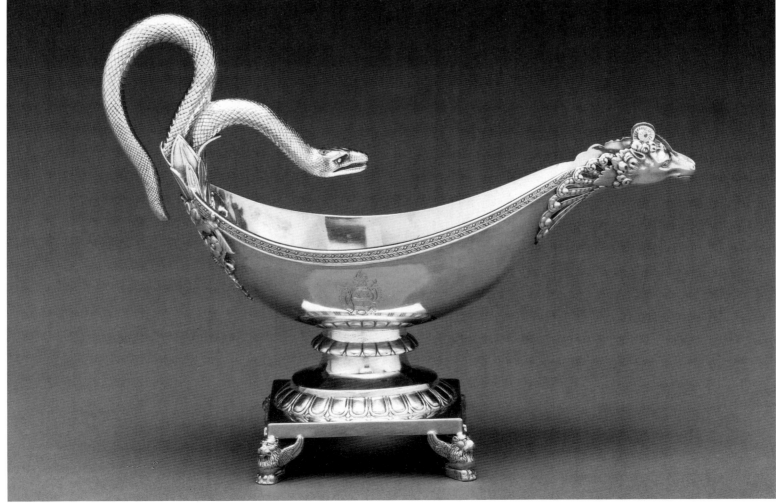

337

**Fig. 338. Presentation vase,** by Thomas Fletcher (1787–1866) and Sidney Gardner (1785–1827), Philadelphia, 1824; silver, height 23½ inches (59.6 cm.), maximum width 20½ inches (52 cm.). Presentation pieces like this elaborate vase and its companion (a promised gift to the Museum) came into vogue about the time of the War of 1812, and their popularity increased throughout the nineteenth century. Based on the form of the famous Warwick Vase, discovered in Italy and taken to England in the late eighteenth century, this piece celebrates the completion of the Erie Canal. Classical motifs like egg-and-dart moldings, anthemia, and lion's-paw feet are combined with views of specific scenes along the canal. Although its sources are disparate, the vase is coherently planned and beautifully executed. It and its mate were presented to DeWitt Clinton in appreciation of his contribution to the Erie Canal project.

Purchase, Louis V. Bell and Rogers Funds; Anonymous and Robert G. Goelet Gifts; and Gifts of Fenton L. B. Brown and of the grandchildren of Mrs. Ranson Spaford Hooker, in her memory, by exchange, 1982 (1982.4)

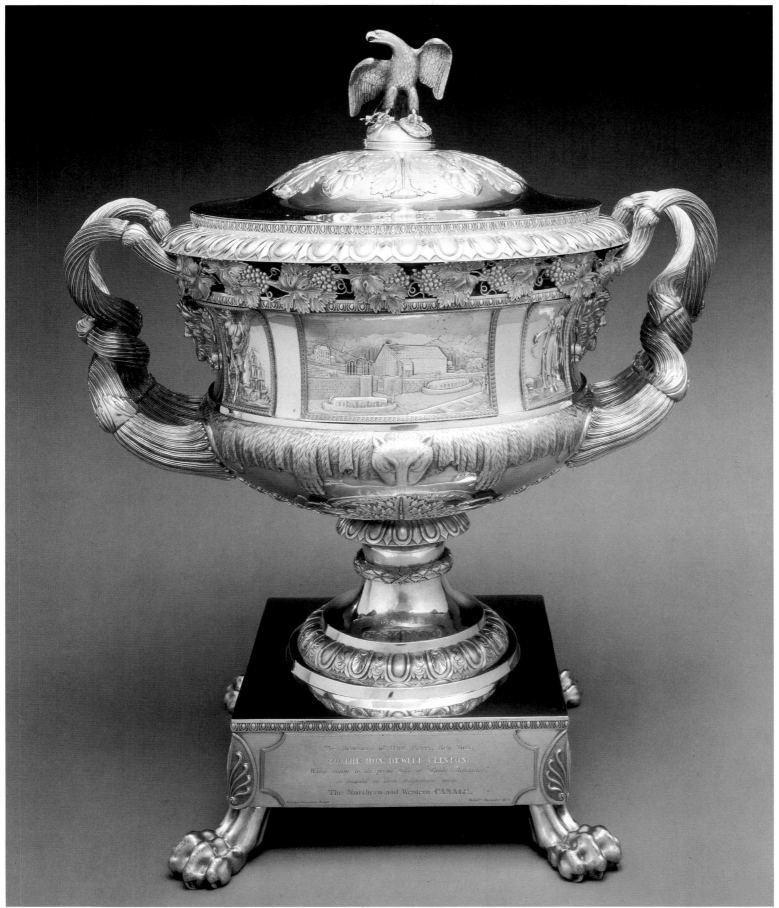

338

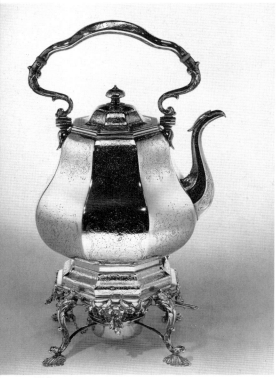

339

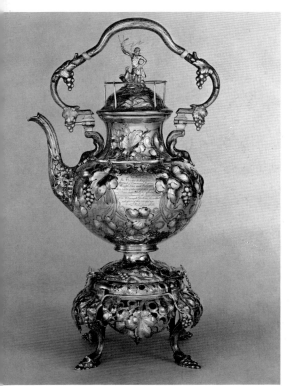

340

**Fig. 339. Kettle on stand,** *made by William Forbes (active 1826–50), and sold by Ball, Tompkins, and Black, New York, about 1840; silver, height 13 inches (33 cm.). The lavish ornament of the kettle illustrated in Fig. 340 is lacking in this example of a few years earlier. The handles of the pots are very much alike, but the delicate chased floral, leaf, and scroll design that ornaments the octagonal panels of this example is much less assertive than the sculptured repoussage of its near contemporary. The taste for scrolling rococo forms is present in both teapots, but it is expressed very differently—proving, perhaps, that lavish ornament was never universally popular, even in periods when it was dominant. This kettle is part of a seven-piece tea set, and although its form and ornament were restrained, the number of its pieces was not. It is particularly unusual in including a hot-milk pot and a covered butter dish.*
Gift of Guerdon Holden Nelson, Cyril Irwin Nelson, Nicholas Macy Nelson and Michael Underhill Nelson, in devoted memory of their grandmother, Elinor Irwin Holden, and of their mother, Elise Macy Nelson, 1981 (1981.22.1)

**Fig. 340. Kettle and stand,** *by John Chandler Moore for Ball, Tompkins, and Black, New York, 1850; silver, height 17 5/16 inches (43.9 cm.). Like the vase presented to DeWitt Clinton, this kettle was made as a presentation piece—in this case to honor the man who installed the first telegraph lines from New York to Boston and Buffalo. Its pear shape, curved legs, and lavish repoussé ornament of grapevines and leaves are characteristic of fully developed Rococo Revival design. The domed lid is engraved with a scene that includes a train, a sailboat, and telegraph lines, and the cast finial depicts Zeus with an eagle. By the middle of the century, firms like Ball, Tompkins, and Black had been formed to sell silver made by others—and were forerunners of our modern jewelry stores.*
Gift of Mrs. F. R. Lefferts, 1969 (69.141.1a-c)

The later years of the nineteenth century saw the revival of a number of other historic styles. Changing fashions that resulted in a bewildering mixture of forms and decoration in furniture and silver were closely related. As with furniture, the labels given to these successive, overlapping silver styles—rococo, Gothic, and Renaissance among them—provided only a vague guide to their appearance.

By mid-century the American Empire style had largely been replaced by what were called rococo and Renaissance patterns. Much hollow ware was almost completely covered with heavy chased C- and S-scrolls and diapers combined with bold repoussé ornament in naturalistic floral designs. The transition from the relative restraint of the Empire style to the lush ornamentation of the Rococo Revival may be seen in two teakettles made within the ten-year period between 1840 and 1850 (Figs. 339 and 340).

**Fig. 341. Presentation vase,** *designed by James H. Whitehouse for Tiffany and Company (1853–present), New York, about 1875; silver, height 33 3/8 inches (84.8 cm.). This and the two succeeding illustrations make it abundantly clear that when it came to presentation pieces money was no object and economy of ornament of no interest. A group of friends of William Cullen Bryant ordered this vase in honor of the poet's eightieth birthday. Above everything else the vase conveys a sense of high aspirations and the good life achieved. Its form is that of a classical vase, and much of its ornament is borrowed from the vocabulary of the Renaissance—for example, the symmetrical diaper pattern of the background and the round medallions containing a profile portrait of Bryant himself and scenes from his life and work. The poet's preoccupation with nature is reflected in the American flora that are interwoven with Renaissance motifs.*
Gift of William Cullen Bryant, 1877 (77.9ab)

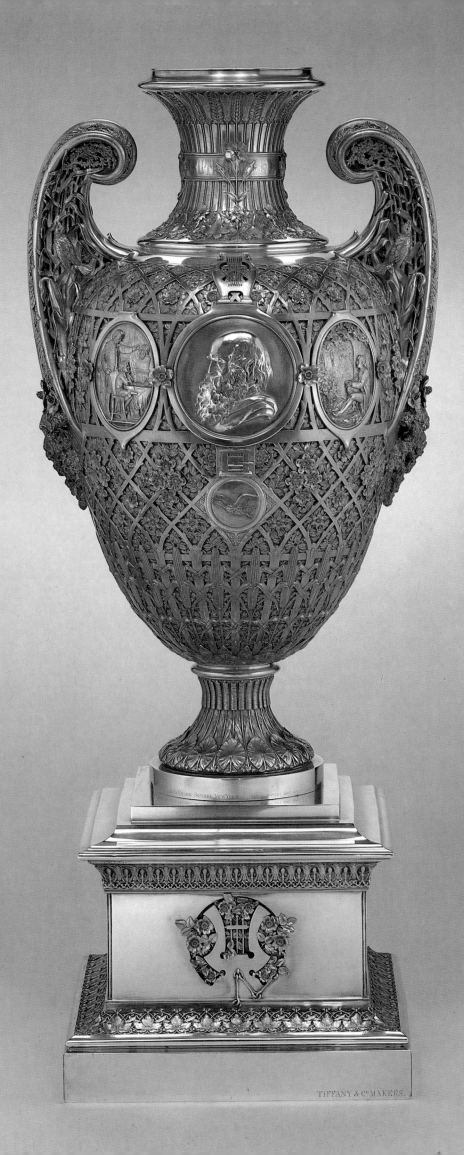

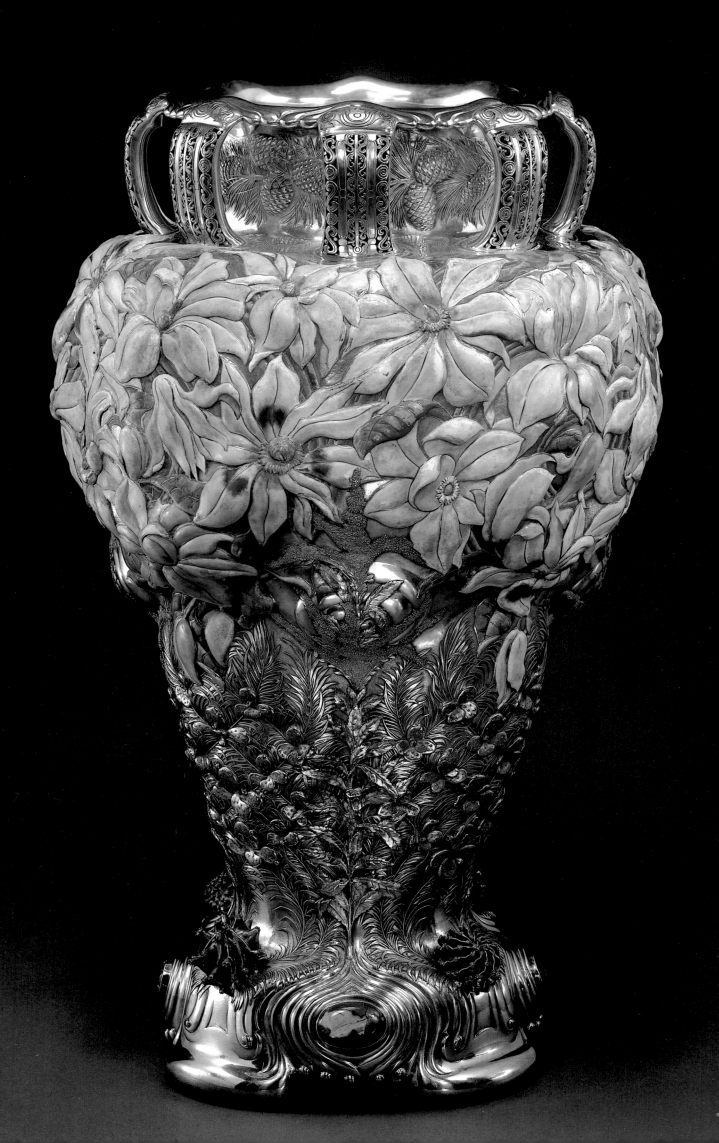

342

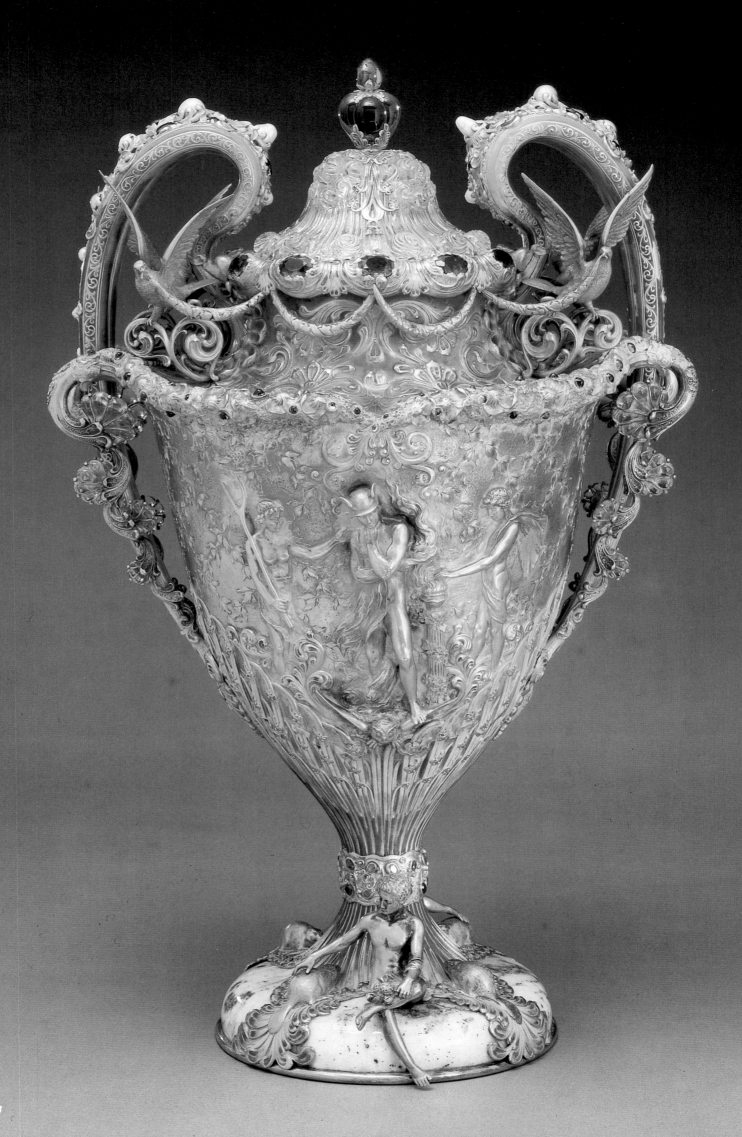

*Overleaf*

**Fig. 342. Vase,** *designed by John T. Curran for Tiffany and Company (1853–present), New York, 1893; silver, gold, and enamel, height 31 inches (78.7 cm.). The opulence characteristic of the highest style objects of the late nineteenth century is exemplified in this piece, made for the World's Columbian Exposition of 1893 and called the "Magnolia vase." Its size is impressive, its materials precious, its ornament lavish and varied. Wildly eclectic design influences are incorporated in it: a contemporary described the piece, saying that its form had been suggested by "pieces of pottery found among the relics of the* ancient cliff-dwellers of the Pueblos," and calling its handles Toltec. Its base employs curves in the Art Nouveau manner, and its ornament is symbolic of American plants and other natural forms. Yet, despite its disparate influences, it is cohesive—it succeeds as a work of art.*
Gift of Mrs. Winthrop Atwell, 1899 (99.2)

**Fig. 343. Presentation vase,** *designed by Paulding Farnham for Tiffany and Company (1853–present), New York, 1893–95; gold, semiprecious stones, and enamel, height 19½ inches (49.5 cm.). The height of lavishness, this vase could have been produced only in a period of prosperity, optimism, and self-confidence. It was commissioned by the stockholders and direc-*tors of the American Cotton Oil Company as a gift to Edward Dean Adams, chairman of the board. Adams had labored ceaselessly to save the company from ruin, refusing all compensation, and this was a thank-you gesture. Its form is that of an ancient Greek vase, and its symbolism is that of traditional mythology, employed here to tell the story of cotton and the American Cotton Oil Company. It was so necessary to have a key to the symbolism that Tiffany published a booklet to explain it and, while they were at it, added remarkable statistics on the large number of specialized craftsmen needed to make this tour de force and emphasized its great cost.*
Gift of Edward D. Adams, 1904 (04.1)

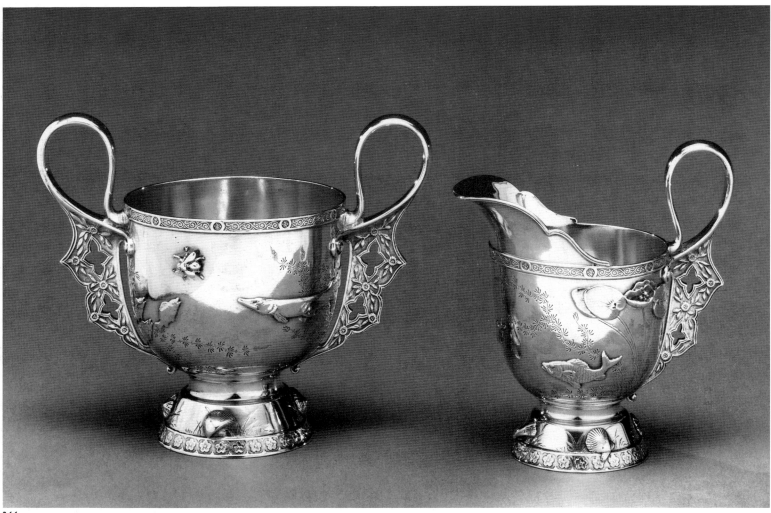

344

In 1874, to honor William Cullen Bryant on the occasion of his eightieth birthday, a group of the poet's friends commissioned James H. Whitehouse of Tiffany and Company to fashion a huge vase in the Renaissance Revival style (Fig. 341). Although this massive piece has the outlines of an antique Greek vase, it is overlaid with complex ornamentation that includes a profile portrait of Bryant, symbolic representations of American flora and fauna, and Renaissance Revival medallions referring to the poet's writings and interests.

Bryant gave the vase to the Museum a few years after it was presented to him.

Tiffany's designers worked in a wide range of styles, often combining influences from several sources in one piece. A creamer and sugar bowl (Fig. 344), for example, add Japanese and "Eastlake" motifs to a basically Renaissance Revival shape.

**Fig. 344. Cream pitcher and sugar bowl,** *by Tiffany and Company (1853–present), New York, 1874; silver, height of sugar bowl 4¹⁵⁄₁₆ inches (12.3 cm.), height of creamer 4⅝ inches (11.2 cm.). The helmet-shaped creamer and the high loop handles of both pieces are characteristic of Renaissance Revival design, but the flat applied fish, lily pads, and shells, as well as the engraved seaweed and lily-pad stems evoke Japanese art—a great influence on Western designers in the 1870s. A further diverse influence is seen in the flat handle supports with cutout designs, for they resemble "Eastlake" furniture motifs.*
Purchase, The Edgar J. Kaufmann Foundation Gift, 1969 (69.128.1,2)

# The Post-Centennial Period 1875–1915

**Fig. 345. Teapot,** *by Tiffany and Company (1853–present), New York, about 1888; silver, enamel, and ivory, length 11 inches (27.9 cm.). Edward C. Moore, Tiffany's chief designer in the 1880s and a partner in the firm, probably designed this pot, which is part of a set that also includes tongs and a sugar bowl and creamer. Moore was among the artists who created an interest in Near Eastern art in this country, both through his own designs and through his fine collection of Near and Far Eastern art. Exotic objects like this, popular especially during the 1880s and 1890s, coordinated well with interiors that included a "Turkish corner" or, as in the case of the Rockefeller house in New York, a whole Moorish room.*
Gift of a Friend of the Museum, 1897 (97.1.1)

**Fig. 346. Tray,** *by Tiffany and Company (1853–present), New York, 1889–91; silver, diameter 12 inches (30.5 cm.). The taste for extremely ornate and exotically decorated objects began to ebb somewhat among some people during the 1890s, and simpler pieces like this one were produced. The trend that had been growing among a small group of reforming architects and designers and that resulted in the Arts and Crafts movement had produced an interest in hand, rather than machine, production. The surface of this tray, with its obvious hammer marks, reflects this interest. The engraved irises and leaves convey an interest in oriental—particularly, in this case, Japanese—design.*
Rogers Fund, 1966 (66.52.1)

By the time the foregoing pieces were made, Tiffany's silverwares were already internationally acclaimed. At the Paris exposition of 1867 the firm had won the first award ever given to a foreigner. In their opulence, eclecticism, and use of symbolism, two other large and impressive vases made by Tiffany and Company represent the extravagant taste of America's Gilded Age. The complexity of design of both the so-called Magnolia vase and the Adams vase (Figs. 342 and 343) is staggering, calling for expert craftsmanship of a kind that could probably not be commanded today. About this same time Tiffany and Company produced a teapot (Fig. 345; part of a so-called tête-à-tête set) that was much less grand than the vases in conception, but of a highly imaginative design. The company described the set as ". . . made . . . entirely by hand . . . without seams . . . each . . . from a single piece of silver. It is enameled, etched and gilded; and is also etched and gilded on the interior, which in itself is a very difficult and remarkable piece of work. . . ." This exotic set was clearly inspired by Islamic art: the colors of the enamels recall those of Turkish rugs and of Syrian Mamluk glass of the fourteenth century. The influence of the East is seen again in a tray ornamented with iris blooms and leaves—a theme taken from Japanese art and used here in combination with a hand-hammered surface that is one of the characteristics of the Arts and Crafts movement (Fig. 346).

A ewer and plateau (Fig. 347) made early in the present century by the Gorham Manufacturing Company of Providence, Rhode Island, were fashioned in the Art Nouveau style. Martelé was Gorham's name for handmade wares of

345

346

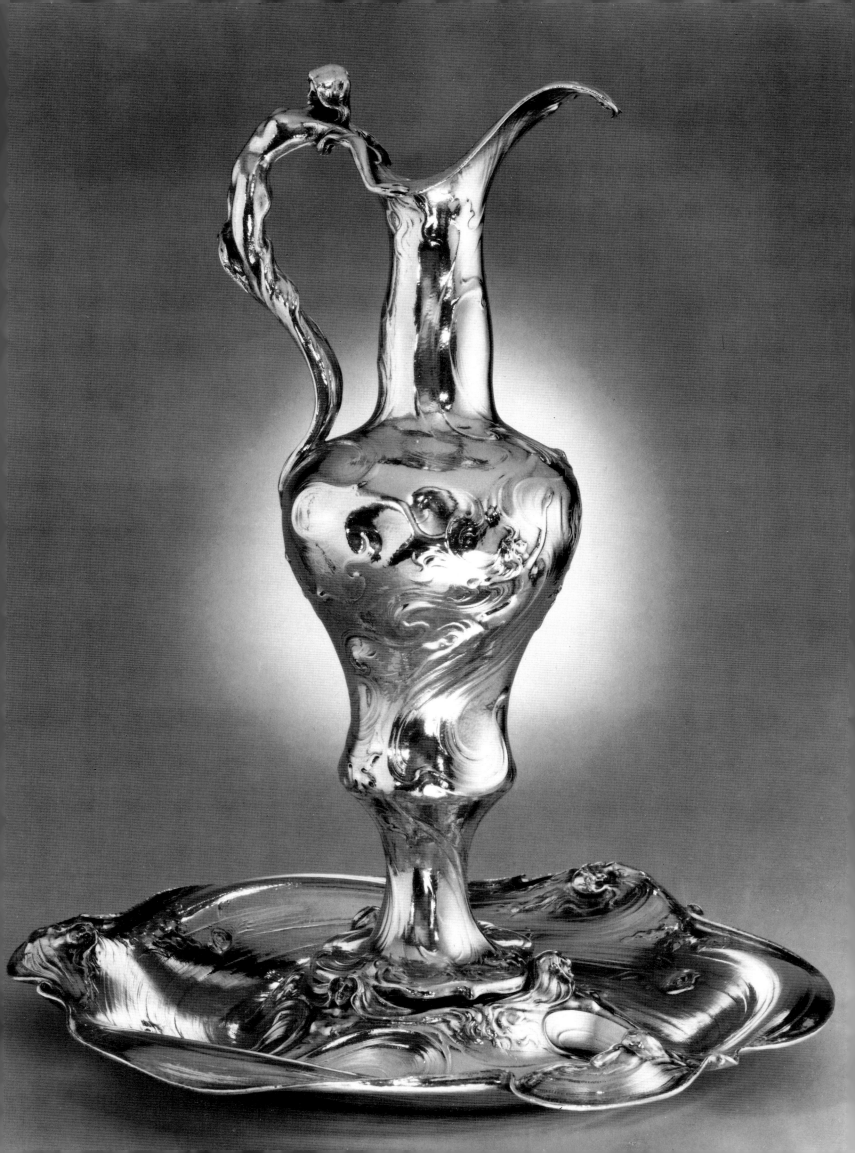

metal purer and softer than sterling silver. The plain surfaces of each piece reveal the marks left in the metal as it was hammered by hand to its unique shape. Here are the freely flowing organic forms and ornaments typical of the Art Nouveau style, and they are seen again in a slender vase of green glass overlaid with sinuously curving silver ornament (Fig. 348). It appeared to many that with the Art Nouveau movement the modern world had finally cast off the bonds of the past, exuberantly turned away from historical precedent, and confidently restated the principles of design in purely contemporary terms. More recently this shift has been viewed as part of a perpetual cycle in which straight-line and curvilinear styles alternate.

**Fig. 347. Ewer and plateau,** *by the Gorham Manufacturing Company (1865–1961), Providence, about 1901; silver, height of ewer 19 inches (48.3 cm.), diameter of plateau 17⅛ inches (43.5 cm.). This impressive set represents the Gorham Company's effort to produce art objects made by hand of silver purer than sterling. The English designer William Codman, who supervised their production, gave these wares the name Martelé. Designed in the flowing Art Nouveau style, they emphasized motifs that lent themselves to sweeping curves, as the female, fish, and leaf forms do on this ewer and plateau. Martelé wares were expensive when they were made and they have remained so, for production was limited and examples rarely come on the market. It was said that no two pieces were alike.*
Gift of Hugh Grant, 1974 (1974.214.26ab)

**Fig. 348. Vase,** *by the Alvin Manufacturing Corporation, Providence, 1900–10; glass and silver, height 14 inches (35.6 cm.). This vase was produced by the silver-deposit process in which silver is electroplated onto glass. The Alvin Corporation specialized in this kind of work, which was most popular between 1890 and 1910. The curves of the vase and of the sinuous Art Nouveau leaves and flowers that decorate it accord well together.*
Sansbury-Mills Fund, 1980 (1980.299)

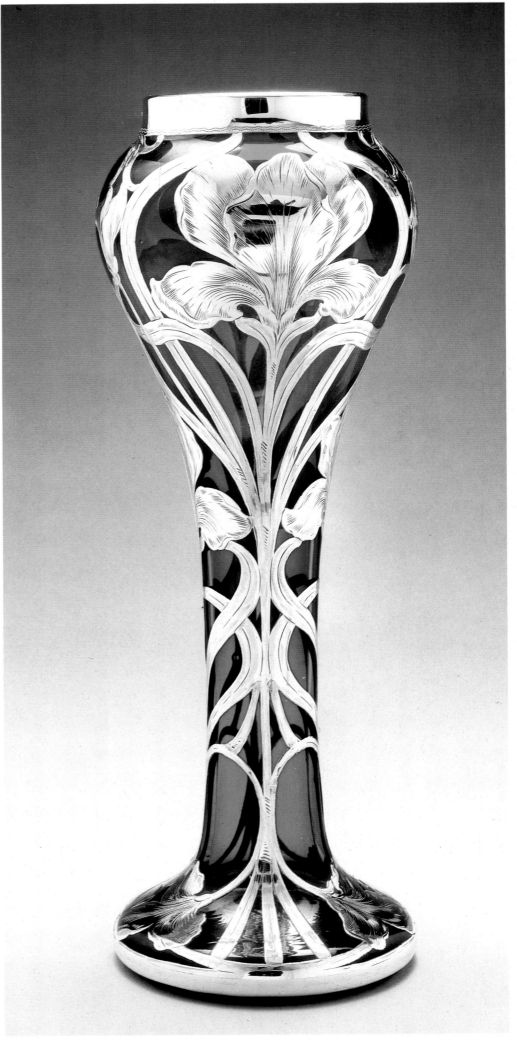

*348*

347

# Pewter

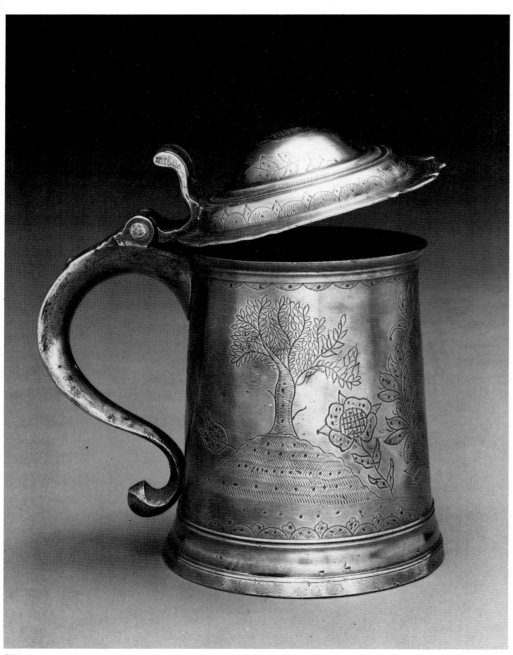

349

**Fig. 349. Tankard,** by John Will (about 1707–about 1774), New York, 1752–74; pewter, height 7⅛ inches (18.1 cm.). Tankards were used in the eighteenth century for the hard cider, ale, and beer that lent warmth and cheer to cold, work-filled days and nights. This example, by a member of the accomplished Will family of pew-terers, is especially rare because it is decorated with naïve engravings ("wriggle work") of trees, leaves, and flowers and trimmed at top and base with scalloping in imitation of the cut-card orna-ment on New York silver tankards.
Gift of Mrs. J. Insley Blair, 1940 (40.184.1)

Throughout the colonial and early Federal periods pewter, made principally of tin with small admixtures of lead and antimony, was a ubiquitous metal, serving in myriad capacities from the nursery to the banquet hall, from the tavern to the Communion table. It is relatively soft and destructible, but it can be easily melted and remolded at small expense. It was the brass molds in which pewter was cast that were costly to make and replace, and they received prolonged use that tended to retard developments in design. Thus, since forms in pewter were often copied from those in silver, the styles of pewter porringers, tankards, teapots, and other vessels persisted long after silversmiths had abandoned them for more fashionable ones. Nevertheless, although forms are more or less standardized because of the reliance on molds, pewter's enduring attraction may be judged by the number of outstanding examples in the Museum's collection.

Probably just before the Revolutionary War, John Will, a New York pewterer, made a tankard whose form was typical but whose ornament—engraved floral designs on body and domed lid—were unusual (Fig. 349). As many as four molds were required to make such a piece of hollow ware: one each for the body, the lid, the thumbpiece for opening the lid, and the handle. Will's slightly earlier contemporary Simon Edgell of Philadelphia fashioned a magnificent fifteen-inch dish of excellent metal strengthened by scrupulous all-over hammering (Fig. 350). In addition to these prime examples are a pear-shaped teapot standing on little curved legs with claw-and-ball feet, by William Will (Fig. 351); a unique christening basin by Joseph Leddell (Fig. 352); and an elegant little creamer by Peter Young (Fig. 353)—simple, satisfying forms typifying what is best and most significant in eighteenth-century American pewter.

Early in the nineteenth century a finer grade of pewter known as britannia was introduced into America. This silver-white alloy contained no lead but some copper to lend hardness and more antimony to give a bright sheen. Because it was a tough alloy that could be rolled into thin sheets and then spun into the desired shape on a lathe or stamped into the needed component parts by a press, britannia was used to make a host of diversified objects. From the 1830s to the 1860s this adaptable metal was at the height of its popularity.

Thomas Danforth Boardman of Hartford, Connecticut, one of a number of related pewterers with the same surname, was among the first Americans to produce britannia ware. During a partnership with Lucius Hart in New York he produced a lidless quart measure of baluster shape (Fig. 354). This unusual American piece (not unlike earlier English models) bears the initials J. D. and the date 1835. The enormous variety and quantity of forms manufactured during britannia's heyday—everything from cuspidors to Communion services, from candlesticks and lamps to picture frames and babies' bottles, from teapots and spoons to earpieces for hearing trumpets—can hardly be suggested here, but it is at least clear that the quality of performance at its best survived the industrialization of this ancient craft.

*Fig. 350. **Dish,** by Simon Edgell (w. Philadelphia 1713–42), Philadelphia, 1713–42; pewter, diameter 14¾ inches (37.5 cm.). Trained in London, Simon Edgell came to Philadelphia in 1713 and apparently achieved success both as a pewterer and a merchant. This splendid dish with hand-hammered decoration certainly testifies to his pewter-making skill. Although hammering is often found on English pewter wares of the period, it is unusual in American work.* Gift of Joseph France, 1943 (43.162.25)

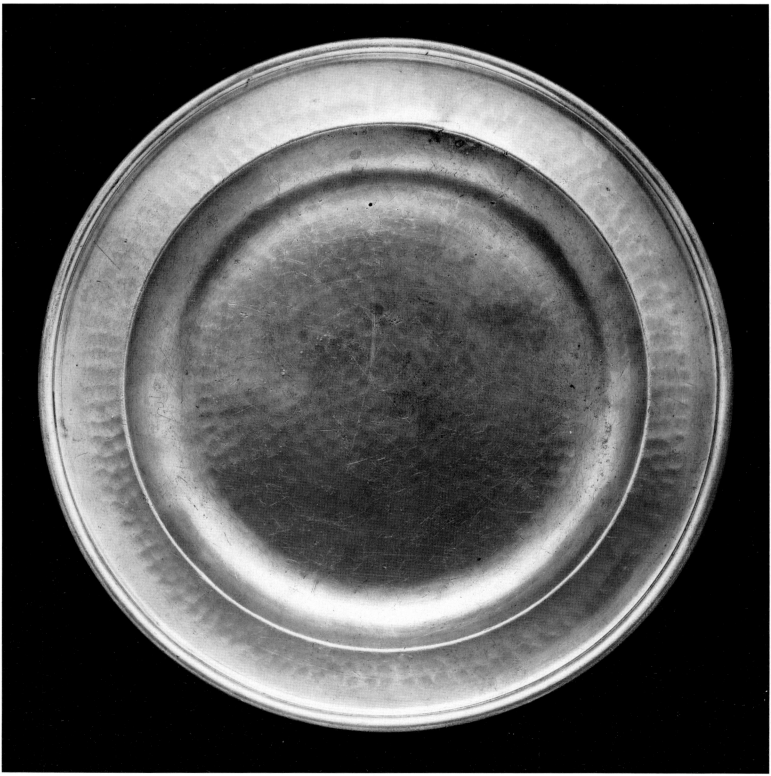

350

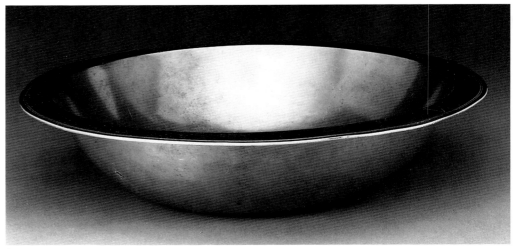

352

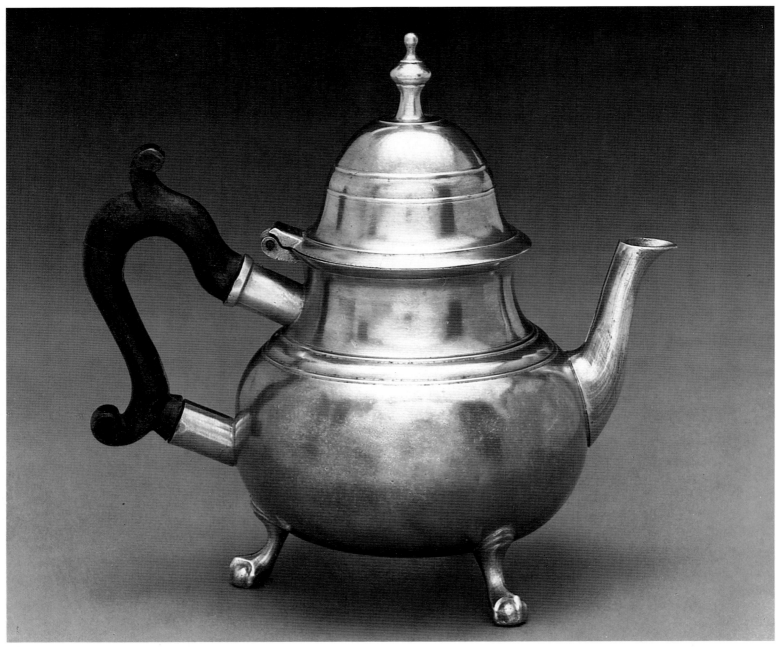

351

**Fig. 351. Teapot,** by William Will (1742–98), Philadelphia, 1764–98; pewter, height 8¼ inches (21 cm.). William is the member of the pewter-making Will family of New York and Philadelphia whose work is most avidly collected today. "Other American pewterers turned out metal of just as fine quality, but very few were ca-pable of such a high order of workmanship and, to the best of my knowledge, none attempted such ambitious designs," wrote authority Ledlie Laughlin in Pewter in America. The pear-shaped pot was the standard form in pewter until the in-troduction of the drum shape about the time of the Revolution. This example has particular charm because of its claw-and-ball feet, which are like those of late colonial furniture.

Gift of Mrs. J. Insley Blair, 1949 (49.2)

**Fig. 352. Basin,** *by Joseph Leddell, Sr. (about 1690–1754) or Joseph Leddell, Jr. (d. 1754), New York, 1712–54; pewter, diameter 12⅞ inches (32.7 cm.). Basins were used in colonial times both for serving food and for baptismal rites. It is not known for which purpose this basin was originally made, but whatever its use, it is a splendid example of its type, rare because it is the earliest form of American basin and because of the perfection of its shape. Joseph Sr. is thought to have been born in England, where he no doubt learned his trade. He was in New York by 1711, conducting business there until his death in 1754. His son, Joseph Jr., who undoubtedly learned the craft from his father, was at work in New York from about 1740 until his death in 1754. He advertised in 1752 that he made "any uncommon Thing in Pewter, in any Shape or Form as shall be order'd. . . ." It is unclear whether the basin was made by father or son, for it is marked simply "I. Leddell."*
Gift of Mrs. J. Insley Blair, 1940 (40.184.2)

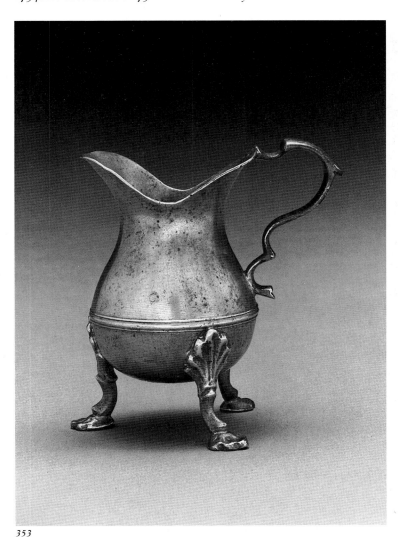

353

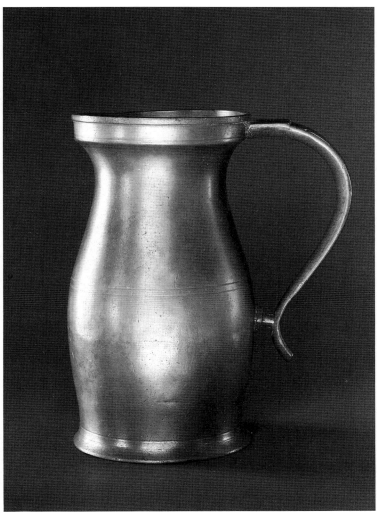

354

**Fig. 353. Creamer,** *by Peter Young (1749–1813), New York and Albany, 1775–95; pewter, height 4½ inches (10.5 cm.). Pear-shaped pitchers like this with scroll handle, cabriole legs, and shell feet are rare in American pewter. They incorporate fashionable rococo features that were seldom seen in pewter, for they necessitated buying costly new molds. Peter Young, wrote Ledlie Laughlin in* Pewter in America, *"was not just another pewterer. He was a maker of taste, ability, and considerable originality."*
Gift of Clara Lloyd-Smith Weber, 1981 (1981.117)

**Fig. 354. Measure,** *by Boardman and Hart (1828–53), New York, 1835; pewter, height 7 inches (17.8 cm.). Although wine measures were advertised by colonial pewterers, none has survived, and even nineteenth-century examples are extremely scarce. This lidless, baluster-shaped measure is therefore not only desirable as a rare form but as a marked example of the work of the well-known pewterers Boardman and Hart.*
Gift of Clara Lloyd-Smith Weber, 1979 (1979.449)

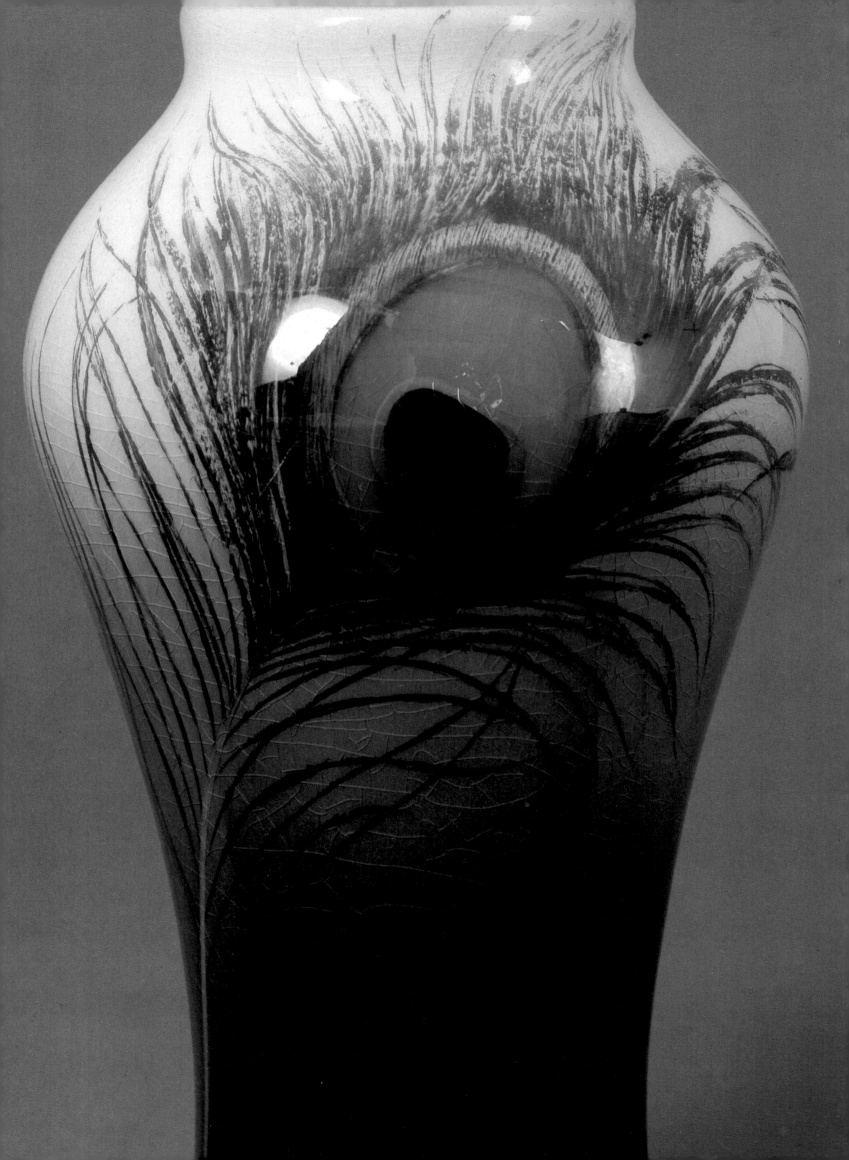

# CERAMICS

# The Colonial and Federal Periods, 1630–1830

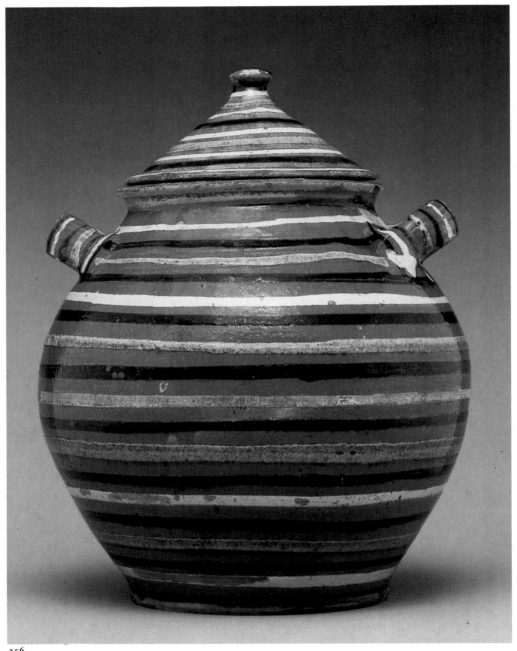

356

**Fig. 356. Covered jar,** *North Carolina, 1785–1830; red earthenware, height 12¾ inches (32.4 cm.). This engaging form is known as a sugar jar in North Carolina, where the Moravians produced many of them from before the middle of the eighteenth century onward. Upon their arrival in America from Germany or Switzerland, most of the Moravians who eventually*

*came to North Carolina lived for a time in Pennsylvania. Their pottery is different from what evolved in Pennsylvania, however, and this jar, decorated simply with bright stripes of slip, contrasts markedly with the Pennsylvania German sgraffito plate opposite.*
Rogers Fund, 1918 (18.95.16)

Clays that could be used for making various types of pottery were plentiful in colonial America, as of course was wood to fire the potters' kilns. Consequently, ceramics were made to serve local needs from the earliest days of colonial settlement. Then and for many years to come, not only bricks, but roof tiles and kitchen, dairy, and table equipment were made of coarse red earthenware. These were simple, utilitarian forms that were usually washed or splashed with protective and sometimes decorative glazes of various colors.

These practical wares were made in many places, with some regional differences in form and decoration. Outstanding was the highly distinctive pottery of the Pennsylvania Germans, with colorful, sprightly designs and inscriptions. A wide variety of forms were made, from pitchers, jugs, plates, and mugs to flowerpots, shaving basins, and toy whistles. Two basic decorative techniques were employed: slip decoration and sgraffito. Both methods were centuries old and both were practiced in other areas of the country. Slip decoration was achieved by drawing with colored liquid clay, or "slip," on the pottery with a goose quill before the final firing (Fig. 356). Sgraffito designs were scratched through a slip coating with a stick, revealing the red-clay base beneath (Figs. 357 and 358). Graphic motifs and inscriptions were commonly taken from folk images and folklore carried over from the Old World to the New.

Stoneware, made of finer and denser clays that were fired at a much higher temperature than ordinary earthenware, was produced as early as the eighteenth century. The harder body of this ware could be glazed merely by throw-

**Fig. 357. Plate,** *possibly by Henry Roudebuth (active about 1790–1816), Pennsylvania, about 1793; red earthenware, diameter 12¼ inches (31.1 cm.). Pennsylvania German pottery is characterized by bright colors and freely and humorously drawn flowers, birds, human figures, and animals—all of which set it apart from New England work. Here a sgraffito peacock struts across a yellow ground toward a tulip-like flower almost as big as he is—both motifs were popular in Pennsylvania German art. The cartouche containing the date 1793 and the initials H. R. is unusual and has led students—cautiously, in the absence of any supporting evidence—to entertain the thought that its maker may have been Henry Roudebuth of Montgomery County. Decorative plates like this were made not to use every day but to give as gifts or to mark special occasions.* Gift of Mrs. Robert W. de Forest, 1933 (34.100.124)

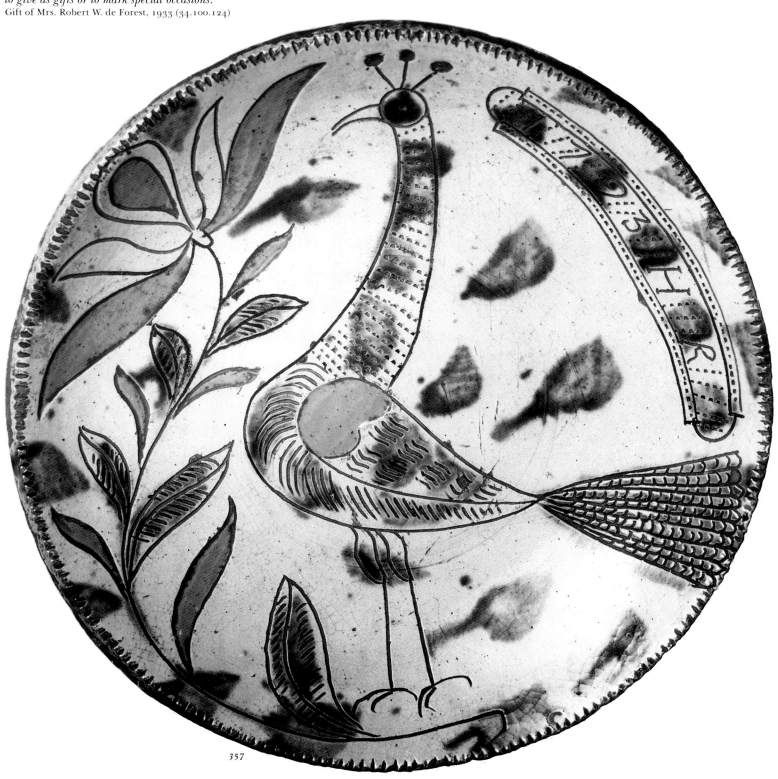

357

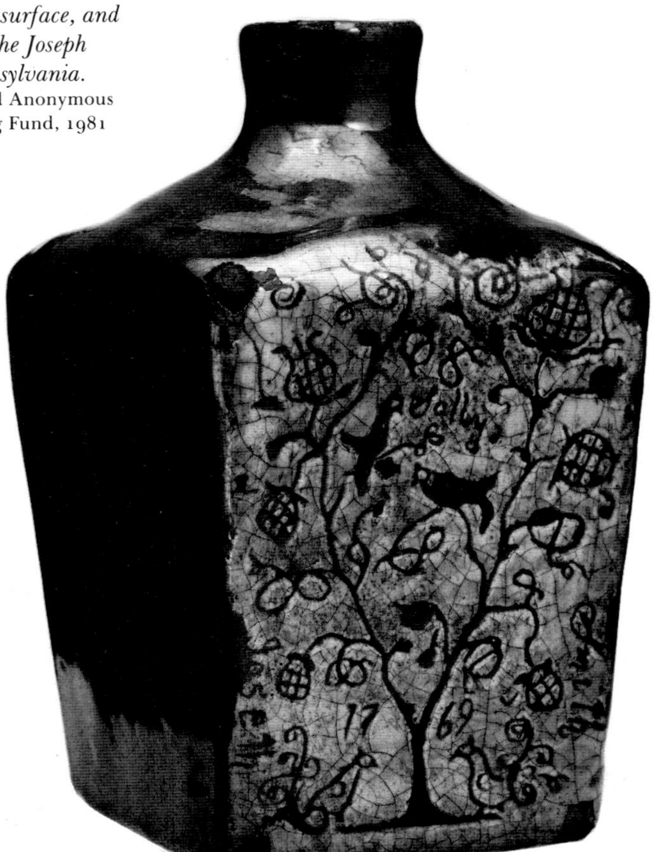

*358*

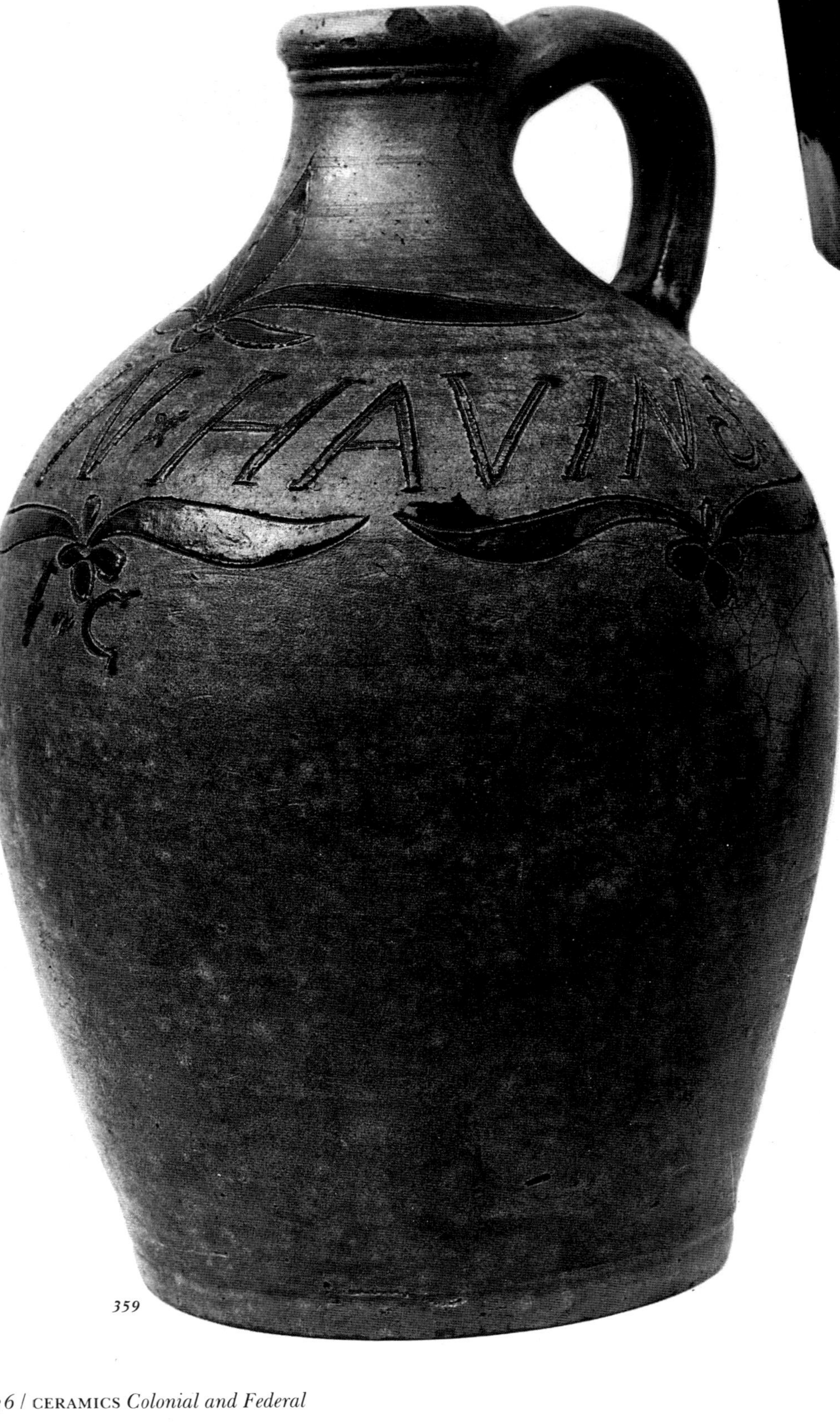

*359*

ing salt into the kiln when the fire was at its hottest. The result was a thin, colorless, very hard coating that was impervious to liquids. It was also resistant to acids, so that salt-glazed stoneware was popular for containers for vinegar, pickles, preserves, and the like. The practical advantages of this type of ware were obvious, and it was produced in various regions of the country throughout the nineteenth century.

Most stoneware was gray with decoration painted freehand in cobalt blue. One jug bears the incised inscription "Iohn Havins. 1775, July 18, N. York" and the mark "I. C.," probably the initials of the potter John Crolius of New York City (Fig. 359). The Crolius family was established in New York in the 1720s and, with the Remmey clan, dominated stoneware production there for most of the eighteenth century. In 1797, however, a pottery was established near Corlear's Hook on the East River near Grand Street, and until 1819 the stonewares made there competed successfully with those of the older potteries. The pleasingly formed and decorated jar shown here (Fig. 360) is one of numerous surviving examples that are stamped "Coerlear's Hook."

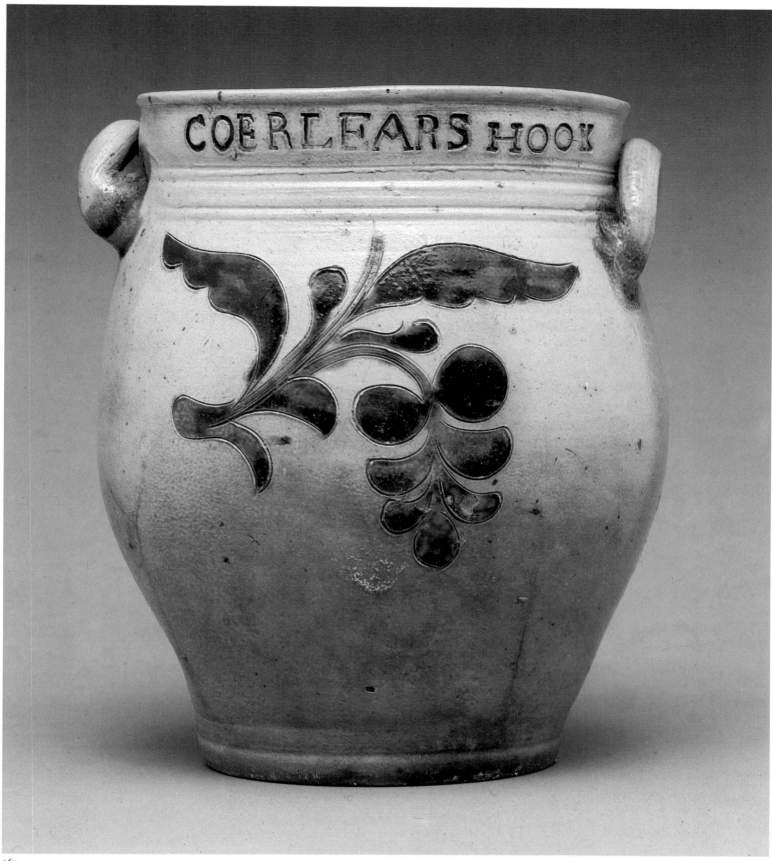

360

**Fig. 359. Jug,** *probably by John Crolius (1733–1812), 1775; stoneware, height 10 inches (25.4 cm.). Made of gray clay and decorated with incised scrolls colored blue, as was usual with such stonewares, this jug is most unusual in bearing the name of its owner, the initials of its maker, and the date and place of its manufacture. It is extremely rare to find stoneware of such an early date and with such complete documentation. During the eighteenth century, fear of the "infamously bad and unwholesome" lead glazes used*

*on common redware led to the widespread promotion of stoneware as a substitute, especially for the storage of acidic foods, which become poisonous when combined with lead. As a result, stoneware crocks and jugs were made in large numbers.*
Rogers Fund, 1934 (34.149)

**Fig. 360. Jar,** *probably by Thomas Commeraw (active 1797–1819) or David Morgan (active 1797–1802), New York, 1797–1819; stoneware, height 9½ inches (24.1 cm.). The smoothly*

*incised flower-and-leaf design colored with a deep cobalt blue glaze is typical of decorations on the wares produced by the pottery established late in the eighteenth century at Corlear's Hook on the East River in downtown Manhattan. Open-mouthed jars of this kind were produced in quantity for use in the kitchen or pantry as storage receptacles for such diverse foods as preserves, cream, and butter. This example bears the incised identification "Coerlears Hook N. York."*
Rogers Fund, 1918 (18.95.13)

**Fig. 361. Pitcher,** *by the American China Man-ufactory (1826–38), established by William Ellis Tucker (1800–32), Philadelphia, 1826–38; porcelain, height 9¼ inches (23.5 cm.). Fashion-able European porcelains provided the inspiration for nearly all the decorative objects and tablewares William Ellis Tucker produced at his* Philadelphia porcelain works, but this pitcher is *an example of the one new form Tucker evolved. Its compact rounded body, high loop handle, and fluted base, although certainly expressive of the late neoclassical period in general, combine in a way that has not been found in pitchers from any other factory. Tucker's venture was short-lived,* but while it lasted it was the first successful porce-lain manufactory in the United States.
Purchase, Mrs. Russell Sage Gift, 1970 (1970.112)

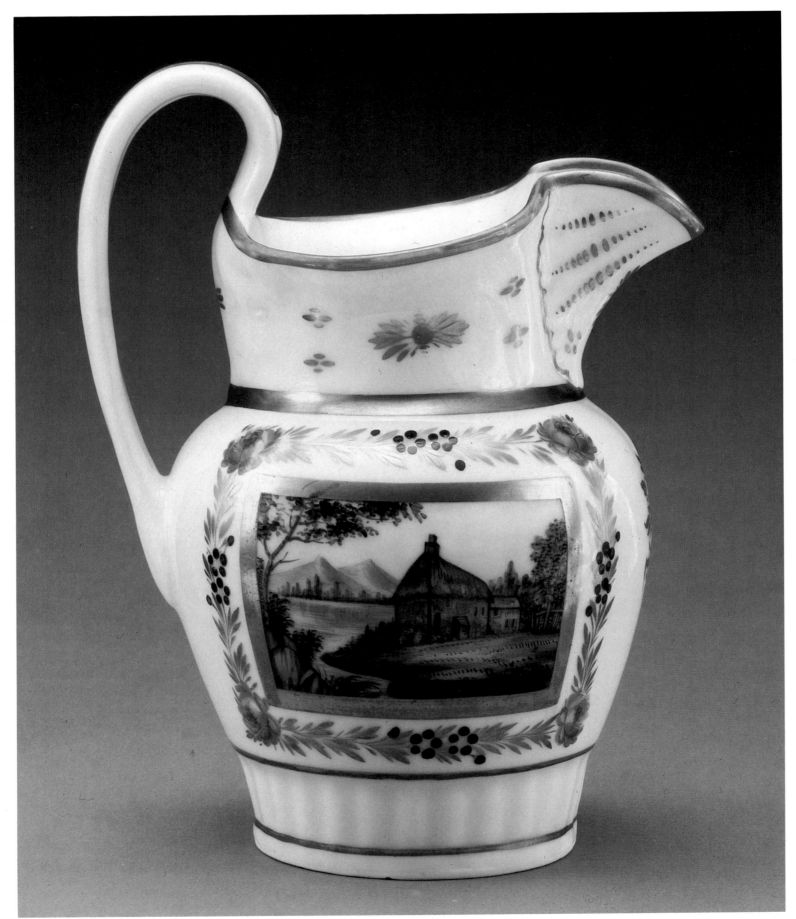

361

# The Pre-Centennial Period
# 1830–75

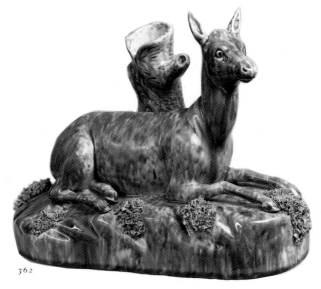

362

O ne of the most extensively produced types of pottery from about
1840 was a more pretentious earthenware that was mottled or streaked with
a lustrous brown glaze often resembling
tortoiseshell. It was known as Rockingham because pottery so glazed was
first made in the eighteenth century at
Swinton, England, on the estate of the
Marquis of Rockingham. This and some
other new types of pottery were shaped
in molds rather than thrown on the
wheel. The technique, like that of pressing glass, shifted the emphasis from the
craftsman to the designer of molds and
opened the door to mass production.
Rockingham ware was molded into a
wide variety of forms: doorknobs, paperweights, cuspidors, picture frames,
pudding bowls, lamp bases, pitchers,
and decorative objects of different sorts.
It was produced at a number of factories in New Jersey, Maryland, Vermont,
and Ohio. The figure of a reclining doe
before a hollow tree trunk (Fig. 362), attributed to designer Daniel Greatbach
at Bennington, Vermont, is a representative example. The new technique lent
itself to more elegant wares as well. A
light and delicate effect was achieved by
the American Pottery Company of Jersey City, New Jersey, in their white teapot with molded decoration of mean-
dering stems and flowers (Fig. 363).

Short-lived attempts to produce true
porcelain were undertaken as early as
the eighteenth century, notably from
1770 to 1772 by Bonnin and Morris of
Philadelphia. Only a rare few of their
works have survived. It was in 1826 that
William Ellis Tucker, also of Philadelphia, opened the first really successful
porcelain factory in America. The enterprise closed in 1838, but in its brief
period of production it produced thin,

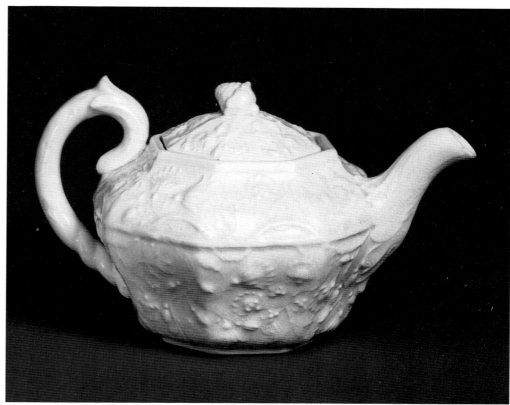

363

*Fig. 362. Figure of a doe, by Lyman, Fenton
and Company (1849–58), Bennington, Vermont, 1849–58; earthenware, height 8½ inches
(21.6 cm.). Like the famous Bennington poodles,
this doe and a recumbent stag were made as a
pair to be used as mantel ornaments. They were
never produced in great quantities and are thus
relatively rare today. The flint-enamel glaze that
covers the doe was a kind of improved Rockingham glaze—mottled brown with blue, green,
and yellow added. This lively surface, developed
by Bennington's genius potter, Christopher Weber
Fenton, and patented in 1849 as Fenton's
Enamel, was used for all kinds of decorative and
utilitarian wares produced at Bennington.*
Rogers Fund, 1938 (38.125.2)

*Fig. 363. Teapot, by the American Pottery Com-
pany, Jersey City, New Jersey, 1843–48; earthenware, height 3¾ inches (9.5 cm.). Until the
second quarter of the nineteenth century European ceramics manufacturers dominated the
American market for fine ceramics, and D. and J.
Henderson's American Pottery Manufacturing
Company was one of the first American potteries
to compete successfully. The firm specialized in
Staffordshire types, and among their borrowings
was the technique of making pottery in molds instead of on the potter's wheel. This was such an
efficient and economical method of fashioning objects with elaborate relief decoration that other
potteries were quick to follow their lead. Like the
Bennington doe, this charming white pottery teapot, which bears the rare mark of its maker, was
produced in a mold. Its decoration of low-relief
vines and flowers and its acorn finial were taken
from the Rococo Revival vocabulary, which was
becoming more and more popular in the 1840s,
when the teapot was made.*
Sansbury-Mills Fund, 1982 (1982.67.1a,b)

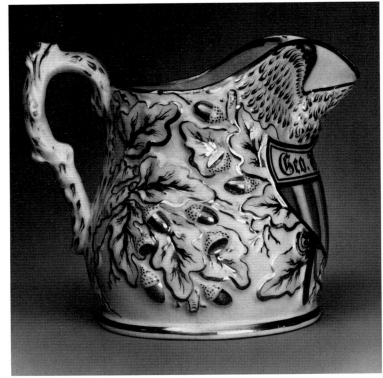

*Fig. 364. Pitcher,* by Charles Cartlidge and Company (1848–56), Greenpoint (Brooklyn), New York, 1848–56; porcelain, height 8⅛ inches (20.6 cm.). A lapse of ten years occurred between the closing of the Tucker porcelain manufactory and the opening of Cartlidge's porcelain works. Beginning with buttons, the firm moved on to produce such novelties as cane heads and doorknobs and then wares like this presentation pitcher. The classicism and restraint of the Tucker pitcher have now given way to Rococo Revival naturalism: sprays of oak leaves complete with acorns have been molded onto the sides of the pitcher; the handle is molded into a knobby branch shape; and the spout is in the form of the head and neck of an eagle. Several such pitchers are known, each bearing a different inscription. Obviously the customer decided on the inscription, which was applied to the pitcher after the order was placed.
Sansbury-Mills Fund, 1979 (1979.67)

364

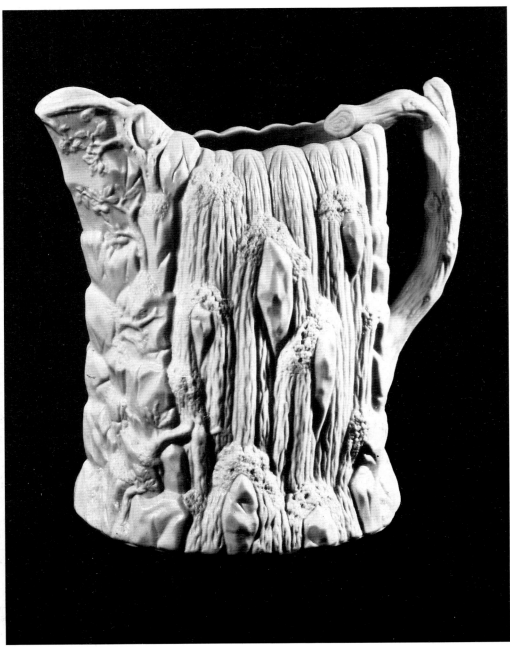

365

white, translucent wares that competed with European imports.

Although with the help of immigrant French craftsmen and some backing from local associates, Tucker (in partnership at various times with various people) turned out some elaborate pieces, most of the firm's output consisted of relatively simple adaptations of fashionable French, German, and English designs. Among them are several pitchers painted with imaginary landscapes in sepia and polychrome and with floral decorations in natural colors (Fig. 361). The shapes of these pieces reflect the neoclassical spirit of the time.

In the decades after the Tucker factory closed new adventures in American porcelain were undertaken. Around the middle of the nineteenth century Charles Cartlidge and Company of Greenpoint, New York, was producing porcelain in a variety of forms. Fashions had changed since the Tucker days, and the Cartlidge output visibly departed from the classical spirit of the earlier wares. A case in point is a robust, somewhat squat pitcher covered with naturalistic relief decorations corresponding to Rococo Revival styles (Fig. 364).

Parian ware, a white, waxy porcelain developed in England for use in unglazed objects, was also introduced into this country around the middle of the last century. It was so named because of its resemblance to marble quarried on the Aegean island of Paros. Indeed, it

**Fig. 365. Pitcher,** by the United States Pottery Company, Bennington, Vermont, about 1853; Parian porcelain, height 8¼ inches (21 cm.). Christopher Weber Fenton, who introduced Fenton's Enamel (see Fig. 362), also introduced Parian ware, a hard, marble-like porcelain that is translucent and has a smooth unglazed surface. It had been developed in Europe for making statues that were much less expensive than stone ones. Fenton quickly found that he could make all sorts of objects in Parian, especially those with highly modeled surfaces like that of this pitcher, on which a landscape in relief showing a waterfall, rocks, and trees is supposed to represent Niagara Falls. The piece combines the romantic mid-century attitude toward nature in general,

the American fascination with its own natural wonders in particular, and the pervasive Victorian interest in oddities.
Gift of Dr. Charles W. Green, 1947 (47.90.15)

**Fig. 366. Vase,** by the Union Porcelain Works (1863–about 1920), Greenpoint (Brooklyn), New York, about 1876; porcelain, height 12¾ inches (32.4 cm.). The Centennial celebration in Philadelphia inspired American manufacturers of all the decorative arts to scale new heights. Among the most attractive and successful were the "Century Vases" designed by Karl Mueller of the Union Porcelain Works. These incorporated patriotic motifs drawn from American history and recorded recent technological achievements

and native plants and animals. This version bears a band, in biscuit (unglazed porcelain), with panels of low-relief historical scenes; just above, on a surface patterned with leaves from native trees, is a profile bust of George Washington; bison heads serve as handles; and more American flowers and birds are drawn on the inner and outer surfaces of the neck of the vase. In praising the Union Porcelain Works's display, the Crockery and Glass Journal, a contemporary publication, encouraged other potteries to follow their lead: "Let American manufacturers make their own designs and leave off copying foreign ones!"
Gift of Mr. and Mrs. Franklin M. Chace, 1969 (69.194.1)

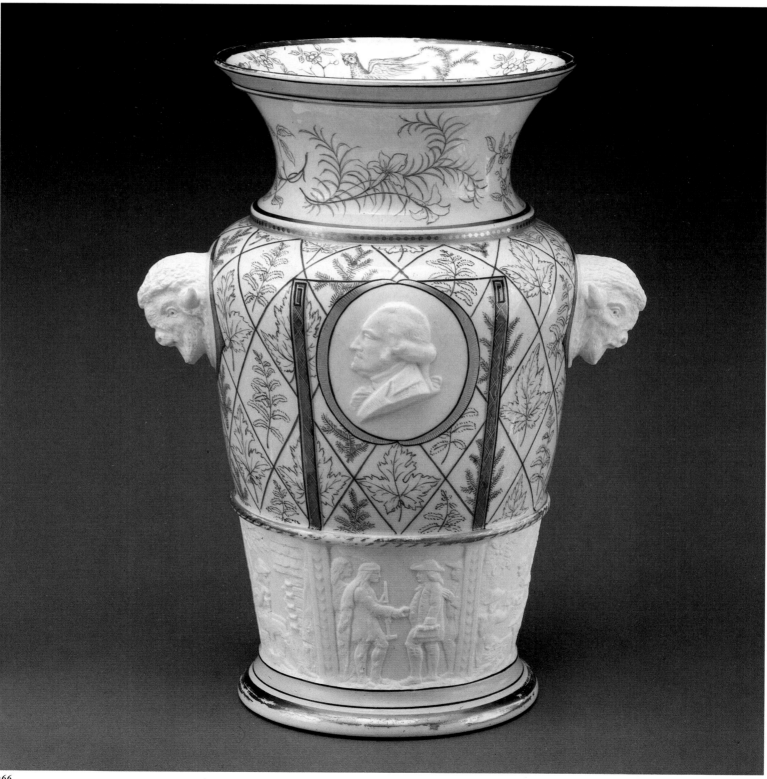

366

# The Post-Centennial Period 1875–1915

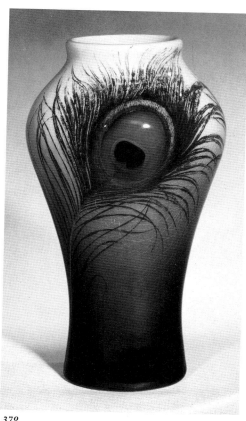

370

*Fig. 370. Vase, decorated by Carl Schmidt, Rookwood Pottery Company (1880–1967), Cincinnati, Ohio, about 1908; earthenware, height 10 inches (25.4 cm.). Rookwood was not the oldest of the American art potteries, but it was the most influential. Remarkably rich colors and glazes were developed there, and the style of decoration gradually evolved from rather amateurish naturalistic designs inspired by Japanese ceramics to the suave professionalism of this peacock feather, executed around the turn of the century when Art Nouveau designs were popular in avant-garde circles.* Purchase, Edward C. Moore, Jr. Gift, 1969 (69.17)

American ceramics came into their own in the years following the Centennial. For the first time the products of American kilns were winning international recognition for their technical quality and artistic interest. As in the case of American glass during the same years, design in ceramics was affected by a craving for what a contemporary referred to as "civilizing, refining, and elevating" objets d'art. One of the finest of the commercial art potteries was Ott and Brewer of Trenton, New Jersey. Their Belleek vase (Fig. 368) shows the influence of several styles—in form it resembles Japanese and Art Nouveau works, while its twiglike handles recall those of rococo examples.

Some of the most distinctive achievements were those of the artist-potters whose commercial output reflected the principles and ideals of the current English Arts and Crafts movement. In other words, the aesthetic qualities of the objects were in accord with their utilitarian forms. The Arts and Crafts philosophy was that art in the broadest sense could and should be part of everyday life.

One of the first establishments to devote its energies to handmade art pottery was the small family-run Chelsea Keramic Art Works in Chelsea, Massachusetts. Founded in 1866, the firm turned to art pottery in 1872. A tea set of 1877–80 whose pieces have blue-green honeycomb surfaces and angular bodies (Fig. 369) is important both in being a very rare example of tableware by this firm and in having a strikingly streamlined, modern appearance at this early date. It is another example of the influence of Japanese design on American work of the late nineteenth century.

In 1880 Maria Longworth Nichols, an art patron and ceramics enthusiast of Cincinnati, founded the Rookwood Pottery. She introduced a painterly tradition that influenced ceramic decoration strongly for nearly fifty years. Within a decade of its founding, Rookwood had won its first gold medal at l'Exposition universelle in Paris. A vase bearing an underglaze peacock feather with an arresting eye (Fig. 370) is an outstanding example of the production of Rookwood, which very soon became the most influential ceramics firm in the country. As might be expected, it had many imitators.

The Grueby Faience Company of Boston, founded in 1897, was another commercial enterprise that successfully employed leading designers and used advanced techniques. A pottery vase with a matte finish, made about 1900, reflects the fashion for Egyptian motifs (Fig. 371). Grueby won prizes at exhibitions both at home and abroad with such objects.

A different mood prevails in a very delicate porcelain bowl (Figs. 372 and 373) made early in the twentieth century at the prestigious Syracuse atelier of Adelaide Alsop Robineau. Its rim and foot are pierced and decorated with colored incised designs—a difficult and demanding feat given the fragility of the porcelain body. Mrs. Robineau attempted to make a dozen such delicate pieces, but completed only three (of which only two survive). She destroyed the other efforts as failed attempts to reach her standards of quality.

About the time of World War 1 rapid industrialization and changing public taste caused most of these distinctive art potteries to cease operation, one after

**Fig. 365. Pitcher,** by the United States Pottery Company, Bennington, Vermont, about 1853; Parian porcelain, height 8¼ inches (21 cm). Christopher Weber Fenton, who introduced Fenton's Enamel (see Fig. 362), also introduced Parian ware, a hard, marble-like porcelain that is translucent and has a smooth unglazed surface. It had been developed in Europe for making statues that were much less expensive than stone ones. Fenton quickly found that he could make all sorts of objects in Parian, especially those with highly modeled surfaces like that of this pitcher, on which a landscape in relief showing a waterfall, rocks, and trees is supposed to represent Niagara Falls. The piece combines the romantic mid-century attitude toward nature in general,

the American fascination with its own natural wonders in particular, and the pervasive Victorian interest in oddities.
Gift of Dr. Charles W. Green, 1947 (47.90.15)

**Fig. 366. Vase,** by the Union Porcelain Works (1863–about 1920), Greenpoint (Brooklyn), New York, about 1876; porcelain, height 12¾ inches (32.4 cm). The Centennial celebration in Philadelphia inspired American manufacturers of all the decorative arts to scale new heights. Among the most attractive and successful were the "Century Vases" designed by Karl Mueller of the Union Porcelain Works. These incorporated patriotic motifs drawn from American history and recorded recent technological achievements

and native plants and animals. This version bears a band, in biscuit (unglazed porcelain), with panels of low-relief historical scenes; just above, on a surface patterned with leaves from native trees, is a profile bust of George Washington; bison heads serve as handles; and more American flowers and birds are drawn on the inner and outer surfaces of the neck of the vase. In praising the Union Porcelain Works's display, the Crockery and Glass Journal, a contemporary publication, encouraged other potteries to follow their lead: "Let American manufacturers make their own designs and leave off copying foreign ones!"
Gift of Mr. and Mrs. Franklin M. Chace, 1969 (69.194.1)

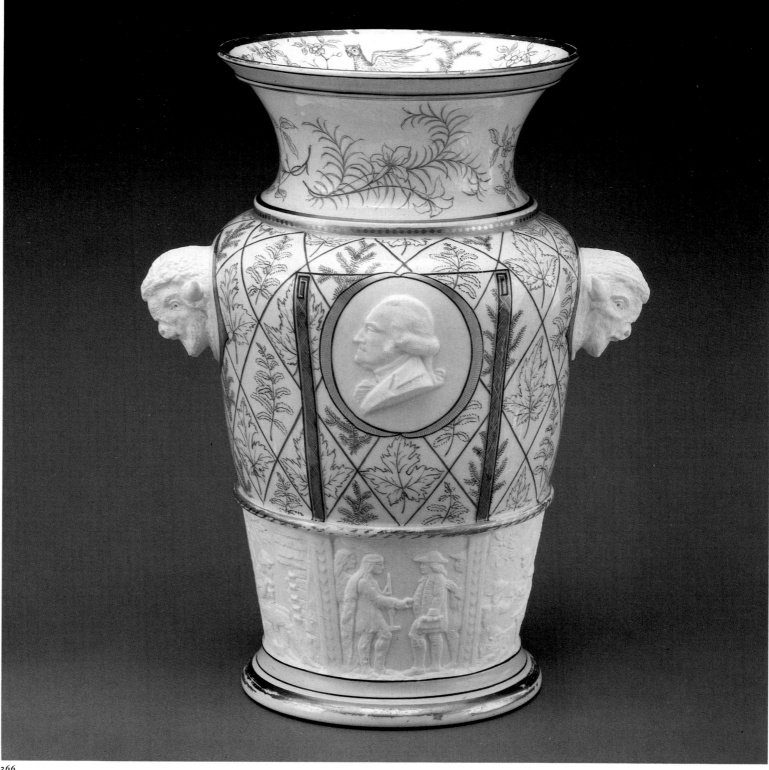

366

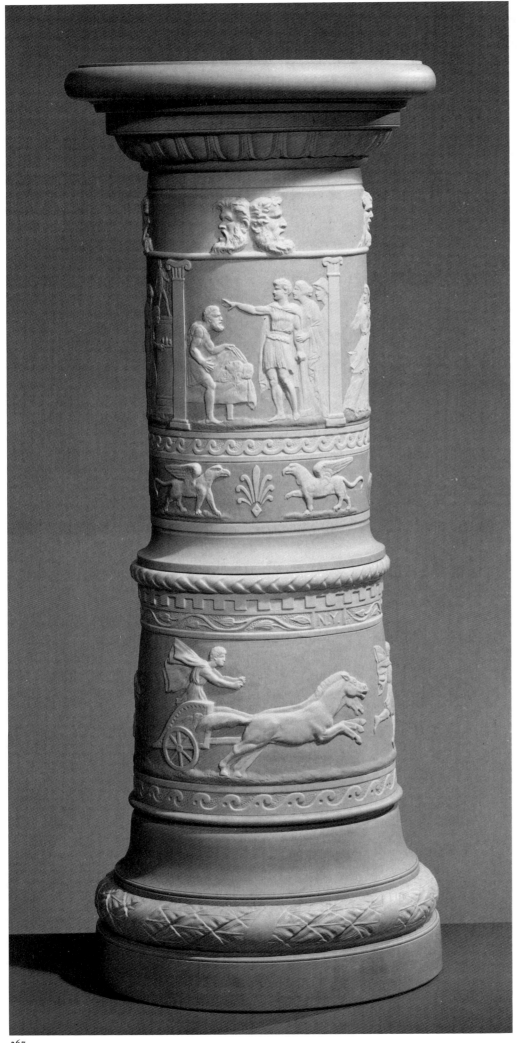

proved a happy substitute for that stone when it was molded into statuettes that were sometimes described as "Parian marble." There is also a sculptural quality to the Niagara Falls pitcher (Fig. 365) made by the United States Pottery Company at Bennington, Vermont, in celebration of America's natural wonders. Unlikely as such a subject was, the resultant form, an extreme expression of the naturalistic rococo decoration favored at the time, was surprisingly effective. Color was often used in Parian ware: a smooth white design stands out in relief against a pitted ground of blue, pink, buff, or green. These pieces were made in molds but finished by hand.

The United States International Exhibition, known as the Centennial, provided an excellent showcase for the improved porcelains that had been developed since mid-century. The Union Porcelain Works of Greenpoint (Brooklyn), New York, showed its "Century Vase" (Fig. 366), designed for the occasion by the gifted German-born sculptor Karl Mueller. A version of this monumental piece in the Museum's collection displays a relief profile of George Washington and has bison heads for handles. Panels in a band around the base contain relief figures recalling various aspects of American history. Mueller was also responsible for an impressive pedestal of biscuit (unglazed) porcelain with neoclassical figures in white relief against an apricot-colored ground (Fig. 367).

**Fig. 367. Pedestal,** by the Union Porcelain Works (1863–about 1920), Greenpoint (Brooklyn), New York, about 1876; porcelain, height 42½ inches (108 cm.). Another display piece designed by Karl Mueller for the Union Porcelain Works to take to the Centennial was this pedestal made of pale apricot and white biscuit porcelain. Americans felt the confidence that prosperity and a century of achievement in many different fields had brought, and they identified themselves with the classical Greek and Roman civilizations, whose accomplishments they admired. Using a classical column form and the classical Greek story of Electra as the decorative theme, the designer allied Americans with both the practical and artistic achievements of those legendary ancient civilizations. A contemporary account describes the Union Porcelain Works display, in which two of these pedestals support two "Century Vases."
Purchase, Anonymous Gift, 1968 (68.99.1a–d)

367

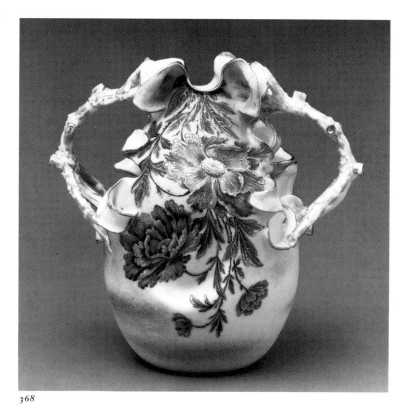

368

**Fig. 368. Vase,** by Ott and Brewer (founded 1871), Trenton, New Jersey, about 1900; Belleek porcelain, height 9½ inches (24.1 cm.). The undulating form and naturalistic decoration of this delicate vase were influenced by Art Nouveau design, its wavy open mouth by Japanese ceramics (which were much admired by Westerners at international exhibitions during the second half of the nineteenth century), and its twiglike handles by Rococo Revival examples. This eclecticism was typical of the late nineteenth century, when Americans couldn't seem to get enough of the exotic. The body is Belleek, an extremely thin porcelain developed in Ireland and copied by American potteries.
Purchase, The Edgar J. Kaufmann Foundation Gift, 1968 (68.103.1)

**Fig. 369. Tea set,** marked by the Chelsea Keramic Art Works (1872–89), Chelsea, Massachusetts, 1877–80; earthenware, height of teapot 4¾ inches (12.1 cm.), of sugar bowl 4¼ inches (10.8 cm.), of teacup 2½ inches (6.4 cm.). Made at one of the earliest American art potteries, these very unusual pieces were apparently influenced by oriental metalwork. Their angular shapes, produced in molds and actually hammered like metal while the clay was still moist, were probably inspired by displays of Japanese and other Eastern decorative arts at the Centennial exhibition of 1876. Their lovely blue-green color, their diminutive size, and their abstract geometrical forms join in making them the antithesis of most contemporary ceramic wares.
Gift of Mr. and Mrs. I. Wistar Morris III, 1982 (1982.440.1–4)

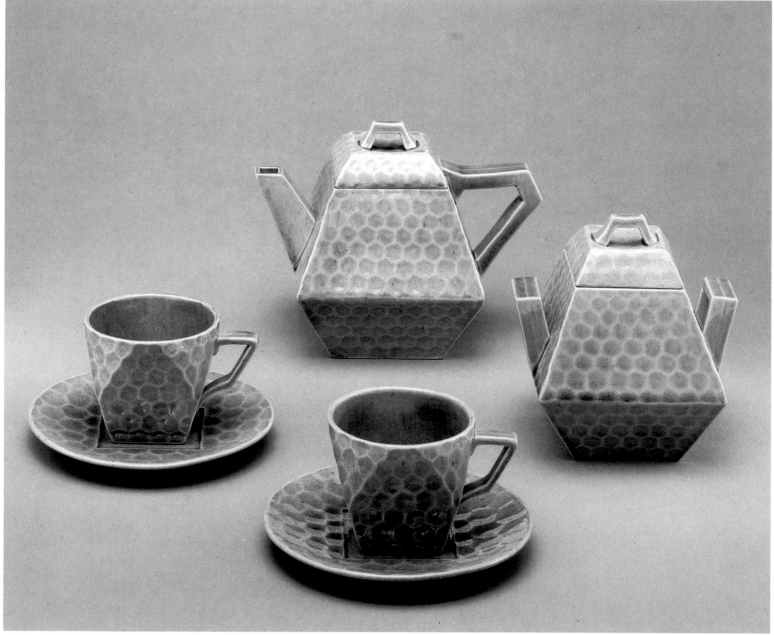

369

# The Post-Centennial Period 1875–1915

*Fig. 371. Vase,* by the Grueby Faience Company (1894–1911), Boston, 1899–1910; earthenware, height 11 inches (27.9 cm.). Grueby was another successful art pottery, with a specialty in simple, heavy, matte-glazed forms with low-relief leaf ornament. The most common color, and the one most clearly recognizable as a Grueby product, is cucumber green, but the pottery did develop other colors, such as the mustard yellow of this vase. This example is characteristic of the pottery's Egyptian-inspired shapes. Grueby forms and colors went very well with other art productions of the time: Gustav Stickley often displayed his furniture with a Grueby vase, and Tiffany ordered Grueby bases for his glass lampshades.
Purchase, The Edgar J. Kaufmann Foundation Gift, 1969 (69.91.2)

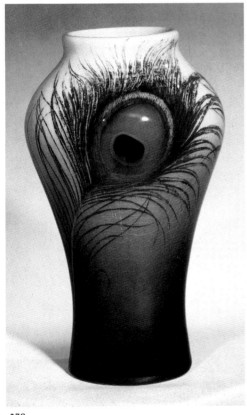

370

*Fig. 370. Vase,* decorated by Carl Schmidt, Rookwood Pottery Company (1880–1967), Cincinnati, Ohio, about 1908; earthenware, height 10 inches (25.4 cm.). Rookwood was not the oldest of the American art potteries, but it was the most influential. Remarkably rich colors and glazes were developed there, and the style of decoration gradually evolved from rather amateurish naturalistic designs inspired by Japanese ceramics to the suave professionalism of this peacock feather, executed around the turn of the century when Art Nouveau designs were popular in avant-garde circles.
Purchase, Edward C. Moore, Jr. Gift, 1969 (69.17)

American ceramics came into their own in the years following the Centennial. For the first time the products of American kilns were winning international recognition for their technical quality and artistic interest. As in the case of American glass during the same years, design in ceramics was affected by a craving for what a contemporary referred to as "civilizing, refining, and elevating" objets d'art. One of the finest of the commercial art potteries was Ott and Brewer of Trenton, New Jersey. Their Belleek vase (Fig. 368) shows the influence of several styles—in form it resembles Japanese and Art Nouveau works, while its twiglike handles recall those of rococo examples.

Some of the most distinctive achievements were those of the artist-potters whose commercial output reflected the principles and ideals of the current English Arts and Crafts movement. In other words, the aesthetic qualities of the objects were in accord with their utilitarian forms. The Arts and Crafts philosophy was that art in the broadest sense could and should be part of everyday life.

One of the first establishments to devote its energies to handmade art pottery was the small family-run Chelsea Keramic Art Works in Chelsea, Massachusetts. Founded in 1866, the firm turned to art pottery in 1872. A tea set of 1877–80 whose pieces have blue-green honeycomb surfaces and angular bodies (Fig. 369) is important both in being a very rare example of tableware by this firm and in having a strikingly streamlined, modern appearance at this early date. It is another example of the influence of Japanese design on American work of the late nineteenth century.

In 1880 Maria Longworth Nichols, an art patron and ceramics enthusiast of Cincinnati, founded the Rookwood Pottery. She introduced a painterly tradition that influenced ceramic decoration strongly for nearly fifty years. Within a decade of its founding, Rookwood had won its first gold medal at l'Exposition universelle in Paris. A vase bearing an underglaze peacock feather with an arresting eye (Fig. 370) is an outstanding example of the production of Rookwood, which very soon became the most influential ceramics firm in the country. As might be expected, it had many imitators.

The Grueby Faience Company of Boston, founded in 1897, was another commercial enterprise that successfully employed leading designers and used advanced techniques. A pottery vase with a matte finish, made about 1900, reflects the fashion for Egyptian motifs (Fig. 371). Grueby won prizes at exhibitions both at home and abroad with such objects.

A different mood prevails in a very delicate porcelain bowl (Figs. 372 and 373) made early in the twentieth century at the prestigious Syracuse atelier of Adelaide Alsop Robineau. Its rim and foot are pierced and decorated with colored incised designs—a difficult and demanding feat given the fragility of the porcelain body. Mrs. Robineau attempted to make a dozen such delicate pieces, but completed only three (of which only two survive). She destroyed the other efforts as failed attempts to reach her standards of quality.

About the time of World War I rapid industrialization and changing public taste caused most of these distinctive art potteries to cease operation, one after

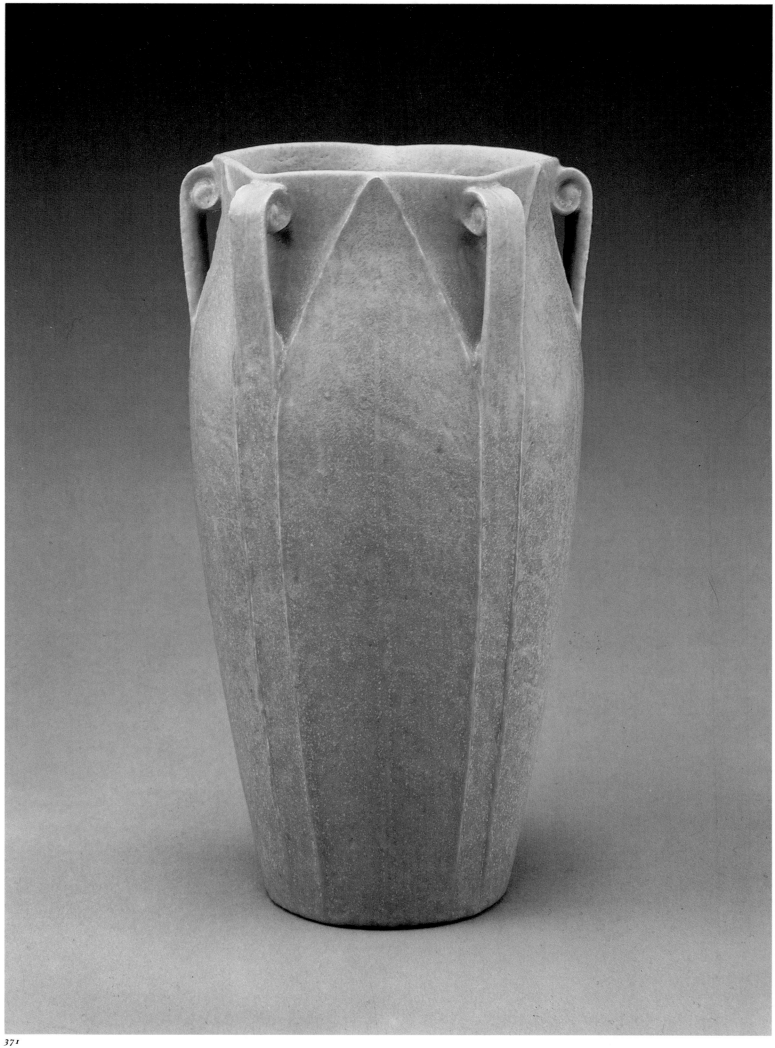

371

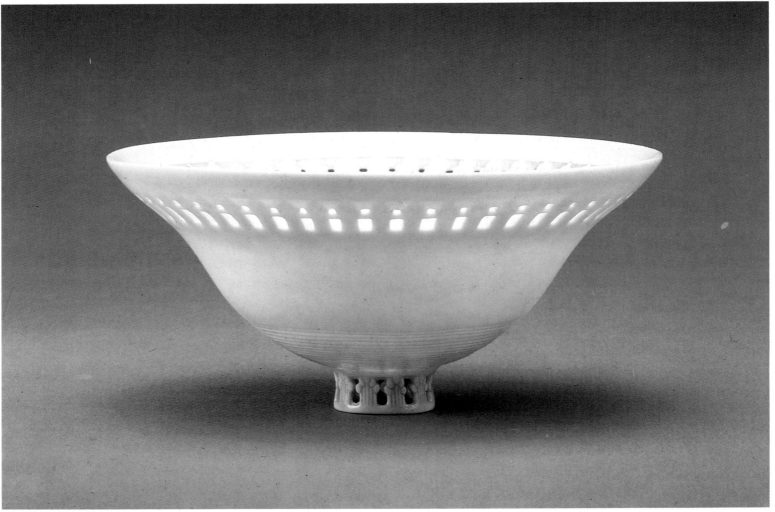

372

**Figs. 372 and 373. Bowl,** *by Adelaide Alsop Robineau (1865–1929), Syracuse, New York, 1924; porcelain, height 2³/₄ inches (7 cm.). Unlike the other art pottery shown here, Adelaide Robineau's bowl was paper thin—so delicate that only one other example of this type survives. Other less fragile Robineau pieces do exist, but this example illustrates a characteristic technique of the potter, that of excising parts of the design and incising others. Robineau worked alone, with her devoted husband as her associate, and her production was thus limited—especially since she worked with fragile porcelain bodies that often required several firings before the shape and glaze were perfect. She received many awards at international exhibitions, and while she never made a profit, her work was from the first acquired by museums for their permanent collections.*
Purchase, Edward C. Moore, Jr. Gift, 1926 (26.37)

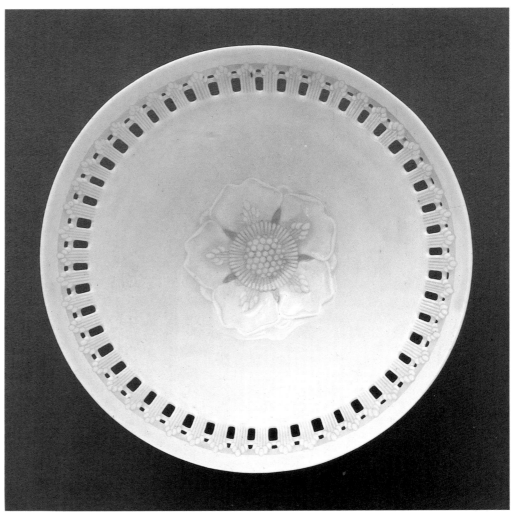

373

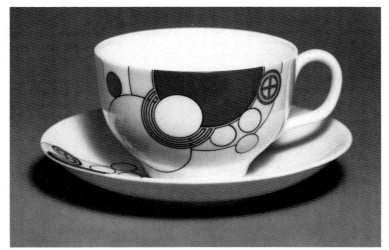

**Fig. 374. Cup and saucer,** *part of the dinner service seen in Fig. 375. Diameter of saucer 5³/₁₆ inches (12.6 cm.), diameter of cup 3⁷/₁₆ inches (8 cm.).*
Gift of Mr. and Mrs. Roger G. Kennedy, 1978 (1978.501.14,16)

374

another. However, they had paved the way for the individual studio potteries of the years ahead.

One of the first to recognize that machines could be put to work in the service of art was Frank Lloyd Wright. As early as 1901 he had written that the duty of dominating the machine "is relentlessly marked out for the artist in this, the Machine Age." His ability to practice what he preached is clearly demonstrated in the china he designed for the Imperial Hotel in Tokyo, one of Wright's best-known commissions. Primary colors and one abstract form—the circle—are combined to create china that is as pleasing to look at as it is practical to stack and use (Figs. 374 and 375).

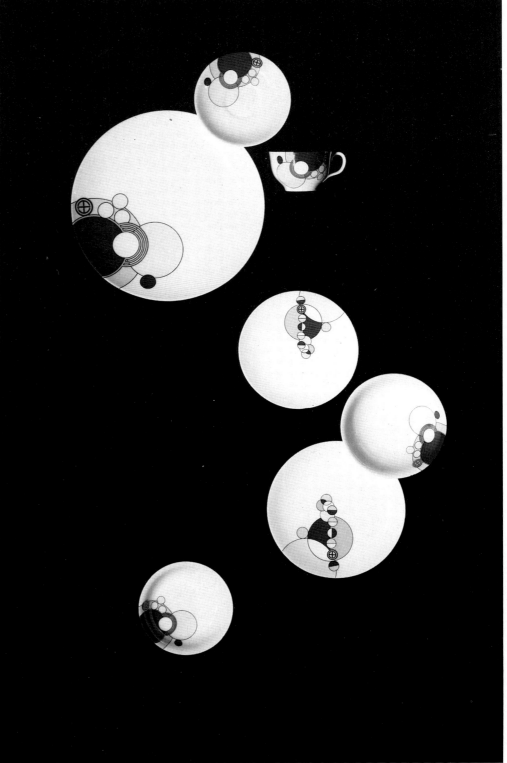

**Fig. 375. Dinner service,** *by Frank Lloyd Wright (1867–1959), about 1922; porcelain, diameter of dinner plate 10⅝ inches (26.3 cm.). Frank Lloyd Wright was one of the first to realize that machines could be used to create honest, yet artistic, furnishings. As early as 1901 in his landmark lecture, "The Art and Craft of the Machine," delivered at Hull House in Chicago, Wright advanced his belief in mass production. These plates, bowls, and cups, which he designed for use at his great Imperial Hotel in Tokyo, prove that he was correct. In both form and ornament they make use of the circles that were to become an important element of Wright's designs for both buildings and furnishings, and they were easily produced by machine in whatever numbers were necessary.*
Gift of Mr. and Mrs. Roger G. Kennedy, 1978 (1978.501.14,16,4,8,10,6,12)

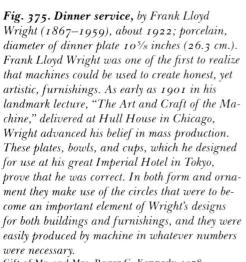

375

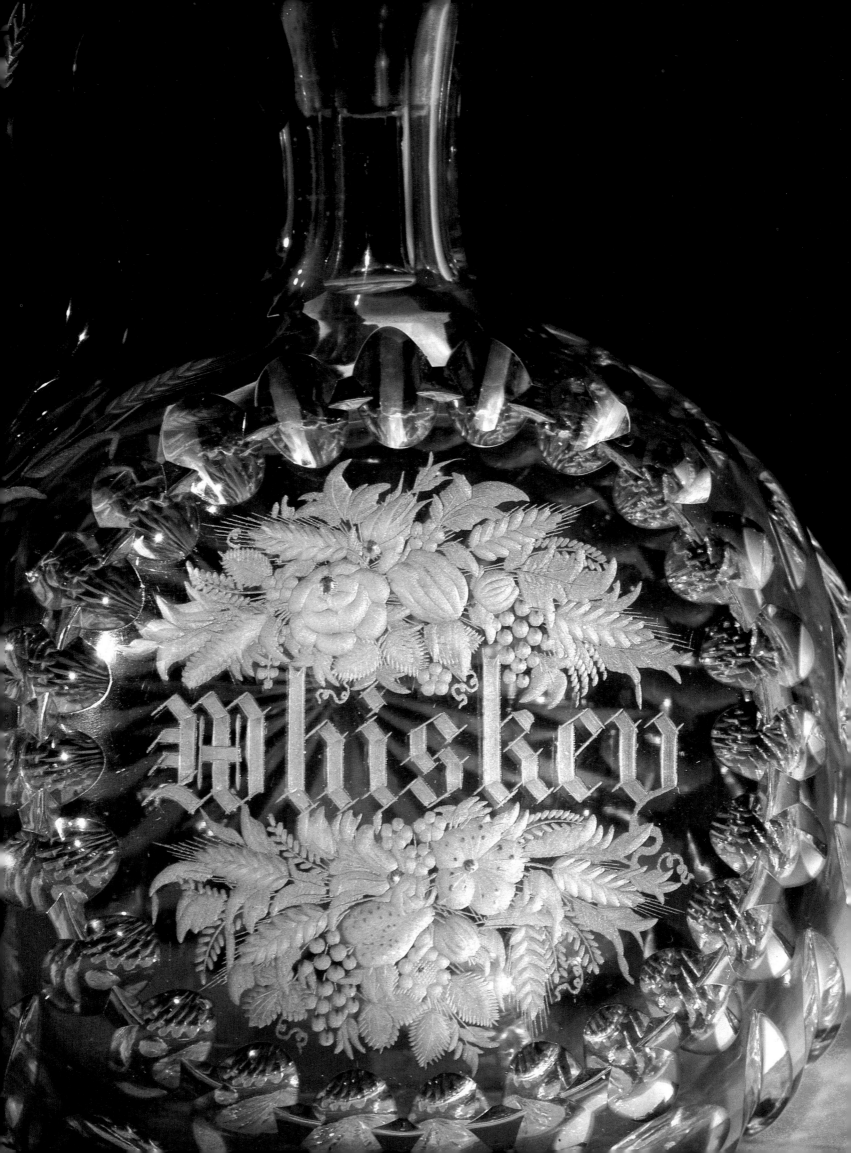

# GLASS

Fig. 376. Detail, decanter from the Boston and Sandwich Glass Company, see Fig. 399.

# The Colonial and Federal Periods
## 1630–1830

Of the many materials used in the decorative arts, glass lends itself to the greatest variety of treatment. It can be freely blown and tooled to any conceivable form; it can be fashioned into a film of gossamer thinness or a solid of weighty bulk; it can be blown or pressed into patterned molds of many different shapes; it can be cut and engraved into glittering textures; it can be given gem-like colors that range the spectrum or endowed with crystalline clarity; it can be enameled with colorful designs. Over the past two centuries American glassmakers have taken advantage of all these possibilities.

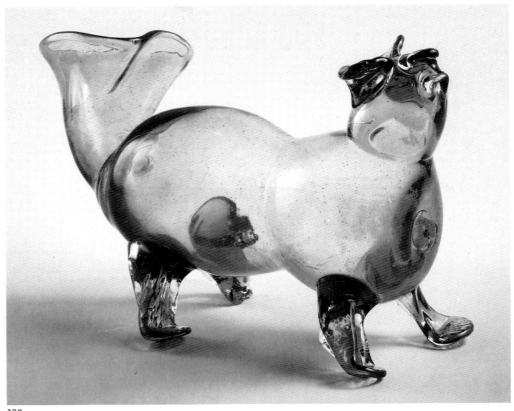

377

Glassmakers were included among the earliest immigrants, from Jamestown on, but the craft achieved a significant output only when the eighteenth century was well advanced and when artisans, Germans for the most part, established furnaces in several different colonies. Among the more enduring of these was the factory Caspar Wistar established in 1739 near Alloway in southern New Jersey with the aid of craftsmen brought to America from the Continent. German influence is clearly evident in the glassware produced by this factory, which operated for about forty years. Here, as at most American glasshouses until well into the nineteenth century, the commercial product consisted primarily of green ("common") glass bottles and windowpanes.

Wistar's factory also produced amusing decorative pieces and simple tablewares such as vases, bowls, sugar bowls, and pitchers. A frisky green-glass *Schnapshunde*, or bottle in the shape of a dog, attributed to Wistar (Fig. 377) is the sort of informal, or "offhand," piece that collectors seek. It has the charm that results from a glassblower's turning his skill to the pleasant task of creating amusing or useful objects for family and friends, having no reason to stick to conventional or predictable paths.

During the dozen years before the Revolution the Pennsylvania glasshouses of the fabulous "Baron" Henry William Stiegel, another German entrepreneur, advertised products as good as any imported from abroad. The pattern-molded sugar bowls, creamers, salts, syllabub and jelly glasses, and other forms often attributed to Stiegel's several furnaces were in fact expertly made of good metal (a technical word for molten glass). In nearly all cases these attractive bright-colored pieces are indistinguishable from examples known to have been made abroad. The technique by which Stiegel-type wares were produced involved the use of small open pattern molds. A gather of molten glass was inserted into the mold, then withdrawn, and blown into whatever larger shape was desired. The subtly graduated pattern formed by the expansion of the design, greater in one area than another (like the figures on a toy balloon as it is blown up), resulted in surfaces whose effect is that of rippling movement in changing light. An amethyst-colored flask thus produced and impressed with what is known as a diamond-daisy pattern may well have been a Stiegel product (Fig. 378).

Among the finest fully identified surviving examples of eighteenth-century American glass are two handsomely engraved presentation goblets made in the New Bremen, Maryland, manufactory of John Frederick Amelung. The first, dated 1788 (Fig. 379), was very likely presented by Amelung to his German financial backers to prove his success with his New World glass factory. The other goblet (Fig. 380), engraved with the arms of the state of Pennsylvania, was presented by Amelung to Thomas Mifflin when he became governor of that state in 1791.

Amelung had arrived in America from Bremen, Germany, in 1784. He was accompanied by sixty-eight experienced workmen and armed with letters of recommendation from John Adams and Benjamin Franklin, both of whom

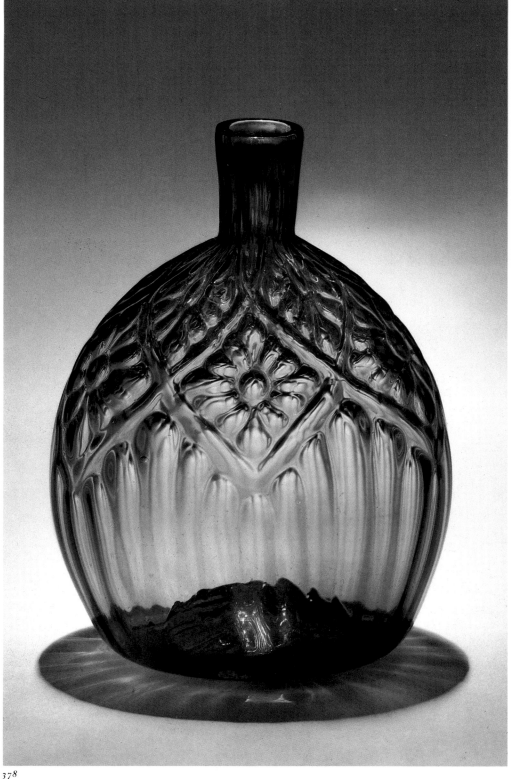

378

**Fig. 379. Goblet with cover,** *New Bremen Glass Manufactory (1787–95), established by John Frederick Amelung, New Bremen, Frederick County, Maryland, about 1788; glass, height with cover 11¼ inches (28.6 cm.). Amelung arrived from Bremen, Germany, with the equipment to build a substantial glassworks and sixty-eight craftsmen to staff it. He produced a great range of wares from glasses and tumblers to sugar bowls with ornamental handles and the usual bottles and window glass. Then, because of fires and other catastrophes at the factory, and because of a serious lack of buyers, he went bankrupt in 1795. This covered goblet is perhaps the most important piece Amelung produced, for it is not only finely proportioned and well made, but it is*

*the earliest signed glass object produced by an American glasshouse. Amelung is thought to have made it to present to the German stockholders in the company that had backed his American enterprise, for it bears the inscription "Old Bremen Success and the New Progress"; on the reverse is "New Bremen Glassmanufactory 1788/ North America, State of Maryland." The goblet was discovered in Bremen, Germany, in 1928.* Rogers Fund, 1928 (28.52)

**Fig. 380. Goblet,** *New Bremen Glass Manufactory (1787–95), established by John Frederick Amelung, New Bremen, Frederick County, Maryland, 1791; glass, with replaced foot of wood, height 10 inches (25.4 cm.). Although it*

*has lost its original cover and foot, this goblet is a splendid example of the work that Amelung's craftsmen could turn out when the occasion arose. Engraved presentation pieces like this and the goblet in Fig. 379 were by no means Amelung's main product, but he was partial to making them and giving them—perhaps partly for publicity purposes—to cities, organizations, and important personages. This goblet was presented to Thomas Mifflin when he became governor of Pennsylvania in 1791. The arms of Pennsylvania are engraved on one side, and "New Bremen Glassmanufactory / 1791" on the other.* Rogers Fund, 1937 (37.101)

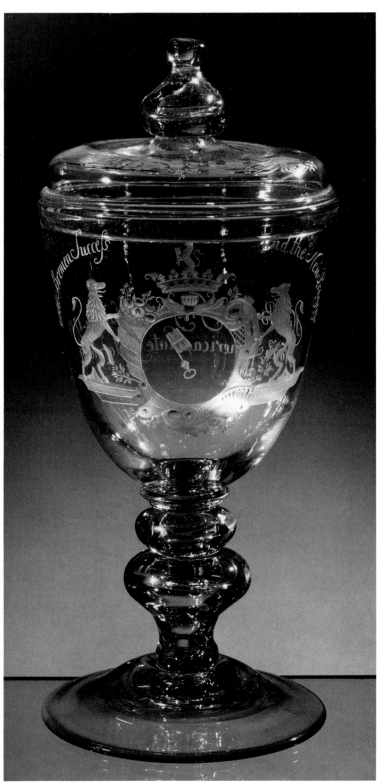

379

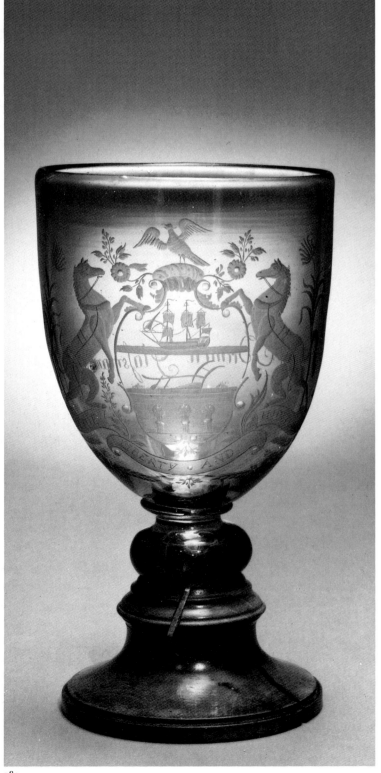

380

**Fig. 381. Decanter,** *possibly by Bakewell, Page, and Bakewell (1808–40), founded by Benjamin Bakewell, Pittsburgh, 1820–40; lead glass, height with stopper 10¼ inches (26 cm.). If Stiegel and Amelung didn't quite succeed in capturing the American market for European-type glass, Bakewell did. His aim was to make cut and engraved flint (lead) glass as fine as that imported from England and France, and the fact that he was called "the father of the flint-glass business" by a report on glass in the census of 1880 indicates that he was successful. In 1817 he produced a service of engraved- and cut-glass tableware for President Monroe. The strawberry diamond-and-fan pattern that decorates this decanter was the most popular cut design in early nineteenth-century America and is characteristic of Bakewell's work in the 1820s.*
Purchase, Paul Peralta Ramos Gift, 1974 (1974.145)

were then in Europe. His enterprise soon won the notice of George Washington. Despite these advantages, his venture collapsed in 1795, and Amelung's craftsmen moved on to factories elsewhere in the new nation. Glassblowers were peripatetic craftsmen anyway, and the influence of the earliest is to be seen in glass made later in New York, New England, Pennsylvania, Ohio, and elsewhere, whither they and their descendants migrated from those pioneering factories.

Throughout the colonial and early Federal periods, no American product could compete with the fine, clear glass imported from Europe. The first venture to do so successfully was launched in 1808 when Benjamin Bakewell established a glasshouse at Pittsburgh that produced clear lead glass, deeply and brilliantly cut in the English fashion. At the time, it was said, New Yorkers supposed Pittsburgh "to be at the farther end of the world." The development of a successful and sophisticated glasshouse in Pittsburgh was therefore surprising and was an early indication of the booming economic potential of the American Midwest. A few years later President James Monroe ordered from Bakewell a large service engraved with the arms of the United States for the White House. Typical of the workmanship of Pittsburgh's craftsmen in the 1820s is a decanter embellished with a cut diamond-and-fan pattern (Fig. 381) in the manner of contemporary English and Irish designs.

In 1818, ten years after the Bakewell plant opened, Deming Jarves of the New England Glass Company undertook similar productions in cut glass, continuing them at the Boston and Sandwich Glass Company, which he

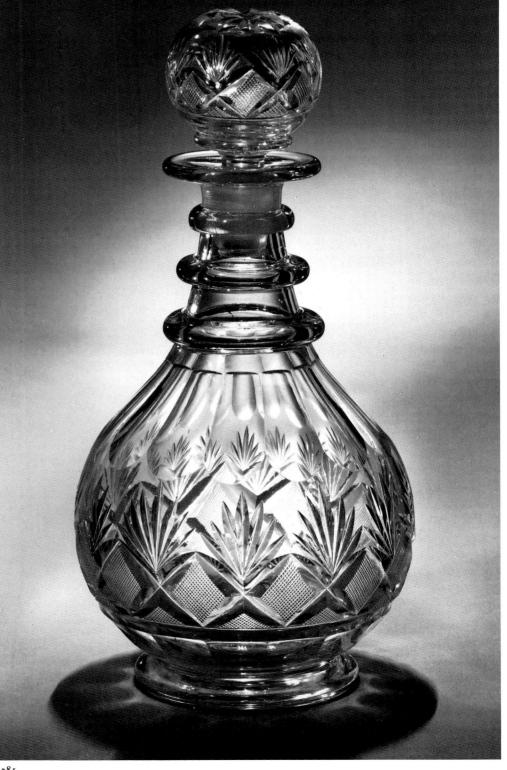

381

*Figs. 382 and 383. Vase, *New England Glass Company (1818–88), East Cambridge, Massachusetts, about 1843; lead glass, height 13 inches (33 cm.). The New England Glass Company produced a great variety of table and ornamental wares both for the domestic market and for export to the West Indies and South America. The firm's preeminence in the area of flint, or lead, glass is noteworthy, and this vase, presented to the company's foremost glassblower and superintendant, perhaps upon the occasion of his twentieth year with the company and his sixtieth birthday, displays outstanding metal, form, and ornament. The inscription on one side reads, "From/Henry Whitney/to/Thomas Leighton/East Cambridje/August·1843/A token of grateful remembrance," and on the other side there is an engraved view of the New England Glass Works itself. The use of such a view on an important object is most unusual and makes the vase doubly significant—as an example of the finest work the New England Glass Company could produce in the 1840s and as a document showing what the factory looked like during those years.*

Purchase, Robert G. Goelet and Mr. and Mrs. William H. Hernstadt Gifts, 1980 (1980.69)

founded in 1825. At this time other successful furnaces that produced fine wares were operating at Pittsburgh and elsewhere in Pennsylvania, New England, New York, and New Jersey. The New England Glass Company operated continuously for seventy years and produced some of the finest glassware made in America during that time. One of the most important examples is a presentation vase (Figs. 382 and 383) engraved with a view of the factory itself and the inscription "From/Henry Whitney / to / Thomas Leighton / East Cambridje / August. 1843 / A token of grateful remembrance." Leighton was superintendent of the glassworks until his death in 1849. His six sons also held positions of importance in the company, and as a dynasty the family made an unparalleled contribution to the history of glassmaking in America. In 1888 this prestigious company moved to Toledo, Ohio, where inexpensive fuel to feed the furnaces was abundant. Its arrival in that city was hailed with a parade and an open-air banquet. At this point the name was changed to Libbey Glass Company.

At numerous factories, designs very roughly approximating those of cut glass were produced by blowing a gather of glass into full-size patterned molds with two, three, or four hinged sections. The result was a relatively inexpensive tableware now commonly referred to as "blown-three-mold" glass. The practice was an ancient one, although American craftsmen did not know of the early precedents. This method could not duplicate the sharp facets of cut glass, but it produced engaging objects (Fig. 384). Patterns cut into the molds were not so sharply geometric as those of cut glass but branched out into baroque and other more freely flowing styles.

Another technique commonly practiced in nineteenth-century America was that of pattern molding, the earliest examples of which we associate with Stiegel's pre-Revolutionary operation. It was employed at other early glass factories as well, and again in the Midwest during the 1830s and 1840s (Fig. 385).

Other types of molds, with two hinged sections, were used to produce patterned whiskey flasks and bottles.

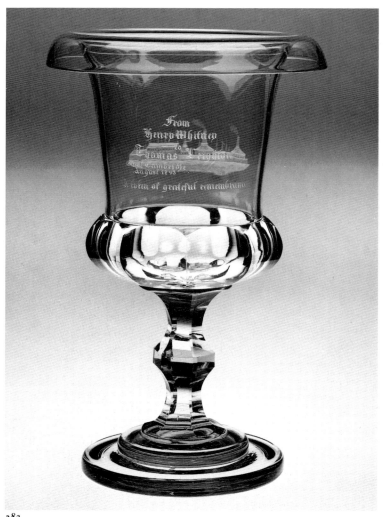

382

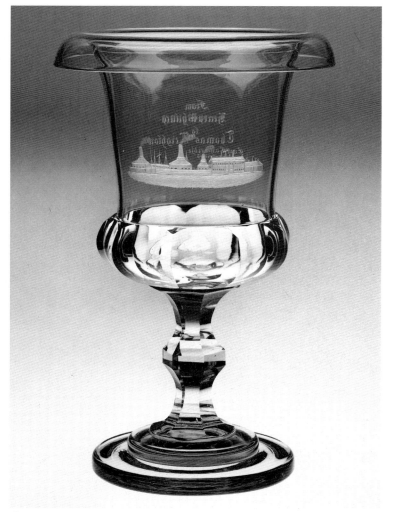

383

The molded designs often celebrated some important occasion or prominent public figure, providing an informal pictorial commentary on the passing national scene from about the time of the War of 1812 to the Civil War. One of the most colorful producers of such convenient vessels was Thomas W. Dyott (Fig. 386), a self-styled doctor and purveyor of nostrums. Craftsmen at the factories that turned out these and other inexpensive commonplace products, including window glass, in commercial quantities, continued to produce tablewares

**Fig. 384. Group of blown-three-mold objects.** Left to right: cream pitcher, *New England, probably Boston and Sandwich Glass Company (1825–88), Sandwich, Massachusetts, 1825–40; glass, height 4 inches (10.2 cm.);* decanter, *probably Boston and Sandwich Glass Company (1825–88), Sandwich, Massachusetts, 1825–40; glass, height 11¼ inches (28.6 cm.);* sugar bowl, *probably Midwest, 1820–40; glass, height 6 inches (15.2 cm.). Blown-three-mold glass was developed in an effort to produce an inexpensive but attractive alternative to imported cut glass. Since it was made in a mold, it was much cheaper to produce than the English and Irish cut glass it imitated, and since these molds didn't turn out sharply faceted pieces that looked cut, a* new category was born. *The different parts of the pattern flow together, smoothing the edges that look sharp and sparkly in cut glass. Also, because the full-size molds produced pieces that had the pattern impressed both inside and out, it has a rather bumpy charm all its own. Many forms were produced by this technique, mainly at eastern factories; some, like the sugar bowl in this group, are rare. Decanters have survived in the greatest numbers.*

Gift of Henry G. Schiff, 1980 (1980.502.32); Paul Peralta Ramos Gift, 1970 (1970.188.1a,b); Gift of R. Thornton Wilson, 1939 (39.18.7a,b)

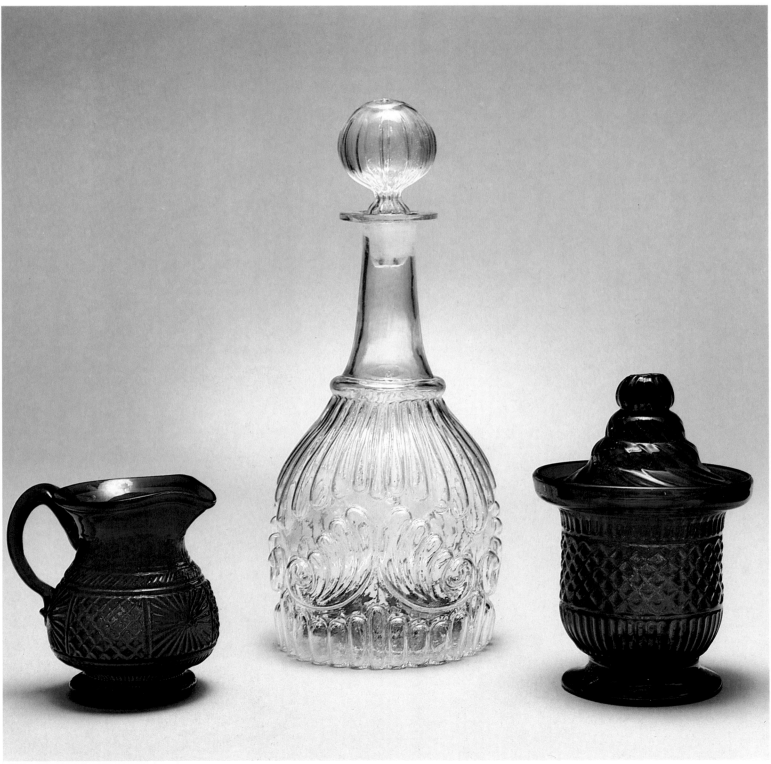

384

**Fig. 385. Pattern-molded wares.** Left to right: bottle, *Midwest, probably Zanesville, Ohio, 1815–40; glass, height 8 inches (20.3 cm.);* sugar bowl, *Midwest, 1815–40; glass, height 4½ inches (11.4 cm.).* The tradition of forming objects in an open mold, removing them, and blowing them so that they become larger, begun at Stiegel's eighteenth-century Pennsylvania glasshouse, was carried into the Midwest by glass-workers looking for jobs when Stiegel's enterprise failed. Nowhere else, wrote George and Helen McKearin (*American Glass*) were "The brilliant ambers, golden yellows, and delicate shadings in greens which are rarely encountered in the products of any other glass houses in America, England, or on the Continent . . ." the rule. These two pieces, with their characteristic shapes and lovely colors, exemplify the best of the midwestern output.
Gift of Henry G. Schiff, 1980 (1980.502.69,85ab)

**Fig. 386. Flask,** *Kensington Glass Works (1818–38), established by Thomas W. Dyott, Philadelphia, 1824–28; glass, height 7 inches (17.8 cm.).* Whiskey flasks like this were produced in full-size two-part molds from the early years of the nineteenth century onward. The pictures that decorate them range from portraits of important people like Benjamin Franklin to symbols such as the eagle and cornucopia and on to geometric sunburst patterns like those found on blown-three-mold wares. The enterprising and ambitious "Dr." Dyott of Philadelphia was a major producer of the flasks, which were also a staple of many other glasshouses, and he had no qualms about molding his own portrait on the side opposite the great Franklin. Because of their historic interest, these flasks have been collected for many years.
Bequest of Helen Hay Whitney, 1944 (45.35.7)

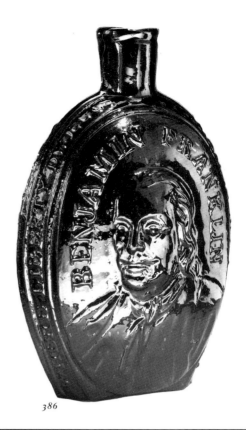

*386*

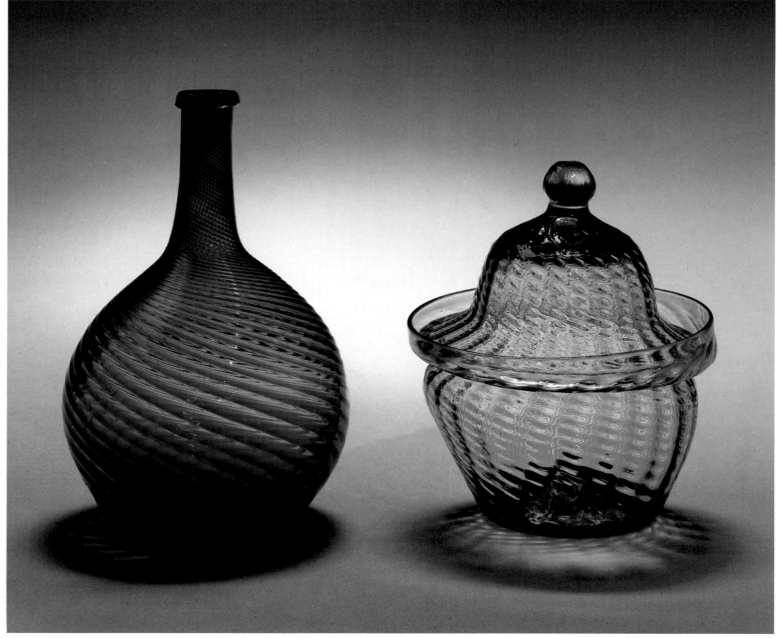

*385*

of some distinction as well. Using the same unrefined glass, they produced objects for their own purposes and for sale to local customers. A pair of exceptionally handsome candlesticks, a pitcher, and a footed compote (Fig. 387), the last two overlaid with decorative loops or "lily pads," are presumably pieces of this sort. These forms are in the traditional vernacular of the glassblower freely manipulating his material with age-old techniques. Because the shapes and decorative techniques were characteristic of wares first produced by glasshouses in southern New Jersey, such pieces are called "South Jersey"— although the tradition spread to New York and New England. These wares were made from the late eighteenth century to the 1870s, when the glass industry was almost completely mechanized.

**Fig. 387. Group of "South Jersey" type objects.** Left to right: compote, *probably New York State, 1830–50; glass, height 3¾ inches (9.5 cm.); pitcher, mid-Atlantic states, 1830–60; glass, height 7¼ inches (18.4 cm.); pair of candlesticks, southern New Jersey, 1825–50; glass, height of each 9⅛ inches (23.2 cm.).* Glassworkers who had come to America to work for Caspar Wistar passed their skills along to the next generation and gradually, as glasshouses were opened throughout New York and New England, the tradition that has become known as "South Jersey" (the site of Wistar's factory) flourished. It was a tradition rooted in common glass fashioned for the most part into bottles and windows. But South Jersey workmen had always enjoyed the privilege of also making useful or decorative objects for their friends and families, and these objects are prized by collectors today. They were most often of bottle and window-glass colors: pale aquamarine to dark amber and olive, and are characterized by free-blown shapes and ornament made of glass tooled into swirls and other abstract forms. "Lilypad" decoration, seen here on both the pitcher and the unusual footed

compote, is one of the most characteristic, and it seems to be uniquely American, for no European example is known. The swirls that surround the lower sockets and contrast with the smoothly curving balusters of the candlesticks are another characteristic type of South Jersey ornament.

Gift of Henry G. Schiff, 1980 (1980.502.10); Rogers Fund, 1922 (22.224.2); Rogers Fund, 1935 (35.124.1,2)

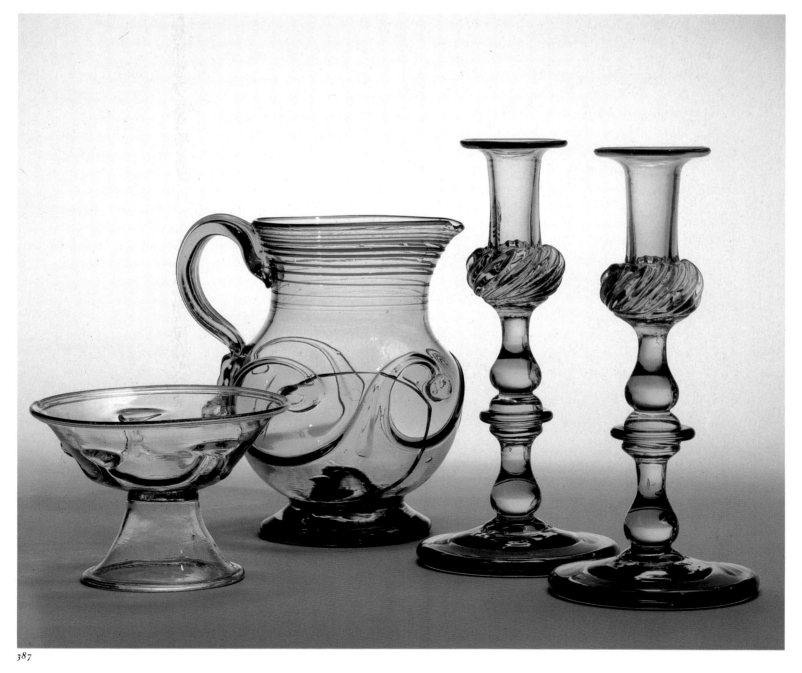

387

# The Pre-Centennial Period, 1830–75

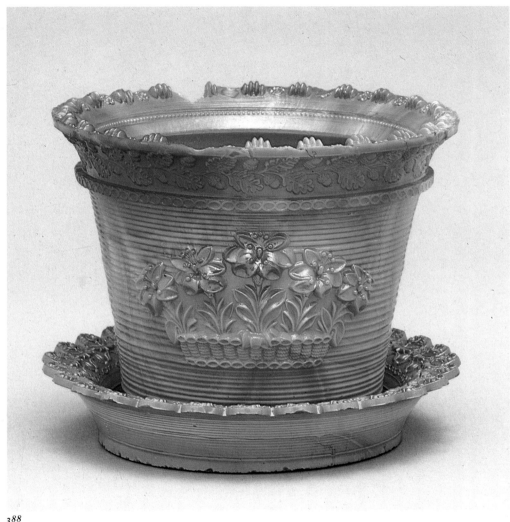

388

The first important change in the fashioning of glass since the beginning of the pre-Christian era was that of mechanically pressing the molten glass into patterned molds. This technique enabled various forms with intricate designs to be mass manufactured quickly and at moderate cost. Deming Jarves introduced the process in the early nineteenth century at the Boston and Sandwich Glass Company, and it was soon put to use in a number of other glasshouses both east and west of the Allegheny Mountains. Although the mechanically pressed ware was at first meant to imitate cut glass, the iron-and-brass molds into which the molten glass was forced could be modeled with more precise, minute detail than a glass-cutter's wheel could achieve. Backgrounds of delicate stippling that caught, reflected, and refracted any light that played against them gave this earliest, so-called "lacy," glass a novel and distinctive character. It found a large appreciative audience from the beginning—and it still does. As in the case of blown-three-mold glass, designers of pressed-glass molds in the 1830s and 1840s departed from geometrical cut-glass prototypes and used rococo, Gothic, and classical motifs with patriotic symbols in highly original combinations (Figs. 388, 389, and 390).

The pressing process also made it feasible to produce forms of a sort no glassblower could duplicate. This possibility, clearly demonstrated in a variety of novel lacy-glass shapes, became even more manifest in the 1860s and 1870s when a number of glasshouses converted to the manufacture of pressed wares of cheaper glass. By then, improved pressing techniques made possible a still wider variety of designs and

**Figs. 388, 389, and 390. "Lacy" pressed wares.** Left to right: flowerpot and saucer, *probably New England, 1830–35; glass, height 3¹¹⁄₁₆ inches (9.4 cm.)*; lamp, *pressed stem and lacy base, blown font, New England, 1830–35; glass, height 8⅞ inches (22.5 cm.)*; dish, *possibly New England, 1830–50; glass, length 9⁵⁄₁₆ inches (23.7 cm.).* Once the technique for pressing glass had been developed, many factories began to employ it. At first, since the molten glass usually contained impurities, the pressed object was stippled in all areas not covered by the primary design, giving the background a lacy appearance. This group of the very earliest pressed wares is thus called lacy glass. It includes the rare shell dish, a lamp that combines a pressed base

with a free-blown font, and a flowerpot and saucer. The blue color of the flowerpot is most unusual, and the form itself has no known counterpart. Lacy glass, like blown-three-mold, was developed as an inexpensive substitute for cut glass, but, also like the other molded ware, it has become a desirable category in itself in collectors' eyes. As the McKearins point out (American Glass), "While many of the pressed glass patterns included decorative motifs characteristic of cut glass, the intricacy and delicacy of most patterns, particularly in the Lacy category, could not possibly have been achieved by a cutting wheel."
Bequest of Anna G. W. Green, in memory of her husband, Dr. Charles W. Green, 1957 (57.131.11,12); 1951 (51.171.28); and 1951 (51.171.160)

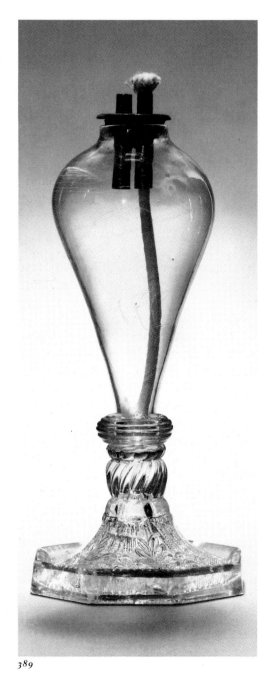

389

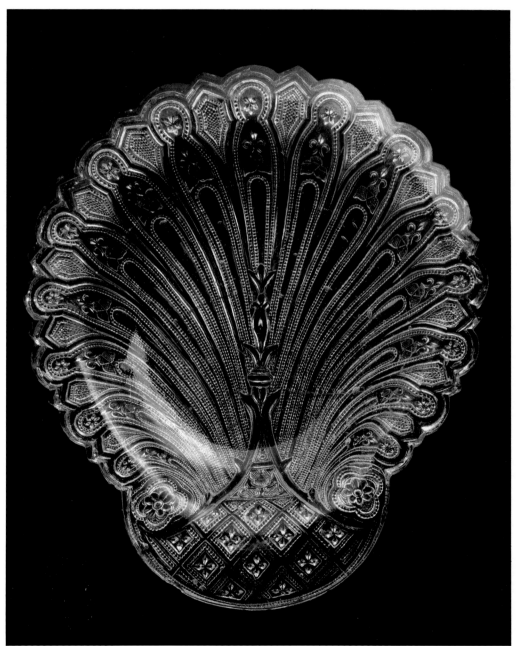

390

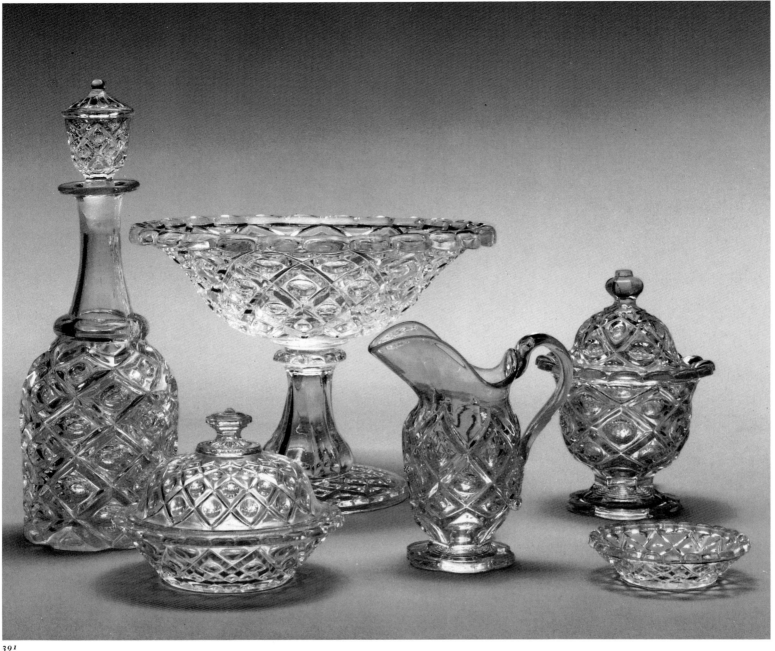

391

**Fig. 391. Pattern-glass objects.** Left to right: decanter, butter dish, footed compote, creamer, sugar bowl, sauce dish *in the Diamond Thumbprint pattern, probably Pittsburgh, 1850–60; glass, heights 13¾ inches (34.9 cm.), 6¼ inches (15.9 cm.), 8½ inches (21.6 cm.), 6⅛ inches (15.6 cm.), 9 inches (22.9 cm.); diameter 4⅜ inches (10.6 cm.). By about 1840 a new category of pressed glass, now called pattern glass, came on the market. Perhaps because people like new styles, or because of new discoveries in the manufacturing process, the new wares turned away from the elaborate lacy patterns to simpler, more geometric ones that were pressed into large* matching sets of tablewares. Wine glasses, tumblers, saucers, sugar bowls, creamers, and a wide variety of other forms were made up in the same design, which often came also in special serving dishes such as compotes (see Fig. 392), celery vases, decanters, fruit bowls, water pitchers, and so on. It was in this period, too, that large sets were produced in many other mediums: ceramic tablewares; furniture suites for parlors, dining rooms, and bedrooms; and silver place settings and serving pieces.*

Gift of Mrs. Emily Winthrop Miles, 1946 (46.140.1,12,22,24a,b,30a,b,77)

forms, and the trend toward producing glassware in complete table settings was established (Fig. 391). This so-called pattern glass, given such suggestive trade names as Westward-Ho, Ashburton, Lincoln Drape, and so on, made attractive tableware available to a large public at low prices. The lower quality of the glass used was sometimes camouflaged by partly frosting the surface and by other devices. A splendid compote, for example, is pressed in what was known as the Thumbprint pattern (Fig. 392), an allover design of oval facets whose highly reflective surfaces, while simulating the effect of good cut glass, tend at the same time to disguise any imperfections in the material used. Popular favorites from about the 1840s to the 1870s were figural subjects in the round, such as candlesticks in the shape of dolphins (Fig. 393).

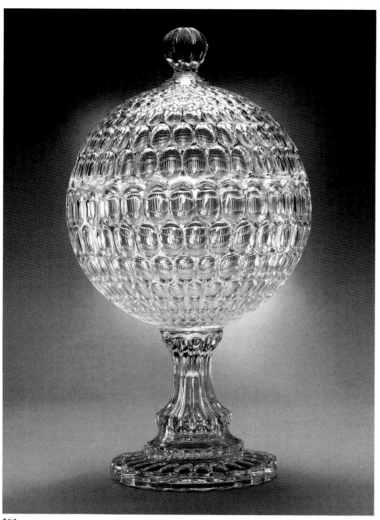

**Fig. 392. Compote with cover** in the Thumb-print pattern, by Bakewell, Pears and Company (1836–82), Pittsburgh, 1860–70; glass, height with cover 14⅛ inches (35.9 cm.).
Gift of Mrs. Emily Winthrop Miles, 1946 (46.140.83ab)

**Fig. 393. Pressed dolphin candlesticks.** *All are New England, probably Boston and Sandwich Glass Company (1825–88), Sandwich, Massachusetts; glass. Left: about 1840, height 8½ inches (21.6 cm.); center: 1845–65, height 10⅜ inches (26.4 cm.); right: about 1840, height 10⅜ inches (26.4 cm.). Dolphin candlesticks were among the pressed wares that were made from about 1840 to 1870, and they have been popular among collectors for many years. Fortunately, they were made in sizable numbers, in both short and tall versions, and in several colors or combinations of colors, sometimes with gilding. Although pressed wares in general, and dolphin candlesticks in particular, are often assumed to have been made at the well-known Sandwich factory, they were in fact made at a number of other glasshouses as well.*
Gift of Mrs. Emily Winthrop Miles, 1946 (46.140.360); Bequest of Anna G. W. Green, in memory of her husband, Dr. Charles W. Green, 1957 (57.131.3); Rogers Fund, 1936 (36.148.1)

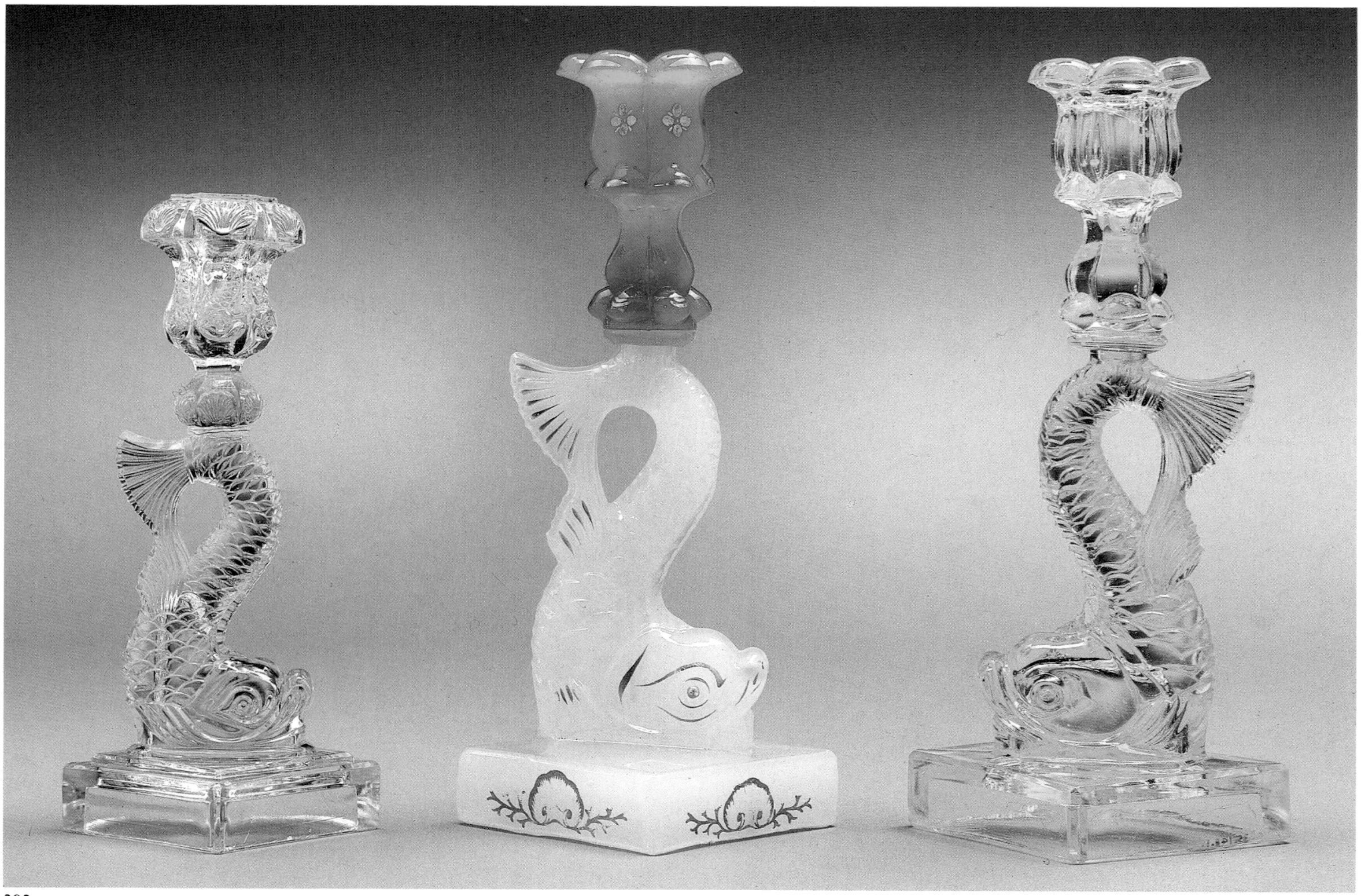

392

393

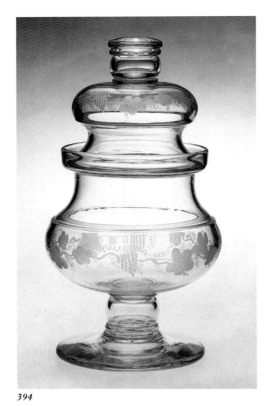

394

*Figs. 394–97.* While innovations in glass making processes were regularly introduced, traditional methods continued to be employed as well. Free-blown tablewares in the South Jersey tradition were offered along with pressed, molded, cut, and engraved wares by factories in New England and New York.

*Fig. 394. Sugar bowl,* New England, probably South Boston Flint Glass Works (1812–about 1820) or Phoenix Glass Works (about 1820–70), established by Thomas Cains, South Boston, Massachusetts, 1815–35; glass, height 9¹¹/₁₆ inches (24.6 cm.).
Gift of Ethelinda and Lowell Inness, 1980 (1980.421.1)

*Fig. 395. Pitcher,* probably New England Glass Company (1818–88), East Cambridge, Massachusetts, 1817–40; glass, height 11½ inches (29.2 cm.).
Rogers Fund, 1910 (10.60.26)

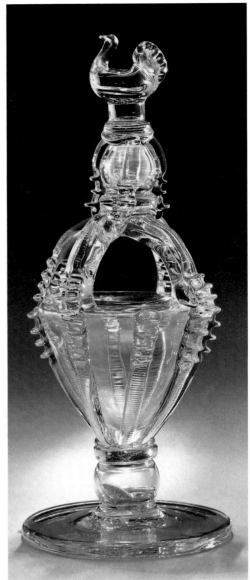

396

*Fig. 396. Bank,* New England, possibly Boston and Sandwich Glass Company (1825–88), Sandwich, Massachusetts, 1833–50; glass, height 10¼ inches (26 cm.).
The Sylmaris Collection, Gift of George Coe Graves, 1930 (30.120.308)

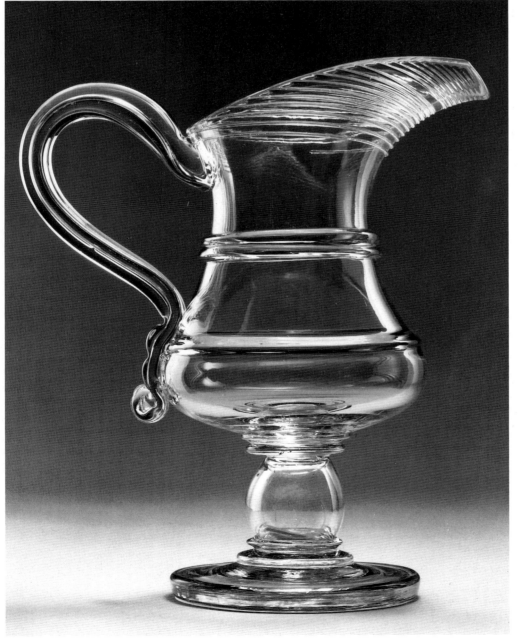

395

During much of the nineteenth century, free-blown glass of fine quality continued to be made in quantity. Cases in point are a handsome clear-glass pitcher decorated with applied threading and mid-bands and with an English shilling of 1817 in the hollow knop of its stem (Fig. 395). It was probably made by the New England Glass Company. A bank, also of clear glass and possibly a product of the Sandwich factory, has a bird finial and five- and ten-cent United States coins in the hollow knops beneath the finial and at the base, respectively (Fig. 396). An exceptionally fine compote engraved with a version of the United States seal and a band of decorative motifs (Fig. 397) was made in 1861 at the Greenpoint Glassworks in

**Fig. 397. Compote,** *Greenpoint Glassworks*
*(1852–63), established by Christian Dorflinger,*
*Brooklyn, New York, 1861; glass, height 7½*
*inches (19 cm.). Part of a state service ordered*
*for the White House by Mrs. Lincoln in 1861,*
*this compote was designed, cut, and engraved by*
*Christian Dorflinger.*
Gift of Kathryn Hait Dorflinger Manchee, 1972
(1972.232.1)

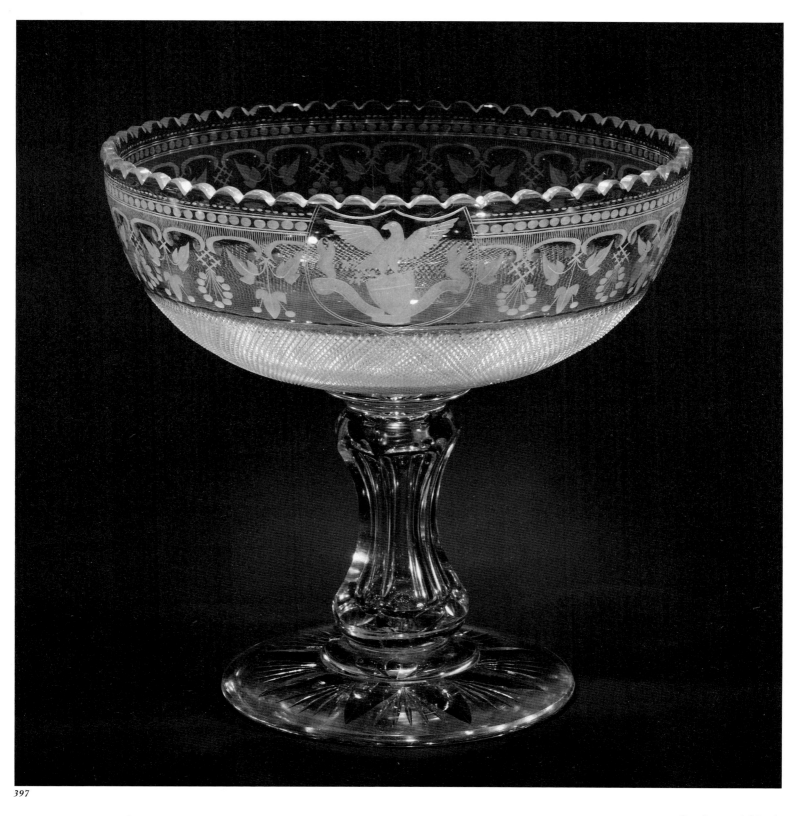

397

**Figs. 398, 399, and 400. Overlay and cased glass.** *Techniques associated with glassmaking in Bohemia became popular about mid-century, and the colorful wares that resulted are called Bohemian-style glass. The techniques involved layering glass of different colors on one object and decorating by means of cutting. Three varieties of American glass in the Bohemian style are seen here, Figs. 399 and 400 with "overlay," or outer layers of glass of a different color from that of the basic object that have been cut through to reveal the layer beneath, and Fig. 398, which is "cased," or covered by uncut layers of different colors.*

**Fig. 398. Pitcher,** *probably Pittsburgh, 1850–60; cased glass: amethyst inside, white over it, clear outside; height 9½ inches (24.1 cm.).* Purchase, Mr. and Mrs. William H. Hernstadt Gift, 1980 (1980.355.1)

**Fig. 399. Decanter,** *inscribed "March 27ith/Sandwich Mass/1867/G.F. Lapham Eng," Boston and Sandwich Glass Company (1825–88), Sandwich, Massachusetts; clear glass overlaid with ruby, height 10⅛ inches (25.7 cm.).* Funds from various donors, 1967 (67.7.22ab)

**Fig. 400. Lamp,** *Boston and Sandwich Glass Company (1825–88), Sandwich, Massachusetts, 1855–67; ruby glass overlaid with white, height 19 inches (48.3 cm.).* Funds from various donors, 1967 (67.7.23)

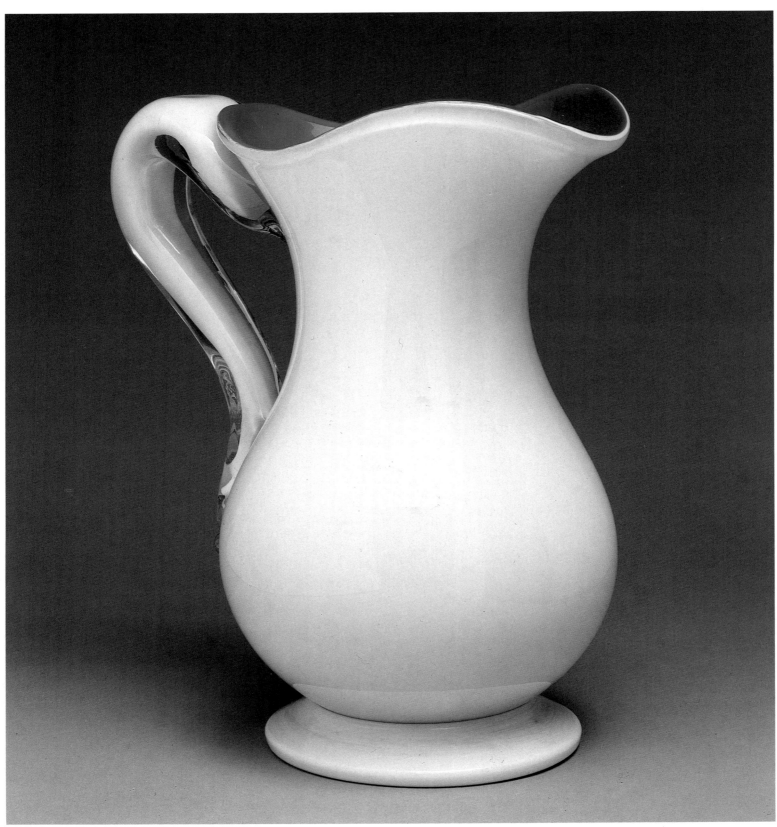

*398*

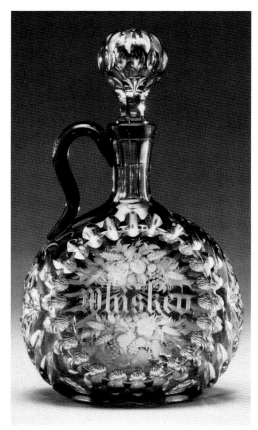

399

Brooklyn, New York, by Christian Dorflinger, a French émigré. It is part of a
state service ordered for the White
House by Mrs. Lincoln.

Throughout the last half of the nineteenth century, a wide variety of innovations in glassmaking succeeded one
another. One outstanding technical
achievement perfected during these
years was that of coating clear glass
forms with thin layers of colored glass,
then cutting through the latter to leave
a pattern in the clear glass beneath;
such pieces were also sometimes engraved. This technique, copied from
wares produced in Bohemia, is brilliantly represented here in a ruby-
colored decanter made at the Sandwich
factory in 1867 (Fig. 399). In another
example, a lamp possibly made at the
same factory, an opaque white overlay is
cut away in attractive patterns to expose
the ruby glass underneath (Fig. 400). A
large and exceptionally handsome
pitcher probably made in Pittsburgh
has on the inside a layer of amethyst
covered with opaque white and is cased
on the outside with clear glass (Fig.
398). The gracefully shaped handle has
a thumb rest as an aid to lifting and
tilting the capacious piece. Expert
craftsmen recently immigrated from
Germany and France contributed importantly to the development and use of
such techniques in America.

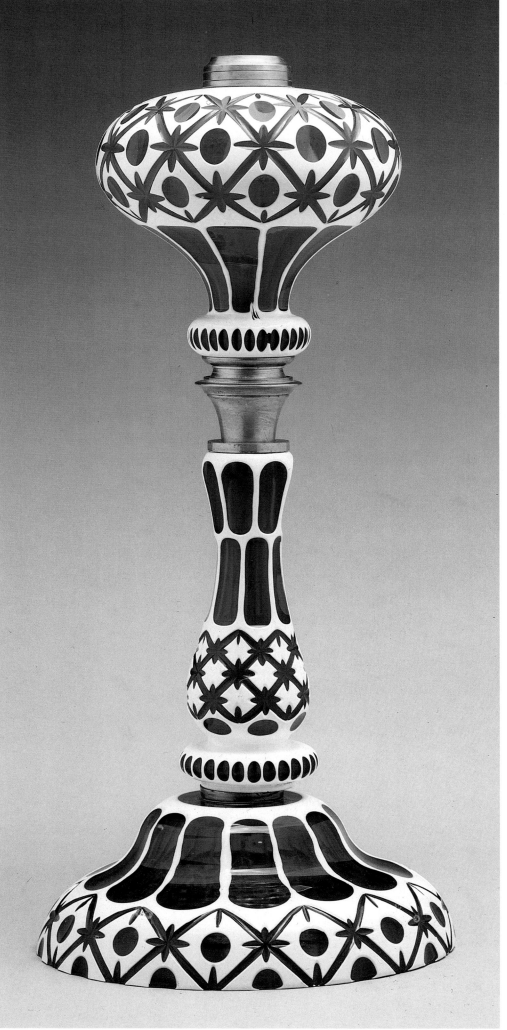

400

# The Post-Centennial Period, 1875–1915

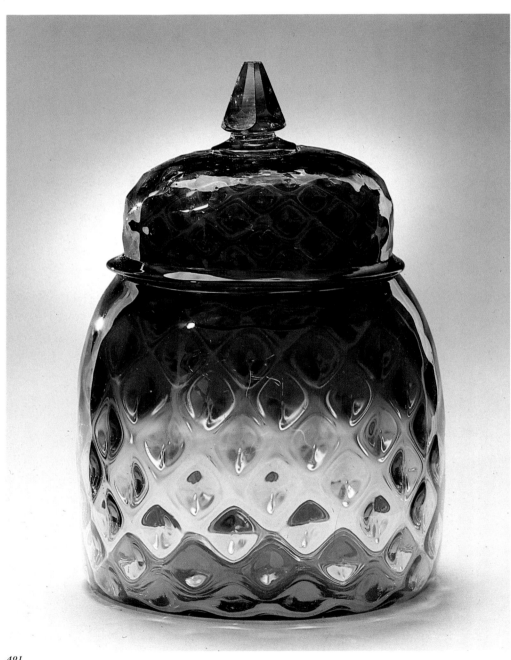

***Fig. 401. Cracker jar,*** *labeled "N E G W/AM-BERINA/PAT'D/July 24, 1883," by the New England Glass Company (1818–88), East Cambridge, Massachusetts, 1883; glass shaded from amber at the bottom to ruby at the top, height 8³/₈ inches (21.3 cm.).*
Gift of Mrs. Emily Winthrop Miles, 1946 (46.140.483)

In the last quarter of the century a great demand for "artistic glass" encouraged glassmakers to make even greater efforts to produce what now seems an almost bewildering abundance of richly colored and textured and fancifully shaped wares. It was a period of constant invention and innovation that brought forth many-colored and variously ornamented forms. These were patented at different factories under such suggestive trade names as Burmese, Peachblow, Pomona, Amberina, and Agate—appealing to the contemporary taste for the exotic in all sorts of household furnishings. Various examples of these popular but short-lived fashions indicate the high degree of virtuosity that contributed to their success (Figs. 401 and 402).

The last years of the century also saw the development of cut glass on an unprecedented scale. During this so-called brilliant period, the glass was made of heavy, lustrous metal precisely cut into any one of innumerable patterns (Figs. 403 and 404). Housewives were reminded that such glassware constituted the "most showy, and in many respects, choicest of table equipments." Another fashion of the period was glass on which a pattern in a thin silver coating was deposited, then further defined by engraved or etched details (see Fig. 348).

By far the most influential innovator of these years, and an active proponent of the Art Nouveau movement, was Louis Comfort Tiffany. His work, particularly in glass, was as well known abroad as at home—and it was often copied. Tiffany had experimented with glass as early as the 1870s, and his interest in this medium grew with the years. By the most intricate and inventive techniques he achieved an astonishingly

**Figs. 401 and 402. Art glass,** *as it was called,
was the response to a demand for wares that were
more colorful, more exotic, and more unusual
than ever before. Color was the key, and the art
glass made from about 1880 to 1900 is a
triumph of the glassmaker's art. Shading from
one color to another or from very pale to deeply
hued was an important aspect of art glass, as can
be seen in the Amberina cracker jar (Fig. 401)
and the Peachblow vase (Fig. 402, left). The
vase in Fig. 402 (right),* cased in gold and brown
and etched with twisting Art Nouveau streamers
against a frosted ground, *was inspired by the
glass of far-off Islam.*

**Fig. 402. Vases.** Left: *probably New England
Glass Company (1818–88), East Cambridge,
Massachusetts, 1886–88; glass shading from
cream to rose, height 14⅜ inches (36.5 cm.);*
right: *marked "Honesdale," by the Honesdale
Glass Works (1901–32), Honesdale, Pennsylva-
nia, about 1901; glass, height 14⅜ inches
(36.5 cm.).*
Rogers Fund, 1973 (1973.16); Purchase, Anonymous
Gift, 1969 (69.91.1)

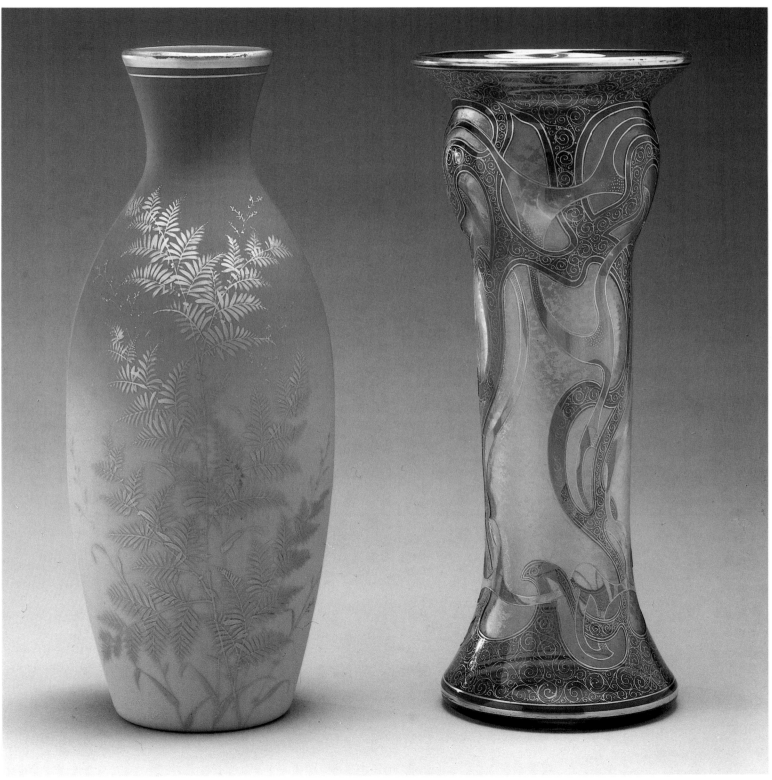

402

**Figs. 403, 404, and 405.** *The leading American glass factories exhibited elaborate cut and engraved wares at both the Centennial exhibition in Philadelphia in 1876 and at the Columbian exhibition in Chicago in 1893, creating a demand among the public that they were then only too happy to supply. The heavy cut glass, in the "brilliant" style, was made of very high quality lead glass by such firms as C. Dorflinger and Sons and T. G. Hawkes and Company in Corning. Nearly every conceivable form was made in the brilliant style, from imposing bowls like that in Fig. 403 to diminutive egg cups. A more delicate but no less elaborate type was engraved glass of the kind seen in Fig. 405.*

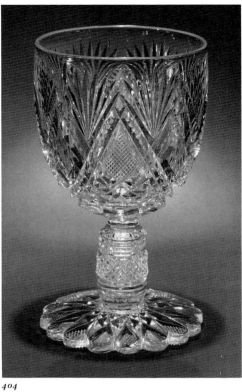

**Fig. 404. Goblet,** *by C. Dorflinger and Sons (1865–1921), White Mills, Pennsylvania, 1886–90; glass cut in the Parisian design, height 5½ inches (14 cm.).*
Gift of Kathryn Hait Dorflinger Manchee, 1972 (1972.232.2)

**Fig. 403. Punch bowl,** *possibly C. Dorflinger and Sons (1865–1921), White Mills, Pennsylvania, 1895–1910; glass, height 9¹¹⁄₁₆ inches (24.6 cm.).*
Funds from various donors, 1970 (1970.17)

**Fig. 405. Wine glass,** *Steuben Glass Works (1903–present), Corning, New York, 1903–10; glass, clear flashed with orchid, height 8⅞ inches (22.5 cm.).*
Gift of Mr. and Mrs. Samuel B. Feld, 1968 (68.209.1)

404

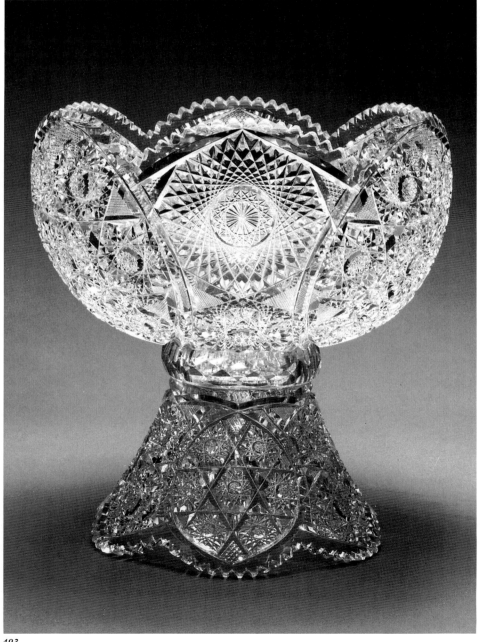

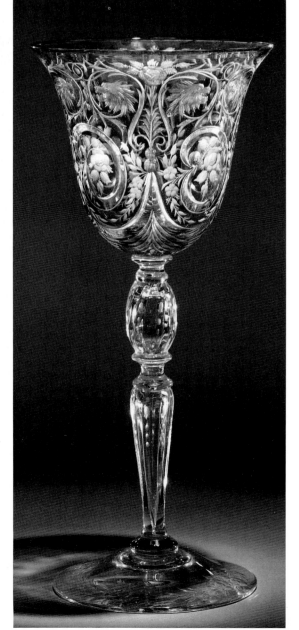

403

405

wide range of novel and colorful effects. For a score of years and more his products won awards at virtually every important international fair. The Museum first acquired examples of his work in 1896.

A lamp with a green bronze base of lily pads and stems rising to support a leaded-glass lotus-flower shade is another exquisite example of the Art Nouveau style (Fig. 406). In connection with this piece it should be remembered that, for the first time in history, brightness from fixtures could be directed downward as well as up because of the invention of electric lighting.

It has been estimated that by 1898 Tiffany had created 5,000 colors and varieties of his famous "favrile" glass, an innovation that was hailed by *House Beautiful* as "a distinctively American product that is recognized wherever it is shown as an achievement in art." The report went on to observe that Tiffany's favrile vases had "all the splendor of opals, emeralds, aquamarines, and chrysoprus . . . colors stolen from hyacinths, tulips, and roses, from garnets, corals, and turquoise. Iridescence . . . [is] irradiated with purple and gold" (Figs. 407 and 408).

About 1905 Tiffany designed a superb stained-glass window panel for the New York residence of William Skinner (see Fig. 5). "The skill with which this glass is designed and executed," one critic wrote recently, "layered and tinted in subtle gradation to suggest distant mountains, sky, and water, is art and craft at its best." The view, a depiction of Oyster Bay, Long Island, is framed by wisteria vines bearing clusters of lustrous blue blossoms recalling Tiffany's wisteria lampshades. These were extremely highly regarded about the turn

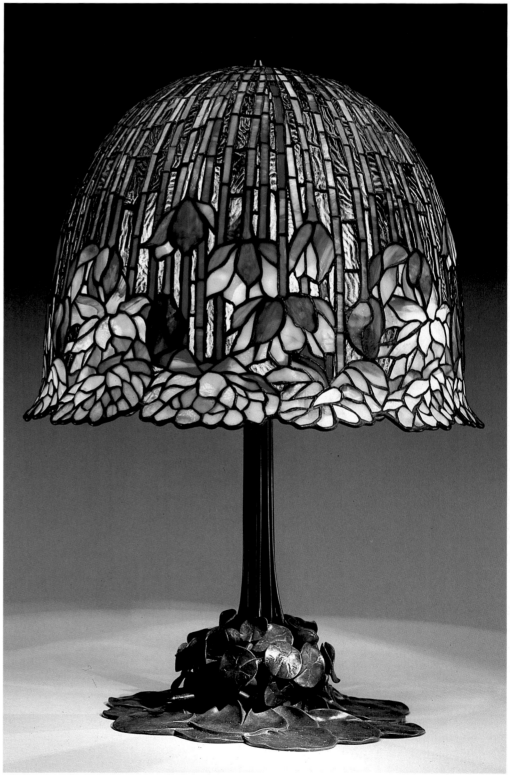

406

**Figs. 407 and 408. Favrile glass.** *Of all the producers of art glass during the final years of the nineteenth century and the early years of the twentieth, no one was more imaginative and inventive than Louis Comfort Tiffany (1848–1933). After considerable experiment, he produced his famous "favrile" glass (the name is taken from the word fabrile, or handmade). Glass of different colors was combined while still molten; blown; and sometimes twisted and twirled on the gather to achieve effects suggestive of flowers, paperweights, lava, and marble. Iridescence was important, and was achieved by exposing the still-hot glass to metallic vapors.*

**Fig. 407. Vases,** *both Tiffany Glass and Decorating Company (1892–1902), established by Louis Comfort Tiffany, Corona, New York.* Left: *"paperweight" glass, blue on a black background suggesting an iris, 1897; height 11³⁄16 inches (28.4 cm.).* Right: *iridescent favrile glass suggestive of a peacock feather, 1893–96; height 14⅛ inches (35.9 cm.).*
Gift of Louis Comfort Tiffany Foundation, 1951 (51.121.8); Gift of H. O. Havemeyer, 1896 (96.17.10)

**Fig. 408. Vases.** Left and center: *both Tiffany Glass and Decorating Company (1892–1902), established by Louis Comfort Tiffany, Corona, New York.* Left: *iridescent favrile glass, flower-form vase, 1898; height 18¹¹⁄16 inches (47.4 cm.).* Center: *opalescent favrile glass, flower-form vase, height 16¼ inches (41.3 cm.).* Right: *bowl, Tiffany Studios (1902–38), established by Louis Comfort Tiffany, Corona, New York, 1908; iridescent favrile glass, volcano or lava bowl, height 6⁵⁄16 inches (16 cm.).*
*Left to right:* Gift of Louis Comfort Tiffany Foundation, 1951 (51.121.17); Anonymous Gift, 1955 (55.213.28); Gift of Louis Comfort Tiffany Foundation, 1951 (51.121.13)

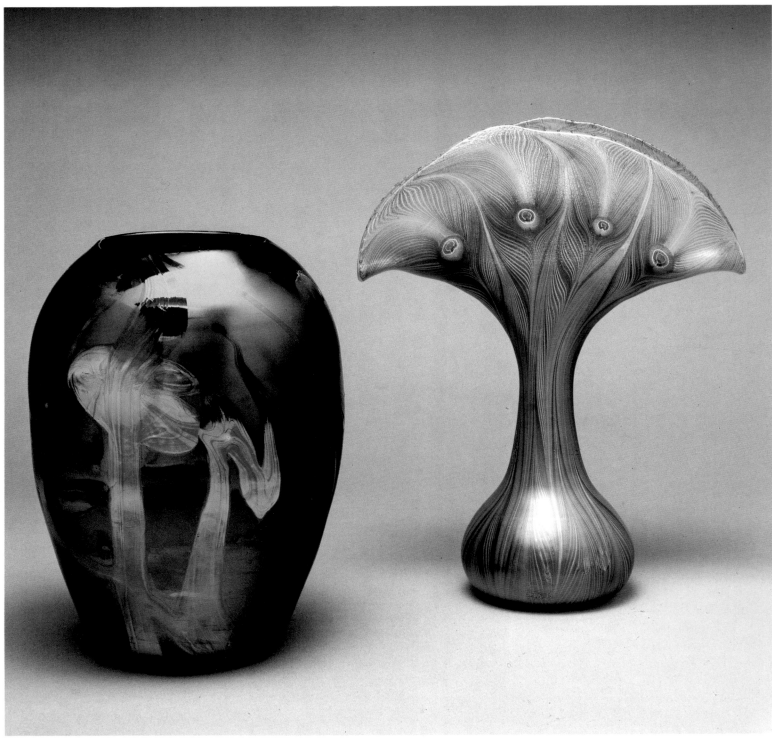

407

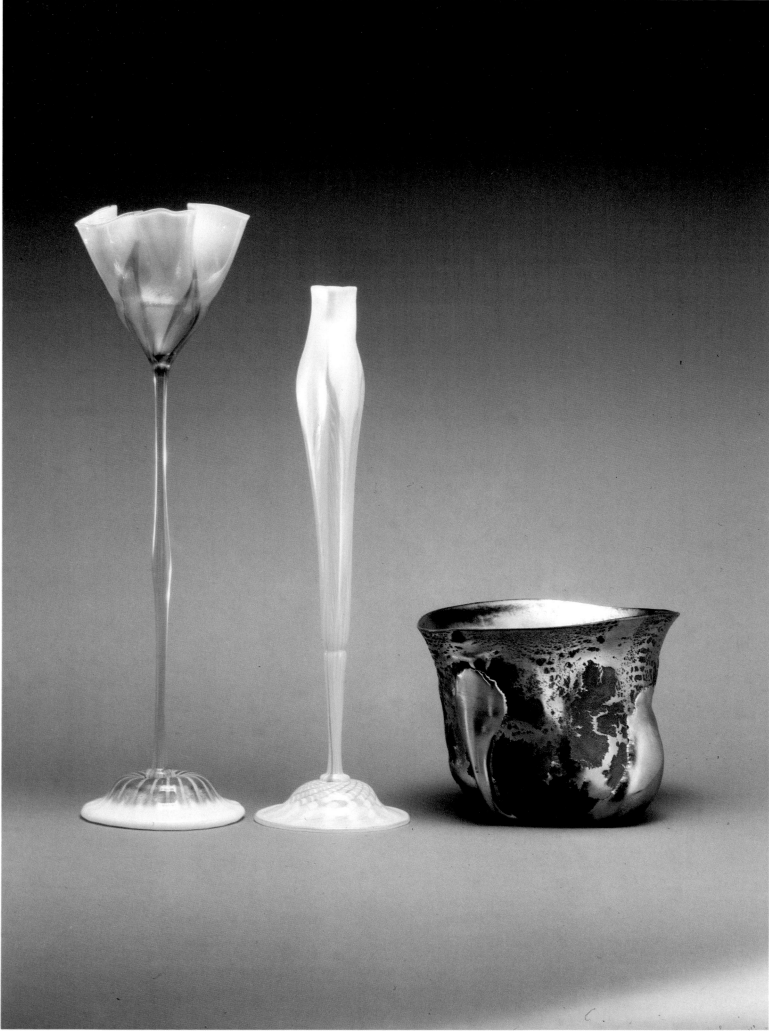

408

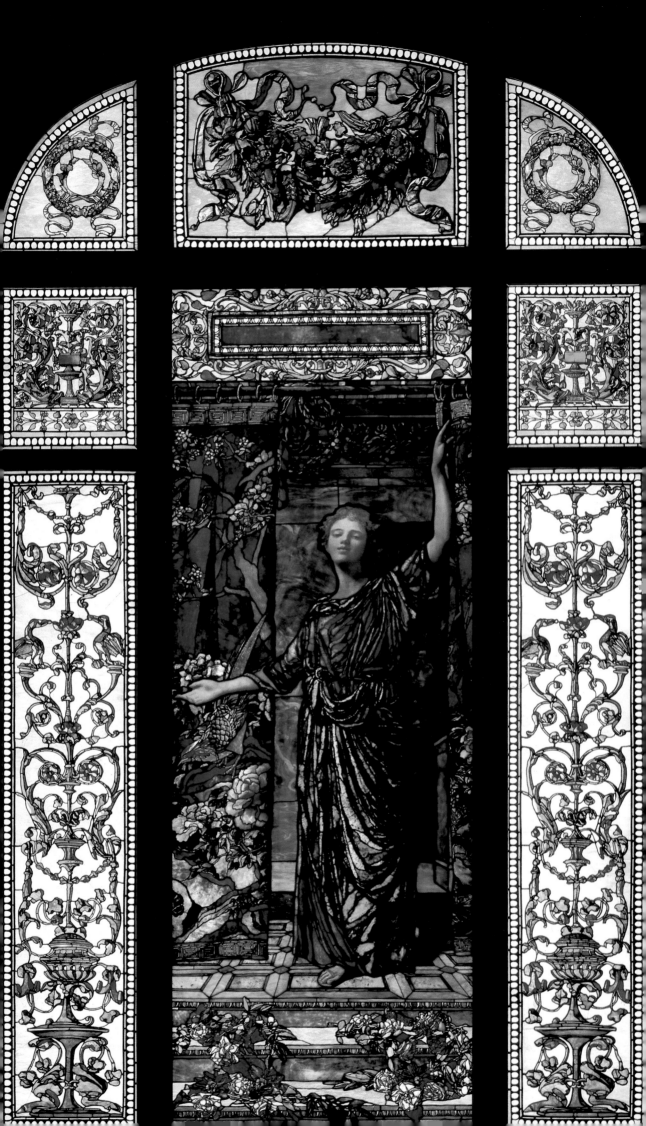

**Fig. 409.** *"Welcome" window, by John La Farge (1835–1910), New York, 1909; stained glass, 13 by 8 feet (4 by 2.4 m.). In the last two decades of the nineteenth century when art glass was at its most popular, with its emphasis on brilliant and unusual color effects, stained-glass windows were incorporated into many "artistic" houses. La Farge, who was internationally acclaimed for his contributions to the art of stained glass, made this richly colored window for the home of Mrs. George T. Bliss at 9 East Sixty-eighth Street in New York. In it he made use of his "American glass"—opaque, translucent, iridescent, and very much in keeping with the opulent interior his window graced.*
Gift of Susan Dwight Bliss, 1944 (44.90)

of the century, and they are today eagerly sought by those who can afford the very high prices that examples command—when they can be found.

Like Tiffany, the artist-designer-craftsman John La Farge used stained glass to create deeply and richly colored paintings in glass (Fig. 409). Like Tiffany too, La Farge was famous both at home and abroad as a pioneer practitioner of the art of stained glass. The rich hues that both men worked so hard to achieve—adding layer after layer to arrive at just the right texture and tone—contrasted markedly with the simpler colored and stained glasses that architects George Elmslie and Frank Lloyd Wright used in their windows. Choosing much lighter shades and neatly delineated shapes, they created leaded-glass windows whose abstract patterns repeated and reinforced the lines of the houses for which the windows were designed (Fig. 410). As Elmslie wrote of his own work in *Western Architect* for January 1913: "It is all intensely organic, proceeding from main motif to minor motifs, interrelating and to the last terminal, all of a piece. . . ."

Wright's most successful stained-glass windows were those made in 1912 for the Avery Coonley playhouse (see Fig. 4, really a kindergarten run by Mrs. Coonley). Wright had completed the Coonley residence at Riverside, Illinois, a few years earlier and thought it was the best work he had done up to that time. Here all reference to the naturalistic themes and tints typical of so much of Tiffany's glass have given way to abstract, geometric patterns ultimately based on the shapes of things children play with at parties—balloons, flags, and confetti—expressed almost starkly in primary colors. Wright dubbed the

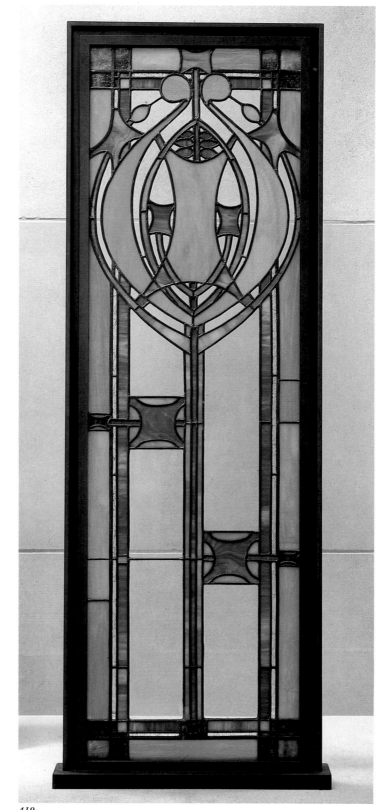

*410*

triptych window a "kinder-symphony," but its abstract design also inevitably recalls the nonobjective experiments with paint and canvas that were being undertaken about the same time by the avant-garde Dutch painter Piet Mondrian.

**Fig. 410.** *Window, by George Grant Elmslie (1871–1953) of Purcell, Feick and Elmslie (1909–13), Minneapolis, 1911; clear and stained leaded glass, height 60 inches (152.4 cm.). The Arts and Crafts approach to stained glass was of course very different from that of Beaux-Arts and Art Nouveau designers such as La Farge and Tiffany. Like Wright (see Fig 4), Elmslie used colored-glass windows in severely stylized and geometric patterns composed of clear glass combined with stained glass in cool, light colors. The window shown here is from the stair hall of the J. C. Cross house in Minneapolis, which Elmslie's firm remodeled in 1911.*
Gift of Roger G. Kennedy, 1972 (1972.20.2)

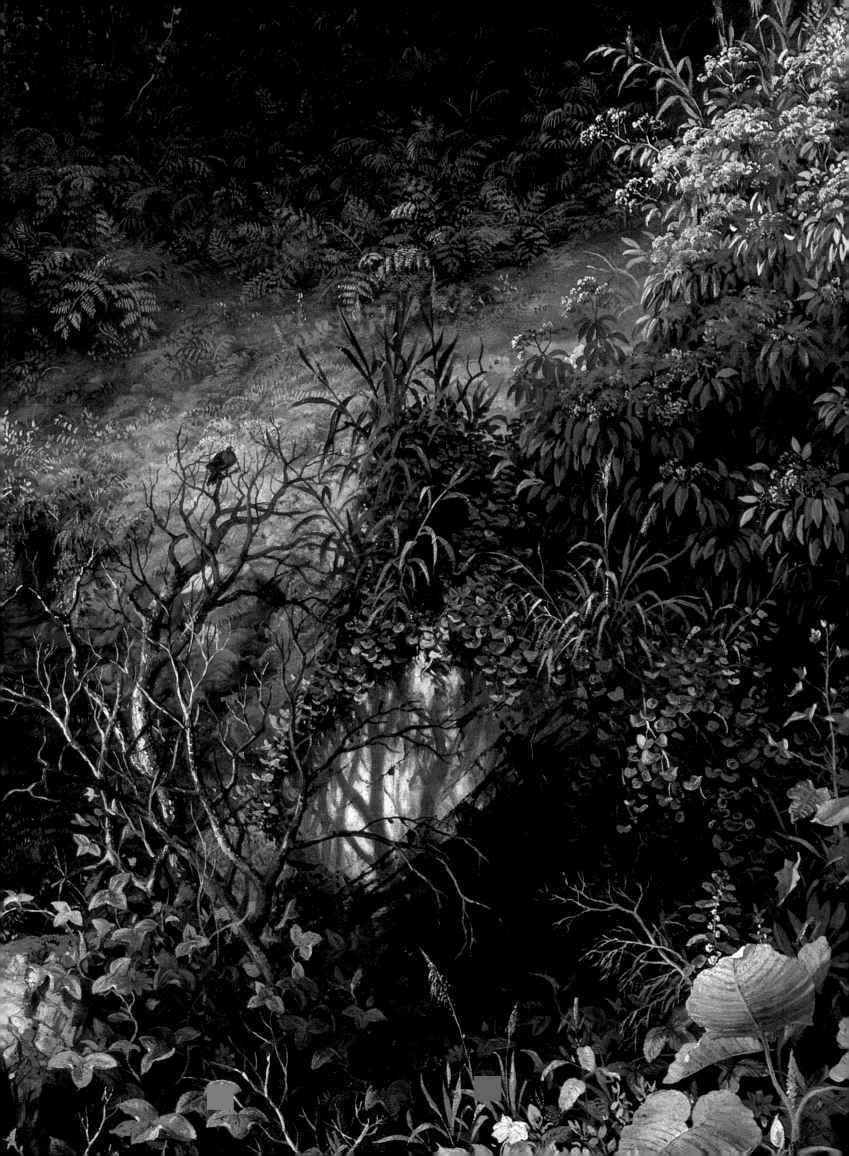

# PAINTINGS
# PRINTS
# DRAWINGS AND
# WATERCOLORS

**Fig. 411.** *Detail,* Heart of the Andes, *by Frederic Edwin Church, see Fig. 463.*

# The Colonial Period, 1630–1790

Under the terms of its charter, drawn up in 1870, the Metropolitan Museum has been committed to American art, and the collection of paintings now includes about 1,600 examples. The great proportion of those shown here are works from the eighteenth and nineteenth centuries.

The collection is constantly being enlarged and improved by new acquisitions. Virtually every artist whose work is important in the history of American art is represented by at least one example—in many instances by an outstanding one.

For all practical purposes the story of painting along the eastern seaboard of America starts with the seventeenth century. Some artist-explorers were on the scene earlier, but they did not contribute directly to the mainstream of American painting.

A number of artists of limited talent but commendable zeal worked in several colonies in the 1600s. What they produced is hardly distinguishable from paintings the colonists brought with them from overseas—rude, provincial approximations of fashionable European portraiture of the time. Conditions of life in colonial America did not encourage specialization in any form of work, and little or no distinction was drawn between the crafts and the fine arts. With or without formal training, the professed artist might well turn his hand to producing shop signs or decorations for home or ship as need and occasion arose. Among the earliest paintings in The American Wing, indeed, are the colored designs applied to various forms of furniture and to wall panels in the period rooms—floral and geometric patterns, landscapes, an occasional still life, and some religious subjects. Local craftsmen with no schooling or serious practice in art might on demand turn their homespun skills to limning the features of their neighbors. The eighteenth century was well along before any painter managed to live solely on his earnings as an artist.

More than a dozen men, foreign-born and native, whose work typifies the best efforts of the colonial artist, are represented in the collection. How competent they could be in spite of all the difficulties of their situation is demonstrated by John Smibert's portraits of Francis Brinley and of his wife with their infant son (Fig. 412). Brinley was a wealthy and prominent New Englander who came to the colonies from England in 1710. Smibert painted these likenesses in 1729, shortly after his arrival in America. He presented his subjects with some authority and, despite their conventional poses, with some style. The artist was a Scot who had earlier been a house painter, plasterer, and coach painter. In London he received some formal training, which he supplemented with a three-year tour of Italy. There he copied the old masters and painted some life portraits. He turned to America because "he was warmed with imaginations of the . . . pleasures of a finer Country & Air more healthful. . . ."

One does not find originality in most colonial portraits. The artist tried his best to approximate the modes and standards of European art, as his patrons expected him to do. Thus, following the usual practice of the period, Smibert based his compositions on engravings after fashionable portraits and on paintings by prominent English artists. In the 1730s and early 1740s English portraiture followed the international baroque style popularized by Sir Godfrey Kneller and his school, whose works were reproduced in widely distributed mezzotints.

Smibert organized the first art exhibition known to have been held in America. It consisted of both his original portraits and his copies of old masters, and of prints and casts of ancient sculptures (including one of the Venus de Medici) that he had acquired abroad. For more than a generation after his death in 1751, aspiring artists continued to visit the studio where these works were on view and to learn from them what they could. In a sense, it was a classroom for American painters.

Peter Pelham, another artist who had emigrated from London, became Smibert's friend and neighbor in Boston. Pelham had been trained not as a portraitist, but as a mezzotint engraver—who copied other people's portraits—and it has been pointed out that he was probably delighted at Smibert's arrival in Boston because at last someone would be painting portraits for him to engrave. The mezzotint of Cotton Mather (Fig. 413) was done from a portrait of the legendary Puritan that Pel-

ham had been forced to paint himself before Smibert arrived on the scene.

Portraits by others of Smibert's contemporaries and immediate followers—Robert Feke, Joseph Badger, John Wollaston, and Joseph Blackburn among them—further illustrate the manner in which these provincials strove to satisfy those who sat for them. The prominence of most of their patrons indicates that their work was not without appreciation in their own day.

John Singleton Copley was one of the first colonial artists to make a living by

his brush alone. Although he was essentially self-taught, this native-born Bostonian had a surpassing natural talent that enabled him to paint better pictures than any he had ever seen. When he was barely out of his teens, Copley had already established himself as a competent and well-known portraitist who enjoyed the patronage of prominent New Englanders.

In 1765 he drew a charming pastel portrait of *Mrs. Edward Green* (Fig. 414). The brilliant blue of the sitter's dress and of the background drapery com-

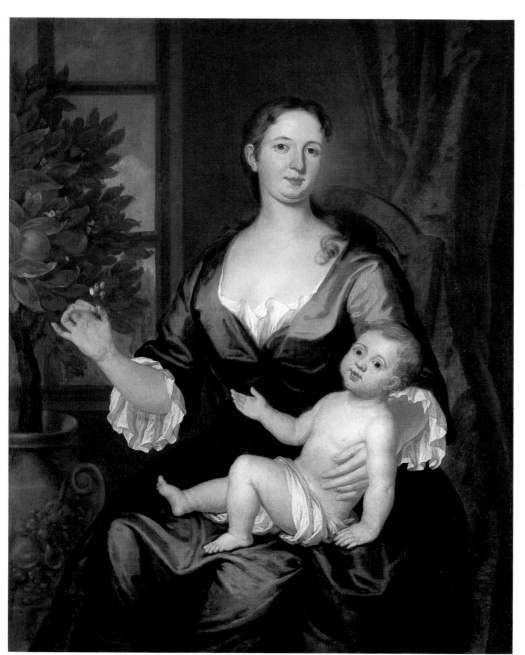

412

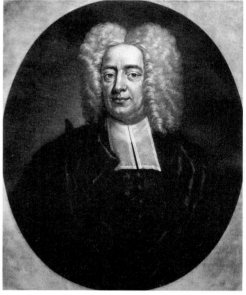

413

*Fig. 413.* **Cotton Mather,** *by Peter Pelham (about 1695–1751), 1728; mezzotint, 13⅝ by 9¾ inches (34.6 by 24.8 cm.). Peter Pelham was trained in London by John Simon, one of that city's leading mezzotint engravers. He emigrated to Boston in 1727 and the next year produced this realistic likeness of the noted Puritan clergyman Cotton Mather. Thought to be the first mezzotint produced in America, it is considered the best of this artist's fourteen portrait engravings of American subjects. Pelham was a friend and neighbor of John Smibert (see Fig. 412); stepfather, teacher, and mentor of America's greatest colonial artist, John Singleton Copley; and father of the artist Henry Pelham. He thus exerted an influence on the development of the arts in colonial America through his family and associations as much as through his work.*
Bequest of Charles Allen Munn, 1924 (24.90.14)

*Fig. 412.* **Mrs. Francis Brinley and Her Infant Son,** *by John Smibert (1688–1751), 1729; oil on canvas, 50 by 39¼ inches (127 by 99.7 cm.). Smibert was among the earliest trained artists to emigrate from England to the colonies, and Mrs. Brinley was one of his first American subjects. Of distinguished family herself, she married one of the wealthiest men in Massachusetts, and that*

*fact is referred to by the orange tree in the background of her portrait. This exotic plant, which had become fashionable when Louis XIV filled Versailles with hundreds of specimens, could be grown in the cold New England climate only in a greenhouse—and it was therefore a sign of wealth.*
Rogers Fund, 1962 (62.79.2)

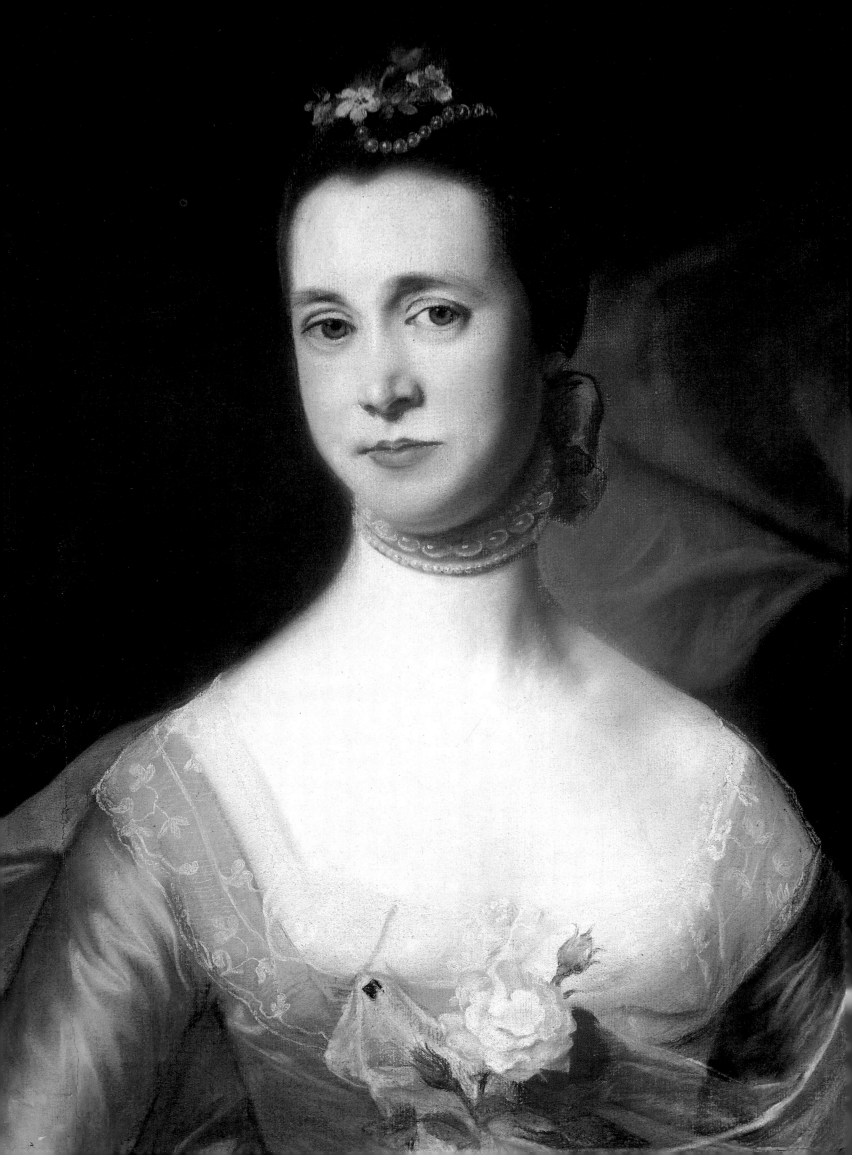

**Fig. 414. Mrs. Edward Green,** *by John Singleton Copley (1738–1815), 1765; pastel, 23 by 17½ inches (58.4 by 44.5 cm.). Copley was the first native American painter of undisputed genius, and his pastel portraits are among his finest works. Although he was an amazingly quick study, observing and absorbing techniques of the artists around him, Copley's mastery of the art of pastel is puzzling, for the medium was not much employed in America. Copley's handling of color, always sure and sometimes startlingly effective, is at its most enchanting here. The resonant blue of Mrs. Green's dress, which is picked up in a slightly deeper shade in the background drapery, is given piquancy by the single blushing rose she wears.*
Curtis Fund, 1908 (1908.08.1)

**Fig. 415. Mrs. John Winthrop,** *by John Single-ton Copley (1738–1815), 1773; oil on canvas, 35½ by 28¾ inches (90.2 by 73 cm.). This is among Copley's best portraits. Here, as in so many others, he has caught Mrs. Winthrop "in the midst of life, speaking with characteristic expression and lively gesture." Copley's rendering of the textures of things is remarkable too—of the richness and sheen of the fabric, ribbons, and laces of Mrs. Winthrop's costume and of her hands and their reflection in the satiny tabletop. These details are conveyed so sensitively and skill-fully that they amount to visual poetry.*
Morris K. Jesup Fund, 1931 (31.109)

bine with her rose-tinted lace and shoulders to produce a striking painting. His portrait of *Mrs. John Winthrop* (Fig. 415), painted in 1773 when he was thirty-five years old, represents Copley's American work at its best. Here is demonstrated his skill at translating textures of surfaces into paint—the intricate composition of lace, the sheen of silk, and the polished mahogany of the reflecting tabletop. These, along with the strong characterization of subject and the effect of immediate presence, won Copley such prestige that he complained he hardly had time to eat his victuals as he fulfilled commissions on a journey from Boston to New York and Philadelphia. Of such brilliantly realistic likenesses John Adams once said, "You can scarcely help discussing with them, asking questions and receiving answers."

As so many other American artists were to do, Copley gravitated to the London studio of Benjamin West just before the outbreak of the Revolution. West was exactly Copley's age, a self-taught Pennsylvanian who had earlier quit his native land to find greater opportunities abroad. In 1782, seven years after he arrived in England, Copley painted the portrait of twelve-year-old

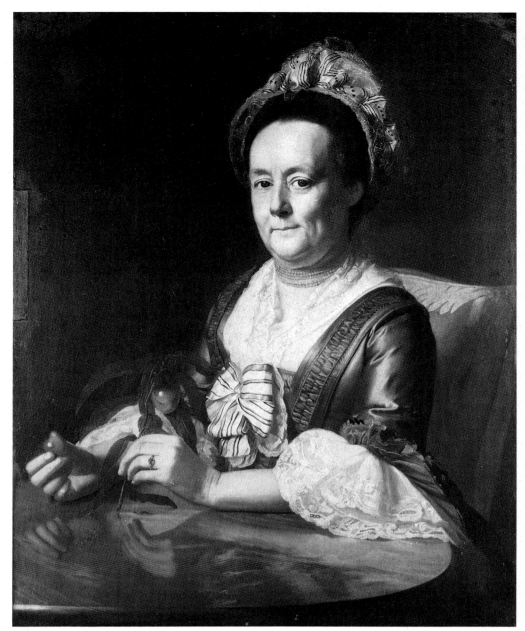

415

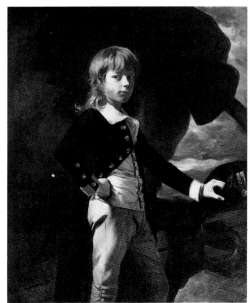

416

**Fig. 416. Midshipman Augustus Brine,** *by John Singleton Copley (1738–1815), 1782; oil on canvas, 50 by 40 inches (127 by 101.6 cm.). Copley went to Europe to study in 1774, settled in London in 1775, and never returned to America. He painted this bold little boy, son of Admiral James Brine, the year the youth was thirteen and was appointed midshipman in the British Royal Navy. Although the portrait shares the strong characterization and feeling of immediacy of Copley's American portraits, it reveals as well a new freedom of expression acquired from his study of the old masters and his firsthand observation of his English and Continental contemporaries. It is one of his best English works.*
Bequest of Richard De Wolfe Brixey, 1943 (43.86.4)

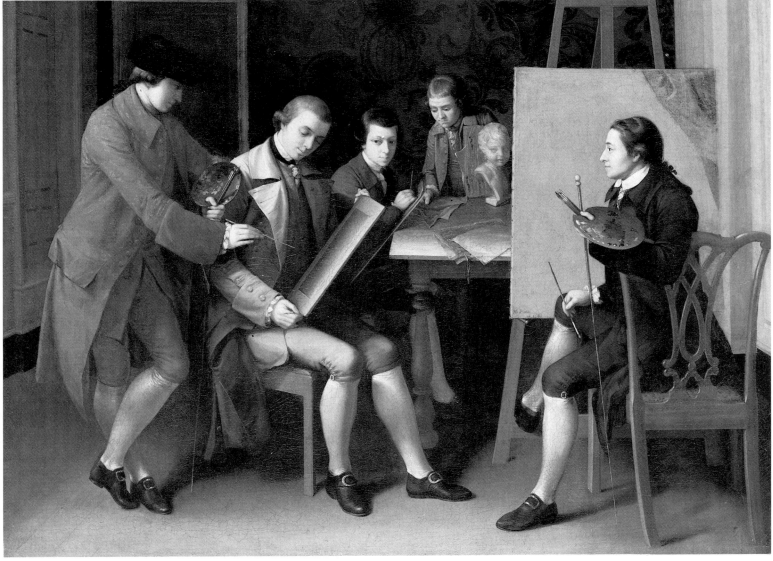

417

Augustus Brine (Fig. 416), midshipman in the British Royal Navy. In this winsome likeness, the freer brushwork and the dramatic lighting and ambience are early results of Copley's European study. The artist never returned to America.

West, meanwhile, found in London all the opportunities he had looked for. In 1792 he succeeded the eminent Sir Joshua Reynolds as president of the Royal Academy. He was in some respects the most advanced painter of his day (although not by any means the best). He was a major proponent of the neoclassical mode in painting and he also pointed the way to the romantic style of later years. He was possibly the most widely known American artist in history, at least until James McNeill Whistler won international renown toward the end of the nineteenth century.

Another of West's American pupils, Matthew Pratt, a fellow Pennsylvanian who as a youth had been apprenticed to a sign painter, had come and gone before Copley arrived in London. Had he

not painted *The American School* (Fig. 417), it is likely that Pratt would be all but forgotten. As it is, his conversation piece remains one of the major documents of colonial painting. It represents a group of young American artists working in West's studio under the direct supervision of the master, who stands, palette in hand, criticizing a work by one of the young men (possibly Pratt himself). This is no masterpiece, but it is a unique and intimate record of the "school" that gave such impetus to the development of American art. Three generations of aspiring American artists flocked to West's studio to learn from him.

The distinction between academic art and folk art is often blurred. This point is very clearly demonstrated in the case of Ralph Earl, a dissolute bigamist, spendthrift, and drunkard from New England who had set himself up in Connecticut as a portraitist before the Revolution. During the war he fled to London—probably to study with Benjamin

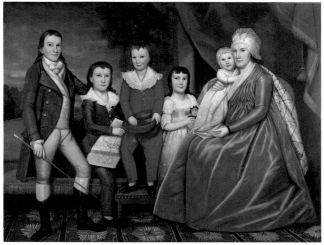

418

**Fig. 418. Mrs. Noah Smith and Her Children,**
*by Ralph Earl (1751–1801), 1798; oil on canvas, 64 by 85¾ inches (162.6 by 217.8 cm.).
Stiffly posed, proper, and prosperous looking, the Smith family represent the well-to-do New England gentry that Earl recorded often and faithfully from 1785 (when he returned to America from England, where he had spent the war years) through the 1790s. After 1794 his alcoholism got the better of him and his painting often suffered, though this portrait is sharply focused and neatly painted. The textures of the Smiths' clothes are skillfully conveyed, and the variety of colors touched here and there with white create lively accents.*
Gift of Edgar William and Bernice Chrysler Garbisch, 1964 (64.309.1)

West. He stayed in England for seven years, and even exhibited at the Royal Academy. He returned to America, however, to paint as an itinerant artist in a relatively severe and simple style that was well suited to the taste of his compatriots in rural Connecticut. One authority has written that Earl "may be taken as either the most notable of 'untrained professionals' or the most unskilled of the professional painters, as you prefer." The relatively homespun quality in much of Earl's work is apparent in his engaging group portrait of *Mrs. Noah Smith and Her Children* (Fig. 418). With full regard for visual truth, Earl depicts dry-goods merchant *Elijah Boardman* (Fig. 419) standing before his bookcase of leather-bound volumes (whose titles can be read) with bolts of variously patterned cloth neatly displayed in the background. It is forthright, explicit, and detailed, with no unnecessary artifice to distract the eye from the painter's direct statement. This wayward artist died of intemperance at the age of fifty.

**Fig. 419. Elijah Boardman,** *by Ralph Earl (1751–1801), 1789; oil on canvas, 83 by 51 inches (210.8 by 129.5 cm.). Earl's practice of showing his sitters surrounded by their own belongings creates a particularly fascinating picture in this instance. Elegantly clad Elijah Boardman stands at his desk in the dry-goods store that he owned with his brother Daniel. The titles of the books on the shelves beneath his desk are legible and include Shakespeare, Milton, and Johnson's dictionary, giving us an idea of his intellectual tastes. His mercantile tastes are apparent from the neatly stacked bolts of brightly colored fabrics that we can see through the open door just beyond the desk. A notice in the Litchfield* Weekly Monitor *for May 18, 1796, stated that "Mr. Earle's price for a Portrait of full length is Sixty Dollars . . . the Painter finding his own support and materials."*
Bequest of Susan W. Tyler, 1979 (1979.395)

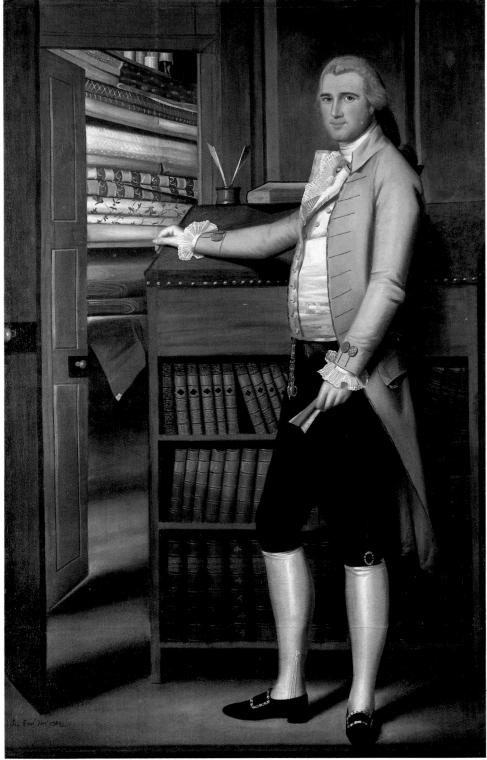

419

# The Revolutionary Period, 1770–90

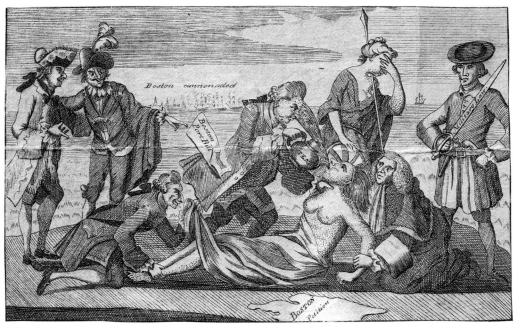

420

**Fig. 420. The Able Doctor, or America Swallowing the Bitter Draught,** *by Paul Revere II (1735–1818), 1774; engraving, 3⅝ by 5¹³⁄₁₆ inches (9.2 by 14.8 cm.). This satirical print shows Lord North, British prime minister, pouring tea down the throat of a female representing America, who shows her scorn by spitting the tea out again. The scene refers to the Boston Tea Party, an incident during which a group of colonists disguised as Indians boarded a British ship and in protest against the duty on tea emptied its 343 chests of that beverage into Boston Harbor. Lively satirical prints referring to topical political or social situations were very popular in England, where they were quickly drawn and widely distributed, but the machinery for mass production did not exist in eighteenth-century America, so such cartoons were printed in smaller quantities and are today very rare. This print was published in the June 1774 number of the* Royal American Magazine; *it was copied almost line for line from an English print.*
Bequest of Charles Allen Munn, 1924 (24.90.644)

**Fig. 421. Miniature portraits,** *by Charles Willson Peale (1741–1827), of* (left to right) General Arthur St. Clair, *1779, 1¾ by 1⅜ inches (4.5 by 3.5 cm.);* General Henry Knox, *1778, 2¹³⁄₁₆ by 2 inches (7.1 by 5.1 cm.); and* George Washington, *1777, 1½ by 1⅛ inches (3.8 by 2.9 cm.); all are watercolor on ivory. The amazingly versatile Charles Willson Peale joined the Continental Army in 1776 and saw active service in the battle of Princeton where, he wrote, "Balls . . . whistled their thousand different notes around our heads. . . ." During this period Peale painted the miniatures of Washington and his officers shown here because, as he pointed out, miniatures were easily portable if it was necessary to flee the enemy. Later on, large replicas of his portraits of Revolutionary War officers became the nucleus of the collection he displayed to the public in a gallery next door to his house in Philadelphia.*
Morris K. Jesup Fund, 1932 (32.110); Gift of J. William Middendorf II, 1968 (68.222.5); Gift of William H. Huntington, 1883 (83.2.122)

American art frequently reflected American political and patriotic life during the Revolutionary War years. Before hostilities were formally acknowledged a few cartoons and broadsides like the one Paul Revere engraved for the *Royal American Magazine* (Fig. 420) publicized—and often magnified—insults and outrages. During the war, American artists made portraits of the men who led the fight. And when it was over American heroes, symbols, landmarks, and eventually, landscapes, dominated both artistic and public imaginations.

Charles Willson Peale, another of West's colonial students, returned to his native land in plenty of time to join the Revolutionary forces in the field of battle, taking his painting kit along with him. Later to become known as the first painter of the American Revolution, Peale relied on miniatures he made at this time to develop the large portraits of Continental Army officers that he painted after the war (Fig. 421). These formed the nucleus of a gallery he established in 1782 near his Philadelphia home. In 1779 Peale accepted a commission from the Supreme Executive Council of Pennsylvania to paint a full-length portrait of his commander in chief, General George Washington. The result was a great success. Peale made numerous replicas of the work, some for royal palaces abroad. The Museum owns one of these much coveted copies, one that may have been made on order from Martha Washington. Illustrated here is another version of Peale's *Washington*, this one a mezzotint engraving (Fig. 423).

George Washington had become a remarkably popular public figure, and there was no question that he was the

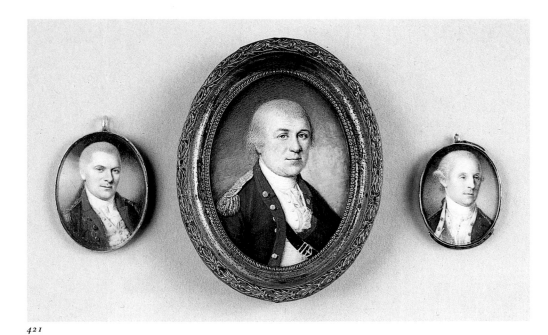

421

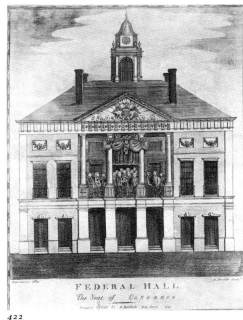

422

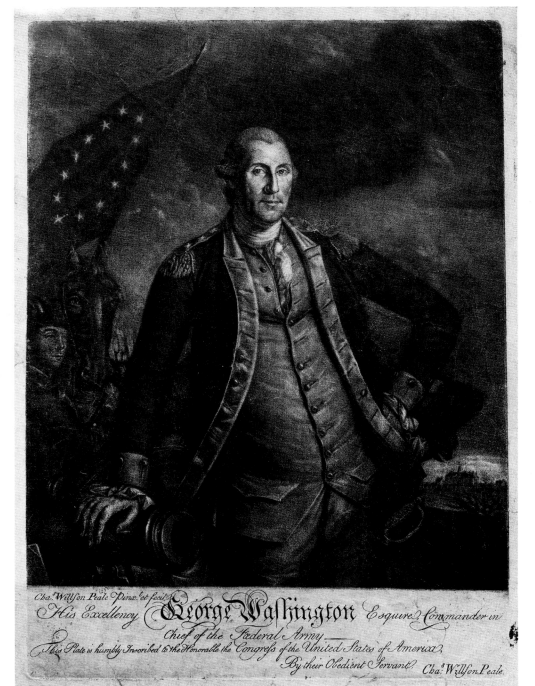

423

**Fig. 424. New York (New York as Washington Knew It),** *by Archibald Robertson (1765–1835), 1794–97; hand-colored engraving, 20¹⁵/₁₆ by 15⅛ inches (53.1 by 38.4 cm.). Beyond the bow of the French vessel in the foreground of this peaceful view of New York is lower Manhattan from Trinity Church at left to Bowling Green at the tip of the island. In the center is Government House, newly erected in the fashionable Federal style; it was planned as the presidential mansion, but Congress and the president moved to Philadelphia before Washington could occupy it.*
The Edward W. C. Arnold Collection of New York Prints, Maps and Pictures, Bequest of Edward W. C. Arnold, 1954 (54.90.612)

**Fig. 425. The City of New York,** *by Samuel Seymour (active 1796–1823), after William Birch (1755–1834), 1803; hand-colored engraving, 24 by 18¾ inches (61 by 47.6 cm.). A few years after Robertson engraved his view of New York, Seymour produced this view from the opposite shore—that is, looking at the lower part of the island from Brooklyn rather than from New Jersey. Although Manhattan seems completely covered with houses, rooftops, and steeples, the foreground scene, with its lazy grazing horse and motionless tree, creates the same feeling of tranquility that dominates the Robertson scene.*
The Edward W. C. Arnold Collection of New York Prints, Maps and Pictures, Bequest of Edward W. C. Arnold, 1954 (54.90.673)

ideal candidate for the office of president. He was inaugurated on April 30, 1789, in New York's newly renovated Federal Hall. Amos Doolittle's engraving of Peter Lacour's eye-witness sketch is the only record we have of that event (Fig. 422).

After the Revolution New York City made a rapid ascent to the position it has held ever since as America's greatest metropolis. Naturally, its being chosen as the first United States capital added to its luster and increased its importance, but *New York as Washington Knew It* (Fig. 424) shows that, although the city was growing, it was still of manageable size when this print was made. A slightly later print, of a view taken across the East River from Brooklyn Heights, shows a more crowded skyline (Fig. 425). An observer wrote of New York in 1800: "The progress of this city is, as usual, beyond all calculations—700 buildings erected in the last twelve months; and Broadway, beyond all dispute, is the best street for length, width, position, and buildings in America."

John Trumbull, son of a governor of Connecticut and a young Harvard graduate, also served in the Revolution, as an aide-de-camp to Washington. In the first year of the war, however, he quit the army over what he considered a point of honor; subsequently he went to London and the studio of Benjamin West. His historical paintings and those memorializing the events of the Revolution that decorate the rotunda of the Capitol at Washington are the most conspicuous examples of his art. For the latter series Thomas Jefferson and John Adams helped Trumbull select twelve decisive episodes in the creation of the new nation. The final renderings were done long after the events. They were rather heavy handed and did the artist's fading reputation little good. However, they were based on earlier studies including sensitive portraits of the principal actors in his scenes, done from life whenever possible. Such portraits, including the Museum's likenesses of Washington, Jefferson (Fig. 426), and Hamilton, bring us close to the founding fathers of the new nation. Trumbull was personally acquainted with many of these outstanding patriots.

What is possibly Trumbull's most successful historical painting, *The Sortie Made by the Garrison at Gibraltar* (Fig.

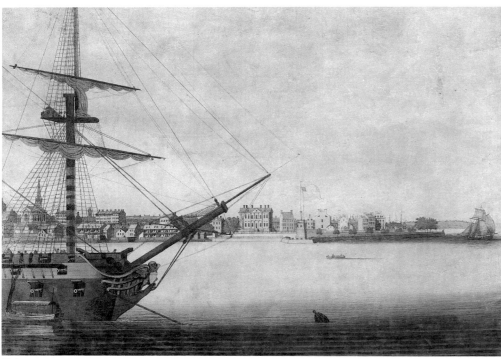

424

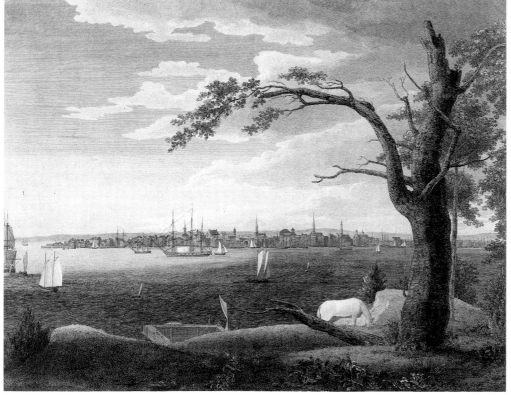

425

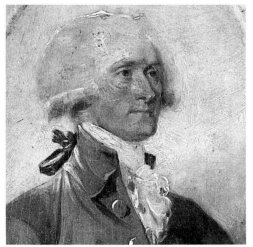

**Fig. 426. Thomas Jefferson** (detail), by John Trumbull (1765–1843), about 1788; oil on wood, 4½ by 3¼ inches (11.4 by 8.3 cm.). When the two men were in Paris in 1786, Trumbull first painted Jefferson's portrait to include in his best-known work, The Declaration of Independence. Later, Trumbull painted three small modified versions of that portrait, of which this is one. It was owned originally by Jefferson's good friend Angelica Church, who wrote him in 1788 that their mutual friend Maria Cosway's similar portrait (now at Yale) ". . . is a better likeness than mine, but then I have a better elsewhere and so I console myself."
Bequest of Cornelia Cruger, 1924 (24.19.1)

426

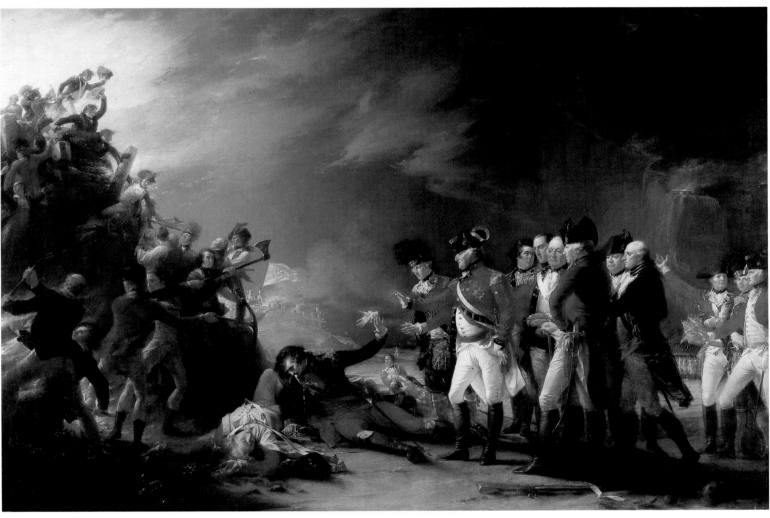

427

427), painted in 1789 when he was in London, does not relate to American history, but depicts an episode during the three-year siege of the English fortress by French and Spanish forces. In 1781 General George Elliot led a nighttime foray during which the British destroyed an entire line of the enemy's counterworks. Trumbull chose to dramatize the moment when the gallant Spaniard Don José de Barboza, although mortally wounded, refused British help because that would have meant complete surrender to the

**Fig. 427. The Sortie Made by the Garrison at Gibraltar,** by John Trumbull (1765–1843), 1789; oil on canvas, 70½ by 106 inches (179.1 by 269.2 cm.). Instead of focusing on the momentous events that had recently taken place in his own country, Trumbull chose, in this eminently successful history painting, to show an episode at Gibraltar in which the British defeated a Spanish attempt to take over their garrison. At center is a Spanish officer fatally wounded in the encounter, but refusing help from the British, who are portrayed as dignified and magnanimous in victory. Trumbull was criticized by his countrymen for portraying the British in a heroic light when they had so recently been at war with America, but he replied that nobility and heroism,

wherever they were found, were worthy subjects. He further explained in his autobiography: "I was pleased with the subject, as offering, in the gallant conduct and death of the Spanish commander, a scene of deep interest to the feelings, and in the contrast of the darkness of night, with the illumination of an extensive conflagration, great splendor of effect and color."
Purchase, Pauline V. Fullerton Bequest, Mr. and Mrs. Walter Carter Gift, Mr. and Mrs. Raymond J. Horowitz Gift, Erving Wolf Foundation Gift, Vain and Harry Fish Foundation, Inc. Gift, Gift of Hanson K. Corning, by exchange, and Maria DeWitt Jesup and Morris K. Jesup Funds, 1976 (1976.332)

**Fig. 428. George Washington,** *by Gilbert Stuart (1755–1828), about 1795; oil on canvas, 30¼ by 25¼ inches (76.8 by 64.1 cm). Stuart returned to America in 1793 after years of living abroad, and soon found a market for his portraits, which were far better than those of any of his American contemporaries. Likenesses of George Washington shortly became his stock in trade, and this, named the Gibbs-Channing-Avery portrait after its former owners, is considered one of the best versions. It is modeled on his first Washington portrait, called the Vaughan Washington, after Washington's good friend Samuel Vaughan, who commissioned it in 1795. That portrait was so well received that Stuart was* deluged *with requests for copies, of which this is one. Because this portrait is remarkably lifelike, with vivid facial color and a calm, penetrating gaze, it is thought that Stuart painted some of it, at least, from life.*
Rogers Fund, 1907 (07.160)

**Fig. 429. An Osage Warrior** *(detail), by Charles Balthazar-Julien Fevret de Saint-Mémin (1770–1852), about 1804; watercolor, 7¼ by 6⁵⁄₁₆ inches (18.4 by 16 cm). Although this watercolor portrait is small, it is very impressive, stressing the warrior's strength and dignity through his bold profile and steadfast expression. His blanket-like wrap, distinctive native hair treatment, and jewelry add color and character to a likeness dominated by monumental impassivity.*
The Elisha Whittlesey Collection, The Elisha Whittlesey Fund, 1954 (54.82)

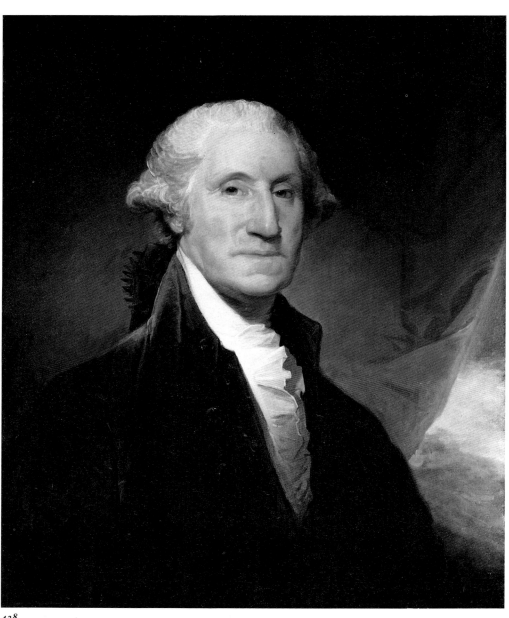

428

traits, often skimping even on bodies and backgrounds. One early critic remarked that Stuart could not, in fact, paint "below the fifth button"; Stuart himself said that he left such accessories to the tailor. "He paints very fast," observed one Russian visitor to the United States about 1812, "and his portraits are more like excellent sketches than like completed paintings."

Stuart claimed that he returned to America to paint a portrait of George Washington, although one of the compelling reasons for his leaving the British Isles was to avoid the very real horrors of the debtors' prison to which his gross extravagance had made him vulnerable.

Of the innumerable portraits of Washington he did produce, the Museum has, among others, a fine early example that represents Stuart's classical American style in its pure form (Fig. 428). Apparently done in part from life, this canvas, the Gibbs-Channing-Avery Washington, is known by the names of its former owners. So well known have such likenesses of the first president become that if he should return to earth he would have to resemble Stuart's portraits to be recognized.

An even more archetypal American than George Washington is seen in Fig. 429—*An Osage Warrior.* The portraitist, Charles Balthazar-Julien Fevret de Saint-Mémin, was a Frenchman who worked in America from the 1790s to 1814, when he returned to France permanently. He is well known for his more than 800 American portraits produced by means of a physionotrace—an instrument invented in 1786 by Gilles Louis Chrétien and improved by Saint-Mémin—that enabled him to record the exact outline of his subject's profile in all its minute details.

enemy. Trumbull explained his choice of a British, rather than an American, subject: "to show that noble and generous actions, by whomsoever performed, were the objects to whose celebration I meant to devote myself."

Most of West's numerous American pupils returned home with developed skills that established fresh standards in post-Revolutionary American art. One

of the most celebrated of these repatriates was the witty, urbane, and bibulous Gilbert Stuart, who mastered a highly distinctive style of portraiture that earned him considerable prestige in England and attracted wide patronage in the new republic. Omitting accessory paraphernalia of the kind that inform and enlighten Copley's paintings, Stuart reduced detail to a minimum in his por-

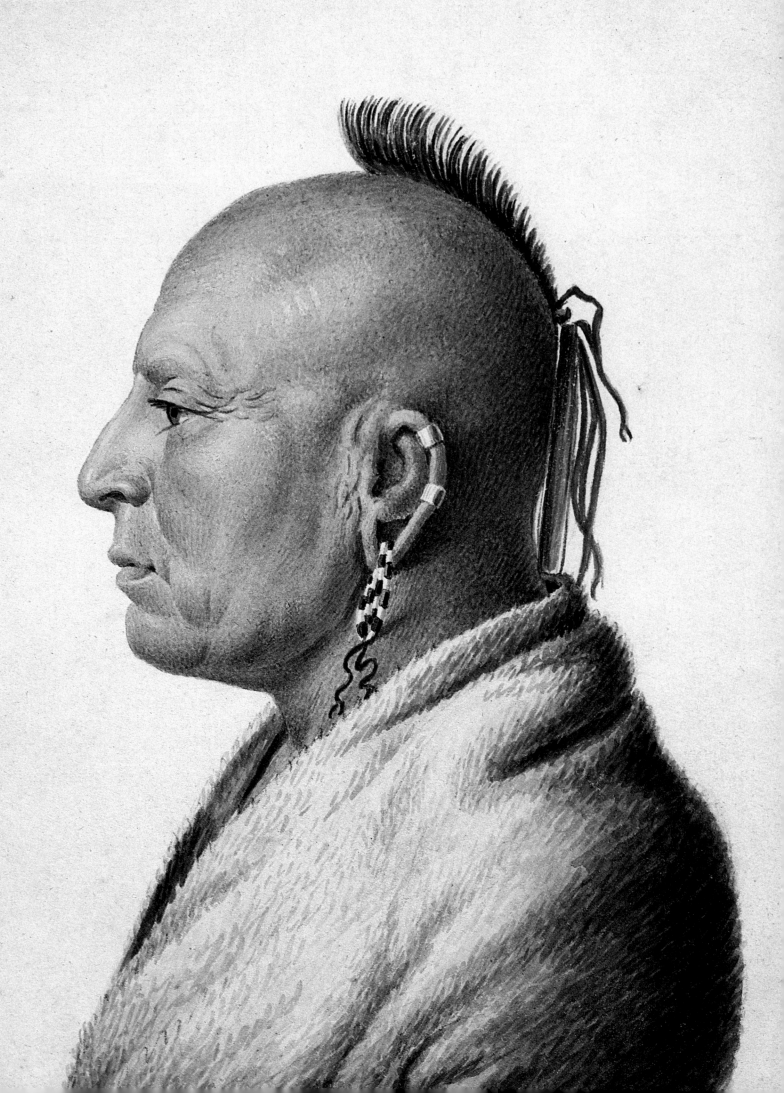

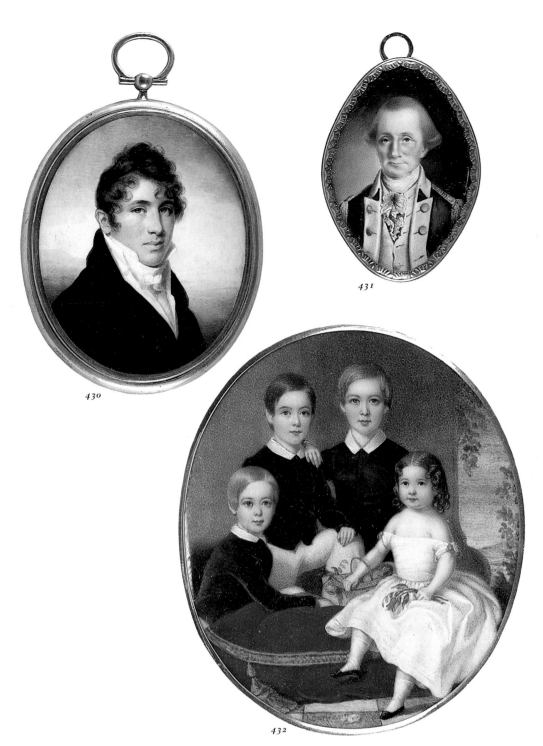

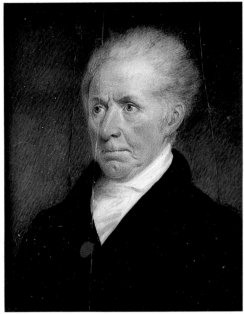

*Figs. 430–37.* **Miniatures.** *The art of painting miniatures was practiced in the colonies from the early decades of the eighteenth century. Over the years many artists best known for their oil paintings on canvas were attracted to this very exacting medium—among them Copley, Charles Willson Peale, and Trumbull. Others specialized in the particular art of painting "in little." Miniature paintings are delicate and fragile, and for this reason, as in the case of watercolors, they cannot long be exposed to strong light without risk.*

*430*

*431*

*432*

*433*

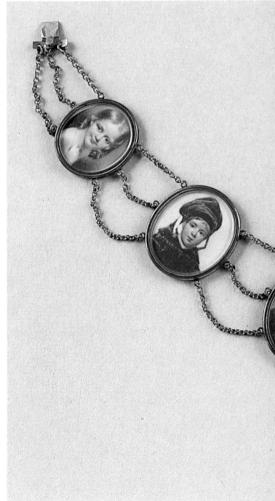

*Fig. 430.* **Robert Macomb,** *by Edward Greene Malbone (1783–1832), about 1806; watercolor on ivory, 3¾ inches by 3 inches (9.5 by 7.6 cm.).* Bequest of Irving S. Olds, 1963 (63.122.1)

*Fig. 431.* **George Washington,** *by John Ramage (about 1748–1802), 1796; watercolor on ivory, 2¹/₁₆ by 1⅜ inches (5.2 by 3.5 cm.).* Bequest of Charles Allen Munn, 1924 (24.109.93)

*Fig. 432.* **The Thompson Children,** *by John Carlin (1813–91), 1846; watercolor on ivory, 4⅛ by 3⅓ inches (10.5 by 8.6 cm.).* Morris K. Jesup and Maria DeWitt Jesup Funds, 1979 (1979.188)

*Fig. 433.* **Gilbert Stuart,** *by Sarah Goodridge (1788–1853), about 1825; watercolor on ivory, 3¼ by 2½ inches (8.3 by 6.4 cm.).* Gift of Misses Sarah and Josephine Lazarus, 1888–95 (95.14.123)

*Fig. 434.* **Jeremiah Lee,** *by John Singleton Copley (1738–1815), 1769; watercolor on ivory, 1½ by 1¼ inches (3.8 by 3.2 cm.).* Harris Brisbane Dick Fund, 1939 (39.174)

*Fig. 435.* **Lieutenant Alexander Murray,** *by James Peale (1749–1831), about 1780; watercolor on ivory, 2½ by 1¹⁵/₁₆ inches (6.4 by 4.9 cm.).* Rogers Fund, 1925 (25.29)

*Fig. 436.* **Miss Ross,** *by James Peale (1749–1831), 1791; watercolor on ivory, 2 by 1⁹/₁₆ inches (5.1 by 4 cm.).* Fletcher Fund, 1941 (41.36)

*Fig. 437.* **Portraits of the Artist's Children,** *by Thomas Seir Cummings (1804–94), about 1841; watercolor on ivory, length 17½ inches (44.5 cm.).* Gift of Mrs. Richard B. Hartshorne and Miss Fanny S. Cummings, 1928 (28.148.1–9)

*437*

A meticulous technique was required to produce these works, many American examples of which, among the best in the world at the time, were painted on ivory especially prepared by stippling or crosshatching. This provided a surface texture that could receive a tiny painted image without so much as a pinhead's area of flaw in the exquisitely thin brushstrokes that were required. There was no room for even a very small mistake in creating the final image and practically none for making corrections after the first washes of color had been laid on the ivory. As in

Homer's watercolors, where the unpainted white surfaces of the paper often served as highlights, so in the case of miniatures the unbleached and undisguised ivory served the same purpose. It provided as well an underlying glow for the thin, transparent coverings of color in other areas. In scrutinizing these works at close range, as must be done to appreciate their special qualities, it is almost literally necessary to hold one's breath for a moment—as indeed the artist probably had to do to create them.

Miniatures are intimate personal documents,

intended to serve as an evocative reminder of a cherished friend, relative, or admirer. Not infrequently the emotional attachment suggested by the precious little work was intensified by a lock of the sitter's hair or a fragment of a written message set in the back of a gold or silver frame. The result had an almost talismanic quality of recalling a distant presence or revivifying a departed soul in fond remembrance.

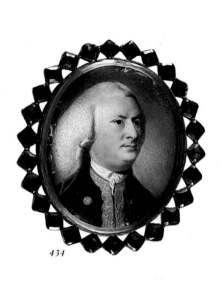

434

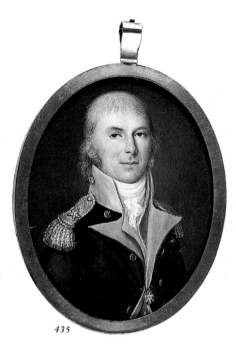

435

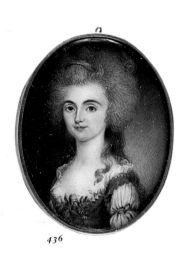

436

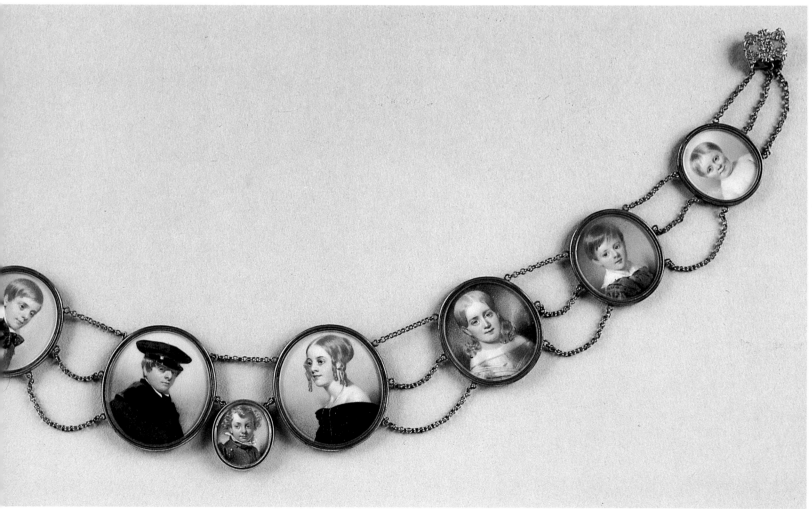

# The Early Nineteenth Century, 1790–1840

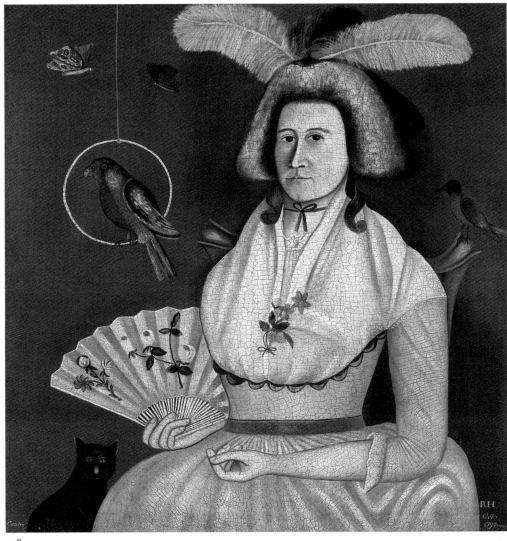

438

**Figs. 438 and 439. Lady with Her Pets,** by Rufus Hathaway (1770–1822), 1790; oil on canvas, 34¼ by 32 inches (87 by 81.3 cm.). One of
the most strikingly decorative of all American
naïve, or folk, portraits, and one of the most successful in terms of composition and characterization, this is Hathaway's earliest known work. The
subject is said to be Molly Whales Leonard of
Marshfield, Massachusetts, and much of her
charm derives from the descriptive details Hathaway included—her feathered headdress, painted
fan, and Chippendale chair. While all these establish Mrs. Leonard as a distinctive character,
her "pets" add even more to her individuality.

There are two birds, one perched beside her on the
crest of the chair and one a parrot in a hoop; two
butterflies; and a cat beside whom is lettered the
word "Canter," which is perhaps his name. The
crackled surface of the painting, which is as
much a distinguishing feature as anything else, is
thought to be the result of Hathaway's improper
combination of materials. The engaging Mrs.
Leonard remains in her original frame, which is
painted in black and ivory to simulate marble.
Gift of Edgar William and Bernice Chrysler Garbisch,
1963 (63.201.1)

"The signing of the Declaration of
Independence in 1776," wrote
folk-art authority Jean Lipman, "also
signaled the beginning of a new independence for American art. The seeds
of the native folk tradition, planted with
the founding of the American colonies
in the seventeenth century, sprouted
and throve all along the eastern seaboard from the last quarter of the eighteenth century through the first three
quarters of the nineteenth." And it
wasn't only folk art that flourished after
the Revolution—it was art of all kinds.
West, Copley, and Trumbull were followed to Europe at first by scores and
then by hundreds of aspiring American
artists seeking instruction in the European academic tradition. Although
many European-trained artists were
eventually successful at home, several of
the leading members of this first generation of formally trained painters were
out of tune with their countrymen, and
their work went unappreciated. Folk
artists, on the other hand, were not concerned with the high ideals that bur-
dened their academic brethren. Their
sometimes crazily drawn but always
frank images of people, animals, and
scenes both real and imaginary usually
appealed as much to their clients as they
do to the swelling ranks of modern folk-
art collectors.

"American folk art" is a term that is
loosely used to cover a wide range of
paintings, sculptures, and artifacts of
various descriptions. Sometimes this
highly miscellaneous category is alter-
natively known as primitive art, naïve
art, or the art of the common man. By
whatever name, the material referred to
is typically the output of men and
women who, to the best of their abilities,
adapted their innate skills to the needs,

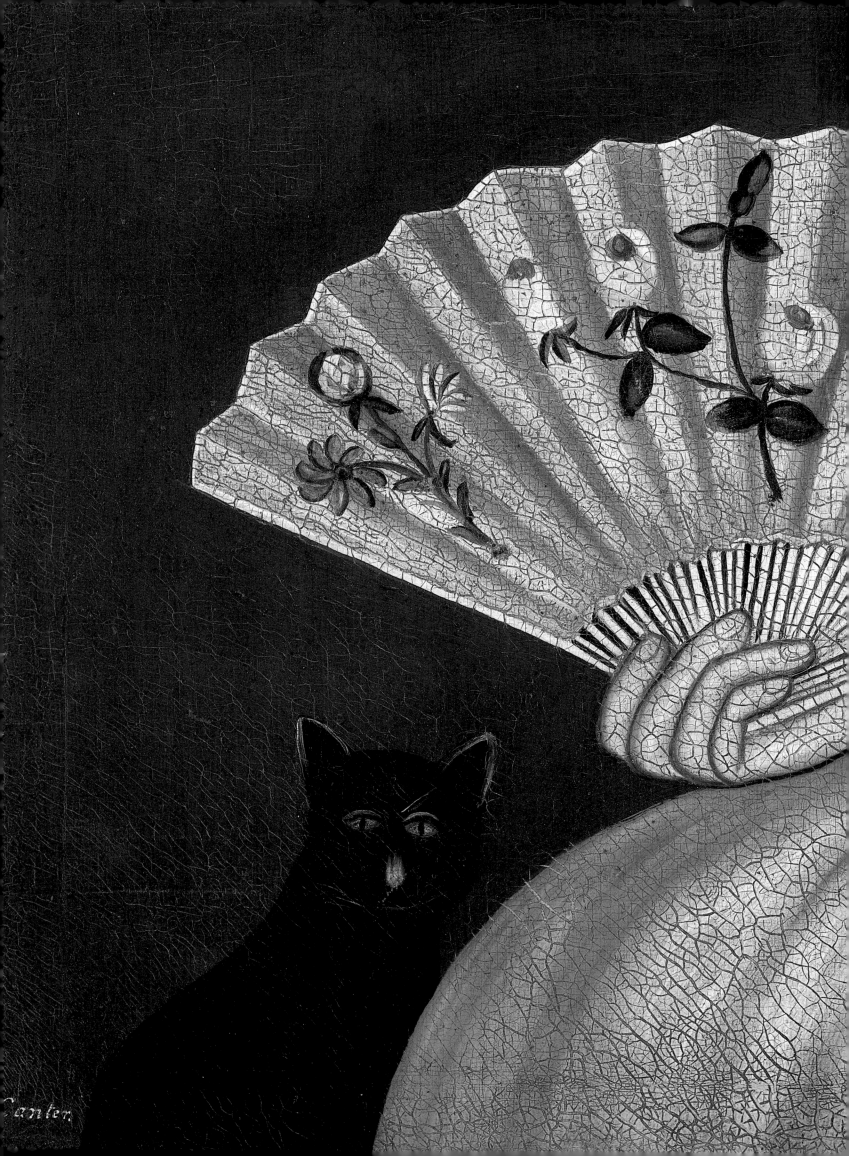

**Fig. 440. The Falls of Niagara,** by Edward
Hicks (1780–1849), 1825; oil on canvas, 31½
by 38 inches (80 by 96.5 cm.). Edward Hicks,
one of America's most notable folk artists, painted
this scene in 1825, six years after he had visited
Niagara Falls. He adapted the composition of his
picture from a vignette on a contemporary map
of North America and took the poetry that frames
the falls from an 1804 poem, but his feeling for
subject matter, color, and atmosphere make the
picture very much his own. Hicks was a coach
and sign painter by profession, so he was trained
to paint flat, two-dimensional surfaces, including
the stylized animals that had decorated signs from
medieval times, and to letter names and mottoes.
His paintings are very much the result of his
professional skills.
Gift of Edgar William and Bernice Chrysler Garbisch,
1962 (62.256.3)

![The Falls of Niagara painting with poetry framing the scene: "Above, below, where'er the astonished eye / Turns to behold, new opening wonders lie," along the top; "Rises on our view, amid a crashing roar / That bids us kneel, and Time's great God adore." along the bottom; "With uproar hideous first the Falls appear, / The stunning tumult thundering on the ear." on the left; "This great o'erwhelming work of awful Time / In all its dread magnificence sublime," on the right; "The Falls of Niagara" labels and the number "18" and "25" in corners]

440

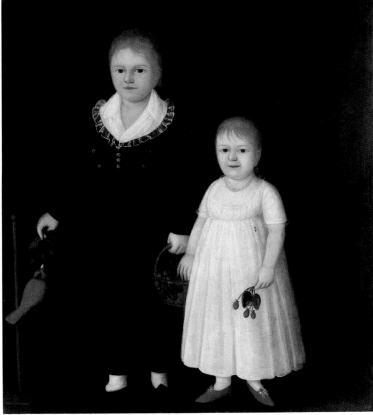

441

While much folk art remains anonymous, the identity of many practitioners has been disclosed through diligent work by students and collectors. *Lady with Her Pets* (Figs. 438 and 439), inscribed "RH Oct' 1790," can be ascribed to one Rufus Hathaway of Massachusetts, who late in the eighteenth century became the town doctor of Duxbury. When he was not engaged in medical pursuits, Hathaway painted portraits, including miniatures, at least one landscape and a still life, and also apparently made picture frames and wood carvings. Whether the feathered bonnet and other costume accessories were the lady's own possessions, studio props, or inventions used to offset the rigid posture and angular face and to create a pleasing pattern, remains conjectural.

A double portrait of *Edward and Sarah Rutter* (Fig. 441), the children of Captain Joshua Rutter of Baltimore, was painted about 1805 by Joshua Johnston (or Johnson), the earliest black artist known to have practiced in this country. More than a score of his portraits have been identified. As here, most of them are characterized by a subtle use of bright color and elegant detail. The Rutter children are shown dressed in their Sunday best for this important occasion, when their likenesses were recorded for the lasting pleasure of their proud parents—and as it turned out, of posterity. Johnston's customary style suggests that he may have been influenced by the work of Charles Peale Polk, a nephew of Charles Willson Peale, who was active in Baltimore during the 1790s.

Although he referred to himself as a "poor, illiterate mechanic," Edward Hicks remains one of the best known and most engaging of American folk artists. He was a cantankerous spirit who once confessed to his diary that his "poor zig-zag nature" predisposed him to extremes. But he succeeded in reconciling his intense religiosity with his artistic proclivities. His favorite theme was the peaceable kingdom, illustrating Isaiah's prophecy of a world at peace under the reign of the Messiah: "The wolf also shall dwell with the lamb, and the leopard shall lie down with the kid; and the calf and the young lion and the fatling together; and a little child shall

circumstances, and possibilities of their daily lives.

***Fig. 441.*** **Edward and Sarah Rutter,** *by Joshua Johnston (or Johnson, active 1789–1824), about 1805; oil on canvas, 36 by 32 inches (91.4 by 81.3 cm.).* Edward Pennington and Sarah Ann were the children of Captain Joshua Rutter of Baltimore, and Johnston has shown them dressed in their Sunday best, regarding us solemnly. Like Hathaway, Johnston painted his subjects' pet bird, and he also placed a colorful cluster of strawberries in Sarah's hand. Johnston is the first black portrait painter known to have worked in America—twenty-two unsigned and undated portraits have been attributed to him.
Gift of Edgar William and Bernice Chrysler Garbisch, 1965 (65.254.3)

***Fig. 442.*** **Mrs. Mayer and Her Daughter,** *by Ammi Phillips (1788–1865), 1830–40; oil on canvas, 37⅞ by 34¼ inches (96.2 by 87 cm.).* Foremost among American painters of the flat, two-dimensional likenesses known as folk portraits was Ammi Phillips, who traveled about rural New York, Connecticut, and Massachusetts painting friends, relatives, and friends of friends from about 1811 to the 1860s. It is not the likenesses that we admire today, for they were remote at best; it is the design—the rhythms and masses—of the composition. In this portrait, painted during the middle of his career, Phillips provides drama and interest through large, simply shaped masses. The faces of Mrs. Mayer

and her child, and her lacy cap, serve as bright counterpoints in an otherwise somber composition.
Gift of Edgar William and Bernice Chrysler Garbisch, 1962 (62.256.2)

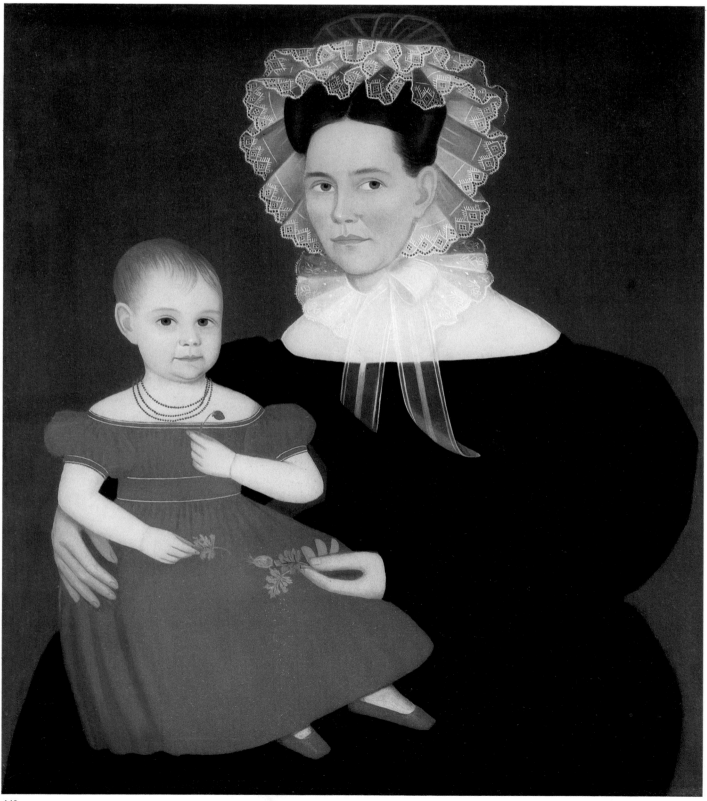

442

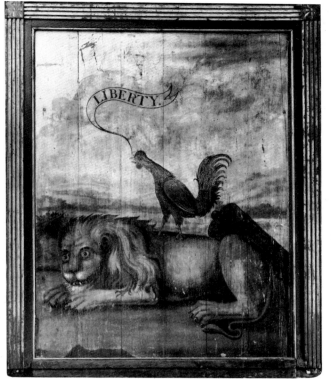

443

*Fig. 443.* ***Tavern sign,*** *United States, 1800–10; white pine, painted, 60 by 41 inches (152.4 by 104.1 cm). Taverns were important in early America not just as providers of food and lodging to travelers, but to local citizens as centers for exchanging news and gossip and for doing business. The same itinerant painters who produced portraits, decorated houses, or enlivened coaches painted tavern signs—one of the earliest forms of commercial advertising. This example, depicting a scrawny rooster perched on a docile lion, probably symbolizes the victory of the colonies (the rooster crowing "Liberty") over England (the defeated lion), as well as informing weary travelers that food, drink, and a clean bed were finally at hand.*
Gift of Mrs. Russell Sage, 1909 (10.125.404)

lead them." Nearly 100 variant versions of this subject, preachments in paint, have survived.

Left an orphan at a tender age, Hicks was raised by a Quaker family, and in time, after a period of relatively free living, he became a dedicated preacher of that faith, for which he received no remuneration. He had early apprenticed himself to a carriage maker, taught himself to paint, and spent most of his life in Newtown, Pennsylvania, making and decorating coaches, designing signs and mileposts, and painting landscapes, including views of his neighbors' farms, and biblical allegories. However, he occasionally traveled many miles on horseback, sometimes in the dead of winter, which for some reason he thought might improve the condition of his ailing lungs. On one of these arduous journeys he visited Niagara Falls. He recorded that visit with a painting of the scene whose composition he copied from a vignette on a map by an earlier artist (Fig. 440). To this he added a decorative border combining verses from the poem "The Foresters" by ornithologist and explorer Alexander Wilson.

Ammi Phillips is another artist who has been rediscovered in fairly recent times. For fifty years this itinerant portraitist worked what was once known as the border country, a limited region of the Berkshires that included New York, Connecticut, and Massachusetts. Over that long period his style varied, as can be told from the hundreds of likenesses attributed to his brush. Phillips would paint portraits of each member of a household, then move on to do the same at the household of a related family in a nearby town. In 1825 the artist John Vanderlyn wrote a letter encouraging his nephew to become a portrait

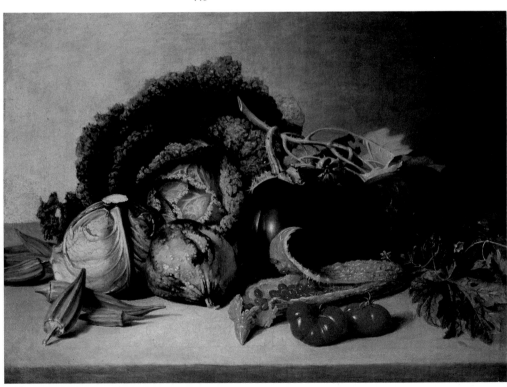

444

*Fig. 444.* **Still Life: Balsam Apple and Vegetables,** *by James Peale (1749–1831), probably 1820s; oil on canvas, 20¼ by 26½ inches (51.4 by 67.3 cm). Although American artists were interested in still life in the eighteenth century, they didn't devote themselves to it until the nineteenth. James and Raphaelle Peale (Charles Willson's brother and eldest son, respectively) led in developing a Philadelphia school of still life. This example, which presents a tempting, colorful assortment of vegetables, including a balsam apple, is a masterpiece of the genre, with a strong and satisfying pyramidal composition and direct, clear illumination.*
Maria DeWitt Jesup Fund, 1939 (39.52)

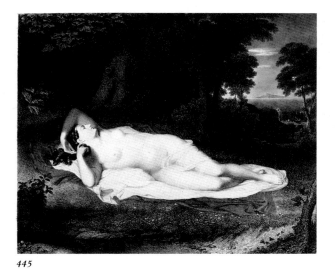

445

painter. "Indeed," Vanderlyn observed, "moving about the country as Phillips did and probably still does, must be an agreeable way of passing one's time." *Mrs. Mayer and Her Daughter* represents one phase of his sizable output (Fig. 442).

For almost a century, one member or another of the extraordinary family headed by Charles Willson Peale was painting pictures. In the 1820s, when he was in his seventies, Charles Willson's brother James Peale, who also had served in the Revolutionary army, produced *Balsam Apple and Vegetables* (Fig. 444). In this remarkably convincing still life the varied shapes, textures, colors, and all but the very taste of cabbage, eggplant, okra, tomatoes, and the balsam apple are presented in an opulent composition.

In the years following the War of 1812, the scene had shifted to a generation of artists who were too young to remember the Revolution and who, for the most part, had the advantage of solid professional training. It was these painters who sowed the seeds of romanticism that eventually found fertile ground in America and produced a wide and varied flowering of talent as the nation spread across the continent. The high level of competence of these men is demonstrated in the canvases of Washington Allston, John Vanderlyn, Samuel F. B. Morse, Thomas Sully, Charles C. Ingham, George P. A. Healy, and a score of others whose work is represented in the Museum's collection.

John Vanderlyn was the first American painter to look to France rather than to England for professional experience. He was the protégé of Aaron Burr, who sent him to Philadelphia to study with Gilbert Stuart for a year and then, in 1796, when Vanderlyn was twenty-one years old, to Paris for further study. There he spent the next five years. After a brief return visit to the United States, he recrossed the Atlantic and went to Paris in the company of Washington Allston, who was to be his lifelong friend. Vanderlyn spent the best part of twenty years in Europe and won some distinction there: in 1808 Napoleon awarded one of his paintings a gold medal.

Back in America once again after his extended European stay, Vanderlyn undertook his most ambitious work, a panoramic view of the palace and gardens of Versailles (Figs. 446, 447, and 448). It is the largest and in some ways the most unusual painting that has ever been exhibited in the Museum. The subject, designed as a continuous circular panorama, covers almost 2,000 square feet of canvas. It is a spectacular tour de force contrived by an accomplished draftsman—though Vanderlyn employed assistants to help him complete this prodigious job. The perspective has been ingeniously adjusted to the circular shape so that the spectator standing at dead center finds convincing vistas leading off in all directions. Onto this deceptively real stage Vanderlyn has introduced a crowd of tourists colorfully clad for a holiday amid the splendors of the world's most famous palace.

The painting was originally planned for exhibition in the Rotunda (Fig. 449), a building at the northeast corner of New York's City Hall Park, erected by the artist with the financial help of his friends. City officials rented Vanderlyn the plot of land for one peppercorn a year. Although he never thought of the panorama as being in the same class with his less extravagant creations, Vanderlyn hoped that it would attract large crowds of paying visitors and that it would lead them to appreciate the "higher branches" of art. These were represented in neighboring galleries by paintings by Vanderlyn and some of his fellow artists. Neither objective was achieved to his satisfaction. One of his own paintings, "Ariadne asleep, naked and abandoned by Theseus," as he described it, was not approved by the public in this country. It was one of the earliest and perhaps the most successful nudes by an American artist of the neoclassical period, and it was finally sold for $600 to Vanderlyn's fellow artist Asher Durand, who made engraved copies that popularized the subject and marked the culmination of Durand's high reputation as an engraver (see Fig. 445). In the end Vanderlyn died alone, embittered, and reduced to virtual beggary in a rented tavern room.

While Vanderlyn concentrated on Europe, other artists were taking a close look at the common American man in his eastern habitats, both rural and village, and on the western rivers and plains, and were reporting him at work and play in a spirit of flattering candor. Hardly any aspect of daily life escaped their brushes—and daily life in America around mid-century was more richly varied than it had ever been before. In William Sidney Mount's quiet and genial pictures of his Long Island neighbors, as in his *Cider Making* (Fig. 450), completed in 1841 during the burgeoning days of democracy, there is an intimacy and at times a humor that reflect a bond between the artist and a broad public. *Raffling for the Goose* and *Long Island Farmhouses*, both in the Museum's collection along with numerous other

**Figs. 446, 447, and 448.** The Palace and Gardens of Versailles, *by John Vanderlyn (1775–1852), 1816–19; oil on canvas, 12 by 165 feet (3.6 by 50 m.). In a day when long-distance travel was much more arduous than it is today, panoramas showing distant and exotic parts of the world were popular. The scenes were painted on huge canvas strips that could be rolled up and taken about the countryside for the entertainment of the populace. Vanderlyn's panorama of Versailles is a unique survival from that period, for the rough and careless handling these canvases received as they were carted from city to city, and the damp, rodent- and insect-infested storage spaces they were consigned to, meant that most were eventually damaged beyond repair.*

*Vanderlyn's hope, in offering his grand view of Europe's most magnificent palace, was that viewers would be impressed and inspired enough by this example of monumental artistic achievement to become interested in the art of their own country—and particularly in Vanderlyn's own portrait and history paintings, which hung in a gallery near the panorama. His hope was never realized, for Americans were not attracted by his ambitious, but rather sterile, formal view of Versailles. Although Vanderlyn later decided that his American audience would have preferred a panorama of New York, it may be that they simply wanted more detail—a livelier, richer depiction of the human scene in and about the palace. At any rate, in 1824 Vanderlyn wrote that "on the*

*whole the exhibition of this picture failed altogether in the success I anticipated. . . ." Apparently as a result, his whole career went steadily downhill, and he died impoverished and embittered.*

Gift of the Senate House Association, Kingston, New York, 1952 (52.184)

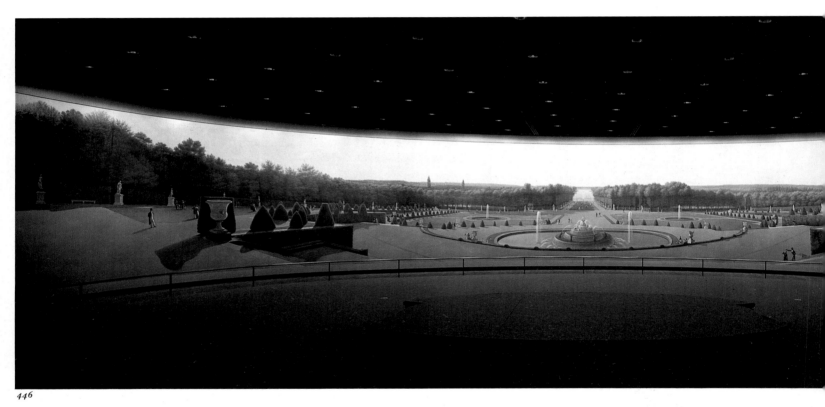

446

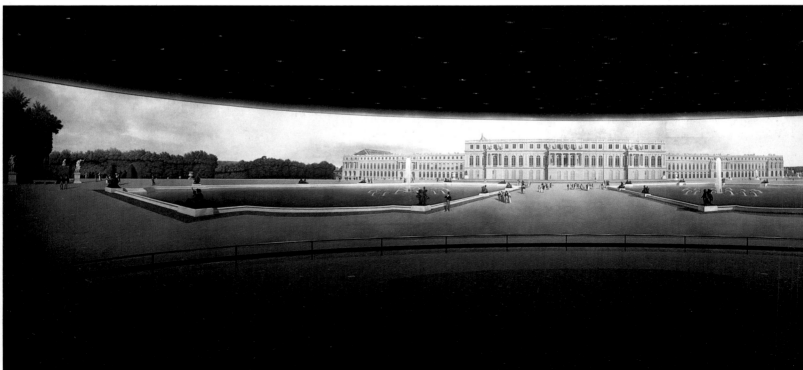

447

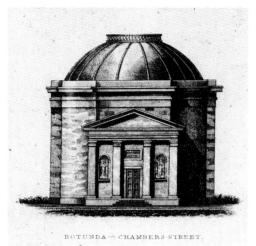

**Fig. 449. The Rotunda,** *from an engraving in the* New York Mirror, *1829. This elegant neo-classical rotunda shows the scope of Vanderlyn's vision. By housing his panorama in such an imposing formal building he hoped to impart to visitors his own sense of the dignity and importance of art.*
Bequest of Charles Allen Munn, 1924 (24.90.1248)

449

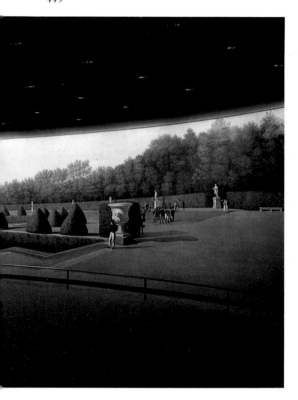

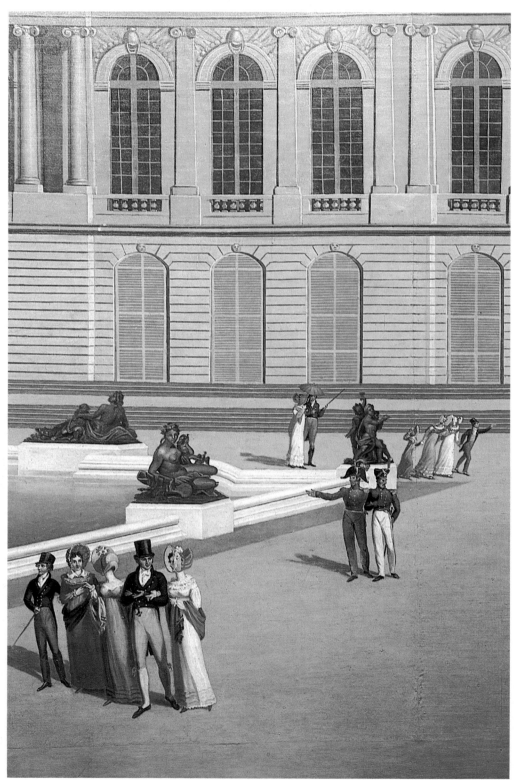

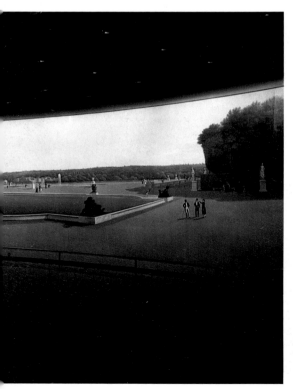

448

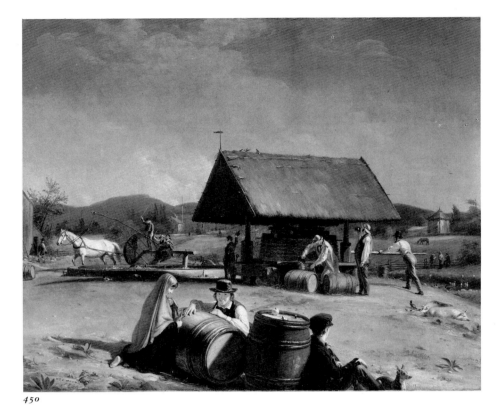

450

**Fig. 450. Cider Making,** *by William Sidney Mount (1807–68), 1841; oil on canvas, 27 by 34⅛ inches (68.6 by 86.7 cm.). This scene, while ostensibly devoted to an idyllic country theme in which a variety of country folks engage in cider making and drinking, has a number of visual references to the presidential campaign of 1840. William Henry Harrison, the successful candidate in that election, had been portrayed as a man who would rather live in a log cabin and drink hard cider than reside among the elegancies of the White House. Such a homespun attitude undoubtedly appealed to Mount, who, unlike so many of his contemporaries, was content to stay home—to study and to seek his subjects in his own backyard on Long Island instead of in Europe. He wanted, in his own words, to "paint pictures that will take with the public—never paint for the few, but the many." Happily, his genius for color and composition and for capturing the immediacy of a specific moment ensured that his paintings have never ceased to "take with the public."*
Charles Allen Munn Bequest, 1966 (66.126)

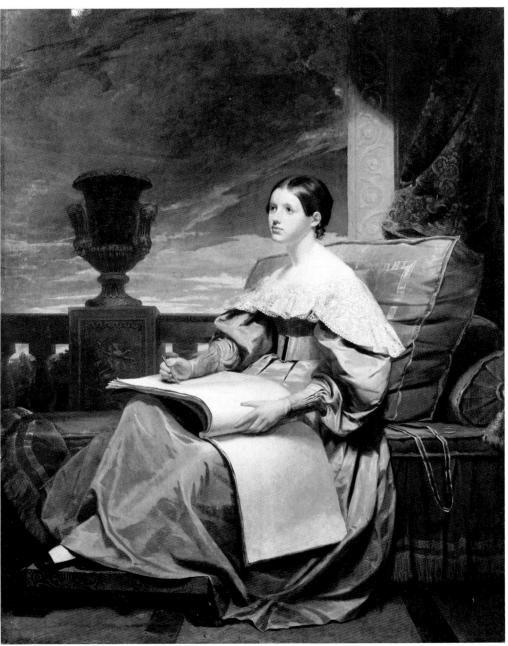

451

**Fig. 451. Susan Walker Morse,** *by Samuel F. B. Morse (1791–1872), about 1835–37; oil on canvas, 73¾ by 57⅝ inches (187.3 by 147.4 cm.). Morse combines in this work a portrait of his oldest daughter, Susan, and symbolism that relates to both art and antiquity. Susan is obviously drawing in a large portfolio, and a classical vase is a prominent feature of the background to her right. The result pleased the critics when the picture was exhibited at the National Academy of Design in New York in 1837. The* New York Mirror *noted that Morse had combined "with portraiture those qualities which belong to historical composition." Nevertheless, Morse suffered from lack of patronage, and he gradually gave up art for inventing. This was his last major work meant for public display, painted at a time when he was in the final stages of experimentation with the telegraph—an invention that brought him the fame that had eluded him as a painter.*
Bequest of Herbert L. Pratt, 1945 (45.62.1)

**Fig. 452. Fur Traders Descending the Missouri,** *by George Caleb Bingham (1811–79), about 1845; oil on canvas, 29 by 36½ inches (73.7 by 92.7 cm.). Although Bingham did eventually go abroad to study, he, like Mount, became a specialist in subjects drawn from the American countryside, his own particular interest being the life of the frontier. From an early age he had apparently settled on detailing "our social and political characteristics." His works dealt with many themes in those areas. All were composed with an unerring eye, beautifully colored, and set in luminous backgrounds, but* Fur Traders *possesses these attributes to such an extent that it rises above the rest. It is an American masterpiece whose subject is the spirit of the still river and its embodiment in the immobile yet alert figures of man, boy, and pet.*
Morris K. Jesup Fund, 1933 (33.61)

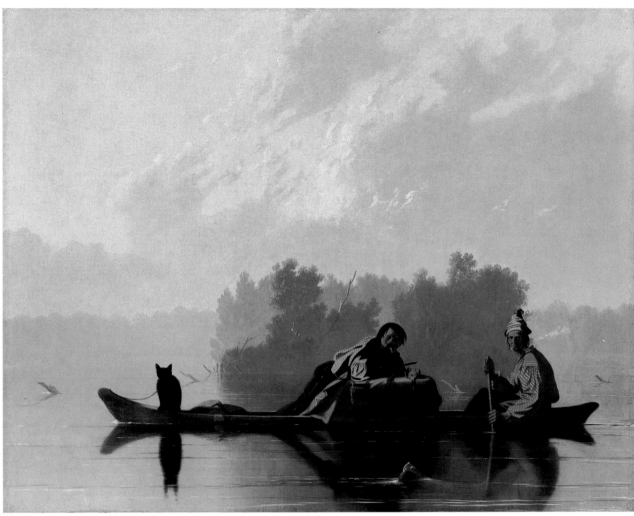

452

paintings in a similar spirit, further demonstrate Mount's commitment to painting *for* the common man as well as about him. As one contemporary newspaper observed, he was better advised to record such domestic and rural scenes than to waste his time and talent on "muffin-faces, or even in portraying gentlemen and ladies."

*The Muse*, Samuel F. B. Morse's sensitive likeness of his eldest daughter, Susan, in a pensive mood (Fig. 451), was one of the last and most skillful of his portraits before this artist put aside his brushes forever to devote himself to photography and to developing the telegraph. The result of that decision was a great loss to American art and a great benefit to American science. Although Morse aspired to be something more than "a mere portrait painter," as he wrote, some of his best work was in this field, and his subjects included a number of prominent persons—John Adams, William Cullen Bryant, and the Marquis de Lafayette. But he wearied of portraiture, and the public showed little interest in his more ambitious paintings. In later years he explained that he had not abandoned art; art had abandoned him.

To the west, George Caleb Bingham recorded the rough habits of the now almost legendary rivermen on their barges and flatboats; the hurly-burly of election activities; and, as in *Fur Traders Descending the Missouri* (Fig. 452), occasional glimpses of a tranquil moment in the life of the frontier. Bingham had grown up in the West, where he received very meager professional training and little exposure to the work of professional artists of any quality. To him it was commonplace to see French Canadian and half-breed *voyageurs* traveling in their piroques and dugouts down the Missouri River—"that savage river . . . ," as Francis Parkman described it, "descending from its mad course through a vast unknown of barbarism. . . ." Here Bingham has chosen to show two trappers and their pet floating downriver on a calm and lazy day. With subtle color and sensitive composition he has created an atmosphere of poetic beauty and of utter tranquility, transmuting the commonplace into something hauntingly beautiful. It is one of his best works and one of the most appealing American paintings of the time.

Men like Mount and Bingham won large and appreciative audiences with their everyday subjects so unpretentiously and realistically construed. For a time, at least, American painting became a popular art. Both Mount and Bingham were among the many artists whose works were bought by the enormously but only briefly successful American Art-Union, shown in the galleries of that organization, and raffled off to subscribers at Christmastime. During its short-lived career the Union distributed some 2,500 works of art at its annual drawings, along with great quantities of engravings of the most popular subjects. In 1851, after seven years of existence, it was forced to close its doors as a violator of the New York State lottery laws. But through its operations, remarked one contemporary, "the people awoke to the fact that art was one of the forces of society."

# The Mid-Nineteenth Century 1840–65

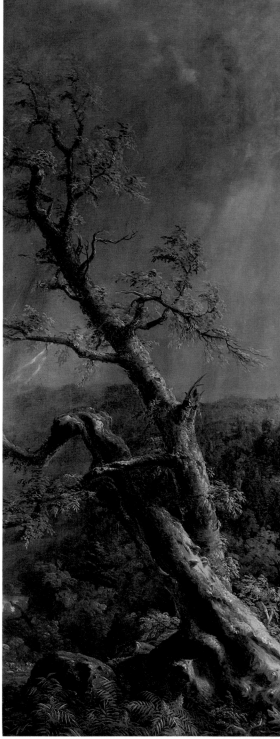

*Fig. 453.* **View from Mount Holyoke, Massachusetts, after a Thunderstorm—The Oxbow,** *by Thomas Cole (1801–48), 1836; oil on canvas, 51½ by 76 inches (130.8 by 193 cm.). Thomas Cole, arriving in America from England at age eighteen, responded immediately to the beauties of the American landscape. He soon bought a house on the Hudson, in the little village of Catskill, and became the founder and leader of the Hudson River school of landscape painting, whose focus was the celebration of the woodlands, streams and rivers, and changing skies of the American wilderness. The Oxbow, not in the Hudson valley but in an equally scenic part of the Northeast near Holyoke, Massachusetts, conveys Cole's romantic vision of the gran-*

In the middle decades of the last century, American artists were opening vistas that had been barely perceived by Stuart, Trumbull, and other early portraitists. These years saw the beginnings of a significant tradition of landscape painting, notably in the canvases of an unorganized fraternity of able painters known as the Hudson River school. In their meticulously detailed yet lyrical pictures of the hills and lakes, the valleys and rivers of their still semiwild continent, these men portrayed the beauty and grandeur of America as Washington Irving, James Fenimore Cooper, and William Cullen Bryant were celebrating it in their writings.

Thomas Cole, a virtually self-taught English immigrant, early developed into a superb landscapist whose work had a strong influence on this group of painters. His panoramic vistas, such as *View from Mount Holyoke, Massachusetts, after a Thunderstorm—The Oxbow* (Fig. 453), are expert and immensely appealing renderings of natural scenes, and they won immediate popular applause. When the aging John Trumbull spied one of Cole's paintings in a New York store window, he remarked, "This youth has done what all my life I have attempted in vain." And he bought the canvas for twenty-four dollars. William Cullen Bryant recalled, too, that the interest young Cole's paintings aroused was like that "awakened by some great discovery." Like other artists of this time, Cole made a European tour, and like the others he returned to paint the American scene with newly opened eyes. With his European experience behind him he also produced a number of large and melodramatic allegorical canvases that were commissioned by well-to-do patrons.

Luman Reed of New York was one of these. A wealthy merchant, he was among the earliest and most influential supporters of the American artists of his time. Generous, discerning, and an enthusiastic connoisseur, Reed was both the friend and the patron of such contemporaries as Cole, Mount, and Durand. One floor of his opulent mansion on Greenwich Street was hung with paintings that he had bought and commissioned from them. This gallery, which was opened to the public one day each week, was thus one of the first public museums in the United States.

Luman Reed's enthusiasm and backing gave a tremendous impetus to the development of American art before his premature death in 1836. It was he who urged Cole to paint *The Oxbow*. To Mount he wrote, "your truth of expression and natural attitudes are to me perfectly delightful and really every day Scenes where the picture tells the story are the kinds most pleasing to me and must be to every true lover of the Art." He bought two exceptionally fine examples of Mount's work.

Asher B. Durand, whose work was well represented in Reed's collection, painted several likenesses of this gentlemanly benefactor (Fig. 454). An engraver (see Fig. 445) turned painter, Durand was primarily a landscapist, a founding member of the Hudson River school who often explored the Catskills with Cole, sketchbook in hand (Fig. 455).

A considerable number of canvases by such capable artists as Frederic Edwin Church, John Frederick Kensett, Sanford Robinson Gifford, Martin Johnson Heade, Fitz Hugh Lane, and George Inness, to name a few, illustrate the further development of landscape

deur of the American countryside. Its wildness—
seen in the thick woods and stark dead tree of the
foreground and in the ominous thunderclouds
above them—provides a dramatic contrast to the
tranquil atmosphere that prevails around the Oxbow. For Cole, this landscape held a message,
which is well expressed in a poem he wrote the
year before he painted it:

I sigh not for a stormless clime,
Where drowsy quiet ever dwells;
Where crystal brooks, with endless chime,
Flow winding through perennial dells.

For storms bring beauty in their train. . . .

Gift of Mrs. Russell Sage, 1908 (08.228)

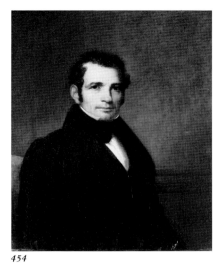

454

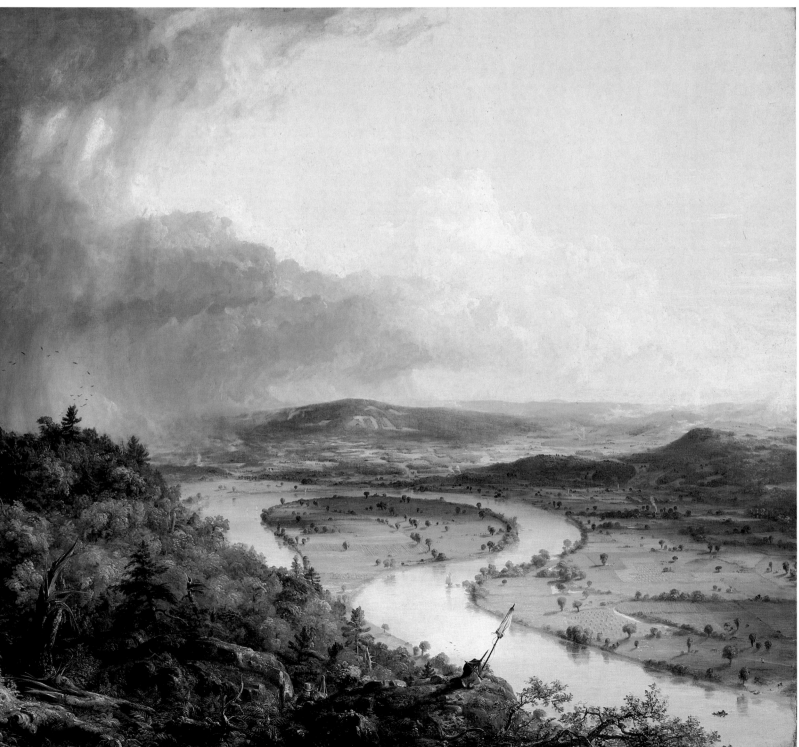

*Fig. 454.* **Luman Reed,** *by Asher B. Durand
(1796–1886), about 1835; oil on canvas, 30⅛
by 25⅜ inches (76.5 by 64.5 cm.). Luman Reed,
wrote Asher Durand's son, was "the first wealthy
and intelligent connoisseur who detected and encouraged native ability in other directions than
portraiture." Besides Durand, Reed patronized
and befriended Thomas Cole and William Sidney
Mount and paid the European travel and study
expenses of several other artists. His house contained a gallery on the top floor—the first such
space designated by an American entirely for the
display of pictures—and the public was admitted
to view his collection one day a week.*
Bequest of Mary Fuller Wilson, 1963 (63.36)

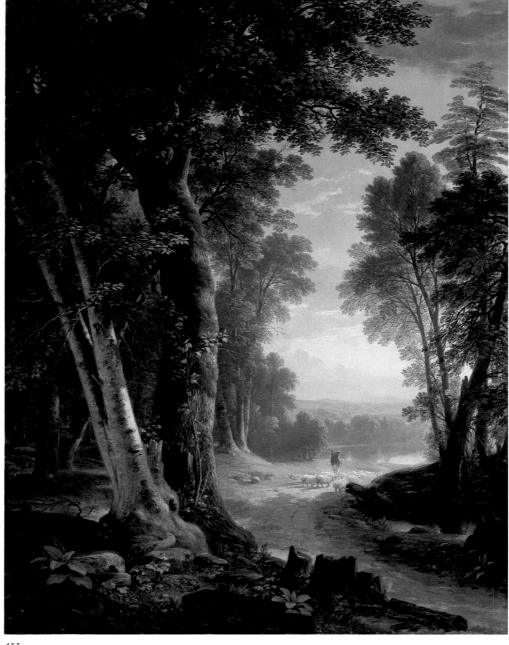

455

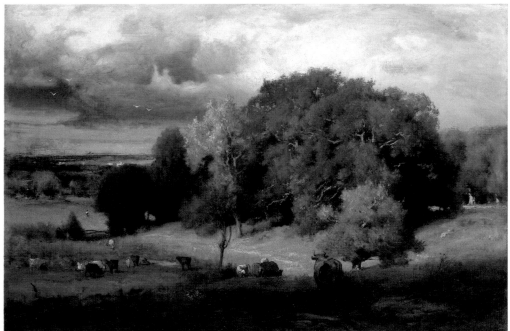

456

*Fig. 455.* **The Beeches,** *by Asher B. Durand (1796–1886), 1846; oil on canvas, 60⅜ by 48⅛ inches (153.4 by 122.2 cm.). At the beginning of his career, Durand was an engraver, becoming one of the most prominent in the country. Among his productions were engravings of views by Thomas Cole and other members of the Hudson River school, and in the 1830s Durand laid down his graver and joined his Hudson River friends as a full-time landscape painter. The need for meticulous observation and attention to detail necessary for superior engravings served Durand well in his paintings. In* The Beeches *the tree stumps and trunks, the leaves growing on and beneath the two trees in the foreground, and the light filtering down and casting shadows, are exceedingly realistically rendered.*
Bequest of Maria DeWitt Jesup, 1915 (15.30.59)

painting in the years surrounding the Civil War. In benign and intensely atmospheric works such as *Autumn Oaks* (Fig. 456), the largely self-taught Inness recorded the smiling aspects of the American countryside after the disasters of the war had passed from the scene. Inness's profoundly spiritual nature shaped his vision of the world about him. From the 1840s to the 1870s he made repeated visits to Europe, and these experiences influenced his artistic development. He was one of the first Americans to admire the work of the Barbizon painters in France, although he neither copied nor imitated any of them. His style was his own, and it changed as he matured.

A preoccupation with the effects of light and atmosphere characterized a sizable group of these later landscapists. In *The Coming Storm* (Fig. 457), Heade reveals an intense love of nature and of light, poetically stated. The two isolated figures and the single white sail under the threatening dark cloud produce an almost surrealistic impression typical of this artist's landscapes.

Fitz Hugh Lane was America's first native-born marine painter of real merit. His *Stage Fort Across Gloucester Harbor* (Fig. 458), recorded in subtle colors and with highly skilled draftsmanship, is characteristic of his serene and spacious views of the New England waterfront he knew so intimately. Lane was sensitive to the changing moods of sea and sky, and he thoroughly understood marine architecture. His work had a strong influence on younger painters of his day.

Kensett's *Lake George*, painted in 1869, is a subtle counterpoint of land,

**Fig. 456. Autumn Oaks,** *by George Inness (1824–94), about 1875; oil on canvas, 21⅛ by 30¼ inches (53.7 by 76.8 cm.). In this scene Inness celebrates both the calm and beauty of the countryside and autumn's glorious colors. By showing the sun streaming down on the flaming foliage in the foreground, Inness makes the color and the trees the dominant notes in his composition. Their brilliance is emphasized further by the deep shadows of the immediate foreground and the purple-gray clouds overhead.*
Gift of George I. Seney, 1887 (87.8.8)

**Fig. 457. The Coming Storm,** *by Martin Johnson Heade (1819–1904), 1859; oil on canvas, 28 by 44 inches (71.1 by 111.8 cm.). Like many other artists of his generation, Heade was fascinated by the ever-changing aspect of nature—by the atmospheric effects produced by an oncoming storm, for example. Here he captures the quiet period that often precedes a storm, when the water and air seem perfectly still. The motionless man and dog in the foreground emphasize nature's transient tranquility.*
Gift of Erving Wolf Foundation and Mr. and Mrs. Erving Wolf, 1975 (1975.160)

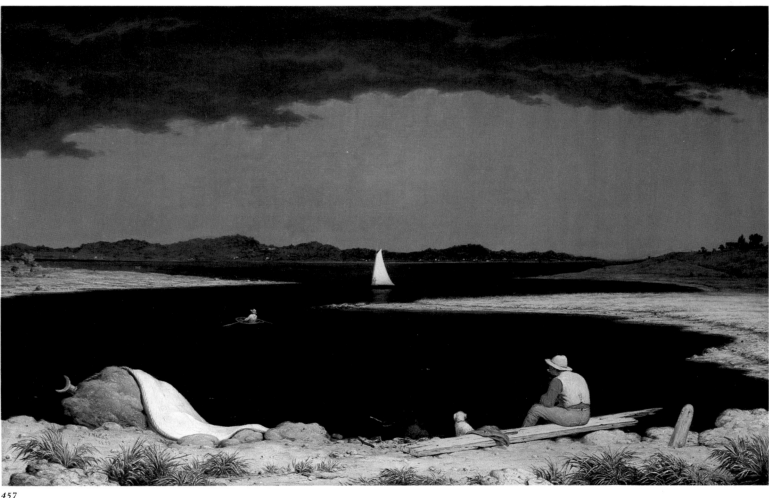

457

water, and shimmering atmosphere (Fig. 459). That much-painted lake has rarely if ever been pictured with the moving expressiveness that pervades Kensett's rendering of it. Like several other prominent artists of the post–Civil War period, Kensett became one of the founders of the Metropolitan Museum.

A very different but equally atmospheric marine subject is Nathaniel Currier's hand-colored lithograph *Clipper Ship "Red Jacket"* (Fig. 460). Produced in 1855, two years before Currier joined with James M. Ives, this print typifies the attitude that was to become standard for Currier and Ives in em-

phasizing American enterprise, accomplishment, and prosperity (Fig. 461). With a few exceptions, the problems and tragedies that accompanied urbanization, war, and massive influxes of immigrants were left to others to portray. At first Currier and Ives's black and white prints were hand colored by teams of women, usually working at home, but later chromolithography, in which several stones with identical images were superimposed in as many basic colors, mechanized the procedure of color reproduction. The firm thus produced untold numbers of inexpensive prints that all but flooded the nation, bringing fair approximations of paint-

ings to the attention of scores of thousands of Americans who had no other means of knowing the originals.

Currier and Ives, along with many of their contemporaries, helped to shape Americans' vision of themselves. Generations of Americans have formed visual impressions of our country's early days from sentimentalized representations of our life and history produced by painters, sculptors, and novelists of the nineteenth century. Emanuel Leutze's *Washington Crossing the Delaware* (Fig. 462), painted in 1851, is a notable example of such romantic imagery. Although it is false in almost every historical detail, this huge canvas has become

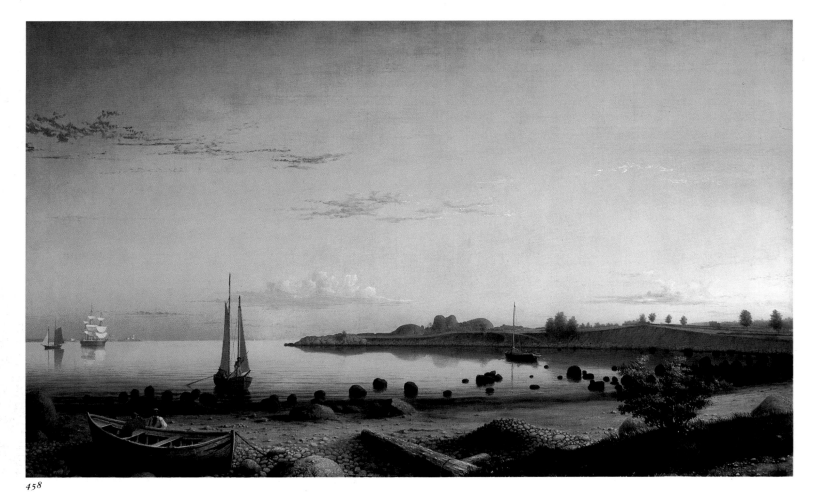

458

***Fig. 458.*** **Stage Fort Across Gloucester Harbor,**
*by Fitz Hugh Lane (1804–65), 1862; oil on
canvas, 38 by 60 inches (95.5 by 152.4 cm.).
Like Heade, Lane concentrated on the effects of
light and atmosphere, most especially as they
manifested themselves in the vicinity of water.
Here Lane paints Gloucester Harbor bathed in
pastel light. The hush that hangs over water and
land alike is almost palpable; nothing moves or
distracts us from the absolute stillness of the scene
and the luminosity of the atmosphere.*
Purchase, Rogers and Fletcher Funds, Erving and
Joyce Wolf Fund, Raymond J. Horowitz Gift, Bequest
of Richard De Wolfe Brixey, by exchange, and John
Osgood and Elizabeth Amis Cameron Blanchard Memorial Fund, 1978 (1978.203)

a widely accepted symbol of Washington's heroic coup on Christmas night of
1776. It is Leutze's most famous picture,
so laden with patriotic sentiment that it
is idle to attempt any aesthetic criticism—except to recall that it is highly
representative of a school of romantic
painting that flourished during the
middle years of the last century at Düsseldorf, Germany, where Leutze was
working at the time he composed this
extraordinary fantasy. In 1851 the president of the American Art-Union claimed that it was "one of the greatest productions of the age, and eminently worthy to commemorate the greatest event
in the military life of the illustrious man
whom all nations delight to honor."

In spite of Leutze's otherwise imaginative rendering of the event, it was in
at least one respect faithful to the facts.
He had taken pains to procure from the
Patent Office in Washington a perfect
copy of the general's clothes. However,
he could not find a German model large
enough to fill them. By the best of fortune the American artist Worthington
Whittredge unexpectedly appeared on
the scene. He was of the required stat-
ure, and Leutze immediately pressed
him into service to pose as the general.
"Spy glass in hand and the other on my

knee," Whittredge recalled, "I stood
and was nearly dead when the operation was over. They poured champagne
down my throat and I lived through it."
He also posed, sitting down, for the
steersman.

In his dynamic depictions of the rugged western mountains, which he made
familiar to most Americans for the first
time, Albert Bierstadt strove for spectacular effects. Such grandiose panoramas as *The Rocky Mountains* (Fig. 464),
freely worked up in his New York studio
from studies made in the field, brought
Bierstadt higher prices than any other
American artist had yet received for his
work. When it was first shown in New
York, this more or less synthetic creation received a tumultuous public welcome.

With such huge, impressive visions of
the western scene it might be said that
the discovery of America by its artists
was almost complete. To satisfy his wish
to record more remote and exotic natural spectacles, Frederic Edwin Church,
a pupil of Thomas Cole, journeyed to
many parts of the world. In South
America he sketched volcanic mountains and such panoramic views as *Heart
of the Andes* (Fig. 463; this painting and
Bierstadt's *Rocky Mountains* are hung to-

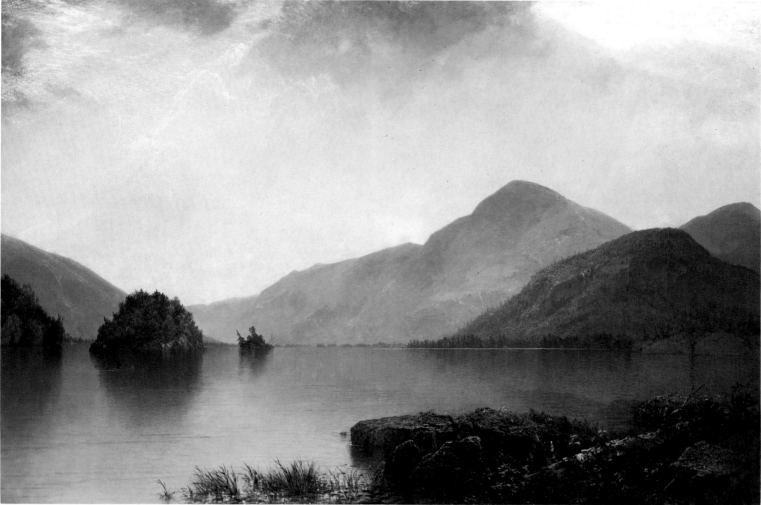

459

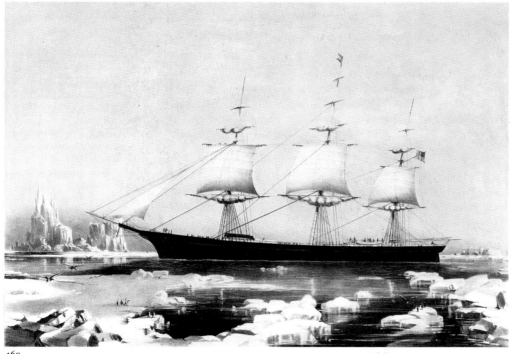

460

*Fig. 459.* **Lake George,** *by John Frederick Kensett (1816–72), 1869; oil on canvas, 44 by 66¼ inches (111.8 by 168.3 cm.). Kensett captured here, in his best painting, the poignant stillness of the lake and surrounding landscape. The misty light and the sheen of the water as it reflects the sky and shoreline are conveyed so convincingly that the viewer is drawn into the hushed atmosphere of the painting. Lake George was painted to order for Morris Jesup of New York; the price was a sizable $3,000, the second highest amount Kensett ever received for a painting—and a bargain for Jesup.*
Bequest of Maria DeWitt Jesup, 1915 (15.30.61)

*Fig. 460.* **Clipper Ship "Red Jacket,"** *by Nathaniel Currier (1813–88), 1855; hand-colored lithograph, 16⅛ by 23¹¹/₁₆ inches (41 by 62.7 cm.). During their long partnership Currier and Ives published over 7,000 different subjects—all relating to life in America. As news was made by boats, trains, and even fire engines, Currier and Ives recorded the occasion. Here an incident in which one clipper ship was trapped in the ice calls to mind the whole era during which the phenomenally beautiful and incredibly fast clippers revolutionized shipping. Currier and Ives prints sold for from 5¢ to $3.00—rarely more. This was truly democratic art for a democratic people.*
Bequest of Adele S. Colgate, 1962 (63.550.17)

gether, as they were at the New York Sanitary Fair of 1864). Church also traveled to the Arctic, with its frozen wastes and mountains of ice, and to distant Greece, where he sketched the Parthenon, among other subjects. All of this he worked into finished canvases upon returning to his studio. Now, however, the almost photographic detail of these immense compositions, so dear to the Hudson River school, begins to seem a little too insistent.

*Fig. 461.* **Winter in the Country. A Cold Morning,** *by Currier and Ives after George H. Durrie, 1864; hand-colored lithograph, 18⁹⁄₁₆ by 27 inches (47.5 by 68.6 cm.). When most people think of Currier and Ives they think of engaging and homey prints like this, showing lovely rural scenery populated by cheerful folks engaged in such traditional tasks as splitting and stacking wood. Currier and Ives prided themselves on providing prints on such a wide range of subjects that no one could fail to find one—or many more than one—of interest. They described themselves as publishers of "Colored Engravings for the People," and according to their biographer Harry T. Peters, "In their heyday Currier prints were to be found adorning the walls of barrooms, barbershops, firehouses, and hotels, as well as of the homes of rich and poor alike."*
Bequest of Adele S. Colgate, 1962 (63.550.502)

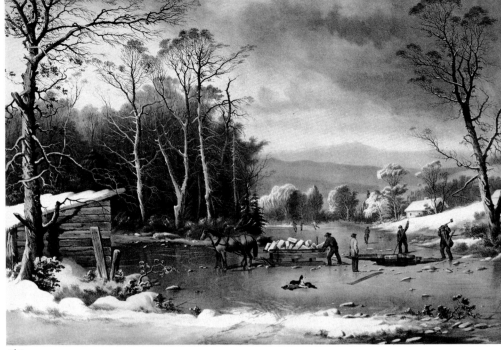

461

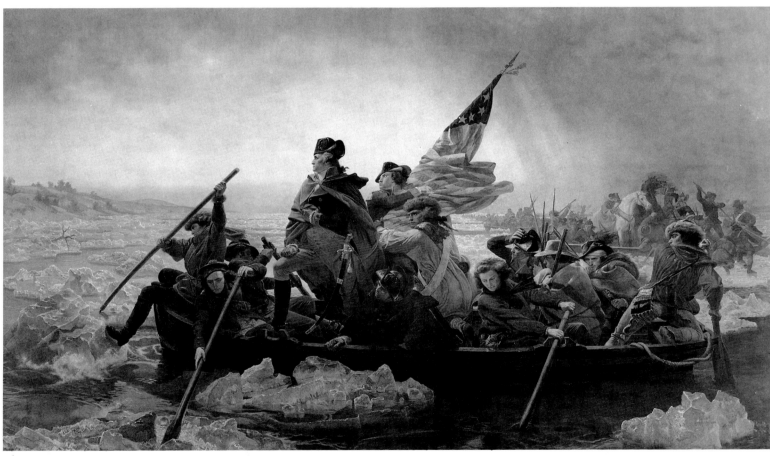

462

*Fig. 462.* **Washington Crossing the Delaware,** *by Emanuel Leutze (1816–68), 1851; oil on canvas, 149 by 255 inches (378.5 by 647.7 cm.). Leutze, born in Germany and brought to America as a baby, returned to Düsseldorf to study painting in 1841. Düsseldorf was very popular with art students in those days, for its stress on correct drawing and melodramatic historical subjects appealed to would-be artists all over Europe and America. Leutze chose as the subject for this painting the night in December 1776 when General George Washington and a ragged band of troops crossed the Delaware River bound for* Trenton, New Jersey. Arriving early the next morning, they surprised the Hessian troops, won the ensuing battle, and thus turned the tide of the war.

Numerous errors in historical details have been identified in this painting, and the heroic poses of General Washington and other central figures undoubtedly serve the purposes of artistic composition with more fidelity than those of historical accuracy. Nevertheless, this is a picture that, because it has been reproduced more often than almost any other American painting, has shaped more Americans' concept of the Revolutionary War than any other. Its importance is in capturing something of the commitment and determination that characterized Washington and other leaders of the period. The drama of this episode, despite the melodrama, rings true.
Gift of John Stewart Kennedy, 1897 (97.34)

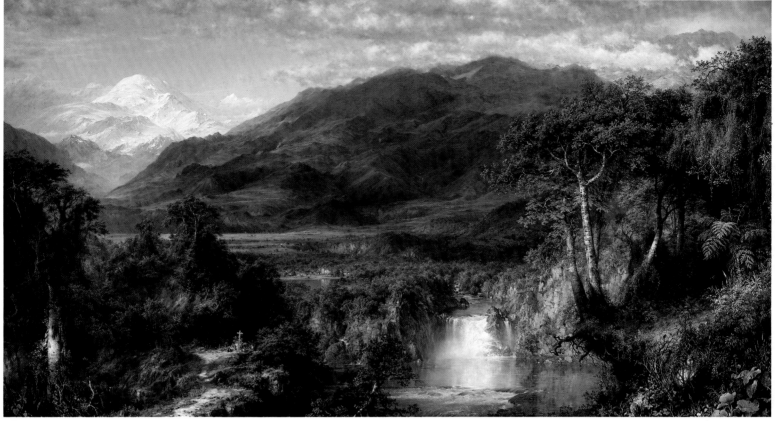

463

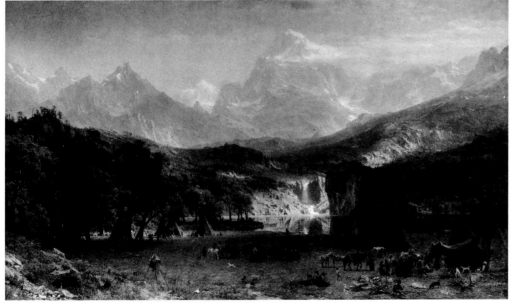

464

**Fig. 463. Heart of the Andes,** *by Frederic Edwin Church (1826–1900), 1859; oil on canvas, 66⅛ by 119¼ inches (168 by 302.9 cm.). Church, who was one of Thomas Cole's few students, painted this monumental scene after two trips to South America. He made sketches and studies in the field, but painted the final oil version in his studio. When he was finished, he placed it in a darkened room surrounded by tropical plants and hidden gaslights, and it caused a sensation. His contemporaries regarded it as a masterpiece in its powerful portrayal of the atmosphere, color, and variety of the Andean landscape.*
Bequest of Margaret E. Dows, 1909 (09.95)

**Fig. 464. The Rocky Mountains, Lander's Peak,** *by Albert Bierstadt (1830–1902), 1863; oil on canvas, 73¼ by 120¾ inches (186.1 by 306.7 cm.). As the American frontier moved westward, so did our artists. The first was Albert Bierstadt, who accompanied an expedition to Wyoming in 1859. He spent the summer sketching the awesome mountains, the lakes, the valleys, and the Indians who lived among them. When he returned to his New York studio, Bierstadt used his sketches to paint scenes such as this. His work was an immediate and enormous success, and he became more famous and commanded more money per picture than almost any other living American artist. Here we see the western slope of the Rockies in the distance; the Green River and a band of Shoshone Indians occupy the foreground. Bierstadt's appeal in such scenes was* twofold: *first, he showed Easterners panoramic views of a whole new part of their land; they were stunned by its magnificence and delighted by the artist's huge dramatic rendering. Secondly, he provided the wealth of minute details his literal-minded public loved.*
Rogers Fund, 1907 (07.123)

# The Late Nineteenth and Early Twentieth Centuries 1865–1915

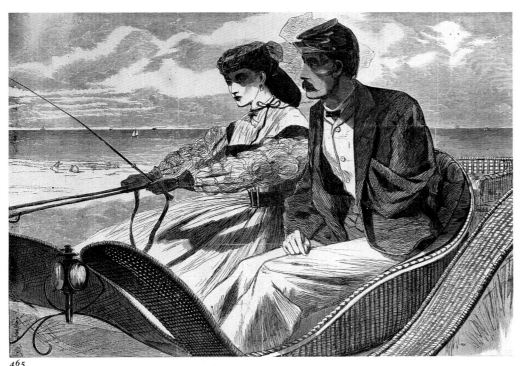

465

**Fig. 465. Our Watering Places—The Empty Sleeve at Newport,** *after Winslow Homer (1836–1910), 1865; wood engraving, 9¼ by 13¾ inches (23.5 by 34.9 cm.). Homer had trained in a lithographer's shop in Boston, his hometown, before giving up nine-to-five work for a freelance life in New York. From 1859, when he moved there, until 1875 he worked steadily on assignments for Harper's Weekly, including a period in 1861 covering the Civil War at the front. Homer is noted for his refusal to concentrate on the grand tragedies of the war and his preference for showing the boredom, the discomforts, and the lower-key sadnesses. In this scene, for example, he shows a side effect of war—the man whose life is radically altered but not necessarily ruined. The man's Civil War kepi (cap) indicates that he is an ex-soldier. His empty sleeve, which gives the picture its name, tells more eloquently than words of the loss of his arm—a point reinforced by the fact that the woman, not he, is driving.*
Harris Brisbane Dick Fund, 1936 (36.13.11[1])

**Fig. 466. Prisoners from the Front,** *by Winslow Homer (1836–1910), 1866; oil on canvas, 24 by 38 inches (61 by 96.5 cm.). When Homer arrived in New York, he took a night-school course and a few private lessons to learn how to paint in oils. His aptitude was such that seven years later, when he painted this scene, it was recognized as the most penetrating and truthful view of the war yet created. The Union and Confederate leaders, the victor and the captor, regard one another levelly, each exhibiting pride and even arrogance. Their stances and expressions indicate the characters of each of the other foreground figures. The somber colors of the soldiers' uniforms and of the ravaged landscape convey the grim sadness of the event.*
Gift of Mrs. Frank B. Porter, 1922 (22.207)

**Fig. 467. Snap the Whip,** *by Winslow Homer (1836–1910), 1872; oil on canvas, 12 by 20 inches (30.5 by 50.8 cm.). In the face of relentless sentimentalism after the Civil War, Homer refused to budge in his commitment to realism. Most contemporary artists would not have been able to resist the opportunity to exploit these children as symbols of a new beginning after the tragic conflict or of innocence and youth regained, but Homer celebrates the summer day and the children's carefree energy straightforwardly, without a touch of sentiment. Henry James, who deplored Homer's lack of polish, nevertheless wrote that "Mr. Homer goes in, as the phrase is, for perfect realism. . . . He is a genuine painter; that is, to see, and to reproduce what he sees, is his only care. . . ."*
Gift of Christian A. Zabriskie, 1950 (50.41)

During the post–Civil War decades two entirely different, strongly independent painters, each utterly candid in his vision of the world about him, were producing pictures whose interest has continued to grow with time. Canvases painted by Winslow Homer and Thomas Eakins are today rated among the finest the New World has produced. Homer started his career in a lithographer's shop, taught himself to draw and paint, and became a magazine illustrator. In his illustration *Our Watering Places—The Empty Sleeve at Newport* (Fig. 465) Homer makes the decidedly unromantic point that the effects of war are felt throughout the country—not just on the battlefield. His early paintings of Civil War scenes such as *Prisoners from the Front* (Fig. 466) and of rural life such as *Snap the Whip* (Fig. 467) are realistic reporting that seemed rough and homely to some critics of the time, straightforward and powerful to others. The former, painted in 1866 and showing a group of bedraggled but proud Confederate prisoners facing their Union captors, is a very sensitive reflection on an episode that Homer had observed as a war correspondent at the front during the tragic conflict. The second conveys equally realistically the playful outdoor antics of freckle-faced Yankee children during a recess from more serious activities within their one-room schoolhouse.

The Museum's collection covers virtually the entire range of Homer's changing vision and technique. In his later works he tended toward greater austerity and more impressionistic rendering. The rude strength that often showed in his work, the down-to-earth honesty of his vision, and his revelation of the elemental forces of nature are all remarkably demonstrated in *Northeaster* (Fig. 468), with its turbulent foaming ocean waves beating against a lonely rockbound shore under a leaden sky. In *The Gulf Stream* (Fig. 469), his theme is the contest between man and the immense, powerful sea. Homer was ut-

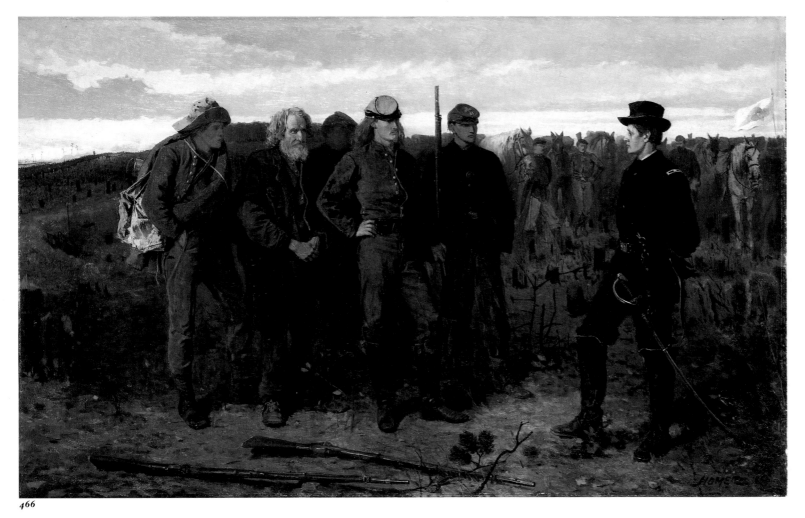

466

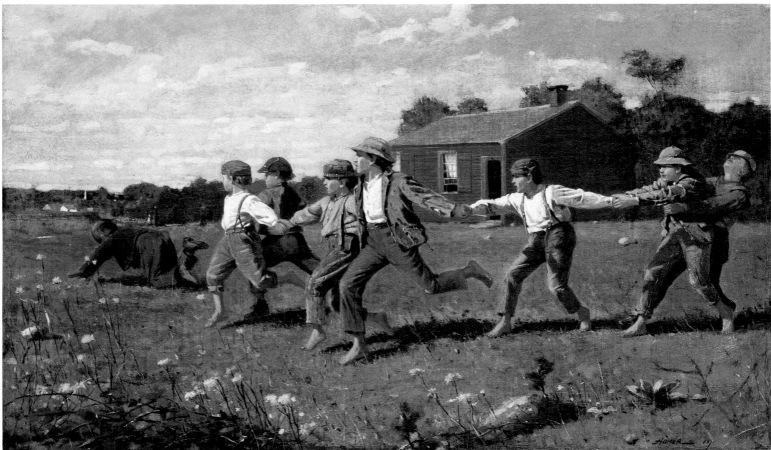

467

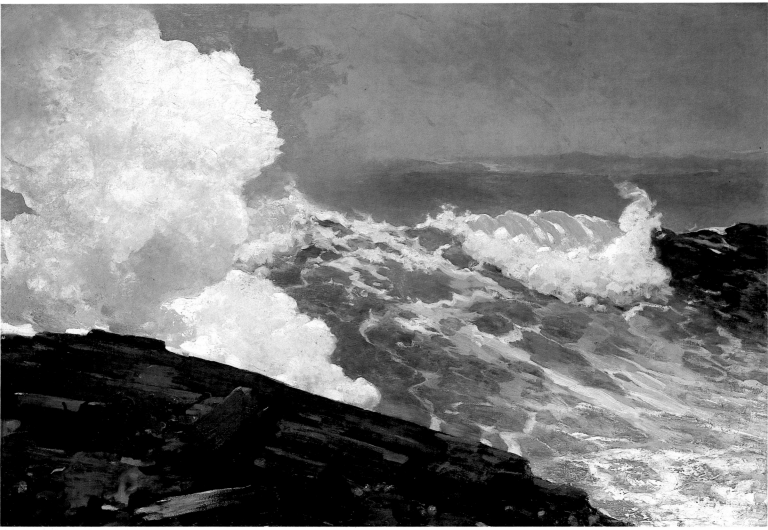

468

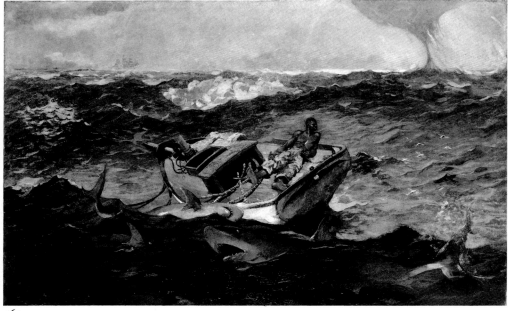

469

ing themes—the interaction of man and nature—is the focus here. A black man, alone and
apparently adrift, is borne along on the powerful
Gulf Stream. The contest seems startlingly un-
even—one lone man in a broken boat against the
limitless, capricious sea and a horde of man-
eating sharks. Yet the man seems curiously expres-
sionless; he has, it seems, faced the probability
that he will lose this battle, and he awaits the end
with dignity.
Wolfe Fund, Catharine Lorillard Wolfe Collection,
1906 (06.1234)

*Fig. 470.* **A Wall, Nassau** (detail), by Winslow
Homer (1836–1910), 1898; watercolor and
pencil, 14¾ by 21½ inches (37.5 by 54.6 cm.).
Here Homer captures the brilliance of a sunny
day in the tropics—the cloudless blue sky, the intensely red poinsettia blossoms, the gray wall with
dazzling white highlights. The choice of watercolor is perfect for this subject—and Homer did
many such scenes on his visits to Cuba, Nassau,
Bermuda, and Florida during the 1880s and
1890s—for the fresh, clear colors of the paint
and the nubbly surface of the paper accord well
with the casual, uncomplicated life of the tropics.
Homer's mastery of the medium is manifest in his
sure combination of densely applied shades for the
shrubbery and flowers with transparent washes
for the wall and sky. His leaving areas of white
paper showing through the wall suggests, simply
and cleverly, the brilliant sun pouring down.
Amelia B. Lazarus Fund, 1910 (10.228.9)

*Fig. 468.* **Northeaster,** by Winslow Homer
(1836–1910), 1895; oil on canvas, 34⅜ by
50¼ inches (87.3 by 127.6 cm.). Homer was a
man with an enormously perceptive eye and a
distinctive vision, and Northeaster is one of his
masterpieces. It captures the essence of the wind-
whipped waves and rocky coast, comments on the
vast power of the sea, and on the implacability of
Nature herself.
Gift of George A. Hearn, 1910 (10.64.5)

*Fig. 469.* **The Gulf Stream,** by Winslow Homer
(1836–1910), 1899; oil on canvas, 28⅛ by
49⅛ inches (71.4 by 124.8 cm.). In later life,
Homer went south to Florida or the Caribbean
for the winter, and this picture is based on
sketches he made in the Bahamas. The sea is
calmer here than in Northeaster, but its vast loneliness is clear, and the bloodthirsty sharks that
practically swim up onto the boat are an explicit
reference to its dangers. One of Homer's endur-

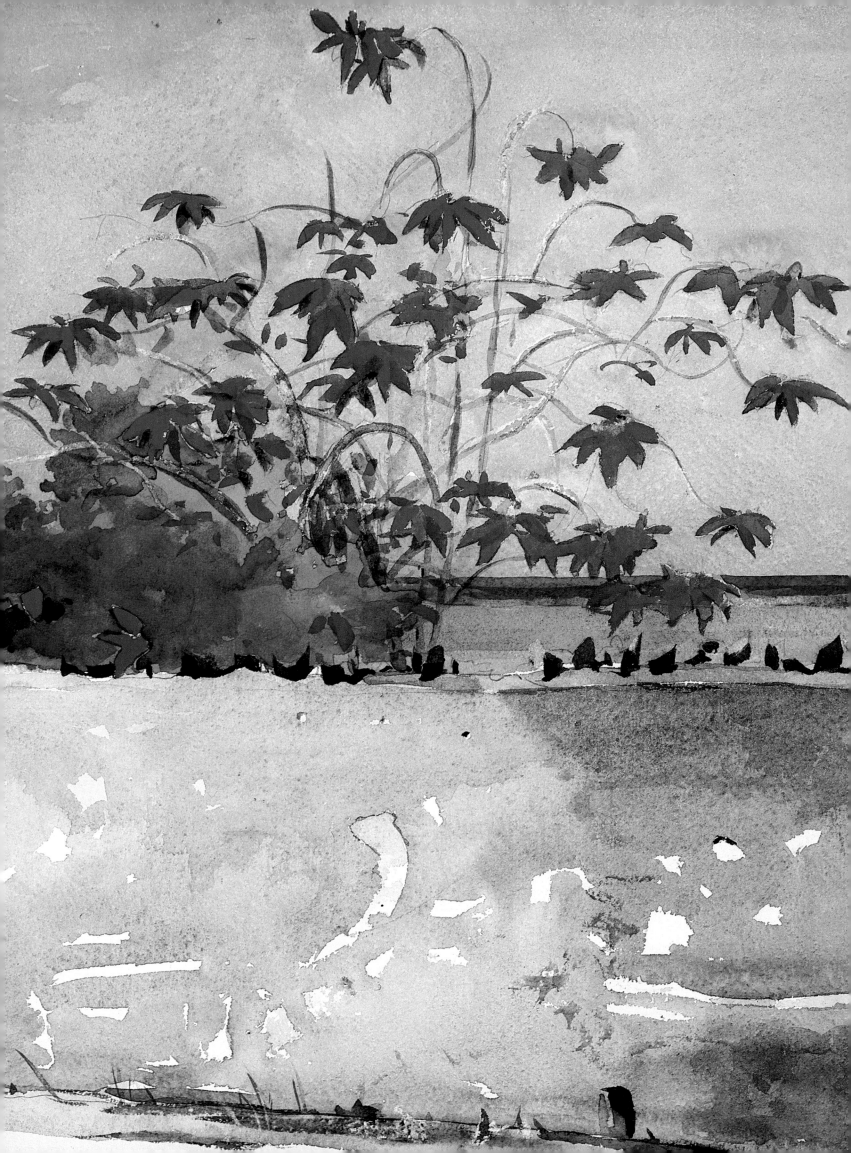

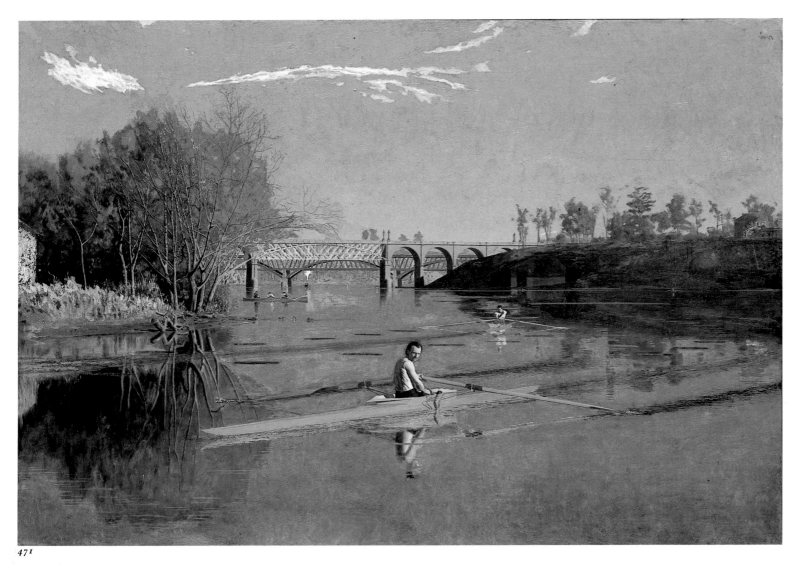

471

terly free of the poses and cant that make art such a precious mystery in some circles. For him the practice of art was an almost instinctive activity that, like mending the fence and gathering the hay, had its right moment.

Homer's *A Wall, Nassau* (Fig. 470) suggests why he was considered a leader in the American watercolor movement. With a relatively limited palette he realized a variety of textures, sometimes achieving a dazzling effect by reserving areas of bare paper for highlights. The visiting English dramatist and novelist Arnold Bennett once wrote of Homer's watercolors that they were "clearly the productions of a master. . . . They thrilled: they were genuine America; there is nothing else like them." He had no teachers of consequence and no pupils—he was the sole great independent artist of his day to win recognition in his own lifetime.

Thomas Eakins of Philadelphia, Homer's very close contemporary, was another resolutely individualistic artist. Indeed, his stubborn persistence in painting people and things as he saw

them—largely in portraits of his fellow Philadelphians—was more uncompromising than most critics of his day could accept. When he died in 1916 his work was relatively unknown. During his lifetime he was thought of more as a scientist and teacher—and he was an excellent one—than as an artist. His interest in capturing the total reality of life led him to serious experiments in photography. He worked out problems of perspective with mathematical precision. To understand better the anatomy of the human body he dissected cadavers. He believed the living human body was "the most beautiful thing there is," and when he insisted that his students, women included, learn to draw from nude figures, public prejudice led to his dismissal from several teaching posts.

He has been termed a "scientific realist," and it was this very quality that led Walt Whitman to remark, "I never knew but one artist, and that's Tom Eakins, who could resist the temptation to see what they thought ought to be rather than what is." The Museum owns an impressive collection of paintings by Eak-

**Fig. 472. The Thinker: Portrait of Louis N. Kenton,** *by Thomas Eakins (1844–1916), 1900; oil on canvas, 82 by 42 inches (208.3 by 106.7 cm.). It was the stark, unsentimental realism of portraits such as this that disturbed Eakins's contemporaries—and that today gives this artist a place among America's foremost painters. The dark figure stands dramatically against a light background, seemingly self-absorbed. His stance is that of a man with his mind not on the artist or on potential viewers but on matters far from the present moment—and, one infers, far more important. Company manners are not important here. The spirit of the moment and of the man are.*

John Stewart Kennedy Fund, 1917 (17.172)

**Fig. 473. The Pathetic Song,** *by Thomas Eakins (1844–1916), 1881; watercolor on paper, 16¾ by 11⅜ inches (42.6 by 28.9 cm.). While many of his contemporaries were concentrating on the light, bright colors associated with sunshine and the out-of-doors, Eakins preferred the dark, rich tones of the old masters. Like those powerful though long-dead mentors, he was interested mainly in character, and his portraits are so penetratingly truthful in relating what he observed of his sitters' characters that they often either refused to take the portrait as a gift or accepted it and took it home to bury it in a closet or up in the attic. The painter Edwin Austin Abbey, explaining why he had refused to sit for Eakins, said "Because he would bring out all the traits of my character that I have been trying to hide from the public for years." The singer here, in a watercolor version of the oil portrait now at the Corcoran Gallery, is Margaret Alexina Harrison, caught, as so many of Eakins's subjects were, at a specific moment. Scholar Donelson F. Hoopes suggests that she has just ". . . reached a sustained note, perhaps the end of the song, and lowers the score to gaze sadly across the room. . . ."*

Bequest of Joan Whitney Payson, 1975 (1976.201.1)

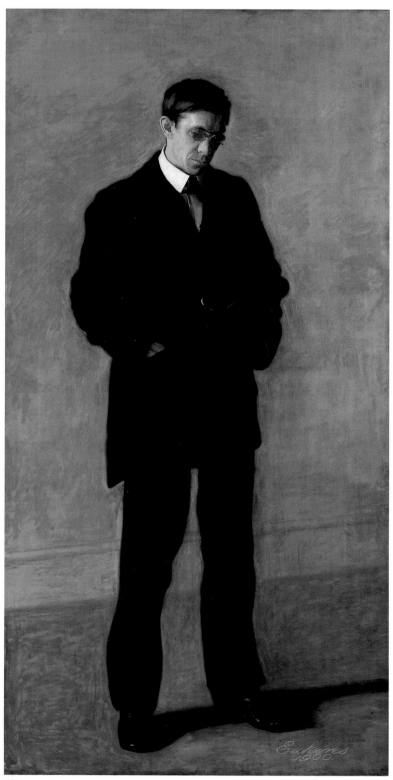

472

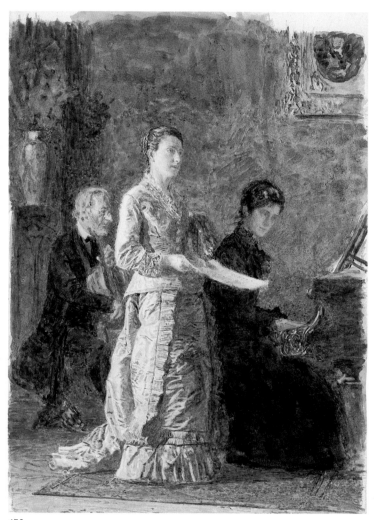

473

ins, the nucleus of which was purchased from the artist and his wife, Susan Hannah Macdowell Eakins, who was also a painter. *Max Schmitt in a Single Scull* (Fig. 471), the reflective full-length portrait of Louis Kenton entitled *The Thinker* (Fig. 472), and *The Pathetic Song* (Fig. 473) brilliantly demonstrate the absolute integrity and high degree of technical competence with which he reproduced his chosen subjects and which sent his reputation soaring after he was in his grave.

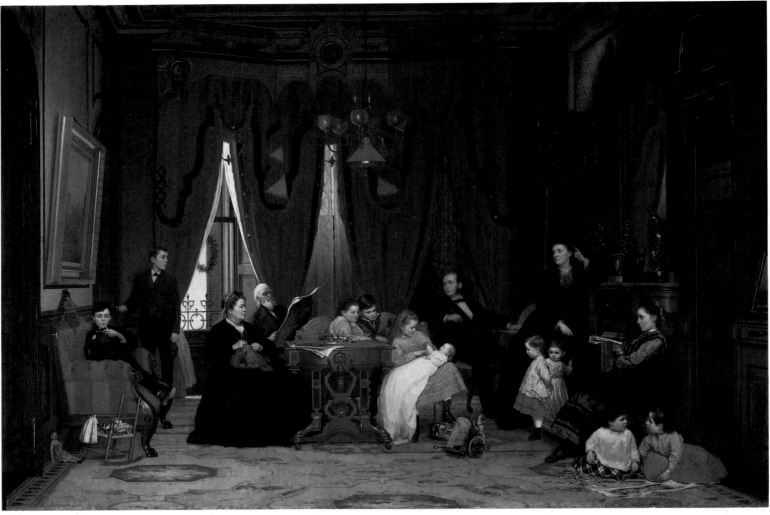

474

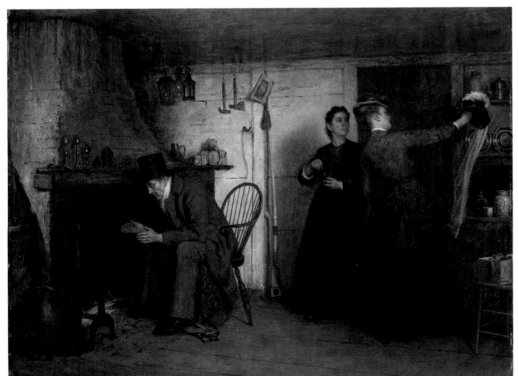

475

*Fig. 474.* **The Hatch Family,** *by Eastman Johnson (1824–1906), 1871; oil on canvas, 48 by
73⅜ inches (121.9 by 186.4 cm.). Like Leutze,
Johnson studied in Düsseldorf, where he learned
to draw with minutely detailed accuracy. Unlike
Leutze, however, Johnson chose to paint his contemporary native scene, both indoors and out,
joining realism with shrewd observation of character to produce outstanding paintings.* The
Hatch Family *shows the extended family of Wall
Street broker Alfrederick Smith Hatch in the library of his richly furnished Park Avenue house.
As a document it is invaluable, for it shows, de-
tail by minute detail, how an upper-middle-class
Victorian family lived in the early seventies.
Johnson, according to a member of the Hatch
family, considered it "the best of his works."*
Gift of Frederic H. Hatch, 1926 (26.97)

*Fig. 475.* **The New Bonnet,** *by Eastman Johnson
(1824–1906), 1876; oil on canvas, 20¾ by 27
inches (52.7 by 68.6 cm.). To judge from his
paintings, Eastman Johnson liked a good story,
and he liked people. This scene, set in a farm-
house on Nantucket, where Johnson summered
for many years, relates to a specific anecdote—the
showing off of a new bonnet—but it also gives us*
an idea of the everyday life of the ordinary people
who lived and worked on the island. Details are
important, here as in all Johnson's paintings, in
describing the character and his world. Aspects of
daily life are suggested by the whale-oil lamps on
the mantelpiece and the lanterns hanging just
above them, and by the tools to the left of the door.
We can see that this is the household of hardwork-

*ing, practical people who live among plain and
serviceable furnishings. The contrast between this
modestly furnished room and the frivolous hat,
with its feathers and veil, add flavor to Johnson's
story.*
Bequest of Collis P. Huntington, 1900 (25.110.11)

In the years following the Civil War many American artists swarmed to Europe to savor a rich variety of experience in countries of the Old World, there to find fresh inspiration and instruction in their art. They returned to America from Munich, Paris, and other Continental art centers with new techniques and more cosmopolitan outlooks and with confidence that, upon their return, they would form the advance guard of important new developments in American painting.

Eastman Johnson had gone to study in Düsseldorf—a center that spawned an international style that was, in some part at least, carried back to the homelands of those who learned there. Later on, when he was working in The Hague, Johnson was hailed as the "American Rembrandt" and was offered the post of court painter. However, he chose to return to his native land, where his particular talents quickly won him wide recognition and steady patronage for both his portraits and his genre paintings. In *The Hatch Family* (Fig. 474), painted in 1871, no detail is neglected to create a realistic group portrait of fifteen members of this prominent New York family gathered in the opulently furnished library of their Park Avenue residence. (The baby, born after the picture was finished, was added later by the artist.) Johnson considered this his masterpiece, although *Cornhusking at Nantucket* and *The New Bonnet* (Fig. 475), to name but two of his other works, would secure him a firm reputation.

Louis Moeller, one of our Munich-trained artists, shows a similar concern with realism. In his *Sculptor's Studio* (Fig. 476), the sculptural casts that stand about the room and the drawings pinned to the wall are so clearly and accurately rendered that they can be identified.

The ultimate in painterly realism was achieved by such artists as William Michael Harnett and John Haberle. For much of the history of painting in the Western world, artists have striven to create an illusion of three-dimensional reality on a flat painted surface. During the last quarter of the nineteenth century such virtuoso American artists as Harnett and Haberle depicted commonplace and disparate objects seemingly selected at random to carry this

*Fig. 476.* **Sculptor's Studio,** *by Louis Moeller (1855–1930), 1880s; oil on canvas, 23 by 30 inches (58.4 by 76.2 cm.). Moeller studied at the National Academy in New York and then in Munich. When he returned home at the end of the 1870s he began to produce interiors, often inhabited by the people who lived or worked there, that show typical American Victorian rooms, furnishings, and human occupations. This painting, however, shows an unoccupied room whose emptiness is emphasized by the expanse of bare floor in the foreground. The owner of the studio is as yet unknown, but some of the prints and sculptural casts in the room have been identified—mainly as copies of European and oriental works.*
Purchase, The Bertram F. and Susie Brummer Foundation, Inc. Gift, 1967 (67.70)

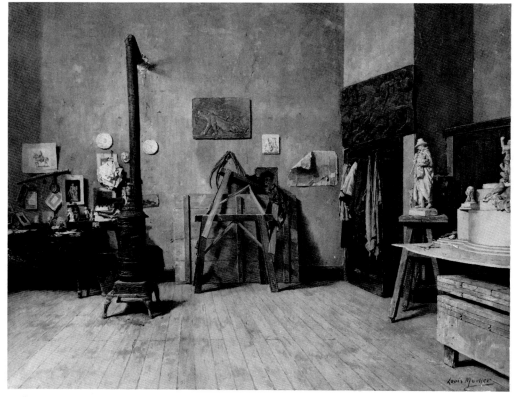
476

sort of visual trickery to a point that almost deceives the eye. The French term *trompe l'oeil* ("fool the eye") is commonly applied to these ingenious exercises in simulated textures, faithfully rendered colors, precise drawing, and meticulously observed perspective. The miscellaneous paraphernalia so artfully represented in Harnett's *The Artist's Letter Rack* (Fig. 477) and Haberle's *A Bachelor's Drawer* (Fig. 478) truly seem to be real and tangible rather than flat depictions of things.

The objective and realistic art of the foregoing artists found a complete antithesis in the brooding, visionary canvases of Ralph Blakelock, Albert Pinkham Ryder, and Elihu Vedder. As Blakelock's vision was haunted by the forest, Ryder's was haunted by the sea—

the sea in its awesome and somber loneliness, as it had never before been painted. His *The Toilers of the Sea* (Fig. 479) has a lyrical intensity that gives an emotional force to this stark view of a small phantom vessel cutting through the sea beneath a vast clouded sky. Ryder paid little heed to external realism or to detail. His seascapes derived from a subjective, deeply personal inner vision. He often worked for years on a single picture, even reworking some he had already sold, in an endless struggle to make some final satisfactory statement.

Munich was one European training ground for young artists that became popular in the 1870s. Characteristic of this school is an interest in the tech-

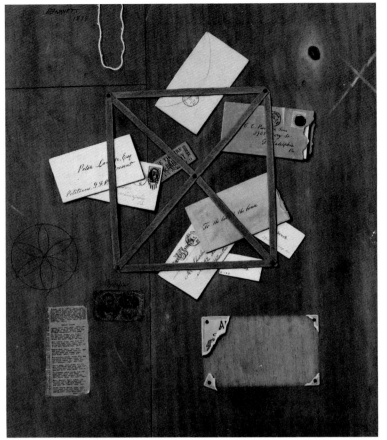

477

**Fig. 477. The Artist's Letter Rack,** *by William Michael Harnett (1848–92), 1879; oil on canvas, 30 by 25 inches (76.2 by 63.5 cm.). Harnett was the leader of a group of still-life painters during the last quarter of the nineteenth century. His work was influenced by that of James and Raphaelle Peale of Philadelphia, his hometown, and later by the seventeenth-century Dutch still-life painters, whom he studied when he lived in Munich in the 1880s. Harnett's device of painting a vertical surface such as a door or, as here, a board, is highly successful in creating a trompe l'oeil effect. The pink tape that has been tacked to the board to create a homemade letter rack holds a seemingly miscellaneous assortment of cards and letters. They are amazingly realistic—one nearly reaches out to pluck a letter from the rack—and recent study has suggested that the names and addresses shown were not selected at random but probably refer to the Philadelphia family firm that commissioned the picture. The name C. C. Peirson & Sons appears on the blue letter; other names and references may be to business associates of the Peirsons.*
Morris K. Jesup Fund, 1966 (66.13)

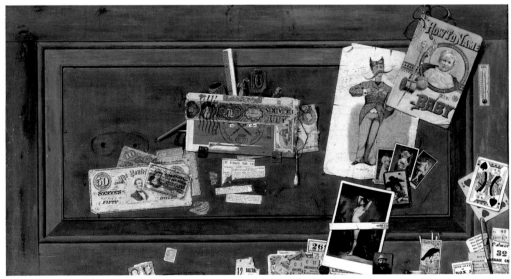

478

**Fig. 478. A Bachelor's Drawer,** *by John Haberle (1856–1933), 1890–94; oil on canvas, 20 by 36 inches (50.8 by 91.4 cm.). Although Haberle's trompe l'oeil work was popular in the 1880s and 1890s, it gradually sank into oblivion, not to be rescued until the early 1950s. Haberle's ability to make the bills, pictures, and clippings tacked to the drawer front seem real was extraordinary. One friend who came to his studio when the work was almost finished mistook the oil for the model and inquired when Haberle intended to begin the painting. Fragments of newspaper clippings seen here refer to the enthusiastic public reception of others of Haberle's paintings. But the main theme of this witty picture seems to be the passing of the bachelor's salad days. Juxtaposed with symbols of bachelor freedom—girlie pictures, theater tickets, cards—is the prominently displayed indication that marriage and responsi-* bility are on the horizon—"How to Name the Baby." *Haberle's eyes were so sorely taxed by his work on this and other minutely detailed paintings like it that he declared this his last* trompe l'oeil *effort.*
Purchase, Henry R. Luce Gift, 1970 (1970.193)

niques of such old masters as Hals, Rubens, and Rembrandt. Louis Moeller studied in Munich, as did Frank Duveneck, who is among the best known of our Munich-trained painters. Of Duveneck's *Lady with Fan* (Fig. 480) Henry James wrote, "it is hard to imagine a more discriminating realism, a more impressive rendering of the special, individual countenance." A similar subject was painted by Abbott H. Thayer, who studied in New York and Paris. The influence of the old masters is clearly visible in Thayer's *Mrs. William F. Milton* (Fig. 481), whose pose and costume are like those of a woman in a Rubens painting.

After attending West Point, James McNeill Whistler worked briefly for the U. S. Coastal Survey. There he received instruction in drawing and etching, before going to Paris to study art in 1855. In 1859 he proceeded to London, where he became a great celebrity. This elegant wit and accomplished painter insisted that art was for its own sake, that painting was based on the intrinsic interest of formal, decorative, and significant designs in color. To disassociate them from their ostensible subjects, he termed his paintings "arrangements," "nocturnes," and "symphonies." Thus he referred to his painting of Cremorne Gardens (Fig. 482)—"seen by starlight and the fitful gleam of fireworks"—as a nocturne, to his portrait of Théodore Duret as *Arrangement in Flesh Colour and*

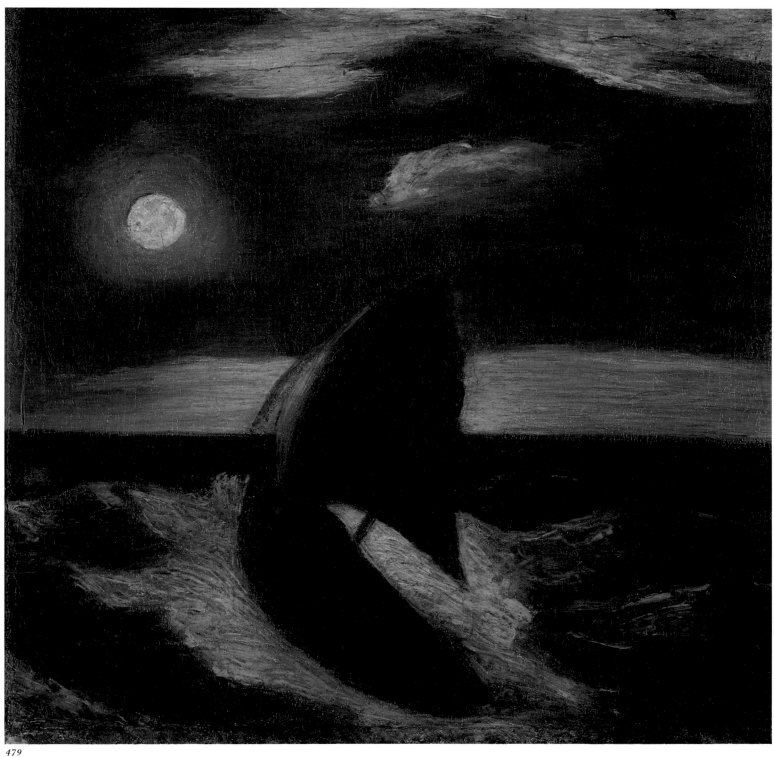

479

*Black* (Fig. 483), and to his most popular portrait of his own aging parent, commonly known as "Whistler's Mother," as *Arrangement in Grey and Black*. He was deeply interested in oriental art, elements of which he adapted to his personal style. Whistler's portrait of Duret, a well-known Parisian art critic and collector as well as a friend and admirer of Monet, immensely pleased that very discerning subject, who proudly showed it to his visitors after he took it home. It is still considered one of Whistler's most accomplished likenesses.

A quite separate phase of Whistler's artistic activity appears in the quantity

**Fig. 479. The Toilers of the Sea,** *by Albert Pinkham Ryder (1847–1917), probably early 1880s; oil on wood, 11½ by 12 inches (29.2 by 30.5 cm.). The subject of this arresting painting, its title probably taken from Victor Hugo's novel of the same name, has less to do with the story of a young sailor and his boat than with Ryder's inner vision. He had grown up with the sea in New Bedford and it possessed his imagination, as did clouds and the moon in a dark sky. In an effort to make tangible his visions, Ryder worked long and laboriously on his canvases, experimenting with color and with layer after layer of paint and glazes. Although his canvases have deteriorated as a result of his painting and repainting, Ryder achieved deep glowing colors and textures so smooth that they have been compared to enamels or semiprecious stones. The colors here range* *from gray to black to gold touched with green. The luminous, though dark, palette and the simple shape of the boat against the sea and sky combine to produce a painting that is as forceful as it is mysterious.*
George A. Hearn Fund, 1915 (15.32)

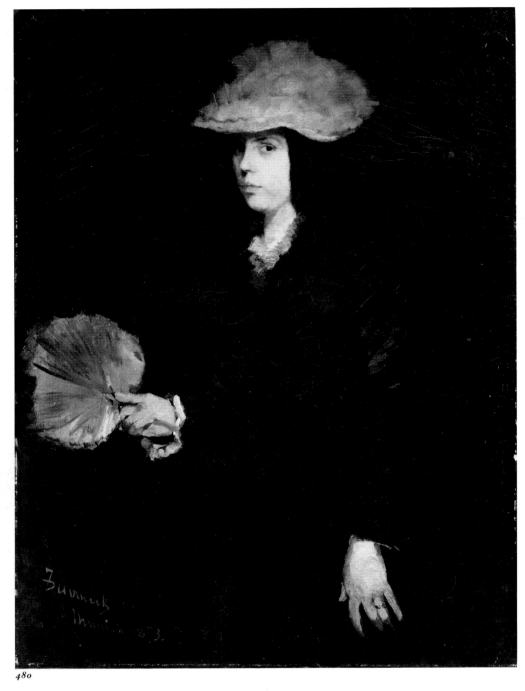

**Fig. 480. Lady with Fan,** *by Frank Duveneck (1848–1919), 1873; oil on canvas, 42³/₄ by 32¹/₄ inches (108.6 by 81.9 cm.). Early in the 1870s, Duveneck left Ohio to study art in Munich, then an exciting and progressive art center. Study of such old masters as Hals, Rembrandt, and Velázquez influenced members of the Munich school to forsake a detailed approach for a sketchy one and to concentrate on the most important features of the subject—in this case the woman's face. In Munich Duveneck also acquired the dark palette he used in this painting. When Duveneck's paintings were exhibited in Boston in 1875 the discerning Henry James remarked on "their extreme naturalness, their unmixed, unredeemed reality." He went on to note of this painting: "This face strikes us as a very considerable achievement. The consummate expressiveness of the eyes, the magnificent rendering of flush and bloom, warmth and relief, pulpy blood-tinted, carnal substance in the cheeks and brow, are something of which a more famous master than Mr. Duveneck might be proud."*
Gift of the Charles F. Williams Family, 1966 (66.19)

480

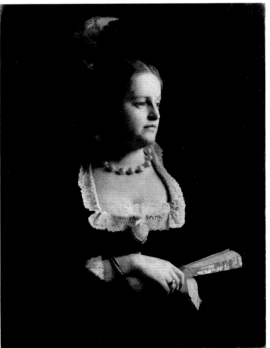

481

**Fig. 481. Mrs. William F. Milton,** *by Abbott H. Thayer (1849–1921), 1881; oil on canvas, 32 by 24 inches (81.3 by 61 cm.). Like so many of his contemporaries, Thayer, after beginning study in Boston and New York, continued his artistic education abroad. In Paris, where he lived from 1875 to 1879, he studied at the Ecole des Beaux-Arts, with Henri Lehmann and Jean Léon Gérôme. In* Mrs. Milton *his use of a somber palette and a pose reminiscent of that of a woman in a Rubens portrait indicate his admiration for the old masters.*
Gift of Mrs. William F. Milton, 1923 (23.77.3)

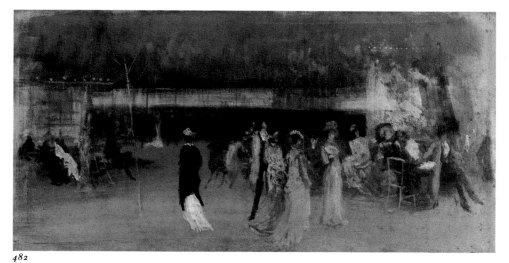

482

**Fig. 482. Cremorne Gardens, No. 2,** *by James McNeill Whistler (1834–1903), about 1875; oil on canvas, 27 by 58⅛ inches (68.6 by 134.9 cm.). Whistler's interest in paintings as exercises in formal harmonies led him to do a series of night pieces, which he called nocturnes. The pleasure gardens that give this painting its name flourished briefly in the mid-nineteenth century in the Chelsea section of London where Whistler lived. Fashionably dressed guests stroll about, exchange a word or two, and gather at a table to enjoy refreshments in a painting that captures the essence of a summer night. Light pierces the darkness or highlights a figure, but much of the garden and most of its inhabitants remain lost in the darkness.*
John Stewart Kennedy Fund, 1912 (12.32)

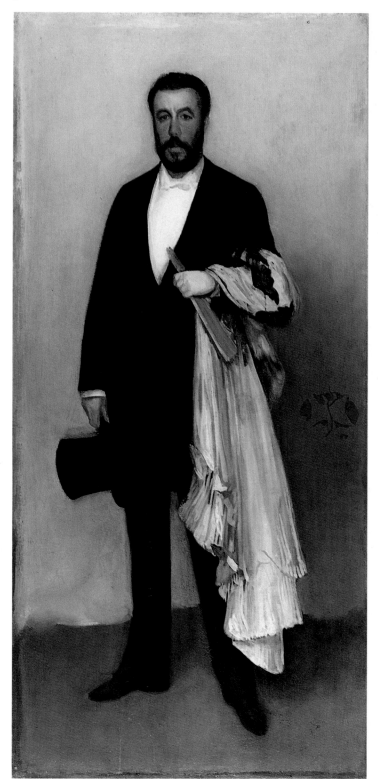

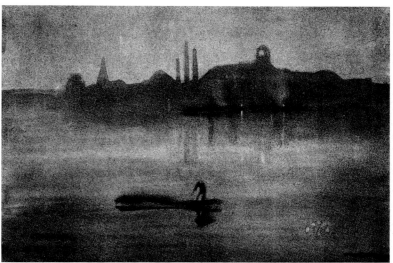

484

**Fig. 483. Arrangement in Flesh Colour and Black: Portrait of Théodore Duret,** *by James McNeill Whistler (1834–1903), about 1883; oil on canvas, 76⅛ by 35¾ inches (193.4 by 90.8 cm.). Unlike Eakins, whose portrait of Louis N. Kenton this resembles superficially, Whistler's foremost concern was not portraiture. He was more interested in pure composition, its tensions and its harmonies. Here Duret's boldly painted black suit and snowy shirt and tie stand out sharply against the background, exemplifying American art historian Edgar P. Richardson's description of Whistler's portraits as having broad areas of color "(whose mere breadth was shocking then), without reflections from one to the other, but with long, clean edges, presenting bold contrasts of warm against cool, light against dark, hue against hue."*
Wolfe Fund, Catharine Lorillard Wolfe Collection, 1913 (13.20)

**Fig. 484. Nocturne,** *by James McNeill Whistler (1834–1903), 1878 (printed in 1887); lithotint, 6¾ by 10¼ inches (17.2 by 26 cm.). Whistler was one of the most important printmakers of the nineteenth century; his etchings and lithographs, produced from the late 1850s onward, influenced his contemporaries to revive those arts. Here Whistler uses a grainy texture to convey the quality of the night light—dark and light mixed together to create a dusk-verging-on-dark atmosphere. The river and the land merge, one or two lights twinkle, and the whole composition, as the title suggests, evokes a dreamy, pensive piece for the piano.*
Harris Brisbane Dick Fund, 1917 (17.3.159)

483

**Fig. 485. Madame X (Madame Pierre Gautreau),** *by John Singer Sargent (1856–1925), 1884; oil on canvas, 82⅛ by 43¼ inches (208.6 by 109.9 cm.). Sargent was born in Florence and studied art in Italy and Paris, but, despite foreign training, he brought to his work an American freshness and willingness to flout tradition. Early in his career he lived in Paris, where he painted Madame Gautreau, an American married to a Paris banker. The finished portrait was exhibited at the Paris Salon of 1884, where it precipitated an uproar. The stark simplicity startled a public not yet exposed to "less is more" aesthetics, and Madame Gautreau's daring décolletage provided a further shock. The subject's mother asked Sargent to remove the painting* from exhibition, but he refused. What seemed barbarous to a genteel public seemed fine and bold to hardier viewers, however. In 1887 Henry James wrote of the portrait: *"It is full of audacity of experiment and science of execution; it has singular beauty of line, and certainly in the body and arms we feel the pulse of life as strongly as the brush can give it."*
Arthur Hoppock Hearn Fund, 1916 (16.53)

**Fig. 486. Mr. and Mrs. I. N. Phelps Stokes,** *by John Singer Sargent (1856–1925), 1897; oil on canvas, 84¼ by 39¾ inches (214 by 101 cm.). Sargent painted this handsome New York couple in London. The portrait was originally to be only of Mrs. Stokes, and many years later* Stokes wrote of the occasion that settled her dress and pose in Sargent's mind: *"Edith had on a starched white piqué skirt, and a light shirt-waist under her blue serge, tailor-made, jacket. As she came into the studio, full of energy, and her cheeks aglow from the brisk walk, Sargent exclaimed at once: 'I want to paint you just as you are.'" Later it was decided to add Mr. Stokes to the portrait, and although his wife remains the central figure, he is very much a presence in the composition, his tall form echoing and emphasizing hers. The elongation of figures, which makes them so striking, and the emphasis on Mrs. Stokes's costume, with its sharp contrast between white skirt and dark jacket, were criticized when the portrait was exhibited in America. More em-*

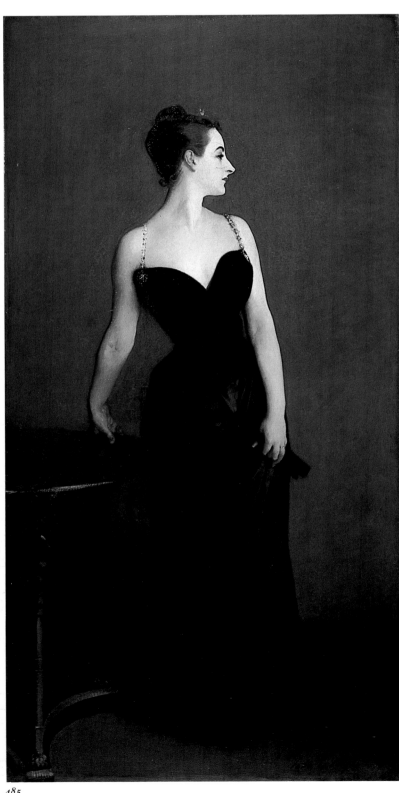

485

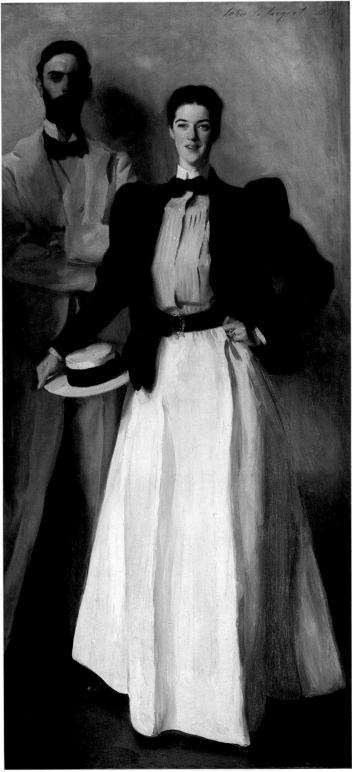

486

*Fig. 487.* **The Escutcheon of Charles v of Spain,** *by John Singer Sargent (1856–1925), about 1912; watercolor and pencil, 11⅞ by 17¾ inches (30.2 by 45.1 cm.). The intense light of a summer day is seen here shimmering on a carved stone escutcheon; the strong molded arch that encloses the carving provides structure in a composition that might otherwise be difficult to read. The impressionistic works on this page contrast strongly with the more substantial images of Madame Gautreau and Mrs. Stokes on the opposite page.*
Purchase, Joseph Pulitzer Bequest, 1915 (15.142.11)

*Fig. 488.* **Two Girls with Parasols at Fladbury,** *by John Singer Sargent (1856–1925), 1889; oil on canvas, 29½ by 25 inches (74.9 by 63.5 cm.). Although Sargent was much sought-after as a painter of formal portraits, he was happier doing impressionistic landscape studies and sketches. This vivid outdoor scene reveals Monet's influence in both subject matter and brushwork, for here Sargent, as if in revolt from the demands of portraiture, concentrates on color and light, leaving the girls' faces featureless. In fact, by 1909 his discontent had increased to the point where he all but gave up painting portraits to concentrate on capturing the vibrant outdoor light in watercolors.*
Gift of Mrs. Francis Ormond, 1950 (50.130.13)

of superb etchings and lithographs he produced throughout his career (Fig. 484). Whistler had many followers, and the influence of his aesthetic theories was considerable.

Whistler was but one of a number of exceptional American artists who preferred to live abroad during their professional careers. His younger contemporary John Singer Sargent, a complete cosmopolitan, chose to remain in London after studying and working in Paris for a period of years. His success as a fashionable portraitist was extraordinary; to be "done" by Sargent at $5,000 and up was considered a distinction and a privilege, well worth the very high fee. His portrait of Madame Pierre Gautreau, entitled *Madame X* (Fig. 485), is a striking characterization of a celebrated beauty and a masterpiece of economical expression. When Sargent offered to sell the canvas to the Museum, he wrote, "I suppose it is the best thing I have done." The Museum has acquired more than a dozen other examples of this artist's work, some of which, such as *Mr. and Mrs. I. N. Phelps Stokes* (Fig. 486), show Sargent's talent for psychological penetration of his subjects. Although it resulted in an admirably fresh and vivid portrait, Sargent labored long and hard on the Stokes painting. He redid the head of Mrs. Stokes nine times before he was satisfied with it.

Later in life he found welcome relief from fashionable portraiture in landscapes such as *Two Girls with Parasols at Fladbury* (Fig. 488), and in watercolors of dazzling charm (Fig. 487). The latter are represented in the Museum's collection by numerous examples. It is no heresy to prefer these private exercises of Sargent's to his commissioned por-

487

488

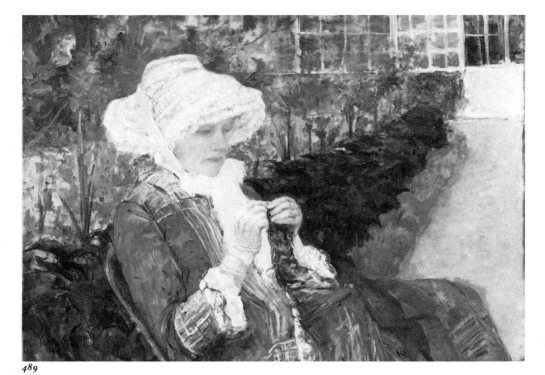

489

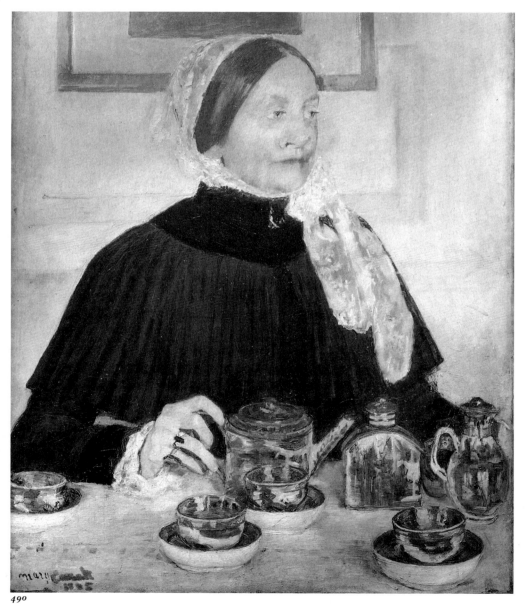

490

*Fig. 489.* **Lydia Crocheting in the Garden at Marly,** *by Mary Cassatt (1844–1926), 1880; oil on canvas, 32 by 42 inches (81.3 by 106.7 cm.). Many of Cassatt's paintings are of women—or of mothers and children—and frequently her model was her beloved sister Lydia, as is the case here. The vibrancy of the colors of the garden and the brilliance of Lydia's bonnet emphasize her pallor, which foreshadows her death two years later. A good deal of Cassatt's importance lies in the in- fluence she had on her wealthy art-oriented coun- trymen, for she imparted her enthusiasm for French impressionist paintings to them and was therefore responsible for some wonderful canvases finding a home in America at an early date. The Havemeyer collection, now at the Metropolitan Museum, is a major example.*
Gift of Mrs. Gardner Cassatt, 1965 (65.184)

*Fig. 490.* **Lady at the Tea Table,** *by Mary Cas- satt (1844–1926), 1885; oil on canvas, 29 by 24 inches (73.7 by 61 cm.). Mary Cassatt was brought up in Pennsylvania and studied at the Pennsylvania Academy of the Fine Arts, but from young womanhood onward she preferred to live in Europe. She established a studio in Paris, be- came friends with Degas and other members of the still very new impressionist group, and grad- ually created a style of her own. She and Berthe Morisot were the only women asked to exhibit with the impressionists, and from the 1870s Cas- satt showed with them rather than with the more traditional artists at the Paris Salon. In this por- trait she places Philadelphia aristocrat Mrs. Rob- ert Moore Riddle in an ambiguous setting—fore- ground and background are the same color, revealing her debt to Degas, Manet, and Japa- nese prints, and the bold color scheme emphasizes and repeats the blue and white of the Chinese porcelain tea set. Whistler was among the first to collect this oriental ware as just one aspect of his great appreciation of Eastern art.*
Gift of Mary Cassatt, 1923 (23.101)

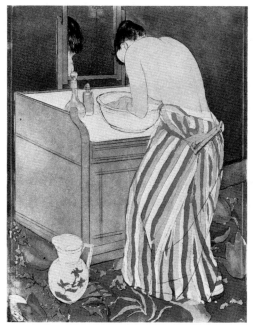

491

Fig. 491. Woman Bathing, by Mary Cassatt
(1844–1926), 1891; drypoint, soft-ground etching, and aquatint, 14⁵⁄₁₆ by 10⁹⁄₁₆ inches (36.5
by 26.8 cm.). In 1890 Cassatt attended an exhibition of Japanese wood-block prints at the Ecole
des Beaux-Arts in Paris with her friends Manet
and Degas. Like them, she was enormously impressed with the prints, and, besides acquiring
some for her own collection, she set about incorporating such elements as their two dimensional-
ity, coloring, and asymmetry into her own work.
After much careful experimentation Cassatt produced a series of color prints, of which this is one,
that demonstrate her success in closely duplicating
the effects of Japanese printmaking.
Gift of Paul J. Sachs, 1916 (16.2.2)

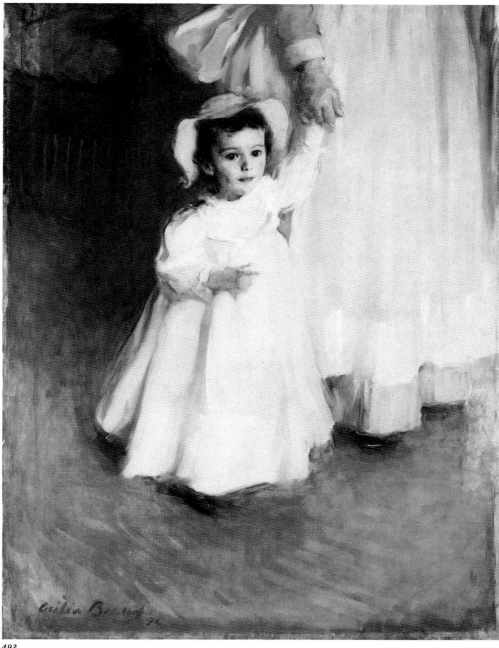

492

traits. Painting for himself for a change,
unhampered by the need to satisfy a
client, and working in a medium natural to his quick and fluid style of recording impressions, his responses were so
personal and immediate that it is impossible to remain indifferent to them.

Although Sargent spent most of his
life abroad, like Whistler he always considered himself an American at heart
and in fact. He refused a British knight-
hood rather than give up his United
States citizenship, which he treasured to
the end of his days.

Conspicuous among other American
artists abroad was Mary Cassatt, a Pennsylvanian with impeccable social creden-
tials. The first really important American woman artist, she remains among
the best. She was, as well, the only
American artist who became an established member of the impressionist

group in Paris. She worked with Degas
and learned from him, Manet, Renoir,
and other French impressionists, but
she imitated none of them. She was not
interested in painting important people
and treated her sitters so impersonally
that, except for some members of her
own family, few are identified. Apparently she never did a commissioned
portrait. The subject in Lydia Crocheting
in the Garden at Marly (Fig. 489) is the
artist's sister, Lydia Cassatt, and Lady at
the Tea Table (Fig. 490) represents Mrs.
Robert Moore Riddle. Cassatt never
married and had no children, but she
created numerous glowing depictions
of mothers and their small children.

Mary Cassatt had an important influence on the development of American
taste—at least on the taste of wealthy
compatriots whom she introduced to
the works of many significant European

Fig. 492. Ernesta with Nurse, by Cecilia Beaux
(1855–1942), 1894; oil on canvas, 49 by 37
inches (124.5 by 94 cm.). Cecilia Beaux was
from a genteel Philadelphia family. Her best
work was done around the turn of the century,
and here she combines interests in abstract pattern and portraiture to create an unusual and
arresting canvas. It is possibly her best-known
painting, and one that has always been very popular with viewers. By the end of her long life,
Beaux had achieved many honors, though she
never became a trend setter.
Maria DeWitt Jesup Fund, 1965 (65.49)

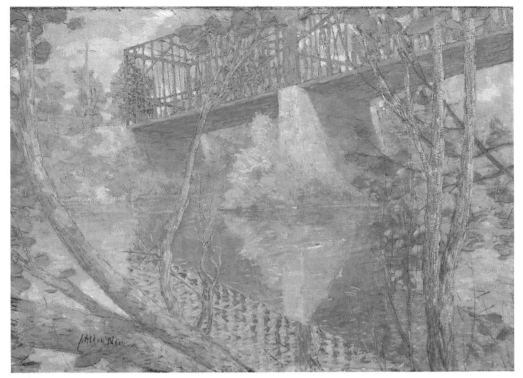

493

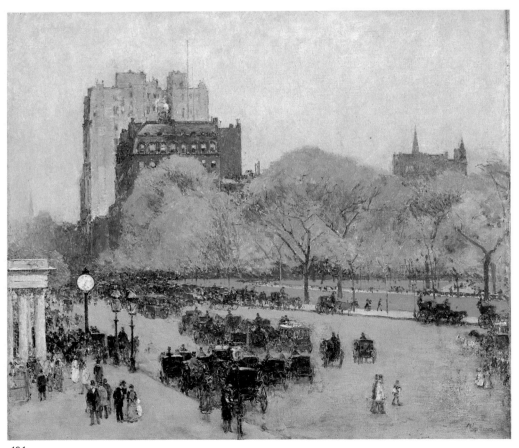

494

**Fig. 493.** The Red Bridge, by J. Alden Weir (1852–1919), 1895; oil on canvas, 24¼ by 33¾ inches (61.6 by 85.7 cm.). Both Weir's father and older brother were artists; he studied under his father at West Point, at the Pennsylvania Academy, and in Paris under Gérôme and Bastien-Lepage. By the 1890s he had begun to experiment with impressionism, and this outstanding canvas is one of the results. The soft greens and blues of the foliage, sky, and water contrast markedly but somehow lyrically with the red of the new iron bridge. In 1898 Weir joined with nine other eminent painters with impressionist leanings to form The Ten, and for twenty years the group exhibited together.
Gift of Mrs. John A. Rutherford, 1914 (14.141)

artists of the past and present and whom she advised in their purchases. Like Whistler, Cassatt was deeply impressed by Japanese prints and, again like Whistler, had she never painted a canvas she would be well remembered for her superb prints (Fig. 491). Her respect for Japanese art is especially evident in these, many colored examples of which are in the Museum's collection.

Cecilia Beaux, another woman artist of Cassatt's generation and also a Pennsylvanian, specialized in portraits, which she executed with imagination and verve. The striking painting *Ernesta with Nurse* (Fig. 492), in which a voluminous skirt, sleeve, and hand are all that is visible of the nurse, shows the spirited composition and bold brushwork for which Beaux was noted.

In his book *Crumbling Idols*, published in 1894, Hamlin Garland wrote that the French impressionists had taught him to see colors everywhere. Their work, he explained, conveyed a "momentary concept of the sense of sight; the stayed and reproduced effect of a single section of the world of color upon the eye." He urged his compatriots to look at their own land in this novel and illuminating way. However, the American artist returning from France had to adjust his sights to the different realities of his native scene and atmosphere. The light in this country was different from that in France, and to those grown accustomed to the picturesquely costumed natives and clustered stone dwellings of Normandy and Brittany, America in its progressive commotion seemed to offer only prosaic counterparts.

J. Alden Weir studied art first with his father, who was professor of drawing at West Point, and then in New York and Paris. In 1895, when he and his family

**Fig. 494.** **Spring Morning in the Heart of the City,** by Childe Hassam (1859–1935), painted 1890 and reworked before 1899; oil on canvas, 18⅛ by 20¾ inches (46 by 52.7 cm.). Born in Boston, Hassam studied art both there and in Paris, where he went for the first time in 1886. He became a popular artist in America, having settled in New York, where from the 1890s onward he practiced a solid version of impressionism that Americans found comfortable. This view of New York City, showing Madison Square Park, exemplifies Hassam's conservative brand of impressionism. A reviewer wrote in 1893 that the painting provided a "vivid instantaneous glimpse of seething streets," causing the viewer to imagine "that muffled roar of traffic which is the incessant voice of the metropolis."
Gift of Ethelyn McKinney, in memory of her brother, Glenn Ford McKinney, 1943 (43.116.1)

**Fig. 495. The White Kimono,** *by Childe Hassam (1859–1935), 1915; etching and drypoint, 7⁷/₁₆ by 10¹³/₁₆ inches (18.9 by 27.5 cm.). Turning to printmaking for the first time in 1915 at the age of fifty-six, Hassam became outstanding in that field. In this example, a woman clad in a kimono stands lost in contemplation before a fireplace—a subject influenced by Japanese art and the work of Whistler. This was a new departure for Hassam, who until now had been in the habit of portraying city scenes and country landscapes.*
Harris Brisbane Dick Fund, 1917 (17.3.494)

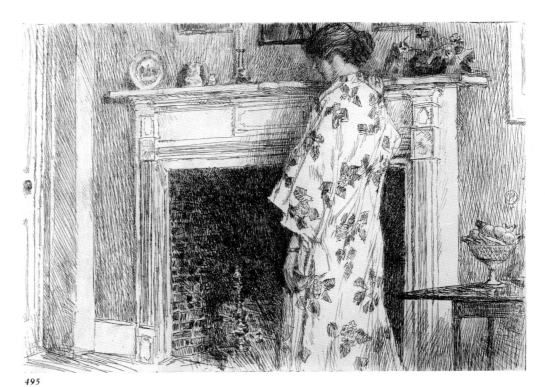

495

arrived in Windham, Connecticut, for their annual visit, Weir was at first dismayed to find a new cast-iron construction replacing the old covered wooden bridge that spanned the Shetucket River near his house. Then, in a moment of revelation he saw in that stark red-coated replacement the subject of a luminous painting in a setting of summer verdure. He labeled it quite simply *The Red Bridge* (Fig. 493).

During his sojourn in France, Childe Hassam learned the technique and the palette of the impressionists, to lay on his canvases the brilliant synthetic pigments that were then available in separate, small flecks for the eye of the observer to mix in its own way. This he did in his painting *Spring Morning in the Heart of the City* (Fig. 494), although here as in other examples of his work he did not emphasize color vibrations at the expense of the forms he depicted. As he grew older Hassam's interest in printmaking grew stronger (Fig. 495), finally taking precedence over his painting.

The contingent of American impressionists and post-impressionists included such other disparate and talented artists as Maurice Prendergast, Edmund C. Tarbell, John H. Twachtman, and, among still others represented in the collection, William Merritt Chase. Chase was the most influential of the group, for in his lifetime he probably instructed more art students than any other American, including Benjamin West. Early in his professional career on the Continent he worked very successfully in a broad manner that recalled the slashing brushstrokes of Hals, Rubens, and Velázquez. As he approached middle age back in America, Chase lightened his palette, and in

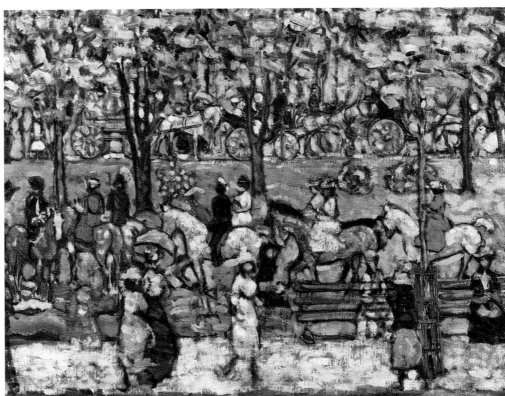

496

**Fig. 496. Central Park,** *by Maurice Prendergast (1859–1924), 1908–10; oil on canvas, 20³/₄ by 27 inches (52.7 by 68.6 cm.). This cheerful, supremely colorful scene in New York's Central Park is the result of years of European travel and study. Early in his career Prendergast worked in watercolor, developing a fresh, personal style. When he turned to painting in oils, he adapted many of his watercolor scenes to the new medium, often reworking them over and over, as he has done here. This scene is thought to date from 1903, but Prendergast's assured handling of the oils would place the date of this particular canvas at about 1908–10. His technique is based on the French post-impressionist one of applying dots and blobs of color, one next to the other, so that* the scene seems to shimmer on the canvas. The picture is held in place by the strong horizontal and vertical lines, however, created by the benches and roadway and by the trees that thrust upward across the canvas.
George A. Hearn Fund, 1950 (50.25)

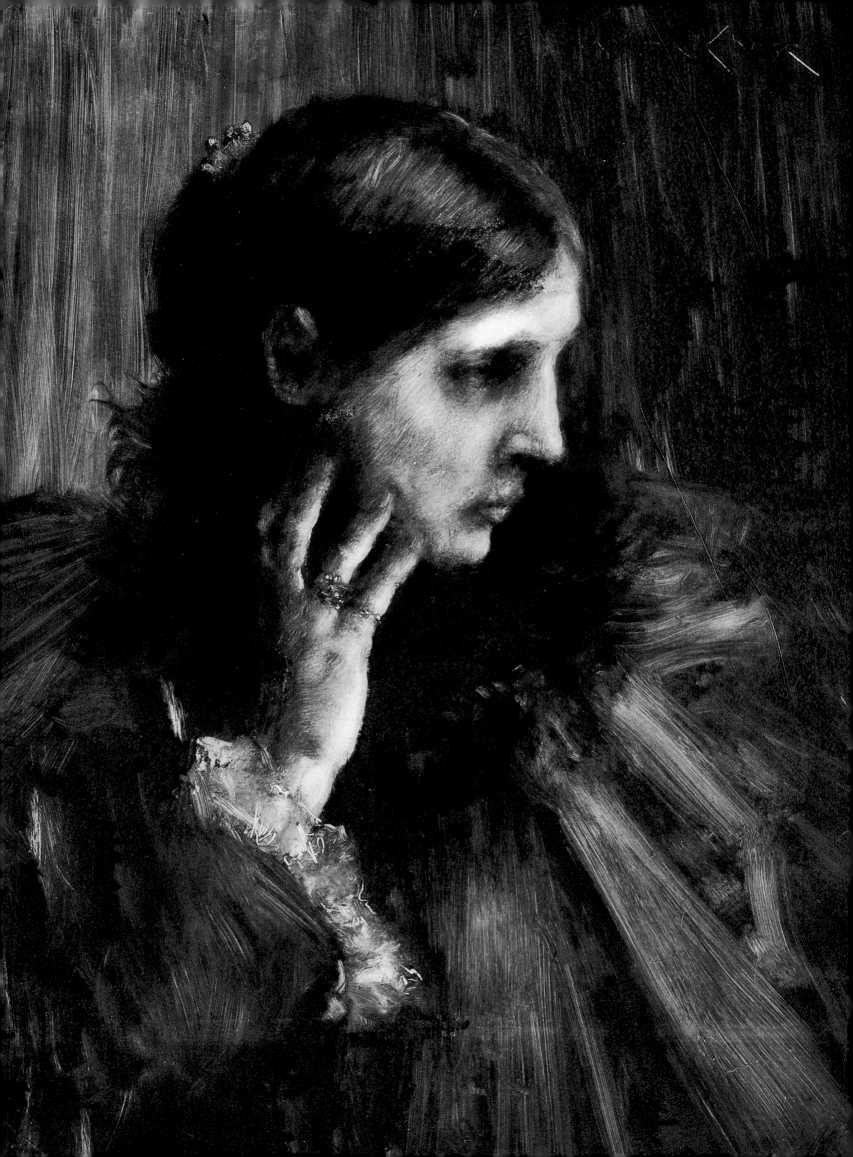

**Fig. 497.** **Reverie: A Portrait of a Woman,** *by William Merritt Chase (1844–1916), 1890–95; monotype, 19½ by 15¾ inches (49.5 by 40 cm.). The monotype was a medium introduced in the seventeenth century and revived by artists in the last quarter of the nineteenth. Basically, the process involves painting on the printing plate without etching or engraving lines on it. Because there is no way to hold the image after the first printing, only one impression can be made—although if enough ink remained on the plate, a second image could be printed. This moving and sensitive portrait, of unusually large size, is thought to be of Chase's wife.*
Purchase, Louis V. Bell, William E. Dodge, and Fletcher Funds; Murray Rafsky Gift; and funds from various donors, 1974 (1974.544)

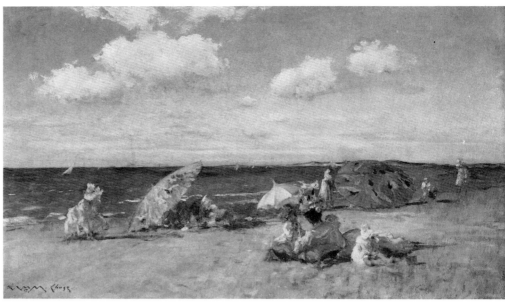

498

scenes such as *At the Seaside* and *For the Little One* (Figs. 498 and 499) he applied brilliant colors with a masterful technique and with enormous zest. Chase experimented with printmaking too, and *Reverie* (Fig. 497) is a monotype that has the richness of a painting.

John H. Twachtman, occasional painting companion and friend of most of the men just mentioned, pictured *Arques-la-Bataille* (Fig. 503), a site near Dieppe on the Normandy coast, in a subtle orchestration of subdued colors. Delicate grays, greens, and blues are thinly and broadly applied in a manner that evokes an image of the landscape rather than defines it and is reminiscent of the tonal harmonies of Whistler.

The post-impressionist style was represented in America by Maurice Prendergast, who had been particularly influenced by the work of Pierre Bonnard and Edouard Vuillard when he studied in France. His work reflects his fascination with brilliant primary colors and surface texture. Art historian Jules Prown's observation that Prendergast's "delight in blobs of color manifested itself in a fascination with balloons, parasols and banners" is borne out by the Museum's *Central Park* (Fig. 496).

John White Alexander, yet another American who studied and lived in Europe, was one of our leading artists at the turn of the century. His *Repose* (Fig. 504), a strikingly elegant recumbent female figure, shows the influence of his friend Whistler in its delicate brushwork and thin paint surfaces as well as of the Art Nouveau movement in its composition.

The present century has witnessed extraordinary changes in the arts as in everything else, and they have been at times both violent and confusing. At the

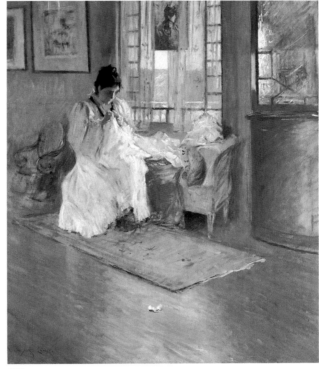

499

**Fig. 498.** **At the Seaside,** *by William Merritt Chase (1844–1916), about 1892; oil on canvas, 20 by 34 inches (50.8 by 86.4 cm.). A native of Indiana, Chase studied there and in New York and St. Louis before being sent to Europe by a group of St. Louis businessmen. (When they inquired whether Chase would like such a trip, he responded "I'd rather go to Europe than go to heaven.") Returning to America in 1878, he took a studio at 51 West Tenth Street in New York and embarked on his successful career as prolific painter and printmaker and extremely influential teacher. For many years he conducted summer art classes at Shinnecock on Long Island, where he had a house and where this impressionist beach scene was painted. The freely disposed brushstrokes and bright, clear colors represent Chase's response to French impressionist painting; it was this response that he passed along to a generation of American artists who studied with him.*
Bequest of Miss Adelaide Milton de Groot (1876–1967), 1967 (67.187.123)

**Fig. 499.** **For the Little One,** *by William Merritt Chase (1844–1916), about 1895; oil on canvas, 40 by 35¼ inches (101.6 by 89.5 cm.). As was often his custom in the nineties, Chase here depicts an intimate family picture, showing Mrs. Chase sewing beside a window in their Shinnecock house. Light pours onto the crumpled fabric Mrs. Chase is working and onto the expanse of bare polished floor in the foreground—an unusual innovation. The flood of light from the window creates a diagonal line from the foreground to Mrs. Chase and to the space between the slightly parted curtains. In the center of the window Chase hung a monotype very like the one illustrated in Fig. 497.*
Amelia B. Lazarus Fund, by exchange, 1913 (13.90)

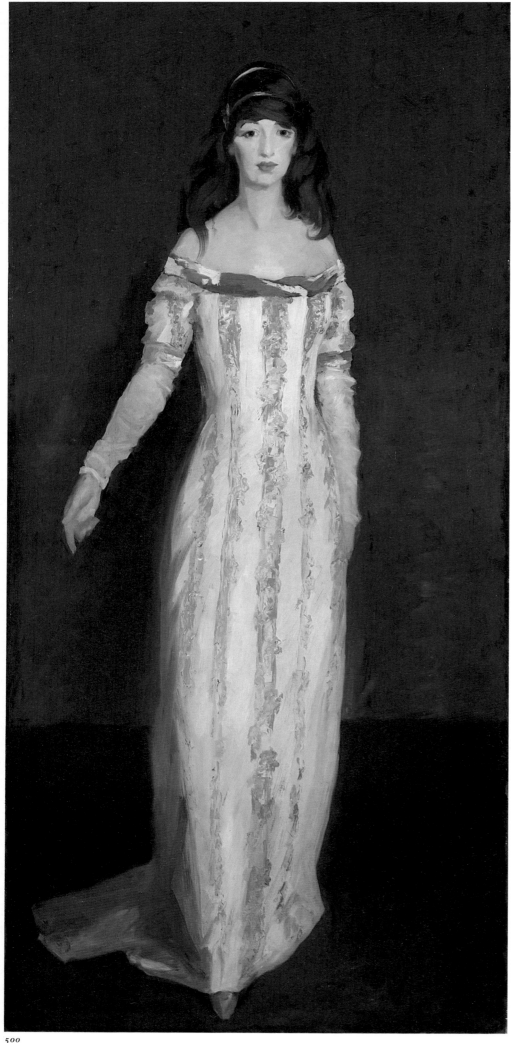

**Fig. 500. The Masquerade Dress: Portrait of Mrs. Robert Henri,** *by Robert Henri (1865–1929), 1911; oil on canvas, 76½ by 36¼ inches (194.2 by 92 cm.). Henri studied art both in Philadelphia and in Paris, becoming a force in the art world first of Philadelphia and later of New York. He had advanced notions about art and artists, believing that work of all kinds should be shown in exhibitions without the formality of jury selection. He was an original member of the group later known as the Ash Can school, whose members believed that beauty is everywhere, even among the ash cans of teeming big-city streets. This portrait of his wife is a more conventional subject, however. Striking in its verticality, emphasized by the stripes of Mrs. Henri's dress, and in its juxtaposition of dark and light, it has, as well, an oriental aspect.* Arthur Hoppock Hearn Fund, 1958 (58.157)

start, new and challenging forces were making themselves felt in American art. In 1908 eight artists showed their work at the Macbeth Gallery in New York; their exhibition was a revolt of sorts. They were all more or less familiar with advanced trends in European painting and with the work of the older Continental masters as well, but while they did not exile themselves in Paris or London, they did take issue with the current artistic trends of the academies. The Eight, as they named themselves and as they will probably always be called—Robert Henri, John Sloan, George Luks, Maurice Prendergast, Ernest Lawson, Everett Shinn, Arthur B. Davies, and William Glackens—were all individuals in their styles and techniques. They were determined that the artist should have freedom and opportunity to express his message in his own way and, for the most part, they saw in the ordinary person and the commonplace scene, even among the ash cans of the teeming cities, a poetry worthy of the artist's brush. It was their choice of subject matter rather than their technical approach that set them apart from the approved academic art of their time. Following Eakins's counsel to artists, they peered deep into the heart of American life to give vital meaning to their work. Several of them had been newspaper and magazine illustrators and were thus practiced in realistic portrayals of daily urban life as they came across it in the course of their reportorial rounds. Collectively they are commonly referred to as the "Ash Can

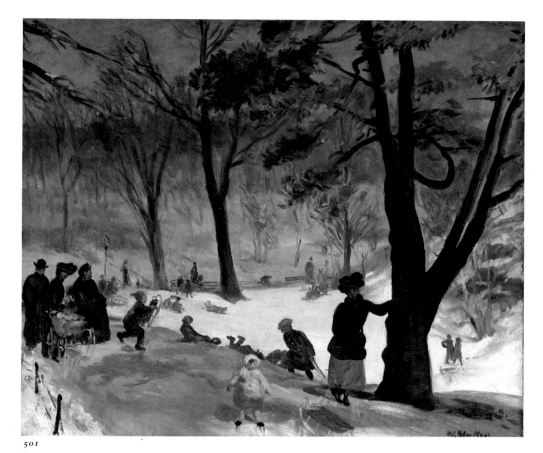

501

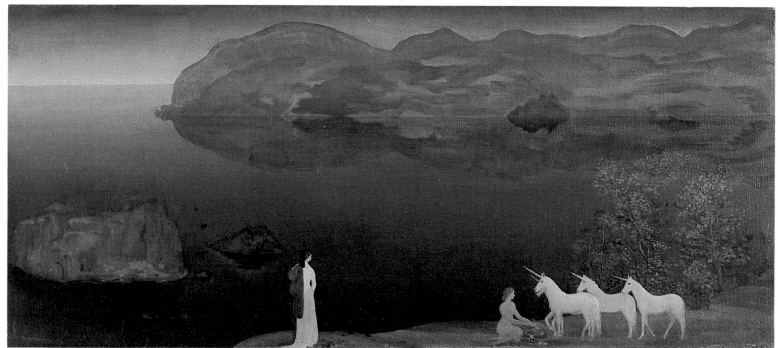

502

**Fig. 501. Central Park in Winter,** *by William James Glackens (1870–1938), 1905; oil on canvas, 25 by 30 inches (63.5 by 76.2 cm.).* "William Glackens," *wrote curator Henry Geldzahler,* "produced the most consistently happy paintings of his period." *Using approaches borrowed widely from American and French artists he admired, Glackens created this cheery view of activists and onlookers on a snowy day in Central Park. Applying small, feathery strokes in the manner of Renoir, the artist produced in this early period impressionistic scenes that focused on anecdotal details. Glackens was a graphic artist and illustrator whose only formal training took place in night classes. He worked for several newspapers during his career, meeting there such contemporaries as John Sloan, George Luks, and Everett Shinn, all eventual members of the iconoclastic group now known as The Eight.* George A. Hearn Fund, 1921 (21.164)

school," but, more accurately, they were New York realists.

Paintings by all eight of these men are represented in the Museum's collection. By no means were all their canvases devoted to street scenes. The catholicity they showed in their choices of subject matter, which drew some censure at the time, is revealed in numerous canvases, for example Henri's broadly painted *The Masquerade Dress* (Fig. 500), a portrait of his wife that reflects his admiration for Hals, Velázquez, and Manet.

**Fig. 502. Unicorns (Legend—Sea Calm),** *by Arthur B. Davies (1862–1928), 1906; oil on canvas, 18¼ by 40¼ inches (46.4 by 102.2 cm.). Davies studied art in Chicago and New York, and, like a number of other members of The Eight, worked as an illustrator. He is most famous for his early, dreamlike paintings, as seen in his masterpiece,* Unicorns. *Here the unreal, mythical aspects of Davies's inspiration are emphasized by the unicorns, imaginary creatures attended by equally unworldly maidens. The mountains and smooth, still water heighten the dreamy atmosphere. Davies exhibited with The Eight not because he shared his contemporaries' interest in the hurly-burly of city life, but because he believed* in more freedom to exhibit unconventional works. *He was a major organizer of the revolutionary Armory Show of 1913, presenting to his stunned countrymen the avant-garde styles of European artists.* Bequest of Lillie P. Bliss, 1931 (31.67.12)

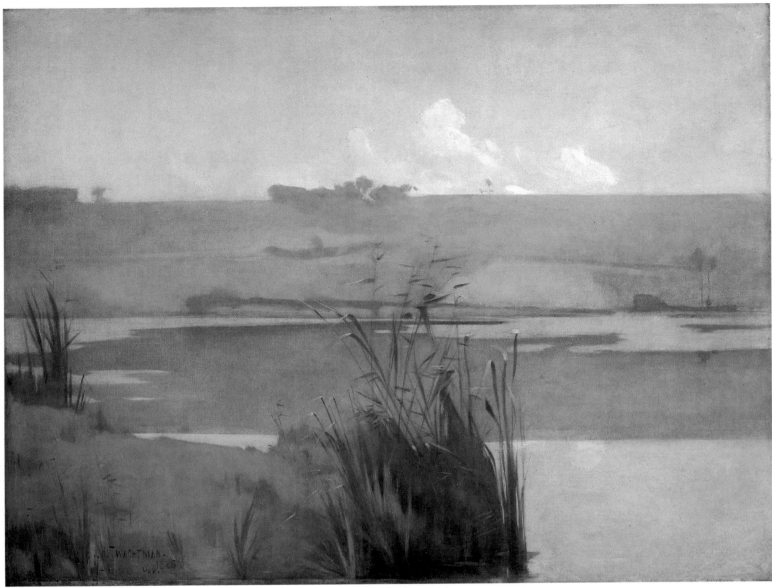

503

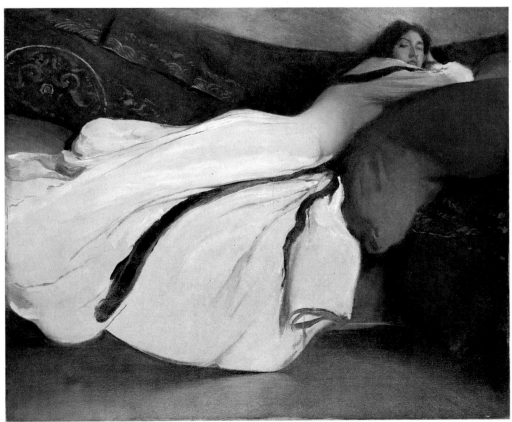

***Fig. 503.*** **Arques-la-Bataille,** *by John H. Twachtman (1853–1902), 1885; oil on canvas, 60 by 78⅞ inches (152.4 by 200.3 cm.). Twachtman was born in Cincinnati and began his career painting floral decorations on window shades in his father's business. He soon moved onward and upward, however, studying with Frank Duveneck and accompanying him to Munich to work there. He met, traveled with, and painted with many of the leading American artists of his generation, including Hassam, Robinson, and Chase. He executed this painting, his greatest work, from a sketch he made during an expedition to the Normandy coast. His interest in the landscape is decorative rather than literal: the strong horizontals, succeeding one another in strata of gray and green from the foreground to the background, are counteracted by clumps of reeds that provide strong, dark vertical accents.* Morris K. Jesup Fund, 1968 (68.52)

504

Central Park in Winter (Fig. 501), painted by Glackens in 1905, tells a happy anecdote of children sleighing. It was quickly apprehended, without resort to unnecessary detail. John Sloan's etching *Turning Out the Light* (Fig. 505) deals with an Ash Can subject—stressing everyday life in all its ordinariness or drabness. Joseph Pennell was a noted illustrator and printmaker who, though not a member of the Ash Can school, shared these urban painters' interest in the world around them—especially in the architecture of cities and factories. In *From Cortlandt Street Ferry* (Fig. 506) he captures the atmosphere of downtown Manhattan at night as it would have appeared to a passenger arriving at the Cortlandt Street slip on the ferry from New Jersey. In an entirely different vein, Arthur B. Davies's *Unicorns* (Fig. 502), probably his most famous work, presents a scene withdrawn from reality into a tranquil, lyrical world of the artist's imagination. The poetic symbolism is too dreamlike for explanation.

At the famous Armory Show of 1913, Arthur B. Davies and Walt Kuhn, with the assistance of other vanguard artists, staged a large exhibition of modern art, both American and foreign. The major impact of that great exhibition came not from the American work but from the international section where, for the first time, Americans at large experienced the shock of fauvism, cubism, expressionism, and other phases of abstract painting and sculpture as those movements had developed in Europe over the preceding twenty or thirty years. From then on, "modern art" became a phrase to conjure with in this country, a battle cry that continues to evoke strong feelings ranging from great enthusiasm to utter revulsion.

Throughout this discussion, we have seen American art develop from a tiny imported seedling into a robust, wide-branching growth of variegated character, constantly invigorated by grafts of alien strains, as it still is, but always sinking its roots deeper into native soil. In later years, American painting and sculpture have spread out in an almost bewildering variety of unprecedented forms. This country, particularly New York City, has become an international capital of art; what is done here is at its best widely accepted as a standard of performance.

**Fig. 504. Repose,** *by John White Alexander (1856–1915), 1895; oil on canvas, 52¼ by 63⅝ inches (132.7 by 161.6 cm.). This daring portrait is one in a series of figure studies that stress the long, sinuous, sensuous lines of the female figure. But like so much work of this period, the design is the important thing, and the figure simply a means to that end. In emphasizing elongated flowing lines, Alexander was reflecting the influence of the Art Nouveau movement. He lived in Paris during the 1890s and belonged to a circle of prominent artists, poets, and writers that included Whistler, Henry James, and Oscar Wilde.*
Gift of Irina A. Reed, 1980 (1980.224)

**Fig. 505. Turning Out the Light,** *by John Sloan (1871–1951), 1906; etching, 5 by 7 inches (12.7 by 17.8 cm.). Sloan moved from Philadelphia to New York City in 1904, and applied his considerable talents as an etcher to the city scene. Turning Out the Light is one of his "New York City Life" series, in which ordinary people are seen leading ordinary lives. The commonness of such subjects offended many people who were used to thinking of art as dealing only with conventional subjects, such as landscapes or people carefully posed in their Sunday best. Sloan's dedication to realism lasted throughout his lifetime, though he shifted his interests from time to time in the kind of realism he portrayed. When the Armory Show revealed the state of art in Europe—cubism, abstraction, for example—Sloan's approach seemed conventional by contrast.*
Gift of Gertrude Vanderbilt Whitney, 1926 (26.30.16)

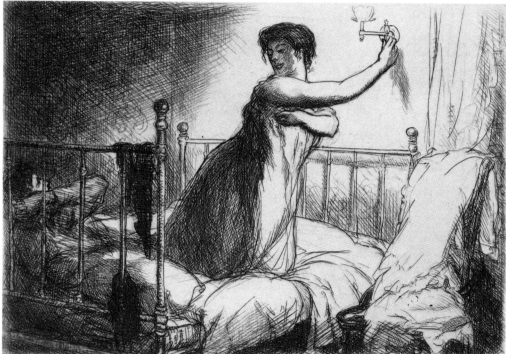

505

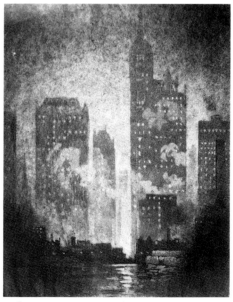

506

**Fig. 506. From Cortlandt Street Ferry,** *by Joseph Pennell (1857–1926), 1908; sandpaper mezzotint, 12¹⁵⁄₁₆ by 9¹³⁄₁₆ inches (32.9 by 24.9 cm.). The artist, who became well known both at home and abroad, was a great friend and admirer of Whistler, and his work was often compared to that of the older artist. Here, in a shadowy night scene reminiscent of Whistler's, Pennell captures the excitement of New York on a rainy night—shimmering light and rain fall between the skyscrapers towering in the foreground, creating a path on the water in front of the oncoming ferry. After the First World War, Pennell settled in New York and established the graphics department at the Art Students League.*
Harris Brisbane Dick Fund, 1917 (17.3.799)

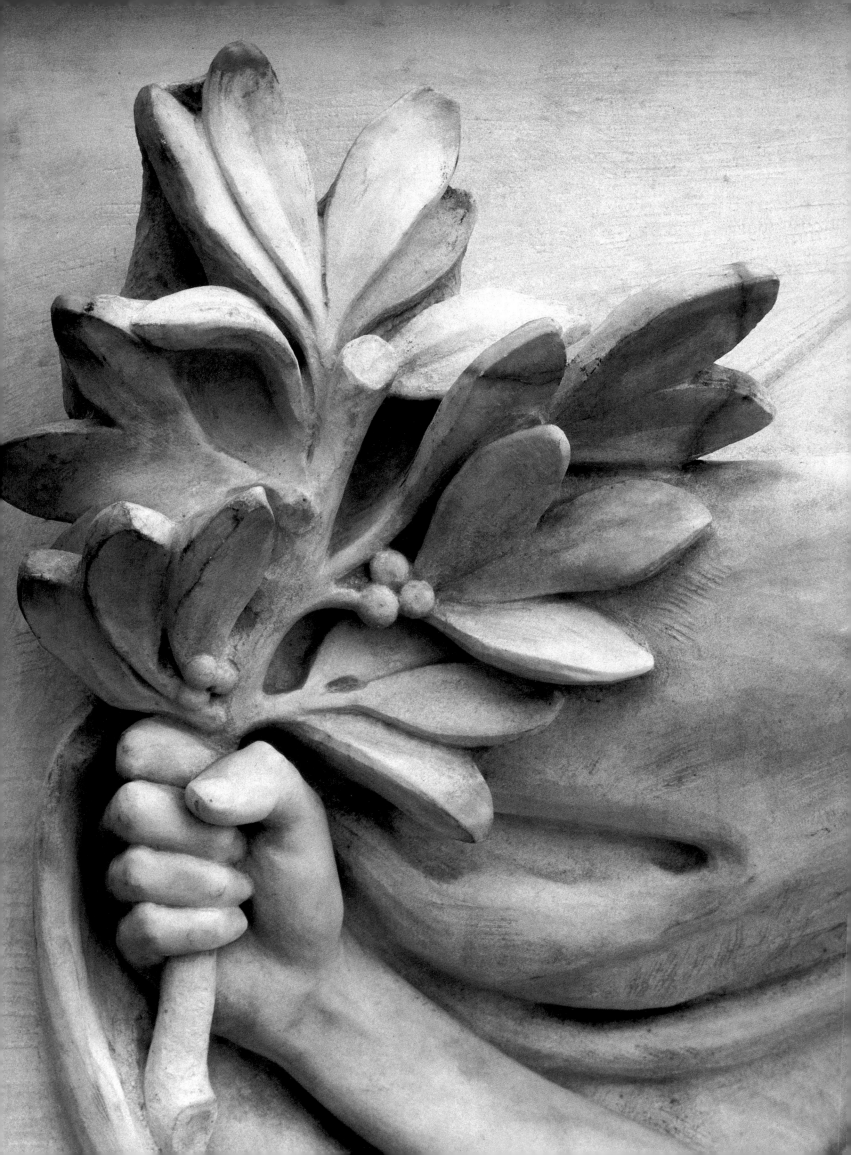

# SCULPTURE

**Fig. 507.** Detail, Mourning Victory, by Daniel
Chester French, see Fig. 519.

# The Colonial and Federal Periods
## 1630–1830

The earliest American sculptors were the skilled woodworkers who in the seventeenth and eighteenth centuries specialized in the ornamental carvings that grace some of the finest examples of furniture in The American Wing collection. Men of similar talents provided figureheads for colonial vessels and occasionally portrait busts and allegorical figures of somewhat primitive character. To these pioneering artists should be added the stonecutters who worked their grim designs on early tombstones.

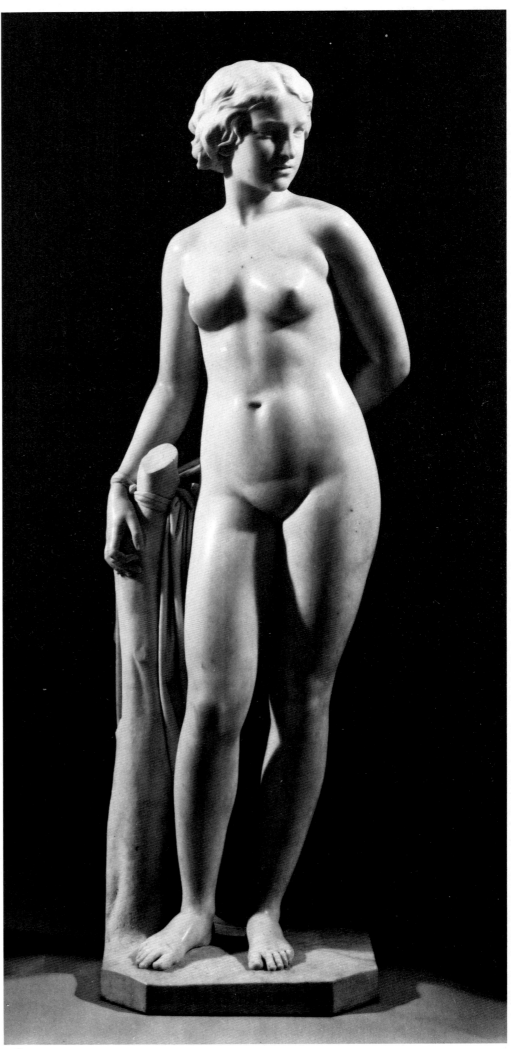

*Fig. 508.* **The White Captive,** *by Erastus Dow Palmer (1817–1904), 1859; marble, height 66 inches (167.6 cm.). While many of his countrymen were going abroad to study sculpture, Palmer remained at home working, for the most part, on American subjects. The White Captive was apparently inspired by stories of abductions of white settlers by the Indians. One critic said that it was among the finest sculptures created in America up to that time, and went on, ". . . nothing so fine had come over the seas from Italy; nothing so original, so dramatic, so human; nothing that could approach it even in charm of workmanship."*
Bequest of Hamilton Fish, 1894 (94.93)

508

# The Mid-Nineteenth Century, 1840–65

Then, in the second third of the nineteenth century an American school of marble sculpture came into sudden and unexpected bloom. The United States had emerged from the War of 1812—the second war for independence, as it has been called—with a self-consciousness and self-confidence that mounted over time. Those were years of ascendant democracy in this country, leading to the election of Andrew Jackson as president in 1828. Americans were eager to identify their own personal and political virtues with those of the republics of antiquity. Among other things, sympathy for contemporary Greeks who, in the 1820s, were engaged in a war of independence from Turkish domination, added zest to an admiration for ancient Greek models and the Roman copies and adaptations they inspired.

It was in Italy that ancient sculptures and copies of them could be seen and studied with profit, and these strongly influenced the first American sculptors who went there to practice their art. Most of these "Yankee stonecutters" went to Italy for experience and guidance, and a number of them remained. There good marble was abundant and wages of expert stonecutters were low. The aspiring sculptor could give a plaster model to a local craftsman and depend upon him to chisel a faithful replica in enduring marble, an operation often not within the capacity of the original artist. It was just one further advantage that in Italy artists could model nudes without suffering the social criticism that greeted such exposures in America—at least unless they were presented in the guise of figures of some acceptable allegorical significance rather than simply as attractive naked fe-

males. As late as the 1860s one French visitor to the United States observed that, generally speaking, the depiction of a woman's natural form was "not permitted . . . beyond the head and the extremities."

A graceful life-size marble nude with decidedly allegorical trappings is *The White Captive* (Fig. 508), fashioned by Erastus Dow Palmer in the neoclassical style—a mode remarkably popular throughout the Western world in the middle years of the last century. Palmer, a self-taught New Yorker, never went abroad for study. He worked from living models, often one of his daughters, and although this was his first attempt at such a subject, *The White Captive* remains one of the finest of its kind made in America in the last century. It seems to have been inspired by tales of the Indians' captives along the colonial frontier, and it quickly won nationwide attention.

When Vermont-born Hiram Powers left for Italy in 1837, John Quincy Adams composed a bit of doggerel urging the artist to:

Go forth, and rival Greece's art sublime;
Return, and bid the statesmen of thy land
Live in thy marble through all after-time!

Powers never did return to America; he spent most of his professional career in Florence, where he acquired an international reputation. His bust of *President Andrew Jackson* (Fig. 509) is a characteristic and outstanding instance of the American approach to portraiture—a solidly realistic likeness in a neoclassic manner. In 1835 Powers modeled the grizzled, toothless, sixty-eight-year-old war veteran and president to the life, as Jackson had requested. And in 1837 he cut the marble version in Italy.

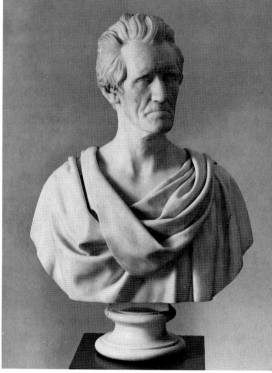

509

**Fig. 509. President Andrew Jackson,** *by Hiram Powers (1805–73), 1837; marble, height 34½ inches (87.6 cm.). Powers considered this moving portrait of Andrew Jackson to be one of his finest works. He was at first reluctant to show the president as he looked at age sixty-eight, but Jackson admonished him, "Make me as I am, Mr. Powers, and be true to nature always. . . . I have no desire to look young as long as I feel old. . . ." Powers carved Jackson's bust in marble himself instead of handing the plaster model over to an Italian stonecutter, as was customary in those days.*
Gift of Mrs. Frances V. Nash, 1894 (94.14)

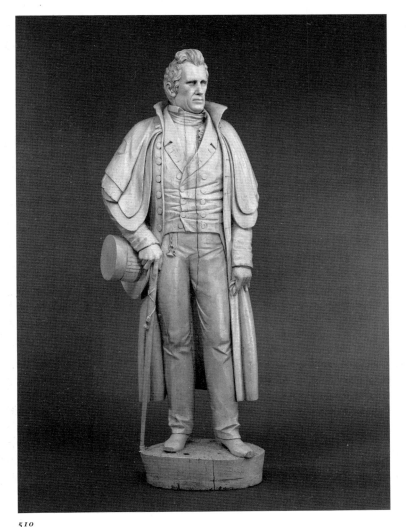

510

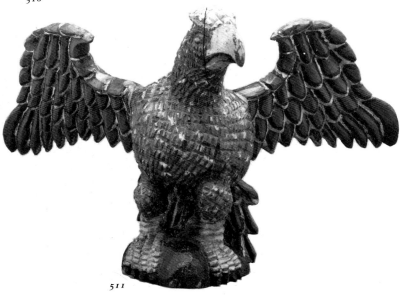

511

**Fig. 512. Cleopatra,** *by William Wetmore Story (1819–95), 1858, this version 1869; marble, height 54½ inches (138.4 cm.). The public that received this statue of Cleopatra with such enthusiasm was interested at least as much in historical and story-telling aspects of works of art as they were in artistic technique and insight. Here Story presents Cleopatra brooding on her life as she faces her death. The glamour of this beautiful and powerful queen's life—the intrigues and stormy affairs—was fascinating to romantically minded Victorians. But didacticism was equally important, and the fact that Cleopatra's recklessly romantic way of life led to her downfall is an important part of the message here.*
Gift of John Taylor Johnson, 1888 (88.5)

Powers's contemporaries ranked him with the greatest sculptors of antiquity and the Renaissance—a judgment that today seems more than extravagant, simply absurd. However that may be, it reminds us that we all too often tend to use the present as an absolute standard for judging the past—a tendency that reduces much that qualified contemporaries once deemed important to the level of seeming merely quaint. This is also absurd for, properly understood, no achievement of the past remains merely quaint. As we are frequently reminded, viewing the past perceptively and for its own sake may lead to better ways of evaluating the present. We can thus, at least, hope to escape from what the late Bertrand Russell referred to as "the parochialism of time." It is one of the large purposes of the Museum, with its enormously varied collections, to provide this escape.

It might be noted in passing that Powers was something more than an artist. To the end of his days he remained as well an "ingenious Yankee mechanic"—an inventor of tools, instruments, and machines that worked well. He was also a strangely farsighted visionary who discussed with his friend Nathaniel Hawthorne the practicalities of an improved plan for laying transatlantic cables, and who prophesied the feasibility of flying machines and the possibility of life on distant planets. Beyond that, he was handsome and a superb conversationalist. Such an uncommon combination of attributes won him the close and cherished friendship of, among others, Robert and Elizabeth Barrett Browning, who knew him in Florence. (Mrs. Browning once observed that his eyes were so commanding that she won-

**Fig. 510. Andrew Jackson,** *by William H. Rumney (1837–1927), about 1860; pine, painted, height 78¼ inches (198.8 cm.). This life-size portrait of the seventh president shows him at his most commanding and dignified, and makes a fine contrast to Powers's portrait. The sculptor was a ship's-figurehead carver, and his work is bold and direct, as a figurehead has to be. Ordered by a prominent shipwright to stand before his East Boston home, the figure is painted white to simulate marble. The pose is taken from a painting of Jackson by Ralph E. W. Earl.*
Purchase, Rogers Fund, The J. M. Kaplan Fund, Inc. and Mrs. Frederick A. Stoughton Gifts, Harris Brisbane Dick and Louis V. Bell Funds, 1978 (1978.57)

**Fig. 511. Eagle,** *attributed to Wilhelm Schimmel (1817–90), nineteenth century; wood, painted, height 12 inches (30.5 cm.). Schimmel's life was as colorful as his carvings. Though details remain sketchy, he is believed to have wandered about the countryside in Cumberland County, Pennsylvania, paying for his food and drink with his carvings. His eagles, produced with a jackknife, smoothed with bits of broken glass, and painted with whatever colors Schimmel could obtain, have a rugged and vigorous liveliness that is lacking in many other wooden toys.*
Gift of Mrs. Robert W. de Forest, 1934 (34.100.169)

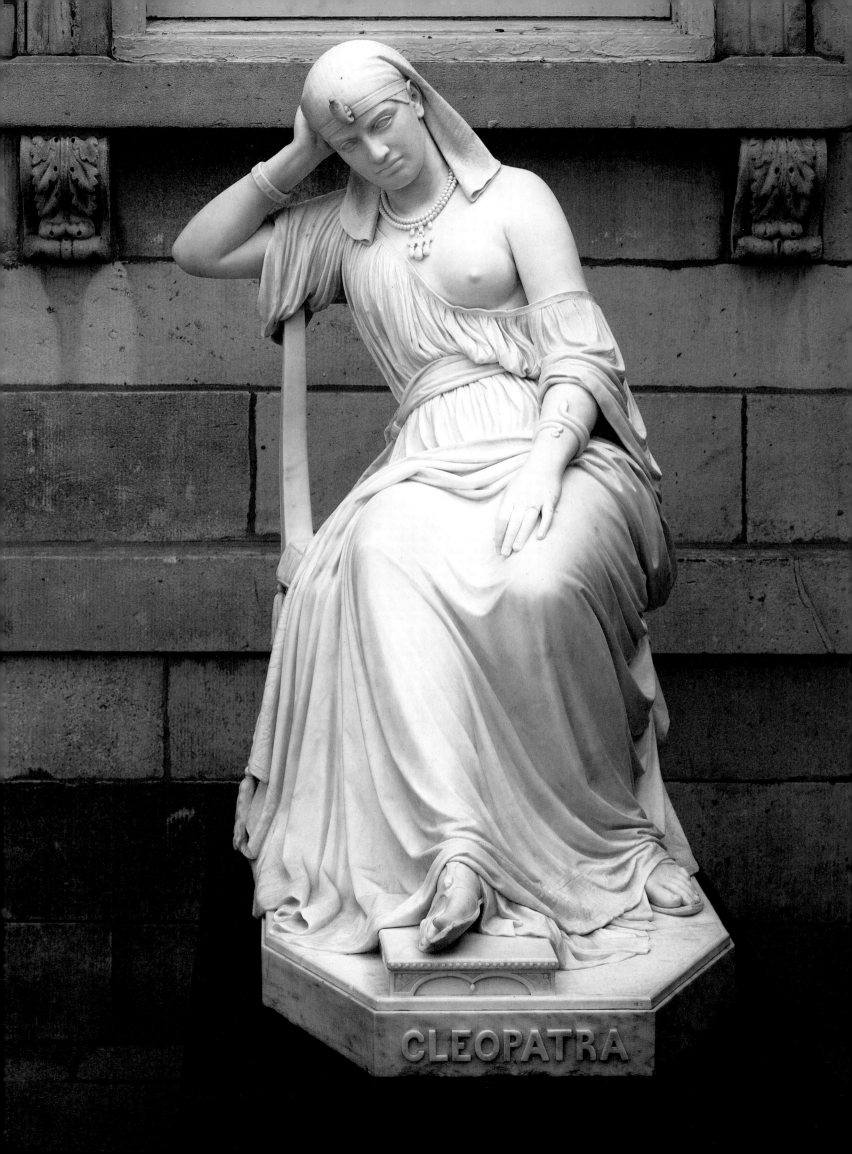

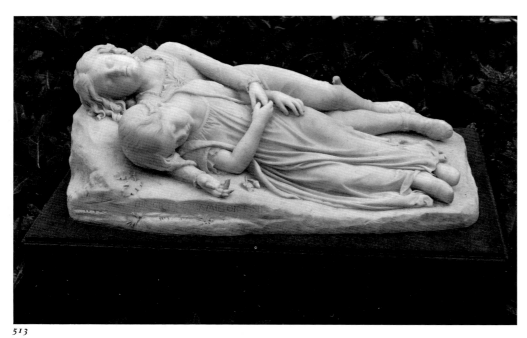

513

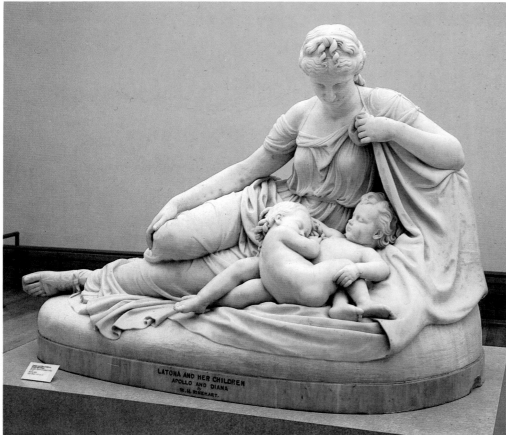

514

dered "if they claved the marble without the help of his hands.")

While most American sculptors were flocking to Italy to have their works chiseled in marble, stay-at-home craftsmen were turning out an abundance of figures carved in wood. Their free-standing portraits are far less numerous than likenesses painted on canvas or paper, but they include examples that are vigorous statements of personality. These efforts have been referred to as "country whittling developed to a fine art." Thus the rugged, almost forbidding presence of Andrew Jackson is strongly expressed in the full-length portrait of the warrior-president carved by one William Rumney (Fig. 510). An interesting comparison can be made between this figure and Hiram Powers's marble bust of Jackson. Another, much more primitive but equally effective, wooden figure is that of a painted eagle by Wilhelm Schimmel. For some years after the Civil War, this itinerant German immigrant whittled toys and mantel ornaments for the inhabitants of snug Cumberland County, Pennsylvania, farmhouses. The businesslike eagle seen here (Fig. 511) is typical of Schimmel's many carvings of the national bird.

Thomas Crawford and William Wetmore Story, both of good family and with influential social and political associations, turned to the practice of sculpture as young men. Working largely in Rome, they earned enviable reputations in the years immediately preceding the Civil War. A typical nineteenth-century romantic, Story infused his subjects with literary allusions. He was a friend of Nathaniel Hawthorne, who described him as a "perplexing variety of talents and accomplishments— . . . being a

**Fig. 515. Indian Hunter,** *by John Quincy Adams Ward (1830–1910), 1860; bronze, height 16 inches (40.6 cm.). Ward was one of the first sculptors to choose American, rather than European, training and to concentrate on native American subjects. By 1849 he was studying with Henry Kirke Brown of Brooklyn, and in 1861 he established his own studio;* Indian Hunter *was his first independent work. His choice of subject and his realistic rendering of the Indian and his dog signified Ward's rejection of fashionable neoclassical treatments, and the work was enthusiastically received by the press. Eleven small statues like this have so far been discovered. A large version, made after Ward journeyed to the Dakotas to observe Indians at first hand, was commissioned by a group of New Yorkers and presented to Central Park—the first sculpture to be placed there.*
Morris K. Jesup Fund, 1973 (1973.257)

poet, a prose writer, a lawyer, a painter, a musician, and a sculptor." In *The Marble Faun*, published in 1860, Hawthorne described Story's seated figure of *Cleopatra* (Fig. 512), giving it a wide popularity among American and English novel readers. Crawford's *The Babes in the Wood* also has a literary association. It illustrates verses from an old English nursery rhyme of the same title that was widely popular with Victorian sentimentalists, some of whom seem to have shed tears at the sight of Crawford's evocation of the subject (Fig. 513).

American sculptors were still going to Italy to study and work and, often enough, to live out their professional lives. William Henry Rinehart, who had early been apprenticed as a stonecutter in a Maryland quarry and settled permanently in Rome in 1858, became one of the best of his generation. At the time of his death in 1874, he was still at work on the marble group of *Latona*, goddess of the night, with Apollo and Diana, her children by Jupiter, which was completed later (Fig. 514). Although still in the neoclassic mode, Rinehart's work shows a regard for realism that was in keeping with the stylistic developments of post–Civil War times.

The increasing trend toward realism was carried a long step forward by John Quincy Adams Ward in his bronze *Indian Hunter* (Fig. 515), depicting a stalking brave with his hunting dog. Ward completed the work in 1860 following a trip west to study native Indians on their own heath. A few years later, an enlarged version of this statuette was placed in Central Park, where it may still be seen.

*The Falling Gladiator* (Fig. 516) is one of several works by William Rimmer

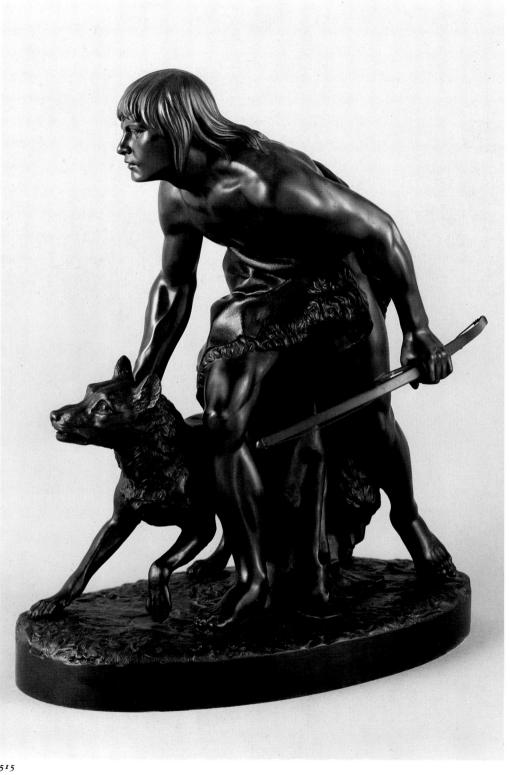

515

owned by the Museum. Rimmer, another largely self-taught artist, was a practicing doctor without artistic training or a professional degree; he began the serious pursuit of sculpture at the age of about forty-five. When the original plaster model of this bronze was exhibited at Paris in 1862, the striking realism of the anatomy, which contrasted remarkably with conventionally modeled forms of the day, led to the unjust criticism that the figure was cast from life. Aside from this, Rimmer was neglected as an artist in his lifetime, except by a few perceptive critics. In 1864 one of the latter, James Jackson Jarves, contrasted the powerful realism and originality of Rimmer's work with what he considered the sentimental prettiness and lack of technical distinction in the efforts of Crawford, Powers, and the whole group of expatriot American sculptors of the time.

Rimmer was an unusual figure in the history of American art. In addition to being a physician and a sculptor, he was a teacher, a writer, and, as one critic described him, "the strangest historical painter of the American mid-century, and possibly the one possessed of the greatest inborn genius." His paintings, like his sculpture, represent tense, dramatic action, anguish, and struggle. His father seriously believed himself to be the son of the Lost Dauphin, a delusion that was visited on his son and must have haunted his imagination. (John James Audubon apparently believed that *he* was that mysterious princeling, but neither claim can be taken seriously.) When Rimmer died in 1874 one of his former students, the famous sculptor Daniel Chester French, wrote: "The poor long-suffering doctor! His was an unhappy and unsuccessful life. He just missed being great."

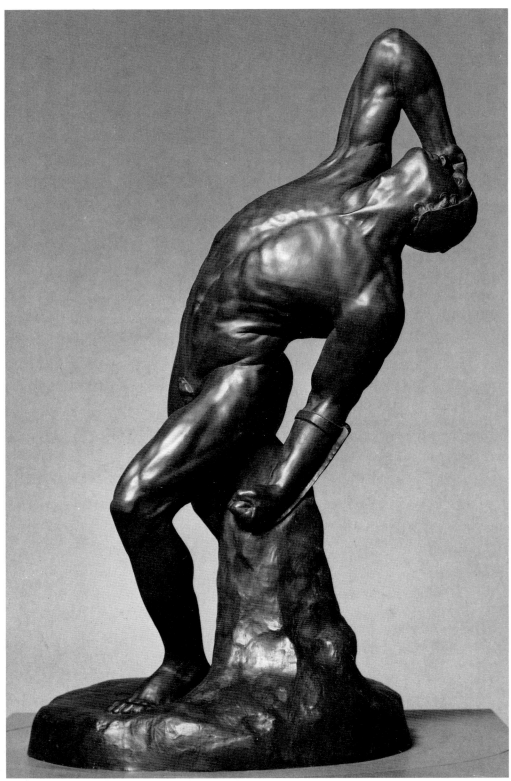

516

**Fig. 516. The Falling Gladiator,** *by William Rimmer (1816–79), 1861, this cast 1907; bronze, height 62¾ inches (159.4 cm.). William Rimmer was a physician by profession, with no training in the art of sculpture. He pursued his avocation in time stolen from a full medical practice, carving this extraordinarily vivid portrait from clay in an unheated basement. With no model but himself, Rimmer achieved an anatomically accurate expression of the agony of a powerful gladiator who has just been delivered a stunning—killing—blow. The figure was sent to Paris for exhibition in 1863 and attracted a good deal of attention, though the public was so unfamiliar with such expressive realism as that created by the gladiator's straining muscles that it refused to believe that Rimmer could have made the figure without the aid of a cast taken from a human body.*
Rogers Fund, 1907 (07.224)

# The Late Nineteenth and Early Twentieth Centuries 1865–1915

Events and circumstances attending the Civil War loosed titanic forces in the United States, forces that in a remarkably short time imposed a new order on American society and culture, as they did on our economy and politics. To the saviors of the Union all things seemed possible. New enterprises were undertaken on an unprecedented scale, and new leaders arose from the ranks of industrial, civil, and military life. The public monuments that were raised to these prominent figures were cast in bronze to withstand exposure to the out-of-doors in all seasons. The romantic idealization of earlier years gave way to a forthright naturalism in the post–Civil War years. Contemporary costumes, realistically rendered, replaced the classical togas of prewar sculptures.

In the last decades of the nineteenth century, America seemed more than ever a land of unlimited opportunities. Here was a world of bigger, more crowded cities, a world that beckoned to great hordes of immigrants, each with a golden gleam in his eye. Business and industry were reorganized as mammoth corporations were planned and inaugurated. Agriculture itself was becoming a big business. With its wheatlands and cattle ranges, the United States had become the world's greatest single source of food. New fortunes were made; old ones increased—and some were lost in extravagant speculations. It was the period of unbridled acquisitiveness and corrupt practices that Mark Twain branded the "Gilded Age." Men of great wealth but often of limited cultural background spent lavishly on their mansions and art collections.

Meanwhile, American sculptors turned away from Florence and Rome to Paris as the capital of art, to study there

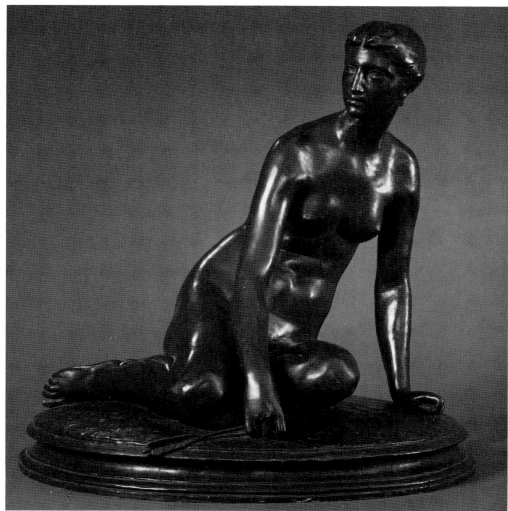

517

*Fig. 517.* **Diana,** *by Olin Levi Warner (1844–96), 1887; bronze, height 23½ inches (59.7 cm.). Unlike Rimmer's tortured gladiator, Warner's smoothly modeled Diana conveys a sense of serenity. Warner's training also differed from that of the self-taught Rimmer, for he had gone to Paris to study at the prestigious Ecole des Beaux-Arts and had there absorbed the sophisticated neoclassicism conveyed by this figure. Warner's* Diana *is not without vitality, however; the huntress turns, startled in the midst of her bath by the approach of Actaeon. In the words of critic Charles Caffin, her pose reflects the "suspense between absolute repose and projected movement."* Gift of National Sculpture Society, 1898 (98.9.5)

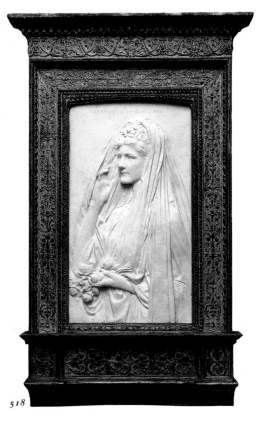

518

*Fig. 518. Mrs. Stanford White, by Augustus Saint-Gaudens (1848–1907), 1884; marble, 23 by 12¾ inches (58.4 by 32.4 cm.). This bas-relief portrait of Mrs. Stanford White was a wedding gift from the sculptor to the bridegroom. Mrs. White is portrayed in her wedding dress, and Saint-Gaudens has heightened the bridal effect by choosing to model her in delicate low relief on pure white marble. Both the sculptor's training at the Ecole des Beaux-Arts in Paris, where lively and decorative classicism was taught, and his admiration for sculpture of the early Renaissance are apparent here. Saint-Gaudens often worked with White on decorating houses designed by the latter's firm, McKim, Mead, and White, and the eminent architect collaborated with the celebrated sculptor again by designing the Renaissance Revival frame that encloses this portrait.*
Gift of Erving Wolf Foundation, 1976 (1976.388)

*Fig. 519. Mourning Victory, by Daniel Chester French (1850–1931), 1915; marble, height 146 inches (370.8 cm.). This figure of Victory in mourning was created as the central focus of* The Melvin Memorial, *erected in Concord, Massachusetts, in 1909 as a tribute to the three Melvin brothers who had died in the Civil War. Their surviving brother commissioned the monument, and then expressed his approval and appreciation of the completed work by ordering this reduced version as a gift to the Metropolitan Museum, of which the sculptor was a trustee. Considered one of French's masterpieces, the figure of Victory seems to be emerging from the depths of the marble she is carved from. She lifts an American flag from her forehead and carries laurel leaves in her right hand, signifying both the heroism of dying for one's country and the victory that resulted from the deaths of martyred soldiers like the three Melvin brothers.*
Gift of James C. Melvin, 1912 (15.75)

at the Ecole des Beaux-Arts and in the studios of Parisian sculptors. Among the first was Olin Levi Warner, who modeled the tranquil seated *Diana* (Fig. 517). Although Warner was gifted and well trained by his French teachers, his work was not immediately appreciated by his countrymen. Just as it was beginning to catch on, he was killed in a bicycle accident in Central Park. Among Warner's friends when he studied in Paris was Augustus Saint-Gaudens. As early as 1867, at the age of nineteen, this artist had left his New York home for a three-year stay in France and a further sojourn in Italy. The son of a French shoemaker, Saint-Gaudens was born in Ireland and brought to America as an infant. After his European experiences he returned to this country to become undisputed leader of the first generation of American artists in the Beaux-Arts tradition. With his suave and powerful style he revitalized the current trend of naturalism. The richly modeled surfaces of his compositions and their restrained, elegant designs, and the sure felicity with which he integrated a variety of arts, brought him fame surpassing that of any other American sculptor.

Indeed, Saint-Gaudens was a towering figure in the American art world of the late nineteenth century and was showered with commissions and honors. The Museum owns several dozen examples of his work in relief and in the round, a number of them portraits of such personages as Robert Louis Stevenson, Admiral Farragut, General Sherman, and others, in addition to allegorical figures designed largely for public monuments. Among the latter group is a replica of his figure of Diana, goddess of the hunt (see Fig. 6), designed in 1892 as a weather vane for the

tower of the old Madison Square Garden; it was the only nude Saint-Gaudens ever produced, a memorable but unapproachable figure. Equally remote is the low-relief profile of Mrs. Stanford White (Fig. 518), sensitively carved in marble and beautifully framed by her husband, the famed architect.

In 1881–82, in collaboration with John La Farge, another artist who enjoyed a high reputation at the time, Saint-Gaudens fashioned the monumental marble and mosaic mantelpiece shown against the eastern wall of the courtyard. This was originally installed in the entrance hall of the Cornelius Vanderbilt mansion at the corner of Fifth Avenue and Fifty-seventh Street, when that New York neighborhood was burgeoning with palatial homes of the very rich. Peace and Love, Saint-Gaudens's two heroic caryatids carved of Numidian marble, support a lintel over which is a mosaic designed by La Farge. On either side of La Farge's central figure is a Latin inscription that reads, in translation: "The house at its threshold gives evidence of the master's good will. Welcome to the guest who arrives; farewell and helpfulness to him who departs." La Farge was a highly respected artist in his lifetime, and his work in mosaic represents but one facet of his talent. Among other things, he was a superb muralist. (His *Ascension* in the Church of the Ascension in New York was considered by some the greatest contemporary painting of its kind produced anywhere.) Although La Farge had studied painting with William Morris Hunt, a devotee of the Barbizon school and an important influence on many of his countrymen through his paintings in that style, La Farge developed his own manner of painting. He once wrote, "I wished to

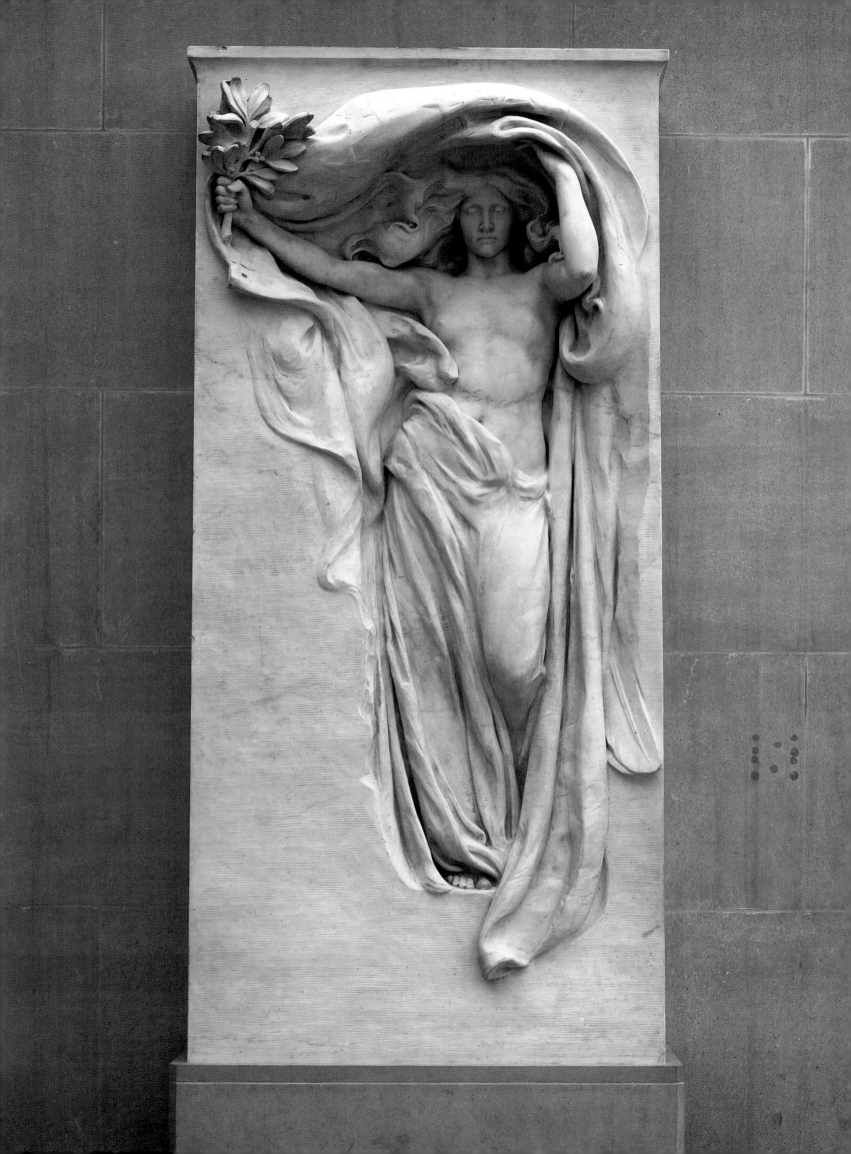

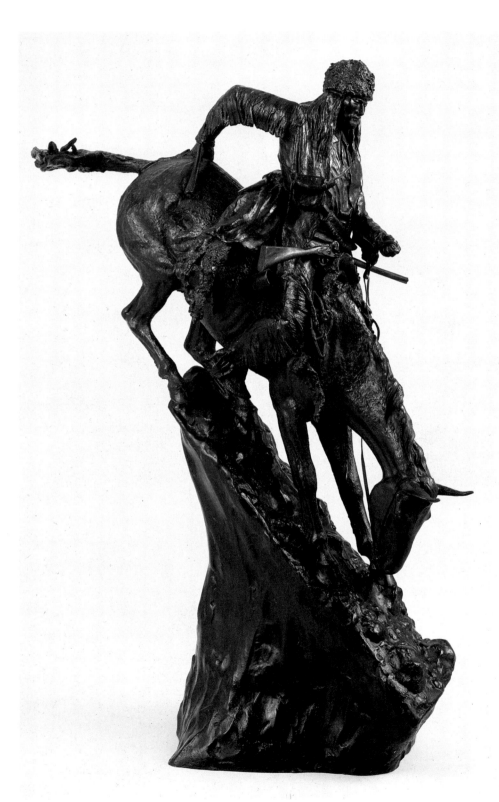

520

apply principles of light and color . . . to indicate very carefully in every part, the exact time of day and circumstance of light." Today he is best remembered as the first American master of the fusion of decorative art and architecture. Before Tiffany, he worked with stained glass as no American had before him. His "Welcome" window (see Fig. 409), completed in 1909 and now on display in the southwest corner of the courtyard, has been termed one of the crowning achievements of his career. In it, his passionate interest in light and color came into full play.

The only contemporary sculptor to approach Saint-Gaudens's fame was Daniel Chester French, who had once studied anatomy with Rimmer. His approach to art was relatively conservative and upheld the academic tradition of his time with elegant style. French's Melvin Memorial, commonly known as *Mourning Victory* (Fig. 519), is a marble copy of a monument he created in 1909 as a memorial to three brothers of the Melvin family who had died in the Civil War and who were buried in Sleepy Hollow Cemetery, Concord, Massachusetts, where French's original marks their graves.

French enjoyed a long and illustrious professional career: in 1873, when he was in his early twenties and far from proven as an artist, he was commissioned to execute the bronze statue of the minuteman that still stands in Concord. It won him immediate fame, and forty-eight long years later he created the statue of Abraham Lincoln for the famous memorial to that president at Washington.

In the final decades of the last century the American West was completing an epic cycle. The frontier, so long a sig-

**Fig. 521. Dancer and Gazelles**, *by Paul Manship (1885–1966), 1916; bronze, height 32¼ inches (81.9 cm.). Studying in Rome and Greece, Manship was much influenced by Renaissance and archaic Greek sculpture. Here the woman, stylized yet sinuously shaped, is flanked by two gazelles whose arching curves echo the curves of her body. Manship's work in this decorative two-dimensional vein became popular, and he executed numerous commissions for well-known and wealthy patrons, including the Metropolitan Museum.*
Purchase, Bequest of Francis Lathrop, 1959 (59.54)

**Fig. 522. The Peacocks**, *by Gaston Lachaise (1882–1935), about 1918, this cast 1922; gilded bronze, height 23¼ inches (59.1 cm.). Lachaise's use of three interrelated forms whose shapes repeat and reinforce one another is similar to that of Manship (for whom he worked as assistant for several years) in* Dancer and Gazelles. *In creating and sustaining a delicate balance, Lachaise exhibits here the skill that seems even more remarkable in his monumental women (on which he was working at the same time that he was producing such animal sculptures as* Peacocks). *Although he was born in Paris and attended the Ecole des Beaux-Arts, Lachaise eventually abandoned the academic tradition in* favor of a more abstract expressiveness. Here the mood is one of decorative elegance.
Gift of H. N. Slater, 1950 (50.173)

nificant feature of American experience, was officially declared closed in 1890. With some good reason Frederic Sackrider Remington considered himself *the* artist-reporter of the rapidly vanishing ways of life along these vast borderlands where army troopers, cowboys, and Indians acted out the finale of an almost legendary drama. His action-charged paintings remain a vivid guide for those who try to visualize the passing of the Wild West. Theodore Roosevelt predicted that the cowboys would live for all time in the bronze figures of Remington, such as *The Mountain Man* (Fig. 520).

*Struggle of the Two Natures in Man* (see Fig. 7), a freestanding group cut in marble by George Grey Barnard, depicts the divine nature of man casting off his earthly self and reaching for the heavens. Like Saint-Gaudens, Barnard studied at the Ecole des Beaux-Arts, and like Saint-Gaudens he worked in a naturalistic vein. However, his typical subjects show no influence from academic French styles. Rather, they express a passionate romanticism and a rebellious disregard for the canons of art observed by his conservative contemporaries. His *Two Natures* is a dramatic work, with figures considerably larger than life-size. It clearly reveals his admiration for the sculptures of Michelangelo and of Auguste Rodin, Barnard's somewhat older French contemporary and another highly independent spirit. Barnard was a poor and lonely young student in Paris when he modeled this monumental composition in 1891. When the marble version (which he cut himself) was first shown to the public in 1894, it was highly praised by French critics. Predictably, Rodin was among the many who admired the work

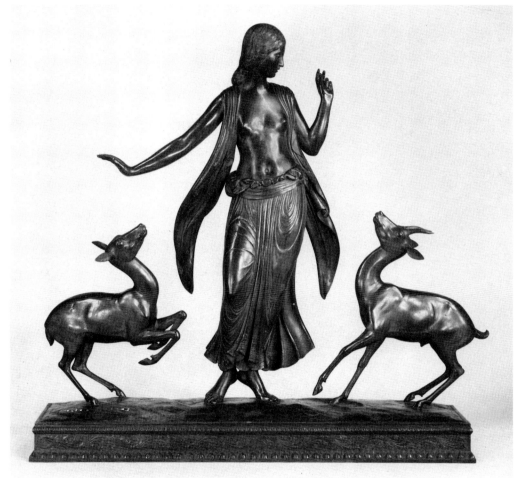

521

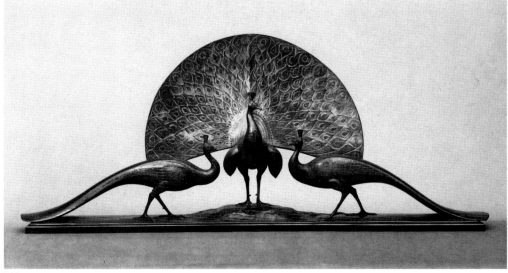

522

**Fig. 523. Figure of Dignity—Irish Mountain Goat,** *by John Bernard Flannagan (1895–1942), granite and aluminum, about 1932; height 53¾ inches with base (136.5 cm.). Largely self-taught, Flannagan progressed from wood to stone carving. He liked to work in the country, selecting stones from the fields and letting their shapes suggest his sculptures. In* Mountain Goat, *the animal and the stone are literally fused, each giving meaning to the other. The rough texture of the granite emphasizes the nature of both the stone and of the hardy mountain goat that arises from it. The cast-aluminum horns that contribute markedly to the effectiveness of the sculpture are a witty touch.*
Gift of The Alexander Shilling Fund, 1941 (41.47)

**Fig. 524. Mother and Child,** *by William Zorach (1889–1966), about 1930; marble, height 65 inches (165.1 cm.). Although he exhibited Fauvist paintings at the 1913 Armory Show, by the 1920s Zorach had decided to concentrate on sculpture. He was among the first (along with Flannagan) to revive the direct-carving method of sculpture, in which the artist works directly on the stone from start to finish with no intermediate models. Here the intertwined figures of mother and child provide an intricate interplay of line and mass. As John Baur wrote in the catalogue to an exhibition of Zorach's works at the Whitney Museum, "the flowing progression of the main forms and of the spaces between them, the relaxed turn of heads and bodies all lead the eye around the piece, up and down, forward and backward with a slow and fugue-like rhythm."*
Fletcher Fund, 1952 (52.143)

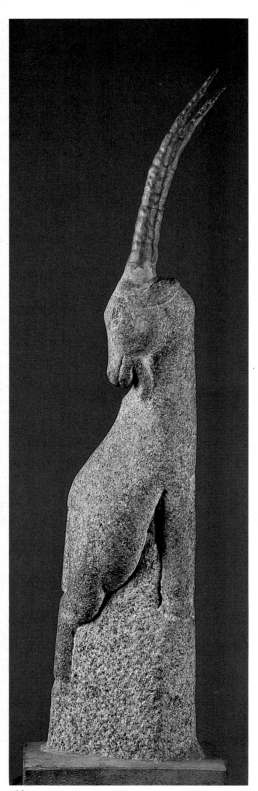

523

and were impressed by its expressive powers. Barnard was just thirty-one years old at the time. In later years he formed a collection of medieval French stonework that became the nucleus of The Cloisters, the Metropolitan Museum's collection of medieval art at Fort Tryon Park in New York City.

As the present century advanced, the quite literal naturalism of the sculptors just mentioned gave way to a simplification of form that is compellingly illustrated by Paul Manship's highly stylized bronze composition, *Dancer and Gazelles* (Fig. 521). When he won the Prix de Rome in 1909—he was twenty-four years old at the time—Paul Manship went to the Academy in Rome for further study, bypassing Paris and the Ecole des Beaux-Arts. There he became fascinated by the examples of archaic Greek art and other works of classical antiquity that he saw in and about that timeless city. The experience strongly influenced Manship's subsequent development as an artist and can be discerned in the graceful curving rhythms, the fastidiously executed drapery folds, and the finely articulated anatomical details of the *Dancer.* However, although Manship used classical subjects for many of his sculptures, his renderings of these were his own and were explicitly modern in spirit. Upon his return to America, Manship enjoyed a great vogue through such works as this one, another entitled *Centaur and Dryad,* and others owned by the Museum. One eminent critic referred to him as "the most hopeful figure in native sculpture." All New Yorkers and visitors to the metropolis are familiar with Manship's prominently displayed *Prometheus,* the soaring gilded bronze figure in the sunken plaza of Rockefeller Center.

In his bronze *The Peacocks* (Fig. 522), the French émigré sculptor Gaston Lachaise, a sometime assistant to Manship, shows a debt to the latter's style in the bold emphasis on linear pattern. (Lachaise worked with Manship on the completion of the stone tablet in memory of John Pierpont Morgan installed in the Great Hall of the Museum.) He soon abandoned such decorative and ornamental mannerisms in favor of forms of voluptuous roundness, and it was with these that he earned a reputation that ranked him among the greatest sculptors of the period. John B. Flannagan's *Irish Mountain Goat* (Fig. 523) rises directly from the rough piece of fieldstone that both serves as the goat's base and is part of its body—a reference to the oneness of things that Flannagan stressed over and over in his work. Both the streamlined form of the goat and the deliberate choice of ordinary yellowish stone instead of the smooth marble or metal favored by Beaux-Arts sculptors mark Flannagan as a modernist.

*Mother and Child* (Fig. 524) was chiseled directly in marble by the Lithuanian-born William Zorach between 1927 and 1930. The freshly aroused interest in direct stone-carving seen in both Flannagan's and Zorach's work brought with it a new emphasis on form and solidity that shows the influence of cubism, a style with which Zorach had become familiar when he first visited France in 1910. However, the relatively abstract quality of the resulting design does not reduce the living expressiveness of the figures here. In the decade following the completion of this work, Zorach became a leader of the modern movement in this country.

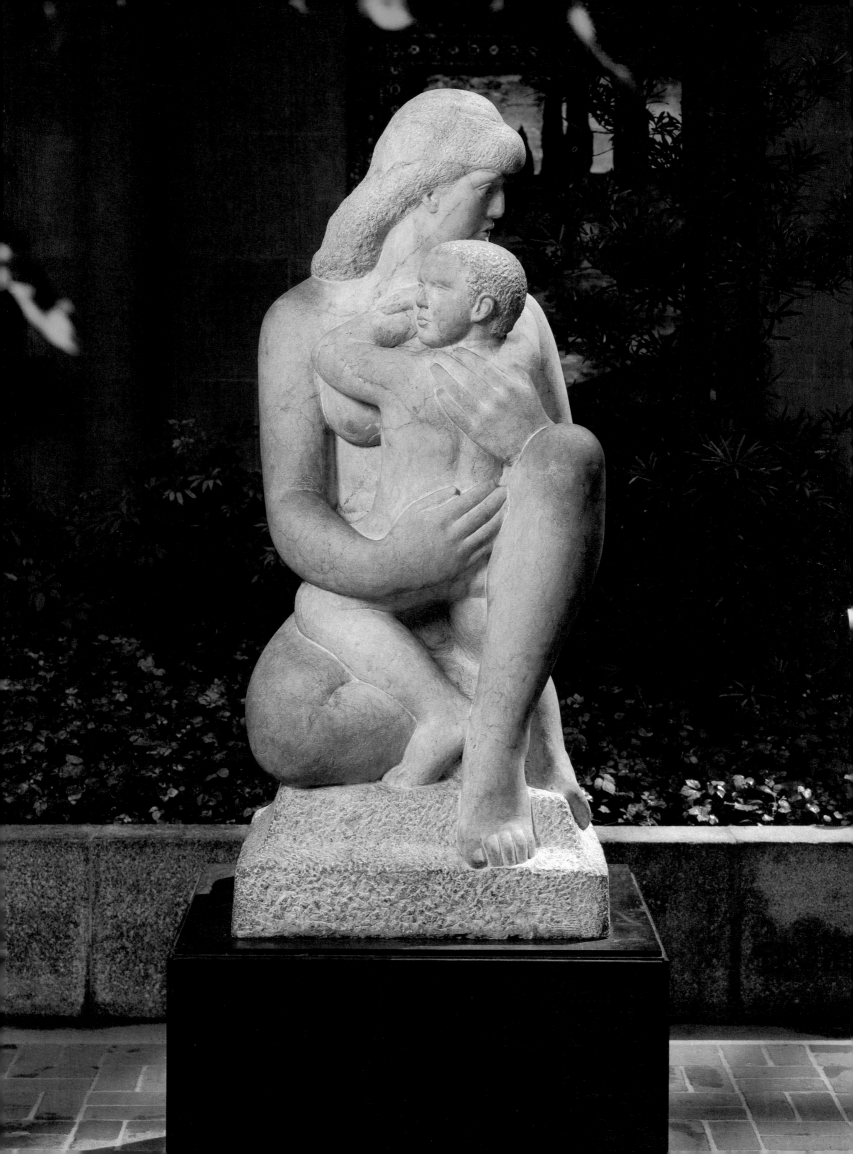

# Selected Bibliography

Besides the following works and consultations with the curators, clippings and unpublished reports in the American Wing files provided material for captions.

## General

Brooklyn Museum. *The American Renaissance, 1875–1917.* New York: Pantheon Books, 1979.

Butler, Joseph T. *American Antiques, 1800–1900.* New York: Odyssey Press, 1965.

Clark, Robert Judson, ed. *The Arts and Crafts Movement in America 1876–1916.* Princeton: Princeton University Press, 1972.

Comstock, Helen, ed. *The Concise Encyclopedia of American Antiques.* 2 vols. New York: Hawthorne Books, n.d.

Cooper, Wendy A. *In Praise of America, American Decorative Arts, 1650–1830 / Fifty Years of Discovery Since the 1929 Girl Scouts Loan Exhibition.* New York: Alfred A. Knopf, 1980.

Davidson, Marshall B., author and editor in charge. *The American Heritage History of Colonial Antiques.* New York: American Heritage Publishing Co., 1967.

———. *The American Heritage History of American Antiques from the Revolution to the Civil War.* New York: American Heritage Publishing Co., 1968.

———. *The American Heritage History of Antiques from the Civil War to World War I.* New York: American Heritage Publishing Co., 1969.

Earle, Alice Morse. *Customs and Fashions in Old New England.* Reprint. Rutland, Vt.: Charles E. Tuttle Co., 1975.

Howe, Katherine S., and Warren, David B. *The Gothic Revival Style in America, 1830–1870.* Houston: Museum of Fine Arts, 1976.

Mayhew, Edgar deN., and Myers, Minor, Jr. *A Documentary History of American Interiors from the Colonial Era to 1915.* New York: Charles Scribner's Sons, 1980.

Sprigg, June. *By Shaker Hands.* New York: Alfred A. Knopf, 1975.

Stillinger, Elizabeth. *The ANTIQUES Guide to Decorative Arts in America, 1600–1875.* New York: E. P. Dutton and Co., 1972.

Tracy, Berry B., and Gerdts, William H. *Classical America, 1815–1845.* Newark, N.J.: The Newark Museum, 1963.

Tracy, Berry B., Johnson, Marilynn, and others. *19th-Century America, Furniture and Other Decorative Arts.* New York: The Metropolitan Museum of Art, 1970.

## Period Rooms and Furniture

Andrews, Edward Deming, and Andrews, Faith. *Shaker Furniture.* New York: Dover Publications, Inc., 1950.

Art and Antiques, ed. *Nineteenth Century Furniture, Innovation, Revival and Reform.* New York: Art and Antiques, 1982.

Baillie, G. H., Clutton, C., and Ilbert, C. A. *Britten's Old Clocks and Watches and Their Makers.* Reprint. New York: Bonanza Books, 1955.

Baltimore Museum of Art. *Baltimore Furniture, The Work of Baltimore Cabinetworkers from 1760 to 1810.* Baltimore, 1947.

———. *Baltimore Painted Furniture 1800–1840.* Baltimore, 1972.

Battison, Edwin A., and Kane, Patricia E. *The American Clock 1725–1865.* Greenwich, Conn.: New York Graphic Society Limited, 1973.

Bishop, Robert. *The American Chair, Three Centuries of Style.* Reprint. New York: Bonanza Books, 1983.

Bishop, Robert, and Coblentz, Patricia. *The World of Antiques, Art, and Architecture in Victorian America.* New York: E. P. Dutton, 1979.

Bjerkoe, Ethel Hall. *The Cabinetmakers of America.* New York: Bonanza Books, 1957.

Blake, Peter. *Frank Lloyd Wright, Architecture and Space.* Baltimore: Penguin Books, 1965.

Bordes, Marilynn Johnson. *Baltimore Federal Furniture.* New York: The Metropolitan Museum of Art, 1972.

Colonial Society of Massachusetts. *Boston Furniture of the Eighteenth Century.* Boston, 1974. Distributor: The University Press of Virginia.

Comstock, Helen. *American Furniture, Seventeenth, Eighteenth, and Nineteenth Century Styles.* New York: The Viking Press, 1962.

Currier Gallery of Art. *The Dunlaps & Their Furniture.* Manchester, N.H., 1970.

Fairbanks, Jonathan L., and Bates, Elizabeth Bidwell. *American Furniture 1620 to the Present.* New York: Richard Marek Publishers, 1981.

Fairbanks, Jonathan L., and Trent, Robert F. *New England Begins: The Seventeenth Century.* 3 vols. Boston: Museum of Fine Arts, 1982.

Fales, Dean A., Jr. *American Painted Furniture 1660–1880.* New York: E. P. Dutton, 1972.

Gruber, Francis. *The Art of Joinery, 17th-Century Case Furniture in The American Wing.* New York: The Metropolitan Museum of Art, 1972.

Hanks, David A. *The Decorative Designs of Frank Lloyd Wright.* New York: E. P. Dutton, 1979.

———. *Innovative Furniture in America from 1800 to the Present.* New York: Horizon Press, 1981.

Heckscher, Morrison H. "Form and Frame: New Thoughts on the American Easy Chair," *The Magazine Antiques,* Dec. 1971, pp. 886–93.

———. "John Townsend's Block-and-Shell Furniture," *The Magazine Antiques,* May 1982, pp. 1144–52.

———. "The New York Serpentine Card Table," *The Magazine Antiques,* May 1973, pp. 974–83.

Hornor, William Macpherson, Jr. *Blue Book, Philadelphia Furniture, William Penn to George Washington.* Reprint. Washington, D.C.: Highland House Publishers, 1977.

Johnston, William R. "Anatomy of the Chair: American Regional Variations in Eighteenth Century Styles," *The Metropolitan Museum of Art Bulletin* n.s. XXI (Nov. 1962), pp. 118–29.

Kane, Patricia E. *300 Years of American Seating Furniture, Chairs and Beds from the Mabel Brady Garvan and Other Collections at Yale University.* Boston: New York Graphic Society, 1976.

Kaufmann, Edgar, Jr. "Frank Lloyd Wright at The Metropolitan Museum of Art," *The Metropolitan Museum of Art Bulletin* XL, no. 2 (Fall 1982).

Landreau, Anthony N. *America Underfoot, A History of Floor Coverings from Colonial Times to the Present.* Washington, D.C.: Smithsonian Institution Press, 1976.

Loth, Calder, and Sadler, Julius Trousdale, Jr. *The Only Proper Style, Gothic Architecture in America.* Boston: New York Graphic Society, 1975.

Miller, Amelia F. *Connecticut River Valley Doorways.* Boston: Boston University, 1983.

Montgomery, Charles F. *American Furniture, The Federal Period.* New York: The Viking Press, 1966.

Montgomery, Florence M. *Textiles in America, 1650–1870.* New York: W. W. Norton & Company, 1984.

Naylor, Gillian. *The Arts and Crafts Movement.* Cambridge, Mass.: The MIT Press, 1971.

O'Donnell, Patricia Chapin. "Grisaille Decorated Kasten of New York," *The Magazine Antiques,* May 1980, pp. 1108–11.

Otto, Celia Jackson. *American Furniture of the Nineteenth Century.* New York: The Viking Press, 1965.

Palmer, Brooks. *The Book of American Clocks.* New York: The Macmillan Co., 1967.

St. George, Robert Blair. *The Wrought Covenant, Source Material for the Study of Craftsmen and Community in Southeastern New England, 1620–1700.* Brockton, Mass.: Brockton Art Center/Fuller Memorial, 1979.

Schwartz, Marvin D., Stanek, Edward J., and True, Douglas K. *The Furniture of John Henry Belter and the Rococo Revival.* New York: E. P. Dutton, 1981.

Smith, Robert C. "Final Busts on Eighteenth-Century Philadelphia Furniture," *The Magazine Antiques,* Dec. 1971, pp. 900–05.

Stoneman, Vernon C. *John and Thomas Seymour, Cabinetmakers in Boston, 1794–1816.* Boston: Special Publications, 1959.

Snyder, John J., Jr., ed. *Philadelphia Furniture and Its Makers.* New York: Main Street/Universe Books, 1975.

Thornton, Peter. *Authentic Decor, The Domestic Interior, 1620–1920.* New York: The Viking Press, 1984.

Tracy, Berry B. "For One of the Most Genteel Residences in the City," *The Metropolitan Museum of Art Bulletin* n.s. XXV (Apr. 1967), pp. 283–91.

Trent, Robert, ed. *Pilgrim Century Furniture, An Historical Survey.* New York: Main Street/Universe Books, 1976.

## Silver

Avery, C. Louise. *Early American Silver.* New York: The Century Co., 1930.

Buhler, Kathryn C. *American Silver, 1655–1825, in the Museum of Fine Arts, Boston.* Greenwich, Conn.: New York Graphic Society Limited, 1972.

Buhler, Kathryn C., and Hood, Graham. *American Silver, Garvan and Other Collections in the Yale University Art Gallery.* 2 vols. New Haven: Yale University Press, 1970.

Carpenter, Charles H., Jr., and Carpenter, Mary Grace. *Tiffany Silver.* New York: Dodd, Mead & Company, 1978.

Fales, Martha Gandy. *Early American Silver for the Cautious Collector.* New York: Funk & Wagnalls, 1970.

Flynt, Henry N., and Fales, Martha Gandy. *The Heritage Foundation Collection of Silver.* Old Deerfield, Mass.: The Heritage Foundation, 1968.

Hood, Graham. *American Silver, A History of Style, 1650–1900.* New York: Praeger Publishers, 1971.

Safford, Frances Gruber. "Colonial Silver in The American Wing," *The Metropolitan Museum of Art Bulletin* XLI, no. 1 (Summer 1983).

Ward, Barbara McLean, and Ward, Gerald W. R., eds. *Silver in American Life.* New York: The American Federation of Arts, 1979.

## Pewter

Laughlin, Ledlie Irwin. *Pewter in America, Its Makers and Their Marks.* Barre, Mass.: Barre Publishers, 1969.

Montgomery, Charles F. *A History of Pewter in America.* New York: E. P. Dutton, 1978.

Jacobs, Carl. *Guide to American Pewter.* New York: The McBride Co., 1957.

Kerfoot, J. B. *American Pewter.* New York: Crown Publishers, 1942.

## Ceramics

Barber, Edwin Atlee. *The Pottery and Porcelain of the United States.* Reprint of combined editions. New York: Feingold & Lewis, 1976.

Barrett, Richard Carter. *Bennington Pottery and Porcelain.* New York: Crown Publishers, 1958.

Evans, Paul. *Art Pottery of the United States.* New York: Charles Scribner's Sons, 1974.

Godden, Geoffrey A. *An Illustrated Encyclopedia of British Pottery and Porcelain.* New York: Crown Publishers, 1966.

Howard, David Sanctuary. *New York and the China Trade.* New York: The New-York Historical Society, 1984.

Hume, Ivor Noël. *A Guide to Artifacts of Colonial America.* New York: Alfred A. Knopf, 1970.

———. *Here Lies Virginia.* New York: Alfred A. Knopf, 1963.

Post, Robert C., ed. *1876, A Centennial Exhibition*. Washington, D.C.: Smithsonian Institution Press, 1976.

Quimby, Ian M. G., ed. *Ceramics in America*. Winterthur Conference Report 1972. Charlottesville: The University Press of Virginia, 1972.

Stradling, J. G. "American Ceramics and the Philadelphia Centennial," *The Magazine Antiques*, July 1976, pp. 146–58.

Watkins, Lura Woodside. *Early New England Potters and Their Wares*. Cambridge, Mass.: Harvard University Press, 1950.

Webster, Donald Blake. *Decorated Stoneware Pottery of North America*. Rutland, Vt.: Charles E. Tuttle Co., 1971.

### Glass

Feld, Stuart P. "'Nature in Her Most Seductive Aspects': Louis Comfort Tiffany's Favrile Glass," *The Metropolitan Museum of Art Bulletin* n.s. XXI (Nov. 1962), pp. 101–12.

Frelinghuysen, Alice Cooney. "A Masterpiece of the New England Glass Company at The Metropolitan Museum of Art," *Journal of Glass Studies* 25 (1983): 225–30.

Hume, Ivor Noël. "The Search for New Bremen and the Glass of John Frederick Amelung," *The Magazine Antiques*, Mar. 1964, pp. 310–13.

McKearin, George S., and McKearin, Helen. *American Glass*. New York: Crown Publishers, 1948.

———. *Two Hundred Years of American Blown Glass*. New York: Doubleday & Company, 1950.

Wilson, Kenneth M. *New England Glass and Glassmaking*. New York: Thomas Y. Crowell Co., 1972.

### Paintings, Prints, Drawings, and Watercolors

Black, Mary, and Lipman, Jean. *American Folk Painting*. New York: Clarkson N. Potter, 1966.

Burke, Doreen Bolger. *American Paintings in The Metropolitan Museum of Art (A Catalogue of Works by Artists Born between 1846 and 1864)*, vol. III. New York: The Metropolitan Museum of Art, 1980.

Comstock, Helen. "Spot News in American Historical Prints, 1755–1800," *The Magazine Antiques*, Nov. 1961, pp. 446–49.

Cooper, Helen A., and others. *John Trumbull, The Hand and Spirit of a Painter*. New Haven: Yale University Art Gallery, 1982.

Gardner, Albert TenEyck, and Feld, Stuart P. *American Paintings, A Catalogue of the Collection of The Metropolitan Museum of Art (Painters Born by 1815)*. New York: The Metropolitan Museum of Art, 1965.

Goodrich, Laurence B. *Ralph Earl, Recorder for an Era*. n.p.: The State University of New York, 1967.

Groce, George C., and Wallace, David H. *The New-York Historical Society's Dictionary of Artists in America*. New Haven and London: Yale University Press, 1957.

Howat, John K. *The Hudson River and Its Painters*. Reprint. New York: Penguin Books, 1978.

Lipman, Jean. *American Primitive Painting*. New York: Oxford University Press, 1942.

Lipman, Jean, and Winchester, Alice. *The Flowering of American Folk Art, 1776–1876*. New York: The Viking Press, 1974.

The Metropolitan Museum of Art. "American Drawings, Watercolors, and Prints," *The Metropolitan Museum of Art Bulletin* XXXVII, no. 4 (Spring 1980).

The Metropolitan Museum of Art. *American Paintings & Historical Prints from the Middendorf Collection*. New York, 1967.

Peters, Harry T. *Currier & Ives, Printmakers to the American People*. Garden City, N.Y.: Doubleday, Doran & Co., 1942.

Prown, Jules David. *American Painting from Its Beginnings to the Armory Show*. New York: Skira/Rizzoli, 1980.

Quimby, Ian M. G., ed. *American Painting to 1776: A Reappraisal*. Winterthur Conference Report

1971. Charlottesville: The University Press of Virginia, 1971.

Richardson, Edgar P., Hindle, Brooke, and Miller, Lillian B. *Charles Willson Peale and His World*. New York: Harry N. Abrams, 1982.

Richardson, E. P. *A Short History of Painting in America*. New York: Thomas Y. Crowell Co., 1956.

Shadwell, Wendy J. *American Printmaking, The First 150 Years*. Washington, D.C.: Smithsonian Institution Press, 1969.

Smith, Helen Burr. "A Portrait by John Mare Identified: 'Uncle Jeremiah,'" *The Magazine Antiques*, June 1973, pp. 1184–87.

Spassky, Natalie. "Winslow Homer at The Metropolitan Museum of Art," *The Metropolitan Museum of Art Bulletin* XXXIX, no. 4 (Spring 1982).

# Index